Fodor's

PATAGONIA

1st Edition

D0063025

**Where to Stay and Eat
for All Budgets**

**Must-See Sights
and Local Secrets**

Ratings You Can Trust

Fodor's Travel Publications   New York, Toronto, London, Sydney, Auckland
www.fodors.com

FODOR'S PATAGONIA

Editor: Josh McIlvain, Laura Kidder, Adam Taplin

Writers: Eddy Ancinas, Ruth Bradley, Brian Byrnes, Andy Footner, Brian Kluepfel, Jimmy Langman, David Miller, Victoria Patience, Tim Patterson, Jonathan Yevin

Editorial Production: Astrid deRidder

Maps & Illustrations: Alan Craig, Craig Cartographic Services, and Ed Jacobus, *cartographers*; Bob Blake, Rebecca Baer, and William Wu *map editors*

Design: Fabrizio LaRocca, *creative director*; Guido Caroti, Siobhan O'Hare, *art directors*; Tina Malaney, Chie Ushio, Ann McBride, Jessica Walsh, *designers*; Melanie Marin, *senior picture editor;* Moon Sun Kim, *cover designer*

Cover Photo (Torres del Paine National Park, Chile): Philip Kramer/Riser/Getty Images

Production/Manufacturing: Amanda Bullock

1st Edition

ISBN 978–1–4000–0684–7

ISSN 1942-7352

SPECIAL SALES

This book is available at special discounts for bulk purchases for sales promotions or premiums. Special editions, including personalized covers, excerpts of existing books, and corporate imprints, can be created in large quantities for special needs. For more information, write to Special Markets/Premium Sales, 1745 Broadway, MD 6-2, New York, New York 10019, or e-mail specialmarkets@randomhouse.com.

AN IMPORTANT TIP & AN INVITATION

Although all prices, opening times, and other details in this book are based on information supplied to us at press time, changes occur all the time in the travel world, and Fodor's cannot accept responsibility for facts that become outdated or for inadvertent errors or omissions. So **always confirm information when it matters,** especially if you're making a detour to visit a specific place. Your experiences—positive and negative— matter to us. If we have missed or misstated something, **please write to us.** We follow up on all suggestions. Contact the Patagonia editor at editors@fodors.com or c/o Fodor's at 1745 Broadway, New York, NY 10019.

PRINTED IN THE UNITED STATES OF AMERICA

10 9 8 7 6 5 4 3 2 1

Be a Fodor's Correspondent

Your opinion matters. It matters to us. It matters to your fellow Fodor's travelers, too. And we'd like to hear it. In fact, we need to hear it.

When you share your experiences and opinions, you become an active member of the Fodor's community. That means we'll not only use your feedback to make our books better, but we'll publish your names and comments whenever possible. Throughout our guides, look for "Word of Mouth," excerpts of your unvarnished feedback.

Here's how you can help improve Fodor's for all of us.

Tell us when we're right. We rely on local writers to give you an insider's perspective. But our writers and staff editors—who are the best in the business—depend on you. Your positive feedback is a vote to renew our recommendations for the next edition.

Tell us when we're wrong. We're proud that we update most of our guides every year. But we're not perfect. Things change. Hotels cut services. Museums change hours. Charming cafés lose charm. If our writer didn't quite capture the essence of a place, tell us how you'd do it differently. If any of our descriptions are inaccurate or inadequate, we'll incorporate your changes in the next edition and will correct factual errors at fodors.com immediately.

Tell us what to include. You probably have had fantastic travel experiences that aren't yet in Fodor's. Why not share them with a community of like-minded travelers? Maybe you chanced upon a beach or bistro or B&B that you don't want to keep to yourself. Tell us why we should include it. And share your discoveries and experiences with everyone directly at fodors.com. Your input may lead us to add a new listing or highlight a place we cover with a "Highly Recommended" star or with our highest rating, "Fodor's Choice."

Give us your opinion instantly at our feedback center at www.fodors.com/feedback. You may also e-mail editors@fodors.com with the subject line "Patagonia Editor." Or send your nominations, comments, and complaints by mail to Patagonia Editor, Fodor's, 1745 Broadway, New York, NY 10019.

You and travelers like you are the heart of the Fodor's community. Make our community richer by sharing your experiences. Be a Fodor's correspondent.

Feliz viaje! (bon voyage!)

Tim Jarrell, Publisher

CONTENTS

MAPS

PATAGONIA IN FOCUS

SOUTHERN ARGENTINE PATAGONIA

CHILEAN LAKE DISTRICT

ABOUT THIS BOOK

Our Ratings

Sometimes you find terrific travel experiences and sometimes they just find you. But usually the burden is on you to select the right combination of experiences. That's where our ratings come in.

As travelers we've all discovered a place so wonderful that its worthiness is obvious. And sometimes that place is so unique that superlatives don't do it justice: you just have to be there to know. These sights, properties, and experiences get our highest rating, **Fodor's Choice**, indicated by orange stars throughout this book.

Black stars highlight sights and properties we deem **Highly Recommended**, places that our writers, editors, and readers praise again and again for consistency and excellence.

By default, there's another category: any place we include in this book is by definition worth your time, unless we say otherwise. And we will.

Disagree with any of our choices? Care to nominate a place or suggest that we rate one more highly? Visit our feedback center at www. fodors.com/feedback.

Budget Well

Hotel and restaurant price categories from ¢ to $$$$ are defined in the opening pages of each chapter. For attractions, we always give standard adult admission fees; reductions are usually available for children, students, and senior citizens. Want to pay with plastic? **AE, DC, MC, V** following restaurant and hotel listings indicate whether American Express, Diners Club, MasterCard, and Visa are accepted. The Discover card is accepted almost nowhere in South America.

Restaurants

Unless we state otherwise, restaurants are open for lunch and dinner daily. We mention dress only when there's a specific requirement and reservations only when they're essential or not accepted—it's always best to book ahead.

Hotels

Hotels have private bath, phone, and TV and operate on the European Plan (aka EP, meaning without meals), unless we specify that they use the Continental Plan (CP, with a Continental breakfast), Breakfast Plan (BP, with a full breakfast), or Modified American Plan (MAP, with breakfast and dinner) or are all-inclusive (including all meals and most activities). We always list facilities but not whether you'll be charged an extra fee to use them, so when pricing accommodations, find out what's included.

Many Listings
★ Fodor's Choice
★ Highly recommended
⊠ Physical address
✦ Directions
⌖ Mailing address
☎ Telephone
🖷 Fax
⊕ On the Web
✍ E-mail
🖃 Admission fee
☉ Open/closed times
Ⓜ Metro stations
⊟ Credit cards

Hotels & Restaurants
🛏 Hotel
⇔ Number of rooms
⚸ Facilities
🍽 Meal plans
✕ Restaurant
⌑ Reservations
↘ Smoking
🎜 BYOB
✕🛏 Hotel with restaurant that warrants a visit

Outdoors
⚐ Golf
⛺ Camping

Other
☾ Family-friendly
⇨ See also
⊠ Branch address
☞ Take note

Experience Patagonia

Gaucho with horse

WORD OF MOUTH

"I have always dreamed of seeing Patagonia. The reality was better than the dream."

—cmcfong

WHAT IS PATAGONIA?

Patagonia. The name fires the imagination. It is often referred to in literature as a faraway, mysterious land at the "end of the world." In geographical terms, it's a region spanning the bottom one-third or so of Chile and Argentina. It extends from the Lake Districts of these countries to Cape Horn Island in the Drake Passage, the strait between the southernmost tip of South America and Antarctica. But most of all, Patagonia represents a land of amazing natural contrasts: it's the forceful winds, the rains, the flowing ice, it's the mountain peaks, fast-flowing rivers, lush forests, barren deserts, diverse birds and wildlife, stunning lakes, and the turbulent seas that pound its coastline.

Magellan Names the Land

The Portuguese explorer Ferdinand Magellan, in 1520, while on his way to becoming the first person to circumnavigate the globe, gave the land its name. When Magellan encountered some Tehuelche Indians on the present-day southern Argentine coast he became enthralled with their enormous-sized feet. He called them "Patagones," after Patagon, the dog-headed giant in a Spanish novel called *Primaleon*. The land soon became known as "Patagonia," thereby feeding a centuries-old myth that this was a land of giants. But those so-called giants, the Tehuelches, along with other indigenous communities, over time were essentially wiped out by slavery, disease, and settlers. In their stead a unique, eclectic culture arose from the mostly European immigrants who came here to begin a new life in what for them was a severely harsh, untamed world.

A Land Remote

Until recently, most of Patagonia was a virtual island because of its remoteness and difficult terrain. In Chile, that began to change in 1976, when the military dictator Augusto Pinochet began to build the Carretera Austral. This highway, largely a dirt road, was completed in 2000 and has helped improve the connections between Patagonia and the rest of the world. The introduction of modern technologies and development projects that have come with improved infrastructure is transforming the region, with mining, oil, fishing, and energy development among the economic initiatives being fostered. Still, only about 5% of the populations of either country actually live in Patagonia—lengthy stretches of awesome nature await the bold, lucky visitor.

OPEN FOR TRAVEL

Not long ago, Patagonia was the domain of *National Geographic* and *Nature* specials, a raw, punishing landscape fit only for nature's climatic and animal fury. Rarely would you see the humans who live here, even though Patagonia has been inhabited for thousands of years. Instead, we glimpsed through the photographer's lens the jagged mountain peaks, massive glaciers, and the beautiful orcas rising from the depths of the ocean. It all seemed so stark, beautiful, and primeval—for naturalists only. Then came the mountain gear and clothing company, which took and branded the name to denote a truly edgy adventure. Modern voyagers began earning the Patagonia feather in their caps, while no doubt wearing the fleece.

Part of the myth of such places is that travel there requires you to have the athleticism of an Olym-

Natural Wonder

In his voyage around the world in the 1830s, the famed naturalist Charles Darwin came away awestruck. Darwin speculated that the reason he was so deeply affected by Patagonia's natural wonders was "the free scope given to the imagination" supplied by this region's "boundless" landscape. Today, Patagonia is still one of the world's last great places to experience pristine nature due to the large number of remaining areas seemingly untouched by the typical destruction that comes along with the human footprint. The Chilean side is a green, lively landscape with endless mountains and snow-capped volcanoes. Northern Argentine Patagonia is much of the same, but as you steer further south on the Argentinean side vast expanses of desert come into view. Along the coast, whales breed, sea lions huddle up, and huge penguin colonies stir. Guanaco roam the hills. The Andean condor, a black-and-white bird with an airplane-like wingspan, soars throughout the long mountain chain that divides the territory.

Andes Split

Patagonia is split by the Andean mountain chain, which separates Chile and Argentina. The mountains began to rise about 60 million years ago as the Nazca plate started sliding underneath the South American plate. On the western (Chilean) side of the Cordillera the climate is wet and the forests lush, but rainfall decreases dramatically as one moves east over the Argentine frontier. The vast majority of Argentine Patagonia is a broad tertiary plateau of barren desert interspersed with shallow pools of brackish water and scoured by incessant winds.

Much of the Patagonian landscape has been sculpted by the advance and retreat of glaciers from the mountains to the sea. These ice fields still cover a large part of the southern Andes, and are now a popular tourist attraction. The action of the ice has eroded parts of the Andes, leaving dramatic spires of pure granite such as Mt. Fitzroy and Cerro Torre, in the northern section of the Parque Nacional Los Glaciares.

What is Patagonia? It's a place to rejoice in wild nature and life in extreme landscapes.

pian, the ability to survive for weeks on roots and shoe leather, and a Ph.D. in anthropology. The reality of travel in Patagonia is much simpler. To cross a steam in Patagonia by stepping on a few stones is no more difficult than to cross a similar stream in Ohio. You'll probably get your feet wet in both places. The only real difference is the spectacular scenery (no offense, Ohio).

Patagonia is still a remote land with isolated cultures, and traveling here requires some serious flying time. But once you get here, distances are no more insurmountable than some of the lonelier spots in the American West. You can choose as isolated and adventuresome a vacation as you wish, but you can also enjoy fantastically peaceful lodges in beautiful settings, with very good food (and plenty of good wine). If you delight in adventure, travel, and wildlife, there is nothing stopping you from enjoying the heart-stopping sights, sounds, and experiences of Patagonia.

WHAT'S WHERE

Numbers correspond to chapter numbers in the book.

3 Argentina Lake District. Pine forests line the shores of crystal lakes painted with the snowy reflections of jagged mountain peaks. The lakeside city of Bariloche is the destination of choice for outdoor sports enthusiasts. For solitude, head to one of the national parks—and pack your fly-rod.

4 Atlantic Patagonia. Atlantic Patagonia is all about whales . . . or is it Wales? The leviathans of the deep are the star attraction for marine wildlife watchers bound for the Valdés Peninsula, but don't miss the cherished Welsh culture in towns like Trelew and Gaiman. Sip a cup of tea in a rose garden for a taste of the old country.

5 Southern Argentine Patagonia. Southern Patagonia is harsh, dramatic, and humbling. Windswept desert gives way to massive lakes dotted with icebergs. Go horseback riding alongside hardy *gaucho* pioneers, breaking at the end of the day for a traditional lamb barbecue, or take to the trails on foot: the area around El Chaltén has great day hikes.

6 **Southern Chilean Patagonia & Tierra del Fuego.** Mountain forests, rumbling glaciers, and stormy seas awe visitors who reach the continent's southernmost tip. Puerto Natales, Chile, is the best base for exploring Parque Nacional Torres del Paine. The former prison colony of Ushuaia, Argentina, now a beautiful vacation town, is near the Tierra del Fuego National Park.

7 **Chilean Lake District.** The austral summer doesn't get more glorious than in this 400-km (250-mi) stretch of land between Temuco and Puerto Montt. It has become Chile's vacation spot, with resort towns such as Pucón, Villarrica, and Puerto Varas. More than 50 snow-covered peaks offer splendid hiking.

8 **Chile's Southern Coast.** The coastline between the Lake District and Patagonia is truly remote. Anchoring the region's spine is the Carretera Austral, a hair-raising, "I survived" road trip. Flying south is easier; while a cruise from Puerto Montt through the fjords to Puerto Natales is more stylish.

9 **& 10** **Starting in Buenos Aires & Santiago.** Chile and Argentina's capital cities are jumping-off points for travelers bound south to Patagonia. Buenos Aires is the more vibrant of the two.

PATAGONIA PLANNER

When to Go

Summer is the busiest season throughout Patagonia, particularly December and January. Summer days are long, with twilight lingering until 11 PM in the far south, and the weather is mild, though the wind is not. Prices rise with the mercury, and the summer crowds who flock to popular destinations can distract from your experience of *remote* Patagonia. At luxury lodges, the high-season crowds won't bother you, because the best establishments are generally outside the towns.

Midrange and budget travelers might consider visiting Patagonia in the shoulder seasons of spring and fall. November can be windy in the south, but March and April are glorious throughout Patagonia—less windy, with fall color on the hillsides and fresh snow high in the mountains. Easter brings a final wave of domestic tourists.

Winter is low season in Patagonia. With the exception of a few ski resorts near Bariloche and the southern city of Ushuaia, most summer hot spots close in the winter.

Safety

For all its end-of-the-world mystique, Patagonia is one of the world's safer destinations. Argentina and Chile have stable governments by Latin American standards, and the local people are friendly and hospitable. Petty theft is a minor problem in tourist destinations like Puerto Natales and El Calafate, but violent crime is rare.

Outside the towns, the biggest danger is sunburn. The combination of long days and the deceptively cooling wind can roast you. Drinking plenty of water is also important—tap water is generally fine, and you can even drink stream water in the national parks.

Getting Around

If you don't have weeks, it's most convenient to fly between base towns such as Bariloche and Ushuaia. With more time, it's worthwhile to take a least one overland journey to appreciate the immensity of the landscape—this kind of travel should appeal to those who have road-tripped on the more remote routes of the American West.

By Air: Flying between the cities of Patagonia is relatively straightforward. Inquire about flights on LADE, which unlike Aerolineas Argentinas does not charge double for foreign nationals.

By Bus: Buses are clean, safe, and comfortable. Don't attempt to bus all the way across Patagonia, unless you enjoy staring at emptiness for days. For short or medium distances, however, buses are often the best option.

By Car: Driving in Patagonia isn't as difficult as you might imagine. Highways are paved. Secondary roads, including those in the more popular parks, are well maintained. Renting a car in Patagonia is not cheap, especially in popular destinations like El Calafate.

By Boat: The ferry from Puerto Montt to Puerto Natales is one of the more memorable ways to get from the Lake District to the far south, while a sightseeing cruise between Punta Arenas and Ushuaia passes through incredible scenery of fjords and glaciers.

1

Crossing the Border

Crossing between Argentine and Chilean Patagonia is straightforward, although it's important to know current regulations. Tourist entry visas are available free of charge at border posts, although Chile charges U.S. citizens a $100 "reciprocity fee." Bringing fresh food into Chile is not allowed.

The most scenic crossing is the combination of ferries and buses from Bariloche, across Lago Nahuel Huapi, over the frontier to the Chilean town of Puerto Montt. This journey can be done in one day, although stopping overnight is a better option. Crossing between El Calafate and Puerto Natales in southern Chile also entails a mountain crossing. Regular buses ply the route, which takes about six hours.

If driving, check road conditions in advance. Crossing the border in a rental car is usually not a problem, but it's essential to have the proper paperwork.

Patagonia's Wildlife

Patagonia's wildlife often plays second fiddle to the spectacular natural scenery, but the weird and wonderful variety of native animals and birds is a delight for observant visitors. Long-necked guanacos are commonly seen loping over the steppe or traversing the steep slopes of Andean foothills, sometimes accompanied by the rhea, a large ostrich-like flightless bird. In the national parks of Chile or Argentina, keep an eye out for the shy huemul, a rare species of native deer.

Avid birders will find Patagonia a paradise; dozens of endemic species await discovery. Even visitors with no previous interest in birds will gasp at the sight of a condor soaring effortlessly over the mountain peaks.

Finally, Patagonia's coastal parks are one of the best places in the world to observe marine wildlife. Whales and penguins are the top attractions, but dolphins, seals, and sea lions are also easy to spot.

Patagonia's Folks

The original inhabitants of Patagonia, indigenous tribal groups such as the Mapuche, were decimated by colonists of European descent, with the most severe population declines occurring in the second half of the 19th century. In some cases the conflict was brutally cold-hearted, with sheep ranchers hunting natives and paying bounties for every man, woman, and child killed. In other areas settlers and natives coexisted and cooperated for a time, but eventually the natives succumbed to disease and displacement.

The settlers who now inhabit Patagonia are of hardy pioneer stock. Some continue to identify with a specific European culture, as in the Welsh communities of Trelew and Gaiman, but most Patagonians are simply Chilean or Argentine regardless of their ancestral country of origin. In recent years, as Patagonia increases in popularity and the tourism economy booms, a new wave of immigrants from Buenos Aires, Santiago, the United States, and Europe has arrived, and wealthy enclaves like Llao Llao (near Bariloche) have a distinctly international feel.

PATAGONIA PLANNER

What to Pack

This list assumes a visit in late spring, summer, or early fall, with tours throughout Patagonia and moderate trekking.

Outerwear: Prepare for changing weather with clothing that layers comfortably. Include: fleece jacket or sweater, windbreaker, light, full-fingered gloves, quick-dry casual pants, and two hats—one for sun and one to cover your ears.

Other Clothing: Patagonia is not formal, but one smart-casual outfit to wear to dinner is good to have. Also remember a swimsuit for heated pools.

Footwear: Go for comfort over fashion, and leave the heels and loafers at home! Include: comfortable walking shoes and/or lightweight hiking boots with synthetic hiking socks.

Gadgets: Camera with zoom, binoculars, electric outlet adaptor, travel alarm clock.

Accessories: Bring your favorite toiletries from home. Include: sunglasses, sunscreen, lip balm, floss (hard to find!).

Optional: Most trekking and outdoor sport equipment can be rented. Include: fishing gear, trekking poles, Spanish dictionary, insect repellent, rain gear, sandals.

Restaurants & Lodging

Patagonian cuisine is excellent, but somewhat lacking in variety. Most restaurants specialize in meat dishes, pizza, and homemade pastas, although the nicer places will usually offer a semi-creative vegetarian option. Estancias and lodges generally have fixed menus, so let the staff know of dietary preferences in advance. In many restaurants meals are ordered à la carte. Ask for the steak and you'll get just that—a hunk of meat with nothing on the side. If you want all the trimmings ask for a dish "completa" or pick your choice of sauces and side dishes.

Lodging options range from all-inclusive luxury estancias and hotels to basic campgrounds and youth hostels. Generally, you get what you pay for, although hotels in popular destinations may jack their prices up significantly in high season. If traveling in peak season, it's essential to book in advance, as the Patagonian tourism boom shows no sign of slowing down.

Note that inflation is picking up speed in Patagonia—mostly in Argentina, but prices are also rising in Chile (which is more expensive to begin with). As always, it's important to check current prices before booking.

The Chile & Argentina Pesos

A 30-peso meal in Argentina will cost around 5,000 pesos in Chile. Most of the price difference is a matter of denomination. The Argentine peso hovers around 3 pesos to 1 U.S. dollar, while in Chile it takes around 470 pesos to buy a dollar. In relative terms Chile is slightly more expensive than Argentina, but prices for high-end accommodation and meals are similar in both countries.

The Wind

The southern section of South America is the only significant landmass between the latitudes of 45 and 48 degrees south, so there is nothing else to block the wind that roars around the world. The ship captains of old learned to trust in the winds of the "Roaring Forties" to speed them across the southern oceans.

Nowadays travelers don't depend on the wind to get to Patagonia. At worst, the wind is an annoyance, but it is also an inherent element of the Patagonian experience. The best way to deal with strong gusts is to simply lean forward and hold on to your hat. Sunglasses are also important for keeping windblown dust out of your eyes.

In northern Patagonia the wind isn't so bad; it's strongest in Santa Cruz province, especially in the mountain town of El Chaltén and along the coast, and in Chile in Torres del Paine down to Punta Arenas. Long, sunny summer days bring the strongest gusts, because as the sun warms the earth the temperature difference sends air masses, particularly from the ice cap, rushing to fill the gap in atmospheric pressure.

Beware of Mines

Tens of thousands of land mines were planted along the Chilean–Argentine frontier in the 1970s and 1980s, during a period of heightened tensions when military governments were in power. Most of these minefields were planted by Chile, and are in extremely remote areas on the Chilean side of the border. Many mines have already been cleared, but many remain.

There have been no reports of land-mine injuries in Argentina, and only seven land-mine casualties in Chile, the last occurring in 2000. Practically speaking, there is no danger to visitors, but it's a good idea to be aware of the issue and stick to marked trails in remote areas. In towns along the frontier in both Chile and Argentina you will see signs and murals portraying the danger of mines. If embarking on a trek into the backcountry along the frontier, ask the locals about mines, and take warnings seriously.

PATAGONIA TODAY

Population

Patagonia covers more than half of Argentina's national territory, and about a third of Chile's. Yet, despite its large size, Patagonia remains sparsely populated, representing but a tiny percentage of the two countries' national populations even as its modest cities and towns have doubled and tripled in size over the past few decades. Sheep and cattle ranching have long been the major form of activity in the rugged landscape here—indeed, it's said that sheep outnumber people in Patagonia by a ratio of more than 10 to 1.

Cowboys

Patagonia's dominant way of life revolves around livestock. In Argentina, the term for cowboys is *gauchos,* while for Chileans, it's *huasos.* The gauchos and huasos are the horseback riders who tend herds of cattle and sheep. The standard Argentine gaucho uniform consists of long leather boots and woolen ponchos, with a bandanna draped around the neck, and often a beret atop the head. Chilean huasos dress similarly, but somewhat more stylishly, usually sporting wide-brimmed cowboy-like hats. The guacho-huaso culture still prevails from Patagonia's dusty roads to distant mountain valleys. Even if you don't have time or inclination to get up on a horse and do some good old-fashioned cattle rustling, you'll still have the chance to enjoy the cowboy culture's tasty asados, meat roasted or barbecued over an open fire.

Remote Villages

In the *campo,* or countryside, of Patagonia, many of the first villages were established just in the last century. These towns were nearly completely roadless up until the 1990s, so residents moved about on horseback. Coastal and river villages also utilized boats, and in some cases were accessible only by airplanes using makeshift landing strips. One particularly striking example of the remoteness of Patagonian life is Caleta Tortel, a picturesque village located were the Río Baker merges with the Pacific Ocean in southern Aysén. For several decades up until 2002, when they welcomed the first paved roads to their town, the residents of Caleta Tortel sent expeditions by horseback each March and October to buy food and other supplies on the Argentinean border. Round-trip, that journey took three weeks to a month.

Today, satellite television dishes appear on every roof in even the most remote regions, right next to the woodstove chimneys that are also ubiquitous. Though many families are still forced to deal with their relative isolation by growing their own food, it's possible to have electrical service in almost every rural village or town. You are as likely to see cows and horseback riders as you are cars and trucks on the gravelly country roads. But the major cities—such as Coyhaique, Punta Arenas, Ushuaia, or Bariloche—are modern communities with five-star hotels and restaurants, department stores, discos and the like.

Business & Industry

Patagonia's abundant natural resources offer many opportunities for profit in an environment of extremes. The Patagonian ice fields contain some of the world's largest freshwater reserves, while the Argentine desert, just over the Andean mountain chain, boasts precious gas and mineral deposits. Pristine waters off the coast in both countries are not just a haven for penguins and sea lions, but an attractive fishing ground as well. For centuries, Patagonia was sheltered from large-scale

development due to its remoteness and inclement climate. Now, as transit connections improve, big business is setting its sights on Patagonia.

While Chilean and Argentine Patagonia both still maintain large-scale agriculture sectors involving livestock, wheat, and sheep farming, they are increasingly expanding into new industries. More than 80% of Argentina's significant oil and gas industry is based in the region. Argentine Patagonia is also rich in minerals, so gold and other mining companies are adding new ventures all the time. Commercial fishing operations along its coast have multiplied. In Chilean Patagonia, meanwhile, several large-scale hydroelectric dam projects are proposed throughout the region. The largest such dam project is planned for the Baker and Pascua rivers in the southern Aysén. Along the Chilean Patagonia coast, the nation's salmon-farming industry, the second-largest of its kind in the world, is expanding fast.

Tourism

Development pressures aside, Patagonia remains a paradise of natural wonders. Just about every feature of nature's glory is at your doorstep here, from luxurious temperate rain forest to forbidding mountain peaks. The immense ice fields are slowly retreating due to global warming, but they continue to astonish onlookers. Patagonia is most ideal for the tourist who likes to hike and camp, and the region's parks—such as Torres del Paine Park in Chile's far south and Nahuel Huapi Park in the Argentine Patagonia Lake District—today boast camping facilities and trails that are fully up to the mark of global standards. Towns such as Puerto Natales, Ushuaia, and Bariloche have become major centers for ecotourism. They usually offer the full slate of tourism services and are the launching points for several skiing, fishing, biking, rafting, and other adventure sports.

Conservation

Patagonians are a proud lot who view their unique region with great affection. While many of the young go on to Santiago or Buenos Aires and other cities to pursue university studies and careers, most stay closer to home. As new development projects arise, such as several large hydroelectric dams being proposed for the region, strong locally based citizen movements have formed. A current refrain in Chilean Patagonia, which you'll find plastered on billboards and posters in storefront windows, is the phrase "Patagonia Without Dams." Notable foreigners such as Ted Turner and Luciano Benetton are buying up large swaths of real estate to protect nature. Douglas Tompkins, American founder of the Esprit and North Face clothing companies, has created Pumalín Park in northern Chilean Patagonia. It's considered the world's largest private nature park.

TOP PATAGONIA ATTRACTIONS

Perito Moreno Glacier

(B) Stand before the majestic immensity and translucent blue face of the Perito Moreno Glacier. With the natural viewing platform formed by the Peninsula Magallanes, Perito Moreno may be the best place to come before one of nature's most ancient, powerful, and fragile wonders. An ice-trekking excursion over the icy ridges of the glacier is an unforgettable experience.

Mt. Fitzroy

(C) Mt. Fitzroy is one of the most visually dramatic peaks on the planet. Sheer granite walls rise to a blunt, spear-head summit surrounded by perpetual wisps of cloud. The peak is impressive from any vantage point, but trekking to the azure lakes at its base provides the most dramatic view of the legendary massif.

Penguin Colonies

(A) In the summer months hundreds of thousands of Magellanic penguins gather in noisy breeding colonies on the shores of Patagonia. The charming creatures wobble about among their nests, curiously craning their necks to greet visitors, but they launch themselves into the water with surprising agility, shooting like feathery torpedoes beneath the waves. The busiest colonies are accessible from Puerto Madryn, Río Gallegos, and Punta Arenas.

El Bolsón Craft Market

In one of the most fertile valleys in the Argentine Lake District, the "ecological municipality" of El Bolsón hosts a lively crafts market thrice weekly in the village square. Village artisans sell hand-carved wooden clocks and cutting boards, elaborate beadwork, and homemade jams. Local microbreweries set up beer stands along the periphery and musicians play to

the crowds, making for one of the most cheery, down-home scenes in Patagonia.

Ushuaia Prison Museum

Today Ushuaia is a bustling port town with a booming tourism economy, but this city at the end of the world was once a far grimmer destination. In the early 20th century, Argentina's most notorious criminals were exiled to Ushuaia. Today the prison building has been converted into a highly informative museum, with many of the original structures left intact.

Torres del Paine

(E) The famous towers that form the Cordillera del Paine are the most striking feature of Chilean Patagonia's magnificent national park. If the weather clears, go directly to a viewpoint in the park for the surreal and breathtaking sight of three colossal granite spires looming over a landscape of blue lakes, shining snowfields, and evergreen forests.

Chilean Fjords

(D) Follow in the wake of the intrepid explorers who first navigated the icy fjords of Tierra del Fuego, passing beneath windswept peaks, dodging icebergs, and embarking on Zodiac cruises to shingle beaches populated by penguins and elephant seals. Cruises depart in the summer months from Ushuaia and Punta Arenas.

Cueva de las Manos

(F) In a red-rock river valley deep in the steppe of northern Santa Cruz province, the ancient rock paintings and handprints on the wall of the Pinturas Canyon are one of the most mysterious sights in Patagonia. Some of the pictographs are more than 9,000 years old but look as if they could have been painted yesterday.

TOP EXPERIENCES

Eat your way through the Feria Artesanal in El Bolsón.

Every weekend the central plaza in El Bolsón transforms into an artisan's fair with local farmers, brewers, bakers, woodworkers, and craftspeople of all types vending every kind of food and craft imaginable. Depending on the season, delicacies range from fine fruits (raspberries, strawberries, cherries) and vegetables of all varieties, to preserves, cheeses, breads, pastries, organic microbrews, honey, and smoked meats. As you eat your way through the fair, check out the work of local artisans—jewelry, woodcarvings, musical instruments—and strike up a conversation with residents, many of whom left Buenos Aires during the '70s to seek a simpler life close to the land, helping to give El Bolsón its unique identity.

Raft down the Río Futaleufú

The Futaleufú River is famous among kayakers and rafters for its sapphire color and gigantic white water, which is similar in volume to the Grand Canyon's, but with certain sections having even steeper and more powerful drops. Although the entire Futaleufú valley is remote, the extensive infrastructure for rafting and paddling—with luxurious accommodations and numerous other activities including yoga, horseback riding, and hiking—makes it possible to tailor a trip just right for you. You can float on mild but exceptionally beautiful white water, or take on some of the world's biggest commercially rafted rapids.

Watch marine wildlife in Península Valdés

No matter what time of year you visit Península Valdés you'll witness something special in the life cycle of Patagonia's marine wildlife. Newborn sea lion pups emerge in January. Penguin chicks take a crash course in swimming mid-February. In April you can see orcas—sometimes storming the beaches in violent and spectacular chases as they hunt sea lions. From June through December, southern right whales are mating and raising offspring here. These whales are between 36 and 59 feet long, and have several endearing behaviors such as "sailing," where they swim upside down, holding their fins up in the air, or when mothers use their flippers to teach calves how to swim.

Hike El Chaltén

Mountaineers come from all over the world to climb Fitzroy and Cerro Torre here in the Parque Nacional Los Glaciares. El Chaltén is a gateway to the base of these mountains and to some of the most spectacular snowfields, glaciers, lakes, and peaks anywhere. The hike to Laguna de los Tres, at the base of Fitzroy, is especially good, as is a stay at Estancia Helsingfors, a luxury ranch uniquely situated in the center of the national park.

Sea-kayak Isla Chiloé

The largest island in Patagonia, Chiloé, along with the smaller islands in the Chiloé Archipelago, makes for a sea-kayaking paradise. Paddle by rich temperate rain forests, stilt houses built above the tidal flats, and wooden churches that date back to Jesuit missionaries who arrived after the first Spanish explorers in the 16th century. Chiloé has a mystical feel, partly because of the thick forests, partly

because of the local lore, which includes goblins and other mythical creatures.

Trek the glacier

From the nearby town of El Calafate, take a glacier trek at Perito Moreno. Unlike nearly all glaciers on Earth, Perito Moreno is actually expanding. Guided treks of an hour (or more) give you access into a netherworld of ice and crevasses, of great silence sporadically punctuated with the roar of ice blocks shearing off into Lake Argentina. Here you'll learn about glaciology and gain a new perspective on planet Earth. The kinds of views you'll see here are usually reserved for mountaineers at the tops of glaciated peaks; however, the guided walks are easy and safe.

Cruise the Strait of Magellan

The famous Strait of Magellan connects the town of Punta Arenas in Chile with Ushuaia in Argentina via a narrow inland passage of full of wild fjords, mammoth glaciers, and some of the most remote terrain anywhere in the world. Some boats sail all the way to Cape Horn, the last headland before Antarctica, where the Atlantic and Pacific oceans join, often with heavy surf.

Ski in July at Cerro Catedral

Cerro Catedral is not only the most developed ski area in South America (with terrain options for beginners through experts) but its location within Nahuel Huapi National Park gives you a constant view of Lake Nahuel Huapi, like a giant emerald crater down below. Local pubs and restaurants serve handcrafted ales and classic Patagonian dishes such as *guiso de lentejas* (lentil soup with sausage), making for an après-ski so com-

plete you'll forget that it's summer back in the Northern Hemisphere.

Drink champagne on the train to the end of the world

Originally used as a train for transporting prisoners and timber in this southernmost city in the world, today the *Tren del Fin del Mundo* offers rides with champagne and dinner service in wood-paneled coaches reminiscent of the golden age of steam locomotives. The narrow-gauge track runs through the Pico Valley in the dense austral forest of Tierra del Fuego National Park.

Fly-fish the Chimehuin River at Junín de los Andes

Junín de los Andes is internationally famous among anglers for the great number of rainbow, brown, and brook trout, as well as landlocked salmon in its nearby rivers and lakes. It's what fishing is supposed to be: the rivers are clean, protected, and there are no dams.

IF YOU LIKE

Natural Wonders

Patagonia's epic natural scenery is among the most stunning in the entire world. Stark mountain vistas, pristine lakes, calving glaciers and the endless blue dome of sky will overwhelm you with a sense of wild beauty. With little human impact on the land, Patagonia is a refuge for a diverse array of wildlife. Along the south Atlantic coast, sea mammals mate and give birth on empty beaches and in protected bays. Inland, guanaco, rhea, and native deer travel miles over Andean trails and across windswept plains, while condors ride thermal winds above their cliff-top aeries.

Glaciar Perito Moreno, Santa Cruz, Argentina. Tons of ice regularly peel off this advancing glacier and crash into Lago Argentino, sending waves rolling against the shore beneath the viewing platform.

Península Valdés, Chubut, Argentina. This is the best place to view southern right whales as they feed, mate, give birth, and nurse their offspring. Orcas are also present, sometimes chasing sea lions and seals right up onto the beach!

Parque Nacional Nahuel Huapi, Bariloche, Argentina. Rich forests surround the sapphire-blue waters of Lake Nahuel Huapi. Countless smaller but equally magnificent bodies of water teeming with trout make this Argentina's lake district.

Parque Nacional Torres del Paine, Chile. Ash-gray, glacier-molded granite spires tower over miles of hiking trails and reflect in the mirror-like surface of turquoise lakes.

Fjords Of The Far South, Chile. Icebergs bob in the misty channels of fjords near Punta Arenas, a remote wilderness best experienced from the deck of a cruise ship.

Adrenaline Rushes

If an eyeful of natural beauty doesn't make your heart pound as fast as you'd like, why not try an adventure sport? Patagonia is great for winter rushes—skiing, snowboarding, and dogsledding among them. In the summertime, you can cool down by white-water rafting or leaping (with a paraglide) into the breeze.

Ice Trekking on the Perito Moreno Glacier. Strap crampons onto your boots and trek over creaking slabs of 1,000-year-old ice, then celebrate your intrepid ascent with cocktails served over cubes carved from the glacier.

Rafting The Río Futaleufú, Chile. The clear waters of the Futaleufú crash through a granite canyon, creating one of the most spectacular white-water thrill rides in the world.

Paragliding Around Bariloche. Soar like a condor over mountains, forests, and lakes, wheeling and banking on wind currents before landing in a meadow with your heart pumping and a smile as wide as the Andes plastered across your face.

Skiing and snowboarding at La Hoya, Catedral, and Chapelco ski areas. Catedral near Bariloche, and Chapelco near San Martín de los Andes offer groomed runs, open bowls, and trails that follow the fall line to cozy inns or luxurious hotels. La Hoya is a hidden jewel, a more rustic ski area near Esquel.

Tierra Mayor, Patagonia. This family-run Nordic center in a scenic mountain valley near Ushuaia has such novelties as dogsled rides, snowcat trips, and wind skiing. Bundle up!

Windows To The Past

Patagonia is rich in ancient and recent history. Paleontologists drool at the chance to scour the steppe for dinosaur fossils, while archaeology buffs search out traces of the indigenous peoples who succumbed to European colonialism. The stories of the hardy European settlers are also fascinating. By visiting museums, one can imagine what it was like for pioneers to carve a living from a remote and unforgiving land. In some places, such as the island of Chiloé, indigenous and European cultures have blended together, creating a unique culture that is still evolving.

Museo Paleontológico, Trelew, Argentina. You can marvel at dinosaur bones and watch archaeologists at work at this impressive paleontology museum. In 2005 the fossilized bones of a 45-foot-long carnivorous dinosaur were unearthed nearby.

Cueva de las Manos, Santa Cruz, Argentina. The Cave of Hands is a fascinating display of handprints and rock art left on the red-rock walls of the remote Pinturas River canyon by aboriginal peoples between 6,000 and 9,000 years ago.

Churches of Chiloé Island, Chile. The bucolic island of Chiloé was one the last places in South America reached by the Spanish colonists, and the wooden churches that dot the landscape reflect the mix of indigenous and European culture.

Pioneer's Museum, Río Gallegos, Argentina. Located in one of the original houses of Río Gallegos, a visit to the Pioneer's Museum offers a taste of the extreme isolation early Patagonian settlers were forced to overcome.

Lodges and Estancias

Do not leave Patagonia without visiting a traditional working farm, or estancia, many of which have been converted to semiluxurious lodges that offer activities such as horseback riding and fishing. Most estancias only take a few guests at a time, so you can enjoy the remote atmosphere and chat with the owners and farmworkers over traditional barbecues.

Estancia San Guillermo, Chubut, Argentina. Head here to experience a Chubut farm filled with snorting pigs, over-friendly guanacos, and strutting roosters. A few miles outside Puerto Madryn, 1,200 sheep roam the 7,400-acre fossil-filled farm, where you stay in roomy, comfortable villas.

Estancia Helsingfors, Santa Cruz, Argentina. Uniquely located on the shore of Lago Viedma between El Calafate and Mt. Fitzroy, Helsingfors is probably the most attractive estancia in Patagonia. Don't miss a Zodiac tour on the lake or the horseback ride to a hidden glacial pool.

Estancia Nibepo Aike, Santa Cruz, Argentina. Sheep graze among fields of purple lupine flowers against a backdrop of stark snowcapped peaks on the Chilean frontier. Ask a gaucho to saddle up a horse for you and ride into the hills behind the estancia for stunning views across to Perito Moreno glacier.

Remota, Puerto Natales, Chile. With a heated swimming pool, modern architecture and even Jacuzzis, a stay at Remota is hardly a typical estancia experience, but guests aren't complaining about the pampering that accompanies adventure at this luxurious lodge.

GREAT ITINERARIES

LAKE DISTRICT

Day 1: Arrival in Bariloche

Inexpensive two-hour flights leave daily from Buenos Aires (Aeroparque Metropolitano) to Bariloche. If you have lots of time, you might consider driving or taking the 20-hour bus ride across the pampas. Rent a vehicle (four-wheel drive strongly recommended) in Bariloche.

Day 2: Bariloche and Circuito Chico

Spend the day exploring the Circuito Chico and Lago Nahuel Huapi. Depending on weather, boat tours are the best way to see the lake.

Day 3: Circuito Grande to Villa La Angostura

Villa La Angostura marks the beginning of the legendary Circuito Grande. The route follows the shores of Lago Nahuel Huapi on R237 and R231. Check into a hotel in Puerto Manzano.

Day 4: Seven Lakes Road to San Martín de los Andes

Head out of Villa La Angostura with a full tank of gas on the Seven Lakes Road (R234), which passes Lago Correntoso, Lago Espejo, Lago Villarino, Lago Falkner, and Lago Hermoso. The Seven Lakes Road is closed in winter, when you have to go through Junín de los Andes (along RN40) to get to San Martín.

Day 5: San Martín de los Andes and Lanín National Park

If it's winter, skiing at Cerro Chapelco near San Martín is some of the best in South America. Also explore Lanín National Park, with its native Araucaria trees—living fossils from the dinosaur age.

Day 6: Return to Bariloche

Get an early start from San Martín de los Andes for the five-hour drive back to Bariloche along the RN40.

Alternatives: Instead of returning to Bariloche, cross from San Martín de los Andes into Chile via Hua Hum Pass, which is open year-round. From here, work your way south approximately 240 km (149 mi) to Osorno, breaking the trip up into three days. Return to Bariloche by way of Villa Langostura on the Puyehue (or Cardenal Samoré) pass—also open year-round.

ATLANTIC PATAGONIA

Day 1: Buenos Aires to Puerto Madryn

Daily flights are available from Aeroparque Metropolitano in Buenos Aires to Trelew. (Also check for direct flights from Buenos Aires to Madryn.) From Trelew take the half-hour shuttle ride north to Puerto Madryn and rent a vehicle there. You'll still have enough time in the evening to enjoy the beach and the shops and restaurants along the waterfront *rambla*. Or head 14 km (9 mi) south along the coast (follow signs toward Punta Ninfas) to the Punta Loma Sea Lion Reserve. A colony of some 600 South American sea lions can be seen at the beach below a tall, crescent-shaped bluff.

Day 2: Puerto Madryn

In the middle of the waterfront, El Vernardino Club Mar offers a variety of instruction and guided activities including scuba diving, snorkeling, kayaking, and windsurfing, as well as rentals for DIY exploration. During the summer they run a camp for kids called the "sea-school." You'll be spending plenty of time driving

the next few days, so park your car, and walk around—most of the good shopping and restaurants (try Margarita Resto-Bar) are within a few blocks of each other in the city center.

Day 3: Península Valdés and Puerto Pirámides
Leaving Madryn and cutting towards the peninsula on the Ruta 2 takes you into the vast open steppe. Take your time on the way in: an hour invested at the visitor center will make for a more informed visit to this magical place, and a better appreciation of the flora, fauna, and landforms. Check in to lodging at Puerto Pirámides; take a local hike, or go sandboarding in the dunes.

Day 4: Península Valdés
Base your second day around a whale-watching excursion (June–December) in the morning or afternoon, with the rest of the day dedicated to exploring Caleta Valdés all the way to Punta Norte. Here you'll find the most remote and largest sea-lion settlement on the peninsula, and on occasion, orcas. From Punta Norte, take RP3 back inland to Pirámides, pass-ing by El Salitral, one of the peninsula's three large salt-lake ecosystems.

Day 5: Gaiman
From Madryn head 40 minutes south on the RN3 towards Trelew, then cut west, and in another 20 minutes you'll enter the green Chubut River valley and the Welsh settlement of Gaiman. For an experience unlike any other in Patagonia, enjoy a tra-ditional Welsh tea service in the afternoon at one of the famous teahouses, such as the Plas y Coed. Head back to Madryn in the early evening.

Day 6: Madryn to Buenos Aires
Most flights leave in the morning. Catch the shuttle back to the airport in Trelew.

CHILEAN PATAGONIA
Days 1, 2, 3 & 4: The Lake District
Head south 675 km (405 mi) from Santi-ago on a fast toll highway to Temuco, the gateway to Chile's Lake District, or even better, take one of the frequent hour-long flights. Temuco and environs are one of the best places to observe the indigenous Mapuche culture. About an hour south, and just 15 minutes apart on the shores of Lago Villarrica, are the twin resort towns

of flashy, glitzy Pucón and pleasant Villarrica. Drive south through the region from the graceful old city of Valdivia to Puerto Montt, stopping at the various resort towns. Frutillar, Puerto Octay, and Puerto Varas still bear testament to the Lake District's German-Austrian-Swiss immigrant history. Make time to relax in one of the region's many hot springs.

Days 5, 6, 7, 8 & 9: Parque Nacional Laguna San Rafael

From Puerto Montt, take a five-day round-trip cruise through the maze of fjords down the coast to the unforgettable cobalt-blue glacier in Parque Nacional Laguna San Rafael. If you're lucky, you'll see the huge glacier calving off pieces of ice that cause noisy, violent waves in the brilliant blue water. Transport runs from the utilitarian passenger–auto ferries offered by Navimag and Transmarchillay to the Skorpios' luxury cruises.

Transportation: A combination of flights, rental cars, and boat works best. From Santiago, drive south to Temuco and then through the various sights and towns of the Lake District. From Puerto Montt, take the boat cruise down to Parque Nacional Laguna San Rafael—book far in advance for January or February—and on your return to Puerto Montt fly into the city of Punta Arenas. From there, drive north to Puerto Natales and Parque Nacional Torres del Paine. Buses can also be used in place of a rental car, or sign on with a tour in Punta Arenas.

SOUTHERN PATAGONIA
Day 1: To Punta Arenas
Flights leave regularly from Santiago to Punta Arenas (about four hours' flying time) or you can fly from Port Montt

if you've already been traveling south. Visit city highlights: the turreted mansions around Plaza de Armas, and the view from the top of Mount of the Cross. For maximum mobility, rent a vehicle in Punta Arenas; however, everywhere on this itinerary can be accessed by bus.

Day 2: Punta Arenas to Torres del Paine National Park
Begin early and drive or take a tour bus 65 km (40 mi) north to the Otway Inlet. Over 100,000 Magellanic penguins return to nest here each year between October and March. Continue north another two hours to Puerto Natales for lunch. Then continue another two hours to Torres del Paine National Park. On the route you

will pass Paine Massif, Almirante Nieto, and Cuernos del Paine. Be on the lookout for condors. Check in to a mountain lodge, or stay in Puerto Natales.

Days 3 & 4: Torres del Paine National Park

Spend the entire first day in excursions through the park. Choose from Salto Grande, Amarga Lagoon, and Lago Grey. Give yourself about 3½ hours to complete each one. On Day 4, now that you're better acclimated to the park, check out more challenging excursions, such as daylong hikes to the towers themselves (made better with overnight camping at one of the many *refugios* such as El Chileno). The two best-known treks are the "W," a four-day, 76-km (47 mi) backpacking adventure, and the Paine Massif, which takes seven days and traverses 93 km (58 mi).

Day 5: Punta Arenas to Santiago or optional crossing to Argentina

The drive or bus ride back to Punta Arenas is five hours, so plan on spending another night in Punta Arenas before flying back to Santiago or extending your trip anywhere else.

Alternatives: Besides extending your stay in Torres del Paine National Park, consider crossing in to Argentina from Puerto Natales via the Casas Viejas Pass, which is open daily all year from 8 AM to 11 PM, or the Cancha Carrera Pass, which is open from December to March. Both put you on RN40 in Argentina, which leads you to El Calafate and allows access to Glaciers National Park, where you can visit Perito Moreno. There are also cruises that go from Punta Arenas to Ushuaia, Argentina, visiting the spectacular sights of the Strait of Magellan en route.

TRAVEL TIPS

1. Visitors to Chile by plane will need to pay a onetime $100 fee upon entry.

2. Punta Arenas and Puerto Natales have Alfgal stores—your best bet for camping supplies, including stoves and fuel.

3. Always check local road conditions, including whether highways are cut off due to *piqueteros* (striking workers).

4. Fill your gas tank at every opportunity. Many stretches of Patagonia have great distances between gas stations.

5. Be aware of wildlife crossing roads at any time, but especially during dawn and dusk hours.

6. On single-lane mountain roads, the climbing vehicle has the right-of-way.

7. Do not count on passable roads in the mountains except from November to May.

8. Similar to all alpine environments, weather in the Patagonian high country can go from extremely cold to extremely hot in a matter of hours. Always carry foul-weather gear and extra warm clothes even in summer.

9. A good pair of binoculars will make all the difference in wildlife viewing, especially on the coast.

10. The one constant in the forecast is wind.

PATAGONIA HISTORY

Patagonia's lively history involves famous navigators, pirates, scientists, and explorers. For some of its illustrious visitors and first settlers, this region at the "uttermost ends of the earth" was a desolate landscape beaten back by violent winds. The rough and difficult sea passage to the Pacific discovered by early navigators at the extreme southern tip of the South American continent was dubbed the "Furious Fifties." It's a chilly mixing spot of three great oceans—the Atlantic, Pacific, and Antarctic—and where sub-Antarctic cyclones are constantly born. The Spanish captain Antonio de Cordoba remarked upon a scientific expedition that he led to Patagonia in 1786 that it was "the most wretched and unfortunate part of the Earth."

For others, though, Patagonia was a land of mystery, riches, opportunity, and natural beauty. In 1520, a Portuguese navigator (he had moved to Spain) named Ferdinand Magellan put the place on the map of the Western world when he became the first sailor to circumnavigate the globe. His tales of the "Patagones," the unusually tall natives he encountered, inspired imagination and fueled literature for ages to come. William Shakespeare's *The Tempest,* Samuel Coleridge's "Rime of the Ancient Mariner," Conan Doyle's *Lost World,* and Edgar Allan Poe's *The Narrative of Arthur Gordon Pym,* are but a few of literature's classics inspired in some fashion by Patagonian lore.

Passage To the Pacific

Magellan's discovery of a route to the Pacific below Patagonia soon attracted all manner of other ships to the zone, including pirates bound to loot golden booty from the Spanish ships departing Peru. One of the most famous pirates was the legendary Englishman Sir Francis Drake. His name adorns the Drake Passage between South America and Antarctica for he discovered the route where the oceans mix. Along his trip to glory, Drake infamously slaughtered 3,000 penguins in one day to replenish provisions on board his ships. It was later believed by several explorers that within Patagonia there existed a city made of gold called Ciudad de los Cesares, or Cesars City. This myth led to several fruitless expeditions over the years in search of the golden city.

Colonists Arrive, Die

Beyond such pirates and explorers, Patagonia slowly but surely became a destination for colonists. In 1579, the Spaniard Pedro Sarmiento de Gamboa led an expedition to southwestern Patagonia in order to set up defense points against the pirates. In a following expedition, in 1584, he founded the region's first nonindigenous settlements. The first, called "Name of Jesus," located in Cabo Virgenes in the Strait of Magellan, survived only about four years. The pirate Thomas Cavendish found the remaining Sarmiento settlement a few years afterward. He dubbed the place "Port Famine," for the 15 people surviving there were suffering from starvation.

Indigenous Population

Patagonia was largely deemed an inhospitable region for colonization up until the 18th century. Meanwhile, there were people already living there. The indigenous groups of the region included the Mapuches, who lived throughout the north, the Huilliches in the northwest, the Tehuelches in the southeast, and on Tierra del Fuego Island and other parts of the far south lived the Onas, Haush, Alcalufes, and Yaghans. The Mapuches and Huilliches practiced some farming, but the Tehuelche relied almost exclusively on hunting. They were said to have indeed been larger than normal, as Magellan intimated, though it's believed that this perception was due to their common practice of adding guanaco wool to their hair. The Yaghans and Alcalufes were a completely different culture altogether moving about the coastal areas on canoes and primarily fishing to survive. When European colonists eventually arrived in greater numbers, they killed off most of the indigenous peoples through disease and violent conflict.

Colonists Take Root

The two most successful early towns in Patagonia were Carmen de Patagones and Viedma, which were founded in 1779 and remain the oldest surviving settlements in the region. Most European colonists entered the region in increasing numbers in the 1830s. The first settlers were missionaries, while others came to hunt, pan for gold, or raise cattle. Later, the Chilean and Argentine governments courted European immigrants to settle the region. In the 1850s, in Chile's Lake District, thousands of Germans arrived and founded towns such as Puerto Varas. In northern Argentina, a Welsh colony was formed in 1865 in the Chubut province, where they established the towns of Rawson, Gaiman, Trelew, and Esquel. There was also a significant influx throughout Patagonia of English, Scottish, and Croatian colonists.

As colonists spread throughout, on both sides of the Andes the national governments made an effort to conquer the last, large indigenous communities in the region. By the end of the 1880s, the Mapuches, the largest and most defiant indigenous group, had been defeated and pushed off their lands.

Natural History

The naturalist Charles Darwin, who wrote his theory of evolution after traveling around Patagonia for two years, came to the region in 1832. While collecting specimens that later contributed to his groundbreaking ideas, he was mesmerized by its desolate yet "boundless" landscape. Near Puerto Montt, Chile, at a place called Monte Verde, archaeologists have uncovered evidence of what they think is the oldest known human community in the Western Hemisphere, dating back some 12,500 years. Many millions of years ago, in the Eocene era, Patagonia was once joined with South Africa, New Zealand, and Australia in a vast supercontinent scientists call Gondwana. Today, the forests in all of these countries have similar characteristics and each are dominated by *Nothofagus* and *Podocarpus* trees. On this supercontinent roamed the dinosaurs; paleontologists in Patagonia excavate their fossils today. In Patagonia, ancient history is unearthed and gives rise to new mysteries of the past.

Choosing Your Cruise & Tour

2

Stream crossing at El Rincon

WORD OF MOUTH

"[We] then drove to Punta Arenas where we connected to the Mare Australis and cruised 4 nights around Tierra del Fuego to Ushuaia. This was also great. The cruise was very well run, excursions excellent (particularly landing on Cape Horn), and the guides and lectures informative."

—lily3

By Celeste
Moure

LARGER-THAN-LIFE PATAGONIA IS HOME TO stunning jagged-edge mountains and monstrous glaciers. The Andean scenery—sweeping panoramas, huge granite peaks soaring above grasslands and beech forests, unusual mammals, and a rich history—attracts adventurous travelers and jetsetters looking to get away from it all. Whether money is no object or you're traveling on a tight budget, have a limited amount of time or all the time in the world, there are countless tour operators to choose from: some offer general itineraries to introduce you to the region, while others focus on specific activities such as mountain biking, birding, or fly-fishing. A number of cruise lines offer trips ranging from three-day sojourns to explore the region's Lake District to luxurious journeys guided by expert naturalists who take you to the far reaches of Antarctica and Tierra del Fuego.

CRUISING IN PATAGONIA

Cruising is a leisurely and comfortable way to take in the rugged marvels of Patagonia and the southernmost region of the world. Sailing through remote channels and reaching islands virtually untouched by man, you'll witness fjords, snowcapped mountains and granite peaks and their reflections dominating the glacial lakes. You'll get a close look at elephant seals, migrating whales, colonies of Magellanic penguins and cormorants from the comfort of your vessel and during shore excursions taken in Zodiacs (small motorized boats) led by naturalist guides. Far from the beaten path, you'll visit small fishing villages only accessible by sea, explore fantastic temperate rain forests, and enjoy the freshest seafood and local wines. Most short cruises depart from Ushuaia, Argentina or Punta Arenas, Chile, while longer and more luxurious itineraries typically depart from either Buenos Aires or Santiago.

WHEN TO GO

In the Southern Hemisphere, where the seasons are reversed, November through March is considered high season. However, the weather in Patagonia is unpredictable: strong winds and sudden storms are common. Summertime (December through February) is the best time to visit. Shoulder months—October, November, March, and April—tend to have cooler temperatures but also less wind.

October (late spring). Best time to witness the whale migration and the immense colonies of elephant seals and sea lions in Península Valdés.

November (early summer). The natural nesting cycle of Magellanic penguins is November to February. Penguins arrive at the rookeries at the beginning of the month. Spring flowers are in full bloom. This is the best time to catch the bird nesting of finches, sparrows, condors, albatrosses, and other species.

December & January (high summer). The warmest months see penguin chicks hatch in Tierra del Fuego. Long daylight hours also mean great photography opportunities all over Patagonia.

February & March (late summer). Receding ice allows for easier exploration farther south. Whale-watching is at its best. Penguin colonies are very active, as the adults feed the chicks.

BOOKING YOUR CRUISE

The majority of cruisers plan their trips four to six months ahead of time. Book a year ahead if you're planning to sail on a small adventure vessel, as popular itineraries may be full six to eight months ahead.

Consider booking shore excursions when you book your cruise to avoid disappointment later. You can even book your spa services pre-cruise to have your pick of popular times, such as sea days.

Although most travel is booked over the Internet nowadays, for cruises, booking with a travel agent who specializes in Patagonia cruises is still your best bet. Agents have strong relationships with the lines, and have a better chance of getting you the cabin you want, and possibly even a free upgrade. Cruise Lines International Association (⊕ *www.cruising. org*) lists recognized agents throughout the United States.

CRUISE ITINERARIES

Choosing an itinerary is as important as choosing a cruise line or tour operator that fits your tastes and budget. We highlight possibilities that focus on specific areas, as well as typical departure points and costs, and the tour operators that can take you there.

ANTARCTIC CRUISES
Founded to promote environmentally responsible travel to Antarctica, the **International Association of Antarctica Tour Operators** (☎ *970/704–1047* ⊕ *www.iaato.org*) is a good source of information, including suggested readings. Most companies operating Antarctica trips are members of this organization and display its logo in their brochures.

Season: November–March.
Location: Most cruises depart from Ushuaia, in Argentine Patagonia.
Cost: From $2,995 (triple-occupancy cabin) for 12 days from Ushuaia; prices can get quite high.
Tour Operators: Abercrombie & Kent; Adventure Center; Big Five Tours & Expeditions; ElderTreks; G.A.P. Adventures; Lindblad Expeditions; Mountain Travel-Sobek; Quark Expeditions; Travcoa; Wilderness Travel; Zegrahm Expeditions.
Overview: Ever since Lars-Eric Lindblad operated the first cruise to the "White Continent" in 1966, Antarctica has exerted an almost magnetic pull for serious travelers. From Ushuaia, the world's southernmost city, you'll sail for two (often rough) days through the Drake Passage. Most visits are to the Antarctic Peninsula, the continent's most accessible region. Accompanied by naturalists, you'll travel ashore in motorized rubber craft called Zodiacs to view penguins and nesting seabirds. Some cruises visit research stations, and many call at the Falkland, South Orkney, South Shetland, or South Georgia islands. Adventure

Center and Big Five Tours & Expeditions offer sea kayaking and, at an extra cost, the chance to camp for a night on the ice.

Expedition vessels have been fitted with ice-strengthened hulls; many originally were built as polar-research vessels. On certain Quark Expeditions itineraries you can travel aboard an icebreaker, the *Kapitan Khlebnikov,* which rides up onto the ice, crushing it with its weight. This vessel carries helicopters for aerial viewing.

It's wise to inquire about the qualifications of the onboard naturalists and historians; the maximum number of passengers carried; the ice-readiness of the vessel; onboard medical facilities; whether there is an open bridge policy, and the number of landings attempted per day.

CRUISING THE TIP OF SOUTH AMERICA

Cruising the southern tip of South America and along Chile's western coast north to the Lake District reveals fjords, glaciers, lagoons, lakes, narrow channels, waterfalls, forested shorelines, fishing villages, and wildlife. While many tour operators include a one- or two-day boating excursion as part of their Patagonia itineraries, the companies listed below offer from four to 12 nights aboard ship.

Season: September–April.
Locations: Chilean fjords; Puerto Montt and Punta Arenas, Chile; Tierra del Fuego and Ushuaia, Argentina.
Cost: From $1,078 for a four-day, three-night cruise between Punta Arenas and Ushuaia.
Tour Operators: Abercrombie & Kent; Adventure Life; Big Five Tours & Expeditions; Cruceros Australis, Explore! Worldwide; International Expeditions; Lindblad Expeditions; Mountain Travel-Sobek; Off the Beaten Path; Wilderness Travel; Wildland Adventures.
Overview: Boarding your vessel in Punta Arenas, Chile, or Ushuaia, Argentina, you'll cruise the Strait of Magellan and the Beagle Channel, visiting glaciers, penguin rookeries, and seal colonies before heading north along the fjords of Chile's western coast. Adventure Life and Lindblad Expeditions include the Chiloé Archipelago, a region rich in folklore about ghost ships, magical sea creatures, and troll-like beings known as the Trauco. With Abercrombie & Kent and Wildland Adventures, you'll savor the mountain scenery of Torres del Paine National Park for several days before or following the cruise, while Lindblad Expeditions, Mountain Travel-Sobek, and International Expeditions visit Tierra del Fuego National Park. Cruceros Australis and some other companies also include Cape Horn National Park. Wilderness Travel allows time for hiking at Volcano Osorno and in Alerce Andino National Park; the latter protects the second-largest temperate rain-forest ecosystem in the world. Following a five-day cruise, Off the Beaten Path travelers fly to Puerto Montt for a three-night stay at nearby Lake Llanquihue with opportunities for hiking in the mountains. Most itineraries begin or end in Santiago, Chile or Buenos Aires, Argentina.

OCEAN CRUISES

Some ships set sail in the Caribbean and stop at one or two islands before heading south; a few transit the Panama Canal en route. West Coast (U.S.) departures might include one or more Mexican ports before reaching South America. 14- to 21-day cruises are the norm. Vessels vary in the degree of comfort or luxury as well as in what is or isn't included in the price. Guided shore excursions, gratuities, dinner beverages, and port taxes are often extra.

Season: October–April.

Locations: Many itineraries visit Argentina (Buenos Aires and Ushuaia), Brazil (Belém, Fortaleza, Rio de Janeiro, and Salvador), and Chile (Antofagasta, Arica, Cape Horn, Coquimbo, Puerto Montt, Punta Arenas, and Valparaíso).

Cost: Prices vary according to the ship, cabin category, and itinerary. Figure $1,950 to $4,495 for a 14-day cruise, excluding international airfare.

Cruise Companies: Celebrity Cruises, Fred.Olsen Cruise Lines, Holland America Line, Norwegian Cruise Line, Oceania Cruises, Princess Cruises, Regent Seven Seas Cruises, Seabourn Cruise Line, Silversea Cruises.

CHOOSING YOUR TOUR

No longer satisfied with being shuttled in an air-conditioned bus from one point to another for a quick snapshot, today's travelers want to experience the natural wonders of a destination—be it by strapping on crampons and a backpack to trek a glacier or climb a mountain, jumping on a horse or mountain bike, or sharing a meal with new friends around a camp fire miles from another living soul. Even the most high-end tour operators have had to adjust to this new trend, even if a decadent spa treatment and gourmet meal await back at the five-star hotel at the end of the day.

Choosing a tour package carefully is always important, but it becomes critical when the focus is adventure or sports. You can rough it or opt for comfortable, sometimes even luxurious, accommodations. You can select easy hiking and canoeing adventures or trekking, rafting, and climbing expeditions that require high degrees of physical endurance and technical skill. Study multiple itineraries to find the trip that's right for you. This chapter describes selected trips offered by some of the best adventure tour operators in today's travel world.

ADVENTURE & SPORTS TOURS ITINERARIES

A sports-focused trip offers a great way to see the country and interact with local people. Some programs are designed for those with a high level of experience while others don't require a high level of skill; however, in either case, your interest in the particular sport should be more than casual. Companies that operate mountaineering programs usually build an extra day or two into their itineraries to allow for weather conditions. If you're wary of your endurance, ask if support vehicles

Choosing a Trip

How strenuous a trip do you want?
Adventure vacations commonly are
split into "soft" and "hard" adventures.
Hard adventures, such as strenuous
treks (often at high altitudes), Class IV
or V rafting, or mountain ascents, generally require excellent physical condition and previous experience. Most
hiking, biking, canoeing/kayaking, and
similar soft adventures can be enjoyed
by people of all ages who are in good
health and are accustomed to a reasonable amount of exercise.

**Is environmental responsibil-
ity important to you?** Does the
company protect the environments
you'll be visiting? Are some of the
company's profits designated for
conservation efforts or put back into
the communities visited? Many of the
companies in this chapter are involved
in environmental organizations and
promote eco-conscious traveling. On
ecotourism programs, check out the
naturalists' credentials.

What sort of group is best for you?
At its best, group travel offers curious, like-minded people with whom
to share the day's experiences. Inquire

about the group size; many companies
have a maximum of 10 to 16 members, but 30 or more is not unknown.
With large groups, expect little flexibility in the published itinerary and
more time spent (or wasted) at rest
stops, meals, and various arrivals and
departures.

If groups aren't your thing, many companies will customize a trip just for
you. This has become a major part of
many tour operators' business. Such
travel offers all the conveniences of a
package tour, but the "group" is composed of only you or you and your
travel companions.

Are there hidden costs? Know what
is and isn't included in basic trip costs.
International airfare is usually extra.
Sometimes, domestic flights are additional. Is trip insurance required, and if
so, is it included? Are airport transfers
included? Departure taxes? Gratuities?
Equipment? Meals? Bottled water? All
excursions? Many factors affect the
price, and the trip that looks cheapest
in the brochure could turn out to be
the most expensive.

accompany the group or if alternate activities or turn-around points are
available on more challenging days.

BICYCLING
Season: October–March.
Locations: Bariloche; Lake District; Mendoza, Argentina; Chiloé Island;
Puerto Montt; Lake District, Chile
Cost: From $1,225 for eight days from Puerto Montt.
Tour Operators: Experience Plus!; Global Adventure Guide; Southwind
Adventures
Overview: Global Adventure's 15-day journey, graded moderate with
some uphill challenges and occasional single-track riding, crisscrosses
the Lower Andes. The itinerary includes the Lake District and Patago-
nia with occasional options for rafting, canyoning, or volcano climbing. With Southwind, bike and hike the Lake District's gently rolling
terrain, visiting Osorno Volcano, Puyehue and Huerquehue national
parks, and the resort town of Pucón. Starting in Bariloche, Experience

Plus! cycles up to 93 km (58 mi) a day around Lake Llanquihue for views of Osorno and Calbuco volcanoes with the opportunity for Class III rafting on Río Petrohué.

CANOEING, KAYAKING & WHITE-WATER RAFTING

White-water rafting and kayaking can be exhilarating experiences. You don't have to be an expert paddler to enjoy many of these adventures, but you should be a strong swimmer. Rivers are rated from Class I to Class V according to difficulty of navigation. Generally speaking, Class I to III rapids are suitable for beginners, while Class IV and V rapids are strictly for the experienced. Canoeing is a gentler river experience.

Season: November–March.
Locations: Chiloé Archipelago; Río Futaleufú; Lake Llanquehue; Petrohué River; Lake District, Chile. Bariloche; Lake Nahuel Huapi, Argentina.
Cost: From $2,800 for nine days from Buenos Aires, Argentina.
Tour Operators: Adventure Life; Earth River Expeditions; Hidden Trails; PanAmerican Travel; BikeHike Adventures; Geographic Expeditions.
Overview: Chile has scenic fjords for sea kayaking and challenging rivers for white-water rafting. With PanAmerican Travel, sea kayakers spend nine days exploring the fjords, waterfalls, hot springs, and wildlife of the country's rugged coast, camping at night in splendid scenery. BikeHike Adventures offers an eight-day multisport adventure that includes paddling sea kayaks along Lake Llanquehue and chasing the current down the wild Class III rapids of Petrohué River in rafts.

For the experienced rafter, the Class IV and V rapids of Río Futaleufú offer many challenges. Its sheer-walled canyons create such well-named rapids as Infierno and Purgatorio. Earth River's 10-day program includes a rock climb up 320-foot Torre de los Vientos and a Tyrolean traverse where, wearing a climbing harness attached to a pulley, you pull yourself across a rope strung above the rapids. With tree houses and riverside hot tubs formed from natural potholes carved in the stone, overnight camping becomes an exotic experience. Earth River also offers a kayaking journey over a chain of three lakes, surrounded by snowcapped mountains. Access is by floatplane. Hidden Trails and Adventure Life have Futaleufú rafting trips; the latter's program, in addition to shooting the rapids, offers kayaking, fishing, and horseback riding in the mountains.

FISHING

Season: September–March.
Locations: Chiloé Island; Lake District, Chile. Challhuaquen; Nahuel Huapi National Park; El Calafate; Morro Lagoon, Argentina.
Cost: From $2,975 for seven days from Balmaceda, Argentina.
Tour Operators: Fishing International; FishQuest; Fly Fishing And; Frontiers; PanAmerican Travel; Rod & Reel Adventures.
Overview: For anglers, Chile is the Southern Hemisphere's Alaska, with world-class trout fishing in clear streams. Added bonuses include the landlocked salmon and golden dorado, known as the "river tiger." Bilingual fishing guides accompany groups, and guests stay in comfort-

able lodges with private baths. While November is the usual opening date for freshwater fishing, the season begins two months earlier at Lago Llanquihue due to the large resident fish population. Rod & Reel bases participants at a lodge near Osorno volcano. With Fly Fishing And, your 10 days will be divided between two lodges. PanAmerican's seven-day program breaks up lodge stays with a night of riverside camping. Fishing International offers a trip based at an *estancia* (ranch) where you can fish two rivers for brown trout weighing up to 15 pounds. FishQuest has four offerings, fishing a variety of rivers for brown and rainbow trout, dorado, giant catfish, and salmon. With Frontiers, you can choose from a great variety of lodges and rivers in Chile.

HIKING, RUNNING & TREKKING

Patagonia's magnificent scenery and varied terrain make it a terrific place for trekkers and hikers. The trips outlined below are organized tours led by qualified guides. Camping is often part of the experience, although on some trips you stay at inns and small hotels.

Season: October–April.
Locations: Lake District; Torres del Paine; Osorno Volcano, Chile; Bariloche; Tierra del Fuego; Los Glaciares National Park, Argentina.
Cost: From $1,065 for 12 days from Salta, Argentina.
Tour Operators: Adventure Life; American Alpine Institute; Andes Adventures; BikeHike Adventures; Butterfield & Robinson; Country Walkers; Geographic Expeditions; KE Adventure Travel; Mountain Travel-Sobek; Southwind Adventures; The World Outdoors; Wilderness Travel; Wildland Adventures; World Expeditions.
Overview: Programs range from relatively easy hikes (Butterfield & Robinson, Country Walkers) to serious treks involving daily elevation gains up to 2,625 feet and ice and snow traverses using crampons (American Alpine Institute). Highlights include Torres del Paine, Los Glaciares, and/or Tierra del Fuego national parks and crossing the Patagonian Ice Cap. Adventure Life's program lets you overnight in igloo-shape tents at EcoCamp in Torres del Paine.

In addition to its hiking trip, Andes Adventures offers an 18-day running itinerary with runs covering as much as 31 km (19 mi) per day. Other options include an Atacama Desert trek with KE Adventure Travel, which includes an ascent of Licancabur Volcano, or a Futaleufú Canyon trek with Wilderness Travel. Adventure Life and Southwind Adventures each offer four different itineraries, while American Alpine Institute, KE Adventure Travel, and Wilderness Travel have three.

HORSEBACK RIDING

Season: October–April.
Locations: Río Hurtado Valley; Puerto Montt; Río Manso Valley, Torres del Paine; Chile. Bariloche; Nahuel Huapi; Fitzroy, Argentina.
Cost: From $305 per night from Bariloche, Argentina.
Tour Operators: Equitours; Hidden Trails; Boojum Expeditions; Off the Beaten Path; BikeHike Adventures.

Overview: Equitours introduces you to Argentina's gaucho culture at a 15,000-acre *estancia* (cattle ranch). You ride through the grasslands and beech forests of Lanin National Park and spend several nights camping. On their 12-day "Patagonia Glacier Ride" you cross the pampas to Torres del Paine National Park. Nights are spent camping or in lodges. Hidden Trails offers more than a dozen itineraries in both Chile and Argentina, exploring the forests, mountains, and lakes of Patagonia, or several *estancia*-based adventures where you'll ride more than 32 km (20 mi) a day and perhaps join the gauchos as they round up cattle and horses. The company's "Glacier Camping Ride" which ventures into remote areas accessible only by foot or horse. From a base at estancia Nahuel Huapai in the Bariloche region, guests with Boojum Expeditions ride high up in the mountains, on rugged trails aboard strong, sure-footed Criollo horses.

MOUNTAINEERING

This is no casual sport, so choose your tour operator carefully, ask questions, and be honest about your level of fitness and experience. Safety should be the company's, and your, first priority. Are the guides certified by professional organizations, such as the American Mountain Guides Association? Are they certified as Wilderness First Responders and trained in technical mountain rescue? What is the company's safety record? What is the climber-to-guide ratio? Are extra days built into the schedule to allow for adverse weather? Is there serious adherence to "leave no trace" environmental ethics? Several of the tour operators mentioned below have their own schools in the United States and/or other countries which offer multilevel courses in mountaineering, ice climbing, rock climbing, and avalanche education.

Season: November–February.
Locations: Cerro Marconi Sur; Gorra Blanca; Patagonian Ice Cap, Argentina. Torres del Paine; Valle Frances, Chile.
Cost: From $2,980 for 11 days from Calafate, Argentina.
Tour Operators: Alpine Ascents International; American Alpine Institute; KE Adventure Travel; Mountain Madness; World Expeditions.
Overview: American Alpine Institute offers an expedition with ascents of Cerro Marconi Sur and Gorra Blanca in southern Patagonia. On this program, you'll also traverse part of the Patagonian Ice Cap. In Chile, the company offers a two-week program that accommodates climbers and trekkers. It includes a trek near the famous high peaks of the Torres del Paine, Paine Grande, and the great black-horned peaks, the Cuernos; views of the Patagonian Ice Cap; and a trek into the magnificent Valle Frances. Mountain Madness offers a 12-day program that takes trekkers to Torres del Paine in Chile to enjoy trekking, glacier hiking, and kayaking.

MULTISPORT

Multisport trips grow in popularity every year and now form an important part of many adventure tour operators' programs. Innovative itineraries combine two or more sports, such as biking, fishing, canoeing, hiking, horseback riding, kayaking, rafting, and trekking.

Season: November–April.

Locations: Lake District; Río Hurtado Valley; Puerto Montt; Río Manso Valley, Torres del Paine; Chile. Bariloche; Nahuel Huapi; Fitzroy, Argentina.

Cost: From $765 for five days from Puerto Montt, Chile.

Tour Operators: American Alpine Institute; BikeHike Adventures; Earth River Expeditions; Fishing International; Hidden Trails; Mountain Madness; Mountain Travel-Sobek; Nature Expeditions International; The World Outdoors; Wilderness Travel; World Expeditions.

Overview: Hidden Trails combines horseback riding with sea kayaking in Patagonia, while Mountain Madness leads hut-to-hut trekking in Torres del Paine along with kayaking on the Río Serrano and an optional ice climb. With Nature Expeditions, you'll have soft-adventure options most days, such as hiking, rafting (Class II and III rapids), and horseback riding. BikeHike has two multisport trips in Argentina and Chile; you can hike, raft, sea kayak, bike, and ride horses in the Lake District or hike, ride horses, and sandboard in northern Chile. If you want to try serious rafting, consider a trip down Río Futaleufú run by Earth River Expeditions and The World Outdoors; these programs also include hiking and horseback riding.

SKIING AND SNOWBOARDING

When ski season's over in the Northern Hemisphere, it's time to pack the gear and head for resorts in Argentina or Chile. In addition to marked trails, there's off-piste terrain, often with steep chutes and deep powder bowls, plus backcountry areas to try, and plenty for the beginner to intermediate skier as well. Those with strong skills could opt for heli-skiing on peaks reaching 13,600 feet as condors soar above. Many of the resorts exude a European ambience with a lively nightlife scene. The tour operators mentioned below have created all-inclusive ski packages covering airport/hotel and hotel/ski-mountain transfers, accommodations, two meals daily, and lift tickets for a number of mountains and resorts in both Argentina and Chile; many packages combine the two countries. Costs vary with the accommodations selected. Prices quoted are per person in a double; costs are even lower if four people share a room. Less expensive packages, while providing the services mentioned, generally are not guided tours. Eight-day guided packages start around $1,795.

CHILE **Season:** June–October.

Locations: Pucón; Chapelco; Villarrica Volcano.

Cost: From $730 for a seven-day nonguided inclusive package from Santiago.

Tour Operators: PowderQuest; Snoventures.

Overview: At the small resort of Pucón, on the edge of Lago Villarrica, ski on the side of Chile's most active volcano. You can hike to the crater to gaze at molten magma, then ski or snowboard back down. Bordering two national parks, Pucón offers great snowshoeing as well as rafting and caving. PowderQuest and Snoventures offer inclusive packages. Ski weeks without guides run in the $730 to $800 range. PowderQuest's main focus is guided tours of eight to 16 days with time spent at as many as seven resorts in both Argentina and Chile.

ARGENTINA **Season:** June–October.

Locations: Catedral Bariloche; Cerro Bayo; Chapelco; National Park Nahuel Huappi; Lake District; La Hoya-Esquel; Las Leñas.

Cost: From $880 for an eight-day nonguided inclusive package from Buenos Aires.

Tour Operators: PowderQuest Tours; Snoventures.

Overview: Argentina's Bariloche, an alpine-style resort town nicknamed "Little Switzerland," is 13 km (8 mi) from the slopes of Cerro Catedral. This ski area offers more than 1,500 skiable acres with 105 km (65 mi) of trails and is a good choice for skiers of all levels. Your lift ticket is valid for skiing both at Catedral and the adjacent resort of Robles. Also accessed by a flight to Bariloche, the ski center of Cerro Bayo on the northwestern tip of Lake Nahuel Huapi is generally not crowded and offers steep powder runs and excellent backcountry hiking. Some packages combine Catedral, Cerro Bayo, and La Hoya; the latter is a resort near the town of Esquel where easy hikes lead to steep bowls and chutes, some reaching 60 degrees.

With 56 km (35 mi) of downhill trails and a vertical drop of 4,000 feet, plus more than 100 couloirs (steep gullies) and vast off-piste and backcountry areas, Las Leñas is considered by many to be South America's premier ski destination. Between Bariloche and Las Leñas near the resort town of San Martín de los Andes, Chapelco offers challenges for skiers and riders at all levels. The mountain claims a high-speed quad, a gondola, and access to great backcountry bowls. PowderQuest and Snoventures have multiple offerings for all ski destinations mentioned. Many of their packages combine stays at two or more ski areas.

SPECIALTY TOUR ITINERARIES

BIRD-WATCHING TOURS

CHILE **Seasons:** October–November.

Locations: Isla Grande; Chiloé National Park; Punta Arenas; Torres del Paine; Lake District; Antillanca.

Cost: From $6,500 for 18 days from Santiago.

Tour Operators: Focus Tours; WINGS.

Overview: Chile spans a number of distinctive vegetational and altitudinal zones, ensuring a varied and abundant avian population. WINGS's itinerary covers the country from Tierra del Fuego to the Atacama Desert in the north, also spending time in the Lake District around Puerto Montt. Focus Tours offers custom programs to Chiloé or to the Lake District to view the impressive Magellanic woodpecker, torrent duck, and Chilean pintail among other species. In Torres del Paine, guests look for lesser (Darwin's) rhea, Andean condor, ashy-headed goose, and the Magellanic woodpecker.

ARGENTINA **Season:** November–December.

Locations: Los Glaciares National Park; Perito Moreno Glacier; Ushuaia; Tierra del Fuego National Park; Martial Glacier.

Cost: From $6,380 for 16 days from Buenos Aires.

Tour Operators: Focus Tours; Victor Emanuel Nature Tours; WINGS.

Overview: In Patagonia expect to see a great variety of species, including many endemics. Focus Tours offers custom tours to the Valdés Peninsula to look for white-chinned and giant petrels, rock, guanay and king cormorants, the striking black-browed albatross, blackish and American oystercatchers, Antarctic skua, the yellow-billed subspecies of sandwich tern, and others. A side trip south to Punta Tombo includes a visit to one of the largest Magellanic penguin colonies, with a population of around 1.5 million. The company also offers itineraries to El Calafate and Los Glaciares National Park to look for the Andean condor, black-chested buzzard eagle, and rare birds such as the Patagonian tinamou, great shrike-tyrant, and bronze-winged (spectacled) duck. Victor Emanuel offers a program that focuses on the scrub desert and rolling grasslands of southwest Patagonia and Tierra del Fuego with a boat trip on the Beagle Channel that promises albatrosses, petrels, and penguins. WINGS takes guests from the subtropical forests around Iguazú Falls to the sub-Antarctic islands of Tierra del Fuego and Los Glaciares National Park to see Perito Moren Glacier and search for a variety of birds from seed-snipe to sierra-finches.

NATURAL HISTORY

Programs provide insight into the importance and fragility of South America's ecological treasures. The itineraries mentioned below take in the deserts, glaciers, rain forests, mountains, and rivers of this continent, as well as the impressive variety of its wildlife.

Season: October–April.

Locations: Lake District; Los Glaciares National Park; Perito Moreno Glacier, Argentina. Torres del Paine; Osorno Volcano, Chile.

Cost: From $1,860 for nine days from Buenos Aires, Argentina.

Tour Operators: Abercrombie & Kent; Adventure Life; Big Five Tours & Expeditions; ElderTreks; G.A.P. Adventures; Geographic Expeditions; Inca; Journeys International; Myths and Mountains; Nature Expeditions International; Off the Beaten Path; PanAmerican Travel; South American Journeys; Southwind Adventures; Wilderness Travel; Wildland Adventures; World Expeditions; Zegrahm Expeditions.

Overview: You'll view the glaciers of Los Glaciares National Park where the Moreno Glacier towers 20 stories high, the soaring peaks of Torres del Paine, the fjords of the Chilean coast, and a Magellanic penguin colony. Most itineraries spend time in the Lake District, and a few visit Alerce Andino National Park and Osorno Volcano. Many programs include day walks and, often, a one- to three-day cruise. Several operators feature a stay at a ranch, *Estancia Helsingfors,* on Lago Viedma. Abercrombie & Kent has a "Fire and Ice" itinerary, combining the deep south with the arid zone of northern Chile's Atacama Desert.

PHOTO SAFARIS

A benefit of photo tours is the amount of time spent at each place. Whether the subject is a rarely spotted animal, a breathtaking waterfall, or villagers in traditional dress, you get a chance to focus both your camera and your mind on the scene. Professional photographers who offer instruction lead the tours listed below. Only consider these trips if you're serious about improving your photographic skills; otherwise, you might find the pace maddeningly slow.

PATAGONIA **Season:** March–April.

Locations: Central Patagonia; Los Glaciares National Park, Argentina. Torres del Paine National Park, Chile.

Cost: From $3,495 for 12 days from Santiago.

Tour Operators: Joseph Van Os Photo Safaris; Myths and Mountains.

Overview: Timed for vibrant fall colors among ice fields, snowcapped mountains, glaciers, and rushing streams, Joseph Van Os has 12- and 13-day departures during Patagonian fall (the Northern Hemisphere's spring). While one trip visits the famed sites of Torres del Paine and Los Glaciares National Parks, the second concentrates on lesser-known regions, such as the Cavernas de Mármol, or Marble Caves. Led by photographer Bill Chapman, Myths and Mountains offers a 15-day program combining Torres del Paine National Park with the desolation and *moais* (giant stone statues) of Easter Island.

ANTARCTIC **Season:** October; February.

Locations: Antarctic Peninsula; Falkland, South Georgia, and South Orkney islands.

Cost: From $8,495 for 16 days from Ushuaia, Argentina.

Tour Operators: Joseph Van Os Photo Safaris; Lindblad Expeditions.

Overview: Photograph seabirds, Adélie and gentoo penguin colonies, albatross nesting areas, elephant and fur seals, plus the spectacular landscapes of the Antarctic. With Joseph Van Os, you'll travel aboard the helicopter-carrying icebreaker, *Kapitan Khlebnikov.* A high point of this trip is the chance to cruise the Weddell Sea and visit the Snow Hill colony of emperor penguins where some 4,000 breeding pairs are found. Lindblad Expeditions has a one 25-day program where you can learn in the field with nature photographer Tom Mangelsen.

CRUISING & LAND TOUR COMPANY PROFILES

As beautiful as it is vast, it's practically impossible to see everything Patagonia has to offer in one visit. It's not surprising that there are hundreds of companies out there that offer various ways to explore, be it land-based touring, sea-cruising, or a combination of both.

While the list below hardly exhausts the number of reputable companies, these were chosen because they're established firms that offer a good selection of itineraries in Patagonia.

The following company profiles are organized by large cruise lines, boutique cruises, companies that combine land and sea, and those companies that are land based. For each cruise line, we list only the ships (grouped by similar configurations) that regularly cruise in Patagonia.

THE MAJOR CRUISE LINES

Celebrity Cruises. Fjords, glaciers, and emerald lakes are the highlight of a cruise down the west coast of Chile. Upon reaching Ushuaia in Argentina, you'll be surrounded by snowcapped mountains rising out of the sea. En route to the Falkland Islands, there will be sightings of penguins, seabirds, sea lions, and whales. The trip ends in Buenos Aires via Montevideo. **Departs:** Valparaíso, Chile or Buenos Aires, Argentina. **Ships:** The 965-foot-long *Infinity* is all prestige and elegance—think polished marble, etched glass, and wood furnishings. It accommodates 2,046 passengers and features Broadway-like shows, sumptuous meals, a spa menu inspired by exotic rituals, and an expansive library. **Route(s):** Buenos Aires, Montevideo, Puerto Madryn, Port Stanley, Falkland Islands, Cape Horn, Chile, Ushuaia, Punta Arenas, Strait Of Magellan, Chilean Fjords, Puerto Montt, Valparaíso. ☎ *800/647–2251* ⊕ *www.celebrity.com.*

Fred.Olsen Cruise Lines. This British company prides itself on being intimate, friendly, and catering to retired couples. During the 23-day cruise from Buenos Aires to Lima guests are introduced to the Argentine capital, tour the Falklands to explore battlefields or meet islanders over a pint of bitter, and spend considerable time exploring the untamed Chilean fjords. **Departs:** Buenos Aires, Argentina. **Ships:** Bright and airy, the *Boudicca* carries up to 850 passengers in 437 cabins. **Route(s):** Puerto Madryn, Port Stanley, Cape Horn, Ushuaia, Punta Arenas, Chilean Fjords, Puerto Montt, Valparaíso, and Coquimbo. The last stop is Lima, Peru. ☎ *800/843–0602* ⊕ *www.fredolsencruises.com.*

Holland America Line. This award-winning cruise line sails with nearly one crew member for every two guests and offers impeccable service, gourmet dining, and modern design that appeal to a well-heeled clientele. Their 16-day South America Explorer focuses mainly on the Chilean Patagonia side. Shore excursions include visits to a penguin rookery in Stanley, an alpine drive in the heart of the Tierra del Fuego mountain range, and kayaking in Chile's Lake District. **Departs:** Rio de Janeiro, Brazil or Valparaíso, Chile. **Ships:** The MS *Rotterdam,* 780 feet in length, sails at 25 knots and can accommodate up to 1,316 guests. **Route(s):** Rio, Buenos Aires, Montevideo, Falkland Islands, Cape Horn, Ushuaia, Punta Arenas, Puerto Montt, Valparaíso. ☎ *877/724–5425* ⊕ *www.hollandamerica.com.*

Norwegian Cruise Line. NCL offers affordable two-week "freestyle cruisings" around the tip of South America. This line appeals to guests who don't like to follow rules or keep schedules—think young couples and hip thirtysomethings traveling solo who might decide at the last minute to visit a penguin colony in Stanley or ride aboard a steam engine–driven train to Tierra del Fuego National Park. **Departs:** Valparaíso,

Chile or Buenos Aires, Argentina. **Ships:** *Norwegian Dream,* 754 feet in length and featuring 10 decks, accommodates 1,748 passengers. **Route(s):** Buenos Aires, Montevideo, Puerto Madryn, Stanley, Ushuaia, Punta Arenas, Strait of Magellan, Chilean Fjords, Puerto Chacabuco, Puerto Montt, Valparaíso. ☎*800/327–7030* ⊕*www.ncl.com.*

Oceania Cruises. These cruises are as relaxed and elegant as a private country club—mahogany décor, plush carpeting and grand, sweeping staircases. Highlights of your Patagonia or Antarctica cruise will likely include English afternoon tea on a private island in the Falklands, and cruising by snowcapped peaks and jagged glaciers while the captain shares age-old tales of dogged whalers. **Departs:** Rio de Janeiro, Brazil, Buenos Aires, Argentina or Valparaíso, Chile. **Ships:** The 594-foot-long *Insignia* can accommodate up to 684 passengers and 386 crew members. **Route(s):** Buenos Aires, Montevideo, Punta del Este, Puerto Madryn, Ushuaia, Punta Arenas, Puerto Montt, Valparaíso. ☎*800/254–5067* ⊕*www.oceaniacruiseline.com.*

Fodor'sChoice **Princess Cruises.** During a 12-day cruise that includes eight ports of
★ call, you'll have the opportunity to partake in an authentic Chilean rodeo, a canopy-gliding tour at Osorno Volcano in Chile, kayaking in Chile's Lake District, and a four-wheel-drive safari to Volunteer Point to visit a colony of king penguins. A Connoisseur Voyage adds additional days to your trip and lets you further explore the Antarctica Peninsula, Cape Horn, or Ushuaia. **Departs:** Santiago, Chile, or Buenos Aires, Argentina. **Ships:** At 950 feet in length, the *Star Princess* accommodates 2,600 passengers and features an entire deck of minisuites and over 700 balcony staterooms. Amenities include 24-hour complimentary room service, afternoon tea, and 24-hour Internet. **Route(s):** Santiago, Puerto Montt, Pio XI Glacier, Punta Arenas, Ushuaia, Cape Horn, Falkland Islands, Montevideo, Buenos Aires. ☎*800/774–6237* ⊕*www.princess.com.*

Regent Seven Seas Cruises. This company attracts an upscale clientele who expect amenities such as butler and 24-hour room service. The Buenos Aires to Valparaíso cruise will have you visiting boutique wineries outside Montevideo, flying in a helicopter over the Falkland Islands, and visiting a colony of breeding elephant seals and Magellanic penguins. Other excursions include horseback riding in Ushuaia, and a chartered flight over the Drake Passage and across the ice fields of the vast White Continent. **Departs:** Buenos Aires and Ushuaia, Argentina. **Ships:** The world's first all-suite, all-balcony ship, the *Seven Seas Mariner* also offers dining by Le Cordon Bleu of Paris. At 709 feet in length, with eight guest decks, and maximum cruising speed of 20 knots, she caters to 700 guests, and has a staff-to-guest ratio of 1 to 1.6. **Route(s):** Buenos Aires, Montevideo, Puerto Madryn, Port Stanley, Ushuaia, Punta Arenas, Laguna San Rafael, Puerto Montt, Valparaíso. ☎*877/505–5370* ⊕*www.rssc.com.*

Seabourn Cruise Line. During their 19-day Patagonia Passage cruise you'll explore the emerald waterways and snowcapped volcanoes of Chile's Lake District; you'll spot dolphins and seals along the Chiloé

Archipelago; and sail past the majestic Pius XI glacier, a highlight of the Chilean fjords. Excursions include flying in a chartered airplane over the White Continent and boarding a catamaran to head off along the Beagle Channel for views of the mountain ranges rising from the sea, and past the historic Les Eclaireurs lighthouse, which marks the "end of the world." Your trip ends in Buenos Aires. **Departs:** Valparaíso, Chile. **Ships:** *Seabourn Pride* carries 208 passengers in über-elegance and comfort (think marble-clad baths, walk-in closets, flat-screen TVs). At 440 feet in length, she cruises at 16 knots, employs a crew of 164 and features a gym, card room, library, casino, business center, two lounges, a club, café, and restaurant. **Route(s):** Valparaíso, Puerto Montt, Castro, Puerto Chacabuco, Puerto Natales, Punta Arenas, Ushuaia, Camarones, Buenos Aires. ☎877/760–9052 ⊕*www.seabourn.com*.

Silversea Cruises. The 16-day voyage with luxurious Silversea will have you sailing up to the 200-foot-high face of the San Rafael glacier aboard a catamaran; learning about award-winning wines produced in Uruguay's Juanico region; visiting the Falkland battlefields with a local expert; exploring Deer Island, located in a fjord and crowned by glaciers and mountains; viewing the sea-wolf colony of Punta Loma; and visiting a sheep estancia in Puerto Madryn. **Departs:** Buenos Aires, Argentina. **Ships:** *Silver Cloud* offers the kind of six-star luxury you'd expect in an elite hotel. The vessel is 514 feet in length, sails at 20.5 knots and accommodates 296 guests and a crew of 212. **Route(s):** Buenos Aires, Montevideo, Punta del Este, Puerto Madryn, Punta Arenas, Ushuaia, Laguna San Rafael, Puerto Chacabuco, Puerto Montt, Santiago. ☎800/722–9955 ⊕*www.silversea.com*.

BOUTIQUE CRUISE & LAND COMBO TOURS

Boutique tour operators often offer what the major cruise lines cannot: personalized service and attention. At sea you might end up seeing or doing similar things as you would during a sailing on a big cruise. But during the land portion of these trips you'll have more chances to explore the region doing the activities you really like—be it mountain biking, horseback riding, or relaxing at a family-run estancia or lodge.

Abercrombie & Kent. A&K has been offering Antarctica adventures for more than a decade. Guests aboard the *Minerva* are treated to outside cabins and suites, all with private windows or portholes. The all-inclusive pricing means everything from meals, gratuities, and ashore expeditions is covered (read: no hidden costs when you disembark). **Who it's for:** Those who like a "non-cruise-ship" atmosphere that is unscripted, spontaneous, and fresh. **Highlights:** The chance to photograph penguins and nesting grounds of seabirds, and cruise iceberg-strewn passageways of spectacular beauty. **Departs:** Buenos Aires, Argentina and Santiago, Chile. **Ships:** *Minerva* (formerly called *Explorer II*) looks like a country-house hotel and accommodates 198 guests (but is designed for up to 300 passengers) and a crew of 146. She is equipped with retractable stabilizers that minimize side-to-side motion in potentially rough seas. **Route(s):** Buenos Aires, Ushuaia, Drake Passage, Elephant Island, South Shetland Islands, Deception Islands. ☎*630/954–2944 or 800/554–7016* ⊕*www.abercrombiekent.com.*

Adventure Center. Groups of 12–16 travelers explore Patagonia by land and sea, staying mainly in four-star boutique-style hotels and aboard the comfortable *Mare Australis.* **Who it's for:** Those who prefer traveling in small groups. **Highlights:** Cruising the labyrinthine archipelagos of the Chilean fjords and hopping on Zodiacs to discover more of the resident wildlife. **Departs:** Buenos Aires, Argentina or Santiago, Chile. **Ships:** M/V *Mare Australis* accommodates up to 130 passengers. **Route(s):** Buenos Aires, Ushuaia, and Tierra del Fuego followed by a four-day voyage along Beagle Channel to Cape Horn, the Chilean Fjords and Gunther Pluschow Glacier. Sail to Magdalena Island penguin colony; disembark at Punta Arenas and drive to Puerto Natales. Drive via Milodon Cave to Torres del Paine for an optional walk to Paine Towers or boat trip on Lake Grey. Drive to Calafate and visit Perito Moreno Glacier. Return to Buenos Aires. ☎*510/654–1879 or 800/227–8747* ⊕*www.adventurecenter.com.*

Adventure Life. They specialize in small-group tours that have a positive impact on the local culture and environment. Their Patagonia options are as varied as the terrain: you can secure crampons and trek a glacier, board a motor yacht and explore the fjords, or grab your packs and head for the towering spires of Chile's Torres del Paine. **Who it's for:** Eco-conscious travelers who enjoy camping and eating under the stars as much as a three-course meal at a local restaurant. **Highlights:** A picnic lunch sitting on the lateral moraine of Perito Moreno Glacier listening to its thunderous concerto of groaning and cracking ice dropping into the lake below. **Departs:** Buenos Aires, Argentina. **Ships:** M/V *Via Australis* accommodates 129 passengers. **Route(s):** El Calafate and Los Glaciares National Park with two nights at a historic hacienda. Overland journey to Torres del Paine in Chile to enjoy the sights of Grey Glacier and the Horns of Paine over fine Chilean wine. The trip ends by boarding the expedition ship *Via Australis* for a sea journey through the Strait of Magellan. ☎*406/541–2677 or 800/344–6118* ⊕*www.adventure-life.com.*

Big Five Tours & Expeditions. They offer everything from custom-designed private vacations to fully escorted special-interest groups; from engaging family-oriented tours to romantic honeymoons. Guests who partake in the 14-day Patagonia Explorer trip are treated to sumptuous meals paired with local wines and stays at designer hotels and resorts including Eolo Lodge, Explora Salto Chico, and Llao Llao. **Who it's for:** Soft-adventure travelers accustomed to comfort and style. **Highlights:** A catamaran crossing of Lake Nahuel Huapi. **Departs:** Buenos Aires, Argentina. **Route(s):** Buenos Aires, El Calafate, Torres del Paine, Punta Arenas, Puerto Varas, Andean lake crossing to Bariloche. ☎*772/287–7995 or 800/244–3483* ⊕*www.bigfive.com.*

Cruceros Australis. They promote and sell ship tickets for the Expedition Cruisers that sail the Magellan Strait and Beagle Channel. Cruceros

Australis offers three- or four-night programs from October to April. **Who it's for:** Travelers with limited time to explore the region. **Highlights:** Navigate through Beagle Channel to disembark near the Pia Glacier; penguin excursions; Cape Horn visit. **Departs:** Punta Arenas, Chile and Ushuaia, Argentina. **Ships:** *Mare Australis* and *Via Australis.* **Route(s):** Punta Arenas, Ainsworth Bay and Tucker Islet, Pia Glacier and Glacier Alley, Cape Horn, Wulaia Bay, Ushuaia. ☏*305/695–9618 or 877/678–3772* ⊕*www.australis.com.*

ElderTreks. This adventure travel company is designed for people 50 and over. Their 15-day Patagonia and the Lake Districts tour accommodates up to 16 guests and includes all meals and one domestic flight. The company also offers a Patagonia trekking trip. **Who it's for:** Active older travelers who prefer a mix of nature and culture. **Highlights:** Navigate by Zodiac along the Perito Moreno Glacier. **Departs:** Buenos Aires, Argentina. **Ships:** Zodiac boats. **Route(s):** Buenos Aires, Ushuaia, Beagle Channel, Tierra del Fuego National Park, Los Glaciares National Park, Perito Moreno Glacier, Torres del Paine National Park, Nordensjkold and Grey lakes, Puerto Natales, Puerto Varas, Laguna Verde, Valparaíso and Viña del Mar, Maipo Valley wine region, Santiago. ☏*416/588–5000 or 800/741–7956* ⊕*www.eldertreks.com.*

Explore! Worldwide. The 15-day Patagonia & Chilean fjords trip features a four-day expedition cruise hosted by specialist guides who take guests on shore excursions by Zodiac boats. Evenings aboard the ship offer a chance to take knot-tying lessons, cooking demonstrations, wine tastings and more. The land portion focuses on Tierra del Fuego and Torres del Paine, where accommodations are in small, unfussy ranch-style hotels and family-run lodges. **Who it's for:** Independent thirtysomething adventurers and families who enjoy simple meals and accommodations and some freedom to explore at their own pace. **Highlights:** A full-day excursion to Perito Moreno Glacier to watch as huge chunks of blue ice calve into the milky waters below. **Departs:** London, England or Buenos Aires, Argentina. **Ships:** M/V *Mare Australis* accommodates up to 130 passengers. **Route(s):** Buenos Aires, Ushuaia, a four-day sailing through Beagle Channel, past Cape Horn, into the Chilean fjords and to Punta Arenas, where the driving tour commences. The drive to Torres del Paine takes guests across the Patagonian Desert, to Calafate and Los Glaciares National Park, Perito Moreno Glacier and ends with a flight to Buenos Aires. ☏*0844/499–0901* ⊕*www.explore.co.uk.*

G.A.P. Adventures. Specializing in small-group outdoor adventure travel, this outfitter takes you off the beaten track to the heart of the destination. Expect anywhere from 12 to 18 travelers on the three-week Wild Patagonia adventure, an exploration of Chile's Lake District and Patagonia's towering fjords. **Who it's for:** Budget-conscious and adventurous spirits who prefer to experience a destination at a grass-roots level. **Highlights:** Spend two days exploring the Lake District of San Martín de los Andes, one of the most northern parts of Patagonia, during hikes, mountain-bike rides, and 4x4 excursions. **Departs:** Buenos Aires, Argentina. **Ships:** Ferry cruise ship. **Route(s):** Buenos Aires, San Martín de los Andes, Bariloche, Puerto Varas, ferry cruise of Chilean

Fjords, Puerto Natales, Torres del Paine, Perito Moreno, Buenos Aires. ☎416/260–0999 or 800/465–5600 ⊕www.gapadventures.com.

International Expeditions. One of the pioneers in environmentally responsible travel, IE aims to preserve the natural habitats they visit and to improve the welfare of local communities. Exploring on foot, by ship, and by vehicle, you visit the remote regions of Chile's Patagonia accompanied by naturalist guide Claudio Vidal, a native Chilean photographer and author of books on birds and penguins. **Who it's for:** Active travelers who take pleasure in relaxing by a crackling fire with a glass of merlot as much as walking a mile to snap the perfect photo of Austral parakeets. **Highlights:** A sail along the 15-mi-long Grey Glacier, the final tongue of the 300-mi-long Southern Patagonia Ice Field, and then a walk on 20,000-year-old ice before enjoying cocktails back on board. **Departs:** Santiago, Chile. **Ships:** *Alberto de Agostini* accommodates 80 passengers. **Route(s):** From Santiago, you fly into Punta Arenas and depart for Puerto Natales to watch Andean condors. Cruise through Last Hope Fjord and explore Torres Del Paine, Grey Glacier, Paine Waterfalls on foot. Returning to Punta Arenas, you stop at a private gaucho farm for lunch and continue on to the Otway Magellanic penguin colony. Fly back to Santiago. A three-day extension to the Chilean fjords aboard *Via Australis* includes exploring Cape Horn. ☎205/428–1700 or 800/633–4734 ⊕www.ietravel.com.

Lindblad Expeditions. Back in 1966, Lars-Eric Lindblad operated the first cruise to Antarctica and has since directed hundreds of expeditions to the region, all of which carry two National Geographic Society–supported penguin researchers. You'll kayak among icebergs and witness the raucous courtship behavior of penguins. **Who it's for:** Amateur environmentalists and eco-conscious types who appreciate traveling with the most experienced ice masters and expedition leaders. **Highlights:** Join penguin researchers in their ongoing studies and be entertained with stories of their work at dinnertime. **Departs:** Santiago, Chile. **Ships:** *National Geographic Endeavour* is 295 feet long and can hold 110 passengers, with a ratio of one staff member for every eight guests. **Route(s):** Santiago, Ushuaia, Antarctica, Elephant Island, South Orkney Island, South Georgia, Falkland Islands, Ushuaia, Santiago. ☎212/765–7740 or 800/397–3348 ⊕www.expeditions.com.

Mountain Travel-Sobek. During MTS's Patagonia Explorer trip, guests hike the trails of Los Glaciares and Paine national parks and take a relaxing shipboard cruise of the fjords and inlets of the honeycombed Chilean coastline, marvel at calving glaciers and snowcapped peaks, and come to appreciate (in the words of Herman Melville) "all the attending marvels of a thousand Patagonia sights and sounds." **Who it's for:** Anyone from the twentysomething solo traveler to retired couples and families interested in adrenaline-fueled activities. **Highlights:** Cruise through a maze of channels and fjords and up the Beagle Channel, stopping for walks near the Marinelli and Pia glaciers to visit an elephant seal colony and penguin rookeries. **Departs:** Santiago, Chile. **Ships:** *Mare Australis*—accommodates up to 130 passengers. **Route(s):** Santiago, Punta Arenas, Strait of Magellan, Beagle Channel, Cape

Horn National Park, Ushuaia, Calafate, Los Glaciares National Park, Punta Arenas, Santiago. ☎*510/594–6000 or 888/687–6235* ⊕*www. mtsobek.com.*

Quark Expeditions. One of the leading operators of polar expedition cruises aboard comfortable but powerful Russian polar icebreakers. **Who it's for:** They offer three ways to travel: Icebreaker Adventures take you to regions inaccessible to traditional expedition vessels, with aerial sightseeing by onboard helicopters; Active Adventures offer landings for camping, cross-country skiing, kayaking, overnight kayaking and mountaineering; and leisure travelers can opt for Adventures in Comfort, which explore the region at a more relaxed pace. **Highlights:** The Icebreaker Adventure takes you to an emperor penguin rookery while the chicks are very young. **Departs:** Ushuaia, Argentina. **Ships:** The Icebreaker Kapitan Khlebnikov is equipped with helicopters and Zodiacs for shore landings. Former research vessels *Professor Multanovskiy* and *Akademik Shokalskiy* accommodate up to 50 guests each. *Lyubov Orlova* (110 guests) and *Ocean Nova* (82 guests) are Expedition Ships that provide softer adventures in a comfortable environment. **Route(s):** The 11-day Classic Antarctica itinerary sails from Ushuaia through the Drake Passage, to the Antarctic Peninsula and South Shetland Islands before returning to Ushuaia. ☎*203/656–0499 or 800/356–5699* ⊕*www.quarkexpeditions.com.*

Travcoa. This luxury outfitter offers escorted, custom journeys and private-jet expeditions. **Who it's for:** Active adventure travelers who expect the best in comfort. **Highlights:** Taking a swim in the thermally heated seawater at Deception Island. **Departs:** Buenos Aires, Argentina. **Ships:** The *Clipper Adventurer* is equipped with stabilizers and an ice-hardened hull, ideal for navigating Antarctica's rugged environment. At 328 feet, the ship accommodates 122 guests and features a 2:1 passenger-to-crew ratio. **Route(s):** Buenos Aires, Ushuaia, Falkland Islands, Drake Passage, Antarctic Peninsula, Deception Island, Brown Bluff, Paradise Bay, Elephant Island, Ushuaia, El Calafate, Buenos Aires. ☎*949/476–2800 or 800/992–2003* ⊕*www.travcoa.com.*

Wilderness Travel. Knowledgeable guides lead journeys at an appropriate pace while accommodations are in well-located inns that offer the opportunity to meet locals and make off-the-beaten-path discoveries. Their lodge-based adventure, In Patagonia, takes guests to the granite and glacier worlds of Paine and Fitzroy, Tierra del Fuego, and the Beagle Channel by Zodiac. **Who it's for:** Travelers who like to take it slow, even when hiking four to six hours. **Highlights:** Exploring the massive Perito Moreno Glacier by boat and on foot. **Departs:** Buenos Aires, Argentina. **Ships:** Zodiac boats. **Route(s):** Buenos Aires, Ushuaia, Los Glaciares National Park, Perito Moreno, Lago Argentino, Paine National Park, Grey Glacier, Punta Arenas. ☎*510/558–2488 or 800/368–2794* ⊕*www.wildernesstravel.com.*

Wildland Adventures. Authentic travel is this outfitter's priority and they help you choose the right trip and itinerary that meets your personal style and interests. During their 14-day adventure, In the Wake of Magellan: Patagonia by Land & Sea, guests are led by naturalist guides in the national parks and then embark on a five-day voyage through the Strait of Magellan and the Beagle Channel. **Who it's for:** Soft-adventure travelers and families who appreciate being guided by locals. **Highlights:** Hike on guanaco trails though Patagonian steppe to the spectacular Salto Grande waterfall in Torres del Paine. **Departs:** Santiago, Chile. **Ships:** *Mare Australis* accommodates up to 129 passengers. **Route(s):** Santiago, Punta Arenas, Milodon Cave and Torres del Paine, Grey Glacier, Ainsworth Bay, Marinelli Glacier, Brookes Glacier, Pia Glacier, Cape Horn, Puerto Williams, Ushuaia, El Calafate. ☎*206/365–0686 or 800/345–4453* ⊕*www.wildland.com.*

BOUTIQUE LAND TOURS

Alpine Ascents International. This mountaineering school offers two alpine journeys: skiing the South Pole's Mount Vinson, and a Patagonia mountaineering course for fit beginners. It's for fit beginners, those looking to enhance their skills as well as experienced climbers. **Specialty:** Getting you to the top. This company claims a summit success rate of 98%. ☎*206/378–1927* ⊕*www.AlpineAscents.com.*

American Alpine Institute. AAI's philosophy is to teach people to become self-sufficient climbers and skiers. They offer three trips in Patagonia, which are generally limited to 35 to 60 beginner to intermediate hikers: an expedition across portions of the huge ice cap of southern Patagonia; a thorough exploration of Cerro Torre and Fitzroy massifs while viewing exotic wildlife from lakeside camps; and a trek through the dramatic peaks and pastoral lakes of Torres del Paine. Expert guides provide meals in the mountains, climbing equipment, and admissions to museums and national parks. New in 2008 is a five-day trek from Paso Viento to Paso Huemul with a side trip that visits the Ice Cap for a day. **Specialty:** Rock, snow, ice, glacier, and high-altitude climbing. ☎*360/671–1505* ⊕*www.aai.cc.*

Andes Adventures. Led by local bilingual guides with in-depth knowledge of the culture and history of the region, this company features all-inclusive trips for 12 to 20 participants. The Patagonia Hiking Adventure explores the three national parks in the region (Torres del Paine, Los Glaciares, and Tierra del Fuego) with hikes to the base of the Towers of Paine, Cerro Torre, and Fitzroy. During the trip you'll tour Punta Arenas, Ushuaia, and Buenos Aires, and spot penguins, guanacos, flamingos, and other wildlife. You'll like these trips if your days at hostels may be over, but you still enjoy traveling in a group, eating simple but hearty meals, and staying in rustic mountain lodgings with shared bathrooms. **Specialty:** Their running adventures are geared for fit adventurers who can comfortably run 10–15 mi in rolling terrain. ☎*310/395–5265 or 800/289–9470* ⊕*www.andesadventures.com.*

BikeHike Adventures. Focusing on small-group, multisport adventures, this company can customize a dream trip for as few as two travelers. They also attract single travelers (75% on most trips) who are okay with sharing a room (with someone of the same sex). Accommodations are in small, family-run hotels and idyllic camping sites. The action-packed trips take place in Chile's Lake District with biking, hiking, rafting, kayaking, and horseback riding; in Torres del Paine for seven days of mostly hiking; and 12 days of the Best of Patagonia, in both Chile and Argentina, combining hikes, bike rides, paddles, and ice treks. Depending on the trip you choose, you will also see Perito Moreno Glacier, Grey Glacier, Puerto Montt, Osorno Volcano and Los Glaciares National Park. **Specialty:** Multisport adventures for social types. ☎604/731–2442 or 888/805–0061 ⊕ *www.bikehike.com.*

Boojum Expeditions. Gaucho, or cowboy, culture is the focus of their Patagonia trip, which takes nine experienced horseback riders across private parks and Nahuel Huapi National Park in Bariloche, Argentina. From base camps, riders explore rugged, steep mountains, cross rivers teeming with trout, and stop for lunchtime asados (local speak for barbecue). Fishermen can have a go in the cold streams while others view wildlife and chat around a campfire. All land transport, hotel in Bariloche, camping gear and tents, horses and tack, wranglers, guides, and meals are included. You'll see red deer, condors, guanacos, and rheas. **Specialty:** Horseback riding with gauchos on Criollo horses. ☎406/587–0125 or 800/287–0125 ⊕ *www.boojum.com.*

Butterfield & Robinson. Well-heeled travelers with B&R trade in their Chanel coats for North Face fleece jackets; they hike between wine tastings and meals at Michelin-starred restaurants; and rest their weary heads at super-luxe hotels. During their Patagonia Walking tour, guests check out the rare and unusual trees of the Bosque de Arrayanes, strap on crampons for an ice climb in Perito Moreno Glacier, hike in Torres del Paine, and enjoy a glass of great local wine while taking in spectacular glacier views from a hotel room at Los Notros in Los Glaciares National Park. **Specialty:** Taking it slow during walking and biking trips. ☎416/864–1354 or 866/551–9090 ⊕ *www.butterfield.com.*

Country Walkers. After spending time in Buenos Aires and Mendoza, guests head to Argentina's spectacular Lake District. Parque Nacional Nahuel Huapi, with its emerald-green lakes flanked by snowcapped peaks, is an extraordinary walking destination of rare woodlands with Arrayán trees. Days end at boutique hotels and lakeside inns with meals featuring regional cuisine and wines. In Chile, the 11-day trip focuses on the Lake District, Chiloé Island, a onetime Spanish colonial outpost, as well as Patagonia's fjords, glacial lakes, and pampas. **Specialty:** Walking on easy to moderate terrain, superb accommodations, and good food. ☎802/244–1387 or 800/464–9255 ⊕ *www.country walkers.com.*

Doug McClelland's FlyFishingAnd. A trip with this company will have guests fishing for large rainbows and browns with views of majestic mountains, volcanoes, and glaciers. Accommodations are at two fishing lodges near Bariloche, where local guides steer participants to the best rivers. Trip includes ground transfers, all meals, four days of guided fishing and two days of nonfishing activities, including bird-watching, hiking, riding, and sightseeing. **Specialty:** The chance to catch a trophy fish. ⊕*www.flyfishingand.com.*

Dragoman Overland. Their Overland to Tierra del Fuego journey takes guests from Santiago to Ushuaia. In between, travelers discover Chile's vineyards and valleys, the stunning Chilean and Argentine Lake Districts, the glaciated lands of national parks, and Perito Moreno Glacier during a full-day guided trip. Highlights include trekking up through the snow and ice to the summit of Volcano Villarrica and relaxing in the hot pools near Pucón. This company is represented in North America by Adventure Center (⇨*above*). **Specialty:** Freedom and flexibility for budget-conscious and young travelers. ⊕*www.dragoman.com.*

Earth River Expeditions. Using a combination of sea kayaks and hiking, guests with this company explore rarely visited areas of Chile's Patagonia, such as the Futaleufú River for Class IV and V rapids. Accommodations are in private riverfront camps that feature swimming holes, hand-hewn wooden cliff dwellings, cliff-side hot tubs, and a masseuse. Trips include rafting training camp, meals, and transportation. **Specialty:** White-water rafting and multisport trips in the rapids of Patagonia. ☎*845/626–2665 or 800/643–2784* ⊕*www.earthriver.com.*

Equitours. During this company's Patagonia Frontier Trek, guests visit three working estancias where the riding is fast, the distances long, and the views vast. During rides guests see red deer, guanacos, and South American rheas roaming the vast grasslands. The Glacier Camping Ride in Chile offers the opportunity to traverse the Torres del Paine Park, with views of snowcapped mountains towering above. **Specialty:** Horseback riding while immersing in the local traditions and cuisine. ☎*307/455–3363 or 800/545–0019* ⊕*www.equitours.com.*

Exodus. The MO at this company is getting below the surface when exploring the people, wildlife, culture, and scenery of a place. During their Patagonia Highlights trip, guests go to the wild, mountainous south of Argentina, with its rugged, snowy mountains fringed by huge lakes and windswept grasslands inhabited only by shy guanacos and a few hardy gauchos tending sheep. Other trips focus on the Lake Districts of Chile and Argentina, trekking Fitzroy and Paine and crossing Tierra del Fuego. This company is represented in North America by Adventure Center (⇨*above*). ⊕*www.exodustravel.com.*

Experience Plus!. This biking outfitter offers five different tours that allow all types of riders an opportunity to explore Argentina and Chile and get off the beaten path in Patagonia. Their 18-day ExpeditionPlus! Coast to Coast trip begins on the Island of Chiloé off the Pacific coast of Chile and travels across the Andes and Argentina to the Atlantic. Guests use mountain-bike frames for this trip and install knobby tires for part of the ride, switching to slicks when they hit the pavement. Their eight-day Pedaling the Andes trip begins in Bariloche and takes guests through the magnificent Lake District. **Specialty:** In Patagonia, their trips are all about mountain biking off the beaten path. ☎*970/484–8489 or 800/685–4565* ⊕*www.ExperiencePlus.com.*

Fishing International. Accompanied by an bilingual guide, guests explore the hills, canyons, forests, pampas, and waters of the estancias. The all-inclusive fly-fishing programs take care of lodge transfers, all meals paired with fine Argentine wines, two massages per day, a tango show, guides, transportation to/from fishing areas, and fishing license. **Specialty:** Fly-fishing, river, stream, creek, lake and lagoon fishing. ☎707/542–4242 or 800/950–4242 ⊕www.fishinginternational.com.

FishQuest. This outfitter helps guests plan their trip and organize travel arrangements. They'll tell you what tackle to bring, what to leave home, and how to dress for angling in Patagonia. Accommodations are in private guest ranches where experienced local guides lead custom-tailored fishing and hunting excursions. Packages include all meals and drinks, daily guided fishing, and ground transportation from airports to the ranches. **Specialty:** Wade fishing and float fishing for trout and salmon in streams, rivers, and lakes. ☎706/896–1403 or 888/891–3474 ⊕www.fishquest.com.

Focus Tours. English-speaking naturalists guide all of this company's birding tours. They also carry the equipment: a spotting telescope, tape recorder and microphone to bring rare animals into view, and a powerful spotlight for night viewing. A checklist of the birds, mammals, reptiles, and amphibians of each area they tour, with common English and Latin names, helps participants keep track and learn the animals they see. They offer custom tours to the Valdés Peninsula, El Calafate, Tierra del Fuego, Bariloche, and Chile's Lake District. **Specialty:** Wildlife- and bird-watching tours. ☎505/989–7193 ⊕www.focustours.com.

Frontiers. Travel counselors help design and execute deluxe travel arrangements for well-heeled clientele. In Patagonia, that means staying at the luxurious Explora Salto Chico lodge in Chile's Torres del Paine National Park for ice trekking, hiking, and cruising the Lake District. ☎724/935–1577 or 800/245–1950 ⊕www.frontierstravel.com.

Gecko's. This outfitter's trips are aimed at younger independent travelers who seek the freedom of backpacking without the hassles. Their 12-day Antarctica adventure starts and ends in Ushuaia, with crossings through the Beagle Channel and Drake Passage, and features activities ashore on the Antarctic Peninsula and South Shetland Islands and informative presentations. This company is represented in North America by Adventure Center (⇨*above*). **Specialty:** Affordable adventures led by local guides. ⊕www.geckosadventures.com.

Geographic Expeditions. Expect accommodations in superb hotels and estancias, intimate group sizes, and leaders intimate with the corners of Patagonia. Travelers hike among the astounding granite monoliths, forests, and blue lakes of the Torres del Paine and Fitzroy. Tours farther afield go to the Aysén Glacier region in Chile, kayaking in the Pumalín Reserve, and fishing in Lago Yungue in Bariloche. **Specialty:** Luxurious private itineraries. ☎415/922–0448 or 800/777–8183 ⊕www.geoex.com.

Global Adventure Guide. During their 12-day Argentina Mountain Biking tour, which begins in Bariloche and is ideal for intermediate bikers, guests cross the Andes twice, mostly on gravel roads and trails. Guests ride across Los Lagos, a region featuring snow-covered volcanoes, embedded in a vast plain with countless lakes, partly covered in thick rain forest. An escort vehicle assists with luggage and shuttling exhausted riders. At the end of the tour participants can explore the rough landscape of Los Glaciares National Park. **Specialty:** Graded mountain-bike tours tailored to people of all ages. ☎800/732–0861 ⊕www.globaladventureguide.com.

Hidden Trails. Led by nature lovers who love horses, this company's trips let guests gallop across endless pampas, forging rivers, cantering through forests, trotting along age-old trails, and gazing at beautiful vistas. Rates include accommodations, meals, an English-speaking guide, and daily activities. Guests range from 30 to 60 years old and encompass a good mix of single travelers and couples. **Specialty:** Horseback-riding vacations for riders of all levels. ☎604/323–1141 or 888/987–2457 ⊕www.hiddentrails.com.

Inca. This outfitter offers three Patagonia itineraries, each highlighting a different aspect of Patagonia but all including four days in Torres del Paine at the deluxe Explora Salto Chico lodge. Patagonia, The Wild South includes a cruise through the Strait of Magellan aboard the *Mare Australis* to see elephant seals, penguins, seabirds, and glaciers. During the Patagonia Spring trip, you'll witness the annual migration of whales, learn to tango in Buenos Aires, and enjoy a minitrek on Perito Moreno Glacier. Their Christmas in Patagonia escape includes a night in Santiago, seeing nesting penguins in Punta Arenas, and spending a week of horseback riding, hiking, and enjoying spa treatments at Explora in Chile. ☎510/420–1550 ⊕www.inca1.com.

Joseph Van Os Photo Safaris. The Patagonia tour focuses on panoramic landscape and wildlife imagery. The journey takes place during the Patagonian autumn, when beech forests provide a fiery multihued contrast to the landscape and the tumultuous weather offers a wide range of dramatic lighting situations. Participants shoot in the mountainous Los Glaciares National Park, with outstanding photo opportunities at the Fitzroy Massif and Cerro Torre, and spend days at the foot of the peaks of the "Towers" and "Horns" of Torres del Paine National Park. **Specialty:** In-depth photo explorations led by professionals. ☎206/463–5383 ⊕www.photosafaris.com.

Journeys International. Trips, which may be combined with Antarctic cruises, offer opportunities to hike, kayak, climb on a glacier, and get up close to penguins. In Chile, they offer a nine-day Torres del Paine trek suitable for active travelers able to make demanding hikes of five to six hours per day. In Argentina, they offer a two-week Patagonia Nature Safari that begins in Buenos Aires and travels along the Atlantic coast to Bahia Bustamante, for bird-watching, sailing, trekking, and mountain biking. Guests venture to Gaiman, a traditional Welsh village, the Valdés Peninsula, Tierra del Fuego National Park, and Los

Glaciares National Park, including a trek on Perito Moreno Glacier. ☎*734/665–4407 or 800/255–8735* ⊕*www.journeys-intl.com.*

KE Adventure Travel. In Chile, KE offers a moderate trekking holiday exploring Torres del Paine and Fitzroy, with eco-camp accommodations, sightseeing in Santiago, and ice trekking on Perito Moreno. Their more demanding 60-mi Paine Circuit trip involves six days of continuous hiking, by way of several lakeside camps and the remote John Garner Pass. It includes a support team of packhorses, porters, and most meals. **Specialty:** Mountain trekking. KE also organizes tailor-made private expeditions, trips for school groups, and charity treks. ☎*970/384–0001 or 800/497–9675* ⊕*www.keadventure.com.*

Ladatco Tours. Offers more than 35 years of experience planning and operating tours in South America. In Patagonia they offer eight different programs, which vary from a two-day journey crossing the Lake District, from Puerto Montt to Bariloche, and exploring the Inland Fjords of Chile, known for pristine forests, lakes, and national parks, to exploring Tierra del Fuego and Los Glaciares National Park in Argentina. They can tailor a trip that follows your wish list. ☎*305/854–8422 or 800/327–6162* ⊕*www.ladatco.com.*

Mountain Madness. During their Patagonia Exploration trip, participants enjoy trekking, glacier hiking, and kayaking with breathtaking views of wild granite spires, pristine lakes, and powerful rivers. Guests are treated to porter-supported trekking, hiking three to seven hours a day at moderate elevations and walking 4–12 mi a day in Torres del Paine and Los Glaciares Park. Cost includes meals, park entrance fees, airport transfers, group gear for trekking, ice climbing, and kayaking. **Specialty:** Multisport adventures for active travelers. ☎*206/937–8389 or 800/328–5925* ⊕*www.mountainmadness.com.*

Myths and Mountains. Offering 10-day trips to either Argentina or Chile, this company takes care of the details. Group size is 6–10 guests; average age is 45. In Argentina, guests hike and canoe in Tierra del Fuego National Park, navigate the massive ice blocks aboard a Zodiac boat in Los Glaciares National Park, and hike the beech forests of El Mirador del Beagle in Ushuaia. The base in Chile is Torres del Paine National Park, where guests choose from a number of hikes and horseback rides, and explore the Blue Lagoon. ☎*775/832–5454 or 800/670–6984* ⊕*www.mythsandmountains.com.*

Nature Expeditions International. This outfitter specializes in low-intensity adventures tailored for active, healthy persons over 40. NEI also offers plenty of cultural or sightseeing excursions. Highlights of their Journey to Patagonia and The Southern Cone trips include a private tango lesson, glacier cruising and hiking in Los Glaciares National Park, hiking near a penguin colony, bicycling, and white-water rafting or horseback riding in Bariloche's Lake District. Also included are lectures on Patagonia's wildlife, Patagonia historical expeditions, wine tasting and more. ☎*954/693–8852 or 800/869–0639* ⊕*www.naturexp.com.*

Off the Beaten Path. OBP provides custom journeys for independent travelers and guided group journeys for those who prefer traveling with a small group. The Exploring Patagonia tour focuses on hiking, glacier treks, and horseback riding in Fitzroy, Perito Moreno Glacier, and Torres del Paine. Highlights include horseback riding with gauchos across the vast pampas of El Chaltén and crossing the Andes between Chile and Argentina via buses and boats. ☎406/586–1311 or 800/445–2995 ⊕www.offthebeatenpath.com.

PanAmerican Travel Services After getting to know a client over the phone and through e-mail, this company's travel advisors sketch an itinerary and come up with a travel plan. Every trip is unique, varying by destination, choice of accommodations, season, and activities. In Patagonia, that might mean a fly-fishing adventure in the Futaleufú River, and a visit to Chiloé Island. **Specialty:** Custom-tailored itineraries. ☎801/364–4300 or 800/364–4359 ⊕www.panamtours.com.

PowderQuest Tours. Ski trips are led by expert, bilingual guides, who get you there safely and introduce you to the local culture. Ski Patagonia tours focus on the charming Argentine ski towns of Bariloche, San Martín, and Villa La Angostura and backcountry hut-to-hut guided ski tours in Nahuel Huapi Park in Argentina's Lake District. **Specialty:** Guided backcountry ski adventures deep in Argentina's Patagonia. ☎206/203–6065 or 888/565–7158 ⊕www.powderquest.com.

Rod & Reel Adventures. Their one-week fly-fishing adventure and ecotourism expedition program accommodates a maximum of 18 fishing guests and 10 nonfishing guests aboard a ship designed for the area. The ship journeys through gentle fjords and channels, through untouched natural parks and reserves. Guests fish for brown trout, brook trout, rainbows, salmon, steelhead and a few other species. **Specialty:** Fly fishing adventures. ☎541/349–0777 or 800/356–6982 ⊕www.rodreeladventures.com.

Snoventures. To plan your ideal skiing or boarding holiday, Snoventures works directly with the Chilean ski resorts and carefully selected local operators in both Chile and Argentina, including Catedral Bariloche in the Patagonian Lake District and Chapelco Ski Resort near San Martín de los Andes. **Specialty:** Snowboarding and skiing vacations. ☎775/586–9133 in North America ⊕www.snoventures.com.

South American Journeys. Trips focus on yoga, writing, culinary, photography, music, and nature workshops. Their Yoga in Patagonia trip takes guests through Llanquihue Lake to Petrohué. When not meditating or doing downward dogs, guests can hike in Las Torres del Paine National Park and sail Río Serrano for views of Monte Balmaceda and its glaciers. **Specialty:** Workshops for the body and soul, and women-only journeys. ☎818/951–8986 ⊕www.southamericanjourneys.com.

Southwind Adventures. Their programs attract thoughtful world travelers who don't like being herded from site to site. Most guests are in their mid-30s to mid-50s. Trips emphasize native cultures, natural history, and outdoor activities such as walking, trekking, and biking. Customized adventures for four to six people are also offered. Their classic trip is the Hiking the Patagonian Andes (15 days), which features day hikes beneath Mt. Fitzroy, Cerro Torre, and Perito Moreno Glacier in Argentina and then crosses to Chile to hike beneath the famous spires of Torres del Paine National Park. Nights are spent in guest ranches, country inns, and hotels. ☎303/972–0701 or 800/377–9463 ⊕www. southwindadventures.com.

Victor Emanuel Nature Tours. Strong advocates of supporting local conservation organizations, using local drivers and guides, and using in-country tourism operators, this company takes bird enthusiasts to the scrub deserts of Patagonia in search of Burrowing Parrots, canasteros, and secretive marsh-dwellers. In the region's rolling grasslands, guests spot Andean Condors, Rufous-backed Negrito as well as various species of orchids. The trip concludes with a boat trip on the Beagle Channel to view albatrosses, petrels, and penguins. The trip is limited to 14 guests and includes all meals, accommodations, ground transportation, and guide services by tour leaders. **Specialty:** Birding tours. ☎512/328–5221 or 800/328–8368 ⊕www.ventbird.com.

WINGS. Guests explore the Valdés Peninsula, with its dry stony plains covered in xerophytic bushes and occupied by tinamous and rheas, remote beaches teeming with elephant seals and sea lions, whales, and colonies of seabirds. In Los Glaciares National Park, search the forests and steppes for seed-snipe and sierra-finches. In the southern beech forests of Tierra del Fuego the search is for Magellanic woodpeckers followed by a ferry trip down the Beagle Channel amongst albatrosses, penguins, and sea lions. The tour requires gentle walking, sometimes for up to six hours, accommodates four to 16 people plus a guide, includes transportation, and lodging in comfortable hotels/motels. **Specialty:** Tours are strongly oriented toward birds and led by guides with varied interests in natural history. ☎520/320–9868 or 888/293–6443 ⊕www.wingsbirds.com.

World Expeditions. This adventure outfitter focuses on trekking, mountaineering, and nature trips. They offer a number of Patagonia itineraries, such as Parks & Wildlife, which includes the Lake District of Argentina, Torres del Paine, Los Glaciares, and a cruise down the Beagle Channel from Ushuaia. Their two-week Paine Circuit or Paine & Fitzroy Trek trips are for fit travelers used to roughing it. The three-day Perito Moreno or Walking in Fitzroy itineraries are perfect for leisure travelers. ☎415/989–2212 or 888/464–8735 ⊕www.world-expeditions.com.

The World Outdoors. Guided by a local English-speaking naturalist, guests hike amid enormous glaciers, pristine lakes, vast plateaus, and ancient forests of Torres del Paine National Park during a six-day inn-and-hut hiking adventure. Extend the stay by five to six days for a multisport exploration of Chile's Lake District and Osorno Volcano. Who it's for: Adventurous hikers who are comfortable being active up to nine hours a day. ☎303/413–0938 or 800/488–8483 ⊕www. theworldoutdoors.com.

Argentina Lake District

View from Cerro Lindo, El Bolson

WORD OF MOUTH

"We had a rental car and did the Circuito Chico drive around the Llao Llao Peninsula. We again had the weather with us and the view from the main panorama point was literally breath taking. We also took the cable car to the top of Cerro Gordo. Beautiful views once again."

—cdale

WELCOME TO ARGENTINA LAKE DISTRICT

TOP REASONS TO GO

★ **Savage Beauty:** One day a lake is silent, a mirror of its surrounding mountains. Another day, waves are crashing on its shores, wind tears limbs from trees.

★ **The Great Outdoors:** Well-marked trails in the national parks lead into a world of strange forests, leaping waterfalls, and magnificent vistas. Commercial river rafting or kayaking might carry you to Chile.

★ **Everywhere Water:** Forty different lakes, seven major rivers flowing into two oceans, and you can spend days just staring at Nahuel Huapi Lake with its shoreline disappearing under distant peaks and volcanoes.

★ **Ski in Summer:** In the northern Lake District of Patagonia, June through September is ski season on the slopes of Cerro Catedral near Bariloche, and Cerro Chapelco, near San Martín de los Andes.

★ **Savage Beauty:** One day a lake is silent, a mirror of its surrounding mountains. Another day, waves are crashing on its shores, wind tears limbs from trees.

1 In & Around San Martín. This Andean town is a good base for exploring Parque Nacional Lanín and nearby rivers and streams. A good variety of accommodations makes this a logical stopover on the Seven Lakes Route.

2 Route of the Seven Lakes. The best part of this 105-km (65-mi) drive is between Villa Angosura and San Martín de los Andes, where the road winds up and around lake after lake—all of them different in shape, size, and setting.

3 Bariloche. Full of shops, shoppers, and skiers in winter, this unashamedly touristy city on the southeastern shore of Nahuel Huapi Lake welcomes the world with all levels of hostelry, restaurants, and tour offices. The best part of Bariloche is beyond the city limits.

4 Parque Nacional Nahuel Huapi. It's the oldest (founded in 1934), the biggest (272 square mi), and the most popular national park in Patagonia. Explore high mountain glaciers, hundreds of lakes, and trails.

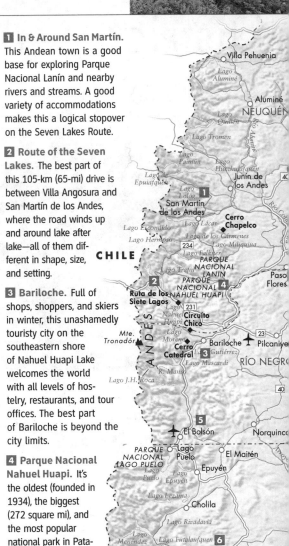

Zapala

22

40

Arroyo Picún Leufú

Sañicó

Piedra del
Aguila

237

Arroyo Limay

Arroyo Collón

Laguna
Blanca

omallo

0   40 miles

0   40 km

Río Chico

CHUBUT

Río Chubut

Gualjaina

25

5 In & Around El Bolsón.
Known to some as a refuge
for hippies and ex-urbanites,
this amiable little town,
in a wide valley between
two high mountain ranges,
straddles RN40 just north of
Parque Nacional Lago Puelo
on the Chilean border. Acres
of hops and berry farms
thrive in the microclimate
along the Río Azul.

6 In & Around Esquel.
With a population of 30,000,
Esquel is the biggest city in
Chubut Province. In nearby
Los Alerces National Park,
giant alerce trees, some of
them 4,000 years old, hide
in the forests that surround
Lake Futalaufquen. South of
Esquel, the town of Trevelín
reveals its Welsh heritage in
tearooms and museums.

Waiting for the boat
at Lake Paimun, Lanín
National Park, Argentina

GETTING
ORIENTED

The Lake District lies in
the folds of the Andes
along the Chilean border
in the provinces of Neu-
quén, Río Negro, and
Chubut, where a myriad
of glacial lakes lap at
the forest's edge beneath
snowcapped peaks.
The area includes four
national parks, with towns
in each. Bariloche is the
base for exploring Parque
Nacional Nahuel Huapi,
and the departure point
for the lake crossing to
Chile. North of Bariloche,
either directly on RN237
or along the Seven Lakes
Route, is Parque Nacional
Lanín with the towns of
San Martín de los Andes
and Junín de los Andes.
The northernmost lake
in the district, Aluminé,
can be approached from
Junín or from Zapala on
RP13. South of Bariloche
and El Bolsón on RN40,
is Parque Nacional
Lago Puelo in the Pacific
watershed, and farther
south, either on RN40
to Esquel, or through the
Cholila Valley, is Parque
Nacional Los Alerces.

ARGENTINA LAKE DISTRICT PLANNER

Health & Safety

Driving in the Lake District is no more harrowing than anywhere else in Argentina, with fast drivers who don't always stop at stop signs. Since distances are great with few services en route, keep your tank filled and tires checked. Never leave anything in your car. Walking on the streets of Bariloche might be more hazardous than driving, as steps and holes in unexpected places are potential ankle-breakers. There are good doctors and clinics in Bariloche, San Martín de los Andes, and Esquel. When the students hit Bariloche during holidays, they go out to party at midnight and leave the clubs and bars in the early morning hours. There has been a rash of serious auto accidents in recent years.

Emergency Services Coast Guard (☎106). **Fire** (☎100). **Forest Fire** (☎103). **Hospital** (☎107). **Police** (☎101).

Eat Well & Rest Easy

Restaurant reservations are seldom needed except during holidays. Attire is informal, and tipping is the same as in the rest of the country (about 10%).

Idyllic lake-view lodges, cozy *cabañas* (cabins), vast *estancias* (ranches), and inexpensive *hospedajes* or *residenciales* (bed-and-breakfasts) are found in towns and in the countryside throughout northern Patagonia. Super-luxurious hotels in Bariloche and Villa La Angostura attract outdoors enthusiasts from all over the world, as do small family-run hostels where backpackers squeeze five to a room. Fishing lodges near San Martín de los Andes, Junín de los Andes, and in the Cholila Valley are not only for anglers; they make great headquarters for hiking, boating, or just getting away. Most of them include all meals and cocktails. Guides are extra. *Apart-hotels* have small, furnished apartments with kitchenettes. Local tourist offices are helpful in finding anything from a room in a residence to a country inn or a downtown hotel. Advance reservations are highly recommended if you're traveling during peak times (December–March; July–August for the ski resorts). Note: lodging prices include tax (IVA—which is 21%) unless otherwise noted.

DINING & LODGING PRICE CATEGORIES (IN ARGENTINA PESOS)

	¢	$	$$	$$$	$$$$
Restaurants					
	under 8 pesos	8 pesos–15 pesos	15 pesos–25 pesos	25 pesos–35 pesos	over 35 pesos
Hotels					
	under 80 pesos	80 pesos–150 pesos	150 pesos–250 pesos	250 pesos–400 pesos	over 400 pesos

Restaurant prices are for one main course at dinner. Hotel prices are for two people in a standard double room in high season.

Getting Here & Around

The most efficient way to get here is by air: from Buenos Aires or Calafate. The most scenic way to arrive is from Puerto Montt, Chile by boat through the lakes. Buses are the new trains—fast, inexpensive, with varying degrees of luxury, including beds, meals, and attendants. A car or bus is the best way to travel between cities in the Lake District, and once you've settled in a destination, you can use local tours, taxis, or a *remis* (car with driver).

Air Travel. Aerolíneas Argentinas (⊕*www.aerolineas.com.ar*) flies from Buenos Aires to Bariloche, Esquel, San Martín de los Andes, and Neuquén; it also connects Bariloche and Calafate. LAN (⊕*www.lan.com*) also flies to Bariloche from Buenos Aires as well as from Santiago, Chile, via Puerto Montt. LADE (⊕ *www.lade.com.ar*) provides service in small planes from Bariloche and Chapelco (San Martín de los Andes) to El Bolsón, Trelew, Puerto Madryn, and Comodoro Rivadavía in Atlantic Patagonia, and El Calafate, Río Gallegos, and Comodoro Rivadavía in the south.

Boat Travel. Traveling between Bariloche, Argentina, and Puerto Montt, Chile, by boat requires three lake crossings and various buses and can be done in a day or overnight. Travel agents and tour operators in Bariloche and Buenos Aires can arrange this trip and many tour companies include it in their itineraries.

Bus Travel. Buses arrive in Bariloche from every corner of Argentina—from Jujuy in the north, Ushuaia in the south, and everywhere in between. Buses are best for shorter trips.

Car Travel. Driving to the Lake region from Buenos Aires is more than 1,500 km (930 mi) and at least three days of interminable stretches with few hotels, gas stations, or restaurants. In Bariloche, renting a car gives you the freedom to stop when and where you want. Keep in mind that the Seven Lakes Road closes when weather is bad. For winter travel, it's a good idea to rent a 4x4. Hiring a remis is another option.

When to Go

You don't have to be a skier to appreciate the snowy peaks reflected in clear blue lakes in the winter months of June through September, when the weather is typical of any alpine region—blowing snowstorms, rain, and fog punctuated by days of brilliant sunshine. August and September are the best months for skiing, as the slopes are crowded with vacationing families and schoolkids in July.

After the windy months of October and November, spring arrives in Patagonia. In December, the weather still might be cool, breezy, overcast, or rainy, but the rewards for bringing an extra sweater and rain gear are great: an abundance of wildflowers and few tourists. January and February are the peak summer months, with long (the sun sets at 10 PM) warm days. March and April are still good months to visit, although rainy, cloudy days and cold nights can curtail some activities, but compensation is fewer crowds and great fall colors.

Money Matters

There are ATMs in all towns and cities—even little villages. Many hotels and shops give a discount for cash (*efectivo*), and give good exchange rates for U.S. dollars. Traveler's checks can be carried as insurance, but cashing them is inconvenient and expensive.

3

Revised by
Eddy Ancinas

HUNDREDS OF SAPPHIRE LAKES LIE hidden amidst the snow-covered peaks of the Andes on the western frontier with Chile, in what has become the most popular tourist area in Patagonia—the Northern Lake District. Bariloche is become the booming vacation town in the center of it all.

Parque Nacional Lanín, in Neuquén Province, and the neighboring Parque Nacional Nahuel Huapi, in Río Negro Province, add up to 2.5 million acres of natural preserve. South of Bariloche and the Cholila Valley and northwest of Esquel, the Parque Nacional los Alerces, named for its 2,000-year-old *alerce* trees, covers 2,630 square km (1,015 square mi) of mountains, forests, and lakes, with only one dirt road leading into it.

Outdoor activities and a wide variety of lodgings in extraordinary settings attract visitors year-round. In winter, skiers come to Cerro Catedral for its size and terrain, superb setting overlooking Nahuel Huapi Lake, and its proximity to Bariloche. Smaller areas such as Chapelco in San Martín de los Andes, La Hoya in Esquel, and Cerro Bayo in Villa La Angostura attract mostly Argentines, and lots of Brazilians.

In spring, ribbons of pink and purple lupine line the roads and fill the mountain meadows along the Seven Lakes Route or Route 40 south to Esquel. Hikers and horseback riders will discover waterfalls cascading from mountaintops into deep, dark canyons. From November to March, fishing enthusiasts revel in the swollen rivers, alive with feisty trout or salmon.

Welsh farmers have grown wheat and raised sheep and cattle on the vast open plains and valleys of Chubut since 1865, and many of their descendants continue to live and work on the land, while preserving their Welsh culture in music, food, and architecture.

IN & AROUND SAN MARTÍN DE LOS ANDES

260 km (161 mi) north of Bariloche on R237, R40, and R234 via Junín de los Andes (a 4-hr drive); 158 km (98 mi) north of Bariloche on R237 and R63 over the Córdoba Pass (69 km [42 mi] is paved); 90 km (56 mi) northeast of Villa La Angostura on R234 (Seven Lakes Rd., partly unpaved and closed for much of winter).

In the southeastern corner of Parque Nacional Lanín, San Martín de los Andes is the largest town within the park, with roads leading south to Bariloche on the Seven Lakes Route, north on a good paved road to Junín de los Andes (41 km [29 mi]), and west on a dirt road to the Hua Hum crossing into Chile (47 km).

Although Junín doesn't have the tourist infrastructure that San Martín has, and it's on the flat Patagonian steppe with no lake in sight, dirt roads leading west take you up the Chimehuin River to Lakes Curruhue, Huechulaufquen, and Paimún—all well known by sports fishermen. As you drive west, the perfect white cone of Lanín Volcano towers in the distance at 12,474 feet. Northwest of Junín, RP60 takes you north of Lanín Volcano to Paso Tromen (67 km [41½ mi]).

SAN MARTÍN DE LOS ANDES

Surrounded by lakes, dense forests, and mountains, San Martín de los Andes lies in a natural basin at the foot of Lago Lácar. It's a small, easygoing town, much like Bariloche was 30 years ago, with many small hotels and houses reflecting the distinctive Andean-Alpine architecture of Bustillo. Wide, flat streets lined with rosebushes run from the town pier on the eastern shore of Lago Lácar to the main square, Plaza San Martín, where two parallel streets—San Martín and General Villegas—teem with block after block of ski and fishing shops, chocolatiers, trinket shops, clothing boutiques, and cafés.

When Lanín National park was founded in 1937, and the ski area at Chapelco developed in the 1970s, tourism replaced forestry as the main source of income, and today, it's the major tourist center in Neuquén Province—the midpoint in the Seven Lakes Route, and the gateway for exploring the Parque Nacional Lanín.

GETTING HERE & AROUND

Aerolíneas Argentinas and LADE have flights from Buenos Aires, but most people arrive from Bariloche via Junín de los Andes or as part of the Seven Lakes Route. Buses from Bariloche are frequent and dependable. San Martín is a pleasant walking town. To access nearby beaches, hiking trails, or the ski area in winter, you need to rent a car, join a tour, or be an energetic cyclist. Taxis are inexpensive and remises can be arranged through your hotel. ■**TIP→** There are no gas stations on the Seven Lakes Route.

ESSENTIALS

BUS **San Martín de los Andes Bus Terminal** (✉ *Villegas at Juez de Valle* ☎ *2972/427–044*).

CURRENCY **Banco de la Nación Argentina** (✉ *Av. San Martín 687* ☎ *2972/427–292*). **Banco Macro Bansud** (✉ *Av. San Martín 850* ☎ *2972/423–962*).

MAIL **Post Office** (✉ *At the Civic Center, General Roca at Pérez*).

MEDICAL **Farmacia del Centro** (✉ *San Martín 896, at Belgrano* ☎ *2972/428–999*). **Hospital Ramón Carillo** (✉ *San Martín at Rodhe* ☎ *107 or 2972/427–211 emergencies*).

REMIS (CAR & DRIVER) **Del Oscar** (✉ *Av. San Martín 1254* ☎ *2972/428–774*).

VISITOR INFO **Dirección Municipal de Turismo** (✉ *J.M. de Rosas 790, at Av. San Martín* ☎ *2972/427–347* ⊕ *www.sanmartindelosandes.gov.ar*) Open daily 8 AM–9 PM.

WHAT TO SEE

The **Museo Pobladores** (Pioneer Museum) is a tiny building next to the tourist office that was the original city council lodge. Dedicated to Mapuche ceramics and weavings, displays of 13,000-year-old tools and fossils give an idea of the ancient life in the region. ✉ *J. M. de*

San Martín
de los Andes

KEY

① Hotels

❶ Restaurants

Rosas 700 ☎*2972/428–676* ▭*1 peso* ☼*Varies—check at the tourist office.*

The former location of the **Intendencia de Parques Nacionales** (National Park Office) is a classic Andean-alpine building in the style of Bustillos, who did the Civic Center in Bariloche and the Llao Llao Hotel. For maps and information on all the parks and trails in the region, as well as fishing permits and information on big-game hunting, visit the new park office at ✉*E. Frey 749* ☎*2972/427–233* ✐*lanin@smandes.com. ar* ☼*Weekdays 8–1:30.*

From town you can walk, mountain bike, or drive to the **Mirador de las Bandurrias** (Bandurrias Overlook). It's a half-day hike round-trip (5 km [3 mi]) up a steep hill through a dense forest of cypress and oak. The reward is a view of town and the lake and a visit to a Mapuche village (**Paraje Trompul**) of about 40 families, most of whom work in town. You can visit the village for a peso, buy refreshments in the *quincho* (café), and see weavings and wood carvings (also for sale). If you're walking, take Avenida San Martín to the lake, turn right, cross the bridge behind the waterworks plant, over Puahullo Creek, and then head uphill on a path around the mountain. By car, leave town on RP48, drive about 4 km (2½ mi) to a turnoff (no sign) on your left.

Take the turn and continue 3 km (2 mi) to the Curruhuinca Community, where you pay a fee to arrive at the lookout.

OUTDOOR ACTIVITIES

The following tour agencies arrange rafting trips on the Hua Hum or Aluminé rivers, guided mountain-biking, horseback-riding, and fishing tours, visits to Mapuche communities, and excursions to lakes near and far, in both Lanín and Nahuel Huapi national parks. Fernando Aguirre, a lifelong resident, offers two- to four-day camping trips with combinations of hiking, riding, rafting, biking, and kayaking. **Siete Lagos Turismo** (⊠ *General Roca 826* 🕿🕿*2972/427–877* 🖃*sietelagostmo@smandes. com.ar*), **El Claro Turismo** (⊠ *Colonel Diaz 751* 🕿🕿*2972/428–876 or 2972/425–876* ⊕*www.elclaroturismo.com.ar* 🖃*elclaro@smandes. com.ar*), and **El Refugio** (⊠ *Tte. Col. Perez 830* 🕿🕿*2972/425–140* ⊕*www.elrefugioturismo.com.ar*) offer similar excursions throughout the area.

BEACHES **Playa Catrite,** 4 km (2½ mi) from San Martín on R234, on the south side of Lago Lácar, is a sandy beach with a campground, a store with picnic items, and a café. **Playa Quila Quina**, 18 km (11 mi) from San Martín, is reached by turning off R234 2 km (1 mi) before the road to Catrite and then getting on R108. On the 12-km (7-mi) drive to the lake you'll pass through Mapuche farmlands and forests. The soft, sandy beach and clear water attract day-trippers and campers, as well as residents with vacation homes. Both beaches can be reached by boat.

BOATING You can rent small boats, canoes, and kayaks at the pier from **Lacar Nonthue** (⊠ *Av. Costanera* 🕿*2972/427–380*). You can also rent a bicycle and take an all-day excursion to the other side of Lake Lácar, where there is a nice beach and woods to explore. Another option is the boat tour to **Hua Hum** at the western end of the lake where the river of the same name runs to the Chilean border.

FISHING During the fishing season (November 15–April 15, extended to the end of May in certain areas), local guides take you to their favorite spots on Lácar, Lolog, Villarino, and Falkner lakes and on the Caleufu, Quiquihue, Malleo, and Hermoso rivers, or farther afield to the Chimehuín River and Lakes Huechulafquen and Paimún. Permits are available at the **Parque Nacional Intendencia** (⊠ *Emilio Frey 749* 🕿*2972/427–233*) or any licensed fishing stores along Avenida San Martín. Most stores and tour operators can suggest guides.

Jorge Cardillo (⊠ *Villegas 1061, behind the casino* 🕿*2972/428–372* 🖃*cardillo@smandes.com.ar*) is a well-known local guide. **Sidy Casa y Pesca** (⊠ *Villegas 570* 🕿*2972/420–646l* 🖃*sidycazapesca@hotmail. com.ar*) rents and sells equipment and offers guidance on wading and trolling for all experience levels as well as fly-fishing trips for experts.

HORSEBACK RIDING (CABALGATAS) Hour-, day-, and weeklong organized and guided rides, often with an *asado* (barbecue) included, can be arranged through local tour offices. **Cabalgatas Abuelo Enrique** (⊠ *Callejón Ginsgins* 🕿*2972/426–465* 🖃*abueloenrique@smandes.com.ar*) offers rides with a guide for two hours or all day, asado included. To get there, take Avenida Dr.

Koessler (R234) toward Zapala, turn left at the polo field and head toward Lago Lolog, then take a right past the military barracks to Callejón Ginsgins.

MOUNTAIN BIKING
San Martín is flat but from there everything goes up. Dirt and paved roads and trails lead through forests to lakes, waterfalls, and high mountain valleys. In town you can rent bikes at **HG Rodados** (⊠ *Av. San Martín 1061* ☎*2972/427–345*). Bikes are also at **Enduro Kawa & Bikes** (⊠ *Elordi at Perito Moreno* ☎*2972/427–093*). **Chapelco Ski Area** has good trails and mountain-biking lessons.

SCENIC DRIVE

The rather long (200 km [124 mi]) round-trip) but rewarding excursion to **Lago Huechulafquen** and **Lago Paimún** can be made via Junín de los Andes. An overnight stay at either lake is recommended. From San Martín, take R234 north to Junín, and then take the dirt road (R61) west. As you speed across the open range following the Río Chimehuín toward the lake, Lanín Volcano plays hide-and-seek on the horizon. This is serious fishing country. Beaches and campsites along the lakeshore are good picnic stops.

SKIING
The ski area and summer resort of **Cerro Chapelco** (⊠ *Information Office: San Martín at Elordi* ☎☎*2972/427–845* ⊕*www.cerro chapelco.com*) is 23 km (14 mi) from town—18 km paved and 5 km of dirt road. Ideal for families and beginner to intermediate skiers, the area has modern facilities and lifts, including a high-speed *telecabina* (gondola) from the base. On a clear day, almost all the runs are visible from the top (6,534 feet), and Lanín Volcano dominates the horizon. Lift tickets run 55 pesos–96 pesos per day, and equipment-rental facilities are available at the base camp (32 pesos–51 pesos per day for skis, boots, and poles). Taxis cost about 35 pesos each way. The summer Adventure Center has mountain biking for experts and classes for beginners, horseback rides, hiking, archery, a swimming pool, an alpine slide, and children's activities.

WHITE-WATER RAFTING
An all-day rafting trip that crosses into Chile on either Río Aluminé or Río Hua Hum can be arranged by **Siete Lagos Turismo** (⊠ *General Roca 826* ☎☎*2972/427–877* ✐*sietelagostmo@smandes.com.ar*), **El Claro Turismo** (⊠ *Colonel Diaz 751* ☎☎*2972/428–876 or 2972/425–876* ⊕*www.elclaroturismo.com.ar* ✐*elclaro@smandes.com.ar*), or **El Refugio** (⊠ *Tte. Col. Perez 830* ☎☎*2972/425–140* ⊕*www.elrefugio turismo.com.ar*).

WHERE TO EAT

$$–$$$
✕**Fondue Betty.** It wouldn't be a ski town without a fondue place. Fondues are uniformly excellent; the cheese fondue is smooth and rich, while the meat fondue comes with cubes of Argentine beef in assorted cuts and up to 12 condiments. The wine list is also great. The two rooms are cozy and intimate, equally well suited to families and honeymooners. ⊠*Villegas 586* ☎*2972/422–522* ⊟*DC, MC, V.*

$$$$
★
✕**Kú.** Dark-wood tables and booths, a friendly staff, and a chalk-board—good building blocks for a restaurant. The smoked-meat plate with deer, boar, trout, salmon, and cheese is a good starter. Patago-

nian lamb *al asador* (on the open fire), plus a good assortment of parrilla classics are paired with a fine wine list. ⊠*Av. San Martín 1053* ☎*2972/427–039* ⊟*AE, DC, MC, V.*

$–$$ ✕**Mendieta.** This may be the friendliest parrilla in Patagonia: cooks, waiters, and even the owners scurry about with sizzling meats and fresh steaming pasta with various sauces. By 2 PM the tables are filled with chatty locals. Pine racks around the dining room display a good selection of Argentina wines, and you can watch three or more Patagonian lambs being slowly roasted *a la cruz* (on the cross) in the street-side window. ⊠*Av. San Martín 713* ☎*2972/429–301* ⊟*DC, MC, V.*

$$–$$$$ ✕**La Reserva.** A couple of blocks from the main drag, this restaurant's elaborate place settings and proper service nod toward formality, but booth seating and warm lighting provide a relaxed touch. Fresh trout is a treat, but you can skip the shellfish. Homemade pastas are more interesting than the norm—try the artichoke ravioli. ⊠*Belgrano 940* ☎*2972/428–734* ⊟*AE, DC, MC, V.*

$–$$$$ ✕**La Tasca.** This is one of the traditional top-end choices in town. With tables scattered about the black-stone floor, and wine barrels, shelves, and every other imaginable surface stacked with pickled vegetables, smoked meats, cheese rounds, dried mushrooms and herbs, olive oils in cans and bottles, and wine bottles, you might think you're in a Patagonian deli. Diners should try local wild game dishes; especially good is the "La Tasca" appetizer platter of smoked salmon, deer, boar, and trout pâté. ⊠*Moreno 866* ☎*2972/428–663* ⊟*AE, MC, V.*

WHERE TO STAY

Most of the 5,000 hotel beds in town are in small hotels, bed-and-breakfasts, and cabin complexes. Two beach campgrounds have electricity, hot water, showers, restrooms, and a store: **Playa Catrite** (⊠*R234, Km 4* ☎*2972/423–091*), and **Quila Quina** (⊠*R108, Km 12* ☎*2972/426–919*), which also has a dining room and some water-sports equipment rentals.

$$$ ⊡**Hosteria Anay.** Inside this small, white stucco–and-log house, guests gather around the fireplace for tea in the cozy sitting area or in the bright, cheerful breakfast room. Rooms have simple whitewashed walls, beamed ceilings, and carpeted floors. **Pros:** Good value. **Cons:** Small rooms. ⊠*Cap. Drury 841,* ☎*2972/427–514* ⊕*www.inter patagonia.com/anay* ⤴*15 rooms* ♨*In-hotel: laundry service, public Wi-Fi, no elevator, parking (no fee)* ⊟*No credit cards* ⦿*CP.*

$$$$ ⊡**Hotel la Cheminée.** Two blocks from the main street is this comfort-
★ able inn with pink-floral chintz and lace curtains. Plump pillows, fresh flowers, and fireplaces in some rooms add to the coziness. A sumptuous breakfast and an afternoon tea of homemade breads, scones, cakes, cookies, and jams are served. **Pros:** Great breakfast, helpful tour options on bulletin board. **Cons:** No bar. ⊠*M. Moreno at General Roca,* ☎*2972/427–617* ✉*lacheminee@smandes.com.ar* ⤴*15 rooms, 3 suites, 1 cottage* ♨*In-hotel: bar, pool, public Wi-Fi, parking (no fee)* ⊟*AE, MC, V* ⦿*CP.*

$$$–$$$$ ⊡**Patagonia Plaza Hotel.** Good-bye genteel rusticity. Hello modern downtown hotel with all the amenities. Shops, tourist offices, and restaurants are around the corner from this centrally located oasis with a lobby fireplace and soaring atrium full of light and plants. Note the paintings on display—each floor represents a different local artist. The friendly and informative staff caters well to the frequent fishermen, families, business travelers, and pleasure-types who stop here. **Pros:** Location, big rooms with modern bathrooms. **Cons:** Atmosphere deficient in restaurant. ⊠ *Av. San Martín at Rivadavia,* ☎☎*2972/422–280* ⊕*www.hotelpatagoniaplaza.com.ar* ⇨*15 rooms* ⟡*In-hotel: bar, restaurant, public Wi-Fi, pool, laundry service, parking (no fee)* ⊟*AE, DC, MC, V* ⦿*CP.*

PARQUE NACIONAL LANÍN

The dramatically beautiful **Parque Nacional Lanín** has 35 mountain lakes, countless rivers, ancient forests, and the Lanín Volcano. Tucked into the folds of the Andes along the Chilean border, it stretches 150 km (93 mi) north–south, covering 3,920 square km (1,508 square mi), and is the third-largest national park in Argentina. The area is home to the Mapuche and you can learn about their history and buy their handicrafts in one of the 50 communities throughout the park.

GETTING HERE & AROUND
Three towns have access to the park. The northernmost section is reached from the town of Aluminé (145 km [90 mi] west of Zapala on RP46), a typical Andean town with no paved streets, but an abundance of nearby lakes (Aluminé, Quillén, and Mohquehue being the most accessible). The Pehuenia resort here is a good base for exploring. Junín de los Andes, in the middle section, is at the end of the paved roads from either San Martín or Bariloche. San Martín, the major town in the park, is in the southern portion. All three towns have roads leading to the border with Chile (⇨ *Chilean Lakes Crossing box, below.*)

Buses connect all three towns with each other and with Bariloche, and tours out of San Martín offer excursions throughout the park.

WHAT TO SEE
Found only in this part of the Andes, the ancient **Araucaria Araucana** tree grows to 100 feet, and has long spiny branches. Cones the size of bowling balls full of piñon nuts provided nourishment to the Mapuche who call these trees *Pehuenes.* The northern portion of the park near Lago Huechulaufquen and Aluminé is the best place to view these peculiar giants.

Volcán Lanín rises 12,378 feet in solitary snow-clad splendor on the western horizon, towering over the entire park and visible from every direction. The closest access is from Junín, but the northern route to Paso Tromen also offers endless photo ops through the tangled branches of the araucaria trees. You can climb Lanín in four days round-trip with a guide—or fly over it with **Aero Club de Los Andes** (⊠ *Chapelco in San Martín de los Andes* ☎*2972/491–379*).

Parque Nacional Lanín

Cunco

Caren-Ruminañi

La Angostura

Ville Pehuenia

23

Lago Aluminé

13

Moquehue

Lonco Luán

RESERVA NATIONAL VILLARICA

CORDILLERA DE LOS ANDES

11

Relem

Picudo

Impodi

Colorado

Lago Colico

Lago Caburgua

Norquinco

11

23

Clucnu Chumpiru

18

Aluminé

Caburgua

Rucachoroi

Lago Villarrica

Puncón

Redondo

Rucachoroi

Pichi Rucachoroi

Villarrica

Curarrehue

Viboras

Lago Quillén

119

Lican Ray

Villarrica

Rincón de las Tres Lagunas

Lago Calafquén

Quetrupillan

Lago Tromen

Arroyo Nahuel Mapi

Coñaripe

Paso Tromen

A. Aica Pam

Panguipulli

201

De Quilchica

Volcán Lanín

Rodeo Grande

Chiquilihuin

Lago Panguipulli

203

Liquiñe

201

Lago Paimún

Pampa Grande

Lago Huechulafquen

Río Alumine

Riñihue

Lago Riñihue

CHILE

Termas de Lahuan

ARGENTINA

Junín de los Andes

Endo

RESERVA NACIONAL MOCHO-CHOSHUENCO

Colo Huincill

Río Currhué

Puerto Pirihueico

Lago Lolog

Río Chimehuin

Futrono

Hua Hum

San Martín de los Andes

Lolog

Arroyo Quemquemtreu

Lago Ranco

Baños de Queñi

Lago Lacar

Quila Quina

A. Chuchuima

Lago Maihue

Escondido

Lago Meliquina

Río Caleufú

Lago Ranco

PARQUE NACIONAL PUYEHUE

Lago Hermoso

Espeleta

Colorado

Estacion Tres Lagos

Piedra Sola

Puyehue

Pichi Traful

234

Brazo Norte

Embalse se Alicura

Lago Puyehue

215

El Portezuelo

Ruca Malen

Lago Traful

Villa Traful

Confluencia

10 miles

10 kilometers

231

PARQUE NACIONAL NAHUEL HUAPI

Villa La Angostura

OUTDOOR ACTIVITIES

BOATING You won't find piers or marinas on any of these lakes, except at designated resorts. At Puerto Canoa on Lake Huechulafquen, a catamaran takes about 50 passengers on a three-hour excursion to Lake Epulafquen, where you can view huge deposits of lava covered with vegetation at the end of the lake. The culprit, a large volcano minus its cone, looms in the distance. The fishing lodge at Paimún Lake has a dock, and in Villa Pehuenia you can rent boats and kayaks.

FISHING Professional fishing guides in San Martín de los Andes, Junín, and Aluminé have their favorite fishing spots, and they offer excursions for a day or a week. To contact a guide, go to ⊕*www.neuquentur.gov.ar*. Fishing lodges lie concealed along the Chimihín River near Junín de los Andes and deeper into the lakes at Paimún. Smaller rivers such as the Malleo, Quillén, Meliquina, and Hua Hum are ideal for wading.

HIKING Besides climbing Lanín Volcano, trails throughout the park wind around lakes and streams, mostly at lower elevations. Signs are intermittent so hiking with a guide is recommended. The best hikes are out of Lago Paimún to a waterfall, Lago Quillén near Aluminé, and Lácar near San Martín.

RAFTING From San Martín, you can run the Caleufu River from October through November, then move on to the Hua Hum in December through March. Both are Class II rivers. *Aluminé* in the Mapuche language means "clear" and this wide river in the northern section of the park provides a thrilling descent through dense vegetation and a deep canyon.

JUNÍN DE LOS ANDES

41 km (25 mi) northeast of San Martín on paved R234; 219 km (136 mi) north of Bariloche on paved R234, R40, and R237.

The quickest route between San Martín de los Andes and Bariloche—and the only route for much of winter—is the paved road that runs through this typical agricultural town, where gauchos ride along the road with their dogs trotting faithfully behind. Once a fort in a region inhabited by the Mapuche, Junín de los Andes became a town during the last phase (1882–83) of the Conquista del Desierto, making it the oldest town in Neuquén Province. For centuries the valley was the trading route of the Mapuche between mountainous Chile and the fertile plains of Argentina. Today Mapuche descendants sell handicrafts and weavings in local shops and fairs. Junín also claims to be the trout capital of Patagonia, and you'll notice street signs adorned with little trouts.

The **Dirección Municipal de Turismo** (⊠*Coronel Suárez at Padre Milanesio* 🖥🖥*2972/491–160*) has information on lodging, dining, campgrounds, and nearby fishing lodges, which are open November–April.

WHERE TO EAT

$–$$ ╳**Ruca Hueney.** For decades, this parrilla on the corner of the main plaza has been Junín's most popular restaurant, and it's still the big trout in a small pond. There are a few Middle Eastern specialties such as *empanadas arabes.* ✉*Coronel. Suárez at Padre Milanesio* ☎*2972/491–113* ⊕*www.ruca-hueney.com.ar* ▤*AE, MC, V.*

THE SEVEN LAKES ROUTE

The **Ruta de los Siete Lagos** (Seven Lakes Route) is an all-day (10–12 hours) trip of 360 km (223 mi) round-trip. The best part, between Villa La Angostura and San Martín de los Andes (110 km [65 mi]) winds through wild mountain valleys, along rushing streams and uninhabited blue lakes. To fully enjoy the journey, plan to include a night or more in San Martín de los Andes, leaving early the next day on RP63 over Paso Córdoba, along the shore of Lago Meliquina and on to the weird and dramatic rock formations just before Confluéncia, where the road joins R237 and follows the Río Limay through Valle Encantado to Bariloche. If you're reluctant to drive, tour buses are available from Bariloche and Villa La Angostura.

From Bariloche, drive north on R237 for 21 km (13 mi), turn left on R231 and continue 65 km (40 mi) to Villa La Angostura. After passing lakes Correntoso and Espejo (about 11 km [7 mi]), the road joins R234, most of which is unpaved (40 km [25 mi]). Because it's perennially under construction, and often closed during heavy rains or winter storms, inquire about road conditions before you leave Villa La Angostura at your hotel, the Oficina de Parque Nacional Nahuel Huapi (Nahuel Huapi National Park Office), or the local police station. Tempting picnic spots or campsites are all along streams or beaches on lakes Villarino, Falkner, and Hermoso.

Highlights of the Drive: Just past Villa La Angostura, the Río Correntoso (the world's shortest river) flows from the lake of the same name into Nahuel Huapi. This is a classic mouth-of-the-river fishing spot. Just past Pichi Traful between lakes Villarino and Falkner, Cascada Vulignanco, a 66-foot waterfall is visible on the left-hand side of the road, where you can pull off at the *mirador* (overlook). A little farther along, near Lago Escondido, the beach at Laguna Pudú Pudú is ideal for a picnic or overnight camping. Definitely stop for the strange rock formations in the canyons near Confluencia and along the cliffs above Río Limay.

VILLA TRAFUL

60 km (37 mi) north of Villa La Angostura on R231 and R65, 39 km (24 mi) from Confluencia on R65, 100 km (60 mi) northwest of Bariloche on R237 and R65.

If there were a prize for the most beautiful lake in the region, Lago Traful would win for its clarity, serenity, and wild surroundings. Small

log houses peek through the cypress forest along the way to Villa Traful, a village of about 500 inhabitants. The town consists of log cabins, horse corrals, two fishing lodges, shops for picnic and fishing supplies, a school, post office, and a park ranger's office. Well-maintained campgrounds border the lake, and ranches and private fishing lodges are hidden in the surrounding mountains. By day swimmers play on rocky beaches on the lake, a kayak cuts the still blue water, and divers go under to explore the mysteries of a submerged forest. Night brings silence, stars, and the glow of a lakeside campfire.

GETTING AROUND

You can approach Villa Traful from two directions by car, bus, or on the Circuito Grande tour. Take the Seven Lakes Road from Villa La Angostura, passing Lago Espejo and Lago Correntoso on a dirt road that can be slippery (or closed) after storms, then turn off onto RP65 at El Portzuelo. From the opposite direction, turn off RN237 at Confluencia onto RP65. This section also closes in heavy snows. As you approach the lake, you'll understand why Ted Turner chose this spot for his fishing lodge, across the Traful River from **Estancia Arroyo Verde**, a fishing and horseback-riding paradise.

The **Oficina Municipal de Turismo** (⊠ *Across from municipal pier* ☎*2944/479–099* ✐*trafultruismo@ciudad.com.ar*) has maps, lodging and restaurant information, and can help plan excursions.

OUTDOOR ACTIVITIES

Arroyo Blanco and Arroyo Coa Có. Drive, walk, or pedal about 3 km (2 mi) up from the village to the trailhead at Pampa de los Alamos, a clearing where the trail to Arroyo Blanco descends into a forest of 1,000-year-old *coihué* trees with their ghostly naked trunks, gigantic *lenga* (deciduous beech), and *ñires* that grow only at high altitudes. The trail leads to a wooden walkway along a steep cliff—the only way one could possibly view the waterfall that tumbles 66 feet into a deep dark chasm. Follow the wooden trail along the cliff for increasingly frightening glimpses of this wild gorge, then return up the same route. Arroyo Coa Có is in the opposite direction with a view of both the waterfall and Lago Traful.

HIKING A strenuous hike (seven hours) from the village to **Cerro Negro** climbs up through forests of cypress, coihués, lenga, and ñires, passing strange rock formations, then it reaches the summit at 6,000 feet with a splendid view of Lago Trafúl and across the Andes all the way to Lanín.

Casacada Co Lemú thunders with a deafening roar down 20 meters at the end of an arduous trail (19 km [12 mi] round-trip). Drive 8 km (5 mi) west toward the Seven Lakes Road to the bridge over Arroyo Cataratas. Before you cross the stream, on your left, the trail climbs slowly at first, then straight up 1,500 meters to the falls. For the best photo light, do this in the afternoon, and hang on to small children.

Laguna Las Mellizas y Pinturas Rupestres (The Twins Lagoon and Cave paintings). A 15-minute boat trip across the lake from the wharf takes you to a sandy beach on the northern shore. A two-hour walk down a trail into a steep gully leads to the pools. Nearby caves with 600-year-old Tehuelche cave paintings are worth exploring.

Mirador Traful. The lake, its surrounding forests and soaring mountains mirrored in the turquoise water, can be viewed from this lookout on a cliff 5 km (3 mi) east of town toward Confluencia.

FISHING This area is famous for its landlocked salmon and record-breaking-size trout in Lago Traful and the Laguna Las Mellizas (Twins Lagoon), 5 km (3 mi) north of town. Fishing season runs from November 15 to April 15.

Osvaldo Brandeman (⊠ *Villa Traful* ☎*2944/479–048* ✐*pescaosvaldo@ hotmail.com*) is a local fishing guide. **Andrés Quelín** (⊠ *Villa Traful* ☎*2944/479–005*) is a fishing guide, and he rents boats at the marina.

SCUBA DIVING In 1975, a violent earthquake caused half a mountain and its forest of cypress trees to slide to the bottom of the lake, creating the **Bosque Submergido.** You can dive to 98 feet in crystalline water and explore this sunken forest. Boat trips can be arranged at **Cabañas Aiken** (☎*2944/479–048*).

WHERE TO EAT

During the slow season (October–November) some restaurants close, so call first.

$–$$ ✕**Alto Traful.** You'll be ready for a hearty dinner of steak, local game, or trout after you climb the stairs to this hillside aerie built by affable owner-craftsman Daniel. A potbellied wood stove in the middle of the room, and the view from floor-to-ceiling windows inspire guests to linger over homemade cakes and coffee. You can drive up a steep road and park in back. ⊠*R65, Km 32.5,* ✛ *West of town* ☎*2944/479–073* ✑*altotraful@yahoo.com.ar* ▤*MC, V.*

$–$$$ ✕**Ñancú Lahuén.** People stop any time of day at this little log house with a hand-hewn thatched roof, open fireplace, and a floor of trunk rounds. The menu has something for everyone: sandwiches, smoked meats, pastas, homemade ice cream, Black Forest cake, lemon pie, tea, coffee, and anything chocolate—or a full meal of salmon, trout, or beef stew with local mushrooms. ⊠*R65* ✛ *Turn away from the lake by the police station, the carved-wood sign says* TEAHOUSE. ☎*2944/479–017* ⊕*www.interpatagonia.com/nanculahuen* ▤*AE, DC, MC, V.*

$–$$$ ✕**La Terraza.** This is the local parrilla, with Patagonian lamb and goat plus all the usual beef cuts served in a brightly lit dining room that looks through the forest to the lake. ⊠*RP65, Km 35.5, across the bridge, west of town* ☎*2944/479–077* ▤*MC, V.*

WHERE TO STAY

$$–$$$ ▥**Marinas Puerto Traful.** Across the road from the lake is this bright-blue lodge with flower boxes lining the wooden porches of the seven upstairs rooms. Inside, the newly refurbished rooms have quiet beige carpeting, white walls and linens, and a bright-orange Mapuche blanket folded across the bed for a splash of color. All the decoration you need is outside the window. Breakfast is served in an all-purpose room that opens onto the deck facing the lake. **Pros:** Lake views. **Cons:** No telephone, no Internet. ⊠*R65, Villa Traful,* ☎*2944/475–284* ⊕*www.marinaspuertotraful.com.ar* ⇆*16 rooms, 1 suite* ⟁*In-hotel: no elevator* ▤*No credit cards.*

CAMPING   You can pitch a tent and throw your sleeping bag down just about anywhere along the lake. There is a campground at Puerto Arrayanes at the western end of the lake, and at Arroyo Cataratas a little closer to the village. A large campground with everything but a roof over your head, **Camping Vulcanche** (☎*2944/479–061*), is east of the village across the road from the lake.

☾   **Camping Traful Lauquen** (☎*2944/479–030*), set in a forest of old-growth trees, has 1,312 feet of pebbly beach where you can launch your rented windsurfer, kayak, or canoe. Campsites with tables, benches, fire pits, washbasins, showers, and toilets are laid in clusters for 2–10 persons making this an ideal spot for family groups. A dining hall and a huge lawn for volleyball add to the fun.

VILLA LA ANGOSTURA

81 km (50 mi) northwest of Bariloche (a 1-hr drive on R231 around the east end of Lago Nahuel Huapi; also accessible by boat from Bariloche); 90 km (56 mi) southwest of San Martín de los Andes on R234 (the Seven Lakes Rd., partly unpaved and closed for much of winter).

Once a lakeside hamlet on a narrow *angostura* (isthmus) on the northern shore of Lake Nahuel Huapi, this small resort town has benefited from thoughtful planning and strict adherence to business codes, making it the second-most-popular tourist area in the Lake District. Its first hotel was built in 1923, 10 years before the town was founded, and today, some of the most luxurious hotels and resorts in Patagonia look out on the lake from discreet hiding places along its wooded shores. Shops and restaurants line the Av. Arrayanes, where you can stop for homemade ice cream or cakes while window-shopping in the three-block-long commercial area. The tourist office and municipal buildings are at El Cruce (the Crossroads), where R231 from Bariloche to the Chilean border intersects with the road to the port and the Seven Lakes Road, R234, to San Martín de los Andes.

GETTING HERE & AROUND

Buses from Bariloche are fast and frequent, but a car is the best way to get around the area and visit the town, which is creeping slowly from Lago Correntoso to Puerto Manzano, as Argentines and foreigners buy land and build houses in the shrinking spaces in between. Bicycles are often available in hotels or can be rented in town.

ESSENTIALS

VISITOR INFO **Secretaría de Turismo y Cultura** (⊠*Av. Siete Lagos 93, at southern end of Av. Arrayanes* ☎*2944/494–124).* **Villa la Angostura** (⊠*Siete Lagos at Av. Arrayanes* ☎📠*2944/494–124* ⊕*www.villalaangostura.gov.ar).*

WHAT TO SEE

Catamaran Futaleufú (⊠*at the pier, Bahía Manso* ☎*2944/494–004* ⊕*www.bosquelosarrayanes.com.ar)* has weekly excursions to the Parque Nacional los Arrayanes on the Peninsula Quetriué and to Isla Victoria.

Puerto Manzano, 7 km (4½ mi) from El Cruce along R231, is a neighborhood of modern hotels, cabins, and vacation homes on a dark, heavily forested dirt road which twists and turns along the peninsula overlooking the Bahía Manzano. Hotels with indoor-outdoor swimming pools and elaborate spas vie for sun (morning on one side, afternoon on the other) and sandy beaches. The road to Cerro Bayo, the local ski area, is a few kilometers beyond the entrance to Puerto Manzano.

OUTDOOR ACTIVITIES

FISHING The **Río Correntoso,** reputed to be the shortest river in the world (260 meters), flows from Lago Correntoso beneath a bridge into Nahuel Huapi Lake, where fly-fishermen from the world over have been coming since the 1920s to catch and release record-breaking-size trout. Trolling, spinning, or fly-fishing from land or by boat in the lagoons and inlets of Nahuel Huapi will take you to spots of incredible scenic beauty and solitude. To arrange a one- to five-day fishing excursion, to rent or purchase equipment, or to hire a guide, contact **Patagonia Fly** at the **Banana Fly Shop** (⊠ *Av. Arrayanes 282* ☎ *2944/494–634* ⊕ *www.patagonfly.com*).

HORSEBACK RIDING Most trails used for hiking and mountain biking are also used for horseback riding. Picnic stops with a swim in a river, and an asado at the end of the ride are added attractions. Horses are available from **Los Saucos** (⊠ *R231, Km 61.8 [Av. Arrayanes 2500]* ☎ *2944/494–853*). Another good riding outfit is **Cahuel Hueñi** (⊠ *Av. Siete Lagos* ☎ *2944/1561–4034*). **Cabalgatas Correntoso** (⊠ *Cacique Antriao 1850, on the road toward Mirador Belvedere* ☎ *2944/1560–4903 or 2944/1551–0559* ⊕ *www.cabalgatacorrentoso.com.ar*) offers three day trips—a two-hour lakeside jaunt, a 3½-hour waterfall riding-hiking trip, or a nine-hour circuit to the valley of Cajón Negro, which includes lunch and a swim; there are also two- to four-day trips into the mountains.

HIKING Access to the Río Bonito trail is 1 km (½ mi) from the base of the ski area at Cerro Bayo. It climbs 500 meters to a waterfall. The trailhead for a longer hike, to Inacayal Fall, is on the right-hand side of R231 just before you arrive at El Cruce. After climbing ¾ mi, you arrive at a 164-foot-high waterfall. Continue another 300 feet to a lookout over Lake Correntoso.

MOUNTAIN BIKING The area has more bike-rental shops than gas stations. You can easily ride from the village to Laguna Verde, near the port, or off the Seven Lakes Road to Mirador Belvedere and on to the waterfalls at Inacayal. The tourist office has a brochure, *Paseos y Excursiones*, with maps, distances, and descriptions (in Spanish) of mountain biking, hiking, and horseback-riding trails.

Maps, information, and rentals are at **Free Bikes** in Las Cruces (⊠ *Las Fucsias 268* ☎ *2944/495–047* ⊕ *www.freebikes.com.ar*). **IAN Bikes** (⊠ *Topa Topa 102, at Las Fucsias* ☎ *2944/495–005*) rents bikes, too, as does **Mountain Bike Cerro Bayo** at the base of Cerro Bayo (☎ *2944/495–047* ✉ *angosturafreebikes@yahoo.com.ar*).

SKIING **Cerro Bayo** (☎ *2944/494–189* ⊕ *www.cerrobayoweb.com*) is 9 km (5½ mi) from El Cruce via R66. During ski season (July–September), skiers and boarders glide over 12 km (7½ mi) of skiable terrain—most of it on 21 easy to intermediate groomed runs. With a 6,000-foot uninterrupted vertical drop and scenic off-piste skiing, this small ski area is much less crowded than neighboring Bariloche. Six double chair lifts,

---

LOCAL SHOPS

One of the best of the many chocolate shops is **En El Bosque** (⊠ *Av. Arrayanes 218* ☎ *2944/495–738*), a delicious artisanal producer where the smells of homemade sweets waft out onto the sidewalk; this one also doubles as a little teahouse. Delicious homemade jams (*dulces caseros*) are sold in nearly every shop. **Tanino** (⊠ *Av. Arrayanes 172* ☎ *2944/494–411*) has the best selection of furs and leather goods—boots, belts, jackets, bags, and purses—in town.

four tele-ski, and two surface lifts access the midstation and the summit (5,000 feet), where a panoramic trail (open in summer for mountain biking) wends its way down 5 km (3 mi) around the mountain, offering a wide view of Nahuel Huapi Lake. Rental equipment and lessons are at the base facility next to El Refugio Chaltén, where goulash, lamb stew, snacks, and beverages are served. At midmountain, Tronadór café has snacks and lunch—try the waffles with dulce de leche or local jams.

WHERE TO EAT

$–$$$ ✕ **Australis.** This is one of the best microbreweries in Patagonia. The excellent cuisine integrates beer, all the way through to dessert—a memorable flan is made with chocolate and a delicious stout. The restaurant will cook up your own freshly caught fish if you bring it in. ⊠ *Av. Arrayanes (R231) 2490* ☎ *2944/495–645* ▤ *AE, DC, MC, V.*

¢–$ ✕ **La Casita de la Oma.** Between the bay and the main street, this teahouse, with its award-winning garden, serves homemade cakes, pies, and scones. Moist chocolate brownie cake with dulce de leche is a winner, as is a pile of filo leaves with dulce de leche and meringue on top. Jars of jam line the shelves. ⊠ *Cerro Inacayal 303* ☎ *2544/494–602* ▤ *MC, V* ⊗ *Closed May.*

$$–$$$$ ✕ **Tinto Bistró.** A hip new spot in town draws inspiration from Asia, while a spicy *cazuela* (stew) of fresh seafood with coconut milk also has a Brazilian bent. The wine list has many of Argentina's top labels at fair prices. ⊠ *Bv. Nahuel Huapi 34* ☎ *2944/494–924* ▤ *AE, DC, MC, V.*

$$–$$$ ✕ **Waldhaus.** This Hansel and Gretel dark-timbered log house outside of town is open for lunch, tea, and dinner. It serves Argentine food with a Germanic flavor: goulash, spaetzle, fondue, and Patagonian lamb. The interior is a riot of hearts and flowers with Swiss canton shields on the walls and ceilings. ⊠ *Av. Arrayanes (R231) 6431* ☎ *2944/495–123* ▤ *No credit cards* ⊗ *Closed Mar.–June and Mon.–Tues. July–Oct. No lunch Mon.–Thurs. and July–Oct.*

WHERE TO STAY

$$$$ ✕▣ **Las Balsas.** A short drive down a secluded (and unpaved) road
★ brings you to this Relais & Châteaux hotel at the edge of Lago Nahuel Huapi. Rooms are small but all have lake views. The spa features an indoor-outdoor pool overlooking the lake. Afternoon tea and evening cocktails are served in the living room, where a crackling fire (in winter) and a homey blend of wicker, natural wood, and old photographs invite guests to linger. In the candlelit dining room, fresh trout and spectacular game dishes are accompanied by vegetables and spices grown in the hotel's organic garden. Dinner reservations are advised if you're not a guest. **Pros:** Incredible, secluded setting, much pampering, gourmet restaurant. **Cons:** Small rooms for a high price. ⊠ *Bahía las Balsas, Villa La Angostura, , Neuquén* ☎ *2944/494–308* ⊕ *www. lasbalsas.com* ⬐ *10 rooms, 3 suites* ⭄ *In-hotel: restaurant, bar, pool, gym, beachfront, bicycles, laundry service, public Internet* ▤ *AE, MC, V* ⊗ *Closed May 15–June 15* ❏ *CP.*

Chilean Lakes Crossing

Mountain biker overlooking lake in Bariloche, Argentina

There are seven border crossings in the Lake District. Paso Pérez Rosales is part of the popular 12-hour bus-and-boat tour from Bariloche to Puerto Montt, Chile (or Chile to Argentina). The **Cruce a Chile por Los Lagos** (Chile Lake Crossing) is a unique excursion by land and lakes. You can do the tour in one or two days in either direction. Beginning in Bariloche, you board the boat at Puerto Pañuelo, stopping for lunch in Puerto Blest, then travel by bus up to Laguna Frías, a cold glacial lake, frozen in winter. After crossing that lake to Puerto Fríos, you show your passport at Argentine customs; then board another bus that climbs through lush rain forest over a pass, before descending to **Peulla,** where Chilean customs is cleared just before arriving at a lodge by Lago Todos los Santos. You may spend the night (recommended) or continue on to Chile by catamaran from Peulla, across the lake, with views of the volcanoes Puntiagudo (which lost its *punto* [peak]

in an earthquake) and Osorno. The boat trip ends at the port of Petrohué. Another (and final) bus skirts Lago Llanquihue, stopping for a visit at the rockbound Petrohué waterfalls, passing through the town of Puerto Varas, and arriving, at last, at the Chilean port town of Puerto Montt.

■TIP→ Guides on the Argentina side speak little English.. Traveling with a tour group makes crossing easier. ⊠ *In Argentina: Puerto Blest S.A. Mitre 415, 1st fl., Bariloche* ☎ *2944/427–143* ⊠ *In Chile: Puerto Varas/Turismo Peulla San Juan 430 2nd fl., Puerto Varas* ☎ *(52)65/236–150* ⊘ *Daily 8:30–3* ⊕ *www.crucedelagos.com.*

The quickest way to return by paved road from Chile to Bariloche is via Osorno, crossing at Cardenal Samoré (aka Paso Puyehue) to Villa La Angostura (125 km [78 mi] from the border to Bariloche on RN231).

Paso Hua Hum is the only crossing open year-round. It may be the shortest route—only 47 km (29 mi) from San Martín de los Andes on RP48—as the condor flies, but it's the longest journey by road, after factoring in the 1½-hour ferry ride across Lake Pirehueico on the Chilean side. There are three ferries daily, and buses leave regularly from San Martín de los Andes. You can also make this crossing by raft on the river Hua Hum.

Farther north, and accessible via Junín de los Andes, are two passes that require a longer excursion. Mamuil Malal (aka Paso Tromen) is 67 km (41½ mi) northwest of Junín de los Andes on RP60. This dirt road crosses Lanín National Park and passes through a forest of ancient araucaria trees as it heads for the foot of Lanín Volcano. Just before the park office, a road leads to good picnic spots and campsites on Lago Tromen. If you continue on to Chile, you'll see the Villarrica and Quetupillán volcanoes to the south and Pucón to the north.

Paso Icalma is 132 km (82 mi) west of Zapala on RN13. Villa Pehuenia, 10 km (6 mi) before the pass, is a small village on the shore of Lake Alluminé with modern accommodations and restaurants. Rafting or fishing the Alluminé River, a visit to an araucaria nursery, plus horse, bike, and raft rentals might tempt you to stay awhile.

No fresh fruits, meats, or vegetables are allowed across the border, so bring a power bar for long stretches without food. Don't forget your passport, and dress for all kinds of weather—wet, windy, hot, or cold. Lake crossings are not fun in driving rain and high waves. Snow may close some passes in winter. Rental-car companies should give you the proper documents for your car, but it's a good idea to double-check that you have all the necessary paperwork. It's also a good idea to have some Chilean pesos with you as it can be expensive to change them at the border.

—Eddy Ancinas

3

$$$–$$$$ ⚐ **Costa Serena.** Every room at this complex in Puerto Manzano has a
  ⚙ lake view. A-frame *cabañas* (cabins) with decks, kitchens, and outdoor
barbecue sleep up to seven. Suites have huge wooden Jacuzzis with
views to the water. During high season a one-week minimum stay is
required in cabins. A large swimming pool and deck with grill, kay-
aks, and boats are on the lake. **Pros:** Good family-reunion spot. **Cons:**
Far from town and tourist attractions. ⊠ *Los Pinos 435, Puerto Man-
zano,* ☎☎2944/494–053 ⊕*www.costaserenavla.com.ar* ⬎7 *rooms,
3 suites, 4 cabins* ⬧*In-hotel: restaurant, bar, pool, gym, beachfront,
no elevator* ⊟*AE, MC, V* ℚ*CP.*

$$$$ ✕⚐ **Hotel Correntoso.** You can see the fish jump from your bedroom win-
Fodor's Choice dow, your dining table, the glass-paneled deck, or from the refurbished
  ★ 100-year-old fishing bar down by the lake. Perched on a hill where the
Correntoso River runs into Nahuel Huapi Lake, this landmark hotel
celebrates its place in history with old photos, light fixtures made from
coihué branches, handwoven Mapuche fabrics, and custom-made furni-
ture. The bar often has live music, and the restaurant overlooking the
lake serves Patagonian specialties such as hare, wild boar, lamb, beef,
and, of course, fish from local lakes and streams. A downstairs play-
room, conference room, indoor-outdoor pool and spa with a riveting
view from the massage table, all look out onto blue Nahuel Huapi Lake.
Children under 10 who are not hotel guests are not allowed in the dining
room, but they are welcome in the original fisherman's shack on the lake,
which has been converted to a casual café-bar serving snacks and sand-
wiches. **Pros:** Great location, food, spa, well-organized excursions. **Cons:**
Expensive. ⊠ *RN 231, Km 86, Puente Correntoso,* ☎2944/1561–9727,
11/4803–0030 in Buenos Aires ⊕*www.correntoso.com* ⬎16 *rooms,
16 suites* ⬧*In-hotel: restaurant, bar, public Wi-Fi, pool, spa, children's
programs* ⊟*AE, MC, V.*

$$ ⚐ **Naranjo en Flor.** This tranquil mountainside retreat in Puerto Manzano looks like a Norman hunting lodge yet feels like home, with a
fireplace in the living room and a piano bar and playroom for bad-
weather days. The restaurant offers interesting modern French cuisine. The modern carpeted bedrooms have big windows and tasteful
antiques. **Pros:** Personal attention. **Cons:** Off the main route, requires
a car. ⊠*Chucao 62,Puerto Manzano,* ☎☎2955/494–863 ✉*naran-
joenflor@infovia.com.ar* ⬎8 *rooms* ⬧*In-hotel: restaurant, bar, pool*
⊟*AE, V* ℚ*CP.*

$$ ⚐ **Pichi Rincón.** In a grove just beyond the village, this simple two-story
inn looks across a spacious lawn through a forest of coihués to the
lake. Two columns of gray river rock guard the comfortable sitting
area, which has a fireplace. Natural wood and hefty pine furniture
dominate everywhere, from common areas to rooms. **Pros:** Good value,
family oriented. **Cons:** Out of town, no restaurant. ⊠*Off Av. Quetri-
hué, 3 km (2 mi) south of town on R231; just before Correntoso, turn
left on Av. Quetrihué,* ☎☎2944/494–186 ⊕*www.pichirincon.com.ar*
⬎*12 rooms, 3 cabins* ⬧*In-room: no TV. In-hotel: pool, public Inter-
net* ⊟*MC, V* ℚ*CP.*

$$$$
FodorśChoice
★ ⚃ **Puerto Sur.** Stone and wood merge throughout the angular space of this hotel in Puerto Manzano. Built into the side of a hill, with views of the lake and mountains from enormous windows, every room has a lake view, Jacuzzi, and restrained modern art. The spa, indoor-outdoor pool, and private beach, plus impeccable service make the reasonable prices a pleasant surprise—near the bottom of the $$$$ range. A few extra pesos get you a private deck. **Pros:** Quiet, secluded spot. **Cons:** Far from town and tourist activities. ⊠*Los Pinos 221, Puerto Manzano, Villa La Angostura* ☎*2944/475–399* ⊕*www.hosteriapuertosur. com.ar* ⨝*7 rooms, 3 suites, 4 cabins* ⚭*In-hotel: public Wi-Fi, restaurant, bar, pool, gym, beachfront* ⊟*AE, MC, V* ⫣*CP.*

BARILOCHE

1,615 km (1,001 mi) southwest of Buenos Aires (2 hrs by plane); 432 km (268 mi) south of Neuquén on R237; 1,639 km (1,016 mi) north of Río Gallegos; 876 km (543 mi) northwest of Trelew; 357 km (221 mi) east of Puerto Montt, Chile, via lake crossing.

Bariloche is the gateway to all the recreational and scenic splendors of the Northern Lake District and headquarters for 2-million-acre Nahuel Huapi National Park. Although planes, boats, and buses arrive daily, you can escape on land or water—or just by looking out a window—into a dazzling wilderness of lakes, waterfalls, mountain glaciers, forests, and meadows.

The town of Bariloche hugs the southeastern shore of Nahuel Huapi Lake, expanding rapidly east toward the airport and west along the lake toward Llao Llao, as Argentines and foreigners buy and build without any apparent zoning plan. Being the most popular vacation destination in Patagonia has not been kind to the town once called the "Switzerland of the Andes." Traffic barely moves on streets and sidewalks during holidays and the busy months of January–March, July, and August.

Nevertheless, the Centro Cívico (Civic Center), with its gray-green stone-and-log buildings has not lost its architectural integrity. Designed by Alejandro Bustillo, this landmark square, with its view of the lake and mountains, is a good place to begin exploring Bariloche.

EXPLORING BARILOCHE

Whether you choose to stay in town, close to shops, restaurants, tour offices and public transportation, or outside the city on Avenida Bustillo, the Peninsula Llao Llao, or nearby Lago Gutiérrez, you'll find plenty of local tour offices, friendly concierges in hotels, taxis and rental-car agencies to assist you. A good way to get your bearings is to start with the Circuito Chico from Bariloche around the Llao Llao peninsula, or go to the top of Cerro Otto and get a 360-degree view of lakes, mountains, and urban areas.

GETTING HERE & AROUND

For long excursions, such as the Seven Lakes Route, Circuito Grande, or Tronodor (⇨*below*), sign up for a tour through your hotel or with a local tour agency. If you prefer the independence of figuring out maps and driving yourself, rent a car. Tour operators for fishing, rafting, and bike trips will pick you up and transport you to your destination. For good maps and a list of tour operators, look for *Guía Busch* at local bookstores, car-rental agencies, and kiosks. A local bus picks up skiers in Bariloche, and many hotels have their own shuttle.

SAFETY   Driving in Bariloche requires total attention to blind corners, one-way streets, and stop signs where no one stops. Never leave anything in your car. On Bariloche's challenging sidewalks, uneven steps, broken pavement, and unexpected holes are potential ankle-breakers. When students hit Bariloche during holidays, they party until 5 or 6 in the morning, resulting in serious drunk-driving auto accidents.

ESSENTIALS

BUS   **Bariloche Bus Terminal** (⊠ *Av. 12 de Octubre* ☎ *2944/432–860*). **Algarrobal** (☎ *9 de Julio 1800* ☎ *2944/427–698*). **Andesmar** (⊠ *Mitre 385* ☎ *2944/430–211*). **Don Otto** (⊠ *At the bus terminal, Mitre 321* ☎ *2944/429–012*). **VIATAC** (⊠ *Moreno 138* ☎ *2944/434–727*). **El Valle** (⊠ *Av. 12 de Octubre 1884* ☎ *2944/431–444*). **Via Bariloche** (⊠ *Mitre 321* ☎ *2944/432–444*).

CURRENCY   **Banco Frances** (⊠ *Av. San Martín 332* ☎ *2944/430–325*). **Bansud** (⊠ *Mitre 427* ☎ *2944/424–210*).

MAIL   **Post office** (⊠ *Moreno 175*).

MEDICAL   **Angel Gallardo** (⊠ *Gallardo 701* ☎ *2944/427–023*). **Farmacia Detina** (⊠ *Bustillo 12,500* ☎ *2944/525–900*). **Hospital Zonal Ramón Carillo** (⊠ *Moreno 601* ☎ *2944/426–119*). **Hospital Sanatorio del Sol** (⊠ *20 de Febrero 598* ☎ *2944/525–000*).

REMIS   **Patagonia Remises** (⊠ *Av. Pioneros 4400* ☎ *2944/443–700*).
(CAR & DRIVER)

RENTAL CARS   **Baricoche** (⊠ *Moreno 115* ☎ *2944/427–638* ⊕ *www.baricoche.com.ar*). **Localiza** (⊠ *Emilio Frey & V.A. O'Conner* ☎ *2944/435–374, 2944/1562–7708 cell* ⊕ *www. autosurpatagonia.com.ar*).

VISITOR INFO   **Oficina Municipal de Turismo** (⊠ *Centro Cívico, across from clock tower* ☎ *2944/429–850* ⊕ *www.barilochepatagonia.info* ✍ *secturismo@bariloche.com. ar*) is open daily 8:30 AM–9 PM.

WHAT TO SEE

The **Museo de la Patagonia** tells the social and geological history of northern Patagonia through displays of Indian and gaucho artifacts and exhibits on regional flora and fauna. The history of the Mapuche and the Conquista del Desierto (Conquest of the Desert) are explained in detail. ⊠ *Centro Cívico, next to arch over Bartolomé Mitre* ☎ *2944/422–330* 🖙 *2.50 pesos* ⊙ *Mon. and Sat. 10–1, Tues.– Fri. 10–12:30 and 2–7.*

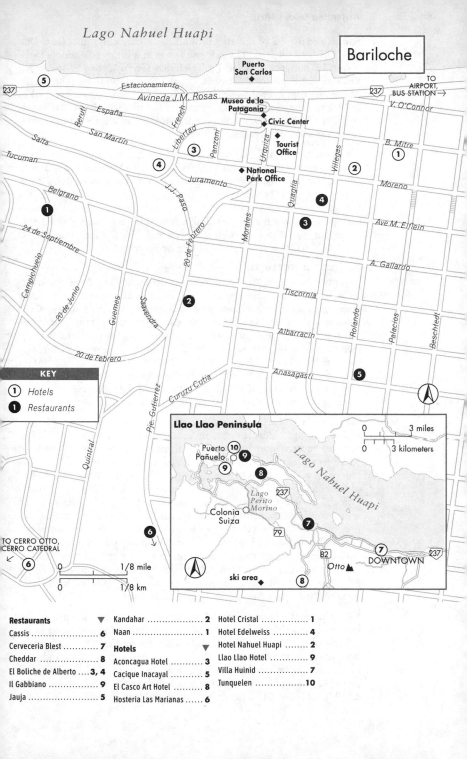

Lago Nahuel Huapi

Bariloche

TO AIRPORT, BUS STATION →

Puerto San Carlos

Museo de la Patagonia

Civic Center

Tourist Office

National Park Office

Estacionamiento

Avineda J.M. Rosas

KEY

① Hotels

❶ Restaurants

TO CERRO OTTO, CERRO CATEDRAL

Llao Llao Peninsula

Lago Nahuel Huapi

Puerto Pañuelo

Lago Perito Morino

Colonia Suiza

DOWNTOWN

Otto

ski area

0   3 miles

0   3 kilometers

0   1/8 mile

0   1/8 km

Restaurants ▼	**Hotels** ▼	
Cassis **6**	Aconcagua Hotel **3**	Hotel Cristal **1**
Cerveceria Blest **7**	Cacique Inacayal **5**	Hotel Edelweiss **4**
Cheddar **8**	El Casco Art Hotel **8**	Hotel Nahuel Huapi **2**
El Boliche de Alberto **3, 4**	Hosteria Las Marianas **6**	Llao Llao Hotel **9**
Il Gabbiano **9**	Kandahar **2**	Villa Huinid **7**
Jauja **5**	Naan **1**	Tunquelen **10**

For an aerial view of the area around Bariloche, don't miss **Cerro Otto** (Mt. Otto; 4,608 feet). The ride to the top in a little red gondola takes about 12 minutes. Owned by **Teleférico Cerro Otto** (⊠*Av. de los Pioneros* ☎*30 pesos* ⊙*Daily 10–5*), all proceeds go to local hospitals. At the very top, a revolving cafeteria with a 360-degree panorama takes in Monte Tronadór, the spiky towers of Catedral Ski Area, Bariloche, and lakes Nahuel Huapi on one side, Moreno on another, and Gutiérrez in yet another direction.

The mountain is 5 km (3 mi) west of town; a free shuttle bus leaves from the corner of Mitre and Villegas, and Perito Moreno and Independencia. You can also hike or mountain bike to the top, or drive 8 km (5 mi) up a gravel road from Bariloche. In winter, cross-country skis and sleds are for rent at the cafeteria. In summer, hiking and mountain biking are the main activities. For a real thrill, try soaring in a paraplane out over the lake with the condors. Call for **information** (☎ 2944/441–035) on schedules and sled or ski rentals.

OUTDOOR ACTIVITIES

HORSEBACK RIDING — Argentine horses are sturdy and well trained, much like American quarter horses. *Tábanas* (horseflies) attack humans and animals in summer months, so wear long sleeves on *cabalgatas* (horseback outings). **Carol Jones** is a the granddaughter of an early pioneering family, and her ranch north of town does day rides and overnights from the Patagonian steppes into the mountains (☎*2944/426–508* ⊕*www.caroljones. com*). **El Manso** (☎*2944/523–641 or 2944/441–378*) combines riding and rafting over the border to Chile. **Tom Wesley** at the **Club Hípico Bariloche** (⊠*Av. Bustillo, Km 15.5* ☎☎*2944/448–193* ⊕*www.cabalgatas tomwesley.com*) does rides lasting from one hour to a week.

SKIING — **Cerro Catedral** (Mt. Cathedral), named for its Gothic-looking spires, is the largest and oldest ski area in South America, with 39 lifts, 4,500 acres of mostly intermediate terrain, and a comfortable altitude of 6,725 feet. The runs are long, varied, and scenic. One side of the mountain has a vertical drop of 3,000 feet, mostly in the fall line. At the top of the highest chair lift, a Poma Lift transports skiers to a weather station at 7,385 feet, where a small restaurant, **Refugio Lynch,** is tucked into a wind-sculpted snow pocket on the edge of an abyss with a stupendous 360-degree view of Nahuel Huapi Lake. To the southwest, Monte Tronadór, a 12,000-foot extinct volcano, straddles the border with Chile, towering above lesser peaks that surround the lake. August and September are the best months to ski. Avoid the first three weeks of July (school vacation). ✛*46 km (28½ mi) west of town on Av. Bustillo (R237); turn left at Km 8.5 just past Playa Bonita.*

Villa Catedral (www.catedralaltapatagonia.com), at the base of the mountain, has ski retail and rental shops, information and ticket sales, ski-school offices, restaurants, and even a disco. Frequent buses transport skiers from Bariloche to the ski area. For information and trail maps, contact **La Secretaría de Turismo de Río Negro** (⊠*12 de Octubre 605* ☎*2944/423–188*). **Club Andino Bariloche** (⊠*20 de Febrero 30* ☎*2944/422–266*) also has information and trail maps.

CLOSE UP

Fishing The Lakes

Fishing season runs November 15–May 1. In some areas, catch-and-release is allowed year-round; catch-and-release is usually compulsory, but in some places catches may be kept. Guides are available by the day or the week. Nahuel Huapi, Gutiérrez, Mascardi, Correntoso, and Traful are the most accessible lakes in the northern Lake District. If you're seeking the perfect pool or secret stream for fly-fishing, you may have to do some hiking, particularly along the banks of the Chimehuín, Limay, Traful, and Correntoso rivers. Near Junín de los Andes, the Malleo and Currihué rivers, and lakes Huechulafquen, Paimún, and Lácar are good fishing grounds. Near El Bolsón and Esquel in the Parque Nacional los Alerces, many remote lakes and streams are accessible only by boat or dirt roads. Fishing lodges offer rustic comfort in beautiful settings; boats, guides, and plenty of fishing tales are usually included. Make reservations early.

Fishing licenses allowing you to catch brown, rainbow, and brook trout as well as perch and *salar sebago* (landlocked salmon) are obtainable in Bariloche at the **Direcciones Provinciales de Pesca** (✉ *Elfleín 10* ☎ *2944/425–160*). You can also get licenses at the Nahuel Huapi National Park office and at most tackle shops. Boats can be rented at **Charlie Lake Rent-A-Boat** (✉ *Av. Ezequiel Bustillo, Km 16.6* ☎☎ *2944/448–562*).

Oscar Baruzzi at **Baruzzi Deportes** (✉ *Urquiza 250* ☎ *2944/424–922*) is a good local fishing guide. **Martín Pescador** (✉ *Rolando 257* ☎ *2944/422–275* ✉ *martinpescador@bariloche.com.ar*) has a shop with fishing and hunting equipment. Ricardo Almeijeiras, also a guide, owns the **Patagonia Fly Shop** (✉ *Quinchahuala 200, Av. Bustillo, Km 6.7* ☎☎ *2944/441–944* ✉ *flyshop@bariloche.com.ar*).

3

ZIPLINE & PARAGLIDING TOURS

Parapente (paragliding) gives you the opportunity to soar with the condors through mountains and out over lakes, lagoons, and valleys. Cerro Otto and Cerro Catedral (both accessible by ski lift) are popular launch sites. For equipment and guide information, contact **Parapente Bariloche** (☎ *2944/462–234, 2944/1555–2403* ✉ *prapente@bariloche.com.ar*). **Canopy** (☎ *2944/1560–7191* ⊕ *www.canopybariloche.com*) allows you to zipline above the forest of Colonia Suiza. Call first, as it doesn't happen every day.

SCENIC JOURNEYS

The **Circuito Chico** (Small Circuit) is a 70-km (43½-mi) half-day scenic trip from Bariloche along the west shore of Lago Nahuel Huapi. As you head west on Avenida Bustillo (R237) toward Península Llao Llao, enjoy the lake views and variety of lodgings on either side of the road until you reach the Península Llao Llao and **Puerto Pañuelo** (Km 25.5) on a little bay on the right—the embarkation point for lake excursions and for the boat crossing to Chile.

Across from the port, the Hotel Llao Llao sits on a knoll surrounded by three different lakes, with a backdrop of sheer rock cliffs and snow-covered mountains. You'll have to admire from afar if you're not a guest (or haven't made a lunch reservation). The Circuito Chico then circumvents the Llao Llao peninsula, following R77 to Bahía Lopez. Following the lake's edge, you glimpse the bay through a forest of ghostly, leafless lenga trees. After crossing the bridge that links Lago Moreno and Lago Nahuel Huapi at Bahía Lopez, the road crosses Arroyo Lopez (Lopez Creek), where you can stop for a hike up to a waterfall, or continue driving above Lago Moreno to Punto Pan-oramico, a scenic overlook worth a photo stop. Just before you cross the bridge that separates Lago Moreno east and west, an unmarked dirt road off to the right leads to the rustic village of **Colonia Suiza,** a good spot to stop for tea or lunch before exploring further. After crossing the Moreno Bridge, and passing Laguna El Trebol (a small lake on your left), R77 joins R237 back to Bariloche.

NEED A BREAK?   **Cheddar Casa de Te.** There's a little log house with a corrugated metal roof, a stone terrace and red umbrellas hanging out over the lake, with views through the gnarly branches of a giant coihué tree to blue water and distant mountains. The trout sorrentinos in pesto sauce are as good as the view. ✉ *Av. Bustillo (R237), Km 25* ☏ *2944/448–152* ☐ *MC, V* ☉ *Closed Tues.*

The **Circuito Grande** (Large Circuit) covers 250 km (155 mi) in an all-day excursion across the lake from Bariloche, and includes two towns where you could spend a night. Leaving Bariloche on R237 heading east, follow the Río Limay into the Valle Encantado (Enchanted Valley), with its magical red-rock formations. Before crossing the bridge at Confluéncia (where the Río Traful joins the Limay), turn left onto R65 to Lago Traful. Five kilometers (3 mi) beyond the turnoff, on a dirt road heading toward Cuyín Manzano, are some astounding sandstone formations. As you follow the shore of Lago Traful, a sign indicates a *mirador* (lookout) on a high rock promontory, which you can climb up to on wooden stairs. The road from Villa Traful dives into a dense forest until it comes to the intersection with the Seven Lakes Circuit (R237). Turn right if you want to add the Seven Lakes Circuit. Otherwise, turn left and follow the shore of Lago Correntoso to the paved road down to the bay at Villa La Angostura.

A less-traveled all-day boat excursion to **Puerto Blest** leaves from Puerto Pañuelo on the Península Llao Llao (accessible by bus, car, or tour). The boat heads west along the shore of Lago Nahuel Huapi to Brazo Blest, a 1-km-long (½-mi-long) fjordlike arm of the lake. Along the way, waterfalls plunge down the face of high rock walls. A Valdivian rain forest of coihués, cypress, lengas, and *arrayanes* (myrtle) covers the canyon walls. After the boat docks at Puerto Blest, a bus transports you over a short pass to Puerto Alegre on **Laguna Frías** (Cold Lagoon), where a launch waits to ferry you across the frosty green water to **Puerto Fríos** on the other side. Monte Tronadór towers like a great white sentinel. The launch returns to the dock at Puerto Alegre, where you can return by foot or by bus to Puerto Blest. From there, the trail to **Cascada Los Cántaros** (Singing Waterfalls) climbs 600 steps to a series of waterfalls cascading from rock to pool to rock. After lunch in **Puerto**

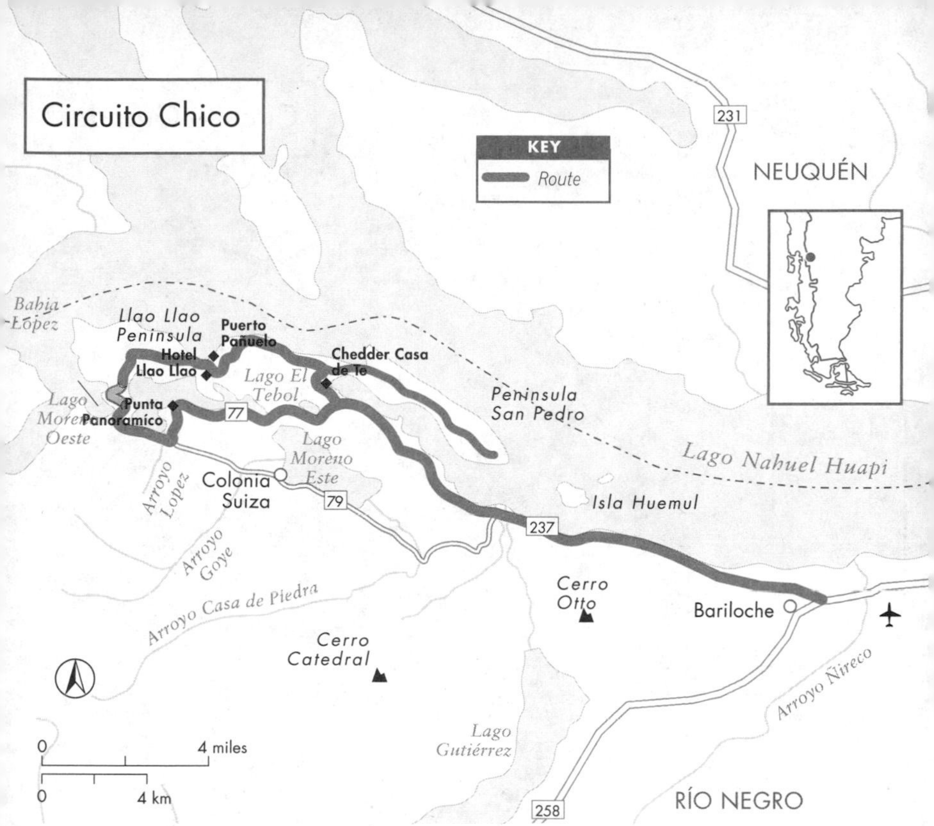
Circuito Chico
KEY
Route
231
NEUQUÉN
Bahia
Lopez
Llao Llao
Peninsula
Puerto
Pañuelo
Hotel
Llao Llao
Chedder Casa
de Te
Lago El
Tebol
Lago
Moreno
Oeste
Punta
Panoramico
77
Peninsula
San Pedro
Lago
Moreno
Este
Colonia
Suiza
79
Arroyo
Lopez
Lago Nahuel Huapi
Isla Huemul
237
Arroyo
Goye
Arroyo Casa de Piedra
Cerro
Otto
Bariloche
Cerro
Catedral
Arroyo Ñireco
0
4 miles
0
4 km
Lago
Gutiérrez
258
RÍO NEGRO

Blest at its venerable old hotel, the boat returns to Bariloche. Note: this is the first leg of the Cruce a Chile por Los Lagos.

WHERE TO EAT

$ ✕**El Boliche de Alberto.** Leather place mats, calfskin menus, and the smell of beef all hint heavily at steak house. Alberto has the best beef in Bariloche. Grilled chicken, lamb, and chorizos all arrive sizzling on a wooden platter, accompanied by empanadas, *provoleta* (fried provolone cheese), salad, fried potatoes, and chimichurri sauce (slather it on the bread). ✉ *Villegas 347* ☎ *2944/431–433* ✉ *Bustillo 8800* ☎ *2944/462–285* 🌐 *www.elbolichedealberto.com* ▭ *AE, DC, MC, V.*

$$ ✕**El Boliche Viejo.** A hundred years ago gauchos stopped here by the Río Limay to eat, drink, and buy supplies, and to catch up on local news. With the same plank floors, grocery shelves from floor to ceiling, and wood siding decorated with pictures from the past—including one of Butch Cassidy and his buddies—this old store-bar-café is worth the 20-minute drive from town. There's a very ungaucho-like salad bar to accompany all the meat cuts, chorizos, and empanadas. Flan with dulce de leche and real whipped cream is the final touch. ✉ *Ruta 237, at Rio Limay Bridge* ☎ *2944/468–452* ▭ *AE, MC, V* ⏲ *No dinner Sun.*

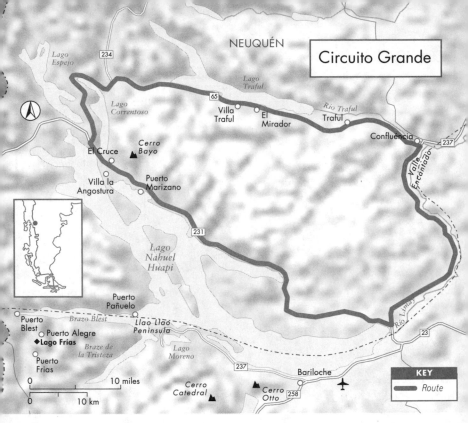

$-$$ ✗ **Cerveceria Blest.** This lively spot claims that it was the first brewpub in Argentina, and its relaxed bustle hits the spot after a day on the slopes. Don't miss the excellent bock beer, with a toasty coffee flavor, or if you prefer hard cider, the Fruto Prohibido. You can come in just for an après-ski beer sampler, or stay for dinner, which might include *costillitas de cerdo ahumadas con chucrut* (smoked pork chops with sauerkraut—is there a more classic beer food than that?). Pizzas, steak potpies, and other Anglophilic options round out the menu. ⊠ *Av. Bustillo, Km 11.6* ☎ *2944/461–026* ▭ *AE, MC, V.*

$$$$ ✗ **Cassis.** Chef Mariana began her culinary career in Argentina's best
Fodor's Choice resorts, until she and her husband found the perfect spot to showcase
★ her considerable talent: on lovely Lago Gutiérrez, across the road from the Arelauquen resort (a 30-minute drive from Bariloche). Together they have created dishes like venison baked in rhubarb and black-currant sauce; carrot, lime, and lemongrass soup; and fantastic desserts such as crispy quince tart with cardamom ice cream or crepes and cakes smothered with fresh berries. The lake views from tall windows, and low candlelight flickering on the beamed ceiling all contribute to a memorable dining experience. ⊠ *R82 Arelauquen Point, Lago Gutiérrez* ☎ *2944/476–167* ⊕ *www.cassis.com.ar* ✍ *Reservations essential* ▭ *No credit cards.*

$$$–$$$$ ✕**Il Gabbiano.** "We don't serve lunch," the folks at this cozy, candlelit house on the Circuito Chico near Llao Llao boast, "because preparing dinner takes all day long." It's hard to argue with that philosophy after you sample the exquisite pastas, which change daily. Look for *tortelli* stuffed with wild boar, or pumpkin ravioli; they also have a way with fresh trout. A beautiful wine cellar is open to guests. ⊠ *Av. Bustillo, Km 24.3* ☎ *2944/448–346* ⚞ *Reservations essential* ⊟ *No credit cards* ☾ *Closed Tues. No lunch.*

$$–$$$ ✕**Jauja.** Big and friendly, Jauja is a favorite with families for its great variety of entrées: meats from Patagonia to the Pampas, fish from both oceans, local game, and pasta dishes are enhanced by fresh vegetables and salads. Take-out food is ordered around the corner at the Quaglia address. ⊠ *Elflein 128* ☎ *2944/429–986* ⊠ *Quaglia 366* ☎ *2944/422– 952* ⊟ *AE, DC, MC, V.*

$$$$ ✕**Kandahar.** A rustic wood building with a woodstove and cozy window seats in alcoves is the perfect setting for sipping a pisco sour, and savoring a plate of smoked trout or salmon and guacamole. Start with the *tarteleta de hongos* (mushroom tart) and *rosa mosqueta* (rose hip) soup, followed by wild game and profiteroles with hot chocolate sauce. ⊠ *20 de Febrero 698* ☎ *2944/424–702* ⊟ *AE, MC, V.*

$$$$ ✕**Naan.** You can go around the world in six courses at this small private home-cum-restaurant in Bariloche's upscale hillside neighborhood, Barrio Belgrano. Vegetarian Viet Nam rolls, Italian panini, French mushroom gratin, Thai soup, Lebanese baba ghanoush—even Tex-Mex quesadillas make great shared appetizers. Then come the main courses: Moroccan pilaf, Chinese beef with shiitake mushrooms and asparagus, a Brazilian seafood plate, Greek lamb kabob, French grilled trout. Desserts are equally creative concoctions of local berries and chocolate whipped, moussed, meringued, or creped. ⊠ *Campichuelo 568, Barrio Belgrano* ☎ *2944/421–785* ⚞ *Reservations essential* ⊟ *AE, MC, V* ☾ *Closed Mon. and 3 weeks in Nov.*

WHERE TO STAY

Accommodations range from family-run *residenciales* (bed-and-breakfasts) to downtown hotels, country inns, resort-spa hotels, fishing lodges, and super-luxurious retreats. If you don't have a car, it's better to stay in town. If you're looking for serenity, consider a lake-view hotel or cabins along the route to the Llao Llao Peninsula. Addresses for out-of-town dining and lodging properties are measured in kilometers from the Bariloche Civic Center.

$$ ☷**Aconcagua Hotel.** A tidy stucco building close to the Civic Center, this four-story hotel has weekly rates for its basic rooms, some of which have lake views. It's neither luxurious nor particularly attractive, but it provides reasonable comfort for little money. **Pros:** Great location close to town. **Cons:** Decor is cold and slightly shabby. ⊠ *Av. San Martín 289,* ☎ *2944/424–718* ⊕ *www.aconcaguahotel.com.ar* ⇌ *32 rooms* ⚑ *In-hotel: parking (no fee)* ⊟ *AE, MC, V* ☷ *CP.*

$$$$ 🎑 **Cacique Inacayal.** Looking out from your bedroom window when
★   the wind whips up the waves on Nahuel Huapi Lake, you'll be glad
you're on land. Perched on a cliff overlooking the lake, Cacique Inacayal has the reception, bar, and an outdoor patio on the top; fine
dining room for hotel guests down one floor; and lake-view rooms on
the three floors below. In the middle of it all, a glass-covered atrium
six stories high allows light into all floors and interior spaces. Dinner
is included in the price and consists of a cold buffet, soup, and two
entrées to choose from. **Pros:** The maître d' makes every dinner seem
like a party. **Cons:** Music in the bar (until 10 PM) could be disturbing
to guests on lower floors, as could be smoke drifting upwards. ⊠*Juan
Manuel de Rosas 625,8400* 🕿🖴*2944/433–888* ⊕*www.hotelinacayal.
com.ar* 🗗*57 rooms* ⚲*In-hotel: bar, parking, public Wi-Fi* ⊟*AE, DC,
MC, V* ⏿*AP.*

$$$$ 🎑 **El Casco Art Hotel.** Intriguing sculptures, perched on marble stands,
Fodor'sChoice   wooden ledges, or freestanding in the garden are part of a collection of
★   over 200 artworks displayed throughout the hotel. All public spaces—
halls, wine bar, gourmet restaurant—even the downstairs gym, indoor-
out swimming pool, and large Jacuzzi—face the lake, where the hotel's
private launch is docked at the pier. The rooms are huge, done in the
same natural colors, with good art and a great view being the major
attractions. The hotel is only 15 minutes from the ski area, Bariloche,
and two 18-hole golf courses. **Pros:** Art everywhere, activities galore,
self-contained luxury. **Cons:** Perhaps too much extravagance for some.
⊠*Av. Bustillo, Km 11.5,* 🕿*2944/463–131* ⊕*www.hotelelcasco.com*
🗗*57 suites* ⚲*In-hotel: restaurant, bar, gym, pool, public Wi-Fi* ⊟*AE,
DC, MC, V* ⏿*FAP.*

$$ 🎑 **Hosteria Las Marianas.** A perfectly proportioned Tyrolean villa, this
B&B on a sunny hillside in Barrio Belgrano, the nicest neighborhood
in town, is only four blocks from the city center, but it's in a world of
its own on a quiet street surrounded by well-tended gardens. The own-
ers are mountaineers and skiers, and their photos decorate the walls
of the breakfast room, where homemade breads and jams are served
to guests who gather at breakfast or tea-time. **Pros:** Away from the
crowds. **Cons:** Uphill haul from city center. ⊠*24 de Septiembre 218,*
🕿🖴*2944/439–876* ⊕*www.hosterialasmarianas.com.ar* 🗗*16 rooms*
⚲*In-hotel: no elevator, public Internet* ⊟*No credit cards* ⏿*CP.*

$–$$ 🎑 **Hotel Cristal.** A basic businesslike downtown hotel, this recycled old
standby in the center of Bariloche has been greatly improved with mod-
ern furnishings and better facilities as tour groups and independent
travelers discover the flavor of being on the street with all the chocolate
shops. The lobby has a nice fireplace and bar. The standard no-frills
rooms are tidy and adequate. **Pros:** Central downtown location, good
value. **Cons:** Small bathrooms, desultory reception, popular with tour
groups. ⊠*Mitre 355,* 🕿🖴*2944/422–442* ⊕*www.hotelcristal.com.ar*
🗗*50 rooms* ⚲*In-hotel: restaurant, bar, public Wi-Fi* ⊟*AE, DC, MC,
V* ⏿*CP.*

$$$$ ✕▦ **Hotel Edelweiss.** Fresh flowers from the owner's nursery are through-out this medium-size hotel, which is within walking distance of every-thing in town. Rooms on the upper floors have lake views from bay windows. Ski and tour buses, whether arranged through the hotel or other travel agencies, pick up passengers at the front door. **Pros:** Great location, helpful staff. **Cons:** Bar has no windows, so-so street-side res-taurant. ✉ *Av. San Martín 202,* ☏ *2944/445–500* ⊕ *www.edelweiss. com.ar* ↻ *94 rooms, 6 suites* ⚷ *In-room: safe. In-hotel: restaurant, bar, pool, gym, parking (no fee), spa, public Wi-Fi* ▭ *AE, DC, MC, V* ⊙*CP.*

$$$–$$$$ ▦ **Hotel Nahuel Huapi.** This slick city hotel on a busy downtown street in Bariloche has a spacious lobby with a wine bar in one corner and a sit-around fireplace in another. Locally made ceramics decorate the interior. Textured beige wallpaper in the large bedrooms shows off the deep reds and browns of the woven bedspreads and upholstered chairs. Some rooms have a nice view into the neighbor's garden. **Pros:** Central location, good accessibility for people with disabilities. **Cons:** Rooms overlooking street might be noisy. ✉ *Moreno 252,* ☏☏ *2944/433–635* ⊕ *www.hotelnahuelhuapi.com.ar* ↻ *86 rooms* ⚷ *In-hotel: restaurant, bar, parking, gym* ▭ *AE, DC, MC, V* ⊙*CP.*

$$$–$$$$ ▦ **Hotel Tunquelen.** The view across the water to distant peaks—from your room, the living room, even from the indoor pool—is the defining feature of this château-like hotel on the lake. The whitewashed rooms trimmed with stucco and native wood open onto the garden or (for an extra US$30 or so) overlook the lake. **Pros:** Tranquil setting. **Cons:** Out of town. ✉ *Av. Bustillo, Km 24.5, 24½ km (13 mi) west of Bariloche on the road to Llao Llao,* ☏☏ *2944/448–600* ⊕ *www.maresur.com* ↻ *31 rooms, 5 suites, 4 apartments* ⚷ *In-hotel: restaurant, bar, pool, gym, bicycles, airport shuttle, parking (no fee), public Wi Fi* ▭ *AE, DC, MC, V* ⊙*CP.*

$$$$ ▦ **Llao Llao Hotel & Resort.** This masterpiece by architect Alejandro Bustillo sits on a grassy knoll surrounded by three lakes with a back-drop of rock cliffs and snow-covered mountains. Local wood—alerce, cypress, and hemlock—has been used for the walls along the 100-yard hallway, where paintings by local artists are displayed. Every room has a view worth keeping the curtains open for. A lunch or dinner reserva-tion will also get you inside to see one of the most beautiful hotels in the world. **Pros:** Beautiful setting, helpful staff, lots of activities. **Cons:** The public is only allowed to visit this landmark hotel on a guided tour on Wednesday at 3 PM. ✉ *Av. Ezequiel Bustillo, Km 25, 25 km (15½ mi) west of Bariloche,* ☏ *2944/448–530* ⊕ *www.llaollao.com* ↻ *153 rooms, 12 suites, 1 cabin* ⚷ *In-room: safe. In-hotel: 2 restaurants, bar, golf course, pool, gym, spa, water sports, bicycles, children's programs (ages 2–12), no-smoking rooms* ▭ *AE, DC, MC, V* ⊙*CP.*

$$$$ ▦ **Villa Huinid.** This peaceful complex of cabins is lorded over by a grand hotel with a lake-view pool and spa. On the lawns below the hotel are older two-story log-and-stucco cottages (one, two, or three bedrooms), with stone chimneys and wooden decks that give the

appearance of private homes with well-tended gardens. You'll enjoy cypress-plank floors with radiant heat, carved wooden counters, and a view of Nahuel Huapi Lake. **Pros:** Like renting a cabin with all the amenities of a hotel. **Cons:** Outdoor hike to breakfast in hotel. ✉*Av. Bustillo, Km 2.6,* ☎*2944/523–523* ⊕*www.villahuinid.com.ar* ⇥*46 rooms, 17 cabins* ⚷*In-room: kitchen. In-hotel: restaurant, bar, pool, gym, public Wi-Fi* ▱*AE, MC, V.*

SHOPPING

Along Bariloche's main streets, calles Mitre and Moreno, and the cross streets from Quaglia to Rolando, you can find shops selling sports equipment, leather goods, hand-knit sweaters, and gourmet food like homemade jams, dried meats, and chocolate. **Ahumadero Familia Weiss** (✉*Palacios 401* ☎*2944/435–789* ✉*Av. Bustillo, Km 20* ☎*2944/435–789*) sells pâtés, cheeses, smoked fish, and wild game.

Chocolate shops, some the size of a supermarket, are on both sides of Mitre. Look for the little Russian-doll faces at **Mamuschka** (✉*Mitre 298* ⊕*www.mamuschka.com*), the bright-red store on the corner, where they hand you a plate of samples to

> ### DISCO DOWN
>
> Three of the town's most popular *discotecas* (discos) are all on the same street, Avenida J. M. de Rosas. Whole families—from children to grandparents—go to discos, though on Saturday night only people 25 and older are admitted. You can dance the night away at **Cerebro** (✉*405 Av. J. M. de Rosas* ☎*2944/424–948*). Bariloche's oldest disco is **El Grisú** (✉*574 Av. J. M. de Rosas* ☎*2944/424–483*). **Roket** (✉*424 Av. J. M. de Rosas* ☎*2944/431–940* ⊕*www.roket.com*) has a cutting-edge sound system.

choose from. You could go down the street sampling the whole block. **Fenoglio** (✉*Mitre and Rolando* ☎*544/423–119*) has ice cream and a café to complement the chocolate confections. **Rapa Nui** (✉*Mitre 202* ☎*944/423–779*) is another high-quality chocolate shop.

Talabarterís sell items for the discerning equestrian or modern gaucho. **Cardon** (✉*Av. San Martín 324*) is a fine leather store whose leather jackets, coats, vests, bags, belts, and boots are sold all over Argentina. At **El Establo** (✉*Mitre 22*), look for shoes, handbags, belts, wallets, and wall coverings with distinctive black-and-white Mapuche designs.

Unusual hand-knit sweaters and hand-painted shirts, skirts, and dresses are at **Mano a Mano** (✉*Mitre 265*).

Cerámica Bariloche (✉*Mitre 112*) has been creating fine ceramics inspired by colorful local flora and fauna for 50 years. **Cultura Libros** (✉*Elfleín 78* ☎*944/420–193*) carries books in English and coffee-table books with superb photos of the Lake District and Patagonia, as well as local guidebooks. **La Barca Libros** (✉*Quaglia 247*) has used books in English and photography and guidebooks.

PARQUE NACIONAL NAHUEL HUAPI

Created in 1943, the Parque Nacional Nahuel Huapi is Argentina's oldest national park. The park extends over 2 million acres along the eastern side of the Andes in the provinces of Neuquén and Río Negro, on the frontier with Chile. It contains the highest concentration of lakes in Argentina. The biggest is Lago Nahuel Huapi, an 897-square-km (346-square-mi) body of water, whose seven long arms (the longest is 96 km [60 mi] long, 12 km [7 mi] wide) reach deep into forests of *coihué* (a native beech tree), *cyprés* (cypress), and *lenga* (deciduous beech) trees. Intensely blue across its vast expanse and aqua green in its shallow bays, the lake meanders into distant lagoons and misty inlets where the mountains, covered with vegetation at their base, rise straight up out of the water. Every water sport invented and tours to islands and other lakes can be arranged through local travel agencies, tour offices, and through hotels. Information offices throughout the park offer help in exploring the miles of mountain and woodland trails and the lakes.

EXPLORING

Having landed in Bariloche, you can explore the park on an organized tour or on your own. Nearby excursions such as the Circuito Chico, Circuito Grande, a trip to Tronodór, or the ski area at Catedral can be done in a day. Since much of the park is covered by Nahuel Huapi Lake (it's 96 km [57 miBC long, covering 346 square mi), some of your exploration will be by boat to islands, down narrow fjords, or to distant shores on organized excursions. Small towns like Villa La Angostura and Villa Traful are excellent destinations for further explorations on foot or by horse to smaller lakes with their connecting streams, waterfalls, and surrounding forests and high peaks. Since most of the park is at a low elevation (under 6,000 feet), getting around in winter is not difficult—just cold. Fall foliage, long, warm summer days, and spring flowers are the rewards of other seasons. Park entry is 12 pesos.

GETTING HERE & AROUND

Most people arrive by plane from Buenos Aires or Calafate, or by boat from Chile. The easy way to get around is to plan your days with a local tour operator or remis, or rent a car, mixing up excursions between land and lake. When planning all-day or overnight trips, remember that distances are long, and unpaved roads slow you down, so you can't pack as much into a day as you would at home.

WHAT TO SEE

The most popular excursion on Lago Nahuel Huapi is the 30-minute boat ride to **Isla Victoria,** the largest island in the lake. A grove of redwoods transplanted from California thrives in the middle of the island. Walk on trails that lead to enchanting views of emerald bays and still lagoons.

The **Parque Nacional los Arrayanes** (✉ *12 km [7½ mi] along a trail from the Península Quetrihué* ☎ *2944/423–111*) is the only forest of arrayanes in the world. These trees absorb so much water through their

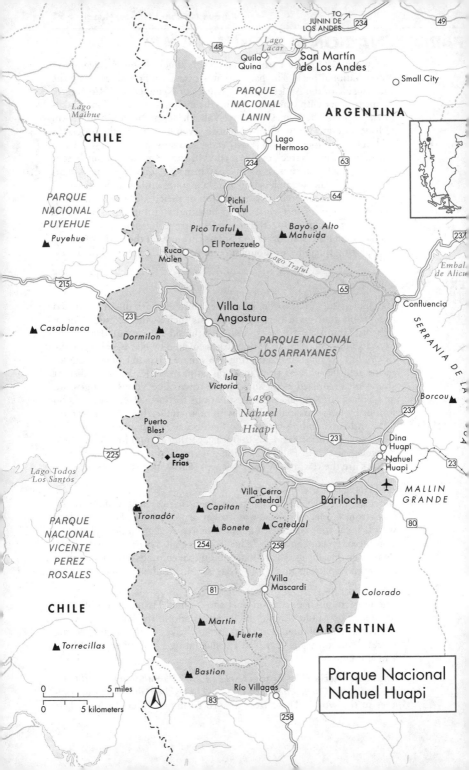

Parque Nacional
Nahuel Huapi

thin skins that all other vegetation around them dies, leaving a barren forest of peeling cinnamon-color trunks. A one-hour stroll up and down wide wooden steps and walkways is a unique experience, as light filters through the twisted naked trunks, reflecting a weird red glow. You can make this excursion from the pier at Bahía Brava in Villa La Angostura (or by boat from Bariloche via Isla Victoria). In summer months you can walk (three hours) or ride a bike, after registering at the *Guardaparque* office (ranger station) near the pier. Leave in the morning, as entrance to the park closes at 2 PM. A nice combination is to go by boat and return by bicycle (it's all downhill that way). If returning by boat, buy your return ticket at the pier before you leave.

Boats to Isla Victoria and Parque Nacional los Arrayanes leave from Puerto Pañuelo, on the Península Llao Llao. They run twice daily (more in high season), at 10 AM and 2 PM. The earlier departure includes time for lunch on the island in a cafeteria-style restaurant. The later departure is a shorter trip. Boats are run by **Cau Cau** (⊠*Mitre 139, Bariloche* ☎*2944/431–372* ⊕*www.islavictoriayarrayanes.com*) and **Turisur** (⊠*Mitre 219, Bariloche* ☎*2944/426–109* ⊕*www.bariloche.com/turisur*).

A visit to **Monte Tronadór** (Thunder Mountain) requires an all-day outing covering 170 km (105 mi) round-trip from Bariloche. The 12,000-foot extinct volcano, the highest mountain in the northern Lake District, straddles the frontier with Chile, with one peak on either side. Take R258 south along the shores of Lago Gutiérrez and Lago Mascardi. Between the two lakes the road crosses from the Atlantic to the Pacific watershed. At Km 35, turn off onto a road marked TRONADÓR and PAMPA LINDA and continue along the shore of Lago Mascardi, passing a village of the same name. Just beyond the village, the road forks and you continue on a gravel road, R254. Near the bridge the road branches left to Lago Hess and Cascada Los Alerces—a detour you might want to take on your way out.

As you bear right after crossing Los Rápidos Bridge, the road narrows to one direction only: it's important to remember this when you set out in the morning, as you can only go up the road before 2 PM and down it after 4 PM. The lake ends in a narrow arm (Brazo Tronadór) at the Hotel Tronadór, which has a dock for tours arriving by boat. The road then follows the Río Manso to **Pampa Linda,** which has a lodge, restaurant, park ranger's office, campsites, and the trailhead for the climb up to the Refugio Otto Meiling at the snow line. Guided horseback rides are organized at the lodge. The road ends 7 km (4½ mi) beyond Pampa Linda in a parking lot that was once at the tip of the now receding **Glaciar Negro** (Black Glacier). As the glacier flows down from the mountain, the dirt and black sediment of its lateral moraines are ground up and cover the ice. At first glance, it's hard to imagine the tons of ice that lie beneath its black cap.

The detour to **Cascada Los Alerces** (Los Alerces Falls), 17 km (10 mi) from the turnoff at the bridge near Mascardi, follows the wild Río Manso, where it branches off to yet another lake, Lago Hess. At this junction are a campground, *refugio* (mountain cabin), restaurant, and trailhead for the 1,000-foot climb to the falls. The path through dense vegetation over wooden bridges crosses a rushing river as it spills over steep, rocky cliffs in a grand finale to a day of viewing nature at its most powerful and beautiful.

OUTDOOR ACTIVITIES

For information on mountain climbing, trails, refugios, and campgrounds, visit the **Intendencia del Parque Nacional Nahuel Huapi** (⊠ *Av. San Martín 24 [at the Civic Center], Bariloche* ☎ *2944/423–111* ⊕ *www.parquesnacionales.gov.ar*).

HIKING

Nahuel Huapi National Park has many forest trails near Bariloche, El Bosón, and Villa La Angostura. For day hikes in the forest along the shore of Nahuel Huapi Lake or to a nearby waterfall, search for trails along the Circuito Chico in the Parque Llao Llao. For altitude and grand panoramas, take the ski lift to the top of Cerro Catedral and follow the ridge trail to Refugio Frey, returning down to the base of the ski area.

West of Bariloche, turn right at Villa Mascardi onto the dirt road to Pampa Linda (⇨ *What to See; Mt. Tronadór, above*). From there you can hike a long day or overnight to Otto Meiling hut, or make shorter forays to the glacier or nearby waterfalls. A three-day trek will take you right past Tronodór and its glacier, along the Alerce River and over the Paso de los Nubes (Clouds Pass) to Puerto Bless, returning to Bariloche by boat. Hiking guides can be recommended through local tour offices. For trail maps and information on all of the Lake District, look for the booklet (in Spanish), *Guía Sendas y Bosques* (Guide to Trails and Forests) sold at kiosks and bookstores. For ambitious treks, mountaineering, or use of mountain huts and climbing permits, contact **Club Andino Bariloche** (⊠ *20 de Febrero 30* ☎ *2944/422–266* ⊕ *www. clubandino.org*). Click on the *mapas* link on the Web site.

MOUNTAIN BIKING

The entire Nahuel Huapi National Park is ripe for all levels of mountain biking. Popular rides go from the parking lot at the Cerro Catedral ski area to Lago Gutiérrez and down from Cerro Otto. Local tour agencies can arrange guided tours by the hour or day and even international excursions to Chile. Rental agencies provide maps and suggestions and sometimes recommend guides.

Dirty Bikes (⊠ *Vice Almirante O'Connor 681* ☎ *2944/425–616* ⊕ *www. dirtybikes.com.ar*) offers local day trips all over the Lake District, including long-distance trips to Chile and back, for all ages and abilities. **La Bolsa del Deporte** (⊠ *Diagonal Capraro 1081* ☎ *944/433–111*) rents and sells bikes.

WHITE-WATER With all the interconnected lakes and rivers in the national park, there's
RAFTING everything from your basic family float down the swift-flowing, scenic Río Limay to a wild and exciting ride down Río Manso (Class II),

which takes you 16 km (10 mi) in three hours. If you're really adventurous, you can take the Manso all the way to Chile (Class IV). **Alunco** (⌧*Moreno 187* ☏*2944/422–283* ⊕*www.aluncoturismo.com.ar*) arranges rafting trips throughout the area. **Aguas Blancas** (⌧*Morales 564* ☏*2944/432–799* ⊕*aguasblancas.com*) specializes in the Manso River and offers an overnight trip to Chile with asado and return by horseback. They also rent inflatable kayaks (*duckies*). **Extremo Sur** (⌧*Morales 765* ☏*2944/427–301* ⊕*www.extremosur.com*) arranges trips on the ríos Limay and Manso.

WHERE TO STAY

✕▦**Isla Victoria Lodge.** On a cliff overlooking the lake and forests of coihués and cypresses, with clean architecture and a quiet interior of white walls, pine trim, leather upholstery, and fine Mapuche woven rugs, this lodge conveys a sense of unity with the natural surroundings. The whole project is a labor of love by its owners who bought the site and transformed it into a unique spa hotel in a tremendously beautiful setting. **Pros:** Total peace in superb surroundings, your own private island after the last boat leaves. **Cons:** Remote, not much to do in bad weather or after a few days. ⊹*Guests arrive by private boat after being transferred to dock at Hotel Tunquelen* ⌧*Reservations: San Martín 523 4th fl. F, Buenos Aires* ☏*11/4394–9605* 🖷*11/4394–9599* ⊕*www.maresur.com* ⬔*20 rooms, 2 suites* ⌂*In-hotel: bar, restaurant, spa, pool, airport shuttle, no kids under 12* ⊟*AE, MC, V* �‖*AI.*

IN & AROUND EL BOLSÓN

EL BOLSÓN

131 km (80 mi) south of Bariloche via R40.

El Bolsón ("the purse") lies in a valley enclosed on either side by the jagged peaks of two mountain ranges. You catch your first glimpse of the valley about 66 km (41 mi) from Bariloche, with the glaciers of Perito Moreno and Hielo Azul (both more than 6,500 feet) on the horizon south and west. Once a Mapuche settlement, Chilean farmers came in the late 1800s in search of arable land. The town remained isolated until the 1930s, when a long, winding dirt road (often closed in winter) connected it to Bariloche. Attracted by the microclimate (about 7 degrees warmer than other Patagonian towns), young Argentines, as well as immigrants from Europe, the Americas, and the Middle East contribute to the cultural identity of this community of about 11,000. The first in Argentina to declare their town a non-nuclear zone, they have preserved the purity of its air, water, and land. Red berry fruits thrive on hillsides and in backyard *chacras* (farms) and are canned and exported in large quantities as jams and syrups. The exploding Patagonian microbrew beer industry is the result of the largest crops of hops planted in Argentina.

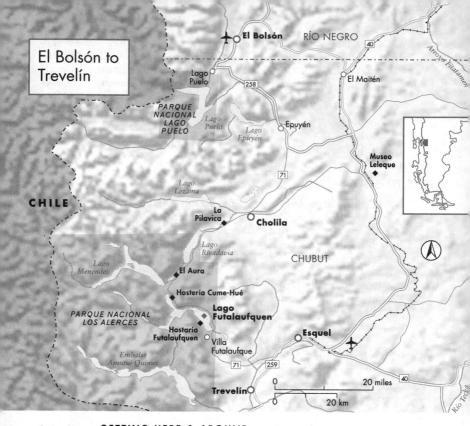

El Bolsón to
Trevelín

GETTING HERE & AROUND

RN40 south from Bariloche or north from Esquel is the only way to
arrive by bus or car. Leaving Bariloche, the road passes Lago Gutiérrez
and enters the Pacific watershed. Lago Mascardi flows into Lago Guil-
lelmo just before the road climbs gently to a pass. There are no public
buses in El Bolsón, so if you're planning an extended stay, you need
to rent a car or hire a taxi. Most of the downtown areas are accessible
on foot.

The main street, San Martín, has shops, restaurants, and some lodgings within a two- to three-block area. A grassy plaza next to the tourist office is the center of activities, with a crafts market on weekends
and some weekdays. The sheer rock face of **Cerro Piltrequitrón** (from a
Mapuche word meaning "hanging from the clouds") dominates the
horizon on the southeast side of town. Trails along the Río Azul or to
nearby waterfalls and mountaintops are a short taxi or bike ride from
the plaza. In spring (late November–December) the roads are lined with
ribbons of lupine in every shade of pink and purple imaginable. Berries
are picked December–March. Summers are warm and lazy and campgrounds at nearby lakes attract backpackers and families.

Huara Viajes y Turismo (✉ *Dorrego 410* ☎ *2944/455–000* ⊕ *www.huara
viajesyturismo.com.ar*) is a full-service travel and tour office that offers

guided hiking, fishing, rafting, horseback, and mountain-bike trips. They also arrange day tours to Lago Puelo that include a boat trip. Rock climbing with rappels is offered on a multi-adventure trip near Lago Puelo.

ESSENTIALS

VISITOR INFO **Secretaría de Turismo** (✉ *Plaza Pagano at Av. San Martín* ☎ *2944/492–604 or 2944/455–336* ⊕ *www.elbolson.gov.ar*).

WHAT TO SEE

The **Cascada de la Virgen** (Waterfall of the Virgin), 18 km (11 mi) north of El Bolsón, is most impressive in spring, when the runoff from the mountain falls in a series of three cascades visible from the road coming from Bariloche. Nearby is a **campground** (☎ *2944/492–610 information*) with cabins, grills, and a restaurant.

The **Cascada Mallín Ahogado** (Drowned Meadow Waterfall), 10 km (6 mi) north of El Bolsón on R258, makes a great picnic spot.

The **Bosque Tallado** (carved forest), about 1 km (½ mi) from the base of Piltriquitrón, is a forest of dry beech trees (resulting from a fire in 1978) that have been carved over the years by 13 of Argentina's notable artists. Thirty-one monumental sculptures transform the dead forest into a living gallery.

The Bolsón International Jazz Festival takes place in December on the streets and in restaurants around town. The Fiesta Nacional de Lúpolo (National hop festival) is celebrated in February.

Don't leave the area of Bolsón or El Hoyo (15 km south) without a jar of jam! You can try all the flavors at **Cabaña Mico** (✉ *Islas Malvinas at Roca* ☎ *2944/492–691* ⊕ *www.mico.com.ar*). Not to be outdone by the beer tasting next door at Otto Tipp, little pots of jam are lined up for sale on a long table with disposable sticks to taste the 40 different flavors.

OUTDOOR ACTIVITIES

Fishing in the nearby lakes and streams can be arranged with guides locally or in Bariloche. Hiking, rock climbing, mountain biking, river rafting, and horseback riding (sometimes all in one trip) lead you to waterfalls, high mountain huts, deep canyons, and hidden lakes. Trips can last a day or up to a week. Boat excursions on nearby Puelo and Epuyén lakes access more hiking trails on the Chilean side of the lake. Some fruit and berry farms welcome visitors to their canning facilities. The tourist office has information on all of the above activities and can supply maps and directions or direct you to local outfitters. Both cross-country and downhill skiing and boarding are at Cerro Perito Moreno, 22 km (13½ mi) north of town on RN40.

HIKING There are 10 *refugios* (mountain huts) with beds and meals in the mountains around Bolsón. A few easy hikes begin but a short taxi ride from the center of town. The Río Azul (Blue River) drops down from the high mountains north of town and runs through the valley to Lago Puelo. Most of the hiking trails are in this area. To reach the Mirador

CLOSE UP

Beer Sampling

This region has long been the biggest producer of hops in Argentina, and with a local population dedicated to agricultural pursuits, it's logical that entrepreneurial *cervezaris artesanales* (artisanal breweries) would become a growing industry. **Otto Tipp** was a German immigrant who opened the first local brewery in 1890. Beers here include the classic triumvirate of blonde, red, and black—plus non-alcoholic malt beer and a fruity wheat beer. You can watch beer being brewed and bottled from a bar stool. This brewery is four blocks from the tourist office. ⊠ *Islas Malvinas at Roca* ☎ *No phone* ☰ *AE, DC, MC, V.*

About 2 km (1 mi) north of town, **Cervezería El Bolsón** is the brewery that started the Patagonian "cerveza artesanal" craze, and even if it's now the least artisanal of the bunch, it has become a local landmark. Every night from December through March, and Friday and Saturday for the rest of the year, the brewery's tasting room turns into a hopping bar and restaurant, where *picadas*, pizzas, sausages with sauerkraut, and a hearty goulash are listed on one side of the menu with suggested beers on the other. For instance, black beer is suggested with smoked meats; chocolate beer with dessert. There are 14 types of beer for you to taste, and descriptions of their ingredients are provided. A large campground is conveniently located by the river in back. ⊠ *RN40, Km 123.9* ☎ *2944/492–595* ⊕ *www.cer-vezaselbolson.com* ☰ *AE, DC, MC, V* ⊗ *Restaurant closed Wed. Apr.–Nov.*

Azul (5 km [3 mi] from the town center), ride or drive west on Azué-naga Street, cross the bridge over the River Quemquemtreu and follow the signs. From here you can look down the valley to Lago Puelo and up at the snow-covered mountains to the West. A 6-km (4-mi) walk will take you to the **Cabeza del Indio** (Indian Head) and **Cascadas Escondidas** (Hidden Falls). A strenuous two-day trek to the **Hielo Azul** (Blue Glacier) climbs through forests to a refugio next to the glacier. Another overnight hike through the forest and past hidden lagoons is to the refugio by the glacier at **Cerro Lindo.** Easier to climb it than to say it, the summit of **Cerro Piltriquitrón** (pronounced pill-tree-quee-tron) offers stupendous views of lakes and mountains all around you, including Tronodór on the Chilean border near Bariloche. There's a refugio at the top with beds and meals. Hang gliding from the top is a singular and hopefully not final experience. **Club Andino Piltriquitrón** (⊠ *Sarmiento at Roca* ☎ *2944/492–600* ⊗ *Nov.–Mar., daily 9* AM*–10* PM) provides information on hikes and trails, arranges guides, and asks that you register when hiking or mountain biking in the area.

MOUNTAIN BIKING Hardy bikers ride all the way from Bariloche, enjoying the long descent into Bolsón. Once there, getting around is pretty easy, as there's not much traffic on the mostly flat dirt roads on the outskirts of town. Most of the waterfall walks and a long trail along the Azul River make pleasant day trips. Epuyén and Puelo lakes require more effort. For guided trips, contact **Huara Viajes y Turismo** (⊠ *Dorrego 410* ☎ *2944/455–000* ⊕ *www.huaraviajesyturismo.com.ar*). To rent a bike and leave it at another destination in the region, contact **Patago-**

nia **Rent a Bike** (☎*2944/1550–6198 or 2944/1567–3347* ✉*lacomarca bike@hotmail.com*).

HORSEBACK RIDING (CABALGATAS) Riding a horse is a fun way to access most of the areas described in the hiking section, especially the area around **Cascada Mallín Ahogado,** or the Río Azul to the Azul Canyon or all the way to the glacier. You can arrange these trips with **Huara Viajes y Turismo** (✉*Dorrego 410* ☎*2944/455–000* ⊕*www.huara viajesyturismo.com.ar*) or **Cabalgatas El Azul** (☎*2944/483–590*).

SKIING The ski area at **Cerro Perito Moreno,** 25 km (15 mi) northwest of El Bolsón, is owned and operated by **Club Andino Piltriquitrón** (✉*Sarmiento at Roca* ☎*2944/492–600*), which also runs a restaurant at the base, where you can rent skis, snowboards, and sleds. The ski area is open from mid-June to mid-October and is used mainly by local families. Four short tows for beginners and one T-bar access the 2,460 feet of skiable terrain on east-facing slopes. Since storms approach from the west, snowfall can be minimal, so it's best to call the tourist office or Club Andino before you go.

WHERE TO EAT

$$$$ ✗**Tsunami70.** The front room is red, the back room chartreuse, bath-
★ rooms blue, and the hallway turquoise—yes, it's colorful! Spanish chef Juan Gonzalez creates seafood selections unheard of in this land of parrillas and asados. His seafood platter (*Degustación de Mariscos*) is a seven-course extravaganza of deliciously prepared seafoods flown in from Patagonia's Atlantic ports. ✉*Av. San Martín 3275* ☎*2944/483–562* ▭*MC, V.*

$$$ ✗**Jauja.** Forty flavors of handmade ice cream attract crowds of schoolkids and tourists to this popular institution next to the tourist office in the middle of town. The restaurant inside is a dependable source of pastas, pizzas, milanesas, and the usual grilled meats. It's the only Wi-Fi café in town. ✉*Av. San Martín 2867* ☎*2944/492–448* ▭*AE, MC, V.*

$$$ ✗**Pasiones Argentinas Resto Bar.** Paintings of passionate tango dancers decorate the brick walls of this popular restaurant near the Villa Turismo. Vegetarian dishes, pastas, pizzas, even hamburgers fall on the menu. Patagonian wine, local beer, Wi-Fi, and take-out food are added attractions. ✉*Av. Belgrano at Berutti* ☎*2944/483–616* ▭*No credit cards.*

$–$$ ✗**Parrilla El Quincho.** About 10 minutes north of town, on the banks of the river Arroyo del Medio, this is the place to try *cordero patagónico al asador* (lamb roasted slowly on a metal cross over a fire), along with sizzling platters of beef. From El Bolsón, follow RN40 north, and get off at the left exit for Catarata Mallín Ahogado. Follow that wind-ing road north, then follow signs for El Quincho; you'll exit to the right after the Catarata exit (if you come to the Iaten K'aik museum, you've gone too far). ⊠*Mallín Ahogado* ☎*2944/492–870* ⊟*No credit cards.*

WHERE TO STAY

The hotel selection in downtown El Bolsón is woefully inadequate. Small guesthouses in and about the town take small groups. The Hotel Amancay is the only full-service hotel worth recommending. About 2 km (1½ mi) south of town off Avenida Belgrano is **Villa Turismo,** a hill-side community of cabins, bed-and-breakfasts, and small inns, most of which have pools, views, and exuberant gardens. Lodges in the sur-rounding mountains open for fishing season in summer (November–April) and close in winter (May–October).

$$ ⊡**Hotel Amancay.** A rose garden and masses of flowers greet you at the door of this yellow-stucco hotel three blocks from the center of town. The lobby has tile floors and dark-wood furniture with bright cush-ions. Rooms are clean but fairly basic, and showers are iffy, but this is about as well as you can do in humble downtown El Bolsón. Hope-fully new owners will remodel. **Pros:** Walk to downtown restaurants. **Cons:** Rooms are small and slightly run-down. ⊠*Av. San Martín 3207,* ☎*2944/492–222* ↩*15 rooms* ⚲*In-hotel: parking (no fee), no eleva-tor* ⊟*AE, DC, MC, V* ⏀*CP.*

$$ ⊡**Lincoln Ranch.** Perched higher than all the other cabin complexes, these modern cottages have plenty of room and all the accoutrements of a vacation home. Mountain views and an opulent garden will soothe your soul while you plan activities in the surrounding areas. **Pros:** Lots of space, easy walk up to Piltriquitrón. **Cons:** Far from restau-rants and downtown shops. ⊠*Villa Turismo, Subida Los Maitenes,* ☎*2944/492–073* ↩*10 1- and 2-bedroom cabins, 1 3-bedroom cabin* ⚲*In-hotel: pool, parking (no fee)* ⊟*MC, V.*

$$ ⊡**La Posada de Hamelin.** Rose bushes and a profusion of flowers cover the arched doorway, while vines climb the walls of this house near the center of town. The rooms are small but with plenty of nooks for stor-age. Guests gather for breakfast in the second-floor breakfast room, which has a refrigerator, books, and games. **Pros:** Friendly, helpful owners, on a quiet street. **Cons:** Small rooms and low ceilings, Pata-gonian shower—water runs freely onto the bathroom floor and has to be squeegeed into drain. ⊠*Int. Granollers 2179,* ☎*2944/492–030* ⊕*www.posadadehamelin.com.ar* ↩*4 rooms* ⚲*In-hotel: parking (no fee), no elevator* ⊟*MC, V.*

$$ ⊡**Posada Rhona Hue.** Anabella Gouchs has converted this former fruit and berry farm headquarters into a B&B where every room is filled with an eclectic mixture of antiques and recycled objects used as furni-ture. Bedrooms are toned-down versions of the three front rooms, and the only sound you'll hear is birdsong. **Pros:** Country living, homemade jams and scones for breakfast, walking distance to Piltriquitrón. **Cons:** Out of town. ⊠*Villa Turismo, Subida de Juan Marqués,* ☎*2944/493–*

717 ⊕*www.interpatagonia.com/rhonahue* ➾*4 rooms, 1 apartment, 1 cabin* ౼*In-hotel: parking (no fee), pool* ⊟*MC, V* �*CP.*

PARQUE NACIONAL LAGO PUELO

19 km (12 mi) south of El Bolsón on RN40 and RP16.

One of the smallest national parks in the southern Andes, Lago Puelo has the warmest water for swimming, the largest salmon (coming all the way from the Pacific Ocean), and many hiking possibilities—the most interesting of which are at the other end of the lake on the Chilean border.

Information is at the **park ranger's office** (☎*2944/499–183* ⊕*www. lagopuelo.gov.ar*), and picnic and fishing supplies can be purchased at the roadside store, 4 km (2½ mi) before you reach the sandy beach at Lago Puelo.

COMARCA ANDINA

The southern portion of the Lake District is known as the **Comarca Andina**, and includes the geographically and historically linked areas of the Río Manso, lakes Puelo and Epuyén, El Maitén, and Cholila in northern Chubut province. The mountains, valleys, lakes, and forests of this region have a particular Andean quality distinct from the lake regions to the north.

OUTDOOR ACTIVITIES

BOAT EXCURSIONS On Lago Puelo, three launches, maintained by the Argentine navy, wait at the dock to take you on one- to three-hour excursions. The trip to El Turbio, an ancient settlement at the southern end of the lake on the Chilean border, is the longest. On the return trip, a branch to the right leads down a narrow arm to a river connecting Lago Puelo with Lago Epuyén. A cruise along the shore of the Brazo Occidental (Western Arm) ends at the Chilean border, where the lake runs into a river bound for the Pacific Ocean. You can return by horse or on foot. One side of the lake is inaccessible, as the Valdivian rain forest grows on steep rocky slopes right down into the water. Campgrounds are at the park entrance by the ranger's station, in a bay on the Brazo Occidental, and at the Turbio and Epuyén river outlets. **Juana de Arco** (⊠*San Martín at Juez Fernández* ☎*2944/493–415 or 2944/1563–3838* ⊕*www.inter patagonia.com/juanadearco*) is one of the boat-tour operators.

HIKING Arriving at the water's edge, you will have three trails to explore: one is an easy stroll in the woods on a wooden walkway; another involves a steep climb to an overlook; and the third is an all-day trek (eight hours round-trip) to **Los Hitos** on the Chilean border, where you can admire the rapids on the Puelo River. It's possible to camp there at **Arroyo Las Lagrimas** and continue on for five or six days across Chile to the Pacific Ocean. You can also take a boat to **El Turbio** at the other end of the lake, where a tough two- to three-day trek climbs to Lago Esperanza. Another option would be to hike to El Turbio from **El Desemboque** on **Lago Epuyén**. For a guide, contact Fabio Barreiro at **Puelo Extremo** (☎*2944/499–588 or 2944/1541–999*) or one of the tour offices in El Bolsón.

IN & AROUND ESQUEL

180 km (112 mi) southeast of El Bolsón via R258 and R71, 285 km (177 mi) south of Bariloche via R259 and R40.

After you leave El Bolsón and enter the Province of Chubut, you cross the Patagonian steppe—with high mountains to the west, and a great expanse of grassland to the east. Along the way, you may see gauchos herding their sheep or "riding the fences" (checking to see that they aren't broken) of their vast ranches. Esquel and Trevelín are good towns from which to visit the Parque Nacional Futalaufquen, or the Corcovado and Futaleufú rivers. The ski area at Cerro Bayo is closer to Esquel.

ESQUEL

In 1906 Esquel was a small village where sheep ranchers, many of them Welsh, came to buy supplies and visit with seldom-seen neighbors from the huge ranches, which still operate on the endless steppes east of the Andes and in verdant valleys closer by. Although Esquel is now the most important town in northern Chubut Province and the gateway to unlimited recreational activities, it retains a frontier-town feeling. There is a notable construction boom going on, however, with new hotels and cabin complexes springing up everywhere.

GETTING HERE & AROUND

Aerolineas Argentinas/Austral has four flights a week from Buenos Aires, but there are no direct flights from Bariloche. Many people fly to Bariloche and travel to Esquel by rental car or bus. Once there, tour operators, local buses, or a remis can get you to most of the popular destinations, but it's hard to beat a rental car for ease and spontaneity in exploring the region. Be sure your tank is full.

ESSENTIALS

VISITOR INFO **Secretaría de Turismo y Medio Ambiente** (⊠ *Alvear at Sarmiento* 🕾🕾 *2945/451–927* ⊕ *www.esquel.gov.ar*).

WHAT TO SEE

In 1905, when Patagonia was still a territory, a railway project was conceived to facilitate the transport of wool, cattle, and lumber from the far-flung villages of El Maitén, Trevelín, and Esquel to Ingeniero Jacobacci, where it would link up with the national railway and the rest of the country. German and American companies worked with the Argentine railroad from 1922 until 1945, when the last section was completed. Today, **La Trochita**, also known as "el trencito" or the Old Patagonia Express, puffs clouds of steam and toots its horn as its 1922 Belgian Baidwin and German Henschell engines pull the vintage wooden cars 402 km (249 mi) from Esquel to **Nahuel Pan**, a Mapuche-Tehuelche community with a museum, typical food, occasional musical events, and a gift shop (20 km [12 mi] round-trip, two departures daily at 9 and 2 PM December–April). Inside the cars, passengers gather around the woodstoves to add wood, sip *mate*, and discuss the merits

Driving to Esquel via Cholila and Parque Nacional Futalaufquen

Turn off RN40 just past Epuyén onto R71 (unpaved all the way to Lago Futalaufquen—about 130 km [81mi]). Enclosed by high Andean peaks on either side, the wild and desolate Cholila Valley is home to some of the finest ranches in Patagonia. You won't see many structures—just miles of grass and contented cows. Perhaps this is the reason why **Butch Cassidy, Etta Place, and the Sundance Kid** chose a site by the river where they lived as "respected citizens" and ranched between 1901 and 1905. They kept a low profile until they attended a Governor's Ball in Esquel. The governor so enjoyed their company, he asked to pose with them in a photograph that later appeared in a Buenos Aires newspaper, where Pinkerton detectives, after years of searching, saw the pictures. After robbing the bank in Río Gallegos, they fled to Bolivia, where they were finally shot. (Or were they? Cue mystery music.) Just north of Cholila, look for the turnoff for the Casa de Piedra teahouse and turn right onto the road

in front of the police station. A path through a gate leads to a group of small log houses in a clump of trees. Farther down the road, the **Casa de Piedra Teahouse** serves tea with Welsh cakes from December through April. The owners are third-generation Cholilans whose grandparents knew and liked their nefarious neighbors.

🏨 **La Pilarica.** Look for the long, green corrugated-metal building with red trim down by the **Río Carrileufu.** Guests will find a welcoming stone fireplace in the great room, where breakfast, cocktails, and dinner are prepared by chef Tilsa, whose homemade bread, jams, and pastas are much appreciated by hungry travelers. Picnic lunches are provided on request. Simple wood rooms have white duvets on sturdy pine beds. ✉ *RP71, Villa Rivadavia, Cholila, Chubut* ☎ *2945/450–159, 2945/1568–6526 cell* ⊕ *www.patagoniaexpress.com/lapilarica.htm* 🛏 *5 rooms* ☼ *In-hotel: restaurant, bar* ▤ *AE, MC, V* ⊙ *FAP.*

of this rolling relic For current schedules and reservations, contact the **Estación Esquel Train Station** (✉ *Urquiza at Roggero* ☎ *2945/451–403*).

El Museo Leleque. In 1910 the British owners of the approximately 2,538,200-square-km (980,000-square-mi) Leleque Ranch (now owned by Benetton) brought merino sheep from Australia to the region, establishing this breed in Patagonia. The museum at the ranch headquarters has four rooms and El Boliche—where refreshments are served in a replica of the old store-café-hangout of the gauchos. Each of the four rooms houses a collection of artifacts and displays illustrating different periods of Patagonian history. First, the Tehuelche-Mapuche era, then the arrival of the Spanish, and finally the pioneers (mainly Welsh). ✉ *RN40* ✛ *90 km (56 mi) from Esquel, 80 km (49½) mi from El Bolsón* ☎ *2945/455–151 Ext. 24* ⊙ *Thurs.–Tues. 11–5.*

NEED A BREAK? Homemade ice cream and pastries, coffee and tea, and two computers with Internet access will keep you busy for an afternoon at Mayor (✉ *Rivadavía 1943, at Sarmiento*). Marí Castaña (✉ *Rivadavía 1943, at 25 de Mayo*

☏ *2945/451–752*), on one of Esquel's busiest street corners, is the classic Argentine *confitería*; locals and tourists flock to the place for its cool buzz, its whiskies and spiked coffee drinks, and its friendly service.

OUTDOOR ACTIVITIES

With all the remote lakes and rivers in both Los Alerces National Park and along the border with Chile, rafting, kayaking, and fishing are obvious pursuits. Hiking in the national park, horseback riding in the mountains or on ranches, and winter sports at Cerro Bayo make this a year-round recreational center.

FISHING   Fishing fanatics from the world over have come to battle with the stubborn trout or catch and release the wily rainbow in the remote lakes, tranquil lagoons, shallow rushing rivers, or deep quiet rivers of Los Alerces National Park. For fishing information on the Río Grande or Río Futaleufú (near Chile), and a list of licensed guides, contact the tourist office in Esquel. Permits are available at gas stations, fishing shops, and at the **Dirección de Pesca Continental** (⊠*Pasteur 538* ☏*2945/42468*).

RAFTING & BOATING   The white-water rafting season begins in November, when the rivers are full and fast, and lasts into March. **Frontera Sur** (⊠*Av. Alvear y Salmiento* ☏*2945/450–505* ⊕*www.fronterasur.net*) organizes rafting trips for a day on the Corcovado or a week on the Futaleufú, ending in Chile; sometimes kayak and canoe instruction is included. **Sol del Sur** (⊠*9 de Julio 1086* ☏☏*2945/42189* ⊕*www.hsoldelsur.com.ar*) also offers rafting trips on the Corcovado and Futaleufú rivers.

SKIING   Only 13 km (8 mi) from Esquel and generally blessed with a long ski season (July–mid-November), La Hoya is a popular ski resort for its reasonable prices and uncrowded slopes—2,200 acres of skiable terrain. A new FlyPark—the largest freestyle park in South America—has three sections for different levels of ability. Four chairlifts and five surface lifts take you up 2,624 feet. Runs are long and above the tree line, and off-piste skiing is often possible. For information about the ski area, contact the Esquel tourist office, or **La Hoya Esquel** (⊠*Rivadavía 1003* ☏*2945/453–018* ✎*diroes@ar.inter.net*).

WHERE TO EAT

$$–$$$ ✕**De Maria Parrilla.** Popular with local ranchers, fishermen, and town folk, this typical grill has a salad bar at dinner and Patagonian lamb is often cooked out back on an *asador*. The room is simple, narrow, and cute, with two rows of tables and an open kitchen in back. The owner, also a ski instructor, studied cooking in Buenos Aires and returned home to open this restaurant. The local lamb, pork, and game dishes are all prepared with a personal touch. ⊠*Rivadavía 1024* ☏*2945/454–247* ▭*AE, DC, MC, V.*

¢–$$ ✕**La Luna.** This terraced "resto bar" is not just the ultimate lively après-ski spot—it's also excellent for an intimate dinner. The food is Argentine to the core, with the occasional modern touch, such as a Guinness sauce on one of the 10 versions of *lomo* (beef tenderloin). Pastas, such as chicken lasagna, are homemade. Argentine-style pizzas include *fugazzeta* (mozzarella, onion, oregano, and green olives). Try the microbrewed Araucana beer, made in nearby El Bolsón. ⊠*Rivadavía 1024* ☏*2945/454–247* ⊟*AE, DC, MC, V.*

WHERE TO STAY

$ ⌂**Hostería Cumbres Blancas.** After skiing, hiking, or exploring the nearby parks, the big carpeted rooms here exude unexpected extravagance. Most have views beyond the ample lawn to windswept plains and lonely mountains. The top-floor suite has a balcony and fireplace. A good restaurant adjoins the hotel. **Pros:** Best accommodations in town. **Cons:** A few blocks from downtown. ⊠*Av. Ameghino 1683,* ☏*2945/455–100* ⤢*19 rooms, 1 suite* ⌂*In-hotel: restaurant, room service, bar, parking (no fee)* ⊟*AE, DC, MC, V* ¶○¶*CP.*

$ ⌂**Hotel Sol del Sur.** This large brick building right in downtown Esquel was once a casino. The building is old and austere, as are the rooms. The convenience of having an adjoining tour agency and ski retail and rental shop makes up for the plain furnishings. **Pros:** Convenient location. **Cons:** A long way from stylish. ⊠*9 de Julio at Sarmiento,* ☏*2945/452–189* ✐*soldelsur@ar.inter.net* ⤢*50 rooms, 2 5-person apartments* ⌂*In-hotel: restaurant, bar* ⊟*AE, DC, MC, V* ¶○¶*CP.*

$$$ ⌂**Ibai Ki Mendi.** A river runs over polished stones through the living room (under glass) of some of these stone-and-log cabins designed by a local architect. Some units have balconies, others have gardens—no two are exactly alike. Roomy enough for a prolonged stay, this is an excellent choice for a family ski vacation. **Pros:** Easy access to ski area. **Cons:** Long walk to town. ⊠*Rivadavia 2965,* ☏*2945/451–503* ⊕*www.ibaikomendi.com.ar* ⤢*3 rooms, 8 cabins sleeping 6* ⌂*In-hotel: gym, pool, public Wi-Fi, parking (no fee), no elevator* ⊟*AE, MC, V* ¶○¶*CP.*

SHOPPING

At **Casa los Vascos** (⊠*25 de Mayo at 9 de Julio*) you can outfit yourself in gaucho attire: black hat, scarf pulled through leather knot, *bombachas* (baggy, pleated pants, gathered at the ankle), and boots.

PARQUE NACIONAL LOS ALERCES

50 km (30 mi) west of Esquel on R259 and R71; 151 km (94 mi) south of El Bolsón on RN40.

The **Parque Nacional los Alerces** is named for its 2,000- to 3,000-year-old *alerces* (*Fitzroya cupressoides*), actually a European larch, but similar in size and age to redwoods. Covering 2,630 square km (1,012 square mi) of lakes, rivers, and forests, most of the park is accessible only by boats and trails. Wild, rugged, and astoundingly beautiful, this park is mostly untouched. The only dirt road into the park takes you to **Villa Futalaufquen** (Futalaufquen Village), on the lake of the same name.

GETTING HERE & AROUND

If you enter at the northern gate on R71, you will drive 55 km (34 mi) through dense forest along Lago Rivadavía and Lago Verde with a glimpse in the distance of Lago Menendez, then along Lago Futalaufquen until you reach Villa Futalaufquen. You can do this in reverse by entering from Esquel or Trevelín.

Tour buses from Bariloche, El Bolsón, or Esquel visit the park on a regular basis. You could also hire a remis in Esquel, but it's hard to beat the independence of your own car. If you're staying in a hotel or fishing lodge, you can depend on them to ferry you around by boat or minibus.

For camping and fishing information, visit the **park information office** (☎*2945/471–020* ⊕*www.parquesnacionales.gov.ar*) in Villa Futalaufquen. Fishing in the 14 lakes and connecting rivers here is legendary; licenses are available in the village at two small shops, Kiosco and Almacén, at the fishing lodges, and the campgrounds at Bahía Rosales.

SAFETY   There are no telephones in Parque Nacional Alerces—only radio contact. Cell phones don't work in most of the park. Fishing excursions in lakes and rivers should always be led by a licensed guide, and hikers should tell park rangers or the hotel when and where they are going. Dirt roads can be slow, tedious, and often under construction, so allow plenty of time (and gas).

OUTDOOR ACTIVITIES

BOATING   An all-day boat excursion begins at Puerto Limonao in Villa Futalaufquen and crosses the lake for 1½ hours to the Arrayanes River, down which the boat will navigate to Puerto Mermoud on Lago Verde where passengers disembark and walk about 1 km (½ mi) to Puerto Chucao on **Lago Menéndez.** There, another boat awaits to take you to a large island in the middle of the lake where you can see the rockbound hanging glacier on **Cerro Torrecillos.** The boat continues down the north branch of the lake to Puerto Sagrario, where a two-hour walk ends in a grove (*alerzal*) of 3,000-year-old alerce trees. A little farther on is Lago Cisne with its abundant waterfalls, then you head back to port after a long day. You can also join this excursion at Lago Verde by crossing the Arrayanes suspension bridge and walking to the dock on Lago Menendez.

Two other lake excursions are possible from Puerto Limonao: one to Lago Krugger with its nearby rapids on the Frei River, and the other to the lagoon at the base of the Torrecillos glacier. Tour operators in Esquel and lodges in the park can arrange these lake excursions, or you can sign up at the dock. Daily excursions from Puerto Limonao run December–April, but check what days of the week they operate.

FISHING   Other than trolling in the lakes, the best spots for fishing within the park are along the Arrayanes River, and at lakes Krugger and Verde. Rainbow and brown trout are abundant and feisty. All fishing is catch-and-release. Permits are obtainable at the small fly shop and at the kiosk in Puerto Limonao, at the Hostería Cume Hue, and at the campground at Bahía Rosales on Lake Futalaufquen.

HIKING The Centro de Informes (Information center) in Villa Futalaufquen has a good trail map (plus a museum and relief map). Five trailheads begin in this area. One is a 30-minute stroll through fields of lupine to a rock wall with barely visible petroglyphs, and two short walks of about 15 minutes each lead to nearby waterfalls. For more serious endeavors, you must register at the Centro de Informes. Most of the longer hikes climb the mountain behind the park office and lead to waterfalls and spectacular overlooks. A 12-hour hike to Lake Krugger requires an overnight at the refugio. In the area around lakes Rivadavía and Verde and the Río Arrayanes, many gentle trails weave through the woods near the water. There are more challenging hikes to Laguna Escondida (four hours), and Cerro Alto el Petiso (seven hours). At the end of the north arm of Lago Menendez, a two-hour hike takes you into the 3,000-year-old alerce forest.

MOUNTAIN The dirt road (R71) around the park is ideal for mountain biking, but
BIKING no rentals are available in the park. You can ride on any of the trails open to hikers.

WHERE TO STAY & EAT

$$$$ 🏨 **El Aura.** The floor-to-ceiling windows in all the cabins and restaurant bring the outdoors inside, where all the modern comforts in stone, slate, wood, and sleek upholstery surround pampered guests in this Patagonian paradise. Travelers come from Cholila and Esquel for the gourmet restaurant. Those desiring a more casual meal find a full menu in **Heur-Heut**, the next-door grill. In-house fishing guide Diego Brand has fished throughout most of the United States and Canada, but his love and enthusiasm for his home territory is contagious. Price includes all meals, tea and wine. **Pros:** Exotic location on a lake, with river, hiking trails, horseback riding, fishing and boat excursions all to yourself. **Cons:** Long trip to get there, could be dismal in bad weather. Reservations: ✉ *Callao 796, piso5, Buenos Aires,* ☎ *2945/1569–5139, 800/528–6069 in U.S. and Canada* ⊕ *www.el-aura.net* 🛏 *3 cabins* 🛎 *In-hotel: restaurant, bar, public Wi-Fi* 🖃 *AE, MC, V* ⊗ *Closed May–Oct.* 🍽 *FAP.*

$$$$ 🏨 **Hostería Futalaufquen.** The stone-and-log lodge sits on a grassy hill with a view through the alamo trees to the lake. Inside, worn leather, wicker furnishings, and polished wood evoke an English hunting lodge. The rooms are simple—with creaky floors, white walls, wood trim, a chair, and a bed—all you need, really, because the place to be is outside. The hotel arranges hiking, fishing, horseback rides, and lake excursions from the nearby Puerto Liminao at Villa Futalaufquen. **Pros:** Rustic comfort, in an incomparable setting with outdoor activities. **Cons:** Bad weather can curtail activities, and there are few indoor alternatives. ✉ *Villa Futalaufquen,* ⚓ *4 km (2 mi) from the village* ☎ *2945/471– 008* 🛏 *12 rooms, 3 cabins* 🛎 *In-hotel: restaurant, bar, bicycles, no elevator* 🖃 *AE, MC, V* 🍽 *FAP.*

$$ 🏨 **Hostería Cume Hué.** Owner Camilo Braese was born in this stucco-and-wood inn overlooking the lake. Having hiked and fished the area since he was a boy, Braese is much sought after as a guide. Breakfast, lunch, and tea are served in the living room, and you have dinner in the *quincho* (a room with a fireplace for asados). Rooms are basic, with small beds and lots of blankets. Some rooms have lake views, and most share a bath. For reservations, contact Daniel Eradura at the number listed below. **Pros:** A unique setting between lake and river. The food is grown and prepared on-site. **Cons:** The owners have been caring for repeat guests for many years and are getting a little tired. ⊠ *Off R71 on Lago Futalaufquen's north shore, 70 km (43½ mi) southwest from Esquel,* ☎ *2945/451–893* ⇨ *13 rooms, 3 with bath* ▭ *No credit cards* ¶◎¶*FAP.*

TREVELÍN

25 km (15½ mi) south of Esquel on R259.

The Welsh came to Trevelín in 1888, when 30 men were sent out to explore the region. Their ancestors, beginning in 1865, had set sail across the Atlantic to escape the economic, religious, and social oppression in their homeland. Expecting to find the Promised Land, they instead found a windswept empty expanse with little or no arable land—nothing like the fertile green valleys they had left behind. Undaunted, these hardy pioneers settled in the Chubut Valley. As the population grew and farmland became scarce, they looked westward toward the Andes. They found their *cwn hyfryd* ("beautiful valley" in Welsh) between the present towns of Esquel and Corcovado. Fifty families settled in the area, building their town around a flour mill; *Trevelín* in Welsh means "mill town." Trevelín is a pleasing alternative to bigger and busier Esquel.

GETTING HERE & AROUND

Whether you arrive from Esquel on R259 or from Parque Nacional los Alerces on R71, you'll end up at the central park in the middle of town where the tourist office is located. Excursions other than fishing and rafting are best done independently by car. Buses arrive daily from Esquel.

WHAT TO SEE

The **Dirección de Turismo** (⊠ *Plaza de la Fontana, [prov]Chubut[/prov]* ☎ *2945/480–120* ⊕ *www.trevelin.org*) has information on the history of the region and its Welsh settlers. Hardworking, honest, faithful, and as proud to be Argentine as they are to have their own traditions, many descendants of those first families still live here, and the tourist office can arrange interviews with some of them. Many family-run *residenciales* and small hotels closed down during the economic crisis in 2000–2002. Check at the tourist office for new ones opening up as the economy stabilizes.

OUTDOOR ACTIVITIES

The rivers Futaleufú (known as Río Grande on the Argentina side) and Corcovado (Carrenleufú in Mapuche), both south of Trevelín and running west to the Pacific, are famous for fishing and rafting.

Reserva Provincial Natural Nant-y-Fall. Seventeen kilometers (11 mi) from Trevelín, signs will tell you when to turn off for this short walk in the woods from waterfall to waterfall. Each one is different and fun to photograph from the little viewing platforms erected along the way.

Route 259 to Futaleufú River and Chile Border is 38 km (23 mi) from Trevelín. As you drive south on R259 across an immense valley, you'll see cattle and sheep graze in fields that go on forever in pastoral splendor beneath spiky peaks that rise straight up on the horizon, marking the border with Chile. Several streams rush under wooden bridges on their way to the river and the Pacific Ocean.

WHERE TO EAT

¢–$ ✗**Casa de Té La Mutisia.** You can't miss the giant teapot and cup firmly planted in the rose bushes outside this Welsh teahouse. Everything is blue and white inside, from ruffled curtains to checkered tablecloths to grandma's best china. A Scottish tune plays in the background as cakes arrive by the plateful: scones, jams, rhubarb pie, nutty spice cake, coconut and chocolate cookies. ⊠*Av. San Martín 170* ☎*2945/480–165* ▤*No credit cards* ☽*No lunch.*

¢–$ ✗**Casa de Te Nain Maggie.** *Nain* (grandma) Maggie (1878–1981) handed down the old family recipes to her granddaughter who, with her own daughter, continues to make the same fruit tarts, cakes, breads, and scones with currant or gooseberry jam—just a few of the confections you'll find in this typical Welsh teahouse. ⊠*Perito Moreno 179, at Sarmiento* ☎*2945/480–232* ⊕*www.patagoniaexpress.com/nainmaggie.htm* ▤*No credit cards.*

$$–$$$ ✗**Restaurante Mi Lugar.** A small brick-and-wood house on a quiet street looks and feels like home, and everything about it is *casera* (homemade)—the pastas, vegetarian crepes, bread, and desserts are all made by the family. ⊠*Sarmiento 551* ☎*2945/480–027* ▤*MC, V.*

WHERE TO STAY

$$ ⊡**Casa de Piedra** (Stone House). Sun streams in through the windows and lights up the fanciful collection of twisted wood, tables, chairs, a bar, and a stairway. In winter, a fire in the stone fireplace invites guests to gather round for tea or a glass of wine. Slate floors, plain white walls, a Mapuche motif in bedspreads and wall hangings, all give a sense of place to this brand-new B&B whose owners have chosen to live and work in a place they love. ⊠*Brown 244,* ☎*2945/480–357* ⊕*www.casadepiedratrevelin.com* ➥*8 rooms, 1 cabin for 6* ♿*In-hotel: lounge* ▤*MC, V* ⏏*CP.*

$ ⊡**Casa Verde.** This hillside hostal, surrounded by a grassy field, is ideal for families and travelers intending to explore the area. Fishing and rafting, mountain-bike and hiking trips can be organized through the hostal with or without other guests. Rooms are basic, with bunk beds and private bathrooms. A common kitchen and outdoor grill are available to guests, although breakfast and tea are served for an extra charge. **Pros:** Casual and friendly, interesting guests. **Cons:** Out of town, service perhaps too casual. ⊠*Los Alerces s/n,* ☎*2945/480–091 or 2945/15691–535* ⊕*casaverdehostel.com.ar* ➥*8 rooms* ♿*In-hotel: bicycles* ▤*No credit cards.*

Atlantic Patagonia

Penguins, Peninsula Valdes

WORD OF MOUTH

"Went to the penguin colony at Punta Tombo one day, which was amazing. Close to half a million penguins—the chicks had just hatched, and were really tiny. The second day trip was to the Valdes Peninsula—took a boat to see the southern right whales and were lucky to see plenty of them."

—lily3

WELCOME TO ATLANTIC PATAGONIA

TOP REASONS TO GO

★ **Marine Wildlife:** Península Valdés is home to sea lions, elephant seals, southern right whales, and orcas. At Punta Pirámides thousands of right whales come to mate and give birth each year from June to mid-December.

★ **Seabirds:** Exceptional populations of seabirds nest here, including arctic terns, blackish oystercatchers, cormorants, southern giant petrels, and steamer ducks. At Punta Tombo, 500,000 penguins waddle to the sea on "penguin highways."

★ **Diving:** Protected from the open sea by the Península Valdés, the tranquil, clear Golfo Nuevo off the coast of Puerto Madryn is the scuba-diving capital of Argentina. Unique dives include diving with sea lions.

★ **Catching up on Your Welsh:** In the largest Welsh colony outside of Wales, Gaiman's citizens have preserved their traditions and language. Historic teahouses serve scones, cakes, and tarts from centuries-old recipes.

1 Puerto Madryn. Although it has the best shopping, restaurants, and hotels in Atlantic Patagonia, Puerto Madryn's slogan is *Naturaleza muy cerca,* or very close to nature. There is easy access to protected wildlife areas and guides to take you there.

2 Península Valdés & Puerto Pirámides. Few places in the world offer better wildlife viewing than Península Valdés. Whale-watching and dive boats explore the peninsula from Puerto Pirámides, a flower-filled, 350-person village built among pyramid-shaped dunes and cliffs at the edge of Golfo Nuevo.

3 Trelew & Gaiman. With its teahouses, rose gardens, and chapels dating back to the original 19th-century Welsh settlers, Gaiman, along with the larger nearby city of Trelew, preserves its culture and traditions with celebrations of Welsh poetry, song, and dance called Eisteddfod, held each fall.

GETTING ORIENTED

Atlantic Patagonia describes the eastern seaboard of Chubut province from Península Valdés to Comodoro Rivadavía, approximately 318 mi from north to south, and extending inland another 90 mi to Sarmiento. Although the Atlantic coast is the least-traveled region of Patagonia, it has become increasingly popular with small group tours from Europe, which has helped establish a good tourist infrastructure (including English-speaking attendants at most information centers), even in remote towns such as Camarones. The local people throughout the region are generally affable and helpful, and visitors who speak Spanish or at least try will be treated with special *cariño* (affection).

4 Punta Tombo to Bahía Bustamante. Traveling from Punta Tombo—the largest penguin rookery in South America—to Bahía Bustamante, a ghost town turned mini-ecoresort, is like having a national park all to yourself.

5 Sarmiento. This small, friendly town is a green oasis in the dry Patagonian steppe. There are stunning petrified forests nearby and a paleontology "park" with life-size dinosaur replicas, plus a weekly artisans' and crafts fair with locally grown produce. It's least touristy place in the region.

ATLANTIC PATAGONIA PLANNER

Health & Safety

Besides using sunscreen (do not underestimate the austral sun), the most important safety consideration is taking precautions around wildlife. Do not approach or let your children approach sea lions, penguins, or any other animals, no matter how docile or curious they might seem. Although tap water is safe to drink throughout the region, most travelers still choose to drink bottled water, just to be on the safe side. Finally, there are hospitals in every town except Bahía Bustamante.

Emergency Services Coast Guard (☎106). **Fire** (☎100). **Forest Fire** (☎103). **Hospital** (☎107). **Police** (☎101).

When to Go

The entire region is in the rain-shadow of the Andean Cordillera, making for a cool, dry climate with temperatures averaging 66°F in January and 45°F in July. It's very windy; bring extra warm clothes regardless of the season.

Newborn sea-lion pups emerge in January. Penguin chicks take a crash course in swimming mid-February. The most popular time is June through December, when southern right whales are mating and raising offspring at Península Valdés. But August to September is when there are whales, low-season prices and there are fewer people.

Eat Well & Rest Easy

Atlantic Patagonia has the best seafood in Argentina. Try *lenguado*, or sole, and salmon, as well as seafood *paella*. *Restaurantes* are generally sit-down-and-take-your-time affairs that don't open for dinner until 8. Most serve excellent meat cooked on the *parilla* as well as rich pasta dishes, and *postres*, or desserts, above all *flan cassera*, or homemade custard. Be on the lookout for *cordero*, roasted lamb, a Patagonian classic. Most bars serve quick bites—hamburgers, sandwiches, etc.—known as *minutas*. The region is also famous for its berries and its various jams.

Although quality and even luxurious hotels exist in Puerto Madryn and Trelew, quaint bed-and-breakfasts and other personalized *hosterías* offer the best deals and often the region's best lodging.

DINING & LODGING PRICE CATEGORIES (IN ARGENTINA PESOS)				
¢	$	$$	$$$	$$$$
Restaurants				
under 8 pesos	8–15 pesos	15–25 pesos	25–35 pesos	over 35 pesos
Hotels				
under 80 pesos	80–140 pesos	140–220 pesos	220–300 pesos	over 300 pesos
Restaurant prices are based on the median main course price at dinner. Hotel prices are for two people in a standard double room in high season.				

Getting Here & Around

Air Travel. The best way to get to Atlantic Patagonia is to fly from Buenos Aires. Aerolíneas Argentinas (⊕ *www.aero lineas.com.ar*) flies (along with its subsidiary Austral) from Buenos Aires to Trelew and Comodoro Rivadavia. From Trelew, Aerolíneas also flies direct, with varying frequency, to El Calafate and Ushuaia in southern Patagonia. LADE (Líneas Aéreas del Estado ⊕ *www.lade.com.ar*), connects Trelew, Puerto Madryn, and Comodoro Rivadavia to other parts of Patagonia, including Bariloche, El Calafate, and Ushuaia. Some of LADE's flights are on small propeller planes, and many routes only run once or twice per week. Andes Líneas Aéreas (⊕ *www.andesonline.com*) now has direct flights from Buenos Aires to Puerto Madryn.

Bus Travel. Buses connect every city in Atlantic Patagonia, and if you have the time and patience you can get just about anywhere in the region except the isolated coastline from Punta Tombo to Bahía Bustamante. Use local tour operators rather than municipal buses for day excursions to Península Valdés.

Car Travel. The towns of Trelew and Gaiman are fairly self-contained, and the central area of Puerto Madryn can be walked easily, but unless you plan on a series of day excursions with tour operators, your best access to Atlantic Patagonia is with a vehicle. Rent a car in Puerto Madryn or Trelew. Renting a vehicle is the easiest way to see Península Valdés and the coastline along RP1, and gas is 30% cheaper in Chubut than in the rest of the country.

Be cautious on the two-lane highway Ruta 3. There are no passing lanes. Also minimize or avoid driving in larger cities such as Trelew and Comodoro Rivadavia. Reduce your speed on dirt roads, as the *ripio,* or gravel surface, is deceptively loose. If you're planning to drive remote coastal roads, take extra food and water (ideally, camping gear as well). Should mechanical problems arise you'll be a long way from help and out of cell-phone range. Stay with your vehicle; a tour-bus or estancia worker will come by eventually. Flat tires are common, but so are *gomerías* (mechanics) who charge about 10 pesos to patch a tire.

Finally, consider paying for a *remis* (car with driver) for a less stressful, if pricier alternative.

Gauchito Gil

Small shrines with red flags and banners—usually snapping in the Patagonian wind—are found along roadsides throughout the region. These are shrines to Gauchito Gil, a farmworker who was killed on January 8, 1878. Although not officially recognized by the Catholic Church, many Argentines considered him a saint.

Legend has it that a rich widow fell in love with Gauchito Gil and when the local chief of police—who was also in love with the woman—found out, he tried to kill him. Gil escaped by joining the army but was eventually caught by the chief of police, who strung him up in a tree, tortured, and killed him. Before dying, Gauchito Gil told the man that his son was sick, and that "if you pray and ask me to save your son, he will live." The man prayed for Gauchito Gil and when he returned to the village, his son got better.

4

by David
Miller

ATLANTIC PATAGONIA IS WHERE THE low windswept pampas meet the ocean. It's a land of immense panoramic horizons and a coastline of bays, inlets, and peninsulas teeming with seabirds and marine wildlife. The region is most famous for Península Valdés, a UNESCO Natural World Heritage site where travelers can see southern right whales, orcas, southern elephant seals, and sea lions. As in the rest of Patagonia, there are seemingly endless dirt roads where you won't see another person or vehicle for hours, only guanacos, rheas, and other animals running across the steppe.

The human history of this region began with the native Tehuelches who fished and hunted the coast and pampas and whose spears and arrowheads are still found along riverbeds and beaches. The first Spanish explorer, Hernando Magallanes, arrived in Golfo Nuevo in 1516, and was followed by several other Spanish expeditions throughout the 17th and 18th centuries. From 1826 to 1836, two English captains, Parker King, of the *Adventure,* and Robert Fitzroy, sailing the *Beagle,* made the first accurate nautical maps of the region.

Inland, a Welsh pioneer named Henry Jones explored the Chubut river valley in 1814. Fifty years later, a small group of Welsh families—fleeing religious persecution in Great Britain—became the first Europeans to move to this area permanently, clearing the way for waves of Welsh immigrants that forged colonies in Gaiman, Trelew, Rawson, and Puerto Madryn. Beginning in the mid-19th century, the Argentinean government courted settlers from all over Europe, including Italy, Spain, and Germany, as well as Boers from South Africa, offering land ownership as a strategy for displacing indigenous populations and fortifying the young nation against neighboring Chile. These settlers adapted their agrarian traditions to the Patagonian terrain, planting windbreaks of Lombardy poplar, along with fruit trees and flower gardens. They set up dairy farms, sheep ranches, and continued their cultural traditions and cuisine, such as Welsh Tea, still found throughout Atlantic Patagonia today.

PUERTO MADRYN

67 km (41½ mi) north of Trelew, 450 km (279 mi) north of Comodoro Rivadavía, 104 km (64 mi) west of Puerto Pirámides.

Approaching from the Ruta 3, it's hard to believe that the horizon-line of buildings perched just beyond the windswept dunes and badlands is the most successful of all coastal Patagonia settlements. But once you get past the outskirts of town, past the tire-repair places and humble barrios, to the city's downtown, and onto the wide coastal road known as the Rambla, you'll see why. The restaurants, bars, cafés, dive shops, multistory houses, and hotels facing the clear and tranquil Golfo Nuevo are full of activity but not yet overcrowded.

When the peso was devalued in the 1990s, Puerto Madryn's local fishing and tourism industries quickly gained international attention. The rapid growth and expansion of infrastructure—which continues each

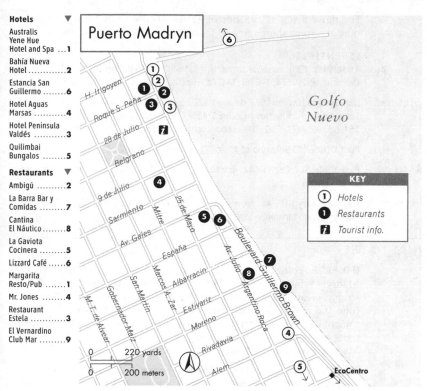

Hotels ▼

Australis
Yene Hue
Hotel and Spa ...**1**

Bahía Nueva
Hotel **2**

Estancia San
Guillermo **6**

Hotel Aguas
Marsas **4**

Hotel Peninsula
Valdés **3**

Quilimbai
Bungalos **5**

Restaurants ▼

Ambigú **2**

La Barra Bar y
Comidas **7**

Cantina
El Náutico **8**

La Gaviota
Cocinera **5**

Lizzard Café **6**

Margarita
Resto/Pub **1**

Mr. Jones **4**

Restaurant
Estela **3**

El Vernardino
Club Mar **9**

Puerto Madryn

Golfo Nuevo

KEY

① *Hotels*

❶ *Restaurants*

🛈 *Tourist info.*

year—occurred on top of an already prosperous economy and booming population growth due to the construction of Argentina's largest aluminum plant, Aluminios Argentinos S.A., in the 1970s.

The first economic boom came in 1886, when the Patagonian railroad was introduced, spurring the town's port activities along with salt and fishing industries. Although it isn't likely the original Welsh settlers who arrived here in 1865 could have imagined just how much Puerto Madryn would evolve, a large part of Madryn's success is owed to their hardworking traditions. The anniversary of their arrival is celebrated every 28th of July here and in other Chubut towns. Only a statue—the Tehuelche Indian Monument—serves as a reminder of the indigenous people who once lived here and who helped the Welsh survive.

GETTING AROUND

Madryn is just small enough to walk, and most of the hotels and residences are on or near the 3½-km-long (2-mi-long) Rambla, or pedestrian walkway along the Golfo Nuevo. A great way to get around is by renting a bicycle. To reach the nature preserves just north and south of town—El Doradillo and Punta Loma—you'll either need to rent a vehicle, travel with a tour, or take a *remis*.

For those flying in and out of Trelew, Transportes Eben-Ezer is the official airport shuttle to and from Puerto Madryn.

ESSENTIALS

BUS   **Andesmar** (⊠ *Terminal de Ómnibus* ☎ *2965/473–764*). **Don Otto** (⊠ *Terminal de Ómnibus* ☎ *2965/451–675*). **TAC** (⊠ *Hipólito Yrigoyen 331* ☎ *2965/451–537*).

CURRENCY   **Banco de la Nación** (⊠ *9 de Julio 127* ☎ *2965/450–465*). **Credicoop** (⊠ *Roque Sanez Peña at 25 de Mayo* ☎ *2965/455–139*). **Banco del Chubut** (⊠ *25 de Mayo 154* ☎ *2965/471-250* ⊕ *www.bancochubut.com.ar*).

MAIL   **Post Office** (⊠ *Belgrano at Maíz* ⊠ *Av. Julio A. Roca 223*).

RENTAL CARS   **Patagonia Sur Car** (⊠ *Av. Rawson 1190* ☎ *2974/466–768* ⊕ *www.patagonia surcar.com.ar*).

VISITOR INFO   **Puerto Madryn** (⊠ *Av. Roca 223* ☎ *2965/453–504 or 2965/456–067* ⊕ *www. madryn.gov.ar/turismo/en/general_information/*).

WHAT TO SEE

El Doradillo. Following the coastal road 14 km (9 mi) north from Puerto Madryn brings you to El Doradillo Beach. The ocean floor drops steeply, creating a special environment where, between the months of June and mid-December, you can walk up to southern right whales, sometimes with mothers teaching their young to swim. During other times of the year, it's just a regular beach similar to the rest of Puerto Madryn's coastline. ⊠ *Free.*

The **Museo Oceanográfico y Ciencias Naturales** *(Oceanographic and Natural Science Museum)* is housed in a lovely 1917 colonial building once owned by the Pujol family of original settlers. The museum focuses on marine life and you can see a giant squid preserved in formaldehyde and learn how fish breathe. ⊠ *Domecq García at Menéndez* ☎ *2965/451–139* ⊕ *www.hostar.com.ar/museo* ⊠ *Free* ☉ *Weekdays 9–7, weekends 2:30–7.*

☾ **EcoCentro.** EcoCentro is a modern hands-on museum and research center that promotes the protection of the sea through education. A whale-sounds exhibit and an invertebrates "touch pool" allow visitors to get a personal appreciation for marine life, and a new cave exhibit is especially good for kids. The center is on a cliff at the north end of the city's beach. ⊠ *Julio Verne 3784* ☎ *2965/457–470* ⊕ *www.ecocentro.org. ar* ⊠ *21 pesos* ☉ *Daily 2:30–7:30.*

Punta Loma Sea Lion Reserve. Just 14 km (9 mi) southeast of the city (follow signs toward Punta Ninfas), Punta Loma might be your first glimpse of the region's spectacular marine mammals. A colony of some 600 South American sea lions can be seen at the beach below a tall, crescent-shaped bluff. ☎ *2965/453–504* ⊠ *20 pesos* ☉ *Visit during low tide—check local paper or tourism office for tide schedule.*

OUTDOOR ACTIVITIES

Bicycling, surf and deep-sea fishing, plus windsurfing and sea kayaking are all great activities in and around Puerto Madryn. Sandboarding, or surfing the dunes, is a lesser-known but really fun and safe activity, as well as being a great way to explore the dunes south of town.

Most importantly, Madryn is Argentina's scuba-diving capital. In an effort to further promote diving, town officials sank the *Albatros,* a large fishing vessel, off the coast in Golfo Nuevo. The real jewel, however, is the marine wildlife.

BIKING

Madryn is just the right size to tour by bike. Several companies rent bicycles for about 20 pesos a day, including **XT Mountain Bike** (⊠ *Av. Gales 439* ☎ *2965/472–232*).

DIVING

One dive shop stands out in particular: **Aquatours** (⊠ *Av. Roca 550* ☎ *2965/451–954* ⊕ *www.aquatours.com.ar*) has dive masters and instructors who have pioneered courses in diving with sea lions, and who offer diving for disabled persons. Several other dive shops are on Boulevard Brown, including **Scuba Duba** (⊠ *Blvd. Brown 893* ☎ *2965/452–699*).

FISHING

Costas Patagonicas (☎ *2965/451–131*) organizes fishing trips. **Jorge Schmid** (☎ *2965/451–511*), a respected guide in the area, offers fishing trips as well as whale-watching and dolphin-viewing trips.

HORSEBACK RIDING

For a completely different view, check out Madryn's beaches from horseback. Rides are available with **Huella y Costas** (⊠ *Blvd. Brown 1900* ☎ *2965/1563–7826*).

KAYAKING & WINDSURFING

☾ **Vernardino Club Mar** rents sea kayaks and windsurfers, and runs a "Sea School" where local instructors work with children aged 6–14 on snorkeling, windsurfing, bait and lure fishing, basic nautical and fishing knots, and identification of local fauna, as well as offering motor- and sailboat excursions. There is also a windsurfing school for adults. (⊠ *Blvd. Brown 860* ☎ *2965/455–633* ⊕ *Main site: www.vernardinoc lubdemar.com.ar/index.html; sea school: www.escueladelmar.com.ar*).

WHERE TO EAT

$$ ✕ Ambigú. This stylish place is across the street from the beach. The menu has 60 pizzas to choose from, as well as entrées like sirloin medallion (*medallón de lomo*) with pumpkin puree. A clean, contemporary style complemented by well-mounted photographs documenting the history of the building (note the art deco detailing, including original iron cresting, on the exterior) lends the restaurant both authenticity and sophistication. ⊠ *Av. Roca at Av. Saénz Peña* ☎ *2965/452–541* ▤ *AE, MC, V.*

$$-$$$ ╳ **La Barra Bar y Comidas.** Usually it's not a good sign when a restaurant tries to do everything at once: *parilla,* pizza, and elaborate meat and seafood dishes. But La Barra does it all well, and the never-ending crowds at this restaurant, just steps from the shore, attest to the quality. Skip the mediocre fried calamari, however. ⊠*Blvd. Brown 779* ☎*2965/455–550* ▭*AE, MC, V.*

$$ ╳ **Cantina El Náutico.** Don't let the corny, yellow-neon sign outside dissuade you; this local favorite run by three generations of a French Basque family serves fantastic homemade pasta and fresh seafood. Even the "butter" that accompanies the bread is a cut above—a mixture of mayonnaise with garlic, parsley, and pepper. For dessert, try the outstanding *macedonia* (fruit salad with ice cream). ⊠*Av. Roca 790* ☎*2965/471–404* ▭*AE, DC, MC, V.*

$$ ╳ **La Gaviota Cocinera.** The secret of this restaurant from husband-and-wife team Pablo and Flavia Tolosa is the combination of cozy rooms and reliable food at very reasonable prices. The three-course set-price meals might feature tenderloin with leek and mustard sauce, or grilled chicken stuffed with olives and dried tomatoes. ⊠*Galles 32* ☎*2965/456–033* ▭*AE, MC, V.*

$$-$$$ ╳ **Lizzard Café** One of the few restaurants open all day which serves consistently good food, the Lizzard Café has become a favorite spot for travelers seeking an early dinner, a late lunch, or an afternoon session of peanuts and beer while watching football matches on one of the large flat-screen TVs. Pool tables, a powerful sound system, and good views of the coast are upstairs. Pizza is your best bet. Vegetarians should try the "San Francisco," with oregano, onions, spinach, green olives, egg, and walnut. ⊠*Roca at Gales* ☎*2965/455–306* ▭*V.*

$$-$$$$ ╳ **Margarita Resto/Pub.** Margarita has long been famous in Puerto
★ Madryn for its cocktails and nightlife. The food here is excellent and it's one of the few places you can find more elaborate vegetarian options. On Wednesday nights at 11 there is live jazz. You can grab a quiet meal at lunchtime, yet the dance-floor lighting, disco ball in the back room, and chill-out beats remind you of the party to come. ⊠*Av. Saénz Peña 15, at Roca* ☎*2965/470–885* ⊕*www.margaritapub.com* ▭*AE, MC, V.*

$-$$ ╳ **Mr. Jones.** It brews its own beer and is the closest thing to an Irish pub in Atlantic Patagonia. Although the beer is good, the food is more than an afterthought with potpies, sausages with kraut, pizzas, and other brew-happy food. It's packed every night. ⊠*9 de Julio 116, at 25 de Mayo* ☎*2965/475–368* ▭*AE, MC, V.*

$-$$ ╳ **Restaurant Estela.** Run lovingly by Estela Guevara, who could easily pass for anybody's favorite aunt; menus come in English, German, French, and Italian. Postcards on the walls sent by former dinner guests from all over the world attest to the owner's popularity. Ms. Guevara, who is of Ukrainian descent and speaks perfect English, tends to all her guests personally and will even offer travel advice. The restau-

CLOSE UP | Tour Options in Atlantic Patagonia

Carlos and Carol de Passera of Causana Viajes have 17 years of experience leading custom and special-interest trips—focusing, for example, on archaeology, birding, botany, natural history, or whale-watching—for American and Canadian adventure-travel companies. Cuyun Co Turismo can arrange all-day tours of the Península Valdés; reserve ahead, especially if you want an English-speaking guide. They can also organize tours to Punta Tombo, Gaiman, the Dique Ameghino, and Camarones. Cuyun Co Turismo and Causana Viajes organize tours to Bahía Bustamante.

At Península Valdés, Jorge Schmid specializes in whale-watching tours; his boat has ample covered space in case it rains. Hydro Sport runs smaller whale-watching boats, which are particularly good for getting up close and personal with the whales. A third option is Bottazzi, which has bilingual staff and small, open boats similar to Hydro Sport's. Aonik'Enk de

Patagonia gives tours of Sarmiento, the Bosque Petrificado, and other nearby destinations; it also rents four-wheel-drive vehicles.

Companies:

Aonik'Enk de Patagonia (⊠ *Av. Rawson 1190, Comodoro Rivadavia* ☎🖳 *2974/466–768 or 2974/461–363* ⊕ *www.aonikenk.com.ar*). **Bottazzi** (⊠ *Complejo La Torre, Blvd. Brown at Martín Fierro, Puerto Madryn* ☎ *2965/474–110* ⊕ *www.titobottazzi. com*). **Causana Viajes** (⊠ *Moreno 390, Puerto Madryn* ☎ *2965/455–044* ⊕ *www.causana.com.ar*). **Cuyun Co Turismo** (⊠ *Julio A. Roca 165, Puerto Madryn* ☎ *2965/454–950 or 2965/451–845* ⊕ *www.cuyunco.com. ar*). **Hydro Sport** (⊠ *Av. Julio A. Roca s/n, Puerto Madryn* ☎ *2965/495–065* ⊕ *www.hydrosport.com.ar*). **Jorge Schmid** (⊠ *Av. Julio A. Roca s/n, Puerto Pirámides* ☎ *2965/495–112 or 2965/495–029* ⊕ *www.puntaballena. com.ar*).

rant serves hearty meals of beef, chicken, and fish at reasonable prices. ⊠ *R. S. Peña 27* ☎ *2965/451–573* ▤ *AE, MC, V* ⊘ *Closed Mon.*

$$-$$$ ✕ **El Vernardino Club Mar.** In the center of the beach, El Vernardino has the best location in Puerto Madryn. Don't let the playground and the stacks of kayaks and windsurfers (El Vernardino also runs a "sea school" and rents equipment) dissuade you from eating here. A diverse menu with twists on classic seafood dishes—like the "wok marino" or seafood stir-fry—makes for some of the best eating in the city. ⊠ *Blvd. Brown 860* ☎ *2965/455–633* ⊕ *www.vernardinoclubdemar.com.ar/ index.html* ▤ *AE, MC, V.*

WHERE TO STAY

$$$$ ▦ **Australis Yene Hue Hotel and Spa.** The Australis Yene Hue is Puerto Madryn's newest luxury hotel. From the cavernous lobby with cascading water garden to the luminous breakfast room, well-equipped (by Argentinean standards) minigym, and rooftop pool, the Yene Hue is modern, spacious, and refined. **Pros:** Brand-new. **Cons:** Young staff still getting organized, rooms not facing the ocean may not be worth the

price. ✉*Roca 33* ☎*2965/471–214* ⊕*www.australiset.com.ar* ⮐*68 rooms* ♿*In-hotel: bar, pool, spa, laundry service, public Wi-Fi* ▭*AE, MC, V* ⏀*CP.*

$$$$ ⛶**Bahía Nueva Hotel.** Clean, spacious rooms and a central location make this hotel a Madryn classic. The Bahía Nueva, with its cozy, brick-walled lobby with fireplace, comfy armchairs, and bookshelves stocked with ecoconscious literature, evinces familiarity and intimacy. **Pros:** Exceptionally friendly English-speaking staff, flat-screen TVs in every room. **Cons:** Rooms are the same price with or without a view; the dark back rooms are not worth the price. ✉*Av. Julio A. Roca 67,* ☎*2965/451–677 or 2965/450–045* ⊕*www.Bahianueva.com.ar* ⮐*40 rooms* ♿*In-hotel: bar, laundry service, public Wi-Fi* ▭*AE, DC, MC, V* ⏀*CP.*

$$$ ✕⛶**Estancia San Guillermo.** If you want to experience a Chubut farm filled with snorting pigs, overfriendly guanacos, and strutting roosters, head for Estancia San Guillermo. A few miles outside Puerto Madryn, owners Alfredo and Cristina Casado welcome you to their home with 1,200 sheep who roam their 7,400-acre fossil-filled farm. Watch Alfredo shear a sheep or his helpers prepare the *parilla* (grill). Stay in roomy, comfortable villas with kitchens and bathrooms; rates include all meals. The estancia has a dining room if you're just coming for the day. **Pros:** You'll have a Patagonian estancia all to yourself. **Cons:** You're isolated from the rest of town once you get there. ✉*Contact info in Puerto Madryn: Av. 28 de Julio 90,* ☎*2965/452–150* ⊕*www. san-guillermo.com* ⮐*3 rooms* ▭*No credit cards* ⊘*Closed mid-May– mid-June* ⏀*FAP.*

$ ⛶**Hotel Aguas Mansas.** This hotel is one block from the beach in a pretty residential neighborhood and a few blocks from the center of town. It's nothing fancy—just clean, quiet rooms and good, personable service. It's one of the few lodgings with a pool, especially in this price range. **Pros:** Pool, friendly staff. **Cons:** Not as elegant as other hotels. ✉*José Hernandez 51,* ☎*2965/473–103* ⊕*www.aguasmansas.com* ⮐*20 rooms* ♿*In-hotel: bar, pool, laundry service* ▭*MC, V* ⏀*CP.*

$$$$ ⛶**Hotel Península Valdés.** After extensive remodeling, the classic Hotel Península Valdés offers a new, elegant cafeteria, new bathrooms throughout the hotel, and modernized elevators. Ask for a *panoramico* (room with a view) on an upper floor for the best experience. **Pros:** Newly remodeled, excellent service. **Cons:** Small, nearly unusable gym by American standards. ✉*Av. Roca 155,* ☎*2965/471–292* ⊕*www. hotelPeninsula.com.ar* ⮐*76 rooms* ♿*In-hotel: restaurant, bar, gym, laundry service, public Wi-Fi* ▭*AE, DC, MC, V* ⏀*BP.*

$$ ⛶**Quilimbai Bungalos.** Staying in bungalows or *cabañas* such as the Quilimbai is a cost-effective alternative for families or for longer-term stays in Madryn, especially if you wish to cook some of your own meals. While not in the center of town, but in the more residential (and quieter) southern end, the clean, comfortable, well-built cabins at Quilimbai (like the majority of short-term apartment or cabin rentals) are in walking distance from an uncrowded, shaded stretch of Madryn's coastline. For a complete list of all the short-term apartment and cabin rentals, check www.madrynalquileres.com.ar. **Pros:** Peaceful setting, family atmosphere, ability to cook your own meals. **Cons:** No services, farther away from center of town. ✉*A. Matthews 2075* ☎*2965/473–665* ⊕*www.quilimbai.com.ar* ⤳*3 cabins* ⚥*In-room: kitchen.*

NIGHTLIFE

For those wanting to dance, the 15-year-old **Rancho Cucamongo** (✉*Brown at Jenkins*) is a *boliche,* or disco, where some of the best DJs in Argentina come to spin their sets.

La Oveja Negra (✉*Irigoyen 144*) is a small, cozy bar and literary café; Thursday through Sunday nights you can attend poetry readings or hear good local bands.

SHOPPING

If you're looking for camping supplies and outdoor gear, check **Montagne** (✉*Roca 235*) next to the visitor center. In the same general complex you'll find **Artesanias Mag** (✉*Portal de Madryn, Av. Roca at Av. 28 de Julio* ☎*2965/474–700*), which makes its own pots and craft items from a local white clay known as *arcilla.* It also sells leather goods, hand-drawn postcards, and custom-made knives. Also in the complex is **El Cardon** (☎*2965/458–200*), a fine clothing boutique. **Barrika** (✉*Av. Roca 109* ☎*2965/450–454*) is an excellent wineshop. The staff will guide you to the choicest Argentinean varietals. On the second floor of Portal de Madryn is **Yenelen,** which sells regional culinary goodies, such as torta *galesa,* chocolates, jellies made from wild Patagonian fruits, and teas.

PENÍNSULA VALDÉS

Fodor's Choice
★

Puerto Pirámides is 104 km (64 mi) northeast of Puerto Madryn.

Designated a UNESCO World Heritage site for its important marine mammal populations, and with its unique landscape—the lowest point (132 feet below sea level) on the South American continent—Península Valdés is one of the most spectacular places in Patagonia. Although full-day tours are available from Puerto Madryn, to properly experience Península Valdés you should plan a minimum of two full days of exploring, spending at least a night, but preferably two, at Puerto Pirámides and/or La Elvira near Caleta Valdés. Bring binoculars.

The biggest attraction is the *Ballena Franca* (southern right whale) population, which feeds, mates, and gives birth here. The protected mammals attract some 120,000 visitors every year from June, when they first arrive, through December. Especially during the peak season of September and October, people crowd into boats at Puerto Pirámides to observe at close range as the 30- to 35-ton whales breach and blast giant V-shaped spouts of water from their blowholes.

CLOSE UP

Calendar of Fauna in Atlantic Patagonia (Península Valdés)

Southern right whale (Eubalaena australis). Valdes Peninsula, Argentina

(Animals are present in months marked with an "X." Note, for example, that birds are present year-round, whereas whales are present only June through December.)

Although few wildlife-viewing experiences are as grandiose as seeing whales breach or witnessing orcas charge the beaches in a hunt for sea lions, there are numerous special moments throughout the yearly cycles of all Atlantic Patagonian fauna. Regardless of what time you visit, you'll be witnessing something memorable.

Birds. Among the many seabirds found in Patagonia—including dolphin gull, kelp goose, southern giant petrel, rock and blue-eyed cormorant, snowy sheathbill, blackish oyster-catcher, and steamer duck—one species, the arctic tern, has the longest migration of any bird. Each year it flies over 21,750 mi (round-trip) from the Arctic to Antarctica. The isolated stretch of coastline near Bahía Busta-mante has the greatest diversity of seabirds in Patagonia.

Penguins. Penguins are the only species of birds that migrate by swimming. At several places in Atlantic Patagonia—most notably Punta Tombo—there are large rookeries of Magellanic penguins, with up to 500,000 birds. The males arrive at the rookery each August. A month later the females arrive and the males begin fighting territorial battles. In October and into November the nesting pairs incubate the eggs. Once the chicks hatch in November, the parents make continual trips to the ocean for food, which they bring back and regurgitate for the chicks to eat. In January the chicks leave the nest, learning to swim in February. Their plumage matures throughout the fall, when the penguins begin migrating north to warmer waters in Brazil.

Southern Right Whales. The first southern right whales arrive in Golfo Nuevo between the end of April and the beginning of May, and can be observed from beaches in and along Puerto Madryn as well as Península Valdés. Your best chance at seeing them will be from a whale-watching point at Puerto Pirámides. These whales are between 36 and 59 feet long, and have several endearing behaviors such as "sailing," where they hold their fins up in the air, and when a mother uses her flippers to teach calves how to swim.

Elephant Seals. Elephant seals are larger mammals than sea lions, and have a different way of moving—using their flippers to waddle along on land, whereas sea lions use both front and back flippers to thrust themselves forward. Adult males can reach up to 6 meters (20 feet) in

	Jan	Feb	Mar	Apr	May	Jun	Jul	Aug	Sep	Oct	Nov	Dec
Fauna	X	X	X	X	X	X	X	X	X	X	X	X
Birds						X	X	X	X	X	X	X
Whales						X	X	X	X	X	X	X
Dolphins	X	X	X									X
Elephant Seals	X	X	X	X	X	X	X	X	X	X	X	X
Sea Lions	X	X	X	X	X	X	X	X	X	X	X	X
Orcas	X	X	X	X					X	X	X	X
Penguins	X	X	X						X	X	X	X

4

length and weigh up to 4 tons, and after four years develop a proboscis, or elephant-like appendage on their noses, which inflates to help produce sounds. The biggest elephant-seal colonies are in Península Valdés, at Punta Cantor and Punta Delgada.

Sea Lions. In January and February, sea lions begin to form "harems," with each dominant male taking up to a dozen females. The fights to maintain these harems can be bloody and violent, and sometimes it's possible to witness an invading male drag off one of the females from the harem with his teeth. Most of the year, however, sea-lion colonies appear peaceful: the animals sun themselves or swim, and the pups are especially curious and playful. They can be observed year-round in dozens of spots, from Península Valdés all along the Atlantic Coast.

Orcas. Summertime (which in the Southern Hemisphere begins on December 21) up until April is when sea lions and elephant seals are reproducing and raising pups. This is when it's possible to see the black fins of orcas cutting through the water along the coastline, occasionally storming the beach in violent and spectacular chases. The best place to see orcas is in Península Valdés, at the extreme northern tip, Punta Norte, in April.

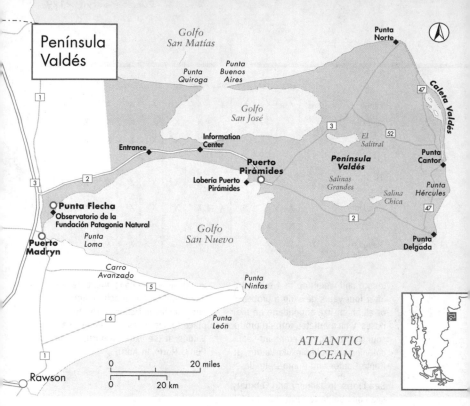

From the visitor center at the entrance to the Peninsula—which is worth an hour just for orientation—a series of interconnected 32- to 64-km (20- to 40-mi) dirt roads take you to several major wildlife-viewing areas. These extend from the cliff-guarded beaches and elephant-seal colonies at Punta Delgada in the south to Punta Norte at the northern tip, where depending on the season, you can see orcas. There are also three salt lakes of varying sizes, and large inland populations of guanacos, foxes, rheas, and partridges in addition to the ubiquitous Patagonian sheep that are ranched here.

Península Valdés was discovered by Hernando de Magallanes in 1520 and later named after Don Antonio Valdés, minister of the Spanish navy in the late 18th century. It is now a protected natural area.

GETTING AROUND
Heading towards the Peninsula on Ruta 2, just before entering the isthmus you'll reach the park entrance where you'll pay a fee of 40 pesos. Some 22 km (14 mi) down the road is the newly remodeled

Information Center and Museum (☎2965/1556–5222 ⊙Daily 8–8). An hour spent here studying the various exhibits on marine, coastal, and continental flora and fauna, as well as fossils, climate, and geology, will make for a more informed visit.

From there you'll continue another 24 km (15 mi) to a junction where you can either go an additional 2 km (1.2 mi) south to Puerto Pirámides, or head 5 km (3 mi) east to where the circuit of interconnected roads taking you around the peninsula begins.

WHAT TO SEE

Puerto Pirámides has only one main street, Avenida de Ballenas, which rolls down Golfo Nuevo with a scattering of tin-roofed buildings among dunes and flowers. For ecological reasons, only 350 people are allowed to live here, but there is a good selection of campsites, hotels, and restaurants. Bring plenty of money with you, as the ATM machine may be out of cash. Aside from whale-watching and lounging around with a beer while looking out on the pyramid-shape cliffs of Valdés Bay, activities include scuba diving, sandboarding, and mountain-biking tours. Whale-watching excursions leave from the little harbor, generally at 8:30 or 9—check with your hotel to reserve with one of the local outfits. Smaller boats, such as the ones operated by Hydro Sport ($\Rightarrow$ *Whale Watching Tours, below*) are preferable to big ones, as they tend to get closer to the whales.

From Puerto Pirámides it's about 5 km (3 mi) along RP2 to the beginning of a circuit around the peninsula. For starters, you'll see the **Lobería Puerto Pirámides**, a sea-lion colony 4 km (2½ mi) from town (on the way to Punta Delgada), but each vista and wildlife-viewing opportunity here is unique, and you'll want to take your time.

From June through November, you can often see whales just 30 meters offshore or so from the **Observatorio de la Fundación Patagonia Natural** (www.patagonianatural.org) at Playa Faro, 12 km (7½ mi) from Puerto Madryn toward Punta Flecha.

Head southeast (with a full tank of gas) along RP2 for about 70 km (43 mi) to get to the elephant-seal and sea-lion colonies at **Punta Delgada**, on the southeastern tip of the peninsula. The elephant seals' breeding season starts in August when the males compete for beach space, after which females arrive, form harems, and give birth. The seals head out to sea in November. There is an old lighthouse, which you can climb to the top of for open-sea views, and guards' quarters that have been turned into an upmarket hotel and restaurant. You have to walk down stairs and paths to get to the animal observation area, which is open 9:30–4:30.

From there, head up the eastern coast of the island (on RP47, though it's unmarked), about another 35 km (22 mi), to the elephant-seal colony at **Punta Cantor.** You can either take RP52 back across the peninsula, reconnecting with RP3 to return to Puerto Pirámides, or continue up the coast another 22 km (14 mi) or so to **Caleta Valdés.** Here you can stop at Parador La Elvira, a complex with a restaurant, gift shop, and cliff-side walkway to another impressive elephant-seal beach—peak activity is in September.

The northeastern corner of the peninsula, **Punta Norte,** has the most remote and largest sea-lion settlement of all; orcas cruise through town from time to time, and Magellanic penguins roam the land from October through March. From Punta Norte, RP3 is an inland shortcut that heads straight back southwest to Pirámides, passing by **El Salitral,** one of the peninsula's three large salt-lake ecosystems.

WHERE TO EAT

$$ ✕**La Estación Pub.** The coolest bar in Pirámides is also the town's best seafood restaurant. Amid the nets and nautical gear is an eclectic collection of music posters leaning heavily towards glam rock—Iggy Pop, David Bowie, Lou Reed, etc.

> **WHALE-WATCHING TOURS**
>
> For whale-watching, **Jorge Schmid** (☎☎ 2965/295–012 or 2965/295–112) is a reliable operator. He also rents scuba equipment. **Hydro Sport** (☎☎ 2965/495–065 ⊕ www. hydrosport.com.ar) is another popular whale-watching operation, and is sponsored by the U.S.-based Whale Conservation Institute.

Owner Mario Gadda is also an avid mountain biker and organizes biking tours. ⊠ *Av. de las Ballenas s/n* ☎ *2965/495–047* ✎ *mariogadda@ gmail.com* ▭ *MC, V.*

$–$$$ ✕**Posada Pirámides.** This family restaurant, which feels like a living room, is across the street from the Hotel Paradise. Its kitchen and delightful staff cook up creative Argentinean cuisine, especially seafood. This is one of the best places to eat in town. Perhaps because it doubles as a hostel (with very basic accommodations), there's a young, informal attitude, but the preparations are serious; don't miss the signature *vieyras gratinadas* (baked scallops with melted cheese) or a heavy but good *lenguado con salsa de camarones* (sole in shrimp sauce) with potatoes noisette. ⊠ *Av. de las Ballenas s/n* ☎ *2965/495–040* ⊕ *www. posadapiramides.com* ▭ *MC, V.*

$$ ✕**La Posta.** A new family restaurant that also serves *minutitias*— hamburgers, sandwiches, and other light fare—La Posta has a great location overlooking the town, and good food. A multitiered patio is on the hillside and next door is an attached mini-mercado where you can buy cold cuts, fruits, vegetables, chips, and drinks. This is a good place to find camping supplies. At night La Posta becomes a resto-bar. ⊠ *Av. de las Ballenas s/n* ☎ *2965/1564–2051* ✎ *lucas_moller84@ hotmail.com* ▭ *No credit cards.*

WHERE TO STAY

$$$ ⌂**Cabañas en el Mar.** These comfortable A-frame cabins have private balconies with views of the ocean, as well as kitchenettes, making them popular with families and biologists here on extended stays. A new ice-cream shop and café is in the lobby. Each unit accommodates up to six people. **Pros:** Inexpensive, and you can cook in your cabin. **Cons:** May be slightly noisy during the day. ⊠ *Av. de las Ballenas s/n,* ☎ *2965/495–049* ⊕ *www.piramides.net/cabanas* ☜ *6 cabañas* ⌂ *In-hotel: laundry service* ▭ *No credit cards.*

$$$$ ⌂**Estancia La Elvira.** This stop along the unpaved RP47 at first seems like a mirage: out of nowhere rises a complex with tour buses, gift

shops, and a grand, picture-windowed roadhouse that overlooks the huge inlet at Caleta Valdés. Estancia La Elvira is the only lodging outside of Punta Delgada and the village at Puerto Pirámides. There are two options available—a half board, which includes breakfast and dinner (designed for those who plan on spending the day exploring on their own), and the full board, which includes breakfast, lunch, and dinner. Both plans include all activities accompanied by English-speaking guides. Choose from guided nature walks down the beach, horseback rides, and mountain biking. The hotel is super-clean and has a comfortable lounge full of books and games. The only drawback is that the peacefulness can be broken when a tour bus pulls up with dozens of guests hungry for a plate of *cordero al asador*. **Pros:** Lots of activities, great views. **Cons:** Tour buses. ⊠*Near Caleta Valdés, along RP47 on the Península Valdés. Office in Puerto Madryn: Av. Hipólito Yrigoyen 257 Local 2,* ☎*2965/474–248 Puerto Madryn, 2965/1540–6183 hotel* ⊕*www.laelvira.com.ar* ➶*8 rooms* ⌂*In hotel: pool* ⊟*No credit cards at hotel, but AE, MC, V accepted for payment at office in Madryn.* ⊘*Closed Apr.–Aug.*

$$$ ▣**The Paradise.** With its bar decorated with postcards and photographs left by visitors, and a fireplace in the back, this hotel is personable and warm. It's a good, if overpriced, choice for those seeking reliability. Rooms are clean and spare, and second-floor rooms have a few more amenities like cable TV. The restaurant ($$–$$$) is okay. **Pros:** The hotel can organize any kind of adventure, from scuba-diving tours to sandboarding. **Cons:** Overpriced rooms. ⊠*Av. Julio A. Roca,* ☎☎*2965/495–030 or 2965/495–003* ⊕*www.puerto-piramides. ar* ➶*12 rooms* ⌂*In-room: no TV (some). In-hotel: restaurant, bar, laundry service* ⊟*AE, MC, V* ⦿*CP.*

$$$ ✕▣**Punta Delgada.** This former lighthouse (along with a navy station,
★ a post office, and a little school for the guards' families) is a sea-lion colony observation point, and an elegant hotel. Punta Delgada's luxuries are simple and aristocratically old-fashioned: comfortable beds, a tennis court, a pleasant pub with pool and darts, starry night skies, board games, and utter tranquility. Excursions are organized by the staff. There are no telephones or even cell service, never mind television; there's no electricity 9–noon and 3–7. Nor are there water views from the rooms, unfortunately; the hotel sits too far inland for that. Still, it's one of the most impressively isolated hotels in Patagonia. Dinner is served for hotel guests only, but nonguests can lunch at the restaurant ($$–$$$$), which features chicken curry, king crab, and *cordero al asador* at midday. Tour groups tend to stop by for lunch in large numbers. **Pros:** Peaceful, good excursions, completely pleasant. **Cons:** Rooms don't have water views, too isolated for some, tour buses. ⊠*Punta Delgadas* ☎*2965/458–444* ⊕*www.puntadelgada.com* ➶*27 rooms* ⌂*In-room: no phone, no TV. In-hotel: restaurant, bar, tennis court* ⊟*AE, MC, V* ⊘*Closed Apr.–July.*

$$$ ▣**Las Restingas.** Built at the very edge of Golfo Nuevo, this is the most
★ luxurious hotel in town, and also the one hotel where it's possible to see whales from your window. Rooms boast crisp linens and huge pic-

ture windows. **Pros:** Beautiful rooms, lobby, overall setting and service. **Cons:** Rooms facing the village are overpriced. ✉*Primera Bajada al Mar at Ribera Marítima* 📠*2965/495–101 or 2965/495–102* ⊕*www. lasrestingas.com* ➾*12 rooms* ♿*In-hotel: restaurant, bar, beachfront, laundry service, pool, spa, public Internet* ⊟*AE, MC, V.*

EN ROUTE Heading north on R3 toward Viedma will take you through the small town of Sierra Grande and its vast supply of iron, said to be among the world's largest. You can tour a mine for 15–20 pesos, hiking 300 feet beneath the earth's crust, rappelling, and rafting in underground waters while learning about iron mining. Contact **Area Natural Recreativa Movil 5** (☎*2934/481–0212 or 2934/481–333*) for information. Other hiking and camping options are nearby; the folks at Area Natural Recreativa Movil 5 can give you more information.

TRELEW & GAIMAN

Where the Chubut River Valley empties into the Atlantic Ocean, you'll find Trelew and Gaiman (along with Rawson, Chubut's capital city), towns that maintain the traditions of the Welsh pioneers who settled the area in the mid-1800s. Each fall Trelew holds a celebration of Welsh poetry, song, and dance called Eisteddfod. Gaiman, with its teahouses, rose gardens, and chapels, is the largest Welsh settlement outside of Wales, and some people are still speaking Welsh.

Trelew has several good restaurants and hotels and a few attractions, such as the MEF (the dinosaur museum). It's also a large city by Patagonian standards (almost 100,000 people), and if you explore the city thoroughly you'll likely encounter *villas miserias* or shantytowns.

Although it's the capital of Chubut province, Rawson is much smaller, with only about 26,000 inhabitants. There isn't much for travelers here. Six kilometers (4 mi) east of Rawson is the small, industrial town of Playa Unión, also with little to offer travelers, unless you're a surfer: the Chubut River deposits sand along the coast here, forming sandbars on the otherwise flat continental shelf, and producing the most consistent surf break in all of Patagonia.

TRELEW

11 km (6 mi) east of Gaiman, 250 km (155 mi) north of Camarones, 67 km (41½ mi) south of Puerto Madryn.

Trelew (pronounced Tre-LEH-ew) is a commercial, industrial, and service hub with hotels, restaurants, gas stations, mechanics, and anything else you might need as you travel from point to point. Its biggest attractions are its paleontology museum and its proximity to the Punta Tombo Reserve and Península Valdés. If you come in the second half of October, you can participate in the Eisteddfod, a Welsh literary and musical festival, first held in Patagonia in 1875. Trelew was founded in 1886 as a result of the construction of the Chubut railway line, which joined the Chubut River valley with the Atlantic coast. It's named after its Welsh founder, Lewis Jones (Tre means "town" in Welsh, and Lew stands for Lewis), who fought to establish the rail line.

GETTING AROUND

If you're driving, from the RN3, take RN25 to Avenida Fontana. If arriving by bus, the terminal is at Urquiza and Lewis Jones, along the Plaza Centenario. Most of what you'll visit is found in the half-dozen blocks between Plaza Centenario and Plaza Independencia, which is also where the tourist office is.

ESSENTIALS

BUS **Andesmar** (✉ *Urquiza at Lewis Jones* ☎ *2944/433–535*). **Don Otto** (✉ *Gales 35* ☎ *2965/423–943*). **TAC** (✉ *Urquiza at Lewis Jones* ☎ *2965/431–452*).

CURRENCY **Banco de la Nación** (✉ *Belgrano at Julio A. Roca* ☎ *2965/449–100*). **Lloyds Bank** (✉ *9 de Julio 102* ☎ *2965/434–264 or 2965/434–058*).

MAIL **Trelew** (✉ *25 de Mayo at Mitre*).

RENTAL CAR **Hertz** (✉ *Aeropuerto de Trelew* ☎ *5411/4816–8001, 0810/2224–3789 central reservations office* ⊕ *www.hertzargentina.com.ar*).

VISITOR INFO **Tourist Office** (✉ *Mitre 387* 📠 *2965/420–139* ⊕ *www.trelew.gov.ar*).

WHAT TO SEE

The town's main square, **Plaza Independencia,** features a central gazebo with intricate woodwork and a steeple. In 1910 the plaza and gazebo were inaugurated on a spot formerly used by the train station's employees to graze their horses.

The **Teatro Español** (Spanish Theater), on the north side of Plaza Independencia, was constructed by the city's Spanish immigrants in 1918. Today it's a cultural center that hosts drama, dance, and musical events. ✉ *Av. 25 de Mayo 237* ☎ *2965/434–336.*

The **Museo de Arte Visuales de Trelew** (Museum of Visual Arts) is east of the plaza and has good monthly contemporary art exhibitions. It's in a Flemish- and German-influenced building designed by a French architect in 1900. From 1913 to 1932, this was the city hall. ✉ *Mitre 385* ☎ *No phone* ⊕ *http://ar.geocities.com/museotw* ⊙ *Daily 8–8.*

🕑 At Trelew's most prominent attraction, the **Museo Paleontológico Egidio**
Fodor'sChoice **Feruglio (MEF),** the most modern display is 2 million years old. This state-
★ of-the-art educational extravaganza features exhibits on extinct dinosaurs from Patagonia. There's a fossil of a 290-million-year-old spider with a 3-foot leg span and the 70-million-year-old petrified dinosaur eggs of a carnotaurus. The museum's tour de force is the bones of a 100-ton, 120-foot-long dinosaur. You can also peek into a workshop where paleontologists study newly unearthed fossils. Tours in English are available. ✉ *Av. Fontana 140* ☎ *2965/432–100 or 2964/420–012* ⊕ *www.mef.org.ar* 🎟 *15 pesos* ⊙ *Daily 10–6.*

Across the street from MEF is Trelew's old train station, which operated from 1889 to 1961, when the government shut down the country's rail service. The national historic landmark now has a small museum of town history, the **Museo Regional Pueblo de Luis** (Lewistown Regional Museum). It has a mishmash of displays on the European influence in the region, the indigenous populations of the area, and wildlife. ⊠ *Av. 9 de Julio at Fontana* ☎ *2965/424–062* ⊒ *2 pesos* ⊙ *Weekdays 8–8, Sun. 2–8.*

WHERE TO STAY & EAT

¢–$ ✕ **Touring Club.** Legend has it that Butch Cassidy and the Sundance Kid once stayed here. This classic old *confitería* was founded in 1907 by the Chubut Railway Company as a restaurant and became Chubut's first hotel in 1926. In its heyday it was one of Patagonia's most luxurious options. Now, the hotel's rooms are too shabby to recommend, but the café staff is proud of its past; the spot is so old-world, the waiters will simply leave a bottle of liquor on your table after only charging you for one drink. Ask to see the old *salón* (dining room). ⊠ *Av. Fontana 240* ☎ *2965/433–997 or 2965/433–998* ⊟ *AE, DC, MC, V.*

$$–$$$ ✕ **El Viejo Molino.** It's fun to find a restaurant that outclasses its city. The
Fodor'sChoice thoughtful design and ultramodern renovation of this 1886 mill have
★ set a new benchmark for dining on the Patagonian coast. Beneath the Alexander Calder–inspired mobiles hanging from the two-story-high ceiling, elegant hostesses and courteous waiters deliver refined service. A glassed-in parilla allows you to watch a cook pour wine over the roast and attend to it lovingly. On Saturday nights there are tango and folklore shows. ⊠ *Gales 250* ☎ *2965/428–019* ⊟ *AE, MC, V.*

$$ ⊡ **Hotel Libertador.** This big hotel has seen better days, but because it caters to tour groups, the English-speaking staff is very reliable. Rooms are clean, get good light, and are reasonably modern. Fourteen "superior" rooms are more recently renovated and are worth the modest increase in price. **Pros:** Only a block from the central plaza. **Cons:** Only the superior rooms are worth the price. ⊠ *Av. Rivadavia 31,* ☎⊟ *2965/420–220* ⊕ *www.hotellibertadortw.com* ⇝ *90 rooms* ⚸ *In-room: dial-up. In-hotel: restaurant, laundry service, parking (no fee)* ⊟ *AE, DC, MC, V* ⧉*CP.*

$$ ⊡ **Rayentray.** The nicest, and most expensive, hotel in Trelew is this 22-year-old building, part of an Argentinean chain. Rayentray, which means "stream of flowers" in Mapuche, has more amenities than any other local hotel. It's a block from Plaza Independencia. **Pros:** Hotel staff can organize excursions. **Cons:** Quality rooms but without any real charm. ⊠ *San Martín 101,* ☎ *2965/434–702* ⊕ *www.cadenaray entray.com.ar* ⇝ *110 rooms* ⚸ *In-hotel: restaurant, pool, laundry service* ⊟ *AE, DC, MC, V* ⧉*CP.*

GAIMAN

17 km (10½ mi) west of Trelew.

The most Welsh of the Atlantic Patagonian settlements, Gaiman (pronounced GUY-mon) is far more charming than nearby Trelew and Rawson. The Welsh colony's history is lovingly preserved in museums and private homes. Welsh can still be heard on the streets (though residents speak Spanish) and a connection to Wales continues with teachers, preachers, and visitors going back and forth frequently (often with copies of family trees in hand). Even the younger generation maintains an interest in the culture and language.

Perhaps the town's greatest draw are its five Welsh teahouses (*casas de té*)—Ty Gwyn, Plas-y-Coed, Ty Nain, Ty Cymraeg, and Ty Te Caerdydd. Each serves a similar menu of tea and home-baked pastries, cakes, and breads for about the same price (around 20 pesos will buy a *completo* sampling, which should serve two). Still, each establishment has its own personal history and atmosphere. Teahouses are usually open daily 3–8; if you're anywhere nearby, they're worth a trip.

GETTING AROUND

Gaiman is self-contained and easily walkable. All of the teahouses and most of the attractions are within a five-block radius of the town square at Avenue Eugenio Tello and M. D. Jones. Those without a vehicle can access the few sites outside of town—such as the Chapel Road or Bryn Gwyn Paleontology Park—by taking an inexpensive remis from one of the *remiserías* on Avenida Eugenio Tello.

As of this writing, the **tourist office** (⊠ *Corner of Rivadavía and Belgrano* ☎ *2965/491–152* ⊙ *Mon.–Sat. 9–8, Sun. 1–8*) was still at the corner of Rivadavía and Belgrano; however, a new tourist office at the corner of Sarmiento and 28 de Julio was nearly completed. Staff members can help point you to sights, but they speak limited English.

ESSENTIALS

CURRENCY **Banco del Chubut** (⊠ *J.E. Evans 115* ☎ *2965/491–044* ⊕ *www.bancochubut. com.ar*).

MAIL **Gaiman** (⊠ *Juan C. Evans 110*).

VISITOR INFO **Tourist Office** (⊠ *Belgrano 234* ☎ *2965/491–571* ⊕ *www.gaiman.gov.ar/turismo*).

WHAT TO SEE

❷ Right beside the original tourist office is the now-unused **train tunnel,** built in 1914 to transport produce and products from Gaiman to the center of the Chubut province. As soon as you cross the tunnel you reach the **Museo Antropológico de Gaiman,** a two-story brick house built in 1910 by the pioneering Nichols family. Inside are pre-Columbian skulls, Patagonian stone tools, and displays of other artifacts from the region. Note that this museum can only be visited with a tour guide. Call the tourist office in advance for reservations.

❶ The **Museo Histórico Regional Galés** (Welsh Regional Historical Museum) is in the old Central Chubut train station. The museum has photographs of Gaiman's original 160 settlers, a library of books in Welsh, and other interesting memorabilia. ⊠ *Av. Sarmiento at Av. 28 de Julio* ☜ *2 pesos* ⊙ *Jan. and Feb., Tues.–Sun. 10–11:30 and 3–6; Mar.–Dec., Tues.–Sun. 3–6.*

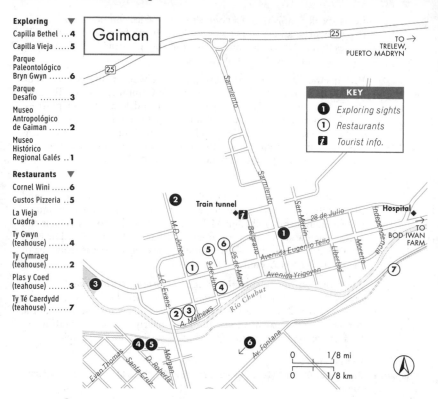

❸ Argentina's weirdest attraction is Gaiman's **Parque Desafío.** Colorful,
★ kitschy, and entirely creative, the park is filled with recycled goods—
80,000 bottles, 15,000 tin cans, and the remains of several automo-
biles—and took over 30,000 hours of work. Its mastermind, Joaquin
R. Alonso, originally began the park in 1980 as a playground for his
grandkids. Alonso and his wife Maria del Carmen Caballero, who live
here, welcome you to the park and invite you to stroll the paths lined
with Alonso's alternately pensive and humorous musings. One reads,
"Cows affirm that artificial insemination is boring." A visit here is
anything but. ⊠ *Av. Brown 52 at Calle Espora* ☎ *2965/491–340* ⌨ *10
pesos* ⊙ *Daily 9–8.*

Throughout the Chubut Valley are three dozen or so chapels where the
Welsh went to school, held meetings, trials, and social events, sang religious hymns, and even had their tea—some still function as teahouses.
❺ Two of these chapels are in Gaiman. The **Capilla Vieja** was built in
1880. Three times a year it's used in a traditional event called Eisteddfod, when townspeople gather to celebrate Welsh traditions with song,
poetry, and dance under the chapel's wooden vaulted ceiling.

❹ Next to the Capilla Vieja is the **Capilla Bethel,** built in 1914 and used
today by Protestants for Sunday service. To reach the chapels take the

first right after the bridge heading out of town and follow the dirt road around several bends.

⑥ The **Parque Paleontológico Bryn Gwyn** (Bryn Gwyn Paleontology Park) is outside town, where the green river valley gives way to the arid steppe. Here you'll find a series of badlands where strata of different formations shows over 40 million years of geological history. Bryn Gwyn is a branch of the Museo Paleontológico Egidio Feruglio in Trelew. Call ahead to arrange a tour. ✉ *11 km (7 mi) south of town* ☎ *2965/1555–5014* ⊕ *www.mef.org.ar/mef/en/institucional/geoparque.php* 💵 *8 pesos* ⊙ *Mar.–Sept., daily 11–5; Oct.–Feb., daily 10–6.*

OFF THE BEATEN PATH

Bod Iwan Farm. Want to spend a day on the same farm where Bruce Chatwin stayed while researching his famed travelogue *In Patagonia*? Contact Waldo Williams at Bod Iwan Farm, a working Welsh farm 15 minutes east of Gaiman, where you can walk among cows, sheep, wagons, and tractors. Waldo will give you a tour of his century-old home, along with the grounds, where he grows fields of alfalfa to feed the Hampshire Down sheep that roam the property. Stick around until dusk; watch the sunset in the Chubut River valley and you'll understand why Patagonia has been a source of both desperation and inspiration for so many. ☎ *2965/491–251 or 2965/1566–1816.*

WHERE TO EAT

$–$$
★ ✕ **Cornel Wini.** Gaiman's newest family restaurant was originally a bar–hotel with a boxing ring in the basement. The Jones family opened it in 1964, calling it the Cornel, or "corner" in Welsh. In 2007 they transformed it into a restaurant, and now the tall-windowed dining room with wooden floors has a hotel-lobby elegance. The cuisine is classic Argentinean. Pastas, pizzas, and parilla are all great; salads and vegetables are mediocre. ✉ *Av. Eugenio Tello 199* ☎ *2965/491–397* ☐ *AE, MC, V.*

$ ✕ **Gustos Pizzeria.** It's not much to look at—a fairly ratty couple of rooms, with a few token chairs and tables outside—and the service is merely perfunctory, but Gustos has surprisingly good pizza. Besides the usual, toppings include Roquefort cheese, ham, hard-boiled eggs, red pepper, onion, and tuna fish. An individual pizza is 8–12 pesos. ✉ *Av. Eugenio Tello 156* ☎ *2965/491–828* ☐ *No credit cards.*

$$ ✕ **Ty Cymraeg.** Photographs of the Thomas family's ancestors guard the walls of the wood-paneled rooms in this teahouse on the banks of the Chubut River. An outdoor patio with tree-shaded benches is at your disposal. ✉ *Av. Matthews 74* ☎ *2965/491–010* ⊕ *www.cpatagonia. com/gaiman/cymraeg* ☐ *AE, DC, MC, V.*

$$
★ ✕ **Ty Té Caerdydd.** Cypress trees, fountains, and sculpted gardens mark the grounds of Gaiman's largest teahouse, which looks like a mini–palatial estate on the south bank of the Chubut River. It succeeds in impressing, though the dining rooms are larger and less homey than the town's other teahouses. A separate *casa de artesanias* is the best place to pick up jams, handicrafts, and souvenirs. ✉ *Finca 202, Zona de Chacras* ☎ *2965/491–510* ☐ *AE, DC, MC, V.*

Gaiman's Teahouses

Each of Gaiman's five teahouses serves up its own unique family recipes for apple tarts, lemon tarts, and a variety of pastries and buns, as well as fresh-churned cream and butter, and homemade marmalade. The tea is always served in fine china with special *cubre teteras*, or covers woven from local Patagonian wool, used to keep the teakettle warm.

Just as the recipes and tastes differ slightly from teahouse to teahouse, so do their interiors. Ty Nain, for example, is like an old antiques shop, with gramophones, carriage lamps, antique radios and coffee grinders on display above each of the four original chimneys, which date back to the building's construction in 1890. Ty Gwyn, with its spacious, high-ceilinged room, feels more like you're eating in some medieval dining hall.

Common to all the teahouses are the collections of skillfully crocheted tapestries, often inscribed with Welsh words or the Welsh alphabet, along with intricate Celtic designs around the borders. You always find love spoons hanging from the walls as well. The tradition of these spoons dates back to 16th-century Wales, where a young man would carve a spoon from a single piece of wood and give it to the girl he wished to marry.

Gaiman's teahouses are owned by descendants of the original Welsh settlers. They are happy to recount this history if you ask about it. There's a strong sense of appreciation for how easy things are today compared to just a couple generations ago. Ana, of Plas y Coed, whose great-grandmother was featured in Bruce Chatwin's book *In Patagonia*, told us, "Imagine making everything from scratch and running this place without refrigerators."

$-$$ ✕**La Vieja Cuadra.** Exposed brick adds character to the town's liveliest
★ restaurant. Some come just for a beer—the place stays lively well into the evening—while others dine on the house specialty: homemade pastas, like spaghetti or ham-and-cheese-stuffed *sorrentinos* (stuffed pasta) with Bolognese meat sauce, or triangular pasta pillows with rabbit confit. Even better are the pizzas. If you crave sirloin, try the *lomo a los tres pimientos* (with three peppers). ⊠*M.D. Jones 418, at Tello on the plaza* ☎*2965/1568–2352* ▤*No credit cards* ⊙*Closed Mon. No lunch Tues.–Sat. No dinner Sun.*

WHERE TO STAY

$ ⊡**Hostería Gwesty Tywi ffarm fach.** After closing the original Gwesty Tywi Hostería on M.D. Jones, Diego Aneiros opened this new bed-and-breakfast out of town. The new location is a beautiful *chacra*, or farm, with a pool for kids, a small playground, fruit trees, and sheep. **Pros:** Good for families, Diego can organize local excursions. **Cons:** Somewhat isolated if you don't have a vehicle. ⊠*Chacra 202 Lote 29,* ☎☎*2965/491–292* ⊕*www.advance.com.ar/usuarios/gwestywi* ➥*6 rooms* ⌂*In-room: no phone, no TV* ▤*AE, MC, V* ⓘ*CP.*

$ ✕⊡**Plas y Coed.** Gaiman's oldest teahouse has is also a bed-and-break-
★ fast. For the inexpensive price you get an immaculate room, plus use of

a comfortable lounge, and the benefit of being able to enjoy Gaiman's oldest rose garden. The majority of these roses are at least 70 years old and roses that arch over the entryway to the teahouse are over 100. **Pros:** Amicable staff and an inclusive, family atmosphere. **Cons:** Not much room for groups larger than six. ⊠ *M. D. Jones 123,* ☎*2965/491–133* ⊕*www.plasycoed.com.ar* ↪*3 rooms* ⚷*In-room: no phone, no TV. In-hotel: restaurant, bar, no elevator* ▭*AE, MC, V* ¶⧵*CP.*

$$$$ ⊡ **Posada Los Mimbres.** This ranch has a fantastic nature trail along the Chubut River. Guests can choose to stay in one of two three-bedroom homes, one of which is a century old. You reach the ranch by following signs from town to the "Zona de Chacras," or farmhouse zone. It's a 5-km (3-mi) ride down a dirt road. **Pros:** Tranquil setting gives a taste of life on the chacra. **Cons:** Isolated from town if you don't have a vehicle, expensive compared to other lodging in Gaiman. ⊠*Chacra 211,* ☎☎*2965/491–299* ⊕*www.posadalosmimbres.com. ar* ↪*2 houses* ⚷*In-room: no a/c, no phone. In-hotel: bicycles* ▭*No credit cards* ¶⧵*BP.*

$ ✕⊡ **Ty Gwyn.** This wood-and-brick teahouse was opened in 1974 by
★ Maria Elena Sanchez Jones, who still directs the kitchen. It serves delicious scones, breads, and jams lovingly made from local fruits, and other elaborate sweets, including the classic Argentine-Welsh tea accompaniment, *torta negra* (black cake), a kind of fruitcake. An interior garden leads to a staircase above which Ms. Sanchez Jones maintains four bedrooms that form the town's best lodging. The quarters are spotless, affordable, and have wood floors, soothing mint-colored walls, and small private balconies with river views. Room 4 has antique furnishings. **Pros:** Best views in Gaiman. **Cons:** Cruise-ship groups arrive regularly in the high season. ⊠*Av. 9 de Julio* ☎*2965/491–009* ⊕*www.cpatagonia.com/gaiman/ty gwyn* ↪*4 rooms* ⚷*In-room: no phone, no TV. In-hotel: restaurant, bar, laundry service, no elevator* ▭*AE, MC, V* ¶⧵*BP.*

FROM PUNTA TOMBO TO BAHÍA BUSTAMANTE

The few travelers willing to stray off Ruta 3 to follow the dirt roads along this stretch of Patagonia's coast will learn a new meaning of "having the place to yourself." If you spend a day traveling from Rawson or Trelew to Camarones (passing Punta Tombo), and the next day drive on from Camarones to Bahía Bustamante—you will literally see nobody on the road.

To some this will seem like a desolate, inhospitable landscape. Yet the land is teeming with both continental and marine wildlife, not to mention the thousands of sheep and goats populating the vast estancias along the way. To others—those who crave open, uncrowded spaces—this area will seem like a paradise. With the exception of Península Valdés, nowhere else in the region yields such a dramatic sense of *endless terrain.*

The only place here with any normal facilities for travelers is Camarones. Punta Tombo is only for viewing wildlife, and Bahía Bustamante is a private—by reservation only—"marine estancia." But each of these stops makes for a convenient, single-day drive, and with good planning and reservations, this area is actually very easy to tour.

PUNTA TOMBO

120 km (74 mi) south of Trelew, 105 km (65 mi) north of Camarones.

Fodor'sChoice   The **Reserva Faunística Punta Tombo** (*Punta Tombo Wildlife Reserve*) has
★   the largest colony of Magellanic penguins in the world and one of the most varied seabird rookeries. Up to half a million penguins live here from the middle of September through March. A trail about a half-mile long takes you to a small point that's intersected by several "penguin highways" linking their nests with the sea. Once you reach the point you'll see how graceful and powerful these creatures (who waddle so awkwardly across the land) become when they enter the water.

Cormorants, guanacos, seals, and Patagonian hares are also in abundance. Although December is the best month to come—that's when the adult penguins actively go back and forth from the sea to feed their newborns—any time is good, except from April through August when the penguins feed at sea. Other than driving, the easiest way to get to Punta Tombo is with a tour from Trelew, Rawson, Gaiman, or even Puerto Madryn. A small restaurant serves good homemade empanadas and also has coffee, cakes, and cold beverages. ☎*30 pesos.*

CAMARONES

252 km (156 mi) south of Trelew, 105 km (65 mi) south of Punta Tombo, 258 km (160 mi) north of Comodoro Rivadavía.

After driving or riding for hours along the empty coastal road (or via RP30 from Ruta 3), the tiny town of Camarones—a collection of brightly colored, tin-roofed buildings with scrollwork fascias, trim, and other curious architectural details—appears like an enchanted village. When you talk to the locals you'll find this to be exactly the case. People here are jovial, happy in their isolation. Most of the stresses found throughout the rest of the country—crime, insecurity, unemployment, pollution—simply don't exist in Camarones. The main debate going on is the battle between the town's two main industries, the production of algae versus salmon fishing. Some species of algae here are invasive, and degrade the native salmon's habitat.

The one main event each year is the Fiesta Nacional de Salmón (National Salmon Festival), with all kinds of events and a fishing contest. Other than that, the main attractions are the beautiful, empty beaches south of town, and the

Cabo Dos Bahías Fauna Reserve, 30 km (19 mi) southeast of town, which is similar to Punta Tombo, and has all kinds of wildlife, including penguins, sea lions, birds, seals, guanacos, rheas, and foxes—but with far fewer human visitors.

GETTING AROUND

Camarones is accessible by public transportation, though only one bus company, Transporte El Ñandú, passes through from Trelew on Monday, Wednesday, and Friday (☎2965/427–499). Once you're in town, if you don't have a vehicle call Ruis Reuben Catriel (☎2971/5418–4077); he can drive you to local destinations, including Cabo Dos Bahías.

> ### FISH AIDE
>
> Local guide **Jorge Kriegel** can set up fishing and diving excursions for you. Call 2974/963–056 or 2971/5418–5567.

Most everything in Camarones is within four blocks of the main plaza, which slopes down to the waterfront and the *puerto*. The **Tourist office** (right at the beach, facing the municipal dock ☎2974/963–040) is attended by Mario Ibarra, a local English-speaking guide.

ESSENTIALS

CURRENCY **Banco del Chubut** (✉ *San Martín 570* ☎ *2974/496-3050* ⊕ *www.bancochubut. com.ar*).

MAIL **Camarones Post Office** (✉ *Roca 100*).

WHERE TO STAY

The **Municipal Campgrounds** in front of the *puerto* have been remodeled and now feature new showers and bathrooms. Each campsite also includes electricity. Call Carlos Vega (☎*2965/1532–2906*) for reservations and information.

$$–$$$ 🛏️**Indalo Inn.** While the Indalo, with its standard block construction and stuffed animals above the television in the lounge–dining room–bar might not seem like the most refined place, it has everything you need for a comfortable stay in Camarones, plus surprising little amenities like a good wine selection and seafood dishes, and Wi-Fi Internet. You can either stay at the hotel, or in one of six cabins right on the waterfront. **Pros:** Friendly, personal atmosphere. **Cons:** Restaurant is hit or miss. ✉*Av. Julio A. Roca at Sarmiento,* ☎*2974/963–004* ⊕*www. indaloinn.com.ar* 🛏️*12 rooms, 6 cabins* ⚖️*In-hotel: bar, restaurant, public Wi-Fi, no elevator* ☰*AE, DC, MC, V* ⏀*CP.*

SHOPPING

Right by the tourist office on the waterfront is **Casa Rabal,** one of the funnest places to shop in all of Patagonia. Originally built in 1898, the shop has everything from locally made cheese to shoes to camping and fishing gear to drywall tools to diapers to bridles for your horse.

BAHÍA BUSTAMANTE

Fodor'sChoice   *89 km (55 mi) south of Camarones, 180 km (110 mi) north of Como-*
★   *doro Rivadavía, 250 km (155 mi) south of Trelew.*

Spending time in Bahía Bustamante is like having your own private Península Valdés. It was founded in 1952 by Lorenzo Soriano, who searched the Patagonian coastline for seaweed to use for extracting colloids. When he found this bay filled with seaweed, he began, along with his sons, to create an entire town including a school, church, auto and boat garage, and housing for more than 400 people who worked harvesting these marine algae.

The operation slowed during the '90s and nearly everyone moved away. In 2004, however, Lorenzo's grandson Matías returned to Bahía Bustamante and began renovating various houses and transforming the place into what he calls an "estancia marina," or marine ranch, with a special focus on ecological sensitivity, observation of marine and continental wildlife, and independence (producing all their own food and electricity). Stays are available for individuals or small groups—only 20 people at a time can stay here—**by reservation only.**

GETTING HERE & AROUND
Bahía Bustamante can only be reached by vehicle. If you don't have a rental car, the only other options are the tour companies Cuyun Co Turismo or Causana Viajes.

Getting to Bahía Bustamante is an adventure. Once you leave Camarones there's not a single sign (or vehicle, usually) along the coastal Ruta 1 for approximately 85 km (52 mi), when you'll see a sign that points to Ruta 3 to the right, or Punto Visser to the left, with a hand-painted sign (invisible at night) saying Bahía Bustamante. Do not take the right toward Ruta 3, but continue left toward Punto Visser/Bahía Bustamante, for another 4 km. You'll cross a small concrete bridge and eventually see a cluster of buildings along the coast. Continue on, passing a sign that says Zona Alguera, Prohibido Pasar, and keep going until you get to a group of single-story buildings, where you'll see a sign that says Administracion.

Once you're in Bahía Bustamante you won't have to drive anywhere. All local transport is handled by Matías or the local guides.

WHERE TO STAY
Bahía Bustamante. Each of the four guesthouses includes twin bedrooms, a living room, bathroom, and kitchen. Activities include bird-watching, visits to a local petrified forest and archaeological sites, and boat excursions to the Malaspina cove where there are sea-lion colonies, plus penguin and seabird rookeries. Other options are trips to local estancias—where you might see demonstrations of old-style sheep shearing using scissors—as well as horseback riding, fishing, mountain-bike excursions, and trekking. Nearly all of the food cooked in the restaurant comes from ingredients grown at the local estancias or fished from the local waters. Bahía Bustamante currently operates between October and April, with other months available by checking

first with Matías. Prices are between $100 and $130 per person per day, including all food and excursions. ⊠*RN3, Km 1676, Chubut* ☎*2971/5625–7500* ⊕*www.Bahiabustamante.com* ➪*4 houses* ⚒*In-hotel: bar, restaurant, public Wi-Fi* ⊟No credit cards ⦿*AI.*

COMODORO RIVADAVÍA

1,854 km (1,149 mi) south of Buenos Aires, 1,726 km (1,070 mi) north of Ushuaia, 945 km (586 mi) north of Río Gallegos, 397 km (246 mi) south of Rawson.

Argentina's answer to Houston, Comodoro Rivadavía is the town that oil built. Argentina's first oil discovery was made here in 1907 during a desperate search for water because of a serious drought. It was an event that led to the formation of Yacimientos Petroliferos Fiscales (YPF), among the world's first vertically integrated oil companies. After YPF's privatization in 1995, however, thousands were laid off, bringing hard times to Comodoro's 130,000 residents. Surrounded by barren hills and sheer cliffs off the Golfo San Jorge, Comodoro looks dramatic from a distance. Up close, it's frayed around the edges. The main commercial streets, where you'll find most restaurants and bars, are San Martín and Comodoro Rivadavía. A relative urban newcomer, Comodoro has little of the old-world charm found in colonial Latin American cities, and it lacks a main central plaza with a traditional church. Residents congregate around the port, with its promenade, park, and basketball and volleyball courts.

Because visiting oil workers occupy rooms for long periods of time, there is a nearly constant shortage of hotel rooms. Do not plan to stay here overnight without a hotel reservation made in advance.

WHERE TO STAY & EAT

$-$$ ✕⛪**Austral Plaza Hotel.** This is really two hotels in one: a 42-room luxury hotel with marble floors and plush towels in the rooms and a modest 108-room hotel adequate for its class. The older portion has the advantage of being cheaper while allowing access to some of the newer portion's amenities, such as fax and Internet services. The Austral also has perhaps the city's finest seafood restaurant, Tunet ($-$$). Pros: Excellent restaurant and dining room. Cons: Gets booked up quickly; make reservations in advance. ⊠*Moreno 725,* ☎*2974/472–200* ⊕*www.australhotel.com.ar* ➪*150 rooms* ⚒*In-hotel: restaurant, gym, parking (no fee)* ⊟AE, DC, MC, V ⦿CP.

¢-$ ✕**La Estancia.** The city's oldest restaurant—made to look like a typical Argentine ranch—has been serving finely prepared, traditionally cooked meats for 34 years. Try the *cordero* (lamb) with chimichurri sauce and mashed potatoes, the seafood, or the homemade pasta. Desserts are extravagant, especially the pancakes with dulce de leche. The owners, the friendly Dos Santos family, provide excellent service. Unlike other restaurants, it has a menu in English. ⊠*Urquiza 863* ☎*2974/474–568* ⊟AE, DC, MC, V.

SARMIENTO & THE BOSQUE PETRIFICADO

150 km (94 mi) west of Comodoro Rivadavía.

Built in a fertile valley formed by the Río Senguer and its two interconnected lakes—Lago Musters and Lago Colhué Huapi—Sarmiento is a green oasis in the middle of the hard Patagonian steppe. This town of 13,000 is relatively new—founded in 1897—and lacks the colonial architecture that might make it more attractive. Yet Sarmiento has its own charm—it's undeniably and unpretentiously the "real Patagonia." Although the lakes and river, petrified forest, and paleontology park are great attractions, and the rolling farmland outside of town—with tall windbreaks of Lombardy poplars usually twisting in the strong wind—is beautiful, relatively few foreign travelers come here.

GETTING HERE & AROUND

Sarmiento is on several bus routes from both Comodoro Rivadavía on the Atlantic side, and Esquel and Bariloche from the Cordillera. Both **Etap** (☎2974/482–750) and **Don Otto** (⊕*www.donotto.com.ar*) provide regular service. Buses arrive on the main street, Avenida San Martín, which runs through the center of town.

Sarmiento is only 15 blocks long and eight blocks wide, and can be walked easily, but if you get tired, or would like to arrange a trip outside of town, there are various *remiserías* along Avenida San Martín.

ESSENTIALS

CURRENCY **Banco de la Nación** (⊠*España at Uruguay* ☎*2974/893–127*). **Banco del Chubut** (⊠*San Martín 756* ⊕ *www.bancochubut.com.ar*).

MAIL **Sarmiento** (⊠*España at Ingeniero Coronel*).

VISITOR INFO **Tourist Office** (⊠*Av. Regimiento de Infantería 25 at Pietrobelli* ☎*2965/454–950 or 2965/451–845* ⊕ *www.coloniasarmiento.gov.ar*).

WHAT TO SEE

❷ Sarmiento is the jumping-off point for the **Monumento Natural Bosque**
★ **Petrificado Sarmiento** (Sarmiento Petrified Forest Natural Monument), about 30 km (19 mi) from Sarmiento on R26. Scattered along a vast and colorfully striated badlands are trunks of conifer and palm trees that were deposited here 75 million years ago when the area was a tropical river delta. Regardless of the time of year, bring a jacket. The wind cools you down quickly even in bright sunlight. ☎*2974/898–282* ⊕*www.coloniasarmiento.gov. ar* ⊡*20 pesos* ⊙*Oct.–Mar., daily 9–8; Apr.–Sept., daily 10–6.*

❶ **Parque Paleontológico Valle de Los**
☁ **Gigantes** (Valley of the Giants Pale-
Fodor's Choice ontology Park) has life-size and sci-
★

> ### FAIR TIME
>
> One of the region's best local fairs, Sarmiento's arts, crafts, and food fair is held every Saturday and Sunday from 9 to 8 year-round, right across from the tourism office at Avenida Regimiento de Infantería 25 and Pietrobelli. Here you can find jams, preserves, honey, woolen garments, and other crafts produced at local *chacras*.

KEY

❶ Exploring sights

① Hotels & Restaurants

🛈 Tourist information

entifically accurate replicas of a dozen different dinosaurs whose fossils were all discovered in the region. Guided visits in English leave directly from the tourist office. ☎2974/898–220 ✉200 meters from the tourist office ☎2965/454–950 or 2965/451–845 ⊕www.coloniasarmiento.gov.ar.

❹ While you're in the area, stop at **Lago Musters,** 7 km (4 mi) from
❸ Sarmiento, and **Lago Colhué Huapi,** a little farther on. At Lago Musters you can swim and there's fishing year-round.

WHERE TO STAY & EAT

$$$–$$$$ ✕**Rancho Grande.** This is where all the locals come to share their *parilladas.* They have excellent Patagonian lamb, plus salads and deserts, and a waitstaff that makes you feel as if you're part of the town. ✉*Av. Estrada 419* ☎*2974/893–513* ▭*No credit cards.*

$$ 🏠**Labrador B & B.** This is a great choice for those wanting to stay in one
Fodor's Choice of the beautiful local *chacras.* Husband and wife Ana Luisa Geritsen
★ (who speaks Dutch and English) and Nicolás Ayling (who speaks English) lovingly tend this working chacra, producing homemade fruit preserves, honey, and cooking huge dinners and breakfasts for their guests. **Pros:** At-home atmosphere, Nicolás can arrange local guided tours. **Cons:** Not for seekers of solitude. ✉*Ruta 20, 1 km (½ mi) before*

the *Río Senguer,* ☎2974/893–329
⊕*www.hosterialabrador.com.ar*
🛏*2 rooms* ⚿*In-room: no phone,
no TV, Internet* ☰*AE, MC, V*
†⊙|*CP.*

$ 🖥 **Los Lagos.** Hotel Los Lagos is
clean, has a decent restaurant, and is
very affordable. It's currently under-
going a full renovation, and when
it's complete all rooms will have
new bathrooms. **Pros:** Affordable,

> **TO SPELUNK?**
>
> Unique in the region, **spelunk-
> ing,** or cave exploration, is
> available through the Agencia
> Santa Teresita at the **Túnel de
> Sarasola,** a natural basalt tunnel
> 45 km (28 mi) west of Sarmiento.
> ☎097/893-238.

some rooms have just been remodeled. **Cons:** Depending on the room,
remodeling can get noisy. ✉*Julio A. Roca at Alberdi,* ☎*2974/893–046*
🛏*20 rooms* ⚿*In-hotel: bar, restaurant, no elevator* †⊙|*CP.*

Southern Argentine Patagonia

Backpacker hiking in Parque Nacional Los Glaciares with Mt. Fitzroy in background, Patagonia, Argentina

WORD OF MOUTH

"I have been to a lot of places around the world but the Glaciers in Calafate has to be one of the most beautiful things to see in this world."

—Apartmentsba

WELCOME TO SOUTHERN ARGENTINE PATAGONIA

TOP REASONS TO GO

★ **Glacier Walk:** The most accessible glacier is Perito Moreno, in the Parque Nacional Los Glaciares near El Calafate. Even little kids can don crampons and cross a stable portion of the behemoth.

★ **The Vastness:** The sheer scale of the unspoiled landscape has a humbling effect. This is a land where human beings are an afterthought, and towns appear like specks against the vast horizon.

★ **Trout Fishing:** Dedicated anglers cast for sea-run brown trout in Río Gallegos or rainbow trout in Lago Roca.

★ **Hiking:** Stark granite peaks planted like spears in the Cordillera beckon mountain climbers and casual trekkers to the village of El Chaltén. Trails lead to lakes, glaciers, and peaks around Cerro Fitzroy and Cerro Torre.

★ **Estancia Stay:** No trip is complete without a visit to an estancia, a working ranch where you can ride horses alongside tough-as-nails gaucho cowboys, and dine under the stars on spit-roasted lamb.

1 Puerto San Julian & Puerto Santa Cruz. The brown monotony of the coast is broken up by these tranquil port towns. Centuries ago, explorers such as Magellan, Drake, and Darwin anchored in protected bays along this coast and marveled at the dolphins and penguins that still delight travelers today.

2 El Calafate & the Parque Nacional los Glaciares. The wild, icy expanse of the Hielo Continental ice cap and the exquisite turquoise surface of Lago Argentino exist in dramatic contrast to the tourist boomtown atmosphere of El Calafate, where international visitors flock to fancy restaurants and modern hotels.

3 El Chaltén & Cerro Fitzroy. El Chaltén is a smaller, rougher, younger, and much less commercial version of El Calafate, and a prime destination for elite mountaineers and casual hikers. Trails lead straight up from town into the foothills of Cerro Torre and Cerro Fitzroy, two of the most sought-after summits in the world.

5

4 Los Antiguos and Perito Moreno Town. In the northwest corner of Santa Cruz province are these two cozy and isolated towns. Perito Moreno—not to be confused with the glacier—is the gateway town to the Cueva de las Manos, a World Heritage site of ancient rock paintings, while Los Antiguos is a pleasant lakeside agricultural village with good fishing and a cherry festival in January.

5 Río Gallegos & Environs. You won't find many trees in the industrial port city of Río Gallegos, one of the windiest settlements in the world. The rather bleak downtown is a celebration of color compared to the utter desolation of the surrounding coastal plain, home to sheep ranchers, oil derricks, and a cacophonous colony of penguins.

GETTING ORIENTED

Most of southern Patagonia is windswept desert steppe, inhabited by rabbits, sheep, guanacos, and a few hardy human beings. The population centers—and attractions—are either along the coast or in a narrow strip of barely fertile land that runs north to south along the base of the Andes mountain range, where massive glaciers spill into large turquoise lakes. Southern Patagonia has seen a dramatic increase in tourism in recent years, which means that prices are high and you should have little trouble communicating in English or finding basic services, especially in popular destinations like El Calafate.

SOUTHERN ARGENTINE PLANNER

Health & Safety

Both Río Gallegos and El Cala-fate have modern medical facil-ities. In more remote areas, like Puerto Santa Cruz or El Chal-tén, you can count on finding a clinic staffed by doctors able to take care of minor problems and arrange transfers for more serious cases. The mountains are not high enough for alti-tude sickness to be a problem, but the weather can turn nasty very quickly, so dress appropri-ately, in layers, and be prepared for whatever the capricious sky chooses to spit down. Long days and a thinning ozone layer mean sunburns are a problem, so lather on the cream. Sun-glasses are essential.

Theft and robbery are not much of a problem in Santa Cruz prov-ince. However, all the wealth spilling into tourist boomtowns like El Calafate is attracting those who, if unable to find a job, might consider an unlocked door or unattended purse too tempting to resist. Take care of your belongings, avoid flaunt-ing expensive jewelry or large sums of cash, take taxis late at night, and you should be fine.

Emergency Services Coast Guard (☎106). **Fire** (☎100). **Forest Fire** (☎103). **Hospital** (☎107). **Police** (☎101).

Eat Well & Rest Easy

Vegetarians will find it tough going in southern Patago-nia—most meals feature red meat, either lamb or beef, with perhaps a salad of grated carrots or iceberg lettuce on the side. El Calafate has a great number of restaurants that offer a relatively wide variety of cuisines, but in the smaller towns your options are largely limited to grilled meat, salty pizza, pasta, and greasy empanadas. Excellent Argentine wine is practically everywhere, and beer is widely con-sumed. If you prefer plain water to the sparkling variety, order it *sin gas* (without bubbles).

El Calafate boasts a wide and growing selection of hotels, hostels, and bed-and-breakfasts geared to international tourists. In less popular areas, you will find utilitarian busi-ness hotels, but as tourism grows the options are expand-ing—even the tiny mountain village of El Chaltén now has its own luxury hotel. In general, hotel prices are higher here than in other areas of Argentina, though deals are available outside of high season. Staying at a working ranch, or estancia, is an essential experience that will give you a true taste of the Patagonian lifestyle. Many ranches, even those in exceptionally remote areas, offer luxurious accommodations and all-inclusive packages for guests.

DINING & LODGING PRICE CATEGORIES (IN ARGENTINA PESOS)

¢	$	$$	$$$	$$$$
Restaurants				
under 8 pesos	8–15 pesos	15–25 pesos	25–35 pesos	over 35 pesos
Hotels				
under 80 pesos	80–140 pesos	140–220 pesos	220–300 pesos	over 300 pesos

Restaurant prices are based on the median main course price at dinner. Hotel prices are for two people in a standard double room (or equiva-lent) in high season, excluding taxes and service charges.

When to Go

Summer lasts from December to February and it's the best time to visit southern Patagonia, when days are long and sunshine is plentiful. Unfortunately, sometimes half the population of Buenos Aires seems to descend on popular towns like El Calafate in the summer, so it's worthwhile to consider a trip in the shoulder seasons of spring and fall, when prices are lower, attractions less crowded, and the weather slightly less cooperative. Many hotels and restaurants close in winter, but visitors intrepid enough to brave frigid temperatures are rewarded with blessed isolation, less wind, and awe-inspiring mountain vistas.

Getting Here & Around

Air Travel. The best way to get to southern Patagonia is to fly from Buenos Aires. Most flights depart from Jorge Newberry airport, a short cab ride from downtown, but double-check ahead of time, because flights are sometimes relocated to Ezezia, the international airport, resulting in a frantic cab ride between airports.

Aerolíneas Argentinas (⊕www.aerolineas.com.ar) flies (along with its subsidiary Austral) from Buenos Aires daily to El Calafate. LADE (Líneas Aéreas del Estado ⊕www.lade.com.ar), in small Fokker F-27 and F-28 and Twin Otter planes, connects Ushuaia and El Calafate on a sparse schedule. Note that although Aerolíneas Argentinas charges double for American nationals, LADE offers tickets at one flat price regardless of nationality.

Bus Travel. Intrepid travelers can get to southern Patagonia by bus but it is much more convenient and often cheaper to fly. More than anywhere else in Patagonia, buses are a major form of transportation within the south. They shuttle passengers across border crossings to Chile as well as between the major cities of Tierra del Fuego and southern Argentina. TAQSA (⊕www.taqsa.com.ar) is the most reliable carrier.

Car Travel. It's possible to rent a car in the far south, but distances are vast, prices are high, and dirt roads are punishing, so it's often more convenient to travel between destinations by bus. If you do rent a car, check the contract carefully and remember that automatic transmissions are few and far between. Thanks to subsidies, gasoline is cheaper in Santa Cruz than in most parts of Argentina.

Literary Patagonia

The literary landscape of Patagonia is as rich as the land itself is barren. The British writer Bruce Chatwin achieved widespread acclaim with his work *In Patagonia* (1977), a lyrical journey many consider among the greatest travel books of all time, despite criticism related to Chatwin's embellishments. Much of Charles Darwin's classic *Voyage of the Beagle* (1839) takes place in Patagonia, where the young naturalist marveled at the region's stark geology during a boat trip up the Río Santa Cruz. *Idle Days In Patagonia* (1893) by the naturalist W.H. Hudson paints an idyllic picture of the author's life as a young man exploring the Patagonian frontier. Finally, the American painter Rockwell Kent's *Voyaging Southward from the Strait of Magellan* (1924) chronicles his boat journey around the continent's tip and contains illustrations by the author.

5

by Tim
Patterson

IMAGINE SAILING ACROSS A BLUE lake full of icebergs, or traversing an advancing glacier in the shadow of the end of the Andes mountain range, watching a valley being formed before your eyes. A trip to southern Patagonia is like a trip back to the Ice Age. Above all it is that glacier, Perito Moreno, that is bringing tourists to Patagonia in unprecedented numbers. In spite of El Calafate's brand-new airport, experiencing southern Argentine Patagonia still means crossing vast deserts to reach oases of isolated population centers. It means taking deep breaths of mountain air and draughts of pure stream water in the shadow of dramatic snowcapped peaks. Most of all, it means being embraced by independent, pioneering souls just beginning to understand the importance of tourism as traditional industries—wool, livestock, fishing, and oil—are drying up.

The culture of southern Patagonia, like that of other parts of the region, is a hybrid of the cultures of primarily European immigrants, who came here in the 19th century, and the cultures of the indigenous peoples, mainly the Tehuelche and Mapuche. The indigenous populations are long gone; they were wiped out by the four-year military campaign (1879–83) led by General Roca and known as the Conquest of the Desert. In summer (December–March), the towns of El Calafate and El Chaltén, in the southern Lake District, come alive with the influx of visitors to the Parque Nacional los Glaciares and climbers headed for Cerro Torre and Cerro Fitzroy.

PUERTO SAN JULIAN & PUERTO SANTA CRUZ

The coast of southern Patagonia is a tale of two worlds—the ocean waters are incredibly rich in marine life, but past the high-tide line the landscape is utterly brown and barren, though not without a certain stark appeal. The small towns of Puerto San Julian and Puerto Santa Cruz break up the bleak monotony of the coastal highway, but offer relatively little in the way of tourist attractions, unless you're exceptionally interested in the history of European expeditions and have the imagination necessary to envision early explorers weighing anchor in the protected bays. South of Puerto Santa Cruz is the Parque Nacional Monte Leon, the newest national park in Argentina, which encompasses over 30 km (19 mi) of untrammeled coastline and vast acres of Patagonian steppe.

GETTING AROUND

The coast of northern Santa Cruz is one part of Patagonia where it's a good idea to rent a car. Regular bus service exists, but the schedules are extremely inconvenient, with most arrivals and departures in the wee hours of the morning. A car is essential for visiting Parque Nacional Monte Leon, whether a rental or a *remise* hired for the day. Puerto San Julian and Puerto Santa Cruz are both laid out on grids and are easy to navigate on foot.

PUERTO SAN JULIAN

Tourists are only just discovering this sleepy port town with its wealth of maritime history and thriving marine ecosystem. This is the shore where sailors in Magellan's fleet encountered the large footprints that led to the exclamation "Patagon!" and the name Patagonia. It's also the place where the English explorer Francis Drake beheaded a rebellious crew member and the young naturalist Charles Darwin hiked over barren hills, searching for freshwater and formulating theories about the geological history of South America. Puerto San Julian is one of the Argentine towns closest to the Malvinas (Falkland Islands) and was severely impacted by the war—don't miss the statue of a fighter jet taking off into the sunset along the waterfront. A boat tour of the bay is an eminently worthwhile excursion, especially for families.

The **Centro de Informes** (⊠ *Av. San Martín* ☎ *2962/454–396* ⊕ *www. sanjulian.gov.ar*) has helpful bilingual attendants.

5

WHAT TO SEE

History buffs will get a kick out of the **Nao Victoria Thematic Museum**, a full-size replica of a ship that sailed in Magellan's armada, which wintered in Puerto San Julian in 1520. Lifelike models of Spanish sailors climb the rigging and discuss mutinies in the mess hall, and there is even a model of a Tehuelche man in guanaco skins. ⊠ *Av. Costanera, by the shore* 🖾 *12 pesos* ⊙ *Daily 9* AM–9 PM.

☾ The **Bahía de San Julian nature reserve** is home to sea lions, penguins, cormorants, and tiny black-and-white striped dolphins. The coastline is carved into cliffs and arches by the incessant waves and wind. **Pinocho Excursiones** is an experienced local tour agency that runs 90-minute boat trips in the bay for 80 pesos per person. Guides speak English and Spanish, can point out numerous species of endemic birds and marine animals, and are knowledgeable about the history of the region. Kids love spotting playful dolphins and visiting a nearby penguin colony. ⊠ *Av. Costanera at Mitre* ☎ *2966/1550–0023 cell* ⊕ *www.pinocho-excursiones.com.ar.*

WHERE TO EAT & STAY

$–$$$ ✕ **Resto Bar La Juliana.** This long-running family-owned establishment is a local favorite for its excellent homemade pasta and fish specialties. The atmosphere is of determined elegance despite downtrodden times. Service is flawless—the waiters wear black tie even at lunch—and the pink tablecloths are pressed and clean, although the floorboards are scuffed and warped and the light in the bathroom was broken at the time of writing. The food and service are so good though, you won't mind the rough edges. ⊠ *Zaballos 1130* ☎ *2962/45–2074* ✎ *lajuli-anarestaurant@hotmail.com* ▤ *No credit cards.*

$$ ⛨ **Hotel Bahia.** The consensus choice for the best hotel in town, the Bahia is comfortable and clean but otherwise unremarkable. This is not a hotel you will remember a month after staying here, but the lobby is pleasantly decorated with green plants, the beds are soft, and the showers are hot. The staff can point you to local attractions and help

A Penguin for President

Nestor Kirchner, a native of Río Gallegos and former governor of Santa Cruz province, was president of Argentina from 2003 until 2007, when he turned the reins of power over to his wife, Cristina. Known informally as "el pinguino" (the penguin), President Kirchner promised to bring "a cold wind of change" upon taking office. As president, the penguin led Argentina's recovery from economic collapse and controversially withdrew amnesty for members of the military government who participated in the "Dirty War."

The penguin also kept a paternal watch over his home territory, directing a great deal of investment to the far south. At least part of the recent tourism boom in Santa Cruz can be traced to his habit of entertaining visiting dignitaries by taking them to see the Perito Moreno Glacier. Although Cristina Kirchner did not grow up in Patagonia, she and her husband keep a home in El Calafate and travel south often to escape the political pressures of the capital.

arrange excursions, but their English is limited. **Pros:** Clean rooms, spacious lobby. **Cons:** Functional but charmless. ⊠ *Av. San Martín 1075,* ☎ *2962/454–028* ⊕ *www.hotelbahiasanjulian.com.ar* ↩ *30 rooms* ♿ *In-hotel: public Wi-Fi, no elevator* ⊟ *AE, MC, V* ⁑⊙⁑ *CP.*

$$ ⌘ **Hotel Miramar.** Locals recommend the newly renovated Miramar for its spotless rooms, good value, and bay views. The sky-blue paint is barely dry on the exterior and the front-desk staff is still getting the hang of the credit-card machine, but already the Miramar is more cozy and appealing than more established alternatives. **Pros:** Clean and homey, water view. **Cons:** Bathrooms are cramped. ⊠ *Av. San Martín 210,* ☎ *2962/454–626* ✎ *miramar146@speedy.com.ar* ↩ *12 rooms* ♿ *In-hotel: bar* ⊟ *MC, V* ⁑⊙⁑ *CP.*

PUERTO SANTA CRUZ

"Far from everywhere," begins the tourism slogan of Puerto Santa Cruz, an example of candor rarely encountered in Argentina's tourist offices. This peaceful little port is indeed a long way from anywhere. As one of the original permanent European settlements in Patagonia, the town is rich in history, and with the creation of the nearby Monte Leon National Park, tourists are slowly filtering in. There is one excellent hotel in town, but a distinct lack of decent restaurants. Don't miss a walk along the shingle beach, where you'll pass fishermen and shipwrecks and perhaps spot dolphins frolicking in the bay.

WHAT TO SEE

For a peek into the colonial history of coastal Santa Cruz, swing by the **Museo Casa de los Pioneros** *(House of the Pioneers)*, which exhibits a broad collection of antiques, old photographs, and mannequins in period dress, some of which seem to have lost their wigs. Don't miss the slightly musty puma skins hanging from a wall in the back room.

Continued on page 166

INTO THE WILD

by Tim Patterson

Patagonia will shatter your sense of scale. You will feel very small, surrounded by an epic expanse of mountains and plains, sea, and sky. Whether facing down an advancing wall of glacial ice, watching an ostrich-like rhea racing across the open steppe, or getting splashed by a breaching right whale off the Valdez Peninsula, prepare to gasp at the majesty of the Patagonian wild.

GLACIERS OF PATAGONIA

The Patagonia ice field covers much of the southern end of the Andean mountain range, straddling the Argentina-Chile border. The glaciers that spill off the high altitude ice field are basically rivers of slowly moving ice and snow that grind and push their way across the mountains, crushing soft rock and sculpting granite peaks.

Most of Patagonia's glaciers spill into lakes, rivers or fjords. Chunks of ice calve off the face of the glacier into the water, a dramatic display of nature's power that you can view at several locations. The larger pieces of ice become icebergs that scud across the water surface like white sailboats blown by the wind.

WEATHER
Weather is unpredictable around glaciers: it's not uncommon to experience sunshine, rain, and snow squalls in a single afternoon.

ICE COLORS
Although clear days are best for panoramas, cloudy days bring out the translucent blue of the glacial ice, creating great opportunities for magical photographs. You'll also see black or gray streaks in the ice caused by sediment picked up by the glacier as it grinds down the mountain valley. When that sediment is deposited into lakes, it hangs suspended in the water, turning the lake a pale milky blue.

ENVIRONMENTAL CONCERN
There's no question that human-induced climate change is taking its toll on Patagonia's glaciers. Although the famous Perito Moreno glacier is still advancing, nearly all the others have shrunk in recent years, some dramatically. The retreat of the Upsala glacier near El Calafate is featured in Al Gore's award-winning documentary, *An Inconvenient Truth*.

Below: Cruise on Lago Argentino, Santa Cruz province, Glaciers National Park, Argentina

TRAVEL SHRINKS

The link between high-impact activities—such as air travel—and climate change is clear, leading to a disturbing irony: the more people come to see the glaciers of Patagonia, the more carbon is released into the atmosphere, and the more the glaciers shrink.

Right: Glacier Grey, Paine Circuit, Torres del Paine National Park, Chile

GLACIERS TO SEE

- Perito Moreno Glacier, Santa Cruz, Argentina

- Upsala Glacier, Santa Cruz, Argentina

- Martial Glacier, Tierra del Fuego, Argentina

- Serrano Glacier, Tierra del Fuego, Chile

- O'Higgins Glacier, Southern Coast, Chile

FIRE & ICE: MOUNTAINS OF PATAGONIA

Trekker, Cerro Torre and Fitz Roy in background, Los Glaciares National Park, Patagonia

In Patagonia, mountains mean the Andes, a relatively young range but a precocious one that stretches for more than 4,000 miles. The Patagonian Andes are of special interest to geologists, who study how fire, water, and ice have shaped the mountains into their present form.

CREATION

Plate tectonics are the most fundamental factor in the formation of the southern Andes, with the oceanic Nazca plate slipping beneath the continental South American plate and forcing the peaks skyward. Volcanic activity is a symptom of this dynamic process, and there are several active volcanoes on the Chilean side of the range.

GLACIAL IMPRINT

Glacial activity has also played an important role in chiseling the most iconic Patagonian peaks. The spires that form the distinctive skylines of Torres del Paine and the Fitzroy range are solid columns that were created when rising glaciers ripped away weaker rock, leaving only hard granite skeletons that stand rigid at the edge of the ice fields.

MOUNTAIN HIGH BORDERS

Because the border between Chile and Argentina cuts through the most impenetrable reaches of the ice field, the actual border line is unclear in areas of the far south. Even in the more temperate north, border crossings are often located at mountain passes, and the officials who stamp visas seem more like mountain guides than bureaucrats.

MOUNTAINS OF THE SEA

Tierra del Fuego and the countless islands off the coast of southern Chile were once connected to the mainland. Over the years the sea swept into the valleys, isolated the peaks, and created an archipelago that, viewed on a map, looks as abstract as a Jackson Pollack painting. From the water these island mountains appear especially dramatic, misty pinnacles of rock and ice rising from the crashing sea.

Right: Mt. Fitzroy

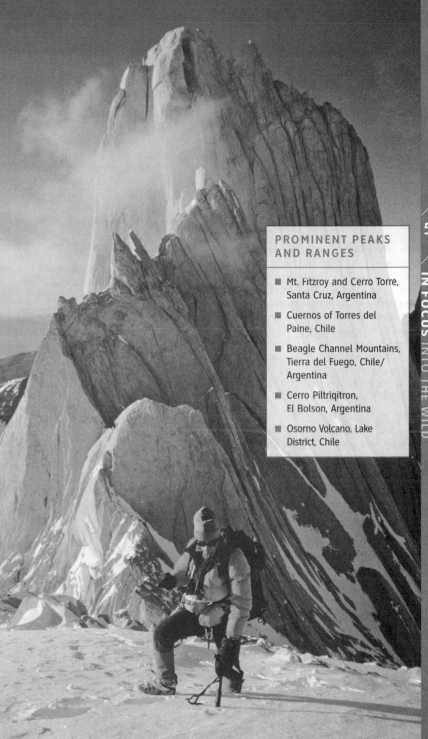

PROMINENT PEAKS AND RANGES

- Mt. Fitzroy and Cerro Torre, Santa Cruz, Argentina
- Cuernos of Torres del Paine, Chile
- Beagle Channel Mountains, Tierra del Fuego, Chile/ Argentina
- Cerro Piltriqitron, El Bolson, Argentina
- Osorno Volcano, Lake District, Chile

YAY, PENGUINOS!

Magellanic Penguin walking to his nest in Peninsula Valdes

Everyone loves penguins. How could you not feel affection for such cute, curious, and loyal little creatures? On land, their awkward waddle is endearing, and you can get close enough to see the inquisitive gaze in their eyes as they turn their heads from side to side for a good look at you. In the water, penguins transform from goofballs into Olympic athletes, streaking through the waves and returning to the nest with mouthfuls of fish and squid for their chicks.

TYPES
Most of the penguins you'll see here are Magellanic penguins, black and white colored birds that gather in large breeding colonies on the beaches of Patagonia in the summer and retreat north to warmer climes during winter. Also keep an eye out for the red-beaked Gentoo penguins that nest among the Magellanics.

If your image of penguins is the large and colorful Emperor penguins of Antarctica that featured in the documentary *March of the Penguins*, you might be slightly underwhelmed by the little Magellanics. Adults stand about 30 inches tall and weigh between 15 and 20 pounds. What they lack in glamor, Patagonia's penguins make up in vanity—and numbers. Many breeding sites are home to tens of thousands of individuals, all preening and strutting as if they were about to walk the red carpet at the Academy Awards.

PENGUIN RELATIONS
Male and female penguins form monogamous pairs and share the task of raising the chicks, which hatch in small burrows that the parents return to year after year. If you sit and observe a pair of penguins for a little while you'll notice how affectionate they appear, grooming each other with their beaks and huddling together on the nest.

HUMAN CONTACT
Although penguins are not shy of humans who keep a respectful distance (about 8 feet is a good rule of thumb), the history of penguin-human relations is not entirely one of peaceful curiosity. Early pioneers and stranded sailors would raid penguin nests for food, and in modern times, oil spills have devastated penguin colonies in Patagonia.

Magellanic Penguins

WHERE & WHEN

The best time to see penguins is from November through February, which coincides with the best weather in coastal Patagonia. Some of the most convenient and impressive colonies to visit are:

■ Punta Tombo, Chubut, Argentina

■ Cabo Virgenes, Santa Cruz, Argentina

■ Isla Madalena, Chile

■ Martillo Island, Tierra del Fuego, Argentina

■ Puerto San Julian, Santa Cruz, Argentina

IN THE SEA

The Patagonian coast teems with marine life, including numerous "charismatic megafauna" such as whales, dolphins, sea lions, and seals.

DOLPHINS

Dolphins are easy to spot on tours, because they're curious and swim up to the boat, sometimes even surfing the bow wake. Commerson's dolphins are a common species in coastal Argentina and the Straights of Magellan. Among the world's tiniest dolphins, their white and black coloring has earned them the nickname "skunk dolphin" and prompted comparisons with their distant cousins, orcas.

WHALES

The Valdez Peninsula is also one of the best places to observe right whales, gentle giants of the ocean. Although the name right whale derives from whalers who designated it as the "right" whale to kill, the right whale is now protected by both national legislation and international agreements.

ORCAS

Orcas aren't as common as dolphins, but you can spot them off the Valdez Peninsula, Argentina, hunting seals and sea lions along the shore. Sometimes hungry orcas will chase their prey a few feet too far and beach themselves above the tide line, where they perish of dehydration.

SEALS & SEA LIONS

In the springtime massive elephant seals and southern sea lions drag themselves onto Patagonian beaches for mating season—hopefully out of range of hungry orcas. These giant pinnipeds form two groups in the breeding colonies. Big, tough alpha bulls have their own harems of breeding females and their young, while so-called bachelor males hang out nearby like freshman boys at a fraternity party, hoping to entice a stray female away from the alpha bull's harem.

Southern Sea Lions
(Otaria flavescens),
Valdes Peninsula, Patagonia

IN THE AIR

Patagonia is a twitcher's paradise. Even non-bird-lovers marvel at the colorful species that squawk, flutter, and soar through Patagonia's skies.

ANDEAN CONDOR

You probably won't see a condor up close. They nest on high-altitude rock ledges and spend their days soaring in circles on high thermals, scanning mountain slopes and plains for carrion. With a wing span of up to 10 feet, however, the king of the Andean skies is impressive even when viewed from a distance. Condors live longer than almost any other bird. Some could qualify for Social Security.

MAGELLANIC WOODPECKER

You can hear the distinctive rat-tat of this enormous woodpecker in nothofagus forests of Chilean Patagonia and parts of Argentina. Males have a bright red head and a black body, while females are almost entirely black.

ALBATROSS

You can spot several species of albatross off the Patagonian coast, gliding on fixed wings above the waves. The albatross lives almost entirely at sea, touching down on land to breed and raise its young. Unless you're visiting Antarctica or the Falklands, your best bet for seeing an albatross is to take a cruise from Punta Arenas or Ushuaia.

RHEA (NANDU)

No, it's not an ostrich. The rhea is an extremely large flightless bird that roams the Patagonian steppe. Although they're not normally aggressive, males have been known to charge humans who get too close to their partner's nests.

KELP GOOSE

As the name implies, kelp geese love kelp. In fact, kelp is the only thing they eat. The geese travel along the rocky shores of Tierra del Fuego in search of their favorite seaweed salad.

⊠*Av. Piedra Buena 704* ☎*No phone* 💲*Free* ⊙*Weekdays 9–7, weekends 9–1 and 5–7.*

WHERE TO EAT & STAY

$–$$$ ✕**Galeria del Sol.** It's not a terribly romantic place to dine, but the Galeria—a sort of food court in a minimall downtown—serves up some of the best pizza, pasta, and calzones in town. Milanesas are also well prepared, and it's a good spot for a midday coffee. ⊠*Av. San Martín 286* ☎*2962/498–742* ▤*MC, V* ⊙*No lunch Sun.*

$–$$ ✕**La Ria.** Large picture windows look out onto the sparkling waters of the river, but La Ria's staff seems more interested in the TV that hangs above those windows and blasts MTV videos and dubbed TNT movies. Whoever chose the lime-green color scheme should be exiled to . . . um . . . southern Patagonia, but the food is decent and fairly priced and the view is excellent—if you can get the waiter to turn off the TV. ⊠*Av. Piedra Buena 650* ☎*2962/498–935* ▤*No credit cards.*

$$ 🏨**Apart Hotel Kawo.** Spacious suites linked by paths lined with colorful flower gardens make the Kawo one of the best hotels on the southern Patagonian coast. Rooms come complete with satellite TV and kitchenettes, and there is a cozy lounge with old National Geographics for when you need to escape the wind. **Pros:** Big rooms with tasteful decoration. **Cons:** Staff does not speak much English. ⊠*Alferez Balestra 468,* ☎*2962/498–037* ✉*kawo04@hotmail.com* ⊕*www.kawoapart-thotel.com.ar* ⮐*12 rooms* ⚐*In-room: kitchen, Wi-Fi, Ethernet* ▤*AE, MC, V* ⦿*CP.*

PARQUE NACIONAL MONTE LEON

Founded in October 2004 on 60,000 hectares of land donated by the Patagonia Land Trust, the Parque Nacional Monte Leon is the newest of Argentina's national parks and the only one on the continental coast. Home to a tremendous array of marine animals and birds, including a large colony of Magellanic penguins, the park attracts visitors in search of wildlife viewing, unmatched isolation, and desolate natural beauty. The main beach is gigantic and nearly always deserted. Like almost all of the Patagonian coast, the landscape is exceedingly bleak. A cavernous natural arch along the shore was briefly a symbol of the park, and still appears in promotional posters, but it collapsed in 2006, leaving the park more or less bereft of scenic symbols.

GETTING AROUND

Infrastructure within Parque Nacional Monte Leon is limited, and the access road can become impassable after heavy storms. It's essential to have your own transportation, which generally means renting a car in Río Gallegos or arranging a remise from Puerto Santa Cruz.

For general information about the park, including current road conditions, contact the **Parques Nacionales Office** in Puerto Santa Cruz (⊠*Belgrano at 9 de Julio,* ☎*2962/498–184*).

Tour Options

In El Calafate, all hotels will arrange excursions to Moreno and Upsala glaciers. Hielo y Aventura specializes in glacier tours, with their showstopping "mini-trekking" (walking on the glacier with crampons) as well as the *safari náutico* (a boat ride next to the glacier). Horseback riding can be arranged by Gustavo Holzman or the tourist office. Alberto del Castillo, owner of El Calafate's Fitzroy Expeditions, has English-speaking guides and organizes glacier and mountain treks.

Interlagos Turismo arranges tours between Río Gallegos and El Calafate and to the glaciers. Tur Aiké Turismo organizes tours around Río Gallegos. In El Chaltén, Cal Tur, Chaltén Travel, and Hielo y Aventura run local tours.

If booking from the United States, Houston, Texas–based **Tours International** (☎ *800/247–7965* ⊕ *www. toursinternational.com*) is a well-established travel agency with extensive experience and local connections in El Calafate.

Cal Tur runs bus tours to destinations across Santa Cruz and down to Tierra del Fuego. ✉ *Av. Libertador 1080, El Calafate* ☎ *2902/491–368.*

Chaltén Travel operates a small empire at the base of Cerro Fitzroy, shuttling a steady stream of backpackers between Bariloche and El Calafate with stops at Perito Moreno and El Chaltén. ✉ *Guemes and Lago del Desierto, El Chaltén* ☎ *2962/491–833* ⊕ *www.chaltentravel.com.*

Fitzroy Expeditions organizes everything from glacier trekking and ice-climbing to kayaking on the Fitzroy River. Recommended. ✉ *Av. San Martín, El Chaltén* ☎ *2962/493–017.*

Gador Viajes is a small agency that operates glacier tours and can arrange visits to estancias around El Calafate. ✉ *Gob. Moyano 1082, El Calafate* ☎ *2962/491–143* ✎ *gadorino@cotecal.com.ar.*

Hielo y Aventura operates mini-trekking and "Big Ice" expeditions on the Perito Moreno glacier. ✉ *Av. Libertador 935, El Calafate* ☎ *2902/492–205* ⊕ *www.hieloyaventura.com.*

René Fernández Campbell is the specialist for boat tours on Lago Argentino and to the Upsala Glacier. ✉ *Av. Libertador 867, El Calafate* ☎ *2902/491–155* ✎ *fernandez_campbell@infovia.com.ar.*

5

WHERE TO STAY

$$$$ 🏠**Estancia Monte Leon.** Before the land that now makes up Parque Nacional Monte Leon was bought by the Patagonia Land Trust, it was an estancia operated by the Braun family since 1920. The original ranch house has been renovated to receive guests, and the Brauns can arrange excursions such as boat rides and fishing. The large central living room is especially appealing after a windy day at the beach, and there is a small museum which exhibits the history of the estancia. **Pros:** Authentic estancia experience, excellent home cooking. **Cons:** Difficult to get to, reservations must be made through the office in Buenos Aires. ✉ *RN3 Parque Nacional Monte Leon* ☎ *2963/432–019, 11/4621–4780 reservations* ✎ *consultas@monteleon-patagonia.com* ⇱ *4 rooms* ▤ *No credit cards* ❑*FAP.*

PERITO MORENO AND LOS ANTIGUOS

Few travelers spend more than one night in this pleasantly laid-back corner of Santa Cruz province. Perito Moreno is the halfway point for buses that ply the lonely Ruta 40 between Bariloche and El Chaltén. Los Antiguos is on the shore of Lago Buenos Aires, 64 km (40 mi) west of Perito Moreno on a good paved road, and only a few kilometers from the Chilean border. The town's relatively mild microclimate enables local farmers to grow excellent cherries and strawberries. Local guides can arrange trout-fishing expeditions in the lake and nearby rivers. The major attraction in this region is the Cueva de las Manos (Cave of Hands), an archeological site of highly evocative rock paintings and handprints located in a scenic canyon near the frontier outpost of Bajo Caracoles, 128 km (80 mi) south of Perito Moreno.

GETTING AROUND

Perito Moreno and Los Antiguos are linked by convenient bus service, with four departures daily Monday–Saturday throughout the year. There is also a cross-border bus connecting Los Antiguos with Chile Chico that leaves daily at noon. Buses ply the Ruta 40 between Perito Moreno and El Calafate in high season (12 hours) and there is also regular service to the major coastal cities of Comodoro Rivadavía and Río Gallegos.

Having your own wheels makes it simple to explore the farms and rivers near Los Antiguos, but think carefully before taking a rental car on the Ruta 40. The road is punishing and remote, so it's essential to have a good map, mechanical knowledge, and emergency supplies.

PERITO MORENO

Perito Moreno is a dusty little crossroads outpost, with little to capture a visitor's attention for more than a day. Most travelers arrive in the evening and depart the next morning, en route between the Lake District and the glaciers of the far south. The main reason to stick around is to visit the nearby Cueva de las Manos, a World Heritage archeological site with rock paintings that are up to 9,000 years old. If headed south to El Chaltén, where there are no banks, stock up on cash before leaving Perito Moreno.

WHAT TO SEE

The **Cuevas de las Manos** (Cave of Hands) is one of the most mysterious and striking sights in all of Patagonia. Located in the beautiful and remote red-rock Pinturas River Canyon, the rock paintings mainly consist of negative images of handprints outlined with red and white pigmentation. There are also drawings of guanacos and lizard-like animals. The ancient handprints, some of which are over 9,000 years old, seem to reach out to the visitor, searching for connection across the millennia. In 1999 these paintings were designated a UNESCO World Heritage site. There are two ways to visit the rock paintings from Perito Moreno. The approach via **Estancia Cuevas de las Manos** involves a moderately difficult trek into the canyon, while the long way around via Bajo Caracoles entails three extra hours in a minibus, but no trekking. If you are in reasonably good shape, the former option is definitely preferable, because the trek through the canyon is nearly as beautiful as the rock paintings. **Zoyen Turismo** (⊠ *Av. San Martín at Saavedra, Perito Moreno* ☎*2963/432–207* ✐*zoyenturismo@yahoo. com.ar*) is an excellent local tour agency that can arrange day trips from Perito Moreno for 140 pesos per person, not including the 15-peso park entrance fee.

WHERE TO STAY

$ ⚑ **Hotel Belgrano.** A Perito Moreno institution, the Hotel Belgrano has received a steady stream of guests for 35 years. It's the best hotel in town, which isn't saying much, as rooms are a bit dilapidated and the carpets worn thin. Still, something about the dusty old atmosphere and wheezing hospitality fits this lonesome frontier town. A fancy hotel wouldn't make much sense in Perito Moreno, and though it's far from luxurious, the Hotel Belgrano feels appropriate, right down to the scuffed linoleum floors. **Pros:** Central location, frontier charm. **Cons:** Some would call frontier charm "dingy." ⊠ *Av. San Martín 1001,* ☎*2963/432–019* ⬅*23 rooms* ⧄*In-hotel: bar, restaurant* ⊟*AE, MC, V* ⊘*Closed July* ⧍*CP.*

LOS ANTIGUOS

Maybe it's a stretch to call Los Antiguos the best-kept secret in Patagonia, but this remote little farming town on the Chilean border is a pleasant spot to relax for a day or two. A fertile slice of land on the windy shore of Lago Buenos Aires, Los Antiguos was historically a retirement home of sorts for elderly members of the indigenous population, who would gather here in their golden years to enjoy the comforts of a relatively warm climate. The name Los Antiguos means "the ancients," in reference to this extinct tradition. The best reasons to visit Los Antiguos are to enjoy the spectacular trout fishing in nearby waters, gorge on ripe cherries in the summertime, and either cross into Chile or break up the journey between Bariloche and the far south.

ESSENTIALS

VISITOR INFO   **Centro de Informes** (⊠*Av. 11 de Julio 446* ☎*2963/491–261* ⊕ *www.losantiguos. gov.ar*) is open daily 8–noon from December to April; from 8 AM–8 PM at other times.

FISHING

The fly-fishing around Los Antiguos is some of the best in Argentina, which means it ranks among the best in the world. Rainbow trout are plentiful in the lake and in Los Antiguos River, and it's also possible to catch native Patagonian fish such as the perca. Catch-and-release is generally mandatory. Local guide **Mario Rodrigo** (⊠*Av. 11 de Julio 853* ☎*2963/491–123, 2966/1551–4923 cell* ✐*pescaaikepatagonico@ yahoo.com.ar*) has several years of experience fishing the rivers and lakes around Los Antiguos and speaks a little "fishing English."

FRUIT FARMS

Dozens of cherry orchards and strawberry farms are around Los Antiguos, and many are open to visitors. One of the most welcoming is **Chacra Don Neno,** located a short walk west of downtown towards the Los Antiguos River. Some English is spoken. ⊠ *Av. San Martín at Tehuelche, ¼ mi from the center of town* ☎ *2963/491–403* ✎ *don_neon_xxi@hotmail.com.*

WHERE TO STAY & EAT

$$–$$$ ✗ **Viva el Viento.** In a large wooden lodge on the main street, this modern restaurant is hands down the best dining option in town. The menu has a broad range of Patagonian specialties and an especially delicious cut of *bife de chorizo* (sirloin steak). Coffee is strong, the bar well stocked, and the staff maintains a good balance between professional service and informal hospitality. Chilean pesos and U.S. dollars are both accepted. ⊠ *Av. 11 de Julio 477* ☎ *2963/491–109* ⊕ *www.vivaelviento.com* ⊟ *MC, V.*

$$$$ ⌂ **Antigua Patagonia.** On the shore of Lago Buenos Aires with expansive views across to the snowcapped Andes, this new hotel offers spacious rooms and large balconies for basking in the Patagonian sun. Fishing trips, horseback riding, and boat excursions on the lake can be arranged at the front desk, and the attached restaurant can prepare fresh-caught trout and a traditional lamb barbecue. **Pros:** Lakeside location, comfortable rooms. **Cons:** A hike from downtown. ⊠ *Ruta 43–Accesso Este,* ☎ *2963/491–005* 🛏 *16 rooms* ⚒ *In-hotel: gym, restaurant, bar* ⊟ *MC, V* ⊗ *Closed May–Sept.* ¶⊙¶ *CP.*

EL CALAFATE & THE PARQUE NACIONAL LOS GLACIARES

320 km (225 mi) north of Río Gallegos via R5, 253 km (157 mi) east of Río Turbio on Chilean border via R40, 213 km (123 mi) south of El Chaltén via R40.

Founded in 1927 as a frontier town, El Calafate is the base for excursions to the Parque Nacional los Glaciares (Glaciers National Park), which was created in 1937 as a showcase for one of South America's most spectacular sights, the Perito Moreno glacier. Because it's on the southern shore of Lago Argentino, the town enjoys a microclimate much milder than the rest of southern Patagonia. During the long summer days between December and February (when the sun sets around 10 PM), and during Easter vacation, tens of thousands of visitors come from all corners of the world and fill the hotels and restaurants. This is the area's high season, so make reservations well in advance. October, November, March, and April are less crowded and less expensive periods to visit. March through May can be rainy and cool, but it's also less windy and often quite pleasant. The only bad time to visit is winter, particularly June, July, and August, when many of the hotels and tour agencies are closed.

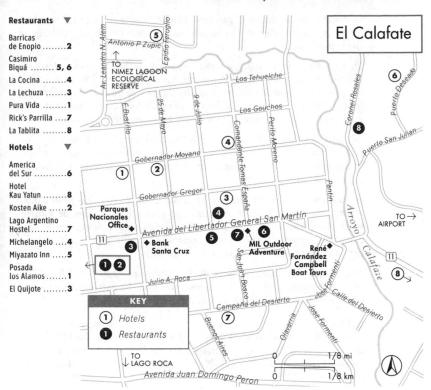

To call El Calafate a boomtown would be to put it mildly. Between 2001 and 2008, the town's population exploded from 4,000 to 22,000, and it shows no signs of slowing down; at every turn you'll see new construction. As a result, the downtown has a very new sheen to it, although most buildings are constructed of wood, with a rustic aesthetic that respects the majestic natural environment. One exception is the brand-new casino in the heart of downtown, the façade of which seems to mock the face of the Perito Moreno glacier. As the paving of the road between El Calafate and the glacier nears completion, the visitors continue to flock in—whether luxury package tourists bound for the legendary Hostería Los Notros, backpackers over from Chile's Parque Nacional Torres del Paine, or *porteños* (those from Buenos Aires) in town for a long weekend.

The booming economy means prices are substantially higher than in most of Patagonia—they seem to rise every other week—and many long-time locals bemoan their hometown's rampant commercialization.

GETTING HERE & AROUND
Daily flights from Buenos Aires, Ushuaia, and Río Gallegos, and direct flights from Bariloche transport tourists to El Calafate's 21st-century glass-and-steel airport with the promise of adventure and discovery

in distant mountains and glaciers. El Calafate is so popular that the flights are selling out weeks in advance, so don't plan on booking at the last minute.

Driving from Río Gallegos takes about four hours across desolate plains, enlivened by occasional sightings of a gaucho, his dogs, and a herd of sheep, and *ñandú* (rheas), shy llama-like guanacos, silver-gray foxes, and fleet-footed hares the size of small deer. **Esperanza** is the only gas, food, and bathroom stop halfway between the two towns.

Avenida del Libertador San Martín (known simply as Libertador, or San Martín) is El Calafate's main street, with tour offices, restaurants, and shops selling regional specialties, sportswear, camping and fishing equipment, and food.

A staircase in the middle of San Martín ascends to Avenida Julio Roca, where you'll find the bus terminal and a very busy **Oficina de Turismo** with a board listing available accommodations and campgrounds; you can also get brochures and maps, and there's a multilingual staff to help plan excursions. It's open daily 7 AM–10 PM.

The **Parques Nacionales Office** (⊠ *Av. Libertador 1302* ☎ *2902/491– 005*), open weekdays 7–2, has information on the entire park, the glaciers, area history, hiking trails, and flora and fauna.

ESSENTIALS

BUS **Bus Sur** (☎ *2966/442–765, 2902/491–631 in El Calafate*). **Cal Tur** (⊠ *Terminal Ómnibus* ☎ *2962/491–842*). **Interlagos** (⊠ *Bus terminal* ☎ *2902/491–179*). **TAQSA** (⊠ *Bus terminal* ☎ *2902/491–843* ⊕ *www.taqsa.com.ar*). **Turismo Zaahj** (☎ *5661/412–260*).

CURRENCY **Provincia de Santa Cruz** (⊠ *Av. Libertador 1285* ☎ *2902/492–320*).

MAIL **Post Office** (⊠ *Av. Libertador 1133*).

MEDICAL **Hospital Distrital** (⊠ *Av. Roca 1487* ☎ *2902/491–001*). **Farmacia El Calafate** (⊠ *Av. Libertador 1190* ☎ *9405/491–407*).

REMIS **El Calafate** (⊠ *Av. Roca* ☎ *2902/492–005*).

RENTAL CARS **Cristina** (⊠ *Av. Libertador 1711* ☎ *2902/491–674* ✉ *crisrent@arnet.com.ar*). **Dollar Rent a Car** (⊠ *Av. Libertador 1341* ☎ *2902/492–634*).

VISITOR INFO **Oficina de Turismo** (⊠ *Av. Roca 1004* ☎ *2902/491–090* ⊕ *www.elcalafate. gov.ar*).

WHAT TO SEE

The Hielo Continental (Continental ice cap) spreads its icy mantle from the Pacific Ocean across Chile and the Andes into Argentina, covering an area of 21,700 square km (8,400 square mi). Approximately 1.5 million acres of it are contained within the **Parque Nacional los Glaciares**, a UNESCO World Heritage site. The park extends along the Chilean border for 350 km (217 mi), and 40% of it is covered by ice fields that branch off into 47 glaciers feeding two enormous lakes—the 15,000-year-old **Lago Argentino** (Argentine Lake, the largest body of water in

Argentina and the third-largest in South America) in the park's south-ern end, and **Lago Viedma** (Lake Viedma) at the northern end near **Cerro Fitzroy,** which rises 11,138 feet. Plan on a minimum of two to three days to see the glaciers and enjoy the town—more if you plan to visit El Chaltén or any of the other lakes. Entrance to the southern sec-tion of the park costs 40 pesos.

The **Glaciar Perito Moreno** lies 80 km (50 mi) away on R11, which is almost entirely paved. From the park entrance, the road winds through hills and forests of lengas and ñires, until suddenly, the startling sight of the glacier comes into full view. Descending like a long white tongue through distant mountains, it ends abruptly in a translucent azure wall 3 km (2 mi) wide and 165 feet high at the edge of frosty green Lago Argentino.

Although it's possible to rent a car and go on your own, virtually every-one visits the park by day-trip tours booked through one of the many travel agents in El Calafate (unless you're staying in Los Notros, the only hotel inside the park—which arranges all excursions). The most basic tours take you to see the glacier from a viewing area composed of a series of platforms wrapped around the point of the Península de Magallanes. The platforms, which offers perhaps the most impressive view of the glacier, allow you to wander back and forth, looking across the Canal de los Tempanos (Iceberg Channel). Here you listen and wait for nature's number-one ice show—first, a cracking sound, followed by tons of ice breaking away and falling with a thunderous crash into the lake. As the glacier creeps across this narrow channel and meets the land on the other side, an ice dam sometimes builds up between the inlet of Brazo Rico on the left and the rest of the lake on the right. As the pressure on the dam increases, everyone waits for the day it will rupture again. The last time was in March 2004, when the whole thing collapsed in a series of explosions that lasted hours and could be heard in El Calafate.

In recent years, the skyrocketing number of visitors to Glaciar Perito Moreno has created a scene that is not always conducive to reflective encounters with nature's majesty. Although the glacier remains spectac-ular, savvy travelers would do well to minimize time at the madhouse that the viewing area becomes at midday in high season, and instead encounter the glacier by boat, on a mini-trekking excursion, or by supplementing Perito Moreno with a visit to one of the less crowded glaciers in the region.

Glaciar Upsala, the largest glacier in South America, is 55 km (35 mi) long and 10 km (6 mi) wide, and accessible only by boat. Daily cruises depart from Puerto Banderas (40 km [25 mi] west of El Calafate via R11) for the 2½-hour trip. While dodging floating icebergs (*tempanos*), some as large as a small island, the boats maneuver as close as they dare to the wall of ice rising from the aqua-green water of Lago Argentino. The seven glaciers that feed the lake deposit their debris into the run-off, causing the water to cloud with minerals ground to fine powder by the glacier's moraine (the accumulation of earth and stones left by the

Shhhh! It's a secret!

Lago Roca is a little-visited lake located inside the national park just south of Brazo Rico, 46 km (29 mi) from El Calafate. This area receives about five times as much annual precipitation as El Calafate, creating a relatively lush climate of green meadows by the lakeshore, where locals come to picnic and cast for trophy rainbow and lake trout. Don't miss a hike into the hills behind Lago Roca—the view of dark-blue Lago Roca backed by a pale-green inlet of Lago Argentino with the Perito Moreno glacier and jagged snowcapped peaks beyond is truly outstanding. "Shhh," said the local who suggested a visit to Lago Roca. "It's the best place in El Calafate. Don't tell everyone." Never trust a guidebook writer.

There are gorgeous campsites, simple cabins, fishing-tackle rentals, hot showers, and a basic restaurant at **Camping Lago Roca** (☎ 2902/499–500 ⊕ www.losglaciares.com/camp-inglagoroca ⊗ Closed May–Sept.). Make reservations in advance if visiting over the Christmas holidays; at other times the campground is seldom crowded. For more comfortable accommodations, you can arrange to stay at the Nibepo Aike Estancia at the western end of Lago Roca, about 5 km (3 mi) past the campground. The national park entrance fee is only collected on the road to Perito Moreno Glacier or at Puerto Banderas, where cruises depart, so admission to the Lago Roca corner of the park is free.

glacier). Condors and black-chested buzzard eagles build their nests in the rocky cliffs above the lake. When the boat stops for lunch at Onelli Bay, don't miss the walk behind the restaurant into a wild landscape of small glaciers and milky rivers carrying chunks of ice from four glaciers into Lago Onelli. Glaciar Upsala has diminished in size in recent years, a trend many attribute to climate change.

The **Nimez Lagoon Ecological Reserve** is a marshy area on the shore of Lago Argentino just a short walk from downtown El Calafate. It's home to many species of waterfowl including black-necked swans, buff-necked ibises, southern lapwings, and the occasional flamingo. Strolling the footpaths among grazing horses and flocks of birds may not be as intense an experience as—say—trekking on a glacier, but a trip to the lagoon provides a good sense of the local landscape. For some reason, the gate is sometimes locked until 9 AM, frustrating early-morning bird enthusiasts. If you get there early go ahead and hop the fence, no one will mind. ⊠ 1 km (½ mi) north of downtown, just off Av. Alem ⊠ 2 pesos.

OUTDOOR ACTIVITIES

BOAT TOURS

The two most popular scenic boat rides in the Parque Nacional los Glaciares are the hour-long **Safari Náutico,** in which your boat cruises a few meters away from the face of the Glaciar Perito Moreno, and the full-day **Upsala Glacier Tour,** in which you navigate through a more extensive selection of glaciers, including Upsala and Onelli, and sec-

Parque Nacional los Glaciares

tions of Lago Argentino that are inaccessible by land. The Safari Náutico costs 35 pesos, not including transportation from El Calafate. **René Fernández Campbell** (✉*Av. Libertador 867, El Calafate* ☎*2902/491–155* ✐*fernandez_campbell@infovia.com.ar*) is currently the only local tour operator that runs boat tours to Upsala and Onelli glaciers. Any hotel can arrange reservations.

HIKING

Although it's possible to find trails along the shore of Lago Argentino and in the hills south and west of town, these hikes traverse a rather barren landscape and are not terribly interesting. The mountain peaks and forests are in the park, an hour by car from El Calafate. If you want to lace up your boots in your hotel, walk outside and hit the trail, go to El Chaltén—it's a much better base than El Calafate for hikes in the national park. Good hiking trails are accessible from the camping areas and cabins by Lago Roca, 50 km (31 mi) from El Calafate.

HORSEBACK RIDING

Anything from a short day ride along Lago Argentino to a weeklong camping excursion in and around the glaciers can be arranged in El Calafate by **Gustavo Holzmann** (✉*Av. Libertador 4315* ☎*2902/493–278* ✐*cabalgataenpatagonia@cotecal.com.ar* ⊕*www.cabalgataenpatagonia.com*) or through the tourist office. *Estancias Turísticas* (tourist ranches) are ideal for a combination of horseback riding, ranch activities, and local excursions. Information on **Estancias de Santa Cruz** is in Buenos Aires at the **Provincial tourist office** (✉*Suipacha 1120* ☎*11/4325–3098* ⊕*www.estanciasdesantacruz.com*). **Estancia El Galpón del Glaciar** (✉*Ruta 11, Km 22* ☎☎*2902/492–509 or 11/4774–1069* ⊕*www.estanciaalice.com.ar*) welcomes guests overnight or for the day—for a horseback ride, bird-watching, or an afternoon program that includes a demonstration of sheep dogs working, a walk to the lake with a naturalist, sheep-shearing, and dinner in the former sheep-shearing barn, served right off the grill and the asador by knife-wielding gauchos. **Estancia Maria Elisa** (☎☎*2902/492–583 or 11/4774–1069* ✐*estanciamariaelisa@cotecal.com.ar*) is an upscale choice among estancias. Other estancias close to El Calafate are **Nibepo Aike** (✉*50 km [31 mi] from El Calafate near Lago Roca* ☎*2966/492–797* ⊕*www.nibepoaike.com.ar*), **Alta Vista** (✉*33 km [20 mi] from El Calafate* ☎*2966/491–247* ✐*altavista@cotecal.com.ar*), and **Huyliche** (✉*3 km [2 mi] from El Calafate* ☎*2902/491–025* ✐*teresanegro@cotecal.com.ar*).

ICE TREKKING

★ A two-hour mini-trek on the Perito Moreno Glacier involves a transfer from El Calafate to Brazo Rico by bus and a short lake crossing to a dock and refugio, where you set off with a guide, put crampons over your shoes, and literally walk across a stable portion of the glacier, scaling ridges of ice, and ducking through bright-blue ice tunnels. It is one of the most unique experiences in Argentina. The entire outing lasts about five hours. Hotels arrange mini-treks through **Hielo y Aventura** (✉*Av. Libertador 935* ☎*2902/492–205* ⊕*www.hieloyaventura.com*), which also organizes much longer, more difficult trips of eight hours to a week to other glaciers; you can arrange the trek directly through their office in downtown El Calafate. Mini-trekking runs about 300 pesos for the day. Hielo y Aventura also runs a longer "Big Ice" trek that traverses a much more extensive area of the glacier and costs 420 pesos. If you're between the ages of 18 and 40 and want a more extreme experience, Big Ice is highly recommended.

MOUNTAIN BIKING

Mountain biking is popular along the dirt roads and mountain paths that lead to the lakes, glaciers, and ranches. Rent bikes and get information at **Alquiler de Bicicletas** (⊠ *Av. Buenos Aires 173* ☎2902/493–806).

LAND ROVER EXCURSIONS

If pedaling uphill sounds like too much work, check out the Land Rover expeditions offered by **MIL Outdoor Adventure.** These trips follow dirt tracks into the hills above town for stunning views of Lago Argentino. On a clear day, you can even see the peaks of Cerro Torre and Cerro Fitzroy on the horizon. MIL's Land Rovers are converted to run on vegetable oil, so environmentalists can enjoy bouncing up the trail with a clean conscience. ⊠ *Av. Libertador 1029* ☎2902/495–446 ⊕ *www.miloutdoor.com.*

WHERE TO EAT

$$$ ✗**Barricas de Enopio.** The emphasis at this restaurant-bar is on the extensive wine list and great cheeses that accompany each glass. A variety of brochettes and dinner entrées are big enough to share. The menu includes eclectic dishes such as pasta stuffed with venison or wild boar. The space is chic, casual, and cozy, with natural-cotton curtains and tablecloths, handmade lamps, and Tehuelche influences. ⊠ *Av. Libertador 1610* ☎2902/493–414 ⊟ *AE, MC, V.*

$$–$$$$ ✗**Casimiro Biguá.** This restaurant and wine bar boasts a hipper-than thou interior and an inventive menu serving such delights as Patagonian lamb with *Calafate* sauce (Calafate is a local wild berry). The **Casimiro Bigua Parrilla,** down the street from the main restaurant, has a similar trendy feel. You can recognize the *parrilla* by the *cordero al asador* (spit-roasted lamb) displayed in the window. ⊠ *Av. Libertador 963* ☎2902/492–590 ⊕ *http://casimirobigua.com* ⊟ *AE, DC, MC, V.*

$$–$$$ ✗**La Cocina.** This casual café on the main shopping street serves homemade pasta, quiches, crepes, and hamburgers. Homemade ice cream and delicious cakes make for good treats. *Postre Chancho* (Pig's Dessert) is ice cream with hot dulce de leche sauce. There is a long siesta from 2 to 7. ⊠ *Av. Libertador 1245* ☎2902/491–758 ⊟ *MC, V.*

$$ ✗**La Lechuza.** This cozy, bustling joint is known for having some of the best pizza in town. The brick oven and thin crust make for a more Italian-style taste and texture than at most spots. ⊠ *Av. Libertador at 1 de Mayo* ☎2902/491–610 ⊟ *No credit cards* ⊗ *No lunch Sun.*

$$–$$$ ✗**Pura Vida.** Modernity merges with tradition at this hippie-ish, veggie-friendly restaurant a few blocks out of the center of El Calafate. It's a treat to find such creative fare, funky decor, cool candles, and

CLOSE UP

A Patagonian Feast

Since sheep and cattle far outnumber humans in Patagonia, expect lamb and beef to appear on almost every menu. Often cooked on a *parrilla* (grill) before your eyes, beef, lamb, and *chorizos* (homemade sausages) are enhanced by a spoonful of *chimichurri* sauce (made from olive oil, garlic, oregano, and sometimes chopped tomatoes and onions). On ranches and in some restaurants, you may have the opportunity to try gaucho-style meat *al asador,* also known as *a la cruz,* where the lamb is attached to a metal cross placed in the ground over hot coals. The heat is adjusted by raking the coals as the meat cooks, and the fat runs down to create a natural marinade. Lamb (*cordero*) and goat (*chivito*) cooked in this manner are delicious, and the camaraderie of standing around the fire sipping *mate* (a traditional Argentine tea) or wine while the meat cooks is part of the gaucho tradition.

Throughout the northern Andean Lake District, local farmed trout, salmon, and *abadejo* (a white fish) are grilled, fried, baked, smoked, and dried. Wild game such as *ciervo* (venison) and *jabalí* (wild boar) is prepared in a variety of ways, from carpaccio to grilled steaks. It's also often smoked; smoked fish (particularly trout) and game from the region are popular appetizers throughout Argentina. Farther south, in Tierra del Fuego, the seafood specialties are black hake (*merluza*

negra), a rich white fish with a texture similar to Patagonian toothfish—which is known in the United States as "Chilean sea bass"—and the legendary *centolla* (king crab or spider crab), which is, curiously, easier to find fresh in Buenos Aires than in Ushuaia. Pizza and empanadas are as popular here as elsewhere in the country, and pasta also appears on every menu—look for *pasta casera* (homemade pasta)—often served with sauces that are listed separately.

Beer and wine are both on the upswing in Patagonia, and you'll stumble across the rather unusual sight of a brewpub inside and outside of most of the region's cities. Dozens of microbreweries now dot the Lakes region in particular. Wine, too, is a growing industry in these parts, with the appropriately named Bodegas del Fin del Mundo, based in the Neuquén province, leading the way with some good pinot noirs and cabernet-malbec blends.

If the 10 PM dinner hour seems too far away from lunch, tea is a welcome break around 5 or 6 PM. Patagonia's Welsh teahouses, a product of Welsh immigration in the 19th century, serve delicious cakes, tarts, and cookies from recipes that have been handed down for generations. Jams made from local berries spread on homemade bread and scones are a welcome treat on a blustery day.

modern art in such a frontier town. The beef stew served inside a *calabaza* (pumpkin) has an irresistible flair and is excellently seasoned, although the beef isn't particularly tender. Even if the cooking isn't quite top-flight, Pura Vida is more than the sum of its parts, drawing in backpackers and older folks alike with an almost mystical allure. ⊠ *Av. Libertador 1876* ☎ *2902/493–356* ▤ *V.*

$$$ ✕**Rick's Parrillá.** It's *tenedor libre* (literally, "free fork," or all you can eat) for 35 pesos at this immensely popular *parrilla* in a big yellow building on El Calafate's main street. The place is packed full of tourists day and night. The room is big and bustling, if not particularly interesting, and the spread includes lamb and *vacío* (flank steak). ⊠*Av. Libertador 1091* ☎*2902/492–148* ▤*MC, V.*

$$–$$$ ✕**La Tablita.** It's a couple of extra blocks from downtown, across a FodorśChoice little white bridge, but this parrilla is where the locals go for a special ★ night out. You can watch your food as it's prepared: Patagonian lamb and beef ribs cooking gaucho-style on an asador, or meat sizzling on the grill, including steaks, chorizos, and excellent *morcilla* (blood sausage). The enormous *parrillada* for two is a great way to sample it all, and the wine list is well priced and well chosen. ⊠*Coronel Rosales 28* ☎*2902/491–065* ⊕*www.interpatagonia.com/latablita* ▤*AE, DC, MC, V* ⊗*No lunch Mon.–Thurs. June and July.*

WHERE TO STAY

¢–$ ▦**América del Sur.** The only downside to this established hostel, which caters to younger backpackers, is its location (a 10-minute uphill walk from downtown). But beautiful views of the lake and mountains and a free shuttle service compensate for the distance. Otherwise, the hostel is simple but spectacular—sparklingly clean and legendarily friendly. There are rooms with two and four beds. It's a particularly cheap deal for groups of four. **Pros:** Great view, friendly staff. **Cons:** A hike from downtown. ⊠*Punto Deseado,* ☎*2902/493–525* ⊕*www.americahostel. com.ar* ♿*In-room: no TV. In-hotel: restaurant, bar, public Wi-Fi, no elevator* ▤*No credit cards.*

$$$$ ▦**Helsingfors.** If we could recommend only one property in southern FodorśChoice Patagonia, it would be Estancia Helsingfors, a luxurious, converted ★ ranch house with an absolutely spectacular location in the middle of the national park on the shore of Lago Viedma. The scenery is straight out of a *Lord of the Rings* movie and knowledgeable guides can point out dozens of species of birds; inside, a cozy fire warms the sitting room, friendly staff serve fine food and delicious house wine, and the beds are perhaps the most comfortable in Patagonia. Don't leave without visiting the jewel of Helsingfors, a breathtaking blue lake at the foot of a glacier that's a three-hour hike or horseback ride from the inn. **Pros:** Unique location, wonderful staff. **Cons:** Three hours by dirt road from El Calafate. ⊠*Reservations in Buenos Aires: Cordoba 827, fl. 11,* ☎*11/4315–1222 in Buenos Aires* ⊕*www.helsingfors.com.ar* ⇋*8 rooms* ♿*In-room: no TV. In-hotel: restaurant* ▤*AE, MC, V* ⊗*Closed May–Sept.* ⎮⊙⎮*FAP.*

$$$$ ✕▦**Hostería los Notros.** Weathered wood buildings cling to the mountainside that overlooks the Perito Moreno Glacier as it descends into Lago Argentino. This inn, seemingly at the end of the world, is 73 km (45 mi) west of El Calafate. The glacier is framed in the windows of every room. A path through the garden and over a bridge spanning a canyon connects rooms to the main lodge. Appetizers and wine are

5

served in full view of sunset (or moonrise) over the glacier, followed by an absolutely spectacular menu that spotlights game, including delicious venison and creative preparations of Argentine classics. A two-night minimum stay is required. This property is extremely expensive; prices include all meals, cocktails, park entry, and a glacier excursion. If you don't feel like spending that much, come just for a meal. **Pros:** Unique location, totally luxurious. **Cons:** Very expensive, crowds bound for Perito Moreno can detract from the secluded atmosphere. ✉ *Reservations in Buenos Aires: Arenales 1457, fl. 7,* ☎ *11/4814–3934 in Buenos Aires, 2902/499–510 in El Calafate* ⊕ *www.losnotros.com* ⇌ *32 rooms* ⬧ *In-room: no phone, no TV. In-hotel: restaurant, bar, airport shuttle, public Wi-Fi, no elevator* ▤ *AE, DC, MC, V* ⊘ *Closed June–mid-Sept.* ⦙○⦙ *FAP.*

$$$$ ✕⊡ **Hotel Kau-Yatun.** From the homemade chocolates and flower bouquets that appear in the rooms each evening to the sweeping backyard complete with swing sets for the kids, every detail of this converted ranch property is tailored to thoughtful hospitality. Guests rave about the attentive staff, the excellent food with a focus on local and organic ingredients, and the building, which feels more well-loved than the newer hotels in town. **Pros:** Great food, loving attention to detail. **Cons:** Water pressure is only adequate. ✉ *25 de Mayo,* ☎ *2902/491–059* ✑ *kauyatun@cotecal.com.ar* ⇌ *44 rooms* ⬧ *In-hotel: restaurant, bar, airport shuttle, bicycles, public Wi-Fi, no elevator* ▤ *AE, MC, V* ⦙○⦙ *CP.*

ⓒ Fodor's Choice ★

$$$$ ⊡ **Kosten Aike.** The wood balconies outside, and the slate floors, wood-beamed ceilings, and unfailing attention to detail inside, will please aficionados of Andean Patagonian architecture. Tehuelche symbols and designs are used on everything from the curtains to the room plaques. A lobby bar and living room with fireplace, card tables, magazines, and a large TV is dangerously conducive to lounging about. **Pros:** Large rooms, central location. **Cons:** Dining room décor is uninspired. ✉ *25 de Mayo 1243, at G. Moyano,* ☎ *2902/492–424, 11/4811–1314 in Buenos Aires* ⊕ *www.kostenaike.com.ar* ⇌ *78 rooms, 2 suites* ⬧ *In-hotel: restaurant, bar, gym, public Wi-Fi* ▤ *AE, DC, MC, V* ⊘ *Closed May–Sept.*

¢–$$ ⊡ **Lago Argentino Hostel.** Just steps from the bus terminal, this chill new hostel is operated by the same family that runs the popular Pura Vida restaurant. Like Pura Vida, the atmosphere is cozy and eclectic. *Amor y paz* (love and peace) reads a sign in the entryway, and the friendly staff would not look out of place at a music festival. Private rooms in an annex across the street from the main building are much nicer, but more expensive, than the functional rooms in the main dorms. **Pros:** Convenient location, pleasant garden. **Cons:** Earplugs recommended, mattresses and pillows could be thicker. ✉ *Campana del desierto 1050,* ☎ *2902/491–423* ⊕ *www.interpatagonia.com/lagoargentino* ⇌ *10 rooms* ⬧ *In-hotel: laundry facilities, public Wi-Fi, no elevator* ▤ *No credit cards.*

$$ 🏠**Michelangelo.** Bright red and yellow native flowers line the front of the low log-and-stucco building with its distinctive A-frames over rooms, restaurant, and lobby. A fine collection of local photographs is displayed next to a sunken lobby, where easy chairs and a banquette surround the fireplace. The restaurant next door is excellent. **Pros:** Good value, convenient location. **Cons:** Limited views. ⊠*Moyano 1020,* ☎*2902/491–045* ⊘*michelangelohotel@cotecal.com.ar* ⤴*20 rooms* ⚒*In-hotel: restaurant, no elevator* ▭*AE, MC, V* ⊗*Closed June* ❉*CP.*

$$ 🏠**Miyazato Inn.** Jorge Miyasato and his wife Elizabeth have brought the flawless hospitality of a traditional Japanese country inn to El Calafate. Comfortably removed from the tourist scene downtown, and only a short walk from the Ecological Preserve, each of the five rooms has hardwood floors and comfortable twin beds. The Miyasatos have two young children, and the family atmosphere makes this cozy inn a refuge of intimacy and calm. **Pros:** Clean, homey, good value. **Cons:** Neighborhood dogs are noisy. ⊠*Egidio Feruglio 150,* ☎*2902/491–953* ⊘*miyazatoinn@cotecal.com.ar* ⊕*www.interpatagonia.com/miyazatoinn* ⤴*5 rooms* ⚒*In-hotel: public Wi-Fi, no elevator* ▭*MC, V* ❉*CP.*

$$$$ 🏠**Nibepo Aike.** This is a lovely estancia within a day trip's distance
★ from El Calafate in a bucolic valley overlooking Lago Roca and backed by snowcapped mountain peaks. Sheep, horses, and cows graze among purple lupine flowers, and friendly gauchos give horse-racing and sheep-shearing demonstrations. The attached restaurant serves up a truly exceptional lamb and beef barbecue. It's possible to visit Nibepo Aike by booking a day-trip at the office in downtown El Calafate but the best way to experience this unique property is with an overnight stay in comfortable rooms decorated with original antiques and ranching memorabilia. The name Nibepo is a combination of the nicknames of the original owner's three daughters—Nini, Bebe, and Porota. All-inclusive packages are available, with mini-trekking and a cruise to the Upsala Glacier. **Pros:** Spectacular scenery, welcoming staff. **Cons:** An hour by dirt road from downtown. ⊠*For reservations: Av. Libertador 1215,* ☎*For reservations: 2902/492–797* ⊕*www.nibepoaike.com.ar* ⤴*11 rooms* ⚒*In-room: no TV. In-hotel: restaurant* ▭*AE, MC, V* ⊗*Closed May–Sept.* ❉*FAP.*

$$$$ 🏠**Posada los Alamos.** Surrounded by tall, leafy alamo trees and con-
★ structed of brick and dark *quebracho* (ironwood), this attractive country manor house uses rich woods, leather, and handwoven fabrics to produce conversation-friendly furniture groupings in the large lobby. Plush comforters and fresh flowers in the rooms, and a deferential staff make this a top-notch hotel. Lovingly tended gardens surround the building and line a walkway through the woods to the restaurant and the shore of Lago Argentino. **Pros:** Nice interiors, beautiful gardens. **Cons:** Staff can be overly formal. ⊠*Moyano 1355, at Bustillo,* ☎*2902/491–144* ⊕*www.posadalosalamos.com* ⤴*140 rooms, 4 suites* ⚒*In-hotel: restaurant, bar, golf course* ▭*AE, MC, V* ❉*CP.*

$$$$ ▦ **El Quijote.** Sun shines through picture windows onto polished slate floors and high beams in this modern hotel next to Sancho restaurant a few blocks from the main street. Rooms are carpeted and have plain white walls (which some readers have reported are paper-thin) and wood furniture. **Pros:** Central location, attentive staff. **Cons:** Lacks personality, uncreative room decor. ⊠*Gregores 1155,* ☎*2902/491–017* ✎*elquijote@cotecal.com.ar* ⬤*80 rooms* ♿*In-hotel: bar, public Wi-Fi* ▤*AE, DC, MC, V* ☾*Closed June and July* ❑*CP.*

EL CHALTÉN & FITZROY

222 km (138 mi) north of El Calafate (35 km [22 mi] east on R11 to R40, then north on R40 on a dirt road to R23 north).

The four-hour one-way car or bus trip to El Chaltén from El Calafate makes staying at least one night here a good idea. The only gas, food, and restroom facilities en route are at La Leona, a historically significant ranch 110 km (68 mi) from El Calafate where Butch Cassidy and the Sundance Kid once hid from the long arm of the law. As you follow the shore of Lago Viedma, look north for the glacier of the same name descending into the lake. Visible for hundreds of miles (weather permitting) on the northern horizon as you approach the frontier village of El Chaltén, the granite hulk of **Cerro Fitzroy** (11,286 feet and named after the captain of the *Beagle,* on which Charles Darwin served as a naturalist) rises like a giant arrowhead next to the slender spires of **Cerro Torre** (10,174 feet). The Tehuelche called Cerro Fitzroy *Chaltén* ("smoke") for the snow constantly blowing off its peak. The village was founded in 1985 as a hiking mecca at the base of the range.

GETTING AROUND

Before you cross the bridge into town over Río Fitzroy, stop at the **Parque Nacional office** (☎☎*2962/493–004*). It's extremely well organized and staffed by bilingual rangers who can help you plan your mountain treks and point you to accommodation and restaurants in town. An essential stop. There is no ATM in town, so get plenty of money before you arrive. The lack of banking facilities is perhaps representative of the noncommercial atmosphere of El Chaltén and the northern section of the national park in general.

WHAT TO SEE

The **Laguna del Desierto** (Lake of the Desert), a lovely lake surrounded by lush forest, complete with orchids and mossy trees, is 37 km (23 mi) north of El Chaltén on R23, a dirt road. Hotels in El Chaltén can arrange trips to Laguna del Desierto for about 90 pesos for the day. There is a simple, family-oriented campground at the lake and the beginnings of an inn that has been under construction for years. Locals recommend visiting Lake of the Desert on a rainy day, when more ambitious hikes are not an option and the dripping green misty forest is extra mysterious.

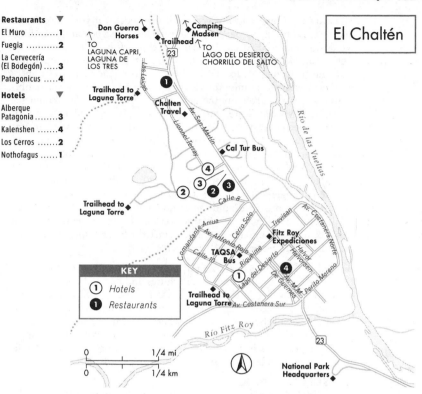

El Chaltén

KEY

① Hotels

❶ Restaurants

The **Chorillo del Salta** (Trickling Falls) is a waterfall just 4 km (2½ mi) north of town on the road to Lago del Desierto. The falls are no Niagara, but the area is extremely pleasant and sheltered from the wind. A short hike uphill leads to secluded river pools and sun-splashed rocks where locals enjoy picnics on their days off. If you don't feel up to a more ambitious hike, the short stroll to the falls is an excellent way to spend the better part of an afternoon. Pack a bottle of wine and a ham sandwich and enjoy the solitude.

OUTDOOR ACTIVITIES

HIKING

Both long and short hikes on well-trodden trails lead to lakes, glaciers, and stunning viewpoints. There are two main hikes, one to the base of Cerro Fitzroy, the other to a windswept glacial lake at the base of Cerro Torre. Both hikes climb into the hills above town and after a little over an hour take you to viewpoints marked El Mirador ("the lookout"). The six-hour round-trip hike to the base camp for Cerro Torre at Laguna Torre has (weather permitting) dramatic views of Torres Standhart, Adelas, Grande, and Solo.

Trails start in town and are very well marked, so if you stick to the main path there is no danger of getting lost. Just be careful of high winds and exposed rocks that can get slippery in bad weather. The eight-hour hike to the base camp for Cerro Fitzroy passes Laguna Capri and ends at Laguna de los Tres, where you can enjoy an utterly spectacular view of the granite tower. If you only have time for one ambitious hike, this is probably the best choice, though the last kilometer of trail is very steep. Water within the park is potable and delicious, so there's no need to start out with more than a liter or two. At campsites in the hills above town hardy souls can pitch a tent for the night and enjoy sunset and dawn views of the mountain peaks. Ask about current camping regulations and advisories at the national park office before setting off with a tent in your rucksack. While hiking, keep an eye out for the endangered Huemul, a type of Patagonian deer. Finally, use latrines where provided, and under no circumstance should you even think about starting a fire—a large section of forest near Cerro Torre was recently devastated by a fire that started when a foolish hiker tried to dispose of toilet paper with a match.

Beyond El Chaltén (37 km [23 mi]), hikes go to and around Lago del Desierto. These are described in brochures and maps obtainable at the national park office in El Chaltén or at the tourist office or national park office in El Calafate. It's possible to continue past Lago del Desierto and hike all the way to Chile, where you can catch a ferry across Lago O'Higgins. Locals recommend this trek as one of the most spectacular experiences in Patagonia, but research up-to-date trail conditions, ferry schedules, and border regulations in advance.

HORSEBACK RIDING
As of 2008, horses are no longer allowed on mountain trails in the park, but there are still pleasant routes around town open to riders. Make arrangements for trail rides through local outfitters and guides, including **Rodolfo Guerra** (⊠ *Northwest of town at Fitzroy trailhead* ☎*2962/493–020*).

MOUNTAIN CLIMBING
Cerro Torre and Cerro Fitzroy are extraordinarily difficult mountains, and expert mountaineers from every corner of the globe come to attempt these elusive peaks. They sometimes camp for weeks, even months, at Laguna Torre, waiting for the wind to die down, the rain to stop, or the clouds to disperse. Climbing permits are available at the **National Park office** (⊠ *Before the bridge into town* ☎☎*2962/493–004*). **Fitzroy Expeditions** (⊠ *Av. San Martín 56, El Chaltén,* ☎*2962/493–017* ⊕*fitzroyexpediciones.com.ar*) has English-speaking guides for glacier and mountain treks, as well as kayaking expeditions. One of the most popular trips is to the glacier at the base of Cerro Torre, where you can even try your hand at ice-climbing. These trips are generally more affordable, less crowded, and arguably more memorable than similar packages offered by tour operators in El Calafate, although you must be in good shape to attempt such ambitious excursions.

For maps, hiking, and lodging information, contact the **Comisión de Fomento** (⊠ *Av. Güemes 174* ☎☎ *2962/493–011* ✍ *comfomel@yahoo.com.ar* ⊕ *www.elchalten.com*).

WHERE TO EAT

¢–$$ ✗ **La Cerveceria.** This artisanal brewpub calls itself a "Hausbrauerei,"
★ but it's not just the delicious pilsner and bock that bring in the crowds. It's also the homey atmosphere—you'll squeeze into one of just a couple of old wooden tables—and the good food. Pizza is made with loving care, but the main attraction is the delicious *locro*: a hearty traditional northern Argentine stew, and this is some of the best in southern Argentina. ⊠ *Av. San Martín s/n* ☎ *2962/493–109* ⊟ *No credit cards* ⊗ *Closed May–Sept.*

$–$$$ ✗ **Fuegia.** This small restaurant, in a grassy field next to the Albergue Patagonia hostel, serves smoked meats, hearty soups, chicken, lamb, beef kabobs, and fresh trout. ⊠ *Av. San Martín 493* ☎ *2962/493–019* ⊟ *MC, V.*

$$–$$$$ ✗ **El Muro.** Cozy coffee-and-pastry shop by day, wine bar and bistro by night, this little family-owned place is a welcome escape when the wind howls down the mountain. In an angular brown cottage with climbing holds on the lee side, just a stone's throw from the Cerro Fitzroy trailhead, the bistro is far enough from new construction downtown to have an expansive river view. ⊠ *San Martín 912* ☎ *2962/493–248* ⊟ *MC, V* ⊗ *Closed Sun.*

$$–$$$$ ✗ **Patagonicus.** Park rangers and trekking guides recommend this long-running restaurant with an extensive collection of black-and-white photos from the 1959 Fitzroy climbing expedition. Excellent homemade pizza and pasta are the main attraction, but Patagonicus is also a nice stop for a midday coffee and a slice of apple pie. ⊠ *Blvd. Martín Güemes* ☎ *2962/493–025* ⊟ *No credit cards* ⊗ *Closed Wed. in Dec., and May–Sept.*

WHERE TO STAY

¢–$$ ▥ **Albergue Patagonia.** Steps from hiking and mountain-biking trails stands this simple wood-frame farm house, with rooms that sleep two to six people. Next door is a new annex with eight rooms, each with its own bathroom. This is the true Chaltén style, popular with the legions of backpackers that trek through town, and it's a good place for solo travelers to meet others. You can cook your meals here, prepare picnic lunches, peruse trail maps, and share information with fellow guests, all for under US$15. The hostel also arranges horseback-riding, hiking, and biking excursions. **Pros:** Congenial atmosphere. **Cons:** New annex rooms are sterile. ⊠ *Av. San Martín 392,* ☎☎ *2962/493–019* ✍ *patagoniahostel@yahoo.com.ar* ⇆ *18 rooms* ⚷ *In-hotel: restaurant, bicycles, laundry facilities, no elevator* ⊟ *No credit cards.*

⊞ **Camping Madsen.** If you have a tent, don't mind windy nights, and want to experience the mountain-climber subculture of Argentina firsthand (or if you're flat broke), the free tent sites at Camping Madsen at the far end of town are an alternative to more traditional accommodation. Local climbing bums sometimes stay in Madsen for a whole season, constructing wooden windbreaks in an atmosphere not unlike the TV show *Survivor*. Although hard-core locals might turn up their noses at tourists infiltrating their anarchic little tent kingdom, in general campers are considerate and it's safe to leave your things in the tent while out trekking. There's also free camping at the other end of town, near the national park office. **Pros:** Can't beat the price. **Cons:** Poorly staked tents blow away on windy days. ⊠ *Just past the Fitzroy trailhead.*

$$$$ ✕⊞ **Los Cerros.** From the high-end group that runs the Hostería Los Notros at the Perito Moreno Glacier comes this sparkling house upon a hill. The lobby has lovely wood details, a fireplace, and lamps that are like works of art. The restaurant ($$$$) is as artful as the hotel, with creative Patagonian cuisine; you can eat here and enjoy the view from a hill atop El Chaltén even if you're not staying—though some hungry diners complain of slow service. Prices are sky-high, but for guests, excursions to Lago Viedma, Glaciar Torre, and Lago del Desierto are included. **Pros:** Spacious common areas, luxurious touches throughout. **Cons:** Pricey, somewhat out of place in this rustic mountain town. ⊠ *El Chaltén,* ☎ *0800/333-7282* ⊕ *www.loscerrosdelchalten.com* ⟳ *44 rooms* ⌂ *In-room: no TV. In-hotel: restaurant, bar, laundry service, spa, public Wi-Fi, no elevator* ⊟ *AE, DC, MC, V* ⧦ *BP.*

$$$ ⊞ **Kalenshen.** This delightful hotel in a pink wooden house has all the creature comforts—not always a given in this backpacker boomtown—plus a pleasant yellow lounge that is great for socializing. *Cabañas,* which sleep four, are an even better deal than the clean, well-kept rooms. The staff is friendly, and the location is perfect, right next to the town's little main street. As of 2008, there is even a heated swimming pool. **Pros:** Comfortable rooms, heated pool. **Cons:** Not much of a view. ⊠ *Lionel Terray 50,* ☎ *2962/493-108* ⊕ *www.kalenshen. ar* ⟳ *17 rooms, 5 cabins* ⌂ *In-hotel: restaurant, bar, pool, no elevator* ⊟ *No credit cards* ⧦ *CP.*

$-$$ ⊞ **Nothofagus.** This family run B&B splits the difference between hostel and hotel, offering simple, spotless rooms in a sky-blue house in the southeast corner of town. Guests are enthusiastic about the value, comfort, and delicious breakfast. The owners have lived in El Chaltén for over 10 years, and can point you to all the best spots. **Pros:** Great value, homey atmosphere. **Cons:** Construction nearby, hot water inconsistent. ⊠ *Hensen s/n,* ☎ *2962/493-087* ⊕ *www.elchalten.com/nothofagus* ⟳ *7 rooms* ⌂ *In-hotel: no elevator* ⊟ *No credit cards* ⧦ *CP.*

RÍO GALLEGOS & ENVIRONS

1,034 km (640 mi) south of Comodoro Rivadavía via R3; 319 km (197 mi) south of El Calafate; 596 km (370 mi) north of Ushuaia; 251 km (157 mi) east of Puerto Natales, Chile, via R40.

Weather-beaten and worn, there's nothing slick about Río Gallegos, the administrative and commercial capital of Santa Cruz Province and one of the windiest cities in the world. Although the downtown could only be considered cosmopolitan when compared to the desolation of the surrounding steppe, there is a gritty charm to this working-class city nonetheless.

Founded in 1885 on the southern shore of the Río Gallegos river mouth in order to establish Argentine sovereignty over the far south, this port city served as the exit point for coal shipments from Río Túrbio, on the Chilean border. Wool and sheepskins from the inland ranches also contributed to the economy, which was heavily dependent on European markets. These days, energy production provides the economic muscle, and those who make the difficult trek south to the penguin colony at Cabo Vírgenes will pass natural-gas derricks that shoot eerie flames against a barren backdrop of windswept plains.

As a gateway city to southern Patagonia, travelers en route south to Ushuaia, north to the Parque Nacional los Glaciares, or west to Chile, are often obliged to spend a night. Although travelers waiting for delayed luggage might complain about "being stuck in this hole," the downtown has a couple of worthwhile museums, comfortable hotels, and decent restaurants. An evening walk along the windswept riverfront promenade is a hair-tousling and soul-awakening experience that might start you humming a mournful Bruce Springsteen song.

GETTING AROUND

The best hotels and restaurants are on Avenue Roca, where you'll also find a smattering of souvenir shops, banks, and camping stores. A taxi to downtown from the airport (5 km [3 mi]) should run no more than 20 pesos. The busy bus station is 2 km (1 mi) from downtown on the way to the airport.

ESSENTIALS

BUS **El Pingüino** (☎ 2966/442–169). **Interlagos** (✉ Bus terminal ☎ 2966/442–080). **TAQSA** (✉ Bus terminal ☎ 2966/442–671 ⊕ www.taqsa.com.ar).

CURRENCY **Bancos de Galicia** (✉ Av. Roca 739). **Banco de Santa Cruz** (✉ Av. Roca 812). **Hipotecario Nacional** (✉ Av. San Martín 801). **Nationale de Lavoro** (✉ Fagnano 44).

MEDICAL **Hospital Regional** (✉ José Ingeniero 98 ☎ 2966/420–025).

REMIS **Centenario** (✉ Maipú 285 ☎ 2966/422–320).

RENTAL CARS **Cristina** (✉ Libertad 123 ☎ 2960/425–709).

VISITOR INFO **Subsecretaría de Turismo** (✉ Av. Roca 863 ☎ 2966/437–412 ⊕ www.epata gonia.gov.ar).

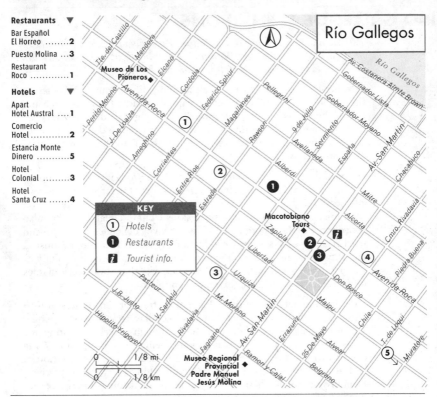

Río Gallegos

KEY

①   *Hotels*

❶   *Restaurants*

🛈   *Tourist info.*

WHAT TO SEE

If you're into dinosaurs, visit the **Museo Regional Provincial Padre Manuel Jesus Molina** (Provincial Museum), which exhibits reconstructed skeletons excavated at sites in Patagonia. Exhibits on biology, geology, history, paleontology, and Tehuelche ethnology are displayed in different sections of the museum, as is an exhibit of contemporary art. ✉*Cajal 51, at Ramón* ☎*2966/423–290* ✉*Free* ☉ *Weekdays 9–7, weekends 11–7.*

Behind a white picket fence near the river is the **Museo de Los Pioneros** (Pioneer Museum) one of the oldest structures in Río Gallegos. Watch your head as you climb the creaky staircase to the second floor, where the rooms are left as they were when the house was inhabited by Dr. Arthur Fenton, the first physician in Santa Cruz, whose descendants now operate the Estancia Monte Dinero near Cabo Virgenes. Exploring the cozy wooden house while wind rattles the shutters gives one a sense of the extreme isolation the earliest settlers were forced to overcome, when the only communication with the outside world was by ship, and a journey to the mountains could take 45 days. ✉*Alberti at El Cano* ☎*2966/437–763* ✉*Free* ☉*Daily 10–8.*

OFF THE BEATEN PATH

Cabo Virgenes. From September through April, this provincial nature preserve hosts 150,000 mating Magellanic penguins—the second-largest penguin colony in Patagonia. A cacophony of screeches and the thump of stubby wings make strolling down the shingle beach feel like standing courtside at an NBA playoff game. A lighthouse guarding the entrance to the Strait of Magellan has a teahouse inside. You can go on an organized tour, or on your own by following the interpretive trail. ✉ *128 km (79 mi) south on RN3. At Km 17, branch left onto RP1, a dirt road, and continue past the ranches to the Reserva Faunística Provincial (Provincial Nature Preserve).*

Macotobiano Turismo (✉ *Av. Roca 998,* ☎ *2966/422–466*) runs tours to Cabo Virgenes when there is enough interest, but be forewarned that their bus has been known to break down, leaving passengers stranded on the barren plain.

Laguna Azul. Surreal volcanic rock formations surround this crater lake next to the Chilean border, about an hour's drive due south of Río Gallegos. Although it's possible to visit with a rental car, the safer option is to contract a remise in town or round up enough people for a group tour. Ask about tour options and current road conditions at the tourism office in Río Gallegos. ✉ *63 km (38 mi) south on RN3. After approximately 60 km (37 mi), branch right onto a dirt road, and continue towards the crumbly hills of the Pali Aike volcanoes.*

5

WHERE TO EAT

$$–$$$$ ✕**Bar Español El Horreo.** A well-heeled clientele fills this rather classy Spanish-looking restaurant around 10:30 PM. Complimentary pisco sours begin your repast. It's hard to beat the local spring lamb, the steaks, or the mountain trout, crab, and seafood—grilled or in homemade sauces. ✉ *Av. Roca 862* ☎ *2966/426–462* ▭ *AE, MC, V.*

$$–$$$ ✕**Puesto Molino.** This pleasant pizza and pasta joint right next door to
☺   El Horreo has a bright-yellow interior, and might be the most cheerful restaurant in town. It's a popular lunch spot and is still crowded with boisterous families at midnight. There's a play area for children and the big clay pizza oven at the back of the room contributes to the inviting atmosphere. ✉ *Av. Roca 854* ☎ *2966/426–462* ▭ *AE, MC, V.*

$$–$$$$ ✕**Restaurant Roco.** The dining room is so spacious, it almost feels like a dining hall at a New England liberal arts college, but the atmosphere is refined, and well-prepared specialties of salmon rosado and lamb grilled at the table, as well as an extensive wine list, make Roco a popular choice among local couples having a special evening out. Try for a table near the big plate-glass windows that look out onto Avenue Roca. ✉ *Av. Roca 1157* ☎ *2966/420–203* ▭ *AE, MC, V.*

WHERE TO STAY

$$ 🏨**Apart Hotel Austral.** Locals recommend the Austral for its good value, central location, and reliability. The compact lobby is unremarkable, but the hallways and rooms are tastefully decorated and the staff is all efficiency and smiles. **Pros:** Good value, friendly staff, artistic touches. **Cons:** Cramped lobby. ☒*Av. Roca 1505,* ☎*2966/420–209* ⊕*www. apartaustral.com* ✍*apartaustral@infovia.com.ar* ⇗*14 rooms, 13 apartment rooms w/ kitchen* ⚿*In-room: kitchen (some). In-hotel: parking (no fee), public Wi-Fi* ☰*AE, MC, V* ⊙❘*CP.*

$$$ 🏨**Comercio Hotel.** The plush red armchairs in the cozy lobby of this well-kept hotel are a balm for tired bones at the end of a long day of travel. Rooms are functional and clean but the bathrooms are on the small side. **Pros:** Bright, comfortable lobby. **Cons:** Front desk staff smoke cigarettes on the job. ☒*Av. Roca 1302,* ☎*2966/420–209* ✍*hotelcomercio@informacionrgl.com.ar* ⇗*53 rooms* ⚿*In-hotel: restaurant, parking (no fee), public Wi-Fi* ☰*AE, MC, V* ⊙❘*CP.*

$$$ 🏨**Estancia Monte Dinero.** If total isolation appeals, this comfortable ranch house near Cabo Virgenes is about as far from the hustle and bustle as it's possible to get without going to the moon. The evangelical Fenton family (the same family who once inhabited the Pioneer Museum House in Río Gallegos) has operated the ranch for five generations, and visitors are invited to participate in horseback rides and observe traditional activities like sheep-shearing. **Pros:** End-of-the-world atmosphere with creature comforts. **Cons:** Difficult to get to. ☒*Cabo Virgenes,* ☎*2966/428–922* ⊕*www.montedinero.com.ar* ⇗*6 rooms* ⚿*In-hotel: public Internet* ☰*AE, MC, V* ⊙*Closed May–Sept.* ⊙❘*AI.*

¢ 🏨**Hotel Colonial.** This long-running hostel is the best budget option in town, not because of its location (a few blocks from downtown) or its paint job (bright pink)—but because Maria Clark, the diminutive proprietor, is an absolute treasure. Señora Clark takes care of her backpacker and working-class Argentinean clientele with grandmotherly solicitude. The bathrooms are shared, but never crowded, and there is plenty of hot water. Senora Clark's son and daughter also run budget hotels in town, so if the original Colonial is full she can no doubt find you a place to sleep. **Pros:** Cheap, friendly. **Cons:** Somewhat scruffy, no private baths. ☒*Rivadavía 212, at Urquiza,* ☎*2966/420–020* ⇗*12 rooms* ☰*No credit cards.*

$$$ 🏨**Hotel Santa Cruz.** This recently renovated property is the best hotel in town. Rooms are clean and comfortable, if a little utilitarian. Intimate seating areas, plants, and a friendly staff make the lobby bar a pleasant retreat on a windy day. A new conference room on the fourth floor has panoramic views of the river and downtown. **Pros:** Central location, cozy lobby bar. **Cons:** Rooms lack charm. ☒*Av. Roca 701,* ☎*2966/420–601* ⊕*www.interpatagonia.com/hotelsanta cruz* ✍*htlscruz @infovia.com.ar* ⇗*53 rooms* ⚿*In-hotel: restaurant, parking (no fee), public Wi-Fi* ☰*AE, MC, V* ⊙❘*CP.*

Chilean Lake District

Lake Llanquihue with Mount Osorno Volcano in background, Puerto Varas, Lake District

WORD OF MOUTH

"Last year my wife and I crossed the lakes from Puerto Varas (Chile) to Bariloche (Argentina) on a boat and bus excursion, and enjoyed it very much. Most of the crossing was by boat, very scenic. Don't think crossing by car or by bus would be as nice."

—caldnj

WELCOME TO CHILEAN LAKE DISTRICT

TOP REASONS TO GO

★ **Volcanoes:** Volcán Villarrica and Volcán Osorno are the conical, iconic symbols of the northern and southern Lake District, respectively, but some 50 other volcanoes loom and fume in this region. Not to worry; eruptions are rare.

★ **Stunning Summer Nights:** Southern Chile's austral summer doesn't get more glorious than January and February, when sunsets don't fade until well after 10 PM, and everyone is out dining, shopping, and enjoying the outdoors.

★ **Lakes and Rivers:** The region may sport a long Pacific coastline, but everyone flocks to the inland lakes to swim, sunbathe, kayak, sail, and more. The region also hosts numerous wild rivers that are, among other things, excellent for fly-fishing.

★ **Soothing Hot Springs:** Chile counts some 280 thermal springs, and a good many of the well-operated ones are in the Lake District, the perfect place to pamper yourself after a day of outdoor adventure and sightseeing.

1 **La Araucanía.** It may not be called Los Lagos, but La Araucanía contains some of Chile's most spectacular lake scenery. Several volcanoes, among them Villarrica and Llaima, two of South America's most active, loom over the region. Burgeoning Pucón, on the shore of Lago Villarrica, has become the tourism hub of southern Chile. Other quieter alternatives exist, however. Lago Calafquén, farther south, begins the seven-lake Siete Lagos chain that stretches across the border to Argentina.

2 **Los Lagos.** Los Lagos, the southern half of the Lake District, is a land of snowcapped volcanoes, rolling farmland, and, of course, the shimmering lakes that give the region its name. This landscape is literally a work in progress, as it's part of the so-called Ring of Fire encircling the Pacific Rim. Most of Chile's 55 active volcanoes are here.

Lake Caburgua

GETTING ORIENTED

The Lake District's altitude descends sharply from the towering peaks of the Andes on the Argentine border, to forests and plains, and finally to sea level, all in the space of about 200 km (120 mi). Throughout the region, big volcanoes burst into view alongside the many large lakes and winding rivers. Architecture and gastronomy here are unlike anywhere else in Chile, much of it heavily influenced by the large-scale German colonization of the 1850s and '60s. The Pan-American Highway (Ruta 5) runs straight down the middle, making travel to most places in the region relatively easy. It connects the major cities of Temuco, Osorno, and Puerto Montt, but bypasses Valdivia by 50 km (30 mi). A drive from Temuco to Puerto Montt should take less than four hours. Flying between the hubs is a reasonable option. The region also now has a passenger train connecting Temuco and Puerto Montt, as well as many towns in between.

CHILEAN LAKE DISTRICT PLANNER

When to Go

Most Chileans not on holiday on the Central Coast head here during southern Chile's glorious summer, between December and March. For fishermen, the official fishing season commences the second Friday of November and runs through the first Sunday of May. Visiting during the off-season is no hardship, though, and lodging prices drop dramatically. An increasing number of smog-weary Santiaguinos flee the capital in winter to enjoy the Lake District's brisk, clear air or to ski and snowboard down volcanoes and Andean hills. Just be prepared for wind and rain.

Festivals & Seasonal Events

Summer, with its better weather and ample presence of vacationers, also means festival season in the Lake District. In late January and early February, Semanas Musicales de Frutillar brings together the best in classical music. Villarrica hosts a Muestra Cultural Mapuche in January and February that shows off Mapuche art and music. During the first week of October, Valdivia hosts a first-class, nationally acclaimed international film festival.

Eat Well & Rest Easy

Meat and potatoes characterize the cuisine of this part of southern Chile. The omnipresent *cazuela* (a plate of rice and potatoes with beef or chicken) and *pastel de choclo* (a corn, meat, and vegetable casserole) are solid, hearty meals. Arguably the greatest gifts from the waves of German immigrants were their tasty *küchen,* rich fruit-filled pastries. (Raspberry is a special favorite here.) Sample them during the late-afternoon *onces,* the coffee breaks locals take to tide them over until dinner. The Germans also brought their beer-making prowess to the New World; Valdivia, in particular, is home base to the popular Kunstmann brand.

If you've traveled in Europe, you may feel at home in the Lake District, where most of the lodgings resemble old-world hotels. Many hostelries, even the newly built ones, are constructed in Bavarian-chalet style echoing the region's Germanic heritage. A handful of lodgings—Temuco's Hotel Continental, Pucón's Hotel Antumalal, and Puerto Octay's Hotel Centinela—are also historic landmarks that shouldn't be missed.

Rates usually include a Continental breakfast of coffee, cheese, bread, and jam. Although most of the places listed here stay open all year, call ahead to make sure the owners haven't decided to take a well-deserved vacation during the March–November off-season.

WHAT IT COSTS IN CHILEAN PESOS (IN THOUSANDS)				
¢	$	$$	$$$	$$$$
RESTAURANTS				
under 3 pesos	3 pesos–5 pesos	5 pesos–8 pesos	8 pesos–11 pesos	over 11 pesos
HOTELS				
under 15 pesos	15 pesos–45 pesos	45 pesos–75 pesos	75 pesos–105 pesos	over 105 pesos

Restaurant prices are based on the median main course price at dinner. Hotel prices are for a double room in high season, excluding tax.

Adventure Travel

Awash in rivers, mountains, forests, gorges, and its namesake lakes, this part of the country is Chile's outdoors capital. Outfitters traditionally are concentrated in the northern resort town of Pucón and the southern Puerto Varas, but firms up and down this 400-km-long (240-mi-long) slice of Chile can rent you equipment or guide your excursions.

The increasing popularity of such excursions means that everybody and their brother and sister seem to want a slice of the adventure küchen. Quality varies widely, especially in everybody's-an-outfitter destinations such as Pucón. Ask questions about safety and guide-to-client ratios. (A few unscrupulous businesses might take 20 climbers up the Villarrica volcano with a single guide.) Also, be brutally frank with yourself about your own capabilities: Are you really in shape for rappelling? Or is bird-watching more your style? This is nature at its best and sometimes at its most powerful.

Sample Itinerary

On your arrival into **Temuco,** spend the afternoon shopping for Mapuche handicrafts at the city's Mercado Municipal. Rise early the next morning and drive to **Villarrica** or **Pucón,** where you can spend the day exploring a beautiful area, maybe taking a dip in one of the nearby thermal springs. The next day take a hike up Volcán Villarrica. Day four means a drive south to **Valdivia,** where you can spend the afternoon visiting the modern-art and history museums on Isla Teja. Catch an evening cruise along the Río Valdivia. Rise early the next day and drive to the Bavarian-style village of **Frutillar** on Lago Llanquihue. Visit the Museo Colonial Alemán and wind up the afternoon partaking of the Chilean onces ritual with a cup of coffee and küchen. Head for **Puerto Varas** the next day for a thrilling rafting excursion on the nearby Río Petrohué. Save **Puerto Montt** for your final day, and spend the afternoon shopping for handicrafts in the Angelmó market stalls. Finish with a seafood dinner at one of the market's lively restaurants.

Getting Here & Around

Air Travel. None of the Lake District's airports—Osorno, Puerto Montt, Temuco, and Valdivia—receives international flights; flying here from another country means connecting in Santiago. Of the four cities, Puerto Montt has the greatest frequency of domestic flights.

Bus Travel. There's no shortage of bus companies traveling the Pan-American Highway (Ruta 5) from Santiago south to the Lake District. The buses, which are very comfortable, have assigned seating and aren't too crowded. Tickets may be purchased in advance.

Car Travel. It's easier to see more of the Lake District if you have your own vehicle. The Pan-American Highway through the region is a well-maintained four-lane toll highway. Bring plenty of small bills for the frequent toll booths you'll encounter.

Train Travel. Chile's State Railway Company, the Empresa de los Ferrocarriles del Estado, has daily service southward from Santiago's Alameda station as far as Temuco on its Terra Sur trains. Trains run daily all year; the overnight trip takes about nine hours. From Temuco, you can board another train south to Puerto Montt and several towns in between. Shuttle-bus service to and from Pucón and Villarrica runs in conjunction with the trains.

6

Updated
by Jimmy
Langman

AS YOU TRAVEL THE WINDING road of the Lake District, the snow-capped shoulders of volcanoes emerge, mysteriously disappear, then materialize again, peeping through trees or towering above valleys. The sometimes difficult journey through breathtaking mountain passes is rewarded by views of a glistening lake, vibrant and blue. You might be tempted to belt out "The hills are alive . . . " With densely forested national parks, a dozen large lakes, easy access to transportation and facilities, and predominantly small, family-run lodgings, this area has come pretty close to perfecting tourism.

The Lake District is the historic homeland of Chile's indigenous Mapuche people, who revolted against the early Spanish colonists in 1598, driving them out of the region. They kept foreigners out of the area for nearly three centuries. Though small pockets of the Lake District were controlled by Chile after it won its independence in 1818, most viewed the forbidding region south of the Río Bío Bío as a separate country. After a treaty ended the last Mapuche war in 1881, Santiago began to recruit waves of German, Austrian, and Swiss immigrants to settle the so-called "empty territory" and offset indigenous domination.

LA ARAUCANÍA

La Araucanía is the historic home of the Araucano, or Mapuche, culture. The Spanish both feared and respected the Mapuche. This nomadic society was a moving target that the Spaniards found impossible to defeat. Beginning with the 1598 battle against European settlers, the Mapuche kept control of the region for almost 300 years. After numerous peace agreements failed, a treaty signed near Temuco ended hostilities in 1881 and paved the way for the German, Swiss, and Austrian immigration that would transform the face of the Lake District.

TEMUCO

675 km (405 mi) south of Santiago on the Pan-American Hwy., Ruta 5.

This northern gateway to the Lake District was the setting for a segment in 2004's *The Motorcycle Diaries,* a film depicting Che Guevara's prerevolutionary travels through South America in the early 1950s. But with its office towers and shopping malls, today's Temuco would hardly be recognizable to Guevara. The city has a more Latin flavor than the communities farther south. (It could be the warmer weather and the palm trees swaying in the pleasant central park.) It's also an odd juxtaposition of modern architecture and indigenous markets, of traditionally clad Mapuche women darting across the street and business executives talking on cell phones, but, oddly enough, it all works.

GETTING HERE & AROUND

At least a dozen bus lines serve Temuco; it's an obligatory stop on the long haul between Santiago and Puerto Montt. The Manquehue airport is 6 km (4 mi) southwest of town, and has daily connections to Santiago and other Chilean cities. At the airport, in addition to taxis,

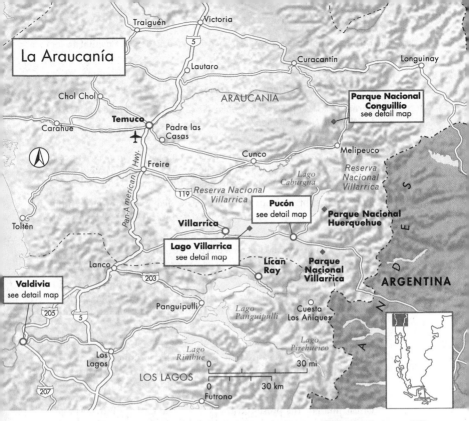

several transfer services can take you into town. If you're going to Villarrica or Pucón, you'll probably come through here as well. The Pan-American Highway, Ruta 5, runs through the city, and is paved, but several of the outlying roads connecting Temuco to smaller, rural towns are two lanes and unpaved. Be careful on such roads, as the Chilean auto accident rate due to passing cars is not very good.

CONAF (⊠ *Bilbao 931* ☎ *45/298–100*) administers Chile's national parks and provides maps and other information about them. In summer it also organizes hikes in Parque Nacional Conguillío. The agency is strict about permits to ascend the nearby volcanoes, so expect to show evidence of your climbing ability and experience.

ESSENTIALS

BUS **Buses JAC** (⊠ *Corner of Balmaceda and Aldunate* ☎ *45/465–500*).**Cruz del Sur** (⊠ *Terminal de Buses, Av. Vicente Pérez Rosales 1609* ☎ *45/730–310*). **Temuco** (⊠ *Av. Rudecindo Ortega* ☎ *45/257–904*). **Tur-Bus** (⊠ *Lagos 538* ☎ *45/278–161*).

CURRENCY **Germaniatour** (⊠ *Manuel Montt 942, Local 5* ☎ *45/958–080*).

INTERNET **Net & Coffee** (⊠ *Portales 873* ☎ *45/940–001*).

MAIL **Correos de Chile** (⊠ *Av. Diego Portales 801*).

MEDICAL   **Farmacias Ahumada** (⊠ *Av. Alemania 505* ☎ *45/246–992*). **Hospital de Temuco** (⊠ *Manuel Montt 115* ☎ *45/212–525*).

RENTAL CARS   **Avis** (⊠ *Vicuña Mackenna 448* ☎ *45/237–575*). **Budget** (⊠ *Vicuña Mackenna 399* ☎ *45/232–715*). **Hertz** (⊠ *Las Heras 999* ☎ *45/318–585*).

VISITOR INFO   **Sernatur** (⊠ *Claro Solar and Bulnes* ☎ *45/312–857*). **Temuco Tourist Office** (⊠ *Mercado Municipal* ☎ *45/203–345*).

WHAT TO SEE

Bustling **Plaza Aníbal Pinto,** Temuco's central square, is ringed with imported palm trees. A monument to the 300-year struggle between the Mapuche and the Spaniards sits in the center.

The small subterranean **Galería de Arte** displays rotating exhibits by Chilean artists. ⊠ *Plaza Aníbal Pinto* ☎ *45/236–785* ☞ *Free* ☉ *Mon.– Sat. 10–8, Sun. 1–8.*

The city's modern **Catedral de Temuco** sits on the northwest corner of the central square, flanked by an office tower emblazoned with a cross.

Lined with lime and oak trees, a shady secondary square called **Plaza Teodoro Schmidt** lies six blocks north of the Plaza Aníbal Pinto. It's ruled over by the 1906 Iglesia Santa Trinidad, an Anglican church that is one of the city's oldest surviving structures.

Housed in a 1924 mansion, the **Museo Regional de la Araucanía** covers the history of the area. It has an eclectic collection of artifacts and relics, including musical instruments, utensils, and the country's best collection of indigenous jewelry. Upstairs, exhibits document the Mapuche people's three-century struggle to keep control of their land. Unfortunately, the presentation glorifies the Central European colonization of this area as the *pacificación de la Araucanía* (taming of the Araucanía territories). But you get a reasonably good Spanish-language introduction to Mapuche history, art, and culture. ⊠ *Av. Alemania 84* ☎ *45/730–062* ☞ *600 pesos* ☉ *Weekdays 9–5:45.*

★   Author Pablo Neruda was Chile's most famous train buff. (Neruda spent his childhood in Temuco and his father was a rail worker.) Accordingly, the city has transformed its old rail yard into the **Museo Nacional Ferroviario Pablo Neruda,** a well-laid-out museum documenting Chile's rail history and dedicated to the author's memory. Thirteen locomotives (one diesel and 12 steam) and nine train carriages are housed in the round engine building. Scattered among the exhibits are snippets from Neruda's writings. "Trains were dreaming in the station, defenseless, sleeping, without locomotives," reads one wistful reflection. Exhibits are labeled in Spanish, but an English-speaking guide is on hand. The museum lies a bit off the beaten path, but if trains fascinate you, as they did Neruda, it's worth the short taxi ride from downtown. Twice-monthly tourist rail excursions to Valdivia use the museum's restored 1940 steam locomotive. ⊠ *Av. Barros Arana 565* ☎ *45/973–940* ☞ *1,000 pesos* ☉ *Tues.–Sun. 9–6.*

The imposing **Monumento Natural Cerro Ñielol** is the hillside site where the 1881 treaty between the Mapuche and the Chilean army was signed, allowing for the city of Temuco to be established. Trails bloom with bright red *copihues* (a bell-like flower with lush green foliage), Chile's national flower, in autumn (March–May). The monument, not far from downtown, is part of Chile's national park system. ⊠ *Av. Arturo Prat, 5 blocks north of Plaza Teodoro Schmidt* 📱*1,000 pesos* ⊙ *Jan.–Mar., daily 8 AM–11 PM; Apr.–Nov., daily 8:30–12:30 and 2:30–6.*

The small **Museo de Chol Chol** in Temuco exhibits a collection of animal-shaped ceramics and textiles with bold rhomboid and zigzag designs—both are distinctively Mapuche specialties—as well as old black-and-white photographs. A *fogón*, the traditional cooking pit, graces the center of the museum. ⊠ *Balmaceda s/n* 📞*45/613–350* 📱*300 pesos* ⊙ *Tues.–Sun. 9–6.*

WHERE TO EAT

$$ ✗ **Centro Español.** The basement dining room of Centro Español, an association that promotes Spanish culture in Temuco, is open for lunch and dinner. You choose from four or five rotating prix-fixe menus. There will always be something Spanish, something seafood, and something meaty to choose from. *Jamón de Serrano*, a salty type of ham, is a specialty. ⊠ *Av. Bulnes 483* 📞*45/210–343* 🍽 *AE, DC, MC, V.*

$ ✗ **Confitería Central.** Coffee and homemade pastries are the specialties of this café, but sandwiches and other simple dishes are also available. Steaming-hot empanadas are served on Sunday and holidays, and during the week you'll swear all of Temuco stops by for lunch among the clattering of dishes and the army of waitresses. ⊠ *Av. Bulnes 442* 📞*45/210–083* 🍽 *DC, MC, V.*

$$ ✗ **El Fogón.** Decorated with primary colors—yellow walls, red tablecloths, and blue dishes—this place certainly stands out in pastel-hue Temuco. The Chilean-style *parrillada*, or grilled beef, is the specialty of the house. Barbecue here has subtler spices than its better-known Argentine counterpart. The friendly owners will gladly take the time to explain the menu to the uninitiated. Even though it's close to downtown, you should splurge on a cab if you're coming to this dark street at night. ⊠ *Aldunate 288* 📞*45/737–061* 🍽 *No credit cards.*

$ ✗ **Mercado Municipal.** In the central market around the produce stalls are small stands offering such typical Chilean meals as cazuela and pastel de choclo. Many have actually taken on the trappings of sit-down restaurants, and a few even have air-conditioning. The complex closes at 8 in summer and 6 the rest of the year, so late-night dining is not an option. ⊠ *Manuel Rodríguez 960* 📞*No phone* 🍽 *No credit cards.*

$$$ ✗ **La Pampa.** Wealthy locals frequent this modern steak house for its huge, delicious cuts of beef and the best *papas fritas* (french fries) in Temuco. Although most Chilean restaurants douse any kind of meat with a creamy sauce, this is one of the few exceptions: the entrées are served with just the simplest of seasonings. ⊠ *Caupolicán 0155* 📞*45/329–999* 🍴*Reservations essential* 🍽 *AE, DC, MC, V* ⊙ *No dinner Sun.*

WHERE TO STAY

$–$$ 🏨 **Don Eduardo Hotel.** Orange inside and out, this pleasant nine-story hotel is made up entirely of cozy furnished apartments, with comfortable chairs and dining areas. All have two or three bedrooms and

The People of the Land

Mapuche woman

The Mapuche profoundly affected the history of southern Chile. For almost 300 years this indigenous group fought to keep colonial, then Chilean powers out of their land. The Spanish referred to these people as the Araucanos, from a word in the Quechua language meaning "brave and valiant warriors." In their own Mapudungun language, today spoken by some 400,000 people, the word *Mapuche* means "people of the land." In colonial times only the Spanish missionaries seemed to grasp what this meant. "There are no people in the world," one of them wrote, "who so love and value the land where they were born."

Chilean schoolchildren learning about the Mapuche are likely to read about Lautaro, a feared and respected young chief whose military tactics were instrumental in driving out the Spanish. He cunningly adopted a know-thy-enemy strategy that proved tremendously successful in fending off the colonists. Students are less likely to hear about the tightly knit family structure or nomadic lifestyle of the Mapuche. Even the region's two museums dedicated to Mapuche culture, in Temuco and Valdivia, traditionally focused on the three-century war with the Spaniards. They toss around terms like *pacificación* (meaning "to pacify" or "to tame") to describe the waves of European immigrants who settled in the Lake District at the end of the 1800s, the beginning of the end of Mapuche dominance in the region.

Life has been difficult for the Mapuche since the signing of a peace treaty in 1881. Some 200,000 Mapuche today are living on 3,000 *reducciones* (literally meaning "reductions"), operated much like the system of reservations in the United States. Other Mapuche have migrated to the cities, in particular fast-growing Temuco, in search of employment.

A resurgence in Mapuche pride has taken several forms, some peaceful, some militant. Mapuche demonstrations in Temuco are now commonplace, many calling attention to deplorable conditions on the reducciones. Some are seeking the return of their land, while others are fighting against encroachment. News reports occasionally recount attacks and counterattacks between indigenous groups and farmers in remote rural areas far off the beaten tourist path.

Awareness of Mapuche history is increasing. (Latest census figures show that about 1 million of Chile's population of 15 million can claim some Mapuche ancestry.)

There is also a newfound interest in the Mapuche language and its seven dialects. Mapudungun poetry movingly describes the sadness and dilemma of integration into modern life and of becoming lost in the anonymity of urban life. Never before really understood by others who shared their land, the Mapuche may finally make their cause known.

–Jeffrey Van Fleet

kitchenettes. Business travelers appreciate the desks and shelves. An eager-to-please staff tends to your needs. **Pros:** Work areas in rooms, spacious. **Cons:** No gym, no safe in room. ⊠*Bello 755* ☎*45/214–133* 📠*45/215–554* ⊕*www.hoteldoneduardo.cl* ➘*46 rooms, 14 suites* ⟁*In-room: no a/c, refrigerator (some), Wi-Fi. In-hotel: restaurant, room service, public Internet, laundry service, public Wi-Fi, parking, no-smoking rooms* ☰*AE, DC, MC, V* ⦿*BP.*

$$ 🖭 **Holiday Inn Express.** If you're looking for something uniquely Chilean about the place, you won't find it, but you will find all the U.S.-style amenities, including the do-it-yourself breakfast for which the chain is known. You're a ways from downtown, but it's a good option if you have a vehicle. **Pros:** Modern, comfortable. **Cons:** Relatively far from the center of Temuco. ⊠*Av. Rudecindo Ortega 1800* ☎*45/223–300* 📠*45/224–100* ⊕*www.hiexpress.com* ➘*62 rooms* ⟁*In-room: no a/c, safe, Wi-Fi. In-hotel: pool, gym, laundry service, parking, no-smoking rooms* ☰*AE, MC, V* ⦿*BP.*

$ 🖭 **Hotel Aitué.** The exterior is unimposing; in fact, its covered drive-up entry, set back from the road, might cause you to drive right past it. Once you're inside, though, you'll find that this small, pleasant business-class hotel has bright, airy rooms. They're on the smallish side, but comfortable, and come with refrigerators and music systems. **Pros:** Well-equipped rooms, comfortable. **Cons:** Hard to find. ⊠*Antonio Varas 1048* ☎*45/211–917* 📠*45/212–608* ⊕*www.hotelaitue.cl* ➘*35 rooms* ⟁*In-room: no a/c, safe, refrigerator, Ethernet, Wi-Fi. In-hotel: no elevator, laundry service, public Internet, parking, no-smoking rooms* ☰*AE, DC, MC, V* ⦿*CP.*

$ ✕🖭 **Hotel Continental.** If you appreciate faded elegance and don't mind
★ an uneven floorboard or two, some peeling paint, and few conveniences, the 1890 Continental is for you. The lobby has leather furniture, antique bronze lamps, and handsome *alerce* and *raulí* (native wood) trims. Rooms have hardwood floors and lofty ceilings. The hotel has hosted Nobel laureates Pablo Neruda and Gabriela Mistral, and former president Salvador Allende. The restaurant ($$) serves delicious French cuisine. Good choices include the steak au poivre and the salade niçoise. **Pros:** A hotel with character, good location, great food. **Cons:** Rooms feel cold and damp, old furniture. ⊠*Antonio Varas 708* ☎*45/238–973* ⊕*www.turismochile.cl/continental/* ➘*40 rooms, 20 with bath* ⟁*In-room: no a/c, no TV (some). In-hotel: restaurant, bar, no elevator, parking* ☰*AE, DC, MC, V* ⦿*CP.*

$$ ✕🖭 **Hotel Frontera.** This lovely old hotel is really two in one, with *nuevo* (new) and *clásico* (classic) wings facing each other across Avenida Bulnes. Tastefully decorated rooms have double-pane windows to keep out the street noise. Opt for the less expensive rooms in the newer wing—they're nicer anyway. La Taberna, the downstairs restaurant on the clásico side ($$), has excellent steak and seafood dining. An orchestra plays and people dance on weekends. **Pros:** Centrally located, good restaurant, nice rooms: **Cons:** No Wi-Fi in rooms. ⊠*Av. Bulnes 733–726* ☎*45/200–400* ⊕*www.hotelfrontera.cl* ➘*90 rooms, 10 suites* ⟁*In-room: no a/c, Ethernet (some), refrigerator, safe (some). In-hotel: restaurant, room service, bar, laundry service, refrigerator, executive floor, public Wi-Fi, parking* ☰*AE, DC, MC, V* ⦿*BP.*

$$–$$$ ⊞**Hotel Terraverde.** Temuco's most luxurious lodging combines all the comforts of a modern hotel with the style of a hunting lodge. The dramatic, glass-enclosed spiral staircase leads off the stone-wall lobby with its huge fireplace and has a view of Cerro Ñielol. Cheerful rooms have lovely wood furnishings. Rates include a huge breakfast buffet, a nice change from the roll and coffee served at many other lodgings in the region. It's part of Chile's Panamericana Hoteles chain. **Pros:** Breakfast buffet, luxurious. **Cons:** Lacks intimacy of smaller hotels. ⊠ *Av. Arturo Prat 220* ☎ *45/239–999, 2/234–9610 in Santiago* ⊕ *www.panamericana hoteles.cl* ⋑ *64 rooms, 6 suites* ⚑ *In-room: no a/c, safe, refrigerator, Ethernet, Wi-Fi. In-hotel: restaurant, room service, bar, pool, laundry service, public Internet, airport shuttle, no-smoking rooms, parking* ⊟ *AE, DC, MC, V* ⍾⍾*BP.*

$ ⊞**Hotel Turismo.** Originally established as a budget accommodation, this three-story hotel retains its bland facade. The interior has been upgraded, however, with a comfortable lobby and rooms with their own music systems, cushy beds, and tables and chairs. **Pros:** Comfortable, nice beds. **Cons:** Lime-green color scheme. ⊠ *Av. Lynch 563* ☎☎ *45/951–090* ⊕ *www.hotelturismotemuco.cl* ⋑ *30 rooms* ⚑ *In-room: no a/c, safe, refrigerator. In-hotel: restaurant, bar, laundry service, parking, public-Wi-Fi* ⊟ *AE, DC, MC, V.*

NIGHTLIFE

Temuco has several universities and has a thriving nightlife. **Geronimo** (⊠ *Antonio Varas 983* ☎ *45/230–041*) is in the center of the city, and has live music mostly oriented toward young adults. **Taberna del Bucanero** (⊠ *Bulnes 315* ☎ *45/214–468*), a pub and disco with a pirate theme, features especially good mixed drinks. **Jalisco Tex-Mex** (⊠ *Hochstetter 435* ☎ *45/243–254*) is a pub-restaurant with Mexican food and lively margaritas.

SHOPPING

Temuco is ground central for the Mapuche Nation. Here you will find the gamut of Mapuche Indian handicrafts, from carpets to sweaters to sculpture. The **Mercado Municipal** (⊠ *Manuel Rodríguez 960* ☎ *No phone*) is one of the best places in the country to find Mapuche woolen ponchos, pullovers, and blankets. The interior of the 1930 structure has been extensively remodeled, and is quite open. The low-key artisan vendors share the complex with butchers, fishmongers, and fruit sellers. There is no bargaining, but the prices are fair. It opens daily at 8, but closes around 3 on Sunday.

A little more rough-and-tumble than the Mercado Municipal is the **Feria Libre** (⊠ *Barros Arana at Miraflores*). You can bargain hard with the Mapuche vendors who sell their crafts and produce in the blocks surrounding the railroad station and bus terminal. Leave the camera behind, as the vendors aren't happy about being photographed. It's open from about 7 to 2 Monday–Saturday.

Casa de la Mujer Mapuche (⊠ *Portales 1190* ☎ *45/233–886*), an indigenous women's center, lets you shop for textiles, ponchos, and jewelry in its display room, with a minimum of fuss. (The organization even

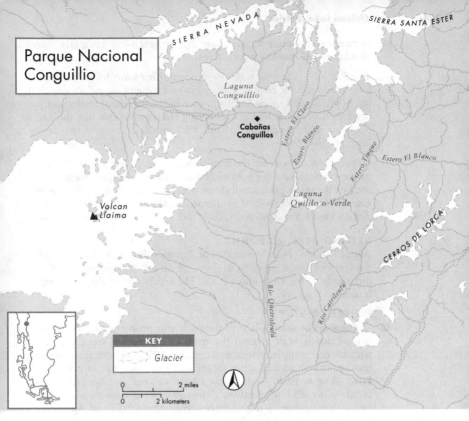

Parque Nacional Conguillío

SIERRA NEVADA

SIERRA SANTA ESTER

Laguna Conguillío

Cabañas Conguillos

Estero El Claro

Estero Blanco

Estero Tisque

Estero El Blanco

Volcán Llaima

Laguna Quililo o Verde

CERROS DE LORCA

Río Quetralcufú

Río Catrileufú

KEY
Glacier

0   2 miles
0   2 kilometers

handles catalog sales.) Proceeds support social development programs. It's open weekdays, 9–1.

Across the Río Cautín from Temuco is the suburb of **Padre Las Casas** (⊠ *2 km [1 mi] southeast of Temuco*), a Mapuche community whose center is populated by artisan vendors selling locally crafted woodwork, textiles, and pottery under the auspices of the town's rural development program. You can purchase crafts here weekdays 9–5. **Farmacia Herbolaria Mapuche Makewelawen** (⊠ *Aldunate 245* ☏ *45/951–620*) offers ancestral Mapuche remedies for everything from a simple head cold to cancers to improving sexual performance.

PARQUE NACIONAL CONGUILLÍO

126 km (78 mi) northeast of Temuco.

Volcán Llaima, which erupted as recently as 1994 and has shown constant, but not dangerous, low levels of activity since 2002, is the brooding centerpiece of Parque Nacional Conguillío. The 10,200-foot monster, one of the continent's most active volcanoes, has altered the landscape—much of the park's southern portion is a moonscape of hardened lava flow. But in the 610-square-km (235-square-mi) park's northern sector there are thousands of umbrella-like araucaria pines, also known as monkey puzzle trees.

The Sierra Nevada trail is the most popular for short hikes. The three-hour trek begins at park headquarters on Laguna Conguillío, continuing northeast to Laguna Captrén. One of the inaugural sections of the Sendero de Chile, a hiking and biking trail, passes through the park. Modeled on the Appalachian Trail, the project will eventually span the length of the country.

Heavy snow can cut off the area in winter, so November to March is the best time to visit the park's eastern sector. Conguillío's western sector, Los Paraguas has a small ski center. ⊠ *Entrances at Melipeuco and Curacautín* ☎ *45/736–200 in Temuco* 🖃 *2,500 pesos* ⊙ *Dec.–Mar., daily 8 AM–10 PM; Apr.–Nov., daily 8–5.*

GETTING HERE & AROUND

About 126 km (78 mi) northeast of Temuco, the roads are paved until the town of Curacautin; from there it's 40 km (25 mi) on gravel and dirt roads to the Conguillío Park. The roads are marked with signs leading to the park.

WHERE TO STAY

$–$$ 🖺 **Cabañas Conguillío.** Close to the park, this property rents basic four-person cabins built around the trunks of araucaria trees. All come with kitchen utensils, stoves, and cooking fuel. Also here are an on-site restaurant and a small store where you can stock up on provisions. **Pros:** Close to park. **Cons:** Closed most of year. ⊠ *Laguna Conguillío* ☎ *45/581–253* 🛏 *6 cabins* ⚴ *In-room: no a/c, no phone, no TV. In-hotel: restaurant, parking* 🖃 *No credit cards* ⊙ *Closed Apr.–Nov.*

VILLARRICA

87 km (52 mi) southeast of Temuco via the Pan-American Hwy. and a paved road southeast from Freire.

Villarrica was founded in 1552, but the Mapuche wars prevented extensive settlement of the area until the early 20th century. Founded by the Spanish conqueror Pedro de Valdivia, it was a Spanish fortress built primarily to serve as a base for gold mining in the area. The fortress's mission succeeded up until 1599, when the Mapuche staged an uprising here and destroyed the original town. On December 31, 1882, a historic meeting between more than 300 Mapuche chiefs and the Chilean government was held in Putue, a few kilometers outside of the town. The next day, the town was refounded. Today this pleasant town of about 40,000 people, situated on the lake of the same name, is in one of the loveliest, least-spoiled areas of the southern Andes, and has stunning views of the Villarrica and Llaima volcanoes. To Villarrica's eternal chagrin, it lives in the shadow of Pucón, a flashier neighbor several miles down the road. But Villarrica has some wonderful hotels that won't give you a case of high-season sticker shock. Well-maintained roads and convenient public transportation make the town a good base for exploring the area.

OUTDOOR ADVENTURES AT A GLANCE

Pucón. Located near a variety of lakes, rivers, forests, and parks, and just 20 minutes from the 9,341-foot-high Villarrica Volcano, Pucón is without doubt one of Chile's top spots for adventure sports. The (active) volcano itself has become an obligatory climb for the many nature- and adventure-seeking tourists who come to Chile. In winter, the volcano is a favorite spot for skiing and snowboarding. Nearby Trancura River is a rafting, kayaking, and fishing paradise. Villarrica Lake and Calburga Lake are two outstanding lakes for fishing, swimming, kayaking, and water-skiing. There are several worthy nature hikes close to Pucón, featuring some of the most beautiful forests in Chile, including the Cani Sanctuary, Huerquehue National Park, and Conguillío National Park.

Puerto Varas. This small, tranquil town on the edge of Lake Llanquihue in the southern Lake District is one of Chile's most popular destinations for adventure-sports enthusiasts. The lake itself frequently boasts strong winds suitable for first-class windsurfing and sailing. At Canopy Lodge of Cascadas, the largest canopy area in Chile, not far from Puerto Varas, you can zip-line through canyons and forest 230 feet high. The Petrohué River offers the opportunity for rafting, and along with numerous other rivers in the area, great fishing. Biking alongside the lake is a popular trip, too. Vicente Pérez Rosales Park and Alerce Andino Park have good trails for hiking and camping. And there is the Osorno Volcano for treks, skiing, and snowboarding. Some two hours from Puerto Varas is Cochamó Valley, a fantastic spot that has drawn comparisons to Yosemite Park in California for its high granite mountain cliffs, waterfalls, and overall landscape. This is a rock-climbing paradise and a hiker's dream, with exceptional horseback-riding trails, too. Just south from Cochamó is Puelo, a river valley in the shadow of the Andes mountains. It's the launching point for some of Chile's best fly-fishing, in addition to great hiking and other outdoors action.

Valdivia. A complex network of 14 rivers cuts through the landscape in and around this southern Chilean city, forming dozens of small islands. About 160 km (99 mi) of the river system are navigable in waters ranging from 16½ to 66 feet deep. That makes ideal territory for kayaking, canoeing, and sailing, among other water sports. Valdivia is also near the Pacific coast. Curinanco beach, 25 km (15½ mi) from Valdivia, is considered a prime spot for fishing. Then there are the intact coastal temperate rain forests on the outskirts of town, secluded areas with beautiful scenery for long hikes and camping trips. At the private nature park Oncol, just 22 km (14 mi) from Valdivia, are hiking trails and an 2,854-foot tree-top canopy course.

Osorno. Osorno itself is no outdoor wonder, but within an hour's drive you can reach Puyehue National Park, one of Chile's best hiking areas, and several lakes for fishing and boating, such as Rupanco. To the west, there is horseback riding, fishing, and hiking along the Pacific coast and at the indigenous network of parks Mapu Lahual, which is managed by Huilluiche Indian communities.

6

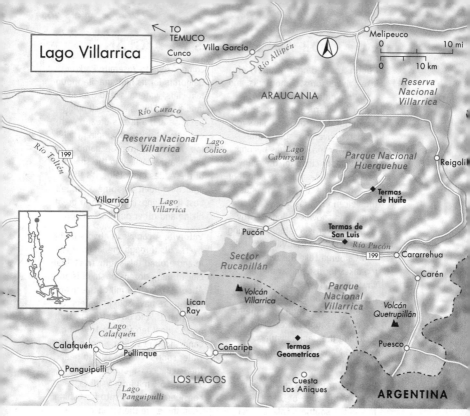

GETTING HERE & AROUND

Located southeast of Temuco, Villarrica can be reached by a paved, two-lane road, from the town of Freire, or farther to the south, from Loncoche. For about 2,000 pesos, buses leave every hour from the Temuco bus terminal and arrive in Villarrica about one hour later.

ESSENTIALS

BUS   **Buses JAC** (✉ *Bilbao 610* ☎ *45/467–777*).

CURRENCY   **Christopher Exchange** (✉ *Pedro Valdivia 1033*). **Turcamb** (✉ *Camilo Henriquez 576*).

INTERNET   **Central de Llamadas** (✉ *Camilo Henriquez 567* ☎ *45/413–640*).

MEDICAL   **Hospital** (✉ *San Martin 460* ☎ *45/411–169*).

RENTAL CARS   **Hertz** (✉ *Picarte 640* ☎ *45/218–316*). **Renta Car Castillo** (✉ *Anfion Munoz 415* ☎ *45/411–618*).

VISITOR INFO   **Villarrica Tourist Office** (✉ *Pedro de Valdivia 1070* ☎ *45/206–618*).

WHAT TO SEE

Feria Mapuche is a fine market featuring some of the best local artisans that make Mapuche handicrafts. You'll find all kinds of items, from sweaters and ponchos to wooden figurines. ⊠ *Corner of Pedro de Valdivia with Julio Zebers* ☉ *Jan. and Feb., daily 9–noon.*

The municipal museum, **Museo Histórico y Arqueológico de Villarrica,** displays an impressive collection of Mapuche ceramics, masks, leather, and jewelry. A replica of a ruca graces the front yard. It's made of thatch so tightly entwined that it's impermeable to rain. ⊠ *Pedro de Valdivia 1050* ☏ *45/415–706* 💲 *200 pesos* ☉ *Jan. and Feb., Mon.–Sat. 9–1 and 6–10; Mar.–Dec., Mon.–Sat. 9–1 and 3–7:30.*

OUTDOOR ACTIVITIES

The friendly, knowledgeable folks at **Flor del Lago** (⊠ *Camino a Pedregoso, Km 9* ☏ *45/415–455* ⊕ *www.flordellago.cl*) will take you on half- or full-day horseback-riding excursions in the forests surrounding Lago Villarrica.

WHERE TO EAT

$$ ✕ **Café 2001.** For a filling sandwich, a homemade küchen, and an espresso or cappuccino brewed from freshly ground beans, this is the place to stop in Villarrica. Pull up around a table in front or slip into one of the quieter booths by the fireplace in the back. The *lomito completo* sandwich—with a slice of pork, avocado, sauerkraut, tomato, and mayonnaise—is one of the best in the south. ⊠ *Camillo Henríquez 379* ☏ *45/411–470* ▭ *AE, DC, MC, V.*

$$ ✕ **La Cava de Roble.** This is a great, elegant grill with exotic and traditional types of meat and an extensive wine list. One standout dish: deer in cranberry sauce, with quinoa, toasted almonds, cabbage, and spinach. ⊠ *Valentin Letelier 658* ☏ *45/416–446* ▭ *AE, DC, MC, V.*

$ ✕ **El Rey de Marisco.** You'll find friendly service and assorted seafood dishes here, such as trout and clams with Parmesan cheese. If you can, call ahead of time to reserve a table with a view of the lake. ⊠ *Valentin Letelier 1030* ☏ *45/412–093* ▭ *AE, DC, MC, V.*

$ ✕ **The Travellers.** Martin Golian and Juan Pereira met by happenstance, and decided to open a place serving food from their homelands—and a few other countries. The result is one or two dishes from Germany, Thailand, China, Italy, Mexico, and many countries in between. While you chow down on an enchilada, your companions might be having spaghetti with meatballs or sweet-and-sour pork. Dining on the front lawn under umbrella-covered tables is the best option on a summer evening. ⊠ *Valentín Letelier 753* ☏ *45/413–617* ▭ *AE, DC, MC, V.*

WHERE TO STAY

$$ **Hostería de la Colina.** The American owners of this hostería, Glen **Fodor'sChoice** and Beverly Aldrich, provide attentive service and special little touches ★ like homemade ice cream. Rooms in the half-century-old main house are a mix of large and small, with carpets and/or hardwood floors, all tastefully decorated with wood furnishings. Two hillside cottages are carpeted and wood paneled and have private patios. There's a hot tub heated by a wood-burning stove, and a serene *vivero* (greenhouse) and

garden that attracts birds. The terrace has stupendous views of Lago Villarrica. **Pros:** Homemade ice cream, friendly service. **Cons:** No TV. ✉ *Las Colinas 115, Casilla 382* 🖨🖨*45/411–503* ⊕*www.hosteriadela colina.com* ◄*10 rooms, 2 cabins* △*In-room: no a/c, no phone, no TV. In-hotel: bar, restaurant, room service, water sports, bicycles, laundry service, public Wi-Fi, parking* ⊟*AE, DC, MC, V* ⦿|*BP.*

$$ 🏨**Hotel El Ciervo.** Villarrica's oldest hotel is in a modest house on a quiet street. Inside are elegant details such as wrought-iron fixtures and wood-burning fireplaces. Spacious rooms, some with fireplaces, have huge beds and sparkling bathrooms. Just outside are a lovely pool and a secluded patio. Rates include an enormous German breakfast with loads of fruit, muesli, and fresh milk. El Ciervo also has all-inclusive seven-day tour packages. **Pros:** Spacious rooms. **Cons:** A bit plain. ✉ *General Körner 241* 🖨*45/411–215* ⊕*www.hotelelciervo.cl* ◄*13 rooms* △*In-room: no a/c, Wi-Fi. In-hotel: restaurant, bar, room service, pool, laundry service, public Internet, public Wi-Fi, no elevator, parking, no-smoking rooms* ⊟*AE, DC, MC, V* ⦿|*BP.*

$$ 🏨**El Parque.** You can take in the commanding views of Lago Villarrica from just about anywhere at this 70-year-old, rustic and quaint retreat—the comfy lobby, the sitting area, the restaurant, or the warmly colored guest rooms. Eleven modern cabins amble down the hill to a private beach and dock. Each cabin, which accommodates two to eight people, comes with a kitchen, fireplace, and terrace. You are on your own here, but lots of personalized attention is yours for the asking. **Pros:** Views of lake, comfortable. **Cons:** Outside of main towns of Pucón and Villarrica. ✉ *Camino Villarrica–Pucón, Km 2.5* 🖨*45/411–120* 🖨*45/411–090* ⊕*www.hotelelparque.cl* ◄*8 rooms, 10 cabins* △*In-room: no a/c, Wi-Fi. In-hotel: restaurant, bar, room service, tennis court, pool, beachfront, laundry service, no elevator, public Wi-Fi, parking, no-smoking rooms* ⊟*AE, DC, MC, V* ⦿|*BP.*

$$$$ 🏨**Villarrica Park Lake Hotel.** This sumptuous old European spa with modern touches is the perfect mix of old-world plush and clean, uncluttered design. There's ample use of hardwood in the bright, spacious common area and the rooms—each with its own balcony and lake view—that descend down a hill toward Lago Villarrica. **Pros:** Lake view, upscale. **Cons:** Expensive, halfway between Pucón and Villarrica. ✉ *13 km (8 mi) east of Villarrica on the road to Pucón* 🖨*45/450–000, 2/207–7070 in Santiago* 🖨*45/450–202, 2/207–7020 in Santiago* ⊕*www.vplh.cl/* ◄*70 rooms, 11 suites* △*In-room: safe, refrigerator, Ethernet. In-hotel: restaurant, room service, bars, pools, gym, spa, beachfront, laundry service, public Internet, public Wi-Fi, airport shuttle, parking, no-smoking rooms* ⊟*AE, DC, MC, V* ⦿|*BP.*H id="d2e1642"SI <LAST.VISIT MONTH="SEP" YEAR="2007"/>R

PUCÓN

25 km (15 mi) east of Villarrica.

The resort town of Pucón, on the southern shore of Lago Villarrica, attracts all manner of Chileans. By day, there are loads of outdoor activities in the area. The beach on Lago Villarrica feels like one of

Chile's popular coastal beach havens near Viña del Mar. By night, the young people flock to the major nightspots and party 'til dawn. The older crowd has a large array of fine restaurants and trendy shops to visit. Pucón has many fans, though some lament the town's meteoric rise to fame. Still, this is the place to have fun all 24 hours of the day in southern Chile. Accommodations are hard to come by in February, which is easily the busiest month. And outside of summer, December to March, most stores, restaurants, and pubs close down.

With Volcán Villarrica looming south of town, a color-coded alert system on the Municipalidad (city hall) on Avenida Bernardo O'Higgins signals volcanic activity, and signs around town explain the colors' meanings: green—that's where the light almost always remains—signifies "normal activity," indicating steam being let off from the summit with sulfuric odors and constant, low-level rumblings; yellow and red indicate more dangerous levels of activity. Remember: the volcano sits 15 km (9 mi) away, and you'll be scarcely aware of any activity. Indeed, ascending the volcano is the area's most popular excursion.

GETTING HERE & AROUND

Pucón has only a small air strip 2 km (1 mi) outside of town for private planes, but the national airlines such as LAN and Sky fly regularly to Temuco. From Temuco, Buses JAC has frequent service to Pucón. Roads that connect Pucón to Ruta 5, the Pan-American Highway, are paved from both Loncoche and Freire. In Pucón, there are several taxis that can move you about but the town itself is small and in most cases you will just need your two feet.

ESSENTIALS

BUS **JAC** (✉ *Corner of Palguin and Uruguay* ☎ *45/443–693*). **Tur-Bus** (✉ *Palguin 383* ☎ *45/481–870*).

CURRENCY **Banco BCI** (✉ *Fresia 174*). **Banco Santander** (✉ *Av. Bernardo O'Higgins 308*).

INTERNET **Unid@d G** (✉ *Av. Bernardo O'Higgins 415* ☎ *45/444–918*).

MAIL **Correos de Chile** (✉ *Fresia 183*).

MEDICAL **Hospital San Francisco** (✉ *Uruguay 325* ☎ *45/441–177*).

RENTAL CARS **Christopher Car** (✉ *Bernardo O'Higgins 335* ☎ *45/449–013*). **Hertz** (✉ *Miguel Ansorena 123* ☎ *45/441–664*). **Pucon Rent A Car** (✉ *Av. Colo Colo 340* ☎ *45/443–052*).

VISITOR INFO **Pucón Tourist Office** (✉ *Av. Bernardo O'Higgins 483* ☎ *45/293–002*).

WHAT TO SEE

Mapuche Museo. A small, private museum, it houses an array of Mapuche artifacts, including musical instruments, masks, rock sculptures, pipes, and other items. ✉ *Capoulican 243* ☎ *45/441–963* ⊕ *www. pucononline.cl/museo* 🖾 *1,000 pesos* ☉ *Jan. and Feb., daily 11–1 and 6–10; Mar.–Dec., daily 11–1 and 3–7.*

Termas Geometricas. Chile is volcano country, and around Pucón are numerous natural hot springs. This is one of the best. Seventeen natu-

Pucón

Lago
Villarrica

Playa Grande

La Peninsula

KEY
① Hotels
● Restaurants

Clemente Holzapfel

Carlos Ansorena

Pasaja Luck

Pedro de Valdivia

Alderete

**Mapuche
Museo** ◆

General Urrutia

O'Higgins

Caupolican

Lincoyan

Fresia

Miguel Ansorena

Palguin

Arauco

Colo Colo

Camino Internacional

Brasil

Chile

Uruguay

Paraguay

Peru

TO ARGENTINA

Ecuador

TO VILLARRICA

⑧ - ⑩

Sebastian Engler

Pablo Nappe

⑪

ral hot-spring pools, many of them secluded, dot the dense native forest. Each thermal bath has its own private bathrooms, lockers, and deck. ⊠*3 km (2 mi) south of Villarrica National Park* ☏*9/7477–1708* ⊕*www.termasgeometricas.cl* ⊠*14,000 pesos* ⊙*Jan. and Feb., daily 10–10; Mar.–Dec., daily 11–8.*

Parque Cuevas Volcanicas. After a short hike uphill, you'll find this cave halfway up Volcán Villarrica, right next to a very basic visitor center. It first opened up in 1968 as a cave for spelunkers to explore, but eventually tourism proved more lucrative. A short tour takes you deep into the electrically illuminated cave via wooden walkways that bring you close to the crystallized basalt formations. Your tour guide may make occasional hokey references to witches and pumas hiding in the rocks, but it's worth a visit. ⊠ *Volcán Villarrica National Park* ⊕*www.cuevas volcanicas.cl* ⊠*12,000 pesos* ⊙*Daily 10–7.*

OUTDOOR ACTIVITIES

At first glance Pucón's myriad outfitters look the same and sell the same slate of activities and rentals; quality varies, however. The firms listed below get high marks for safety, professionalism, and friendly service. Pucón is the center for rafting expeditions in the northern Lake District, with Río Trancura just 15 minutes away, making for easy half-day excursions on Class III–V rapids.

French-owned **Aguaventura** (⊠*Palguín 336* ☏*45/444–246* ⊕*www. aguaventura.com*) outfits for rafting, canoeing, kayaking, snowshoeing, and snowboarding. They specialize in trekking up the volcano for a ski descent, although you should be an expert skier for this. Alex Goly, an accomplished guide to all of Chile, works with Aguaventura and leads informative natural history and geography climbs in the area.

Anden Sport (⊠*Av. Bernardo O'Higgins 535* ☏*45/441–574*) is a good bet for bikes, snowboards, snowshoes, and skis.

Huepil Malal (⊠*Km 27, Carretera a Huife* ☏*09/643–2673 or 09/643– 3204* ⊕*www.huepil-malal.cl*) arranges horseback riding in the nearby Cañi mountains, with everything from half-day to six-day excursions.

Politur (⊠*Av. Bernardo O'Higgins 635* ☏*445/441–373* ⊕*www.politur. com*) can take you rafting on the Río Trancura, trekking in nearby Parque Nacional Huerquehue, on ascents of the Volcán Villarrica, and skydiving.

★ **Sol Y Nieve** (⊠*Av. Bernardo O'Higgins and Lincoyan* ☏☏*45/463–860*) runs rafting trips and hiking and skiing expeditions. It takes groups up Villarrica Volcano.

WHERE TO EAT

$ ✗**Arabian Restaurant.** The Apara family knows how to whip up tasty falafel or *shawarma* (a pita-bread sandwich filled with spicy beef or lamb). Most everyone opts for the outdoor tables over the tiny indoor dining area. ⊠*Fresia 354* ☏*45/443–469* ▤*No credit cards.*

$ ✗**Cassis.** Formerly called the Patagonia Express, at this wonderful café fruit-filled pastries are baked fresh all day long and the coffee is good.

Continued on page 218

FLY FISHING by Jack Trout

Chile and Argentina are the final frontier of fly fishing. With so many unexplored rivers, lakes, and spring creeks—most of which are un-dammed and free flowing to the ocean—every type of fishing is available for all levels of experience. You'll find many different species of fish, including rainbow trout, browns, sea-run browns, brooks, sea-trout, and steelhead.

The Southern Cone has endless—and endlessly evolving—rivers, streams, and lakes, which is why they're so good for fly fishing. These waterways formed millions of years ago, as volcanic eruptions and receding glaciers carved out the paths for riverbeds and lakes that feed into the Pacific or Atlantic Oceans. With more than 2,006 volcanoes in Chile alone (including South America's most active mountain, Volcano Llaima, outside of Temuco), the Lake Districts of both countries are still evolving, creating raw and pristine fishing grounds.

Why choose Chile or Argentina for your next fly fishing adventure? If you're only after huge fish, stick to California. What these two South American countries offer is a chance to combine fishing, culture, and food in a unique package during the northern hemisphere's off season. With the right guide, you just might find yourself two hours down a dirt road, fishing turquoise water in the shadow of a glacial peak, with not a soul in sight but the occasional *gaucho* or *huaso*. It's an experience you will find nowhere else.

Top: Trout angler casts fly to trout/salmon, Llanquihue, Chile.
Right: Tronador Mountain and Hess Lake, Bariloche, Argentina.

NOT NATIVE

Trout, salmon, and other common species aren't indigenous to South America. These fish were introduced during the late 19th century, mostly as a result of demand from European settlers. Germans, Scots, and others needed trout-filled rivers to survive, so they stocked the New World streams in the image of those in the Old World. For more information, consult *Fly Fishing in Chilean Patagonia* by Gonzalo Cortes and Nicolas Piwonka or *Fly Fishing the Best Rivers of Patagonia Argentina* by Francisco Bedeschi.

WHAT TO EXPECT ON THE GROUND

LOGISTICS

You'll probably fly into Bariloche, Argentina, or Chaiten, Chile. You won't need more than two weeks for a good trip, and hiring a guide can make a big difference in the quality of your experience. Since most rivers are un-dammed, you'll need the extra help managing your drift boat or locating foot access for wading that stream you've spotted around the bend. Having the help of someone who knows each section of river can save you a lot of time.

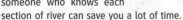
Good fishing near Chaitén, Chile

dict the upcoming season's peak fishing times, since the depth and speed of the streams depends on snow melt. You can safely plan your trip for sometime during February or March.

CHOOSING YOUR GUIDE

When talking to your guide, it is important to describe what type of fishing you enjoy most. Do you prefer to fish out of a boat, allowing you to travel greater distances, or do you prefer the personal zen of wading the river as it rushes by? Also, ask the right questions.

GUIDES VS. LODGES

You can purchase your trip package (usually they run between US $2900 and US $5500) through either an independent guide or a specific lodge property. In both cases, packages usually last one week to 10 days, and include breakfast, lunch, and dinner. If you opt to purchase through a lodge, you have the benefit of property-specific guides who know every nook and cranny of stream surrounding the lodge. On the other hand, hiring an independent guide will give you more power to customize your trip and go farther afield.

TIMING

You should make first contact with your guide or lodge in November, during the southern hemisphere's spring. They will be able to pre-

WHAT TO ASK A GUIDE:

- How early do you start in the morning?
- Do you mainly spin cast or fly fish?
- How long have you been in business?
- Do you always catch and release?
- Will I fish with you or another guide?
- Can I see pictures of your raft or drift boat?
- Do you supply the flies?
- Where do you get your flies?
- Can we fish a river twice if we like it?
- Which rivers and lakes do you float?
- Can we set an itinerary before I arrive?

WHAT TO BRING

5 to 7 Weight Rod: at least 9 foot (consider bringing 9½ foot for larger rivers, windy days, lakes, and sink-tip streamer fishing).

Floating Lines: for dry fly fishing and nymphing.

Streamers: for use while wading to or from the drift boat.

Lines: 15 to 20 foot sink-tip lines with a sink rate of 5.5 to 8 inches per second. It's good to carry two to four different sink rate lines.

Intermediate sink lines: for lakes and shallow depth fishing.

Line Cleaner: because low-ozone areas (the hole in the ozone is close to Antarctica) will eat up lines if you don't treat and clean the lines daily.

Hook sharpener: most guides don't have this very important item.

Small gifts: for the people you meet. Gift-giving can help you gain access to private rivers and lakes. Chocolates, such as Hershey Kisses, or some unique fly pattern, such as a dragon fly, always go over well.

Patagonian brown trout caught on surface fly

Good map: Turistel, in Chile, puts out the best maps and internal information for that country (w www.turistel.cl). Check Argentina Tourism (w www.turismo.gov.ar) for help with that country.

Coffee: Chile has Nescafé instant coffee just about everywhere you go. So if you like a good cup of joe, bring a filter and your favorite coffee. That way all you need is a cup and hot water, and you're all set for your morning fishing.

FLIES

■ Ask your guide where he or she gets flies. Those bought at a discount in countries outside of the United States are often sub-par, so get good guidance on this.

■ If you can, get a list of flies for the time of year you're scheduled to arrive and buy them in the United States before you go. Pay particular attention to the size as well type of insect.

■ The big fish and the quality catches are fooled by the flies that are tied by the guides themselves, because the guides know the hatches and the times they occur.

■ Flies are divided up into similar categories in Chile and Argentina since South America has many of the same insects as we do in North America. Check and see what time each insect is hatching. Note their sizes and colors. You'll need both dry and nymph versions of the following:

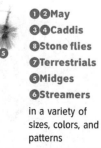

❶❷May
❸❹Caddis
❽Stone flies
❼Terrestrials
❺Midges
❻Streamers

in a variety of sizes, colors, and patterns

ARGENTINA FLY FISHING GUIDES AND RIVERS

Region, Trip Length, Season & Lake or Stream	Guides, Lodges, and Hostel Names	Phone	Web
SAN MARTIN DE LOS ANDES 5 to 7 days December–February	Alejandro Bucannan	2972/424–767	www.flyfishing-sma.com
	Jorge Trucco	2972/427–561 or 429–561	www.jorgetrucco.com
Río Filo Huaum/ Parque y Reserva Nacional Lanin Río Careufu Río Collon Cura Río Quiquihue	Pablo Zaleski / San Huberto Lodge	2972/422–921	www.chimehuinsp.com
	Estancia Tipiliuke	2972/429–466	www.tipiliuke.com
	La Chiminee	2972/427–617	n/a
	Lucas Rodriquez	2972/428–270	n/a
JUNIN DE LOS ANDES 5 to 7 days December–February	Alejandro Bucannan	2972/424–767 or 2944/1530–9469	www.flyfishing-sma.com
	Estancia Quemquemtreu	2972/424–410	www.quemquemtreu.com
Río Malleo Río Chimehuin Río Alumine	Redding Fly Shop Travel	800/669–3474 (in US)	www.flyfishingtravel.com
BARILOCHE 4 to 6 days December–February	Martin Rebora / Montan Cabins	2944/525–314	www.patagoniasinfronteras.com
	Río Manso Lodge	2944/490–546	www.Ríomansolodge.com
Río Limay Río Manso Río Traful Lago Fonk Parque y Reserva Nacional Nahuel Huapi	Estancia Peuma Hue	2944/501–030	www.peuma-hue.com
	Estancia Arroyo Verde	5411/4801–7448	www.estanciaarroyoverde.com.ar
	Hotel Piedras	2944/435–073	www.laspiedrashotel.com.ar
ESQUEL 5 to 7 days December–February	Esquel Outfitters	2944/462–776	www.esqueloutfitters.com
	Guided Connections	307/734–2716 (in US)	www.guidedconnections.com
Río Rivadavia Arroyo Pescado Río Carrileufu Río Pico - Lago Senquer Parque Argentino Los Alerces	Patagonia River Guides	2945/457–020 (in Argentina) or 406/835–3122 (in US)	www.patagoniariverguides.com
	Angelina Hostel	2945/452–763	n/a
	Hotel Tehuelche	2945/452–420	n/a

CHILE FLY FISHING GUIDES AND RIVERS

Region, Trip length, Season & Lake or Stream	Guides, Lodges, and Hostel Names	Phone	Web
PALENA AREA 5 to 7 days December–April Río Palena Río Rosselott Río Yelcho Río Futaleufu Lago Yelcho Parque y Reserva Nacional Palena Parque y Reserva Nacional Corcovado	Jack Trout	530/926–4540 (in US)	www.jacktrout.com
	Chucao Lodge	201–8571	www.chucaolodge.com
	Yelcho Lodge	65/731–337	www.yelcho.cl
	Tres Piedras / Francisco Constano	65/330–157	www.trespiedras.cl
	Martin Pescador Lodge	207/350–8178 (in US)	martinpescadorfishing.com
PUERTO VARAS AREA 4 to 6 days December–March Río Petrohue Río Puelo Río Maullin Parque y Reserva Saltos de Petrohue	Jack Trout	530/926–4540 (in US)	www.jacktrout.com
	Tres Piedras / Francisco Constano	65/330–157	www.trespiedras.cl
	Gray Fly Fishing	65/232–496	www.grayfly.com
	Hotel Licarayen Puerto Varas	65/232–305	www.hotellicarayen.cl
	Hotel Puerto Pilar	65/335–378	www.hotelpuertopilar.cl
	Cabins Río Puelo	90/940–643	www.southernchilexp.com
COYHAIQUE AREA 4 to 7 days December–April Río Simpson Río Nirehuoa Río Paloma Río Azul Río Manihuales Lago Pollux Parque y Reserva Nacional Simpson Parque y Reserva Nacional Cerro Castillo	La Pasarela Lodge & Cabins	67/525–101	www.lapasarela.cl
	Heart of Patagonia Lodge		www.patagoniachileflyfishing.com
	Nicolas Gonzales	98/406–3371	n/a
	Eduardo Otarola	99/946–1943	n/a
	David Federick	98/138–3530	n/a
	Alex PRíor	98/920–9132	www.flyfishingcoyhaique.com
	El Saltamontes Lodge	67/232–779	www.elsaltamonteslodge.com
	Troy Cowles	99/992–3199	n/a
RÍO BAKER & COCHRANE AREAS 4 to 6 days Janurary–April Río Baker Río Cochrane Parque Reserva Nacional Cerro Castillo	David Frederick	406/842–7158 (in US) 98/138–3530 (in Chile)	n/a
	Alex PRíor	98/920–9132	www.flyfishingcoyhaique.com
	Green Baker Lodge - Río Baker	72/491-418	www.flyfishing-baker.com
LAKES DISTRICT: PUCON & VILLARRICA 2 to 4 days Nov.–Dec., then Mar.–May Río Trancura, Parque Villarrica Lago Quillen, Parque Nacional Lanin Río Quillen, Parque Nacional Lanin	MaRío's Fishing Zone	99/760–7280	www.flyfishingpucon.com
	Hostal Aileen Colo	45/441–944	n/a
	Del Volcan Apart Hotel	45/442–055	n/a

There's a varied menu of sandwiches, pizza, and more with an extensive wine list. In summer, this is an especially great ice-cream stop—head for one of the tables outside on the sidewalk. Cassis also stays quite lively on summer nights until about 3 AM. ⊠*Pedro de Valdivia 333* ☎*45/444–715* ⊟*AE, DC, MC, V.*

¢ ✗ **Empanadas y Hamburguesas Lleu-Lleu.** This is the place in Pucón to eat Chile's famous empanadas, a sort of hot pastry filled with diverse ingredients. Try the vegetarian empanada. They also have good sandwiches. They are open every day from 10 AM to 7 AM, which makes it a popular destination for the late-night bar crowd. They can also deliver to your hotel. ⊠*520 General Urrutia* ⊟*No credit cards.*

$$$ ✗ **La Grilla.** The best seafood in Pucón is served here, so don't be frightened off by the nondescript dining room: basic wooden tables and the ubiquitous nautical theme. You'll receive a free pisco sour when you arrive. ⊠*Fresia at Urrutia* ☎*45/442–294* ⊟*AE, DC, MC, V.*

$$$ ✗ **La Maga.** Argentina claims to prepare the perfect parrillada, or grilled beef, but here's evidence that Uruguayans just might do it best. Watch the beef cuts or salmon turn slowly over the wood fire at the entrance. Wood, rather than charcoal, is the key, says the owner, Emiliano Villanil, a transplant from Punta del Este. The product is a wonderfully smoky, natural taste, accented with a hint of spice in the mild *chimichurri* (a tangy steak sauce). ⊠*Fresia 125* ☎*45/444–277* ⊟*AE, DC, MC, V* ⊙*Closed Mon. Apr.–Dec.*

$$ ✗ **Nau Kana.** Come here to sample excellent dishes from Thailand, Japan, Vietnam, Indonesia, and Arabia. Try the Gary Ga, a Vietnamese dish of curried chicken breast with basil, tomato, mushroom, and coconut milk over Arab rice. It's also a good place for cocktails. Open only at night, after 7:30 PM. ⊠*Fresia 236* ☎*45/444–677* ⊟*AE, DC, MC, V.*

$$$ ✗ **¡Viva Perú!** Peruvian cuisine reigns supreme at this restaurant with rustic wooden tables. Try the *ají de gallina* (hen stew with cheese, milk, and peppers) or the ceviche, thoroughly cooked but served cold. You can dine on the porch, a nice option for a pleasant summer night—and take advantage of the two-for-one pisco sours nightly until 9 PM. ⊠*Lincoyan 372* ☎*45/444–025* ⊟*AE, DC, MC, V.*

WHERE TO STAY

$$–$$$$ 🏨 **Apart Hotel Del Volcán.** In keeping with the region's immigrant heritage, the furnishings of this chalet-style hotel look like they come straight from Germany. Checked fabrics cover carefully fluffed duvets in the guest apartments. Many of the generously proportioned apartments also have balconies. Each unit in this centrally located hotel sleeps up to six people. **Pros:** Kitchen, central location, large apartments. **Cons:** No restaurant. ⊠*Fresia 420* ☎*45/442–055* 🖶*45/442–053* ⊕*www.aparthoteldelvolcan.cl* ⇆*18 apartments* ♿*In-room: no a/c, safe, kitchen, refrigerator, Wi-Fi. In-hotel: gym, concierge, parking (no fee), no-smoking rooms* ⊟*AE, DC, MC, V* ⏸◎*BP.*

$$ 🏨 **La Casona de Púcon.** In a beautiful, recently restored 1930s southern-Chile-style mansion made entirely of native woods, this bed-and-breakfast opened in late 2007. The rooms are immaculate, tastefully decorated, and the common areas make you feel at home. It's on the

town plaza, a block from the beach. **Pros:** Tasteful decoration, on the plaza. **Cons:** No restaurant. ⊠ *Lincoyan 48* 🏠 *45/443–179* ⊕ *www. lacasonadepucon.cl* ➣ *11 rooms, 1 suite* ♿ *In-room: no a/c, safe, Ethernet, Wi-Fi. In-hotel: no elevator, laundry service, public Wi-Fi, airport shuttle, parking, no-smoking rooms* ⊟ *AE, DC, MC, V* ❚❘❚ *BP.*

$ ✕🖳 **¡école!** It's part hostel and part beach house—and takes its name
Fodor'sChoice from a Chilean expression meaning "Right on!" Cozy two-, three-, and
★ four-person rooms can be shared or private. The vegetarian restaurant ($), a rarity in the Lake District, merits a trip in itself. You can choose among truly international options, such as lasagna, burritos, and moussaka, and eat in the sunny courtyard or small dining room. The environmentally conscious staff can organize hiking and horseback-riding trips and expeditions to volcanoes and hot springs, as well as arrange for Spanish lessons and massages. **Pros:** Great food in restaurant, easy to meet other travelers, ecoconscious. **Cons:** Some rooms are noisy, toilets don't always work. ⊠ *General Urrutia 592* 🏠🏠 *45/441–675* ⊕ *www. ecole.cl* ➣ *21 rooms, 9 with bath* ♿ *In-room: no a/c, no phone, no TV, Wi-Fi. In-hotel: restaurant, bar, public Wi-Fi, no-smoking rooms, no elevator* ⊟ *AE, DC, MC, V.*

$$$$ 🖳 **Gran Hotel Pucón.** The outside of Pucón's largest hotel is quite *gran*
and imposing in true alpine-lodge style. Its location on the shore provides direct access to the beach. The rooms are scattered among three buildings, and although perfectly acceptable, they're disappointingly contemporary. Depending on which side of the buildings you are on, though, you do get stupendous views of either the lake or Volcán Villarrica. The hotel is enormously popular, so you won't find much peace and quiet, especially in summer. **Pros:** Activities, good location. **Cons:** Noise, rooms aren't especially worth the price. ⊠ *Clemente Holzapfel 190* 🏠 *45/913– 300, 2/429–6100 in Santiago* ⊕ *www.granhotelpucon.cl* ➣ *274 rooms, 141 apartments, 14 suites* ♿ *In-room: no a/c, safe, kitchen (some), refrigerator (some). In-hotel: 2 restaurants, bar, room service, pools, gym, spa, beachfront, water sports, bicycles, children's programs, laundry service, concierge, public Internet, public Wi-Fi, airport shuttle, parking, no-smoking rooms* ⊟ *AE, DC, MC, V* ❚❘❚ *BP, MAP.*

$$ 🖳 **Gudenschwager Hotel.** The Chilean-born, Los Angeles–raised owner
of this property, Pablo Guerra, has taken one of Pucón's oldest lodgings and given it a complete (and much appreciated) overhaul, stripping the paint and exposing the original wood walls and the old radiators. They've placed queen beds in every room and installed little touches, such as safety rails in the bathtubs, which you rarely see in large hotels in Chile, let alone small inns of this size. They bill a few of the more simply furnished rooms on the top floor as "backpacker" rooms, and they are a definite cut above Pucón's typical budget lodgings. Location is everything here: sitting on the peninsula that juts out into Lago Villarrica, the deck affords both lake and volcano views. **Pros:** Great location, good rooms. **Cons:** No phone or TV. ⊠ *Pedro de Valdivia 12* 🏠 *45/442–025* 🏠 *45/442–326* ⊕ *www.hogu.cl* ➣ *20 rooms* ♿ *In-room: no a/c, no phone, no TV. In-hotel: restaurant, bar, public Wi-Fi, no-smoking rooms* ⊟ *AE, DC, MC, V* ❚❘❚ *BP.*

6

$$$$
★
⊞ Hotel Antumalal. A young Queen Elizabeth stayed here in the 1950s, as did actor Jimmy Stewart—and the Antumalal hasn't changed much since. The decor from that decade has been maintained at this family-run hotel. It's perched atop a cliff just outside town above Lago Villarrica, and its cozy rooms have fireplaces and huge windows overlooking the spectacularly landscaped grounds. If you tire of relaxing with a refreshing pisco sour on the wisteria-shaded deck, just ask owner Rony Pollak to arrange an adventure for you. Favorites include fly-fishing, white-water rafting, and volcano climbing. **Pros:** Secluded location, fireplace in room, architecture of hotel. **Cons:** The hotel looks its age. ⊠ *Casilla 84* 🕾 *45/441–011* 🖷 *45/441–013* ⊕ *www.antumalal.com* ⮗ *15 rooms, 3 suites* ⟳ *In-room: no a/c, safe. In-hotel: restaurant, bar, room service, tennis courts, pool, gym, spa, beachfront, water sports, laundry service, public Internet, public Wi-Fi, airport shuttle, parking, no-smoking rooms, no elevator* ═ *AE, DC, MC, V* ⦿ *BP.*

$$$
⊞ Hotel Huincahue. This German-style hotel sits close to the center of town on the main plaza. Lots of windows brighten the lobby and library, which is warmed by a roaring fire. Bright, airy rooms come furnished with wrought-iron and blond-wood furniture. Rooms on the second floor have small balconies. Rates include a hearty American breakfast. **Pros:** Next to plaza, breakfasts. **Cons:** Steep price for what you get. ⊠ *Pedro de Valdivia 375* 🕾 *45/443–540* 🖷 *45/442–728* ⮗ *20 rooms* ⟳ *In-room: no a/c, safe. In-hotel: bar, pool, public Wi-Fi, laundry service, parking, no-smoking rooms* ═ *AE, DC, MC, V* ⦿ *BP.*

$$
⊞ Hotel Los Maitenes. In the center of Pucón, on the most important street for shopping and eating, this is a good quality option. Rooms are clean and comfortable, with pleasantly decorated fresh pine-wood walls, bright colored bed covers, and colorful paintings. Some rooms have good views. Room 11 is slightly bigger, and the best of the lot. **Pros:** Central location. **Cons:** Some rooms on the small side. ⊠ *Fresia 354* 🕾 *45/441–820* ⊕ *www.hotelmaitenes.cl* ⮗ *11 rooms* ⟳ *In-room: no a/c, no phone, safe, Wi-Fi. In-hotel: room service, no elevator, public Wi-Fi, parking, no-smoking rooms* ═ *AE, DC, MC, V.*

$$
Fodor'sChoice
★
⊞ Hotel Malalhue. Dark wood and volcanic rock were used in building this hotel at the edge of Pucón on the road to Calburga. It's about a 15-minute walk from the hubbub of downtown, but Malalhue's many fans see that as a selling point. The cozy sitting room just off the lobby with fireplace and couches is so inviting you may want to linger there for hours. But the guest rooms, with their plush comforters and pillows, beckon, too. The top-floor "superior" rooms under the gables are more spacious and contain vaulted ceilings; they're a few thousand pesos more than the "standard" rooms, which are perfectly acceptable in their own right. **Pros:** Comfortable rooms. **Cons:** 15-minute walk to town. ⊠ *Camino Internacional 1615* 🕾 *45/443–130* 🖷 *45/443–132* ⊕ *www.malalhue.cl* ⮗ *24 rooms* ⟳ *In-room: no a/c, safe. In-hotel: bar, restaurant, room service, laundry service, public Internet, public Wi-Fi, no-smoking rooms, parking, no elevator* ═ *AE, DC, MC, V* ⦿ *BP.*

$
⊞ Kila Leufu and Ruka Rayen. As part of a growing agritourism trend in Chile, a Mapuche family has opened up two guesthouses in the countryside, 15 minutes from Pucón. Kila Leufu provides an authentic

glimpse at Mapuche farming life, complete with authentic Mapuche cooking. Here, you can bake bread and milk the cows if you like, or just relax and read. Ruka Rayen, a second guesthouse next to Palguin River, which is a hot kayaking spot, is run by a Mapuche woman and her Austrian husband. They speak English and a number of other languages and provide not just comfortable lodging but an array of outdoor adventure activities, from horseback rides to hot-springs visits to treks in local nature areas. **Pros:** Mapuche influence, countryside location. **Cons:** No TV, outside of Pucón. ✉️*Camino a Curarrehe, Puente Cabedane* ☎️*09/711–8064* 🌐*www.kilaleufu.cl* 🛏*11 rooms, 5 with bath* 🛎*In-room: no a/c, no phone, no TV. In hotel: bicycles, water sports, parking, laundry service* 🚫*No credit cards* 🍽️*FAP.*

$$$ 🏨**Termas de San Luis.** The famous San Luis hot springs are the main attraction of this hideaway east of Pucón. Here you can rent a rustic cabin that sleeps up to six people. Rates include the option of all or some meals—cabins are not kitchen equipped—and free use of the baths. If you're not staying, 5,500 pesos gets you a day of soaking in the thermal springs and mud baths. **Pros:** Access to hot springs. **Cons:** Distance from Pucón. ✉️*Carretera Internacional, Km 27, Catripulli* ☎️📠*45/412–880* 🌐*www.termasdesanluis.cl* 🛏*6 cabins* 🛎*In-room: no a/c. In-hotel: 2 restaurants, bar, pools, children's programs, no elevator* 🚫*No credit cards* 🍽️*BP, FAP, MAP.*

NIGHTLIFE

Pucón has a fantastic nightlife in summer. There are several bars south of Avenida Bernardo O'Higgins. But a local favorite is the friendly **Mamas & Tapas** (✉️*Av. Bernardo O'Higgins 597* ☎️*45/449–002*). Light Mexican dining morphs into DJ-generated or live music lasting into the wee hours. Across the street is **Bar Esquina** (✉️*Av. Bernardo O'Higgins 630* ☎️*45/441–070*), a popular bar for drinks, food, and dancing. A few kilometers outside of town is the large, fun discotheque **Fire** (✉️*Camino a la Balsa s/n* ☎️*9/275–5362*).

PARQUE NACIONAL HUERQUEHUE

35 km (21 mi) northeast of Pucón.

Unless you have a four-wheel-drive vehicle, this 124-square-km (48-square-mi) park is accessible only in summer. (And even then, a jeep isn't a bad idea.) A two-hour hike on the Lago Verde trail begins at the ranger station near the park entrance. You head up into the Andes through groves of araucaria pines, eventually reaching three startlingly blue lagoons with panoramic views of the whole area, including distant Volcán Villarrica. ☎️*45/298–221 in Temuco* 💰*2,200 pesos* 🕐*Dec.–Mar., daily 8 AM–10 PM; Apr.–Nov., daily 8–6.*

WHERE TO STAY

$$$$ 🏨**Termas de Huife.** Just outside Parque Nacional Huerquehue, this resort lets you relax in three steaming pools set beside an icy mountain stream. At the spa you can enjoy an individual bath, a massage, or both. The complex includes a handful of luxurious cabins, all of which have enormous tubs you can fill with water from the hot springs. Those just visiting for the day—hours are 9 AM–10 PM—pay 9,500 pesos for entry. If you lack your own wheels, the office in Pucón offers twice-daily shuttle service for 14,000 pesos round-trip. There's also a country house past the spa where you can soak in privacy. **Pros:** Access to hot springs and park. **Cons:** Price is steep. ✉ *33 km (20 mi) from Pucón on the road to Caburga* 🕾🕾 *45/197–5666* ⊕ *www.termashuife.cl* ➶ *11 cabins* 🕭 *In-room: no a/c, safe, refrigerator. In-hotel: restaurant, bar, pool, spa, parking, no elevator* 🖃 *AE, DC, MC, V* ⍥*BP.*

PARQUE NACIONAL VILLARRICA

Fodor's Choice ★

15 km (9 mi) south of Pucón.

One of Chile's most popular national parks, Parque Nacional Villarrica has skiing, hiking, and many other outdoor activities. The main draw, however, is the volcano that gives the 610-square-km (235-square-mi) national park its name. You don't need to have any climbing experience to reach Volcán Villarrica's 9,350-foot summit, but a guide is a good idea. The volcano sits in the park's Sector Rucapillán, a Mapuche word meaning "house of the devil." That name is apt, as the perpetually smoldering volcano is one of South America's most active. CONAF closes off access to the trails at the slightest hint of volcanic activity they deem to be out of the ordinary. It's a steep uphill walk to the snow line, but doable any time of year. All equipment will be supplied by any of the Pucón outfitters that organize daylong excursions for about 30,000 pesos per person. Your reward for the six-hour climb is the rare sight of an active crater, which continues to release clouds of sulfur gases and explosions of lava. You're also treated to superb views of the nearby volcanoes, the less-visited Quetrupillán and Lanín. ✉ *15 km (9 mi) south of Pucón* 🕾 *45/298–221 in Temuco* 🖃 *1,100 pesos* ⊙ *Daily 8–6.*

SKIING

The popular **Ski Pucón** (✉ *Parque Nacional Villarrica* 🕾 *45/441–901* ⊕ *www.skipucon.cl*), in the lap of Volcán Villarrica, is one of the best-equipped ski areas in southern Chile, with 20 runs for varying levels of experience, nine rope tows, three double-chair tows, and equipment rental. The facility offers snowboarding, too. The ski season usually begins early July and can sometimes run through mid-October. High-season rates run 18,000 pesos per day; 15,000 pesos per half day. There are also a restaurant, coffee shop, boutique shop for various skiing accessories, and skiing and snowboard classes.

WHERE TO STAY

$ 🛆 **Volcán Villarrica.** This camping area run by CONAF is in the midst of a forest of *coigüe*, Chile's massive red oaks. The site charges 8,800 pesos per person and provides very basic toilets. ✉ *Sector Rucapillán* 🕾 *45/298–221 in Temuco* 🖃 *No credit cards.*

LICAN RAY

30 km (18 mi) south of Villarrica.

In the Mapuche language, Lican Ray means "flower among the stones." This pleasant, unhurried little resort town of 1,688 inhabitants is on Lago Calafquén, the first of a chain of seven lakes that spills over into Argentina. You can rent rowboats and sailboats along the shore, which is also a fine spot to soak up sun. Lican Ray is not as perfectly manicured as Pucón. With but one paved street, a lot of dust gets kicked up on a dry summer day.

GETTING HERE & AROUND

You can reach Lican Ray via the paved Ruta 199 from Temuco and Villarrica. From Valdivia and points south, take Ruta 203 to Panguipulli, then travel on dirt roads north to Lican Ray. There frequent bus service to the town from nearby locales such as Villarrica.

ESSENTIALS

VISITOR INFO **Lican Ray Tourist Office** (✉ *General Urrutia 310* ☎ *45/431–201*).

BEACHES

The peninsula on which Lican Ray sits has two gray-sand beaches. **Playa Chica,** the smaller of the beaches near Lican Ray, is south of town. It's popular for swimming. **Playa Grande** stretches along a few blocks on the west side of Lican Ray and has choppy water. Swimming is best avoided here.

WHERE TO EAT

$$$ ✕**Cábala Restaurant.** Impeccable service is the hallmark of this Italian restaurant on Lican Ray's main street. The brick-and-log building has plenty of windows so you can watch the summer crowds stroll by as you enjoy pizza and pasta. ✉ *General Urrutia 201* ☎ *45/431–176* 🖃 *AE, DC, MC, V* ✆ *Closed Apr.–Nov.*

$$ ✕**The Ñaños.** Hearty meats and stews are cooked up at Lican Ray's most popular eatery. Most people partake of cazuela or pastel de choclo on the terrace on the main street, but the wood-trimmed dining room is a lot cozier, especially if you're having a trout fry on a summer evening. ✉ *General Urrutia 105* ☎ *45/431–021* 🖃 *DC, MC, V.*

WHERE TO STAY

$ ⌂**Hostal Hoffman.** Owner Maria Hoffman keeps watch over this little house just outside town. You can get lost in the plush chairs as you read a book in the sitting room. Equally comfy are the rooms with lots of pillows and thick, colorful quilts on the beds. Rates include a huge breakfast with lots of homemade breads and pastries. **Pros:** Comfy rooms, breakfast. **Cons:** Small. ✉ *Camino a Coñaripe 100* ☎☎ *45/431–109* ➥ *5 rooms* ⌂ *In-room: no a/c, no phone, dial-up. In-hotel: laundry service, public Internet, parking* 🖃 *No credit cards* ❑*BP.*

$ ⌂**Hotel Inaltulafquen.** This rambling old house sits in a garden on a quiet street fronting Playa Grande. The rooms are simple, but bright and airy and filled with plants. The cozy restaurant serves Chilean dishes. **Pros:** Restaurant. **Cons:** A bit quiet. ✉ *Punulef 510* ☎ *45/431–*

6

115 ⤴6 rooms, 2 with bath ⌂In-room: no a/c, no phone, no TV (some). In-hotel: restaurant, bar, laundry service, no elevator ▭DC, MC, V ¶©lBP.

LOS LAGOS

Some of Chile's oldest cities are in Los Lagos, yet you may be disappointed if you come looking for colonial grandeur. Wars with indigenous peoples kept the Spaniards, then Chileans, from building here for 300 years. An earthquake of magnitude 9.5, the largest recorded in history, was centered near Valdivia and rocked the region on May 22, 1960. It destroyed many older buildings in the region and produced a tsunami felt as far away as Japan.

Eager to fill its *tierras baldías* (uncultivated lands) in the 19th century, Chile promoted the country's virtues to German, Austrian, and Swiss immigrants looking to start a new life. The newcomers quickly set up shop, constructing breweries, foundries, shipyards, and lumberyards. By the early part of the 20th century, Valdivia had become the country's foremost industrial center, aided in large part by the construction of a railroad from Santiago. To this day the region retains a distinctly Germanic flair, and you might swear you've taken a wrong turn to Bavaria when you pull into towns such as Frutillar or Puerto Octay.

VALDIVIA

120 km (72 mi) southwest of Villarrica.

If you have time for just one of the Lake District's four hub cities, make it Valdivia. The city gracefully combines Chilean wood-shingle construction with the architectural style of the well-to-do German settlers who colonized the area in the late 1800s. But the historic appearance is a bit of an illusion, as the 1960 earthquake destroyed all but a few old riverfront structures. The city painstakingly rebuilt its downtown area, seamlessly mixing old and new buildings. Today you can enjoy evening strolls through its quaint streets and along its two rivers, the Valdivia and the Calle Calle.

Various tour boats leave from the docks at Muelle Schuster along the Río Valdivia for a one-hour tour around nearby Isla Teja. Expect to⌐ pay about 3,000 pesos. A five-hour excursion takes you to Niebla near the coast for a visit to the colonial-era forts. A four-hour tour north transports you to Puncapa, the site of a 16th-century Jesuit church and a nature sanctuary at San Luis de Alba de Cruces. Most companies charge 10,000–12,000 pesos for either of the longer tours. Each tour company offers all three excursions daily during the December–March high season, and you can always sign on to one at the last minute. Most will not operate tours for fewer than 15 passengers, however.

GETTING HERE & AROUND

Valdivia is served by Ruta 5, the Pan-American Highway. The city also has an airport with frequent flights by national airlines such as LAN,

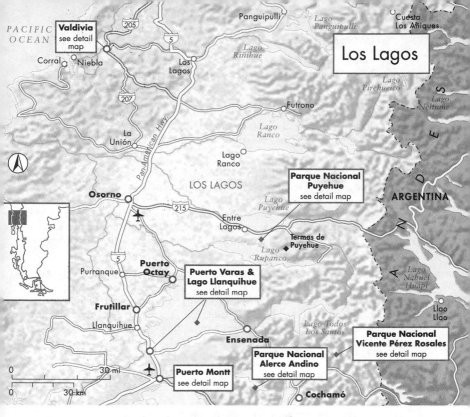

and the nation's bus lines regularly stop here as well. Valdivia's bus terminal is located by the river at the cross section of Munoz and Prat. Some outlying towns and sites around Valdivia you may want to visit, however, are only connected by dirt roads.

ESSENTIALS

BUS **Buses JAC** (✉*Anfión Muñoz 360* ☎*63/333–343*). **Cruz del Sur** (✉*Anfión Muñoz 360* ☎*63/213–840*). **Valdivia Bus Depot** (✉*Anfión Muñoz 360* ☎*63/212–212*).

CURRENCY **Arauco** (✉*Galeria Arauco, Local 24*). **Banco Santander** (✉*Pérez Rosales 505*). **Corp Banca** (✉*Picarte 370*).

INTERNET **Café Phonet** (✉*Libertad 127* ☎*63/341–054*). **Centro Internet Libertad** (✉*Libertad 7*).

MAIL **Correos de Chile** (✉*Av. Bernardo O'Higgins 575*).

MEDICAL **Farmacias Ahumada** (✉*Av. Ramón Picarte 310* ☎*63/257–889*). **Hospital Regional Valdivia** (✉*Simpson 850* ☎*63/297–000*).

RENTAL CARS **Assef y Mendez** (✉*General Lagos 1335* ☎*63/213–205*). **Autovald** (✉*Vicente Pérez Rosales 660* ☎*63/212–786*). **Avis** (✉*Beauchef 619* ☎*63/278–455*). **Budget** (✉*Picarte 1348* ☎*63/340–060*).

VISITOR INFO **Sernatur** (✉*Av. Arturo Prat 555* ☎*63/213–596*). **Valdivia Tourist Office**

(✉ *Terminal de Buses, Anfión Muñoz 360* ☎ *63/212–212*).

WHAT TO SEE

❶ Valdivia's imposing modern **Catedral de Nuestra Señora del Rosario** faces the west side of the central plaza. A small museum inside documents the evangelization of the region's indigenous peoples from the 16th through 19th centuries. ✉ *Independencia 514* ☎ *63/232–040* 💲 *Free* ⊙ *Masses: weekdays 7* AM *and noon, Sat. 8* AM *and 7* PM*, Sun. 10:30* AM*, noon, and 7* PM*; museum: Dec.–Mar., Tues.–Sun. 10–1 and 3–7; Apr.–Nov., Tues.–Fri. 10–1 and 3–7.*

❸ The awning-covered **Mercado Fluvial,** in the southern shadow of the bridge leading to Isla Teja, is a perfect place to soak up the atmosphere of a real fish market. Vendors set up early in the morning; you hear the thwack of fresh trout and the clatter of oyster shells as they're piled on the side of the market's boardwalk fronting the river. Fruit and vegetable vendors line the other side of the walkway opposite the river. ✉ *Av. Arturo Prat at Libertad* ☎ *No phone* ⊙ *Mon.–Sat. 8–3.*

❷ The city's 1918 **Mercado Municipal** barely survived the 1960 earthquake intact, but it thrives again after extensive remodeling and reinforcement as a shopping-dining complex. A few restaurants, mostly hole-in-the-wall seafood joints, but some quite nice, share the three-story building with artisan and souvenir vendors. ✉ *Block bordered by Av. Arturo Prat, Chacabuco, Yungay, and Libertad* ☎ *No phone* ⊙ *Dec.–Mar., daily 8* AM*–10* PM*; Apr.–Nov., daily 8* AM*–8:30* PM*.*

❻ For a historic overview of the region, visit the **Museo Histórico y Antropológico Maurice van de Maele,** on neighboring Isla Teja. The collection focuses on the city's colonial period, during which it was settled by the Spanish, burned by the Mapuche, and invaded by Dutch corsairs. Downstairs, rooms re-create the interior of the late-19th-century Anwandter mansion that belonged to one of Valdivia's first immigrant families; the upper floor delves into Mapuche art and culture. ✉ *Los Laureles, Isla Teja* ☎ *63/212–872* 💲 *1,500 pesos* ⊙ *Daily 10–8.*

❺ The **Museo Philippi,** under construction at this writing, sits behind the
♻ history and anthropology museum. It bears the name of 19th-century Chilean explorer and scientist Bernardo Philippi and will be designed to foster an interest in science among young people. ✉ *Los Laureles, Isla Teja* ☎ *63/212–872* 💲 *1,200 pesos* ⊙ *Dec.–Feb., Tues.–Sun. 10–1 and 2–6; Mar.–Nov., Tues.–Sun. 10–1 and 2–8.*

❹ Known around town as the "MAC," the **Museo de Arte Contemporáneo** is one of Chile's foremost modern-art museums. This Isla Teja complex was built on the site of the old Anwandter brewery destroyed in the 1960 earthquake. The minimalist interior, formerly the brewery's warehouses, contrasts sharply with ongoing construction of a modern glass wall fronting the Río Valdivia, a project slated for completion by 2010, Chile's bicentennial. The museum hosts special exhibitions by contemporary Chilean artists. ✉ *Los Laureles, Isla Teja* ☎ *63/221–968* ⊕ *www.macvaldivia.uach.cl* 💲 *1,200 pesos* ⊙ *Daily 10–2 and 4–8.*

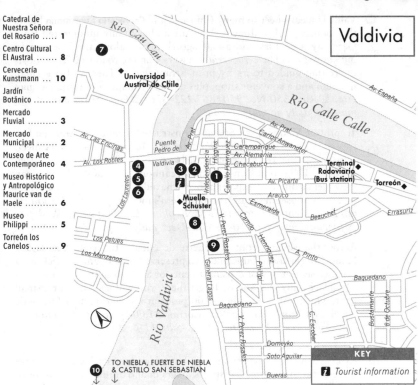

Valdivia

KEY

ℹ️ *Tourist information*

6

❽ A walk south of downtown on Yungay and General Lagos takes you through a neighborhood of late-19th- and early-20th-century houses that were spared the ravages of the 1960 earthquake. The **Centro Cultural El Austral** is in an 1870 house and has period furnishings. ✉️*Yungay 733* ☎️*63/213–6588* ⊕*www.macvaldivia.uach.cl* 💲*Free* ◷*Tues.–Sun. 10–1 and 4–7.*

❾ Just south of the Centro Cultural El Austral lies the **Torreón Los Canelos,** one of two fortress towers constructed in 1774 to defend Valdivia from constant indigenous attacks. Both towers—the other sits on Avenida Picarte between the bus terminal and the bridge entering the city over the Río Calle Calle—were built in the style of those that guarded the coasts of Andalusia, in southern Spain. A wall and moat connected the two Valdivia towers in the colonial era, effectively turning the city into an island. ✉️*General Lagos at Yerbas Buenas.*

❼ The **Jardín Botánico,** north and west of the Universidad Austral campus, is awash with 1,000 species of flowers and plants native to Chile. It's a lovely place to wander among the alerce, cypress, and laurel trees whatever the season—and if you can't make it to Conguillío National Park to see the monkey puzzle trees, this is the place to see them—but it's particularly enjoyable in spring and summer. ✉️*Isla Teja* ☎️*63/221–313* 💲*Free* ◷*Dec.–Feb., daily 8–8; Mar.–Nov., daily 8–4.*

⑩ Valdivia means beer to many Chileans, and **Cervecería Kunstmann** brews the country's beloved lager. The Anwandter family immigrated from Germany a century-and-a-half ago, bringing along their beer-making know-how. The *cervecería* (brewery), on the road to Niebla, hosts interesting guided tours by prior arrangement. There's also a small museum and a souvenir shop, plus a pricey restaurant serving German fare. ⊠ *Ruta 350 No. 950* 🕾 *63/222–570* 🎟 *Free* ⊙ *Restaurant and museum, daily noon–midnight.*

To protect Valdivia, the Spanish constructed a series of strategic fortresses at Niebla, where the Valdivia and Tornagaleones rivers meet. Portions of the 1671 **Fuerte de Niebla** and its 18 cannons have been restored. The ground on which the cannons sit is unstable; you can view them from the ramparts above. The old commander's house serves as a small museum documenting the era's military history. ⊠ *1 km (½ mi) west of entrance to Niebla* 🕾 *No phone* 🎟 *1,000 pesos, Wed. free* ⊙ *Jan. and Feb., daily 10–7; Mar.–Dec., daily 11–6.*

Across the estuary from the Fuerte de Niebla, the 1645 **Castillo San Sebastián de la Cruz** is large and well preserved. In the January–February summer season, historic reenactments of Spanish military maneuvers take place daily at 4 and 6. To get there, you will need to rent a small boat, which only costs about 700 pesos at the marina near Fuerte de Niebla. ⊠ *1 km (½ mi) north of Corral* 🎟 *1,000 pesos* ⊙ *Jan. and Feb., Tues.–Sun. 10–7; Mar.–Dec., Tues.–Sun. 11–6.*

OUTDOOR ACTIVITIES

Rivers, lush coastal temperate rain forests, and the Pacific coastline are some of the attractions for sports lovers in and around Valdivia. Birdwatching is a joy, particularly when you can witness the rare blacknecked swans, one of the world's smallest swans, which have made the Valdivia area their main habitat despite pollution problems from a nearby pulp mill.

Valdivia-based tour operator **Pueblito Expediciones** (⊠ *San Carlos 188* 🕾 *63/245–055* ⊕ *www.pueblitoexpediciones.cl*) organizes marvelous rafting, kayaking, and nature appreciation trips on nearby rivers. An astonishing variety of wetland birds inhabits this part of the country. **Hualamo** (🕾 *09/642–3143* ⊕ *www.hualamo.com*) lets you get a close look if you join its bird-watching and natural-history tours based out of a lodge 20 km (12 mi) upriver from Valdivia.

WHERE TO EAT

¢ ✕**Café Haussmann.** The excellent *crudos* (steak tartare), German-style sandwiches, and delicious küchen are testament to the fact that Valdivia was once a mecca for German immigrants. The place is small—a mere four tables and a bar—but it's that rarest of breeds in Chile: a completely nonsmoking restaurant. ⊠ *Av. Bernardo O'Higgins 394* 🕾 *63/213–878* 🍴 *AE, DC, MC, V* ⊙ *Closed Sun.*

$$ ✕**La Calesa.** Head to this centrally located restaurant for good Peruvian cuisine. Try the *ají* (chicken stew with cheese, milk, and peppers), but be careful not to burn your mouth. Peruvian dishes, particularly the stews,

are spicier than their Chilean counterparts. ✉ *Yungay 735* 📞 *63/225–467* 🍴 *AE, DC, MC, V* 🕐 *Closed Sun. No lunch Sat.*

$$ ✗**Camino de Luna.** The Way of the Moon floats on a barge on the Río Valdivia, just north of the Pedro de Valdivia bridge. As the city is only a few miles from the ocean, it's no surprise that seafood is a specialty here. The *congrío calle calle* (conger eel in a cheese-and-tomato sauce) is particularly good. Tables by the windows offer views of Isla Teja. ✉ *Av. Arturo Prat Costanera s/n* 📞 *63/213–788* 🍴 *AE, DC, MC, V.*

$$$ ✗**Salón de Té Entrelagos.** This swanky café caters to Valdivian business executives, who make deals over sandwiches (try the Isla Teja—with grilled chicken, tomato, artichoke hearts, asparagus, olives, and red peppers), decadent crepes, and desserts. In the evenings, the atmosphere is less formal—the menu is exactly the same—as the Entrelagos becomes a place to meet friends and converse well into the night. ✉ *Vicente Pérez Rosales 640* 📞 *63/218–333* 🍴 *AE, DC, MC, V.*

WHERE TO STAY

$ 🏨**Aires Buenos Hostal.** Near Valdivia's downtown, this renovated, old, and strikingly handsome house is a great find. The price is cheap, but the place is clean, friendly, and warm. It's mostly a backpackers' haven, but there are some private rooms. **Pros:** Price, location. **Cons:** Not many amenities, noise in ground-floor rooms. ✉ *Garcia Reyes 550* 📞 *63/206–304* 🌐 *www.airesbuenos.cl* 🛏 *10 rooms, 5 with bath* 🛋 *In-room: no a/c, no phone, no TV, Wi-Fi. In-hotel: public Internet, public Wi-Fi, parking, no-smoking rooms* 🍴 *AE, DC, MC V* ⭕*BP.*

¢ 🏕**Complejo Turístico Isla Teja.** The campsites at this facility sit in the middle of an apple orchard with an attractive view of the Río Valdivia. There's electricity and hot showers. ✉ *Los Cipreses 1125, Isla Teja* 📞 *63/213–584* 📞 *63/225–855.*

$ 🏨**Hotel El Castillo.** A grand 1920s German-style house sits at Niebla's main intersection on the riverfront and has been converted into this lovely bed-and-breakfast with lots of knickknacks, antiques, and cuckoo clocks in the common areas. Rooms have more modern amenities, but retain the old wood finishing, and overlook either the river or the pool and back gardens. A new wing has been added, but it blends seamlessly with the original house. **Pros:** Nice ambience, good rooms. **Cons:** No restaurant. ✉ *Antonio Ducce* 📞 *63/282–061* 🌐*hotelelcastillo@hotmail.com* 🛏 *11 rooms, 2 cabins* 🛋 *In-room: no a/c. In-hotel: pools, no elevator, parking, no-smoking rooms* 🍴 *AE, DC, MC, V* ⭕*BP.*

$$ 🏨**Hotel Isla Teja.** This affordable hotel doubles as student housing for the Universidad Austral, though a section is open for non-university guests. The rooms are quiet and comfortable, with modern amenities. **Pros:** Comfortable rooms. **Cons:** Not close to town. ✉ *Las Encinas 220, Isla Teja* 📞 *63/215–014* 🌐*www.hotelislateja.cl* 🛏 *90 rooms* 🛋 *In-room: no a/c, Wi-Fi (some). In-hotel: restaurant, bar, room service, no elevator, laundry service, concierge, executive floor, public Internet, public Wi-Fi, airport shuttle, parking* 🍴 *AE, DC, MC, V* ⭕*CP.*

$$–$$$ 🏨**Hotel Naguilán.** You can relax at this charming hotel's poolside gar-
★ den while watching the boats pass by on the Río Valdivia. Rooms in the property's newer building are bigger, with balconies and more modern

furnishings; the older rooms, in a building that dates from 1890, are smaller and have lime-green carpeting, but they have more character, and are cheaper. Service-wise, you're in good hands—as soon as you check in, a waiter will appear to offer you a welcome pisco sour. **Pros:** Good service, river location. **Cons:** No Wi-Fi in rooms. ⊠*General Lagos 1927*☎*63/212–851* ⊕*www.hotelnaguilan.com* ⇖*33 rooms, 3 suites* ⌂*In-room: no a/c, refrigerator (some), dial-up. In-hotel: restaurant, bar, room service, pool, laundry service, no elevator, public Wi-Fi, parking, no-smoking rooms* ⊟*AE, DC, MC, V* ⏇*BP.*

$$$ ⊡**Hotel Puerta del Sur.** Expect lavish pampering with top-notch service at this highly regarded lodging. Spacious rooms, all with river views, are decorated in soft lavender tones. Play a few games of tennis, then hit the pool or relax in the hot tub. You're near the edge of town, so it's good to have your own car. **Pros:** Good service, lots of activities. **Cons:** At edge of town. ⊠*Los Lingues 950, Isla Teja*☎*63/224–500* ⊕*www.hotelpuertadelsur.com* ⇖*45 rooms, 3 suites* ⌂*In-room: safe, refrigerator, DVD, Wi-Fi. In-hotel: restaurant, bars, room service, tennis court, pool, gym, spa, bicycles, laundry service, concierge, executive floor, public Internet, public Wi-Fi, parking* ⊟*AE, DC, MC, V* ⏇*BP.*

$ ⊡**Los Renovales.** In a renovated home on the banks of the Calle Calle River, just a seven-minute drive from the center of Valdivia, this relatively new hotel offers hospitality in a setting you may not want to leave. The rooms are ample, with lots of natural light, and many have a nice view of the river. The quality of the service and facilities in relation to price is excellent. **Pros:** Good value, river setting, homey environment. **Cons:** No pool or other luxuries. ⊠*Pedro Aguirre Cerda 1415*☎*63/278–562* ⊕*www.losrenovales.cl* ⇖*9 rooms, 2 suites* ⌂*In-room: safe, Ethernet, Wi-Fi. In-hotel: restaurant, room service, bar, no elevator, laundry service, public Internet, public Wi-Fi, parking* ⊟*AE, DC, MC, V* ⏇*BP.*

NIGHTLIFE

New York Discotheque (⊠*Km 6 Camino a Niebla* ☎*63/299–999*) is an upbeat discotheque for mostly the younger crowd. **El Legado Bar** (⊠*Esmeralda 657*☎*63/207–546*) is a very cool jazz bar in the heart of the Esmeralda bar scene. **Papadaki's** (⊠*Esmeralda 677*☎*63/246–700*), a combination bar-disco, is a popular hangout that also sometimes has live music.

EN ROUTE   **Isla Huapi.** Some 20% of Chile's 1 million Mapuche live on *reducciones,* or reservations. One of the most welcoming communities is on Isla Huapi, a leafy island in the middle of deep-blue Lago Ranco. It's out of the way—about 80 km (48 mi) southeast of Valdivia—but worth the trip for those interested in Mapuche culture. A boat departs from Futorno, on the northern shore of the lake, at 7 AM Monday, Wednesday, and Friday, returning at 5 PM. The pastoral quiet of Isla Huapi is broken once a year in January or February with the convening of the island council, in conjunction with the Lepún harvest festival. You are welcome during the festival, but be courteous with your camera.

CLOSE UP

Hier ist alles so Deutsch

You'll meet people in the Lake District with names like María Schmidt or Pablo Gudenschwager. At first, such juxtapositions sound odd, but, remember, this melting pot of a country was liberated by a man, good Irishman that he was, named Bernardo O'Higgins.

The Lake District's Germanic origins can be traced to one Vicente Pérez Rosales. (Every town and city in the region names a street for him, and one of Puerto Montt's more fabulous lodgings carries his name.) Armed with photos of the region, Don Vicente, as everyone knew him in his day, made several trips on behalf of the Chilean government to Germany, Switzerland, and Austria in the mid-19th century. His mission? To recruit

waves of European immigrants to settle the Lake District and end 300 years of Mapuche domination in the region once and for all.

Thousands signed on the dotted line and made the long journey to start a new life in southern Chile. It was a giant leap of faith for the original settlers, but it didn't hurt that the region looked just like the parts of Central Europe that they'd come from. The result was *küchen,* sausage, and a good old-fashioned work ethic mixed with a Latin-spirited, oom-pah-pah gemütlichkeit. But don't bother to dust off that high-school German for your trip here; few people speak it these days.

—Jeffrey Van Fleet

6

OSORNO

107 km (65 mi) southeast of Valdivia, via Ruta 5, Pan-American Hwy.

Workaday Osorno is the least visited of the Lake District's four major cities. Like other communities in the region, it bears the imprint of the German settlers who arrived in the 1880s. Osorno, in a bend of the Río Rahue, is convenient for exploring the nearby national parks.

GETTING HERE & AROUND

Osorno is a 1½-hour flight from Santiago. By car, Osorno is reached by the paved Ruta 5, or Pan-American Highway. There is also passenger train service via Temuco. All the main bus lines serve Osorno.

ESSENTIALS

BUS **Buses Vía Octay** (✉ *Errázuriz 1400* ☎ *64/237–043*). **Osorno Bus Depot** (✉ *Errázuriz 1400* ☎ *64/234–149*).

CURRENCY **Banco BCI** (✉ *MacKenna 801*). **Cambiotur** (✉ *MacKenna 1010*).

INTERNET **Chat-Mail-MP3** (✉ *Patricio Lynch 1334*). **Internet Skype** (✉ *MacKenna 939* ☎ *64/319–707*).

MAIL **Correos de Chile** (✉ *Av. Bernardo O'Higgins 645*).

MEDICAL **Farmacias Ahumada** (✉ *Eleuterio Ramírez 981* ☎ *64/421–561*). **Hospital Base Osorno** (✉ *Dr. Guillermo Bühler 1765* ☎ *64/235–571*).

Osorno Tourist Office (⊠ *Plaza de Armas* ☎ *64/218–714*).**Sernatur** (⊠ *Bernardo O'Higgins 667* ☎ *64/237–575*).

WHAT TO SEE

Mapu Lahual. This network of indigenous parks spreads over nine Huilluiche Indian communities on the Pacific coast, amid 123,553 acres of temperate rain forest. The communities offer four tour programs, from one to seven days in duration. However you choose to see these parks, you will find some of the most spectacular nature areas in Chile. In addition, you will get a first-hand look at indigenous culture and have the opportunity to buy native handicrafts. ⊠ *Ramirez 116, oficina 7, Osorno* ☎ *08/186–3083* ⊕ *www.mapulahual.cl.*

Osorno's **tourist office** arranges free daily tours in summer. Each day has a different focus: walks around the city, fruit orchards, or nearby farms are a few of the offerings. ⊠ *North side of Plaza de Armas* ☎ *64/264– 250* ⊑ *Free* ☉ *Office: Dec.–Feb., daily 8–8; Mar.–Nov., weekdays 9–1 and 2:30–6. Tours: daily 10:30.*

The 1960 earthquake left Osorno with little historic architecture, but a row of **19th-century houses** miraculously survived on Calle Juan Mackenna between Lord Cochrane and Freire. Their distinctively sloped roofs, which allow adequate drainage of rain and snow, are replicated in many of Osorno's newer houses.

The modern **Catedral de San Mateo Apostol** fronts the Plaza de Armas and is topped with a tower resembling a bishop's mitre. "Turn off your cell phone," the sign at the door admonishes those who enter. "You don't need it to communicate with God." ⊠ *Plaza de Armas* ☎ *No phone* ☉ *Mass: Mon.–Sat. 7:15 PM; Sun. 10:30, noon, and 8:15.*

The **Museo Municipal Osorno** contains a decent collection of Mapuche artifacts, Chilean and Spanish firearms, and exhibits devoted to the German settlement of Osorno. Housed in a pink neoclassical building dating from 1929, this is one of the few older structures in the city center. ⊠ *Manuel Antonio Matta 809* ☎ *64/238–615* ⊑ *Free* ☉ *Mon.– Thurs. 9:30–5:30, Fri. 9:30–4:30, Sat. 2–6.*

WHERE TO EAT

$ ✕ **Café Central.** You can dig into a hearty American-style breakfast in the morning, and burgers and sandwiches the rest of the day, at this diner on the Plaza de Armas. The friendly, bustling staff speaks no English, but an English menu will be presented to you on request. ⊠ *Av. Bernardo O'Higgins 610* ☎ *64/257–711* ⊟ *DC, MC, V.*

$$ ✕ **Club Alemán.** This was the first in a network of German associations in southern Chile. Established in 1862, it predated the first big waves of European immigration. Despite the exclusive-sounding name, anyone can dine here. There's usually a choice of four or five rotating prix-fixe menus for lunch and dinner, often including a seafood stew or a hearty cazuela, and lots of tasty küchen and other pastries for dessert. ⊠ *Av. Bernardo O'Higgins 563* ☎ *64/232–784* ⊟ *AE, DC, MC, V.*

WHERE TO STAY

$ ⊞ **Gran Hotel Osorno.** Osorno's grande dame, built in the era when art deco was all the rage, has stood the test of time. The five-story hotel has an unbeatable location on the Plaza de Armas. The rooms, although a tad dark, are clean and comfortable. Mercifully, the hotel's Power Disco has closed, though the neon sign still blinks out front. **Pros:** Great location. **Cons:** Tired interior. ⊠ *Av. Bernardo O'Higgins 615* ☏ *64/232–171* 🖷 *64/239–311* ✍ *granhotelosorno@entelchile.net* 📧 *70 rooms* ⚘ *In-room: no a/c, safe, refrigerator. In-hotel: restaurant, bar, laundry service, public Wi-Fi* ☱ *AE, DC, MC, V.*

$$$ ⊞ **Hotel García Hurtado de Mendoza.** This stately hotel two blocks from the Plaza de Armas is one of Osorno's nicest lodgings. Classical lines grace the traditional furnishings and complement the subdued fabrics of the bright and airy guest rooms. **Pros:** Good location, rooms are pleasant. **Cons:** Dated-looking common spaces. ⊠ *Juan Mackenna 1040* ☏ *64/237–111* 🖷 *64/237–115* ⊕ *www.hotelgarciahurtado.cl* 📧 *31 rooms* ⚘ *In-room: no a/c, Ethernet, Wi-Fi. In-hotel: restaurant, bar, room service, laundry service, public Internet, public Wi-Fi, parking, no-smoking rooms* ☱ *AE, DC, MC, V* ⎀ *BP.*

$ ⊞ **Hotel Innsbruck.** Osorno's most Germanic hotel, the Innsbruck has half-timbered walls and flower boxes in the windows. Rooms are small and simply furnished with little more than beds, nightstands, and televisions, but the vaulted ceilings make them seem spacious. **Pros:** Classic Patagonia. **Cons: Small rooms.** ⊠ *Manuel Rodríguez 941* ☏ *64/242–000* ✍ *hinnsbruck@telsur.cl* 📧 *16 rooms* ⚘ *In-room: no a/c. In-hotel: bar, no elevator, laundry service, parking* ☱ *AE, DC, MC, V* ⎀ *CP.*

$$ ⊞ **Hotel Lagos del Sur.** This hotel near the Plaza de Armas provides attentive service and a quiet place to work. Warm golds and greens make a splash in sparkling white guest rooms. The color scheme echoes the building's dark-green exterior. Doubles include a small sitting room off to one side. **Pros:** Good for business travel. **Cons:** A bit tattered. ⊠ *Av. Bernardo O'Higgins 564* ☏ *64/243–244* 🖷 *64/243–696* ⊕ *www.hotelagosdelsur.cl* 📧 *20 rooms* ⚘ *In-room: no a/c, Wi-Fi. In-hotel: bar, laundry service, no elevator, parking, public Internet, public Wi-Fi* ☱ *AE, DC, MC, V* ⎀ *CP.*

EN ROUTE An Osorno business executive's love for tail fins and V-8 engines led him to establish the **Auto Museum Moncopulli.** His particular passion is the little-respected Studebaker, which accounts for 50 of the 80 vehicles on display. ⊠ *Ruta 215, 25 km (16 mi) east of Osorno, Puyehue* ☏ *64/210–744* ⊕ *www.moncopulli.cl* 🎟 *2,000 pesos* ⊙ *Dec.–Mar., daily 10–8; Apr.–Nov., daily 10–6.*

PARQUE NACIONAL PUYEHUE

81 km (49 mi) east of Osorno, via Ruta 215.

Chile's most popular national park, Parque Nacional Puyehue draws crowds who come to bask in its famed hot springs. Most never venture beyond them, and that's a shame. A dozen miles east of the Aguas Cali-

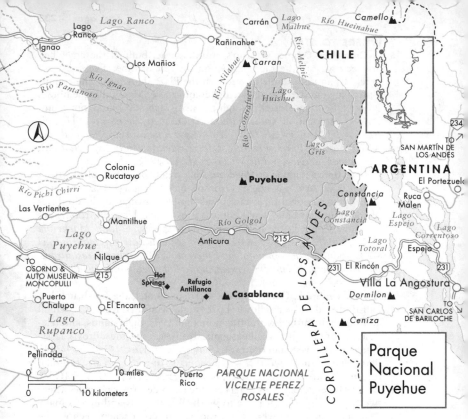

entes sector lies a network of short trails leading to evergreen forests with dramatic waterfalls.

Truly adventurous types attempt the five-hour hike to the summit of 7,350-foot Volcán Puyehue. As with most climbs in this region, CONAF rangers insist on ample documentation of experience before allowing you to set out. Access to the 1,070-square-km (413-square-mi) park is easy: head due east from Osorno on the highway leading to Argentina. ⊠ *Ruta 215* ☎ *64/197–4572* 🖼 *800 pesos* ☉ *Dec.–Feb., daily 8 AM–9 PM; Apr.–Oct., daily 8–8.*

WHERE TO STAY

$$ 📠 **Termas Aguas Calientes.** Just a few kilometers up the road from Termas Puyehue, this is a more affordable, somewhat more independent way to enjoy hot springs and see Puyehue Park. The triangular-shaped cabins are comfortable and well-equipped, and there are two campgrounds costing 6,000 or 10,000 pesos per day. The use of thermal pools costs 6,000 pesos. Their spa offers massages (including a chocolate massage) and facial treatments. ⊠ *Camino Antillanca, Km 4, Puyehue National Park* ☎ *64/331–710* ⊕ *www.termasaguascalientes.com* 🛏 *26 cabins* ♨ *In-room: no a/c, no phone, kitchen, refrigerator. In-hotel: restaurant, pools, spa, parking* ▤ *AE, DC, MC, V.*

$$$–$$$$ 🔳 **Termas Puyehue Wellness and Spa Resort.** Probably Chile's most famous
★ hot-springs resort, this grandiose stone-and-wood lodge sits on the edge
of Parque Nacional Puyehue. Make no mistake: the place is enormous,
with a slate of activities to match, offering everything from darts to
skiing. Yet, despite its huge popularity, and the fact that something is
always going on, it can be surprisingly relaxing. Most people come to
soak in the thermal pools. The rooms and common areas mix starkly
modern and 19th-century Germanic features: chrome, hardwoods, and
even some modern art happily share the same space. The hotel recently
changed to all-inclusive, with meals, drinks, excursions, and use of the
pools and thermal baths included in the price. If you're not staying as
a guest, an all-day pass for the use of the springs and pools, with meals
included, is 30,000 pesos weekdays, 35,000 pesos on weekends and
holidays. ⊠ *Ruta 215, Km 76, Puyehue* ☎ *64/232–881, 2/293–6000
in Santiago* ⊕ *www.puyehue.cl* ⟳ *137 rooms* ⌂ *In-room: no a/c, safe,
refrigerator, Wi-Fi. In-hotel: 3 restaurants, room service, bar, tennis
courts, pools, gym, spa, bicycles, water sports, children's programs,
laundry service, concierge, public Internet, public Wi-Fi, airport shut-
tle, parking* ⊟ *AE, DC, MC, V* ⦿ *BP.*

PUERTO OCTAY

*50 km (30 mi) southeast of Osorno, via Ruta 5, the Pan-American
Hwy.*

The story goes that a German merchant named Ochs set up shop in this
community on the northern tip of Lago Llanquihue. A phrase uttered
by customers looking for a particular item, "*¿Ochs, hay . . .?*" ("Ochs,
do you have . . .?"), gradually became "Octay." With spectacular views
of the Osorno and Calbuco volcanoes, the town was the birthplace of
Lake District tourism: a wealthy Santiago businessman constructed a
mansion outside town in 1912, using it as a vacation home to host
his friends. (That structure is now the Hotel Centinela.) Puerto Octay
doesn't have the frenetic energy of neighboring Frutillar and Puerto
Varas, but its many fans enjoy its more-authentic nature.

WHERE TO STAY & EAT

$$ ✕ **Restaurant Baviera.** Because it's on the Plaza de Armas, this is a popular lunch stop for tour groups. Baviera serves solid German fare—
schnitzel, sauerkraut, sausage, and küchen are among the favorites.
Beer steins and other Bavarian paraphernalia lining the walls evoke the
old country. ⊠ *German Wulf 582* ☎ *64/391–460* ⊟ *No credit cards.*

$$$ 🔳 **Hotel Centinela.** Simple and elegant, the venerable 1912 Hotel Centi-
★ nela remains one of Chile's best-known accommodations. This impos-
ing wood-shingled lodge with a dramatic turret sits amid 20 forested
acres at the tip of Península Centinela jutting into Lago Llanquihue.
Britain's Edward VII, then Prince of Wales, was the most famous guest
(but there's some mystery as to whether his future wife, American divor-
cée Wallis Simpson, accompanied him). Imposing beds and armoires fill
the huge rooms in the main building. The cabins, whose rates include
three meals a day delivered to the door, are more modern than the

6

rooms in the lodge. ⊠*Península de Centinela, 5 km (3 mi) south of Puerto Octay* 🏨🏨*64/391–326* ⊕*www.hotelcentinela.cl* ➽*11 rooms, 1 suite, 18 cabins* ♿*In-room: no a/c, no TV (some). In-hotel: restaurant, bar, beachfront, no elevator* ▤*AE, DC, MC, V* ☉❙*BP, FAP.*

$ ⊡ **Zapato Amarillo.** Backpackers make up the majority of the clientele
★ here, but this is no scruffy youth hostel. This modern alerce-shingled house with wood-paneled rooms affords a drop-dead gorgeous view of Volcán Osorno outside town. Armin Dubendorfer and Nadi Muñoz, the eager-to-please Chilean-Swiss couple that owns it, will arrange guided horseback-riding, hiking, and cycling tours, as well as cheese-fondue evening gatherings. Rates include an excellent buffet breakfast that uses local fruits and dairy products. You also have access to the kitchen. ⊠*2 km (1 mi) north of Puerto Octay on road to Osorno* 🏨🏨*64/210–787* ⊕*www.zapatoamarillo.cl* ➽*7 rooms, 2 with bath* ♿*In-room: no a/c, no phone, no TV. In-hotel: bicycles, laundry facilities, public Internet, no elevator* ▤*No credit cards* ☉❙*BP.*

FRUTILLAR

30 km (18 mi) southwest of Puerto Octay.

Halfway down the western edge of Lago Llanquihue is the small town of Frutillar, a destination for European immigrants in the late 19th century and, today, arguably the most picturesque Lake District community. The town—actually two adjacent hamlets, Frutillar Alto and Frutillar Bajo—is known for its perfectly preserved German architecture. Don't be disappointed if your first sight of the town is the nondescript neighborhood (the Alto) on the top of the hill; head down to the charming streets of Frutillar Bajo that face the lake, with their picture-perfect view of Volcán Osorno.

ESSENTIALS

CURRENCY **Banco Santander** (⊠*Av. Philippi 555* 🕾*65/421–228*).

MEDICAL **Farmacia Frutillar** (⊠*Av. Carlos Richter 170*). **Hospital Frutillar** (⊠*Las Piedras* 🕾*65/421–386*).

VISITOR INFO **Informacion Turistica** (⊠*Costanera Philippi in front of boat dock* 🕾*65/421–080*). **Secretaria Muncipal de Turismo** (⊠*Av. Philippi 753* 🕾*65/421–685*).

WHAT TO SEE

Each year, in late January and early February, the town hosts **Semanas Musicales de Frutillar,** an excellent series of mostly classical concerts (and a little jazz) in the lakeside Centro de Conciertos y Eventos, a semi-outdoor venue. Ticket prices are a reasonable 3,000–10,000 pesos. ⊠*Av. Phillipi 1000* 🕾*65/421–290* ⊕*www.semanasmusicales.cl.*

Culture in Frutillar is not only about Semanas Musicales. In the Centro de Conciertos y Eventos is also housed the **Teatro del Lago,** with a year-round schedule of concerts, art shows, and film. Events take place every week. ⊠*Av. Phillipi 1000* 🕾*65/422–954* ⊕*www.teatrodellago.cl.*

★ You step into the past when you step into one of southern Chile's best museums, the **Museo Colonial Alemán.** Besides displays of the 19th-century agricultural and household implements, this open-air museum has full-scale reconstructions of buildings—a smithy and barn, among others—used by the original German settlers. Exhibits are labeled in Spanish and, *natürlich*, German, but there are also a few signs in English. A short walk from the lake up Avenida Arturo Prat, the museum also has beautifully landscaped grounds and great views of Volcán Osorno. ⊠ *Av. Vicente Pérez Rosales at Av. Arturo Prat* ☎ *65/421–142* ✆ *1,800 pesos* ⊘ *Dec.–Feb., daily 10–7; Mar.–Nov., daily 10–2 and 3–5.*

WHERE TO EAT

¢ ✕ **Café Capuccini.** Sink into one of the plush couches here and write some postcards while you nurse a gourmet coffee drink on a chilly evening. If the couches are taken—they are in demand—grab one of the small tables adorned with a musical-score lamp shade. All have superb lake and volcano views out the curving, sweeping picture window. This café in the new Centro de Conciertos y Eventos complex caters mostly to a pre- and post-theater crowd, but it serves up light fare (sandwiches, küchen, and desserts) on brown stoneware to anyone, any day. ⊠ *Av. Phillipi 1000* ☎ *65/422–900* ☐ *No credit cards.*

$$ ✕ **Club Alemán.** This German restaurant in the center of town has a selection of four or five rotating prix-fixe menus that cost 3,500 pesos. There will always be a meat and seafood option—often steak and salmon—with soup, salad, and dessert. Don't forget the küchen. ⊠ *Philippi 747* ☎ *65/421–249* ☐ *AE, DC, MC, V.*

$$ ✕ **Guten Apetit.** On the waterfront, with tables both outdoors and inside, this is a friendly place with good food. It's the standard southern Chilean menu, from clam stews and Barros Lucos (a classic Chilean sandwich of beef and melted cheese) to large beef and chicken dishes. But they also have a few German imports such as Chuletas Kasler, a German pork chop. In summer, a pianist busts out tunes from 12:30 to 4 PM every day. ⊠ *Balmaceda 98* ☎ *65/421–145* ☐ *AE, DC, MC.*

WHERE TO STAY

$$ 🏨 **Hotel Ayacara.** A beautiful, yellow-and-green house on the lakefront, this bed-and-breakfast is one of Frutillar's best. The service is friendly, the rooms are a delight. **Pros:** Fun and friendly. **Cons:** Not much privacy. ⊠ *Av. Philippi corner of Pedro Aguirre* ☎ *65/421–550, 2/430–7000 in Santiago* ⊕ *www.hotelayacara.cl* ⇆ *8 rooms* △ *In-room: no a/c, Wi-Fi. In-hotel: restaurant, room service, bar, beachfront, no elevator, laundry service, public Wi-Fi, parking, no-smoking rooms* ☐ *AE, DC, MC, V* ⦿ *BP.*

$$ 🏨 **Hotel Elun.** From just about every vantage point at this hillside lodging just south of town—the lobby, the library, and, of course, the guest rooms—you have a spectacular view of Lago Llanquihue. Each room has huge bay windows framing Volcán Osorno. Add the exceptionally attentive owners to the mix, and you have a real find. **Pros:** Great views. **Cons:** A bit homely. ⊠ *Costanera Sur* ☎ *65/420–055* 🖷 *65/420–170* ⊕ *www.hotelelun.cl* ⇆ *14 rooms, 3 suites* △ *In-room: no a/c, safe, refrigerator. In-hotel: restaurant, bar, room service, bicycles, laundry service, no elevator, public Internet, public Wi-Fi, parking, no-smoking rooms* ☐ *AE, DC, MC, V* ⦿ *BP.*

$$ ⊞**Hotel Kaffee Bauernhaus.** Gingerbread cutouts and swirls adorn this pretty 1911 home-turned-inn. You couldn't ask for a much better location—the property is right on the lake, although only one guest room has a lake view. All, however, are wood paneled and tastefully decorated with flowered bedspreads and curtains. The German breakfast is substantial. **Pros:** Great location. **Cons:** Not all rooms have a view. ⊠*Av. Philippi 663* ☏*65/420–003* ⊕*www.interpatagonia.com/bauernhaus* ⊃*8 rooms* ⌂*In-room: no a/c, no TV (some). In-hotel: restaurant, no elevator, public Wi-Fi, parking* ⊟*AE, DC, MC, V* ⦿*BP.*

$$ ⊞**Hotel Serenade.** The names of the guest rooms here reflect musical compositions—like *Fantasia* and *Wedding March*—and each door is painted with the first few sheet-music bars of the work it's named for. Inside are plush quilts and comforters, hardwood floors, and throw rugs. The cozy sitting room, overlooking a quiet side street, is another lovely place to relax. ⊠*Pedro Aguirre Cerda 50* ☏*65/420–332* ⊃*6 rooms* ⌂*In-room: no a/c, no TV. In-hotel: no elevator, laundry service, parking* ⊟*No credit cards* ⦿*CP.*

$–$$ ⊞**Hotel Villa San Francisco.** On a small hill overlooking the lake, the
★   location of this highly recommended hotel could not be better. At the tranquil end of the Costanera, or lakeside road, it has a spectacular view of the town and volcanoes while just a minute's walk from all the sights and sounds of Frutillar. All the rooms have lake views, along with a private terrace. The hotel also has a pleasant pool and a cozy bar and restaurant. This is a place to relax. Francisco Fayula de la Corte, its Spanish owner, took over the hotel in 1999 and has transformed it into Frutillar's top lodging choice. **Pros:** Lakeside view, good value, close to town. **Cons:** Some rooms are small. ⊠*Avda. Phillipi 1503* ☏*65/421–531* ⊕*www.villasanfrancisco.cl* ⊃*15 rooms* ⌂*In-room: no a/c, Wi-Fi. In-hotel: restaurant, room service, bar, pool, gym, beachfront, no elevator, laundry service, public Wi-Fi, parking* ⊟*AE, DC, MC, V* ⦿*BP.*

$$ ✕⊞**Salzburg Hotel & Spa.** Rooms at this Tyrolean-style lodge command excellent views of the lake. Cozy cabins and slightly larger bungalows, all made of native woods, are fully equipped with kitchens and private terraces. The staff will gladly organize fishing trips. The restaurant ($$) serves some of the best smoked salmon in the area. **Pros:** Great view, lots of privacy. **Cons:** Need a car. ⊠*Costanera Norte* ☏*65/421–589* ☏*65/421–599* ⊕*www.salzburg.cl* ⊃*31 rooms, 9 cabins, 5 bungalows* ⌂*In-room: no a/c, no TV. In-hotel: restaurant, bar, pool, spa, laundry service, parking, no elevator* ⊟*AE, DC, MC, V* ⦿*BP.*

BEACHES

Packed with summer crowds, the gray-sand **Playa Frutillar** stretches for 15 blocks along Avenida Philippi. From this point along Lago Llanquihue you have a spectacular view due east of the conical Volcán Osorno, as well as the lopsided Volcán Puntiagudo.

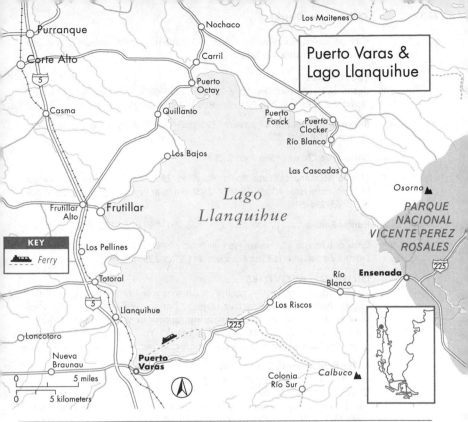

KEY

⛴ Ferry

0 ———— 5 miles

0 ———— 5 kilometers

PUERTO VARAS

27 km (16 mi) south of Frutillar via Ruta 5, Pan-American Hwy.

A small but fast-growing resort town on the edge of Lago Llanquihue, Puerto Varas is renowned for its view of the Osorno and Calbuco volcanoes. Stunning rose arbors and Germanic-style architecture grace the many centuries-old houses and churches that dot this tranquil town. Every year new hotels here crop up as tourism continues to rise significantly. Tons of cafés, trendy restaurants, an excellent casino, and a budding bar scene all point towards Puerto Varas's ascendancy as a serious challenge to Pucón, the region's top vacation spot.

GETTING HERE & AROUND

Puerto Varas is only about a 20-minute drive from the center of nearby Puerto Montt, making it a virtual suburb of that large city. You can get to the Puerto Montt airport via a 40-minute drive south on Ruta 5. Most of the bus lines that serve Puerto Montt make obligatory stops in Puerto Varas on their way north or south. Around town, there are numerous taxis and several minivan buses, which have various stops, the most prominent one on Avenida Salvador near the corner of Calle Santa Rosa. Both taxis and buses can take you to countryside locations such as Ensenada as well as Puerto Montt for a minimal cost. You can cross to Argentina via bus or boat.

ESSENTIALS

BUS **Buses JAC** (✉ *Walker Martinez 227* ☎ *65/236–000*). **Cruz del Sur** (✉ *Walker Martinez 239-B* ☎ *65/231–925*). **Tur-Bus** (✉ *Salvador 1093* ☎ *65/233–787*).

CURRENCY **Banco Santander** (✉ *Del Salvador 399* ☎ *65/237–255*). **Travelsur** (✉ *San Pedro 451* ☎ *65/236–000*).

MAIL **Correos de Chile** (✉ *San José 242*).

MEDICAL **Clinica Alemana** (✉ *Otto Bader 810* ☎ *65/239–100*). **Farmacia Cruz Verde** (✉ *San Francisco 400* ☎ *65/234–293*). **Farmacia Salco** (✉ *Del Salvador 400* ☎ *65/234–544*).

RENTAL CARS **Hunter Rent-a-Car** (✉ *San José 130* ☎ *65/237–950 or 65/522–454*).

VISITOR INFO **Casa del Turista** (✉ *Piedra Plen, in front of Plaza de Armas* ☎ *65/237–956*). **Oficina de Turismo** (✉ *San Francisco 441* ☎ *65/233–477*).

OUTDOOR ACTIVITIES

Fly-fishing is king in the region, with many rivers and the huge Lake Llanquihue making attractive targets. But the region has much more to offer: mountain biking, canyoning, hiking in Vicente Pérez Rosales Park, or just enjoying the lake by kayak. You can also hike up the nearby volcanoes, which makes for an exciting and scenic excursion.

Al Sur Expediciones (✉ *Del Salvador 100* ☎ *65/232–300* ⊕ *www.alsur expeditions.com*) is known for rafting and kayaking trips on the Class III Río Petrohué. It also runs horseback-riding and fly-fishing trips, and handles hotel reservations and guided tours for Pumalin Park. **Aqua Motion** (✉ *San Pedro 422* ☎ *65/232–747* ⊕ *www.aqua-motion. com*) is a longtime provider of rafting and kayaking excursions on the nearby Río Petrohué, as well as trekking, horseback riding, helicopter rides, bird-watching, and fly-fishing tours. **Margouya Tours** (✉ *Santa Rosa 318* ☎ *65/237–640*) specializes in half- and full-day canyoning and rappelling trips near Volcán Calbuco, in addition to kayaking and hiking excursions. **Miralejos** (✉ *San Pedro 311* ☎ *65/234–892* ⊕ *www. miralejos.com*) offers trekking, kayaking, mountaineering, horseback-riding trips throughout the region.

For fly-fishing in Puerto Varas, try **Tres Piedras** (✉ *Ruta 225, Km 22, Los Riscos* ☎ *65/330–157* ⊕ *www.trespiedras.cl*).

WHERE TO EAT

$ ✗ **Café Danes.** A friendly café-restaurant next to Santa Isabel Supermarket on Puerto Varas's main drag, Calle Del Salvador, the restaurant offers a set lunch menu as well as a range of plates, from sandwiches to beef and chicken dishes served up the Chilean way. The large beef and vegetarian empanadas and the illustrious küchen are not to be missed. ✉ *Del Salvador 441* ☎ *65/232–371* ⊟ *No credit cards.*

$ ✗ **Donde El Gordito.** You'll find great seafood here. Some of the fish is personally caught by the avid fisherman-owner, El Gordito, who is usually on hand with his wife to wait tables and ring up checks. This little eatery, housed inside a downtown fish market, also has entertaining decor, some of it chosen by its owner and some of it given to him by the many tourists that luckily find their way to his food. ⊠*San Bernardo 560* ☎*65/233–425* ▭*AE, DC, MC, V.*

$$ ✕**Mediterraneo.** This gourmet restaurant and bar has a privileged view of the lake and volcanoes. A constantly changing menu of sophisticated beef, chicken, and seafood plates combine the best of the local culinary scene with Mediterranean-style cooking. Reserve a table by the window. ⊠*Santa Rosa 68* ☎*65/237–268* ▭*AE, DC, MC, V.*

$$ ✕**La Olla.** This lakeside restaurant does not look like much, but it serves
★ the best fish and seafood dishes in Chile, according to its legion of fans. The specialties of the house are seafood empanadas and other, more simply elegant preparations. It's almost always full during peak hours, so reserve a table ahead of time. ⊠*Av. Vicente Pérez Rosales 1071* ☎*65/234–605* ⌖*Reservations essential* ▭*AE, DC, MC, V.*

WHERE TO STAY

$$ ⊞**Los Alerces Hotel & Cabanas.** Across the street from the town's most popular beach for swimming and tanning, this is a clean, comfortable option. Wood-paneled walls and paintings of flowers predominate. The cabins on-site are a perfect place for a family stay. The hotel pool is inviting, too. **Pros:** Close to beach, large cabins. **Cons:** It's a hike to walk to town. ⊠*Av. Vicente Pérez Rosales 1281* ☎*65/235–985* ⊕*www.hotellosalerces.cl* ⌗*44 rooms, 10 cabins* ⌂*In-room: no a/c, refrigerator, Wi-Fi. In-hotel: restaurant, room service, bar, pool, no elevator, laundry service, executive floor, public Internet, public Wi-Fi, parking, no-smoking rooms* ▭*AE, DC, MC, V* ⍩*BP.*

$$ ⊞**The Guest House.** The aroma of fresh coffee greets you all day long, and little homemade chocolates wait on your pillow at this B&B, a restored 1926 mansion just a couple of blocks from downtown. Period furnishings and antiques fill the cheery rooms. Vicky Johnson, Guest House's exuberant American owner, is a longtime resident of Chile and a font of information. **Pros:** Good location. **Cons:** Not much privacy. ⊠*Av. Bernardo O'Higgins 608* ☎*65/231–521* ⊕*www.vicki-johnson. com/guesthouse* ⌗*9 rooms* ⌂*In-room: no a/c, no TV, Wi-Fi. In-hotel: room service, no elevator, laundry service, public Internet, public Wi-Fi, airport shuttle, parking, no-smoking rooms* ▭*No credit cards* ⍩*BP.*

$$$ ⊞**Hotel Bellavista.** This hotel, an eclectic mix of traditional Bavarian and modern architectural styles, sits right on the lake. Most of the bright rooms have views of the nearby volcanoes, and some have their own balconies. Stylish contemporary furnishings are upholstered in tailored stripes. **Pros:** Great views. **Cons:** None of the frills you might expect. ⊠*Av. Vicente Pérez Rosales 60* ☎*65/232–011* ☐*65/232–013* ⌗*70 rooms, 3 suites* ⌂*In-room: no a/c, safe, refrigerator, Ethernet, Wi-Fi. In-hotel: restaurant, bar, room service, laundry service, public Internet, public Wi-Fi, airport shuttle, parking* ▭*AE, DC, MC, V* ⍩*BP.*

$$$ ⊞**Hotel Cabañas del Lago.** The pine-paneled cabins, hidden among carefully tended gardens, make this place special. Each A-frame unit, which can accommodate five people, is decorated with lace curtains and floral-pattern bedding, and has a woodstove and full kitchen. Most

rooms in the main hotel are a little on the small side, but they're cozy and have lovely views of Volcán Osorno. **Pros:** Great views. **Cons:** Small rooms. ⊠*Klenner 195* ☎*65/232–291* ⊕*www.cabanasdellago.cl* ⚓*130 rooms, 11 cabins, 3 suites* ⚐*In-room: no a/c, safe, refrigerator (some), Ethernet (some). In-hotel: restaurant, bar, room service, pool, spa, laundry service, public Internet, public Wi-Fi, parking, airport shuttle, no-smoking rooms* ⊟*AE, DC, MC, V.*

$$ ⚏**Hotel El Greco.** In a remodeled German schoolhouse more than a century old, this hotel is a friendly, comfy place to stay. It's also literally a minute from the town center, and its hill setting affords it wonderful views. ⊠*Mirador 134* ☎*65/233–880* ⊕*www.hotelelgreco.cl* ⚓*12 rooms* ⚐*In-room: no a/c. In-hotel: no elevator, laundry service, public Internet, airport shuttle, parking* ⊟*AE, DC, MC, V* ⦿*BP.*

$$ ⚏**Hotel Licarayén.** Balcony rooms overlook Lago Llanquihue at this rambling Bavarian-style chalet. Other rooms are bright, with wood paneling and pleasant views of the garden. The fireplace in the common sitting room keeps things warm. **Pros:** Great locations. **Cons:** Plain. ⊠*San José 114* ☎*65/232–305* ☎*65/232–955* ⊕*www.hotelicarayen.cl* ⚓*23 rooms, 1 suite* ⚐*In-room: no a/c, Ethernet, Wi-Fi. In-hotel: room service, gym, public Internet, public Wi-Fi, laundry service, parking, no elevator* ⊟*AE, DC, MC, V* ⦿*CP.*

$$$ ⚏**Melia Patagonia.** One of the few legitimate five-star hotels in south-
★ ern Chile, this relaxing, comfortable hotel is close to downtown. For the hotel's opening in 2007, the Chilean owners modernized what was once Puerto Varas's most prestigious hotel and casino. Rooms are immaculate, the service attentive, and the views from the hotel terrace superb. A regular happy hour and live music make Bar Kutral a popular town hangout. **Pros:** Excellent service, attention to detail, spacious rooms, bar. **Cons:** Gym and pool are small, not all rooms have lake views. ⊠*Klenner 349* ☎*65/201–000* ⊕*www.solmelia.com* ⚓*91 rooms, 2 suites* ⚐*In-room: safe, refrigerator, Ethernet, Wi-Fi. In-hotel: 2 restaurants, room service, bar, pool, gym, spa, laundry service, executive floor, public Internet, public Wi-Fi, parking* ⊟*AE, DC, MC, V* ⦿*BP.*

NIGHTLIFE

The flashy **Casino de Puerto Varas** (⊠*Del Salvador 21* ☎*65/346–600*) dominates the center of town. It has all the Vegas-style trappings, from slot machines to roulette, along with weekly Vegas-style entertainment. The **Barómetro** (⊠*Walker Martinez 584* ☎*65/346–100*) is the town's most lively bar. Expect a DJ most nights, and often live music. On Friday nights, the live jazz at **The Garage** (⊠*Walker Martinez 220*) is an uplifting event and the beer flows fast at the long bar. Young people in their teens or twenties in search of a place to dance the night away go to **La Playa** (⊠*Av. Vicente Pérez Rosales 1400* ☎*8/839–8577*), in Puerto Chico across the street from the town's main beach.

ENSENADA

47 km (28 mi) east of Puerto Varas.

A drive along the southern shore of Lago Llanquihue to Ensenada takes you through the heart of Chile's *murta*-growing country. Queen Victoria is said to have developed a fondness for these tart, red berries, and today you'll find them used as ingredients in the region's syrups, jams, and küchen. Frutillar, Puerto Varas, and Puerto Octay might all boast about their views of Volcán Osorno, but you can really feel up close and personal with the volcano when you arrive in the town of Ensenada, which also neighbors the jagged Volcán Calbuca. The lake drive also illustrates how volcanoes play hide-and-seek on you: you'll see neither along a given stretch of road; then suddenly, you round a bend, or the clouds will part, and there they are.

WHERE TO STAY & EAT

$$ 🏨 **Hotel Puerto Pilar.** On the shore of Lago Llanquihue, this hotel's many activities and perfect volcano views make it immensely popular. If you want the get-away-from-it-all feel for which the place was originally known, opt for one of the fully furnished cabins. Eight of them are constructed in *palafito*-style, held up with stilts right on the lakeshore (a style most commonly seen on the island of Chiloé); you can even fish right from your deck. Carpeted rooms in the main lodge all come with king beds and enormous windows. ⊠ *Ruta 225, Km 27* ☎ *65/335–378, 2/650–8118 in Santiago* ⊕ *www.hotelpuertopilar.cl* ➡ *18 rooms, 2 suites, 13 cabins* ⟷ *In-room: no a/c, safe, refrigerator, Wi-Fi. In-hotel: restaurant, bar, room service, tennis court, pool, beachfront, laundry service, public Internet, public Wi-Fi, parking, no-smoking rooms* ⊟ *AE, DC, MC, V* ⓘ*BP.*

$$ ✕🏨 **Onces de Bellavista.** If you're traveling by car in the afternoon near
★ Ensenada, be sure to stop here. They only serve "onces," which is a sort of Chilean teatime. For 6,500 pesos you get great küchen, cake, bread, cheese, salami, coffee, tea, chocolate, and more. You'll have a panoramic view of the volcanoes and lake while you dine. There is also a minizoo with animals such as llamas and guanaco, a tennis court, and a private lakeside beach. They have six well-equipped cabins if you want to stay overnight. In summer, onces are served every day from 4 PM to 9 PM. The rest of the year they only serve onces on weekends and holidays. ⊠ *Ruta 225, Km 34* ☎ *65/335–323* ⊕ *www.oncesbellavista. cl* ➡ *6 cabins* ⟷ *In-room: no a/c, kitchen, refrigerator. In-hotel: restaurant, beachfront, tennis court, parking* ⊟ *No credit cards.*

$$$$ ✕🏨 **Yan Kee Way.** With a striking view of Volcán Osorno and Lago
Fodor'sChoice Lllanquihue as its backdrop, this fly-fishing lodge and hotel has first-
★ class rooms and cabins. Central heating and goose-down comforters are unheard-of amenities for this part of the world, and Yan Kee Way has them. Moreover, the restaurant, Latitude 42, is outstanding. Unique artwork from around the world adorns rooms and common spaces. And there is the "cave," a one-of-a-kind cigar smoker's haven carved out of ancient, volcanic boulders. **Pros:** Great all-around amenities. **Cons:** Expensive. ⊠ *Ruta 225, Km 42* ☎ *65/212–030* ⊕ *www. southernchilexp.com* ➡ *19 rooms, 8 bungalows, 2 chalets* ⟷ *In-room:*

6

no a/c, safe, refrigerator, no TV, Wi-Fi. In-hotel: restaurant, room service, bar, gym, spa, beachfront, water sports, bicycles, laundry service, public Internet, public Wi-Fi, airport shuttle, parking, no-smoking rooms ☰AE, DC, MC, V ⎥◎⎢BP.

PARQUE NACIONAL VICENTE PÉREZ ROSALES

3 km (2 mi) east of Ensenada.

GETTING HERE & AROUND

Take a one-hour drive along Ruta 224, Camino a Ensenada, from Puerto Varas. Several agencies in Puerto Varas offer guided trips and transport to the park.

WHAT TO SEE

Chile's oldest national park, Parque Nacional Vicente Pérez Rosales was established in 1926. South of Parque Nacional Puyehue, the 2,538-square-km (980-square-mi) preserve includes the Osorno and lesser-known Puntiagudo volcanoes, and the deep-blue Lago Todos los Santos. The visitor center opposite the Hotel Petrohué has access to some fairly easy hikes. The Rincón del Osorno trail hugs the lake; the Saltos de Petrohué trail runs parallel to the river of the same name. Rudimentary campsites cost 10,000 pesos per person. ☎65/290–711 ⎚1,000 pesos ◷Dec.–Feb., daily 9–8; Mar.–Nov., daily 9–6.

The Volcán Osorno begins to appear in your car window soon after you drive south from Osorno and doesn't disappear until shortly before your arrival in Puerto Montt.

The mountain forms the foundation for Chile's newest ski area, **Ski & Outdoors Volcán Osorno** (✉*San Francisco 333, Puerto Varas* ☎65/233–445 *or* 09/262-3323 ⊕*www.volcanosorno.com*), which offers ski and snowboard rentals and lessons. Adults pay 16,500 pesos for a full day of skiing; 12,000 pesos for a half day, with transportation offered from the office in the center of Puerto Varas.

One of the Lake District's signature excursions is a binational one. The **Cruce de Lagos** takes in a combination of bus and boat transport from Puerto Varas to San Carlos de Bariloche, Argentina, via the park's Lago Todos los Santos and Argentina's Lago Nahuel Huapi. **Andina del Sud** (✉*Del Salvador 72, Puerto Varas* ☎65/232–811 ⊕*www.crucedelagos. cl*) offers the trip starting from Puerto Varas or Puerto Montt.

OUTDOOR ACTIVITIES

Make like Tarzan (or Jane) and swing through the treetops in the shadow of Volcán Osorno with **Canopy Chile** (☎65/330–922 *or* 09/638-2644 ⊕*www.canopychile.cl*). A helmet, a very secure harness, 2 km (1 mi) of zip line strung out over 12 platforms, and experienced guides give you a bird's-eye view of the forest below.

WHERE TO STAY

$$$$ ⛺ **Hotel Petrohué.** The common areas in this stately, rustic, orange chalet have vaulted ceilings and huge fireplaces. Guest rooms are a mix of dark woods and stone and have brightly colored drapes and spreads.

Parque Nacional
Vicente Perez Rosales

Cabins echo the design of the main building and have their own fire-places. The hotel's tour office can set you up with cruises on nearby lakes, take you to scale Volcán Osorno if you're an experienced climber, or send you on guided hikes in the park. ⊠ *Ruta 225, Km 64, Petrohué s/n* 🕿 *65/212–025* 🌐 *www.petrohue.com* 🛏️ *20 rooms, 4 cabins* 🔥 *In-room: no a/c, no phone, safe, no TV. In-hotel: restaurant, bar, pool, bicycles, water sports, beachfront, no elevator, laundry service, parking, no-smoking rooms* 🟰 *AE, DC, MC, V* 🍴 *AI, BP, MAP.*

PUERTO MONTT

20 km (12 mi) south of Puerto Varas via Ruta 5, Pan-American Hwy.

For most of its history, windy Puerto Montt was the end of the line for just about everyone traveling in the Lake District. Now the Carretera Austral carries on southward, but Puerto Montt remains the region's last significant outpost, a provincial city that is the hub of local fishing, textile, and tourist activity. Today the city center is sprouting malls, condos, and office towers—it's the fastest-growing city in Chile—but away from downtown, Puerto Montt consists mainly of low clapboard houses perched above its bay, the Seno de Reloncaví. If it's a sunny day, head east to Playa Pelluco or one of the city's other beaches. If you're

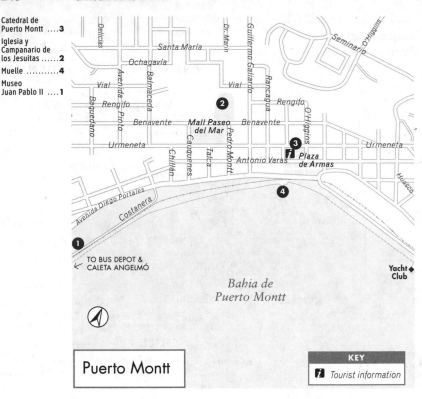

Puerto Montt

KEY
🛈 Tourist information

more interested in exploring the countryside, drive along the shore for a good view of the surrounding hills.

GETTING HERE & AROUND

Puerto Montt is a main transit hub in the region. Buses from Santiago and all points in southern Chile ramble through here, while many cruise ships dock at the port. Puerto Montt's El Tepual Airport has daily air traffic from all the major airlines that serve Chile. The Pan-American Highway also stops here, while the mostly unpaved Carretera Austral, which winds its way through Chilean Patagonia, begins south of the city. To cross over into Argentina by boat, buses leave from here and from Puerto Varas. Chiloé Island is less than two hours' drive from Puerto Montt. Take the last part of Ruta 5, or the Pan-American Highway to Pargua, where two ferries cross the Chacao Channel every hour.

ESSENTIALS

BUS **Cruz del Sur** (⊠ *Av. Diego Portales* 🕾 *65/254–731*). **Puerto Montt Bus Depot** (⊠ *Av. Diego Portales* 🕾 *65/349–010*). **Tas-Choapa** (⊠ *Av. Diego Portales* 🕾 *65/259–320*). **Tur-Bus** (⊠ *Av. Diego Portales* 🕾 *65/259–320*).

CURRENCY **Eureka Turismo** (⊠ *Guillermo Gallardo 65* 🕾 *65/250–412*). **Inter Money Exchange** (⊠ *Talca 84* 🕾 *65/253–745*).

Internet **Cybercafé Navegante** (⊠ *Illapel 10, Local 304A, Mall Paseo Costanera* ☎ *65/435–858).* **Mundosur** (⊠ *San Martin 232* ☎ *65/295–415).*

MEDICAL **Farmacias Ahumada** (⊠ *Antonio Varas 651, Puerto Montt* ☎ *65/344–419).* **Hospital Base Puerto Montt** (⊠ *Seminario s/n* ☎ *65/261–100).*

MAIL **Correos de Chile** (⊠ *Av. Rancagua 126).*

RENTAL CARS **Avis** (⊠ *Benavente 570* ☎ *65/253–307* ⊠ *Urmeneta1037* ☎ *65/255–065).* **Budget** (⊠ *Antonio Varas 162* ☎ *65/286–277* ⊠ *Aeropuerto El Tepual* ☎ *65/294–100).* **Hertz** (⊠ *Calle de Servicio 1431, Parque Industrial Tyrol* ☎ *65/313–445* ⊠ *Aeropuerto El Tepual* ☎ *65/268–944).*

VISITOR INFO **Puerto Montt Tourist Office** (⊠ *Plaza de Armas* ☎ *65/261–823).* **Sernatur** (⊠ *Av. de la Décima Región 480* ☎ *65/254–850).*

WHAT TO SEE

Latin America's ornate church architecture is nowhere to be found in the Lake District. More typical of the region is Puerto Montt's stark ❸ 1856 **Catedral.** The alerce-wood structure, modeled on the Pantheon in Paris, is the city's oldest surviving building. ⊠ *Plaza de Armas* ☎ *No phone* ☉ *Mass: Mon.–Sat. noon and 7* PM*, Sun. 8:30, 10, and noon.*

❶ The **Museo Juan Pablo II,** east of the city's bus terminal, has a collection of crafts and relics from the archipelago of Chiloé. Historical photos of Puerto Montt itself give a sense of the area's slow and often difficult growth and the impact of the 1960 earthquake, which virtually destroyed the port. Pope John Paul II celebrated Mass on the grounds during his 1987 visit. ⊠ *Av. Diego Portales 991* ☎ *65/261–822* ☜ *250 pesos* ☉ *Jan. and Feb., daily 9–7; Mar.–Dec., daily 9–noon and 2–6.*

About 3 km (2 mi) west of downtown along the coastal road lies the **Caleta Angelmó,** Puerto Montt's fishing cove. This busy port serves small fishing boats, large ferries, and cruisers carrying travelers and cargo southward through the straits and fjords that form much of Chile's shoreline. On weekdays small launches from Isla Tenglo and other outlying islands arrive early in the morning and leave late in the afternoon. The fish market here has one of the most varied selections of seafood in all of Chile.

Beaches at Maullín. About 70 km (43 mi) southwest of Puerto Montt, at this small town near Pargua—the ferry crossing to Chiloé—the Maullín River merges with the Pacific Ocean. It's a spectacular setting. Pangal Beach, an extensive beach with large sand dunes, is teeming with birds. If you stay overnight, there are cabins and a campground. ⊠ *Ruta 5 south from Puerto Montt, about a 1-hr drive.*

Barely a stone's throw from Cochamó, the mountainous 398-square-km (154-square-mi) **Parque Nacional Alerce Andino,** with more than 40 small lakes, was established to protect some 20,000 endangered alerce trees. Comparable to California's hardy sequoia, alerce grow to average heights of 130 feet, and can reach 13 feet in diameter. Immensely popular as a building material for houses in southern Chile, they are quickly disappearing from the landscape. Many of these are 3,000–

6

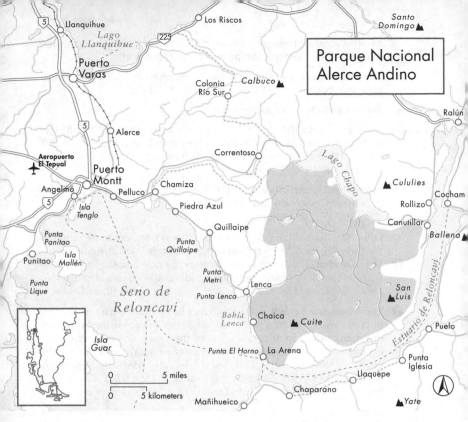

Parque Nacional
Alerce Andino

4,000 years old. ⊠*Carretera Austral, 35 km (21 mi) east of Puerto Montt* ☎*65/212–036* ⊞*1,700 pesos* ⊘*Daily 9–6.*

WHERE TO EAT

$ ✕ **Café Central.** This old-style café in the heart of Puerto Montt retains the spirit of the 1920s and 1930s. It's a good place for a filling afternoon tea, with its menu of sandwiches, ice cream, and pastries. The raspberry küchen is a particular favorite. ⊠*Rancagua 117* ☎*65/482– 888* ⊟*AE, DC, MC, V.*

$$ ✕ **Café Haussmann.** Its pale-wood-and-chrome decor might make this place seem trendy, but it's actually fun and friendly. The great sandwiches and light meals of crudos, cakes, and küchen make it a great destination for late-night noshing. ⊠*San Martín 185* ☎*65/293–380* ⊟*AE, DC, MC, V.*

$ ✕ **Dino's.** Part of a chain of similar restaurants in southern Chile, for years this centrally located spot has been the place for locals to meet and be seen. Sandwiches can be served up extra big if you like. Standard Chilean beef and chicken plates are served, and diverse salads (such as the calamari salad) are excellent. The place also doubles as a coffee shop, so don't hesitate to inquire about the cakes and other desserts. ⊠*Antonio Varas 550* ☎*65/252–785* ⊟*AE, DC, MC, V.*

$$ ✗**Feria Artesanal Angelmó.** Several kitchens here prepare *mariscal* (shell-fish soup) and *caldillo* (seafood chowder), as well as *almejas* (clams), *machas* (razor clams), and *ostiones* (scallops) with Parmesan cheese. Separate tables and counters are at each kitchen in this enclosed market, which is 3 km (2 mi) west of Puerto Montt along the coast road. Most open around 11 AM for lunch and serve for about three hours, and then from about 6 to 9 PM for dinner every day in the January–March high season. The rest of the year, most close some days of the week. ⊠*Caleta Angelmó* ☎*No phone* ▤*No credit cards.*

$$ ✗**El Fogon de Pepe.** If you need a change of pace from the ubiquitous seafood found in these parts, this is a great option. Exquisite roast beef plates in addition to roasted ribs, chicken, and steaks are all great. ⊠*Rengifo 845* ☎*65/271–527* ▤*AE, DC, MC, V.*

$$ ✗**Pazos.** One of the best things to do in Puerto Montt is to eat curanto, a southern Chilean potpourri of shellfish served together with various meats and potatoes. Pazos, in a large house across the street from the beach in Peulluco, is where you'll want to start. They also have an array of other seafood delicacies, and meat and chicken alternatives if you're not up for fish. ⊠*Juan Soler Manfredini, Pelluco, across the street from beach* ☎*65/252–552* ⌃*Reservations essential* ▤*AE, DC, MC, V.*

Fodor'sChoice
★

$$ ✗**Restaurant Kiel.** Hospitable German-born proprietor Helga Birkir stands guard at this Chilean-Teutonic seafood restaurant on the coast west of Puerto Montt. Helga offers a little bit of everything else, but it's her curanto that draws crowds. Fresh produce from her well-kept garden makes lunch here a delight. ⊠*Camino Chinquihue, Km 8, Chinquihue* ☎*65/255–010* ▤*AE, DC, MC, V.*

WHERE TO STAY

¢ ⌂**Los Alamos.** You can camp here at a site with fine views of the Seno de Reloncaví and Isla Tenglo. Sites have electricity and water, and hot showers are nearby. There's also a dock with boats you can rent. The campground is 11 km (7 mi) west of Caleta Angelmó. **Pros:** Cheap. **Cons:** Bring your own linens. ⊠*Costanera, highway to Chinquihue* ☎*65/264–666* ▤*No credit cards.*

$$–$$$ ⌂**Don Luis Gran Hotel.** This modern lodging down the street from the cathedral, a favorite among upscale business travelers, has panoramic vistas of the Seno de Reloncaví. (Rooms on the seventh and eighth floors have the best views.) The carpeted rooms have undergone a welcome renovation and have either queen-size beds or two full-size beds. A big American-style breakfast, served in a cozy salon, is included in the rate. **Pros:** Good for business travelers. **Cons:** Not all rooms have good views. ⊠*Urmeneta at Quillota* ☎*65/259–001* ⊕*www.hotel donluis.cl* ⇆*60 rooms, 1 suite* ⌃*In-room: no a/c, safe, refrigerator (some), Wi-Fi. In-hotel: restaurant, bar, room service, gym, laundry service, public Internet, public Wi-Fi, parking, no-smoking rooms* ▤*AE, DC, MC, V.*

$$ ⌂**Gran Hotel Vicente Costanera.** The grandest of Puerto Montt's hotels underwent a face-lift a few years back and regained its Gstaad-by-the-sea glory. Its Bavarian-style facade resembles that of countless other Lake District lodgings, but the lobby's huge picture window overlooking the Seno de Reloncaví lets you know this place is something special.

6

The modern guest rooms are comfy, with carpets and contemporary wood furniture—but spring for a standard room, rather than an economy one. The difference in price is tiny, but the difference in quality of the rooms is substantial. **Pros:** Clean and modern. **Cons:** Low on personality. ⊠*Diego Portales 450* ☎*65/432–900* ⊕*www.granhotel vicentecostanera.cl* ⊅*82 rooms, 4 suites* ⭗*In-room: no a/c, safe, refrigerator. In-hotel: restaurant, bar, room service, concierge, laundry service, airport shuttle, public Internet, public Wi-Fi, parking, no-smoking rooms* ⊟*AE, DC, MC, V* �O|*BP.*

$$ 🖼 **Holiday Inn Express.** Stunning views of Puerto Montt Bay and the city
★   itself make this place an excellent choice. Combine the view, which almost all the rooms have (some rooms even have their own private terrace), with modern facilities, and this is easily one of the best hotels in the city. As an added bonus, the hotel sits above a large mall that includes a movie theater with six movie screens. **Pros:** Amazing views. **Cons:** Can be noisy. ⊠*Av. Costanera, above Mall Paseo Costanera* ☎*65/566–000* ⊕*www.holidayinnexpress.cl* ⊅*105 rooms* ⭗*In-room: safe, Ethernet, Wi-Fi. In-hotel: restaurant, bar, gym, public Internet, public Wi-Fi, parking, no-smoking rooms* ⊟*AE, DC, MC, V.*

$ 🖼 **Hostal Pacífico.** European travelers favor this solid budget option up the hill from the bus station. The rooms are small, but they have comfy beds with lots of pillows. Look at a few before you pick one, as some of the interior rooms have skylights rather than windows. The staff is exceptionally friendly and helpful. **Pros:** Great staff. **Cons:** Small rooms. ⊠*Juan J. Mira 1088* ☎☎*65/256–229* ⊕*www.hostalpacifico. cl* ⊅*30 rooms* ⭗*In-room: no a/c, Wi-Fi. In-hotel: restaurant, laundry service, public Internet, public Wi-Fi, airport shuttle, parking, no-smoking rooms* ⊟*No credit cards* O|*CP.*

NIGHTLIFE & THE ARTS

If you do venture out late at night, be careful where you walk as with the city's growth in size has come an increase in street crime.

Sherlock (⊠*Antonio Varas 452* ☎*65/288–888*), a bar-restaurant in the city center, is a good place to drink wine or cocktails. In summer, pull up to a table outside. Downstairs on the bar's ground floor they often have live music or karaoke. **Boule Bar** (⊠*Benavente 435, 2nd fl.* ☎*65/348–973* ⊕*www.boulebar.cl*) is a good drinking hole in the city center. The upbeat disco **Kamikaze** (⊠*Juan Soler Mafredini 1667* ☎*8/499–1262* ⊕*www.kamikazeclub.cl*) fills up with people of all ages. Puerto Montt's biggest disco, **Apache** (⊠*Pelluco* ☎*65/345– 867 or 9/703–5348* ⊕*www.apachepub.com*) also has a separate bar with live music.

The **Casa de Arte Diego Rivera** (⊠*Quillota 116* ☎*65/261–859*), a gift of the government of Mexico, commemorates the famed muralist of the same name. It hosts art exhibitions in the gallery, as well as evening theater productions and occasional music and film festivals.

SHOPPING

An excellent selection of handicrafts is sold at the best prices in the country at the **Feria Artesanal Angelmó,** on the coastal road near Caleta Angelmó. Baskets, ponchos, figures woven from different kinds of grasses and straw, and warm sweaters of raw, hand-spun, and hand-dyed wool are all offered. Haggling is expected. It's open daily 9–dusk.

COCHAMÓ

94 km (59 mi) southwest of Puerto Varas via Ruta 225, Camino a Ensenada, following the signs south to Ralun, which is 15 km (9 mi) north of Cochamó.

The small fishing villages of Cochamó are blessed with friendly people but little infrastructure. Only a few farms dot the countryside. In short, nature with a capital "N" is the real reason to come here. Civilization has barely touched these great, vast nature areas, some of Chile's (and the world's) last. Think of Yosemite National Park in California without the crowds. Granite walls and domes reminiscent of Yosemite are prevalent throughout the valley. At Río Puelo, the emerald-blue water seems like a dream amid the rare, ancient alerce forests and Andean mountain scenery. An old frontier cattle trail in Cochamó Valley, once used as a hideout by Butch Cassidy and the Sundance Kid, reminds the visitor that the only way through this natural wonderland is by foot or horse. You won't find any cars or roads here.

GETTING HERE & AROUND

There are few cars in Cochamó, and even fewer gas stations (though you can get gas by the container). Walking is probably the most efficient way to get around. Nearby Puelo is even smaller than Cochamó. If you must, rent a car in Puerto Montt or Puerto Varas. Roads in the region are mostly gravel and dirt, so four-wheel drive would be good. Buses do service these towns, however. If you take the bus, arrange with a travel agency or outfitter beforehand to help with transport to the nature areas on your wish list.

ESSENTIALS

MEDICAL **Posta Salud Rural Río Puelo** (⊠ *Puelo* ☎ *45/197–2507*).

VISITOR INFO **Cochamó Municipalidad** (⊠ *Calle Santiago Bueras, Puelo* ☎ *65/255–474* ⊕ *www. cochamo.cl*).

OUTDOOR ACTIVITIES

Before you pursue any of the myriad activities in the vast forests, fast-flowing rivers, and mountains, be sure to get your bearings. Unlike national parks, these areas are not formally protected and maintained, and often lack well-marked trails. Check with a local outfitter or agency to get more info.

Campo Aventura (⊠ *San Bernardo 318, Puerto Varas* ☎ *65/232–910* ⊕ *www.campo-aventura.cl*) offers treks, rafting, kayaking, and biking trips in Cochamó and Puelo, but they specialize in horseback-riding trips from one to 14 days.

Miralejos (⊠*San Pedro 311, Puerto Varas* ☏*65/234–892* ⊕*www. miralejos.com*) offers trekking, kayaking, mountaineering, and horse-back-riding trips in both Cochamó and Puelo.

For horseback-riding, boating, hiking, and kayaking trips throughout the Río Puelo area, including ascents of Volcán Yates and hikes to ancient alerce forests and glaciers, check with **Andes Patagonia** (⊠*Río Puelo Alto, Cochamó* ☏*9/9549–1069* ⊕*www.andespatagonia.cl*).

WHERE TO STAY & EAT

$$$ 🏨**Andes Lodge.** Billed as a fly-fishing and outdoors lodge, the Andes Lodge has earned a highly favorable reputation among locals and frequent visitors. The restaurant has a fixed menu that features many of the basics, including salmon and beef. The food is not the focus, though. **Pros:** Great for fly-fishing. **Cons:** No frills. ⊠*Puelo,* ☏*65/234–454 or 08/501–5478* ⊕*www.andeslodge.com* 🛏*8 rooms* ☖*In-room: no a/c, no phone, no TV. In-hotel: restaurant, room service, bar, pool, water sports, bicycles, no elevator, laundry service, public Internet, airport shuttle, parking, no-smoking rooms* ▤*AE, DC, MC, V* ❙◎❙*BP.*

$ 🏨**Campo Aventura.** Although most guests of this hostal are also clients of the Campo Aventura tour company, you can still stay here without any touring commitments. Campo Aventura has horseback riding, trekking, rafting, or canyoning excursions. In Cochamó this is the best place to stay. They also have a vegetarian restaurant and camping area. **Pros:** Plenty to do. **Cons:** No frills. ⊠*5 km (3 mi) south of Cochamó on Ruta 225 (Camino a Ensenada)* ☏*65/232–910* ⊕*www. campo-aventura.cl* 🛏*3 rooms, 1 cabin* ☖*In-room: no a/c, no phone, no TV. In-hotel: restaurant, beachfront, no elevator, laundry service, parking* ▤*AE, DC, MC, V* ❙◎❙*BP.*

$ ✕🏨**Domo Camp and Tique Restaurant.** Five extra-large, dome-like tents with wooden floors, a woodstove, and mattresses are connected by wooden walkways that twist through a lovely forest. A cedar-wood hot tub is available. Nearby there are hiking trails. The Tique Restaurant serves up good food, with an eclectic array of dishes such as roasted salmon, steak and fries, roast lamb, spicy pork, or zucchini pie. **Pros:** Unique concept. **Cons:** Rustic! ⊠*Río Puelo Alto, Cochamó* ☏*9/9549–1069* ⊕*www.andespatagonia.cl* 🛏*5 cabins* ☖*In-room: no a/c, no phone, no TV. In-hotel: restaurant, bar, no elevator, parking* ▤*No credit cards* ❙◎❙*BP.*

Chile's Southern Coast

Quetén, Chiloé Island

WORD OF MOUTH

"Patagonia would probably be one of the safest places to drive. From El Calafate to Torres del Paine, we only saw a hand full of cars and everyone was really courteous of one another and even waved hello!"

—oceania

WELCOME TO THE SOUTHERN COAST

TOP REASONS TO GO

★ **Scenery:** The Carretera Austral, a dusty dirt road blazed through southern Chile by Augusto Pinochet, has opened up one of the most beautiful places in the world to tourists. Rent a four-wheel-drive truck or jeep, or bring a mountain bike, and soak it all in.

★ **Glaciers:** To watch a chunk of ice break off the glaciers near Mt. San Valentín, and fall with a thundering splash into the lake below, is reason enough for a trip to Laguna San Rafael National Park (which has 19 different glaciers).

★ **Fishing:** Fly-fishing fanatics were among the first to explore this area thoroughly. You'll be able to step right outside your door for great fishing at any number of lodges. A short boat trip will bring you to isolated spots where you won't run into another soul for the entire day.

★ **Rafting and Kayaking:** The Futalefeu River is Class V-plus. That's raft speak for very fast-moving water. In fact, this river is considered one of the fastest in the world.

1 Chaitén & Puerto Puyuhuapi. Although Chaitén itself isn't much to see, you will find yourself passing through it on the way from Chiloé or the Lake District. It's a perfect spot from which to explore Parque Pumalín, Futaleufú, and Puerto Puyuhuapi.

2 Coyhaique & Environs. Where Río Simpson and Río Coyhaique come together you'll find Coyhaique, the only community of any size on the Carretera Austral. Calling itself "the capital of Patagonia," Coyhaique has some 50,000 residents— more than half of the region's population.

Parque Nacional Chiloé

Cucao

Isla Grande de Chiloé

Isla Guafo

Isla Grar Guaitecc

PACIFIC OCEAN

AISEN DEL GENERAL CARLOS IBANEZ DEL CAMPO

Golfo de Penas

Parque Nacional Laguna San Rafael

Parque Nacional Laguna San Rafael

| 0 | 30 mi |
| 0 | 30 km |

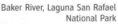

Baker River, Laguna San Rafael National Park

GETTING ORIENTED

The Southern Coast is a tranquil, expansive region covered with pristine nature, much of it protected in national parks and reserves. By and large, this is territory for people who love the outdoors. Here you will find unparalleled fishing, kayaking, white-water rafting, and a road through natural beauty that is ideal for a long mountain-bike trip. Intrepid explorers will be rewarded with relatively untrammeled trails and rarely viewed vistas.

7

Baker River, Laguna San Rafael National Park

CHILE'S SOUTHERN COAST PLANNER

When to Go

Late spring through summer—late November to mid-March—is considered high season in this part of southern Chile. It's highly recommended that you make advance reservations if your intention is to stay at high-end hotels or resorts during this time. Although the weather is likely to be cooler and rainier in the spring (September into November) and fall (March to May), it's also a fine time for travel here.

Money Matters

Converting cash can be a bureaucratic headache, particularly in smaller towns like Chaitén. A better option is using your ATM card at numerous local banks connected to Cirrus or Plus networks.

When you're anticipating smaller purchases, try to have coins and small bills on hand at all times. Small vendors do not always have change for large bills.

Eat Well & Rest Easy

All manner of fish, lamb, beef, and chicken dishes are available in the Southern Coast. By and large, entrées are simple and hearty. Given the area's great distance from Chile's Central Valley, where most of Chile's fruits and vegetables are grown, most things that appear on your plate probably grew somewhere nearby. Many dishes are prepared from scratch when you order.

Traveling by road throughout the region, you may see crudely printed signs with an arrow pointing to a nearby farmhouse advertising *küchen* (rich, fruit-filled pastries)—clear evidence of the many pockets of German influence.

This region offers a surprisingly wide choice of accommodations. What you won't find is the blandness of chain hotels. Most of the region's establishments reflect the distinct personalities and idiosyncrasies of their owners.

Some of the most humble homes in villages along the Carretera Austral are supplementing their family income by becoming bed-and-breakfasts. A stay in one of these *hospedajes* is an ideal way to meet the people and experience the culture. These accommodations are not regulated, so inquire about the availability of hot water and confirm that breakfast is included. Don't hesitate to ask to see the room—you may even get a choice.

WHAT IT COSTS IN CHILEAN PESOS (IN THOUSANDS)				
¢	$	$$	$$$	$$$$
RESTAURANTS				
under 3 pesos	3 pesos–5 pesos	5 pesos–8 pesos	8 pesos–11 pesos	over 11 pesos
HOTELS				
under 15 pesos	15 pesos–45 pesos	45 pesos–75 pesos	75 pesos–105 pesos	over 105 pesos

Restaurant prices are based on the median main course price at dinner. Hotel prices are for a double room in high season, excluding tax.

The Carretera Austral

As you drive south along the Carretera Austral, Chile's southernmost reaches seem to simply disintegrate into a tangle of sounds and straits, channels and fjords. Here you'll find lands laden with lush vegetation or layered in fields of ice. The road struggles valiantly along this route, connecting tiny fishing towns and farming villages all the way from Puerto Montt to Villa O'Higgins. There, the huge Campo de Hielo Sur (Southern Ice Field) forces it to a halt.

Navigating the Carretera Austral requires some planning, as communities along the way are few and far between. Some parts of the highway, especially in the southernmost reaches, are deserted. Check out your car thoroughly, especially the air in the spare tire. Make sure you have a jack and jumper cables. Bring along enough food in case you find yourself stuck far from the nearest restaurant.

Sample Itinerary

On your first day head to the port town of **Chaitén** by ferry from Puerto Montt. Devote a day or two to visiting **Parque Pumalín**, which has some of the most pristine landscape in the region. Then, spend a day going down the Carretera Austral, or Southern Highway, to **Puerto Puyuhuapi,** preferably doing so in your own rented, four-wheel-drive truck or jeep to give you more flexibility. A stay at Puyuhuapi Lodge & Spa, a resort accessible only by boat, is a great way to relax and recharge for the next phase of your journey. While in Puyuhuapi, consider spending an extra day there to visit the "hanging glacier" at **Parque Nacional Queulat.** Afterward, go to **Coyhaique,** located about five hours south. The largest city in the region, Coyhaique will be a good place for shopping and eating a nice meal before heading to nearby **Puerto Chacabuco,** where you can board a boat bound for the unforgettable glaciers at **Parque Nacional Laguna San Rafael.** If you lack the time to continue farther south to see still more of Patagonia's incredible landscape, return to Puerto Montt by a ferry boat that departs from Puerto Chacabuco.

Getting Here & Around

Air Travel. LAN has flights to the region from Santiago, Puerto Montt, and Punta Arenas. They arrive at the Southern Coast's only major airport, 55 km (34 mi) south of Coyhaique, in the town of Balmaceda. Other carriers serving southern Chile include Aerolineas del Sur, Empresa CieloMarAustral, and Empresa Aero Taxi.

Boat & Ferry Travel. Be warned that ferries in southern Chile are slow and not always scenic, particularly if skies are the least bit clouded, but they are reliable. If you're touring the region by car, the ferry is a good choice. The main companies serving this area are Navimag and Transmarchilay.

Bus Travel. Service between Puerto Montt and Cochrane is by private operators such as Tur-Bus. Travel along the Carretera Austral is often agonizingly and inexplicably slow, so don't plan on getting anywhere on schedule.

Car Travel. You can drive the northern part of the Southern Coast without the aid of a ferry, but you'll need to spend some time in Argentina along the way, eventually crossing back into Chile near Futaleufú. The best route takes you to Bariloche, crossing the Argentina border near Osorno and Puyehue, just north of Puerto Montt.

7

Updated
by Jimmy
Langman

THE SLIVER OF LAND KNOWN as the Southern Coast stretches for more than 1,000 km (620 mi), from the southernmost part of the administrative district of Los Lagos through the northern part of Aisén (locally spelled Aysén). Sandwiched between the tranquil valleys of the Lake District and the wondrous ice fields of Patagonia, it largely consists of heavily forested mountains, some of which rise dramatically from the shores of shimmering lakes, others directly out of the Pacific Ocean. Slender waterfalls and nearly vertical streams, often seeming to emerge from the rock itself, tumble and slide from neck-craning heights. Some dissipate into misty nothingness before touching the ground, others flow into the innumerable rivers—large and small, wild and gentle—heading westward to the sea. Chile has designated vast tracts of this truly magnificent landscape as national parks and reserves, but most are accessible only on foot. The few roads available to vehicles are slightly widened trails or the occasional logging route navigable only by the most rugged of four-wheel-drive vehicles.

The Southern Coast is one of the least-populated areas remaining in South America: the population density here is said to be lower than that of the Sahara Desert. The infrequent hamlets scattered along the low-lying areas of this rugged region subsist as fishing villages or small farming centers. The gradual increase of boat and ferry service to some of these towns and the expansion of the major highway called the Carretera Austral have begun to encourage migration to the region. Coyhaique, the only town here of any size, with a population of 50,000, has lots of dining, lodging, and shopping. Meanwhile, a few intrepid entrepreneurs have established world-class accommodations in remote locations near spectacular mountain peaks, ancient volcanoes, and glaciers, with their concomitant fjords and lakes.

Planning a visit to the region's widely separated points of interest can be challenging, as getting from place to place is often difficult. Creating a logical itinerary in southern Chile is as much about choosing how to get here as it is about choosing where you want to go. The most rewarding mode of transport through this area is a combination of travel by boat and by plane, with an occasional car rental if you want to journey a little deeper into the hinterlands.

CHAITÉN & PUERTO PUYUHUAPI

CHAITÉN

201 km (125 mi) south of Puerto Montt.

A century ago, Chaitén wasn't even on the map. Today it's a small port town, with a population of barely more than 3,000. Although it's not really a destination itself, Chaitén serves as a convenient base for exploring the area, including Parque Pumalín.

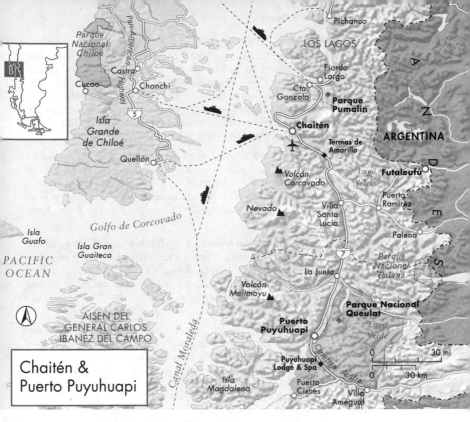

Chaitén &
Puerto Puyuhuapi

GETTING HERE & AROUND

Getting here is fairly easy: both Navimag (⊕*www.navimag.com*) and
Transmarchilay (⊕*www.transmarchilay.com*) operate regular ferry
service between Chaitén and Puerto Montt in the Lake District and
Quellón on Chiloé. Flying is also an option; a few small airlines offer
flights between Chaitén and Puerto Montt.

It's also possible to drive to Chaitén from Puerto Montt via the Carretera Austral, but you have to make use of two car ferries. The first is
fine, as Transmarchilay ferries make nine daily trips between La Arena
and Puelche all year. The second leg is tougher because Transmarchilay's ferries between Hornopirén and Caleta Gonzalo operate only in
January and February.

ESSENTIALS

CURRENCY **Banco del Estado** (⊠*Calle Libertad 298* ☎*65/565–540*).

MEDICAL **Hospital de Chaitén** (⊠*Ignacio Carrera Pinto 153* ☎*65/731–244*).

VISITOR INFO **Chaitur** (⊠*Terminal de Buses, O'Higgins 67* ☎*65/731–429* ⊕ *www.chaitur.
com*). **Sernatur** (⊠*Edificio del Gobernacion, 1st fl., Av. Bernardo O'Higgins 254*
☎*65/731–280*).

WHAT TO SEE

Michimahuida Volcano. Take a day hike through dense temperate rain forest dotted with waterfalls and rare native trees like coihue and canelo to enjoy spectacular views of the 8,000-foot-high Michimahuida. For those more ambitious and physically fit, an overnight camping trip to the glacier at the summit rewards you with tremendous, bird's-eye views of the surrounding area. One local outfitter for trips like this is **Chaitur Excursions** (⊕ www.chaitur.com).

The emerald-green **Lago Yelcho,** one of the best places in the region to fish for brown trout, runs along the Carretera Austral south of Chaitén. Just past the village of Puerto Cárdenas is Puente Ventisquero Yelcho (Glacier Bridge), the beginning of a challenging two-hour hike to Ventisquero Cavi (Hanging Glacier). ⊠ *Off Carretera Austral, 2 km (1 mi) past Puerto Cardenas.*

The much-lauded **Termas del Amarillo,** a modest hot springs about 25 km (16 mi) southeast of Chaitén, offers a nice respite for weary muscles. The setting, along a river running through a heavily forested valley, is lovely. ⊠ *Off Carretera Austral, 6 km (4 mi) inland from Puerto Cardenas* ☎ *No phone* ⊠ *2,000 pesos* ⊙ *Daily 8 AM–9 PM.*

WHERE TO EAT

$$ ✕**Brisas del Mar.** This cheerful little eatery overlooks the sea. The sheer number of items on the menu is astounding. Try excellent fish dishes such as *salmón en mantequilla* (salmon braised in butter), *congrio* (conger eel), and *loco* (abalone). They also have six cabins available for weary tourists. ⊠ *Corcovado 278* ☎ *65/731–284* ⊟ *No credit cards.*

$ ✕**Corcovado.** Here's one place where you won't leave hungry: the portions of the seafood dishes and *asado a la brasa* (mixed grilled meats), served with a baked potato and salad, are huge, but the prices are small. This wooden building sits near the water, so you are treated to great views. The restaurant also adjoins a small hotel under the same ownership. ⊠ *Corcovado 408* ☎ *65/731–221* ⊟ *No credit cards.*

WHERE TO STAY

$ ⊞**Hosteria Puma Verde.** This adorable, wood-shingled B&B is run by
★ Parque Pumalín, which explains why it's in a class of its own. Locally crafted furniture sits atop polished wood floors. Woolen blankets and piles of pillows add to the coziness. Puma Verde has three rooms (one double, two triples), and one apartment that sleeps five. The large apartment, filled with hand-carved wood furniture, rents for a bargain 60,000 pesos without breakfast. **Pros:** Tastefully decorated, cozy. **Cons:** Not a lot of rooms, no TV. ⊠ *Av. Bernardo O'Higgins 54* ☎ *65/731–184* ⊕ *www.parquepumalin.cl* ⇆ *3 rooms, 1 apartment* ⅋ *In-room: no a/c, no phone, no TV. In-hotel: no elevator* ⊟ *AE, DC, MC, V* ⅋O⅋*BP.*

$ ⊞**Hotel Mi Casa.** This friendly hotel has spectacular views of the bay and town from its large, wooden terrace. The restaurant has good regional and international dishes. And the staff goes out of its way to cater to your specific needs. **Pros:** Terrace views, friendly service, good restaurant. **Cons:** Somewhat outside of town, no phone, no TV in some rooms. ⊠ *Av. Norte 206* ☎ *65/731–285* ⊕ *www.hotelmicasa.*

CLOSE UP

Chile's Road to Riches

The Pan-American Highway, which snakes its way through the northern half of Chile, never quite makes it to the Southern Coast. To connect this remote region with the rest of the country, former President Augusto Pinochet proposed a massive public works project to construct a highway called the Carretera Austral. But the $300 million venture had another purpose as well. Pinochet was afraid that without a strong military presence in the region, neighboring Argentina could begin chipping away at Chile's territory. The highway would allow the army easier access to an area that until then was accessible only by boat.

Ground was broken on the Carretera Austral in 1976, and in 1982 the first section, running from Chaitén to Coyhaique, opened to great fanfare. The only trouble was that you still couldn't get there from the mainland. It took another five years for the extension from Chaitén north to Puerto Montt to be completed. An extension from Coyhaique south to Cochrane was finished the following year.

The word *finished* is misleading, as construction continues to this day. Although the Carretera Austral is nicely paved near Puerto Montt, it soon reveals its true nature as a two-lane gravel surface that crawls inexorably southward for 1,156 km (718 mi) toward the outpost of Villa O'Higgins. And the highway isn't even contiguous. In places the road actually ends abruptly at water's edge—ferries link these broken stretches of highway. The segment from Chaitén to Coyhaique is mostly gravel road, but every year the paved sections grow longer.

The Carretera Austral is lauded in tourism brochures as "a beautiful road studded with rivers, waterfalls, forests, lakes, glaciers, and the occasional hamlet." This description is accurate—you may live the rest of your life and never see anything half as beautiful as the scenery. However, the highway itself is far from perfection. The mostly unpaved road has dozens of single-lane, wide-board bridges over streams and rivers. Shoulders are nonexistent or made of soft, wheel-grabbing gravel. Periodically, traffic must wend its way through construction, amid heavy equipment and workers.

What the Carretera Austral offers adventurous travelers is a chance to see a part of the world where few have ventured. The views from the highway are truly amazing, from the conical top of Volcán Corcovado near Chaitén to the sprawling valleys around Coyhaique. Here you'll find national parks where the trails are virtually deserted, such as Parque Nacional Queulat and Reserva Nacional Río Simpson. The region's crowning glory, of course, is the vast glacier at Laguna San Rafael. It may be a tough journey today, but when it is eventually finished, the Carretera Austral could rival the most spectacular scenic roadways in the world.

—Pete Nelson

7

cl ⮌*20 rooms* ⌂*In-room: no phone, no TV (some). In-hotel: restaurant, room service, bar, gym, laundry service, public Internet, public Wi-Fi, no elevator, airport shuttle, parking, no-smoking rooms* ⊟*No credit cards* ⦿*|BP.*

$ 🖵**Hotel Schilling.** Of the town's numerous family-run hospedajes, Hotel Schilling is the most professional and hospitable. Rooms are enlivened by bedspreads in a rainbow of colors. Its location, just across from the ocean, is a major draw. **Pros:** Location, good service. **Cons:** Simple rooms. ⊠*Corcovado 230* ☎*65/731–295* ⦿*www.hotelschilling. patagoniatour.cl* ⮌*12 rooms* ⌂*In-room: no a/c, no phone, Ethernet, Wi-Fi. In hotel: restaurant, parking, no elevator* ⊟*No credit cards* ⦿*|CP.*

PARQUE PUMALÍN

Fodor's Choice ★   *56 km (35 mi) north of Chaitén.*

Parque Pumalín is an extraordinary venture that began when conservationist Douglas Tompkins bought a 42,000-acre *araucaria* (an indigenous evergreen tree) forest south of Puerto Montt. Since 1988, he has spent more than $25 million to purchase the nearly 800,000 acres that make up Parque Pumalín. In addition to araucaria trees, the park shelters one of the largest—and one of the few remaining—intact alerce forests in the world. Alerces, the world's second-longest-lived tree species, which can live up to 4,000 years, are often compared to the equally giant California redwood. The Chilean government declared the park a nature sanctuary in August 2005.

Tompkins, an American who made his fortune founding the clothing companies Esprit and North Face, owns two strips of land that stretch from one side of the country to the other. He tried to buy the parcel between the two halves that would have connected them, but the sale was fiercely opposed by some government officials who questioned whether a foreigner should own so much of Chile. The Pan-American Highway, which trundles all the way north to Alaska, is interrupted here. No public roads, with their accompanying pollution, pass through the preserve, except for a well-maintained road stretching from Chaitén to park headquarters at Caleta Gonzalo.

Parque Pumalín encompasses some of the most pristine landscape in the region, if not the world. There are a dozen or so trails that wind past lakes and waterfalls. Stay in log cabins, at traditional or covered campsites, or put up your tent on one of the local farms scattered across the area that welcome travelers. The entrance to the park is at Caleta Gonzalo, where the ferries from Hornopirén arrive. Buses run from Chaitén in January and February. ⊠*Information centers: Calle Klenner 299, Puerto Varas* ☎*65/250–079* 🖷*65/255–145* ⊠*Av. Bernardo O'Higgins 62, Chaitén* ☎*65/731–341* ⦿*www.parquepumalin. cl* 🎫*Free* ☉*Daily.*

GETTING HERE & AROUND

Caleta Gonzalo, headquarters of Pumalín Park, is about 60 km (37 mi) north of Chaitén. The road from Chaitén to Caleta Gonzalo is well-maintained but not paved. One can also reach Caleta Gonzalo by ferry. To venture to the northernmost areas of the park, such as Cahuelmo hot springs, you will need to rent a boat in Hornopiren, a small town about 110 km (68 mi) southeast of Puerto Montt.

WHERE TO STAY

$$ ★ **Cabañas Caleta Gonzalo.** Nine gray-shingled cabanas, each designed to be distinct from its neighbor, sit high on stilts against the backdrop of the misty mountains. Broad front porches and tall windows let in lots of light. The interiors are rustic yet luxurious, with handcrafted furniture and handwoven woolen blankets. There are also two cabanas, with kitchen and wood stoves for heating, at the Rio Gonzalo Farm. To access these cabanas, you must cross a wooden hanging bridge. The complex includes an attractive visitor center and handicraft shop stocking books, guides, and maps, as well as organic honey and jams. A copper-hooded corner fireplace welcomes you at the adjacent café for meals from early morning until midnight year-round. **Pros:** Unique, close to nature. **Cons:** Remote. ⊠ *Caleta Gonzalo* 🕾 *65/232–300* 🛏 *9 cabins* ⚴ *In-room: no a/c, no TV. In-hotel: restaurant, bar, parking, no elevator* ⊟ *AE, DC, MC, V* ⊙ *BP.*

¢ **Camping in Pumalín.** There are more than a dozen camping sites near Cabañas Caleta Gonzalo. You must cross the hanging bridge over the Gonzalo River and walk to Rio Gonzalo Farm. The campground there includes cold-water showers, bathrooms, and three covered shelters for cooking and eating. There is also a covered shelter for sleeping. Throughout the park, there are several other camping sites at lakes and along trails. Inquire at Caleta Gonzalo.

FUTALEUFÚ

159 km (99 mi) east of Chaitén.

Near the town of Villa Lucia, Ruta 231 branches east from the Carretera Austral and winds around Lago Yelcho. About 159 km (99 mi) later, not far from the Argentine border, it reaches the tiny town of Futaleufú. Despite being barely five square blocks, Futaleufú is on many travelers' itineraries. World-class adventure sports await here, where the Río Espolón and the Río Futaleufú collide. It's the staging center for serious river and sea kayaking, white-water rafting, and mountain biking, as well as fly-fishing, canyon hiking, and horseback riding. Day trips for less-experienced travelers are available.

GETTING HERE & AROUND

The road from Chaitén to Futaleufú, which takes about four hours to drive, is almost entirely unpaved, and conditions are spotty at times. However, it's also possible to enter Futaleufú from Argentina, which is about 190 km (118 mi) southwest of Esquel. From Bariloche, Argentina, proceed south, about four hours' drive, passing through pleasant Argentine tourist towns such as El Bolsón and Esquel. After Esquel you will come upon the road that leads to Futaleufú. The roads are paved throughout the Argentine portion of the trip, and a car rented in Puerto Montt costs less than 40,000 pesos, although better deals can be had in Santiago. Some bus companies offer service to Futaleufú from Puerto Montt and Osorno. Some minivans do make the trip from Chaitén to Futaleufú, but this service is irregular and you may have to wait a day or two.

ESSENTIALS

CURRENCY **Para Ti Store** (⊠ *Pedro Aguirre Cerda 505* ☎ *65/721–215*).

MEDICAL **Hospital de Futaleufú** (⊠ *Juan Manuel Balmaceda 382* ☎ *65/721–231*).

VISITOR INFO **Tourist Office** (⊠ *Av. Bernardo O'Higgins 334* ☎ *65/721–241*).

WHERE TO STAY & EAT

$ ✕🏨 **Hosteria Antigua Casona.** Built in the 1940s, this three-story house is
★ one of the better stays you will find in southern Chile. The Coronado family, who run the place, will quickly make you feel at home. The place has a rustic feel with tasteful decorations throughout, and the restaurant is wonderful. Fine handicrafts are sold on the first floor. The Coronados can help arrange tours and transportation as well. And ask them about staying at their country house, Posada Anchileufu, a good alternative if you want to get a taste of Patagonian country life. **Pros:** Intimate with few other guests, friendly hosts, good food. **Cons:** Not a lot of luxury, no TV, no phone. ⊠ *Manuel Rodriguez 215* ☎ *65/721–311* ⊕ *www.futaleufupatagonia.cl* ⤶ *4 rooms* △ *In-room: no a/c, no phone, no TV, Wi-Fi. In-hotel: restaurant, bar, no elevator, laundry service, public Wi-Fi, parking, no-smoking rooms* ▭ *AE, DC, MC, V.*

$$$ 🏨 **Hostería Río Grande.** This sleek wooden hotel is adventure-travel headquarters for the area. It hosts the Futaleufú Adventure Center, a branch of **Expediciones Chile** (⊕ www.exchile.com), operated by former U.S. Olympic paddler Chris Spelius. December–March it offers four- to seven-night packages that include kayaking, rafting, and hiking trips throughout the region. There is cable TV in the salon. **Pros:** Modern facilities, rafting and other excursions, restaurant. **Cons:** Gets crowded in dining room. ⊠ *Manuel Rodriguez 315; office: Gabriel Mistral 296* ☎ *65/721–320, 888/488–9082 in U.S.* ⊕ *www.pachile.com* ⤶ *12 rooms* △ *In-room: no a/c, no TV. In-hotel: restaurant, room service, bar, laundry service, public Internet, no elevator, parking* ▭ *AE, DC, MC, V* ℹ *BP.*

$$$ 🏨 **Hotel El Barranco.** Easily one of the Futa's best lodging options, it offers first-class rooms and facilities, including a pool. **Pros:** Rooms are comfortable, pool. **Cons:** No business center. ⊠ *Av. Bernardo O'Higgins 172* ☎ *65/721–267* ⊕ *www.elbarrancochile.cl* ⤶ *10 rooms* △ *In-room: no a/c, no TV, Wi-Fi. In-hotel: restaurant, bar, pool, bicycles, no elevator, laundry service, public Wi-Fi, parking* ▭ *AE, DC, MC, V* ℹ *BP.*

PUERTO PUYUHUAPI

196 km (123 mi) south of Chaitén.

This mossy fishing village of about 500 residents is one of the oldest along the Carretera Austral. It was founded in 1935 by German immigrants fleeing the economic ravages of post–World War I Europe. As in much of Patagonia, Chile offered free land to settlers with the idea of making annexation by Argentina more difficult. Those early immigrants ventured into the wilderness to clear the forests and make way for farms.

Today this sleepy town near Quelat National Park is a convenient stopover for those headed farther south in the region. It has a few modest guesthouses, as well as some markets and a gas station.

GETTING HERE & AROUND
The mostly unpaved 210-km (130-mi) drive from Coyhaique along the Carretera Austral, or Southern Highway, can be undertaken by car or bus. Patagonia Connection (⊕*www.patagonia-connection.com*), a Santiago tour company, also gets you here in five hours by boat if you plan to stay at their Puyuhuapi Lodge. A small landing strip nearby serves private planes only.

FISHING
More than 50 rivers are within easy driving distance of Puerto Puyuhuapi, making this a cherished destination among fishing enthusiasts. Here are rainbow and brown trout, silver and steelhead salmon, and local species such as the robalo. The average size is about 6 pounds, but it's not rare to catch monsters twice that size. Daily trips are organized by the staff at the resort hotel, Puyuhuapi Lodge & Spa.

WHERE TO STAY & EAT
$ **Cabanas Aonikenk.** Relatively new to the area, Veronica Gallardo immigrated to this quiet town some five years ago and built this little establishment on her own with few resources. Her hard work has resulted in a more than adequate place to sleep and a great café. **Pros:** Friendly service, good location, affordable price. **Cons:** Facilities are far from luxurious. ⊠*Hamburgo 16* ☎*67/325–208* ↩*2 rooms, 3 cabins* ⌂*In-room: no a/c, no phone. In-hotel: restaurant, no elevator, parking* ⊟*No credit cards* ⍟*BP.*

$ **Hosteria Alemana.** The home of Ursula Flack, the last of the town's original German settlers, is a great choice for budget-minded travelers who want to explore the beautiful countryside. Flack moved here in 1958, 10 years after her husband, who built this large Bavarian-style home with gardens in the middle of town. Rooms with functional baths are simple but charming. Fresh flowers fill the quaint dining room. Ursula also runs perhaps the best eatery in town, Café Rossbach, just a five-minute walk down the road, next to the carpet workshop run by her son, Helmut. **Pros:** Hotel has character, clean. **Cons:** Located outside of town. ⊠*Puerto Puyuhuapi s/n* ☎*67/325–118* ↩*9 rooms* ⌂*In-room: no a/c, no phone, no TV. In-hotel: laundry facilities, laundry service, no elevator, parking, no-smoking rooms* ⊟*AE, MC, V* ⍟*BP.*

$$$–$$$$ ✗🏠 **Puyuhuapi Lodge & Spa.** If you arrive at night, your catamaran sails
Fodor'sChoice   past a dark fjord to a spectacular welcome—drums, bonfires along
★   the shore, and fireworks illuminating the grounds. Accessible only by
water (it's a five-hour boat ride from Puerto Chacabuco to the south),
the property is remote and profoundly secluded. Luckily, your every
need is taken care of here, whether you're in the mood for hiking and
kayaking, excursions to glaciers, or just relaxing with a massage or in
one of the many indoor and outdoor hot-spring pools. Pathways wind
among flower beds, where hummingbirds hover, and between the low-
roofed but spacious accommodations, with decks extending over the
lakefront. The dining room *($$$)* has terrific views of the fjord, and a
wonderful selection of wines. **Pros:** Spa, pool, views. **Cons:** Hard to get
here, no Wi-Fi. ✉*Bahia Dorita s/n, Carretera Austral, 13 km (8 mi)
south of Puerto Puyuhuapi* ☎*67/325–103, 2/225–6489 in Santiago*
🖹*2/274–8111 in Santiago* ⊕*www.patagonia-connection.com* ➥*44
rooms* ⌂*In-room: no TV, safe. In-hotel: restaurant, bar, pools, gym,
spa, laundry service, public Internet, no elevator* ▭*AE, DC, MC, V*
†⊙*BP.*

SHOPPING

Carpets at **Alfombras de Puyuhuapi** (✉*E. Ludwig s/n* ☎*67/325–131*
⊕*www.puyuhuapi.com*) are handwoven by three generations of
women from Chiloé who use only natural wool thread and cotton
fibers. The rustic vertical looms, designed and built specifically for this
shop, allow the weavers to make carpets with a density of 20,000
knots per square meter. Trained by his father and grandfather, who
opened the shop here in the 1940s, proprietor Helmut E. Hopperdietzel
proudly displays the extensive stock of finished carpets of various sizes
and designs. Carpets can be shipped. The shop is closed in June.

PARQUE NACIONAL QUEULAT

175 km (109 mi) south of Chaitén.

The rugged 350,000-acre Parque Nacional Queulat begins to rise and
roll to either side of the Carretera Austral some 20 km (12 mi) south
of the town of La Junta. Rivers and streams that crisscross dense virgin
forests attract fishing aficionados from all over the world. At the higher
altitudes, brilliant blue glaciers can be found in the valleys between
snowcapped peaks. If you're lucky you'll spot a *pudú*, one of the dimin-
utive deer that make their home in the forest.

Less than 1 km (½ mi) off the east side of the Carretera Austral you are
treated to a close-up view of the hanging glacier, **Ventisquero Colgante.**
This sheet of ice slides forward between a pair of gentle rock faces. Several waterfalls cascade down the cliffs to either side of the glacier's foot.
There is an easy 15-minute walk leading to one side of the lake below
the glacier, which is not visible from the overlook. Another, longer hike
takes you deeper into the park's interior.

A short drive farther south, where the Carretera Austral makes one of
its sharp switchback turns as it climbs higher, a small sign points into

the undergrowth, indicating the trailhead for the **Salto Padre García.** There is no parking area, but you can leave your car on the shoulder. This short hike through dense forest is well worth attempting for a close-up view of this waterfall of striking proportions.

There are two CONAF stations (the national forestry service), one at the Ventisquero Colgante overlook, the other a few miles north of the southern park gateway. ✉ *Carretera Austral, 20 km (12 mi) south of La Junta* ☎ *67/231–065 or 67/232–599* 🌐 *www.conaf.cl* 🎫 *1,500 pesos* ⏲ *Daily 8:30–6:30.*

WHERE TO STAY

$$ **Hotel El Pangue.** Follow the driveway to the sprawling complex of reddish buildings on the sheltered shores of Lake Risopatrón. Several shingle-roofed cabanas, all with central heating and ample hot water, were constructed by local craftspeople from native wood. The clubhouse has a fireplace and a panoramic view of the lake. The dining room serves barbecued lamb prepared on a traditional *quincho* (grill). Activities include trolling and fly-fishing on the lake and nearby rivers. Canoes, mountain bikes, and horses are available for exploring the lake and park trails. It's 5 km (3 mi) south of the entrance of Parque Nacional Queulat. **Pros:** Pool, near Queulat Park, helps arrange outdoor activities. **Cons:** Not near town, no TV. ✉ *Carretera Austral, Km 240* ☎ *67/325–128* 🌐 *www.elpangue.cl* *8 rooms, 5 cabanas* *In-room: no a/c, kitchen (some), no TV, Wi-Fi. In-hotel: restaurant, bar, pool, beachfront, water sports, bicycles, laundry service, public Internet, public Wi-Fi, parking, no elevator* 💳 *AE, MC, V* 🍽 *BP.*

7

COYHAIQUE & ENVIRONS

COYHAIQUE

224 km (140 mi) south of Puerto Puyuhuapi.

Ten streets radiate from the central plaza. Horn, one of the most colorful, holds the crafts stands of the Feria Artesanal. Balmaceda connects the central square with the smaller Plaza Prat. Navigating the area around the plaza is confusing at first, but the streets, bearing those traditional names used throughout the country, soon yield to a simple grid system.

GETTING HERE & AROUND

There are regular domestic flights every day to the Southern Coast's only major airport, 55 km (34 mi) south of Coyhaique in the town of Balmaceda. Ferry lines operating in southern Chile sail the interwoven fjords, rivers, and lakes of the region. Navimag (short for "Navigacion Magallanes") operates a cargo and passenger fleet throughout the region. Transmarchilay operates a cargo and passenger ferry fleet similar to that of Navimag, with ships that start in Puerto Montt and sail to nearby Puerto Chacabuco. Tour companies also often offer more luxurious transport that includes stops in Chacabuco.

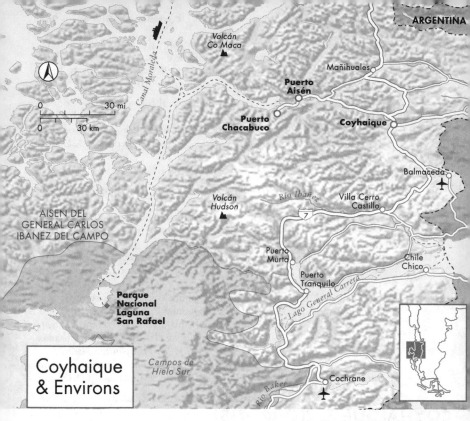

Coyhaique
& Environs

Renting a car, while expensive, is a worthwhile option for getting around. At Balmaceda airport there are several rental agencies. Make sure you understand the extent of your liability for any damage to the vehicle, including routine events such as a chipped or cracked windshield. If you want to visit one of the more popular parks, check out tour prices. They may prove far cheaper than driving yourself. There are also a number of bus companies with offices in Coyhaique that serve most destinations in the area.

ESSENTIALS

BUS **Don Carlos** (⊠ *Subteniente Cruz 63* ☎ *67/232–981*). **Suray** (⊠ *Eleuterio Ramirez 501* ☎ *67/332–779*). **Transfer Valencia** (⊠ *Balmaceda Airport* ☎ *67/233–030*). **Tur-Bus** (⊠ *Magallanes 303* ☎ *67/237–571*).

CURRENCY **Emperador** (⊠ *Bilbao 222, Local 3*). **Turismo Prado** (⊠ *21 de Mayo 417*).

MAIL **Correos** (⊠ *Lord Cochrane 202*).

MEDICAL **Hospital Regional Coyhaique** (⊠ *Dr. Jorge Ibar 068* ☎ *67/233–172*).

RENTAL CARS **AGS Rent A Car** (⊠ *Av. Ugana 1298* ☎ *67/235–354*). **Automotriz Los Carrera** (⊠ *Carrera 330* ☎ *67/231–457*). **Budget** (⊠ *Balmaceda Airport* ☎ *67/255–177*). **Int'l Rent A Car** (⊠ *Balmaceda Airport* ☎ *67/272–220*).

VISITOR INFO   Sernatur (⊠ *Bulnes 35* ☎ *67/231–752*).

WHAT TO SEE

The pentagonal **Plaza de Armas** is the center of town and the nexus for its attractions, including the town's **Catedral** and **Intendencia,** the government building.

The Carretera Austral leads into the northeastern corner of town and to the **Monumento al Ovejero.** On the broad median of the Avenida General Baquedano a solitary shepherd with his horse and his dog lean motionless into the wind behind a plodding flock of sheep. ⊠ *Av. General Baquedano.*

The **Museo Regional de la Patagonia** is worth the small fee for the black-and-white photos of early-20th-century pioneering in this region, as well as for the collections of household, farming, and early industrial artifacts from the same era. To visit is to be reminded of how recently many parts of southern Chile began to develop. ⊠ *Calle Eusebio Lillo 23, Casa de la Cultura* ☎ *No phone* 🎟 *400 pesos* ⊘ *Weekdays 8:30–5:30.*

The 5,313-acre **Reserva Nacional Coyhaique,** about 4 km (2½ mi) north of Coyhaique, provides hikers with some stunning views when the weather cooperates. If it's raining you can drive a 9-km (5½-mi) circuit through the park. ⊠ *54 km (34 mi) east of Coyhaique* ☎ *No phone* ⊕ *www.conaf.cl* 🎟 *800 pesos* ⊘ *Jan. and Feb., daily 8 AM–9 PM; Mar.– Dec., daily 8:30–5.*

The evergreen forests of **Reserva Nacional Río Simpson,** just north of Reserva Nacional Coyhaique, are filled with waterfalls tumbling down steep canyon walls. A lovely waterfall called the Cascada de la Virgen is a 1-km (½-mi) hike from the information center, and another called the Velo de la Novia is 8 km (5 mi) farther. About 1 km from Coyhaique, along the banks of the Simpson River, you can also see the Piedra del Indio, a rock shaped in the profile of an Indian. ⊠ *Carretera Austral, Km 32* ☎ *No phone* ⊕ *www.conaf.cl* 🎟 *800 pesos* ⊘ *Jan. and Feb., daily 8 AM–9 PM; Mar.–Dec., daily 8:30–5.*

The only skiing in northern Patagonia can be had 32 km (20 mi) outside town at **El Fraile.** You can rent equipment for the three trails here. There are no accommodations and it's wise to bring food and water with you. The season runs May–September. ⊠ *Camino Lago Pollux* ☎ *67/232–277.*

OFF THE BEATEN PATH

Lago General Carrera. It takes a 280-km (174-mi) drive from Coyhaique along the rutted, unpaved Carretera Austral to reach this beautiful, almost surreally blue lake, the biggest in Chile (and the second-largest in South America, after Lake Titicaca). But this spectacular place is more than worth the trip. Tourism has only just started developing here, but already, travelers have been making the pilgrimage in four-wheel-drive vehicles to fish, hike, and gasp at the mountains, glaciers, and waterfalls that dot the landscape. A great place to stay in the area is **Terra Luna,** which occupies 15 peaceful acres at the southeastern edge of the lake. The property is serene, with charming (very basic) redwood cabins, grazing horses, and a beautiful main lodge where all meals are served. Excursion packages are offered; you can trek in nearby mountains, raft or kayak on the lake or more lively rivers, or take scenic flights over ice fields and glaciers. The remoteness and changeable weather of the region mean these excursions aren't always guaranteed to happen as planned—but if it's too windy for your plane ride, you can always borrow a mountain bike, or relax in the waterfront hot tub. *⊠Km 1.5, Carretera Austral, Puerto Guadal ☎67/431–263 📠67/431–264 ⊕www.terraluna.cl.*

Cerro Castillo National Reserve. Just 64 km (40 mi) south of Coyhaique, this national reserve is home to one of the most beautiful mountain chains in the region, crowned majestically by the rugged Cerro Castillo. Glacier runoff fills the lakes below the mountain, and the reserve is also home to several species of wildlife. Cerro Castillo could be called one of the best hikes in Patagonia, but it gets perhaps only one-tenth of a percent of visitors compared to its more popular counterpart to the south, Torres del Paine. One excellent hiking route begins at Las Horquetas Grandes, 8 km (5 mi) south of the park entrance. From there, go along La Lima River until Laguna Cerro Castillo, where you can begin your walk around the peak and then head toward the nearby village Villa Cerro Castillo. In addition to hikes, there are some good fishing spots in the area. There is bus service to the reserve from Coyhaique, but it's better to come here in your own rented vehicle. It's also preferable to hike here with a guide, as trails are not always clearly marked. *⊠Km 59, Carretera Austral Villa Cerro Castillo ⊙Daily ⊠Camping at Laguna Chiguay, 2,000 pesos.*

OUTDOOR ACTIVITIES

The principal reason for coming here for many travelers will be to board a boat bound for the spectacular glaciers and ice at Laguna San Rafael Park. To do so, you must arrange with one of four tour operators, or organize your own private boat. But given that it's a 10-hour round-trip deal, organizing your own transportation can be quite expensive. That said, the area around Puerto Aisén is nature-rich and worth checking out too if you have the time. Nearby, for example, is Parque Aiken del Sur, a small private park situated on the banks of Riesco Lake with excellent walks through native flora and strong fly-fishing possibilities. For fishermen, the area is bountiful in prime fishing spots at the numerous rivers and lakes.

Catamaranes del Sur (*⊠Carrera 50, Puerto Chacabuco ☎67/351–112, 2/333–7127 in Santiago ⊕www.catamaranesdelsur.cl*) arranges boat trips to Laguna San Rafael. **Patagonia Connection** (*⊠Puerto Puyuhuapi ☎2/225–6489 ⊕www.patagonia-connection.com*) arranges boat trips to Laguna San Rafael and Puyuhuapi. **Patagonia Green** (*☎67/336–796 ⊕www.patagoniagreen.cl*) can arrange all kinds of excursions to nature attractions around Puerto Aisén, including an overflight of glaciers at nearby Laguna San Rafael Park.

WHERE TO EAT

$ ✕**Casona.** A fire crackles in the corner wood-burning stove in this tidy ★ little restaurant. Vases filled with fresh flowers adorn tables covered with white linen. The place is run by the González family—the mother cooks, her husband and son serve—who exude a genuine warmth to everyone who walks in the door. There's plenty of traditional fare on the menu, including the standout *centolla* (king crab) and *langostino* (lobster), not to mention the hearty *filete casona,* roast beef with bacon, mushrooms, and potatoes. ✉*Obispo Vielmo 77* ☎*67/238–894* ▭*AE, DC, MC, V.*

$ ✕**La Olla.** Starched linen tablecloths lend an unmistakable aura of European gentility to this modest restaurant, operated by a courtly Spaniard and his son. Among the specialties are a fine paella and a hearty *estofado de cordero* (lamb stew). ✉*Av. Arturo Prat 176* ☎*67/234–700* ▭*AE, DC, MC, V.*

$ ✕**Restaurant Histórico Ricer.** Operated by the same family for decades, this popular restaurant is a Coyhaique institution. The stairs in the back lead to a wooden dinner parlor; the walls are covered with fascinating sepia photos from the town's archives. An upper loft here makes a cozy place for tea. Among the most popular items on the extensive menu are salmon, rabbit, and grilled leg of lamb. Lighter fare includes excellent empanadas filled with *locate* (a local mollusk), and a host of sandwiches. The pottery and crocheted hangings that decorate the restaurant were created by the family's matriarch. ✉*Horn 40 at 48* ☎*67/232–920 or 67/237–950* ▭*AE, DC, MC, V.*

WHERE TO STAY

$$ ✕▦**El Reloj.** Simple, very clean, wood-paneled rooms contain just the basic pieces of furniture. But the salon is warmly decorated with antiques and wood furnishings, and it has a large fireplace. Request a second-floor room for a view of the Coyhaique River. The restaurant offers award-winning regional dishes like lamb and salmon. **Pros:** On the river, great food. **Cons:** No frills. ✉*Av. General Baquedano 828* ☎*67/231–108* ⊕*www.elrelojhotel.cl* ⇥*17 rooms* ⬙*In-room: no a/c. In-hotel: restaurant, room service, bar, laundry service, public Internet, no elevator, airport shuttle, no-smoking rooms* ▭*AE, DC, MC, V* ⦿*CP.*

$$ ▦**Hostal Belisario Jara.** You realize how much attention has been paid ★ to the detail here when the proprietor points out that the weather vane on the peak of the single turret is a copy of one at Chilean poet Pablo Neruda's home in Isla Negra. In the quaint lodging's various nooks and crannies, you'll find plenty of wide windows and natural woods. In the small but tasteful rooms, terra-cotta floors complement the rustic carved-pine beds, spread with nubby cream linens. **Pros:** Nice atmosphere, central location. **Cons:** Rooms somewhat small, no credit cards. ✉*Francisco Bilbao 662* ☎*67/234–150* ⊕*www.belisariojara. itgo.com* ⇥*8 rooms* ⬙*In-room: Wi-Fi. In-hotel: bar, no elevator, laundry service, public Internet, airport shuttle, parking* ▭*No credit cards* ⦿*BP.*

$ ▦**Hotel Coyhaique.** This nicely landscaped lodging is in a quiet corner of town, but it's within easy walking distance of the Plaza de Armas.

Rooms are a bit motel-like, with pale-green comforters and drapes, a bed, a TV, and not much else. But they are clean and spacious. **Pros:** Clean, good location, pool. **Cons:** Rooms are underwhelming. ⊠*Magallanes 131* ☎*67/231–137 or 67/231–737* ⊕*www.hotelcoyhaique.cl* ⇆*40 rooms* ⚘*In-room: Wi-Fi. In-hotel: restaurant, room service, bar, pool, laundry service, airport shuttle, public Internet, refrigerator, no elevator* ⊟*AE, MC, V* ⊚|*CP.*

$ ⛄**Minchos Lodge.** A homey place just 656 feet from the Simpson River, the lodge is popular among fishermen because of its fishing guides and boats. There are great views of the mountains and Simpson River Valley. Victoria Moya, the owner, is also a geologist who has detailed knowledge of the regional landscape. **Pros:** Fishing options, views, homey atmosphere. **Cons:** The place is not well-marked and can be hard to find. ⊠*Camino del Bosque 1170,* ☎*67/233–273* ⇆*10 rooms* ⚘*In-room: no phone, no TV (some), Wi-Fi. In-hotel: restaurant, bar, water sports, no elevator, laundry service, public Internet, public Wi-Fi, airport shuttle, parking, no kids under 14, no-smoking rooms* ⊟*AE, MC, V* ⊚|*BP.*

NIGHTLIFE

The outrageous stylishness of **Piel Roja** (⊠*Moraleda 495* ☎*67/236–635*) is given a further boost by its remote location. The bar-disco, whose name translates into "Red Skin," opens relatively early, at 7 PM. Nosh on pizza and explore the four levels of sculptural decor, several bars, a large dance floor, and a private nook. The furnishings are oversize and slightly surreal, a mix of motifs from art nouveau to Chinese. The weekend cover price of 6,000 pesos for men and 3,000 pesos for women is credited toward drinks or food.

Just down the road from Piel Roja, another bar-disco, **El Cuervo** (⊠*Moraleda 420* ☎*67/215–015* ⊕*www.elcuervopub.cl* ⊘*Mon.–Sat. 7 PM–4 AM*), is the new favorite for Coyhaique's young and festive folk. The atmosphere is upbeat and there's plenty of dancing. The weekend cover price at the disco is 6,000 pesos for men, and 3,000 pesos for women.

SHOPPING

Coyhaique is no shopping mecca, but the Feria Artesenal does host some unique handicrafts. As Coyhaique is the largest settlement around, it's also the place to stock up on general supplies if you're heading off on a long exploring expedition.

The **Feria Artesenal** (⊠*Plaza de Armas between Dussen and Horn* ☎*No phone*) has stalls selling woolen clothing, small leather items, and pottery.

PUERTO CHACABUCO & PUERTO AISÉN

68 km (43 mi) northwest of Coyhaique.

It's hard to imagine a drive more beautiful—anywhere in the world—than the one from Coyhaique to the town of Puerto Aisén and its port, Chacabuco. The mist hangs low over farmland, adding a dripping somnolence to the scenery. Dozens of waterfalls and rivers wend their way through mountain formations. Yellow poplars surround charming rustic lodges. And sheep and cattle graze on mossy, vibrant fields. The picture of serenity terminates at the sea, where the nondescript town of Puerto Aisén and its port Chacabuco, Coyhaique's link to the ocean, sits, a conduit to further beauty. This harbor ringed by snowcapped mountains is where you board the ferries that transport you north to Puerto Montt in the Lake District and Quellón on Chiloé, as well as boats headed south to the spectacular Laguna San Rafael.

GETTING HERE & AROUND

Puerto Chacabuco is less than an hour's drive from Coyhaique, and about 10 minutes from nearby Puerto Aisén. Several bus lines in Coyhaique serve Chacabuco. The town is also the jumping-off point for Laguna San Rafael, although the boats that go to the park are almost all luxury tour vessels that you will need to contract in Coyhaique or in Santiago. Consult a travel agent beforehand if you plan to use one of these.

A hanging bridge leads from Chacabuco to **Puerto Aisén,** founded in 1928 to serve the region's burgeoning cattle ranches. Devastating forest fires that swept through the interior in 1955 filled the once-deep harbor with silt, making it all but useless for transoceanic vessels. The busy main street is a good place to stock up on supplies for boat trips to the nearby national parks.

WHERE TO STAY & EAT

$ ⛁**Hotel Caicahues.** Owned by the municipality of Puerto Aisén, this is a quiet, homey place that is frequented by business travelers and tourists in transit to Laguna San Rafael. It's also conveniently in the town center. **Pros:** Quiet, centrally located. **Cons:** Restaurant serves food by a set menu only, no credit cards. ✉*Michimalonco 660* ☎*67/336–326* ✒*20 rooms* ⚙*In-room: no phone, Wi-Fi. In-hotel: restaurant, room service, bar, no elevator, laundry service, public Wi-Fi, parking, no-smoking rooms* ▭*No credit cards* ⦿|*BP.*

$$$$ ✕⛁**Hotel Loberías del Sur.** On a hill overlooking the port, Hotel Loberías del Sur is a luxurious hotel in an unlikely place. The owner, who runs a catamaran service to Parque Nacional Laguna San Rafael, needed a place to pamper foreign vacationers for the night, and so the hotel was born. It provides real comforts after a blustery day at sea, such as firm queen-size beds and separate showers and bathtubs. The restaurant ($$$), as you might expect, has the finest service in town. **Pros:** Luxury, spa, boat tour to the Laguna San Rafael Park. **Cons:** Expensive, nothing to do in port itself. ✉*Carrera 50* ☎*67/351–112* ✇*67/351–188* ⊕*www.catamaranesdelsur.cl* ✒*60 rooms* ⚙*In-room: safe. In-hotel: restaurant, room service, bar, spa, pool, gym, water sports, laundry service, public Internet, public Wi-Fi, airport shuttle, parking, no-smoking rooms* ▭*AE, DC, MC, V* ⦿|*BP.*

$ ⛁**Patagonia Green.** The cabins at Patagonia Green are extremely comfortable, and the nice, attentive owner/manager can help arrange all kinds of excursions to nearby nature areas, including Laguna San Rafael Park. **Pros:** Independent, good location, tour programs. **Cons:**

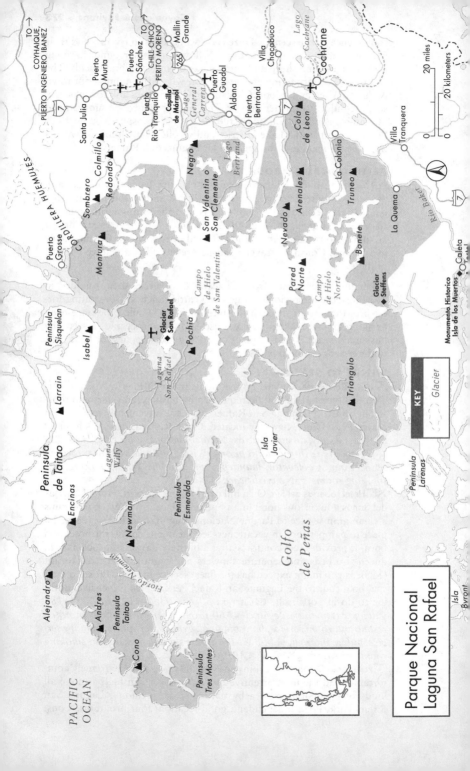

Parque Nacional Laguna San Rafael

KEY

Glacier

20 miles

20 kilometers

PACIFIC OCEAN

Golfo de Peñas

TO →
COYHAIQUE,
PUERTO INGENIERO IBAÑEZ

TO →
CHILE CHICO,
PERITO MORENO

Mallín Grande

Lago Cochrane

Villa Chacabuco

Cochrane

Puerto Murta

Puerto Sánchez

265

Puerto Guadal

Aldana

Puerto Bertrand

Santa Julia

7

Puerto Río Tranquilo

Capilla de Mármol

Lago General Carrera

Lago Bertrand

Villa Tranquera

7

CORDILLERA HUEMULES

Puerto Grosse

Colmillo

Sombrero

Redondo

Negro

San Valentín o San Clemente

Cola de Leon

La Colonia

Río Baker

Montura

Campo de Hielo de San Valentín

Nevado

Arenales

Bonete

Truneo

La Quema

Caleta

Monumento Histórico
Isla de los Muertos

Isabel

Glaciar San Rafael

Pochía

Pared Norte

Campo de Hielo Norte

Glaciar Steffens

Laguna San Rafael

Península Sisquelan

Larraín

Laguna Willy

Isla Javier

Triangulo

Península Taitao

Encinas

Newman

Península Esmeralda

Península Larenas

Alejandro

Andres

Península Taitao

Fiordo Newman

Cono

Península Tres Montes

Isla Byront

No restaurant. ☒ *Located 400 meters from Puerto Aisén bridge, on the Chacabuco side* ☎ *67/336–796* ⊕ *www.patagoniagreen.cl* ⟟ *4 cabins* ⚐ *In-room: no phone, safe, kitchen, refrigerator, Wi-Fi. In-hotel: water sports, laundry service, parking* ⊟ *AE, DC, MC, V* ⎊ *BP (optional).*

PARQUE NACIONAL LAGUNA SAN RAFAEL

Fodor's Choice *5 hrs by boat from Puerto Chacabuco.*

★

Nearly all of the 101,000-acre Parque Nacional Laguna San Rafael is totally inaccessible fields of ice. But only a handful of the people who come here ever set foot on land. Most travel by boat from Puerto Chacabuco or Puerto Montt through the maze of fjords along the coast to the expansive San Rafael Lagoon. Floating on the surface of the brilliant blue water are scores of icebergs that rock from side to side as boats pass. Most surprising is the variety of forms and colors in each iceberg, including a shimmering, translucent cobalt blue.

Massive Ventisquero San Rafael extends 4 km (2½ mi) from end to end. The glacier is receding about 600 feet a year: paint on a bordering mountain marks the location of the glacier in past years. It's a noisy beast, roaring like thunder as the sheets of ice shift. If you're lucky you'll see huge pieces of ice calve off, causing violent waves that should make you glad your boat is at a safe distance.

Wildlife lovers can glimpse black-browed albatross and elegant black-necked swans here, as well as sea lions, dolphins, elephant seals, and *chungungos*—the Chilean version of the sea otter.

Several different companies make the trip to Laguna San Rafael. The cheapest are Navimag and Transmarchilay, which offer both two-night trips from Puerto Chacabuco and four-night trips from Puerto Montt. More luxurious are the three-night cruises from Puerto Chacabuco and the six-night cruises from Puerto Montt run by Skorpios. For those with less time, Patagonia Connection has day trips from Chacabuco on a deluxe catamaran.

7

Southern Chilean Patagonia & Tierra del Fuego

Beacle Channel, Tierra del Fuego

WORD OF MOUTH

"Yes, I'm ready to go back already, looking at some of my photographs of Torres del Paine on a spectacularly sunny day, and can't believe how beautiful it was."

—lily3

WELCOME TO SOUTHERN CHILEAN PATAGONIA & TIERRA DEL FUEGO

TOP REASONS TO GO

★ **Boat Journeys:** Patagonia's unusual topography makes water travel the only way to get to know the extremes of Chile.

★ **Cities at the Bottom of the World:** In Argentina's bygone penal colony Ushuaia and its Chilean counterpart across the Beagle Channel, Puerto Williams, you'll have no trouble finding a good cup of coffee, Internet service, and some tasty eats.

★ **Mad About Ornithology:** Eight species of the largest of all sea birds, the albatross, migrate through Chilean waters. Additionally you can see hawks, owls, woodpeckers, parakeets, and the emblematic condor.

★ **Glaciers:** Set yourself opposite an impossibly massive wall of ice, and contemplate the blue-green-turquoise spectrum trapped within.

★ **Penguins:** Magellanic penguins congregate around the southern Patagonian coast—at the noisy, malodorous colony of Isla Magdalena you'll find a half-burnt lighthouse and over 120,000 waddling friends.

1 **Puerto Natales & Torres del Paine.** Puerto Natales serves as last stop before what many consider the finest national park in South America, Parque Nacional Torres del Paine, 145 km (91 mi) north. A worthy break in your journey is the city itself, commonly called Natales, which has some good restaurants and super-supportive local hosts.

2 **Punta Arenas.** Lord Byron's legendary mariner grandfather gave Chile's southernmost city its name, meaning Sandy Point. At the foot of the Andes, monument-laden Punta Arenas faces the island of Tierra del Fuego, where the Atlantic and Pacific oceans convene—and there it thrived as a key 19th-century refueling port for maritime traffic.

Parque Nacional
Los Glaciares
Lago Argentino

El Calafate

0   50 mi
0   50 km

ARGENTINA

Morro Chico

Villa Tehuelches

Laguna Blanca

Pingüinera de Seno Otway

Isla Magdalena   265

2

Punta Arenas

Puerto Hambre

Fuerte Bulnes

Porvenir

Punta Delgado

San Gregorio

Cerro Sombrero

Punta Catalina   Punta Dungeness

Isla Dawson

Bahía Inútil

Onaisin

Timaukel

3

TIERRA DEL FUEGO

ARGENTINA

Parque Nacional Tierra del Fuego

Puerto Navarino   Ushuaia

Bahía Cook

Cabo de Hornos

Isla Navarino   Puerto Williams

3 **Tierra del Fuego.** The common name of Isla Grande, the largest island of southern Patagonia's archipelago, this is where the world's longest mountain chain peters out to become "el fin del mundo" (the end of the world). Part Chilean, part Argentinean, Tierra del Fuego is synonymous with seclusion and natural beauty, though you will find plenty of company in Ushuaia, the world's most southern *city*.

GETTING ORIENTED

Punta Arenas, almost 2,000 mi south of Santiago, is the provincial capital. The only other settlement of any size in Magallanes province is Puerto Natales, 240 km (150 mi) to the northwest, a well-positioned gateway to Parque Nacional Torres del Paine. A broad expanse of frigid pampas grassland runs between the two cities. At the bottom end of the continent, separated by the Magellan Strait and split between Chile and Argentina, is Tierra del Fuego. Though comprising a number of islands, it's more or less equivalent to Isla Grande. The resort town of Ushuaia ("westward-looking bay" in local Yamana dialect), Argentina, base camp for explorations of the Beagle Channel and the Cordillera Darwin mountain range, is by a long stretch the region's leading tourist attraction.

8

SOUTHERN CHILEAN PATAGONIA & TIERRA DEL FUEGO PLANNER

When to Go

Late November to early March—summer in the Southern Hemisphere—is considered high season in Patagonia. Demand for accommodations is highest in January and February, so advance reservations are vital. Summer weather in these latitudes is by no means warm, but rather pleasantly cool. Bring an extra layer or two, even when the sun is shining. Windbreakers are essential. On or near these Antarctic waters, stiff breezes can be biting. In spring (September to November) and fall (March to May) the weather is usually delightfully mild, but can also be downright cold, depending on clouds and the wind. The region goes into virtual hibernation in the winter months of June, July, and August.

Health & Safety

Emergency services and hospitals are widely available in the cities. At Torres del Paine, there is an emergency clinic during the summer at the national park administration office. The closest hospital is in Puerto Natales. Additionally, every park guide is trained in first aid.

Eat Well & Rest Easy

Two items are considered specialties, especially in Tierra del Fuego: *centolla* (king crab), and *cordero magallánico* (Magellanic lamb). King crab is worth the splurge only if it's fresh. Many Chilean restaurants offer salmon *a la plancha* (grilled), a satisfying local delicacy.

On the Argentina side, you'll find the same fire-roasted centolla and cordero but you can also try the famous Argentine *parrillas* (grilled-meat restaurants). These serve excellent steaks like *bife de chorizo* (bone-in sirloin), as well as *asado de tira* (a rib roast), and delicious *mollejas* (grilled sweetbreads).

Punta Arenas has many historic hotels. For its size, Puerto Natales has a surprising number of options. Several good resorts and lodges skirt Puerto Natales or are within Parque Nacional Torres del Paine. In Argentine Patagonia, hotels tend to be cheaper—but there, too, you'll find a few ultraluxurious options.

The terms *hospedaje* and *hostal* are used interchangeably in the region, so don't make assumptions based on the name.

WHAT IT COSTS IN CHILEAN PESOS (IN THOUSANDS)

¢	$	$$	$$$	$$$$
Restaurants				
under 3 pesos	3 pesos–5 pesos	5 pesos–8 pesos	8 pesos–11 pesos	over 11 pesos
Hotels				
under 15 pesos	15 pesos–45 pesos	45 pesos–75 pesos	75 pesos–105 pesos	over 105 pesos

WHAT IT COSTS IN ARGENTINA PESOS

¢	$	$$	$$$	$$$$
Restaurants				
under 8 pesos	8–15 pesos	15–25 pesos	25–35 pesos	over 35 pesos
Hotels				
under 80 pesos	80–140 pesos	140–220 pesos	220–300 pesos	over 300 pesos

Restaurant prices are based on the median main course price at dinner. Hotel prices are for two people in a standard double room (or equivalent) in high season, excluding taxes and service charges.

Getting Here & Around

To begin your trip in Chile, it's best to fly into Punta Arenas, the region's principal city, or you may drive in from Argentina—if you've been visiting El Calafate—and head directly to Puerto Natales and Torres del Paine. If you'd rather begin in Argentina, head on down to Ushuaia. Many fly or cruise from Punta Arenas to Ushuaia or vice versa.

Air Travel. LAN (⊕www.lan.com) and LANExpress operate flights daily between Punta Arenas and Santiago, Coihaique, and Puerto Montt. Another domestic airline, Sky (⊕www.skyairline.com), covers the same domestic routes for less. Air Comet (⊕www.aircomet.com, also known as Aerolineas del Sur) offers the cheapest flights.

Aerovías DAP (⊕www.aeroviasdap.cl) has regularly scheduled flights exclusively in Patagonia, between Punta Arenas, Porvenir, and Puerto Williams. NanduAir (⊕www.nanduair.com) has daily flights between Punta Arenas and Puerto Natales (November 4–April 30, US$150 each way) in small planes. Aerolíneas Argentinas (⊕www.aerolineas.com.ar) has service between Buenos Aires and Ushuaia, Argentina.

Boat Travel. Boat tours take you to otherwise inaccessible parts of Patagonia and Tierra del Fuego. Cruceros Australis (⊕www.australis.com) runs two ships between Punta Arenas and Ushuaia, Argentina. Navimag (⊕www.navimag.com) runs a service between Puerto Natales and Puerto Montt to the north.

Bus Travel. The four-hour trip between Punta Arenas and Puerto Natales is serviced by small, private companies. One of the best is Buses Fernández, which has a fleet of first-class coaches and its own terminals in both towns. To travel the longer haul between Punta Arenas, Río Gallegos, and Ushuaia, Argentina, your best bet is Tecni-Austral, based in Argentina.

Car Travel. If you truly enjoy the call of the open road, there are few places in the world that can rival Patagonia. In general, those with road-trip experience in the American West should have no trouble. Take a jack and assorted tire-changing tools, with at least one spare. Some stretches are notorious for gas station scarcity.

Taxis are readily available in Punta Arenas, Puerto Natales, and Ushuaia. Ordinary taxis, with yellow roofs, are the easiest. *Colectivos*, with black roofs, run on fixed routes. They cost less, but figuring them out can be tricky if you're not a Spanish speaker.

Border Crossing

The border between Chile and Argentina is strictly maintained, but crossing it doesn't present much difficulty beyond getting out your passport and waiting in a line for the stamp. Most travelers cross by bus, which means getting out of the vehicle for 30–45 minutes to go through the bureaucratic proceedings. (Bring your valuables with you when you leave the bus.) Crossing by car is also quite manageable (check with your car-rental company for restrictions on international travel).

There are three crossings. Dorotea Pass is 27 km (17 mi) along Route CH-250 from Puerto Natales. After going through immigration, there are 14 km (9 mi) to Río Turbio in Argentina. It's open 24 hours from November to March, 8–midnight April–October. Casas Viejas Pass is located 14 km (9 mi) from Puerto Natales. After going through customs, it's about 19 km (12 mi) to Río Turbio (open all year 8 AM–10 PM). From December to March, Cancha Carrera provides access from Puerto Natales through the Cerro Castillo area to El Calafate along National Route 40 in Argentina. From the border crossing, it's 129 km (80 mi) east on PR7 to La Esperanza, then 161 km (100 mi) southeast on RP5 to Río Gallegos.

8

Updated by
Jonathan Yevin

CHILEAN PATAGONIA MAY TRADITIONALLY CLAIM the bottom half of Chile, but the spirit of the region resides in the southernmost province of Magallanes (in honor of 16th-century conquistador Hernando de Magallanes), the waterway of Seno Última Esperanza ("Last Hope Sound"), and the infamous misnomer Tierra del Fuego ("Land of Fire"). It's one of the least inhabited areas in South America, physically cut off from by the rest of the continent by two vast ice caps and the Strait of Magellan. The only links with the north are via air or water—or through Argentina. It's amidst this seclusion that you will find the daunting rocky spires of Torres del Paine, horseback sheep-wrangling gauchos, islands inhabited solely by elephant seals and penguin colonies, and the austere landscapes that captivated everyone from Charles Darwin to Butch Cassidy and the Sundance Kid.

Navigating the channel that today bears his name, conquistador Hernando de Magallanes arrived on these shores in 1520, claiming the region for Spain. Although early attempts at colonization failed, the forbidding landscape continued to fascinate explorers. Naturalist Charles Darwin, who sailed through the Estrecho de Magallanes (Strait of Magellan) in 1833 and 1834, called it a "mountainous land, partly submerged in the sea, so that deep inlets and bays occupy the place where valleys should exist."

The newly formed nation of Chile showed little interest in Patagonia until 1843, when other countries began to eye the region, and Chilean President Manuel Bulnes sent down a ragtag group of soldiers to claim some of it for Chile. Five years later the town of Punta Arenas was founded.

Shortly thereafter, Punta Arenas became a major stop on the trade route around the tip of South America. Steam navigation intensified the city's commercial importance, leading to its short-lived age of splendor from 1892 to 1914, when its population rose from approximately 2,000 to 20,000. The opening of the Panama Canal all but bumped Punta Arenas off the map, and you will still hear Chileans down here bemoaning the loss of shipping. By 1920 many of the founding families had decided to move on, leaving behind the lavish mansions and the impressive public buildings they'd built.

North from Punta Arenas the land is flat and vast; this terrain gave rise to the book of poems *Desolation* by Nobel prize–winning Chilean poet Gabriela Mistral. The road peters out to the north at Parque Nacional Torres del Paine, where snow-covered pillars of stone seem to rise vertically from the plains below. To the east, across the Argentine border, is the only glacier in the world that is still growing after 30,000 years—Glaciar Perito Moreno, one of Argentina's national landmarks. To the south is Tierra del Fuego, the storm-lashed island at the continent's southernmost tip. This bleak wilderness, which still calls out to explorers today, is literally the end of the Earth.

CLOSE UP

Sendero de Chile: Chile's Really Long Trail

The Sendero de Chile ("Chilean path") trail system is one of the most ambitious trekking trail projects in the world, over 9,700 km (6,000 mi) of trails when completed in 2010. This is one of many initiatives the government kicked off to celebrate the 200th anniversary of Chile's 1810 independence from Spain. The aim is to create an ecological connection across the country—through deserts, mountains, valleys, forest, and glaciers—to demonstrate the natural and cultural diversity of Chile. One of the major stated goals underlying the government's initiative is to raise awareness for conservation and the protection of the environment. The path is designed to fill the need for safe public access to natural spaces inside the country for Chileans and tourists. All the infrastructure—signs, refuges, camping areas, bridges—is geared towards reducing human impact on the natural environment. Keep up with the progress at ⊕ *senderodechile.cl.*

PUERTO NATALES

242 km (150 mi) northwest of Punta Arenas.

The land around Puerto Natales held very little interest for Spanish explorers in search of riches. A not-so-warm welcome from the indigenous peoples encouraged them to continue up the coast, leaving only a name for the channel running through it: Seno Última Esperanza (Last Hope Sound).

The town of Puerto Natales wasn't founded until 1911. A community of fading fishing and meat-packing enterprises, with some 20,000 friendly residents, it has recently seen a large increase in tourism and is repositioning itself as a vacation town; it's now rapidly emerging as the staging center for visits to Parque Nacional Torres del Paine, Parque Nacional Bernardo O'Higgins, and other attractions, including the Perito Moreno Glacier across the border in Argentina. A lot of tourism is also generated by the scenic **Navimag cruise** that makes four-day journeys between here and Puerto Montt, to the north.

Hotels and restaurants are simpler than in Punta Arenas, and shops older and more basic. Serious hikers often come to this area and spend four or five days—or more—hiking and camping in **Torres del Paine**, either before or after stopping in Puerto Natales. Others choose to spend a couple of nights in one of the park's luxury hotels, and take in the sights during day hikes from that base.

If you have less time, however, it's quite possible to spend just one day touring the park, as many people do, with Puerto Natales as your base. In that case, rather than drive, you'll want to book a one-day Torres del Paine tour with one of the many tour operators in Natales. Most tours pick you up at your hotel between 8 and 9 AM, and most go along the same route, visiting several lakes and mountain vistas, seeing Lago Grey and its glacier, and stopping for lunch in Hostería

8

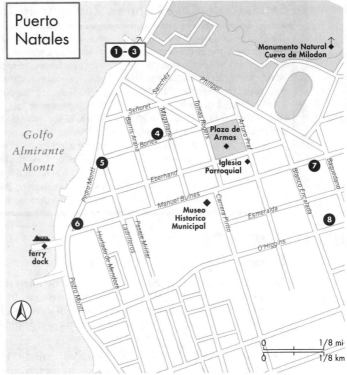

Lago Grey or one of the other hotels inside the park. These tours return around sunset.

Argentina's magnificent **Perito Moreno Glacier,** near El Calafate, can be visited on a popular (long) one-day tour, leaving at the crack of dawn and returning late at night—don't forget your passport. It's a four-hour-plus trip in each direction. (Some tours instead include overnights in El Calafate.) *For some recommended tour agencies, see Chapter 2, Choosing Your Cruise & Tour, but there are many in town, most of them booking the same vans.*

GETTING HERE & AROUND

Puerto Natales centers on the Plaza de Armas, a lovely, well-landscaped sanctuary. A few blocks west of the plaza on Avenida Bulnes you'll find the small Museo Historico Municipal. On a clear day, an early morning walk along Avenida Pedro Montt, which follows the shoreline of the Seno Última Esperanza (or Canal Señoret, as it's called on some maps), can be a soul-cleansing experience. The rising sun gradually casts a glow on the mountain peaks to the west.

ESSENTIALS

BUS **Buses Fernández** (⊠ *Eleuterio Ramirez 399* ☎ *61/411–111* ⊕ *www.buses fernandez.com*).

INTERNET **El Rincón del Tata** (⊠ *Arturo Prat 23* ☎ *61/413–845*).

RENTAL CARS **Avis** (⊠ *Av. Bulnes 632* ☎ *61/410–775*).

VISITOR INFO **Sernatur Puerto Natales** (⊠ *Av. Pedro Montt 19* ☎ *61/412–125*).

WHAT TO SEE

A few blocks east of the Seno Última Esperanza is the not-quite-central **Plaza de Armas.** An incongruous railway engine sits prominently in the middle of the square. ⊠ *Arturo Prat at Eberhard.*

Across from the Plaza de Armas is the squat little **Iglesia Parroquial.** The ornate altarpiece in this church depicts the town's founders, indigenous peoples, and the Virgin Mary all in front of the Torres del Paine.

A highlight in the small but interesting **Museo Historico Municipal** is a room filled with antique prints of Aonikenk and Kaweshkar indigenous peoples. Another room is devoted to the exploits of Hermann Eberhard, a German explorer considered the region's first settler. Check out his celebrated collapsible boat. In an adjacent room you will find some vestiges of the old Bories sheep plant, which processed over 300,000 sheep a year. ⊠ *Av. Bulnes 285* ☎ *61/411–263* 🎟 *1,000 pesos* ⊙ *Weekdays 8:30–12:30 and 2:30–8, weekends 2:30–6.*

In 1896, Hermann Eberhard stumbled upon a gaping cave that extended 650 feet into the earth. Venturing inside, he discovered the bones and dried pieces of hide of an animal he could not identify. It was later determined that what Eberhard had discovered were the extraordinarily well-preserved remains of a prehistoric herbivorous mammal, *mylodon darwini,* about twice the height of a man, which they called a *milodón.* The discovery of a stone wall in the cave, and of neatly cut grass stalks in the animal's feces led researchers to conclude that 10,000 years ago a group of Tehuelche Indians captured this beast. The cave and a somewhat kitschy life-size fiberglass rendering of the creature are at the **Monumento Natural Cueva de Milodón.** ⊠ *5 km (3 mi) off Ruta 9 signpost, 28 km (17 mi) northwest of Puerto Natales* ☎ *No phone* 🎟 *3,000 pesos* ⊙ *Summer, daily 8* AM–9 PM; *winter, daily 9–6.*

8

WHERE TO EAT

$$ ✕ **Asador Patagónico.** This bright spot in the Puerto Natales dining scene
★ is zealous about meat. So zealous, in fact, that there's no seafood on the menu. Incredible care is taken with the excellent *lomo* and other grilled steaks, as well as the steak carpaccio starter. Though the wine list is serious, the atmosphere is less so—the place used to be a pharmacy, and much of the furniture is still labeled with the remedies (*catgut crin* anyone?) they once contained. There's good music, dim lighting, an open fire, and a friendly buzz. ⊠ *Prat 158* ☎ *61/412–197* ▭ *AE, DC, MC, V.*

¢–$ ✕**Café Melissa.** The best espresso in town is found at this café, which also serves pastries and cakes baked on the premises. In the heart of downtown, this is a popular meeting place for residents and visitors, and there's Internet access. It's open until 9 PM. ⊠*Blanco Encalada 258* ☎*61/411–944* ▭*No credit cards.*

$–$$ ✕**Centro Español.** Tables swathed in bright red, and hardwood floors that would be perfect for flamenco dancing create this restaurant's subtly Spanish style. It's a bit formal, but never stuffy. There's a wide selection of simply prepared meat and fish entrées, including succulent squid, served in ample portions. ⊠*Av. Magallanes 247* ☎*61/411–181* ▭*AE, MC, V.*

¢–$$ ✕**Pez Glaciar.** Ecofriendly vibes waft from this bright, newly renovated seafood spot. Marine fossils collected from the adjacent fjord, piles of *National Geographic*s, subtle cuisine, and an English-speaking staff make this restaurant a hit. The fresh lemon-marinated ceviche is amazing, as are the dinner-plate-size sandwiches served on homemade wheat bread. The corner location within the Indigo Hotel, overlooking the water and a backdrop of snowy peaks, makes for a pleasant visit, even if you come just for a cup of coffee. ⊠*Ladrilleros 105* ☎*61/413–609* ⊕*www.indigopatagonia.com* ▭*AE, DC, MC, V* ☯*Closed in winter; months vary.*

$–$$ ✕**Restaurant Última Esperanza.** Named for the strait on which Puerto Natales is located, the Last Hope Restaurant sounds as if it might be a bleak place. It's known, however, for its attentive service and top-quality dishes from chefs Miguel Risco and Manuel Marín. *Cordero* (lamb) and *salmón a la plancha* (grilled salmon) are specialties. The room is big and impersonal. ⊠*Av. Eberhard 354* ☎*61/413–626* ▭*No credit cards.*

¢–$$ ✕**El Rincón del Tata.** It's all about the low-lighting groove at this funky little spot. Artifacts, mainly household items, from the town's early days fill the dining room, which has a working wood-burning stove to keep you warm, and Internet access. Pizza is a specialty, and it's not bad by Chilean standards; the *salmón à la mantequilla* (salmon baked in butter and black pepper) is also decent, and the grilled lamb with garlic sauce is a Patagonian highlight. The waiters' modish tango hats, however, are not. ⊠*Arturo Prat 236* ☎*61/614–291* ▭*AE, DC, MC, V.*

WHERE TO STAY

$–$$ ▥**Hostal Lady Florence Dixie.** Named after an aristocratic English immigrant and tireless traveler, this modern yet long-established hotel with an alpine-inspired facade is on the town's main street. Its bright, spacious lounge is a great people-watching perch. Guest rooms are spartan—not much more than a bed—although the "superior" rooms are bigger and have bathtubs. **Pros:** Very convenient location. **Cons:** Not quite the boutique hotel it purports to be. ⊠*Av. Bulnes 655* ☎*61/411–158* ⊕*www.chileanpatagonia.com/florence* ➷*19 rooms* ♨*In-room: safe. In-hotel: laundry service, public Internet* ▭*AE, MC, V* ℗*CP.*

$ $\boxed{\cdot}$**Hotel Alberto de Agostini.** The Agostini is one of the modern hotels that have cropped up in Puerto Natales in the past few years. Small rooms—some with hot tubs—are unremarkable in decor, but a comfortably furnished lounge on the second floor looks out over the Seno Última Esperanza. **Pros:** Perfectly functional. **Cons:** Rooms small, not distinctive. ✉*Av. Bernardo O'Higgins 632* ☎*61/410–060* ⊕*www. hotelalbertodeagostini.cl* ⤺*25 rooms* ♿*In-hotel: restaurant, room service, bar, laundry service, public Internet* ⊟*AE, DC, MC, V.*

$$$–$$$$ $\boxed{\cdot}$**Hotel CostAustralis.** Designed by a local architect, this venerable three-story hotel is one of the most distinctive buildings in Puerto Natales; its peaked, turreted roof dominates the waterfront. Rooms have wood-paneled entryways, thermo-acoustic windows, and Venetian and Czech furnishings. Some have a majestic view of the Seno Última Esperanza and the snowcapped mountain peaks beyond, and others look out over the city. **Pros:** Great views from bay-facing rooms, good restaurant. **Cons:** Rooms are somewhat bland. ✉*Av. Pedro Montt 262, at Av. Bulnes* ☎*61/412–000* ⊕*www.hoteles-australis.com* ⤺*72 rooms, 2 suites* ♿*In-room: safe. In-hotel: restaurant, room service, bar, laundry service, public Internet* ⊟*AE, DC, MC, V* ❘○❘*BP.*

$–$$$ $\boxed{\cdot}$**Hotel Martín Gusinde.** Part of Chile's modern AustroHoteles chain, this intimate inn possesses an aura of sophistication that contrasts with the laid-back atmosphere of Puerto Natales. The hotel is named after an Austrian ethnologist who studied the native inhabitants of Tierra del Fuego. Rooms are decorated with wood furniture and colorfully patterned wallpaper. It's across from the casino, a block south of the Plaza de Armas. The hotel has the same owners as Hostería Lago Grey in Parque Nacional Torres del Paine, so joint bookings are a good idea. In low season, prices drop by almost two thirds. **Pros:** Atmosphere is urbane. **Cons:** Staff language barrier, seedy casino neighbor. ✉*Carlos Bories 278* ☎*61/412–770* ⊕*www.hotelmartingusinde.com* ⤺*20 rooms* ♿*In-room: safe. In-hotel: restaurant, room service, bar, public Internet* ⊟*AE, MC, V* ❘○❘*CP.*

$$$$ $\boxed{\cdot}$**Indigo Patagonia Hotel & Spa.** Rooms in this completely renovated
★   hotel have amazing views down the Canal Señoret, stretching as far as the Mt. Balmaceda glacier and the Paine Grande. Very minimalist modern natural-wood design abounds. Blankets are made of handwoven wool. With three open-air Jacuzzis and a dry sauna, the rooftop spa is a treat for the senses. Down below common spaces are filled with plush couches and there's a lounge bar where you can enjoy brownies and cappuccinos—or a late-night pisco sour. English is spoken well, as exhibited in the Friday-night shows about Torres del Paine park. Ask for one of the corner rooms, which have windows along two walls. **Pros:** Steeped in ultramodern luxury. **Cons:** Standard rooms do not have bathtubs (though the showers are excellent). ✉*Ladrilleros 105* ☎*61/413–609* ⊕*www.conceptoindigo.com* ⤺*23 rooms, 6 suites* ♿*In-room: no TV. In-hotel: restaurant, bar, laundry service, spa, public Wi-Fi* ⊟*AE, DC, MC, V* ☉*Closed in winter; months vary.*

8

WHERE TO STAY JUST OUTSIDE TOWN

Recently, several lodges have been constructed on a bluff overlooking the Seno Última Esperanza, about a mile outside of town. The views at these hotels are amazing—broad panoramas with unforgettable sunsets. It's too far to walk to town comfortably (about 20 minutes), but there is dependable taxi service for 1,000 pesos.

$$$ ⊞ **Altiplanico Sur.** This is the Patagonian representative of the Altiplanico line of thoughtfully designed ecohotels. Nature takes center stage at Altiplanico Sur. The hotel blends seamlessly with its surroundings due to an interesting construction technique which involves the use of natural materials in its exterior. The roofs are covered with grass and flowers so it looks like the hotel is cascading down the hillside. If you are looking for TVs, Wi-Fi, and other modern-day accoutrements, there are more appropriate choices. Clean, comfortable, and well-designed rooms are in a minimalist style, with great views of the Última Esperanza Sound. The dining area is bright and open. Staff do their best to help, but sometimes language proves a barrier. **Pros:** You couldn't be closer to nature. **Cons:** No mod-cons, staff speaks little English. ⊠ *Ruta 9 Norte, Km 1.5 Huerto 282* ☎ *61/411–919* ⊕ *www. altiplanico.cl* ⬐ *22 rooms* ⌖ *In-room: no TV, safe. In-hotel: restaurant* ⊟ *AE, MC, V.*

$$$$
Fodor'sChoice
★ ⊞ **Remota.** For most of its guests the Remota experience begins a long way off from the hotel, when they are scooped up from the Punta Arenas airport. Not your conventional boring old transfer, however, as the driver stops to point out animals and other items of interest. On arrival you meet what seems like the entire staff, check into your ultramodern room, have a drink from a top-shelf open bar, and run off to the open-air Jacuzzis and impossibly serene infinity pool—before you unpack. The hotel is the paragon of style, deliberately designed in a way that blocks out everything but the exquisite vistas. The various buildings are connected by enclosed walkways in the style that shepherds built for local sheep ranches. The lenga walls are natural and unfinished. The staff feels like family, and all meals and excursions are included in the price. Every day a guide proposes a wide range of activities, demanding various levels of exertion, so you are sure to find something to suit your speed. Equipment is supplied and includes everything from Zodiacs to mountain-climbing gear to bikes. Horseback riding with local gauchos is a hard activity to pass up. The guides are helpful, patient, demonstrate an infectious love for the outdoors, and know how to crack a joke. **Pros:** After a few days the staff feels like family. **Cons:** All-inclusiveness discourages sampling local restaurants. ⊠ *Ruta 9 Norte, Km 1.5, Huerto 279* ☎ *61/414–040* ⊕ *www.remota.cl* ⬐ *72 rooms* ⌖ *In-room: no phone, no TV, safe. In-hotel: spa, pool, bicycles, restaurant, bar* ⊟ *AE, MC, V* ⋔ *AI.*

$$$ ⊞ **Weskar Patagonian Lodge.** Weskar stands for "hill" in the language of the indigenous Kaweskar, the forebears owner Juan José Pantoja, a marine biologist, pays homage to in creating this lodge. Looking over the Última Esperanza fjord, the wooden building is surrounded by parkland and has fabulous views from the terrace. It has a welcoming lounge with rustic fireplaces, ideal when coming back from the windy and cold outdoors. The hotel also boasts a bar and restaurant with a somewhat overpriced standard lunch and dinner menu. The rooms are simply decorated but warm and welcoming—ask for one with a lake view. The staff are unremittingly helpful, and keep the grounds spotless. **Pros:** Great views, helpful staff. **Cons:** Restaurant is so-so given the prices. ⊠*Ruta 9 Norte, Km 1* ☎*61/414–168* ⊕*www.weskar.cl* ⊅*16 rooms, 2 suites* ⚘*In-room: no phone, no TV, safe. In-hotel: restaurant, bar, bicycles, public Internet.*

PARQUE NACIONAL TORRES DEL PAINE

Fodor'sChoice *80 km northwest of Puerto Natales.*
★

A raging inferno broke out in the Parque Nacional Torres del Paine on February 17, 2005, when a Czech trekker's gas camp stove was accidentally knocked over. At the time, he was camped in an unauthorized campsite in an area intended for grazing. The park's famous winds accelerated the blaze, which went on for over a month and required 800 firefighters from Chile and Argentina to rein in. According to reports by CONAF the fire consumed 13,880 hectares, equivalent to 7% of the park. The most ravaged zones were Lake Azul, Lake Cebolla, and the Paine Waterfall. The tourist later apologized in an interview with *El Mercurio* newspaper, was fined $200 by authorities, and donated another $1,000 to the restoration fund. "What happened changed my life … I'll never forget the flames. I would like to express my most profound regret to the Chilean people for the damage caused." The total cost of the damage is estimated to be over $5 million. CONAF's restoration program involved erosion-prevention techniques, reforestation with indigenous species, and transplantation of young samples from neighboring forests. CONAF asks that visitors to the park respect the camping zones and the indications of park staff. The institution posts a series of recommendations for camping, and on how to prevent future disasters, on their Web page.

Some 12 million years ago, lava flows pushed up through the thick sedimentary crust that covered the southwestern coast of South America, cooling to form a granite mass. Glaciers then swept through the region, grinding away all but the twisted ash-gray spires—the "towers" of Paine (pronounced "pie-nay"), the old Tehuelche word for "blue"— that rise over the landscape of one of the world's most beautiful natural phenomena, now the Parque Nacional Torres del Paine (established in 1959). Snow formations dazzle at every turn of road, and the sunset views are spectacular. The 2,420-square-km (934-square-mi) park's most astonishing attractions are its lakes of turquoise, aquamarine, and emerald green waters; and the Cuernos del Paine ("Paine Horns"), the geological showpiece of the immense granite massif.

Another draw is the park's unusual wildlife. Creatures like the guanaco (a woollier version of the llama) and the *ñandú* (a rhea, like a small ostrich) abound. They are used to visitors, and don't seem to be bothered by the proximity of automobile traffic and the snapping of

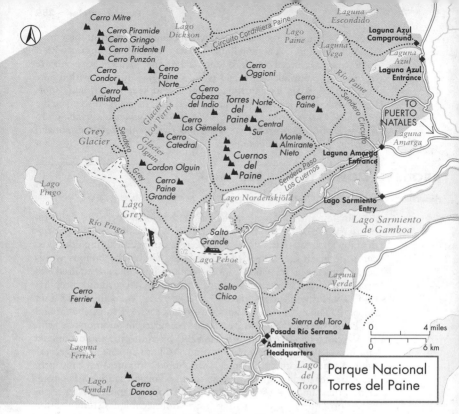

Parque Nacional Torres del Paine

cameras. Predators like the gray fox make less-frequent appearances. You may also spot the dramatic aerobatics of falcons and the graceful soaring of endangered condors. The beautiful puma, celebrated in a National Geographic video filmed here, is especially elusive, but sightings have grown more common. Pumas follow the guanaco herds and eat an estimated 40% of their young, so don't dress as one.

The vast majority of visitors come during the summer months of January and February, which means the trails can get congested. Early spring, when wildflowers add flashes of color to the meadows, is an ideal time to visit because the crowds have not yet arrived. In summer, the winds are incredibly fierce. During the wintertime of June to September, the days are sunnier yet colder (averaging around freezing) and shorter, but the winds all but disappear. The park is open all year, and trails are almost always accessible. Storms can hit without warning, so be prepared for sudden rain or snow. The sight of the Paine peaks in clear weather is stunning; if you have any flexibility in your itinerary, visit the park on the first clear day.

VISITOR INFORMATION

CONAF, the national forestry service, has an office at the northern end of Lago del Toro with a scale model of the park, and numerous exhibits (some in English) about the flora and fauna. ⊠*CONAF station in* *southern section of the park past Hotel Explora* ☎61/247–845 ⊕*www. conaf.cl* ✉*Summer 15,000 pesos, winter 5,000 pesos* ⊙*Ranger station: Nov.–Feb., daily 8–8; Mar.–Oct., daily 8–12:30 and 2–6:30* ✉*Punta Arenas Branch, Av. Bulnes 0309* ☎61/238–581 ✉*Puerto Natales Branch, Av. Bernardo O'Higgins 584* ☎61/411–438.

EXPLORING THE PARK

There are three entrances to the park: Laguna Amarga (all bus arrivals), Lago Sarmiento, and Laguna Azul. You are required to sign in when you arrive. *Guardaparques* (park rangers) staff six stations around the reserve, and can provide a map and up-to-the-day information about the state of various trails. A regular minivan service connects Laguna Amarga with the Hostería Las Torres, 7 km (4½ mi) to the west, for 1,000 pesos. Alternatively, you can walk approximately two hours before reaching the starting point of the hiking circuits.

Although considerable walking is necessary to take full advantage of Parque Nacional Torres del Paine, you need not be a hard-core trekker. Many people choose to hike the **"W" route,** which takes four days, but others prefer to stay in one of the comfortable lodges and hit the trails in the morning or afternoon. **Glaciar Grey,** with its fragmented icebergs, makes a rewarding and easy hike; equally rewarding is the spectacular boat or kayak ride across the lake, past icebergs, and up to the glacier, which leaves from Hostería Lago Grey *(⇨below)*. Another great excursion is the 3,000-foot ascent to the sensational views from **Mirador Las Torres,** four hours one way from Hostería Las Torres *(⇨below)*. Even if you're not staying at the Hostería, you can arrange a morning drop-off there, and a late-afternoon pickup, so that you can see the Mirador while still keeping your base in Puerto Natales or elsewhere in the park; alternatively, you can drive to the Hostería and park there for the day.

If you do the "W," you'll begin (or end, if you reverse the route) at Laguna Amarga and continue to Mirador Las Torres and Los Cuernos, then continue along a breathtaking path to Valle Frances and finally Lago Grey. An even more ambitious route is the "Circuito," which essentially leads around the entire park and takes up to a week. Along the way, some people sleep at the dozen or so humble *refugios* (shelters) found along the trails, and others in tents. Driving is an easier way to enjoy the park: a new road cuts the distance to Puerto Natales from a meandering 140 km (87 mi) to a more direct 80 km. Inside the national park, more than 100 km (62 mi) of roads leading to the most popular sites are safe and well maintained, though unpaved.

You can also hire horses from the Hostería Las Torres and trek to the Torres, the Cuernos, or along the shore of Lago Nordenskjold (which offers the finest views in the park, as the lake's waters reflect the chiseled massif). The hotel offers tours demanding various levels of expertise (prices start at 25,000 pesos). Alternatively, many Puerto Natales–based operators offer multiday horseback tours. Water transport is also available, with numerous tour operators offering sailboat, kayak, and inflatable Zodiac speedboat options along the Río Serrano (prices start around 50,000 pesos for the Zodiac trips) towards the Paine massif and the southern ice field. Additionally, the Hostería Lago Grey operates the *Grey II,* a large catamaran making a three-hour return trip twice daily to Glaciar Grey, at 10 AM and 3 PM; as well as dinghy runs down the Pingo and Grey rivers. Another boat runs between Refugio Pudeto and Refugio Lago Pehoé.

WHERE TO STAY & EAT

$$$$ ⌅**Hostería Lago Grey.** The panoramic view past the lake dappled with floating icebergs and to the glacier beyond is worth the journey here, which doesn't change the fact that this older hotel is overpriced and not very attractive. Rooms seem cheaply built, but are comfortable and have small baths. There's a TV with a VCR in the lounge. The view—and it's one you're not likely to forget—can also be enjoyed through the picture windows in the dining room (breakfast is included; lunch costs about 10,000 pesos per person, and dinner about 20,000 pesos per person with wine). The food is mediocre, though—simple sandwiches are your best bet. The hotel operates its own sightseeing vessel, the *Grey II,* for close-up tours to Glaciar Grey. **Pros:** The views, the location, heated bathroom floors. **Cons:** Thin walls, the price, English-speaking staff is scarce. ⊠*Lago Grey* ☎*61/410–172* ⊕*www.lagogrey.com* ⤺*30 rooms* ⌂*In-room: no TV. In-hotel: restaurant, bar, laundry service* ▭*AE, DC, MC, V* ⍾⎮*BP.*

$$$–$$$$ ⌅**Hosteria Pehoé.** Cross a 100-foot footbridge to get to this hotel on its own island with a volcanic black-sand beach in the middle of glistening Lake Pehoé, across from the beautiful Torres del Paine mountain peaks. Upon seeing the setting, nonguests are often tempted to cancel other reservations. Unfortunately, rooms at Pehoé—built in 1970 as the first hotel in the park—are dark, poorly furnished, windowless, and face an interior lawn. In the new wing, the higher the room number the better the quality. However, it's a delight to walk over the footbridge and have a drink at the ski lodge–like bar, where the views are jaw-dropping. **Pros:** Views are jaw-dropping. **Cons:** Far from attractive grounds, with miserably appointed rooms. ⊠*Lago Pehoé* ☎*61/411–390* 🖷*61/248–052* ⊕*www.pehoe.com* ⤺*40 rooms* ⌂*In-room: no phone, no TV. In-hotel: restaurant, bar, laundry service* ▭*AE, DC, MC, V* ⍾⎮*CP.*

$$$ ⌅**Hosteria Tyndall.** A boat ferries you from the end of the road the few minutes along the Serrano River to this wooden lodge. The simple rooms in the main building are small but cute, with attractive wood paneling. The hallways are poorly lit and the lodge itself can be noisy—a problem solved by renting a log cottage (at $220 a great value for groups of four). There's also a much more basic refugio with dorm-style rooms that are very cheap. Owner Christian Bore is a wildlife enthusiast and bird-watcher; ask him for a tour of the grassy plain looking out toward the central cluster of snowy peaks. Or go fishing—the kitchen staff will cook your catch for free. The prix-fixe lunch costs $14, dinner $25. **Pros:** Cheaper lodging and dining options than other places in the park. **Cons:** Hallways are poorly lit and the lodge itself can get noisy. ⊠*Ladrilleros 256, Lago Tyndall* ☎🖷*61/614–682* ⊕*www.hosteriatyndall.*

com ⇆24 rooms, 6 cottages ⌂In-room: no phone, no TV. In-hotel: restaurant, bar, laundry service ☰AE, DC, MC, V ❢❢CP.

$$$$
Fodor's Choice
★
🏨**Hotel Explora.** On the southeast corner of Lago Pehoé, this lodge is one of the most luxurious—and the most expensive—in Chile. Although there may be some debate about the aesthetics of the hotel's low-slung minimalist exterior, the interior is impeccable: it's Scandinavian in style, with local woods used for ceilings, floors, and furniture. No expense has been spared—even the bed linens were imported from Spain. A dozen full-time guides tailor all-inclusive park outings to guests' interests. A four-night minimum stay is required, for which you'll pay a minimum of US$4,952 for two people, including airport transfers, three meals a day, drinks, and excursions. Rooms with better views go up to almost double that. Yet, as a testament to the value, the place consistently sells out even during the winter. Nonguests may also enjoy a pricey prix-fixe dinner ($60) at the restaurant. **Pros:** The grande dame of Patagonian hospitality and perhaps the best hotel in all South America. **Cons:** A bank breaker. ⊠*Lago Pehoé* ☎*2/206–6060 in Santiago* ☎*2/228–4655 in Santiago* ⊕*www.explora.com* ⇆*44 rooms, 6 suites* ⌂*In-room: no TV. In-hotel: restaurant, bar, pool, gym, laundry service, airport shuttle, public Internet* ☰*AE, DC, MC, V* ❢❢*AI.*

$$$–$$$$
✕🏨**Posada Río Serrano.** A welcoming staff will show you a selection of small, clean rooms with colorful bedspreads. Insist on the ones with lake views. A warm and cheerful salon with a fireplace makes for a nice place to relax. The restaurant serves filling fish dishes, as well as lamb; in summer there might be an outdoor asado. They recently expanded and even added a golf course to the grounds. The inn also has a general store where you can find basic necessities such as batteries and cookies. **Pros:** Good service and location. **Cons:** Rooms a little small—ask for lake views. ⊠*Lago Toro* ☎*61/410–684 for reservations (Puerto Natales)* ⊕*www.hotelrioserrano.cl* ⇆*56 rooms* ⌂*In-hotel: restaurant, bar, golf course* ☰*No credit cards* ❢❢*CP.*

$$$$
★
🏨**Las Torres Patagonia.** Owned by one of the earliest families to settle in what became the park, Las Torres has a long history. Originally an estancia, then a popular hosteria, the facility recently upgraded to three-night-minimum, all-food-and-excursion-inclusive resort, in the style of Remota and Explora. Stretched across several vast fields, the location is perfect if you want to day hike to Mirador Torres, one of the park's highlights. Don't forget to check out the informative minimuseum with the stuffed ñandú. **Pros:** Friendly and efficient, with a homey atmosphere. **Cons:** Not a budget option. ⊠*Lago Amarga* ☎☎*61/360–364* ⊕*www.lastorres.com* ⇆*57 rooms* ⌂*In room: no TV. In-hotel: restaurant, bar, spa* ☰*AE, MC, V.*

PARQUE NACIONAL BERNARDO O'HIGGINS

Southwest of Parque Nacional Torres del Paine.

Bordering the Parque Nacional Torres del Paine on the southwest, Parque Nacional Bernardo O'Higgins is composed primarily of the southern tip of the vast Campo de Hielo Sur (Southern Ice Field). As it is inaccessible by land, the only way to visit the park is to take a boat up the Seno Última Esperanza. The Navimag boat passes through, but only the Puerto Natales–based, family-run outfit Turismo 21 de Mayo (*www.turismo21demayo.cl*) operates boats here—the *21 de Mayo* and the *Alberto de Agostini*. These well-equipped boating day trips are a good option if for some reason you don't have the time to make it to Torres del Paine. On your way to the park you approach a cormorant colony with nests clinging to sheer cliff walls, venture to a glacier at the foot of Mt. Balmaceda, and finally dock at Puerto Toro for a 1-km (½-mi) hike to the foot of the Serrano Glacier. Congratulations, you made it to the least-visited national park in the whole of Chile. In recognition of the feat, on the trip back to Puerto Natales the crew treats you to a pisco sour served over a chunk of glacier ice. As with many full-day tours, you must bring your own lunch. Warm clothing, including gloves, is recommended year-round, particularly if there's even the slightest breeze.

PUNTA ARENAS

Founded a little more than 150 years ago, Punta Arenas ("Sandy Point") was Chile's first permanent settlement in Patagonia. Great developments in cattle-keeping, mining, and wood production led to an economic and social boom at the end of the 19th century; today, though the port is no longer an important stop on trade routes, it exudes an aura of faded grandeur. Plaza Muñoz Gamero, the central square (also known as the Plaza de Armas), is surrounded by evidence of its early prosperity: buildings whose then-opulent brick exteriors recall a time when this was one of Chile's wealthiest cities.

The newer houses here have colorful tin roofs, best appreciated when seen from a high vantage point such as the Mirador Cerro la Cruz. Although the city as a whole is not particularly attractive, look for details: the pink-and-white house on a corner, the bay window full of potted plants, and schoolchildren in identical naval peacoats reminding you how the city's identity is tied to the sea.

Although Punta Arenas is 3,141 km (1,960 mi) from Santiago, daily flights from the capital make it an easy journey. As the transportation hub of southern Patagonia, Punta Arenas is within reach of Chile's Parque Nacional Torres del Paine (about a four- to five-hour drive, thanks to a new road) and Argentina's Parque Nacional los Glaciares. It's also a major base for penguin-watchers and a key point of embarkation for boat travel to Ushuaia and Antarctica.

The sights of Punta Arenas can basically be done in a day or two. The city is mainly a jumping-off point for cruises, or for traveling up to Torres del Paine, which is most pleasantly done by staying in close by Puerto Natales, a town that's gaining ground over Punta Arenas as a vacation destination. Something of a giant service station of a city catering to energy companies, its port, tax-free electronics, the

Seeing it By Sea

The four-day Navimag trips from Puerto Montt to Puerto Natales, which pass the Amalia Glacier, are immensely popular with backpackers and other visitors. The ship isn't luxurious, but it has a restaurant, pub, and lectures on local culture. The boat calls at Puerto Edén, where you can get off and visit the town for a few hours. Navimag tickets can be bought online or at local travel agencies.

If you prefer to travel through the region's natural wonders in comfort, Comapa's affiliate Cruceros Australis runs two ships, the elegant 55-cabin *Mare Australis*, built in 2002, and the even newer 63-cabin *Vía Australis*, constructed in 2005. Both ships have the classic, wood-and-polished-brass design of old-world luxury liners, and both sail round-trip between Punta Arenas and Ushuaia (there are four-day and three-day options). On the way, the ships stop at a number of sights, including the Garibaldi Glacier, a breathtaking mass of blue ice. You also ride smaller motorboats ashore to visit Isla Magdalena's colony of 120,000 penguins, and Ainsworth Bay's family of elephant seals. The cruises include lectures in English, German, and Spanish on the region's geography and history, flora and fauna; all multicourse meals and cocktails (including some formidable pisco sours) are included.

Comapa also runs a ferry three times a week between Punta Arenas and Porvenir, and the *Barcaza Melinka*, which makes thrice-weekly trips to Isla Magdalena (during penguin season).

Turismo 21 de Mayo operates two ships, the *Cutter 21 de Mayo* and the *Alberto de Agostini*, to the Balmaceda and Serrano glaciers in Parque Nacional Bernardo O'Higgins. Passengers on these luxurious boats are treated to lectures about the region as the boat moves up the Seno Última Esperanza.

Lago Grey Tours offers boat trips to Glaciar Grey inside the Parque Nacional Torres del Paine.

BOAT & FERRY LINES

Comapa (✉ *Av. Magallanes 990, Punta Arenas* ☎ *61/200–200* ⊕ *www. comapa.cl* ✉ *Av. Bulnes 533, Puerto Natales* ☎ *61/414–300*).

Cruceros Australis (✉ *Av. El Bosque Norte 0440, Piso 11, Santiago* ☎ *2/442-3110* 🖷 *2/203–5173* ⊕ *www.australis.com*).

Lago Grey Tours (✉ *Lago Grey* 🖷 ☎ *61/225–986* ⊕ *www.lagogrey. com*).

Navimag (✉ *Av. El Bosque Norte 0440, Santiago* ☎ *2/442–3120* 🖷 *2/203–5025* ⊕ *www.navimag.com*).

Turismo 21 de Mayo (✉ *Ladrilleros 171, Puerto Natales* ☎ *61/411–176* ⊕ *www.turismo21demayo.cl*).

8

military, and only some tourism, Punta Arenas seems unable to make up its mind what it wants to be, and it suffers from a lack of cultural activities (a few good museums notwithstanding) and an exodus of its young people.

Numbers in the text correspond to numbers in the margins and on the Punta Arenas map.

GETTING HERE & AROUND

Most travelers will arrive at Aeropuerto Presidente Carlos Ibanez de Campo, a modern terminal approximately 12 mi from town. Public bus service from the airport into the central square of Punta Arenas is 2,000 pesos. Private transfers by small companies running minivans out of the airport (with no other pickup points or call-in service) run 3,000 pesos per person, while a taxi for two or more is your best deal at 5,000 pesos.

> ## MIND THE MINES
>
> On the drive between Punta Arenas and Puerto Natales, Argentina is just a stone's throw away. Chile lined this border with mines in the 1980s, right before the Falklands war when Argentina was threatening to invade Chile over some uninhabitable islands. The mines are just beginning to be removed. Obviously, this is not an area to take a stroll, but there's not much reason to, either—it's just flat, scrubby land with wind-bent trees, and the occasional bomb.

Set on a windy bank of the Magellan Strait, eastward-facing Punta Arenas has four main thoroughfares which were originally planned to be wide enough to accommodate flocks of sheep. Bustling with pedestrians, Avenida Bories is the main drag for shopping. Overall, the city is quite compact, and navigating its central grid of streets is fairly straightforward.

ESSENTIALS

BUS **Buses Fernández** (✉ *Armando Sanhueza 745* ☎ *61/221–429* ⊕ *www.buses fernandez.com*). **Tecni-Austral** (✉ *Lautaro Navarro 975* ☎ *61/222–078 or 61/223–205*).

INTERNET **Austro Internet** (✉ *Croacica 690* ☎ *61/222-297*). **El Calafate** (✉ *Av. Magallanes 922* ☎ *61/241–281*). **Cyber Café** (✉ *Av. Colón 778, 2nd fl.* ☎ *61/200–610*).

MAIL **DHL** (✉ *Pedro Montt 840, Local 4* ☎ *61/228–462* ⊕ *www.dhl.com*). **Post Office** (✉ *Bories 911*).

MEDICAL **Clinica Magallanes Medical Center** (✉ *Av. Bulnes 1448* ☎ *61/211–527*). **Hospital Cirujano Guzman** (✉ *Av. Bulnes at Capitan Guillermos* ☎ *61/207–500*). **Hospital Mutual de Seguridad** (✉ *Av. España 1890* ☎ *61/212–369*).

RENTAL CARS **Avis** (✉ *Roca 1044* ☎ *61/241–182* ✉ *Aeropuerto Presidente Ibáñez*). **Budget** (✉ *Av. Bernardo O'Higgins 964* ☎ *61/241–696* ✉ *Aeropuerto Presidente Ibáñez*). **Hertz** (✉ *Av. Bernardo O'Higgins 987* ☎ *61/248–742* ✉ *Aeropuerto Presidente Ibañez* ☎ *61/210–096*). **International Rent A Car** (✉ *Aeropuerto Presidente Ibañez* ☎ *61/212–401*). **Payne** (✉ *José Menéndez 631* ☎ *61/240–852*). **RUS** (✉ *Av. Colón 614* ☎ *61/221–529*).

VISITOR INFO **Punta Arenas City Tourism** (✉ *Plaza Muñoz Gamero* ☎ *61/200–610* ⊕ *www. puntaarenas.cl*). **Sernatur Punta Arenas** (✉ *Av. Magallanes 960* ☎ *61/225–385* ⊕ *www.sernatur.cl*).

WHAT TO SEE

❼ Cementerio Municipal. The fascinating history of this region is chiseled
★ into stone at the Municipal Cemetery. Bizarrely ornate mausoleums
honoring the original families are crowded together along paths lined
by sculpted cypress trees. In a strange effort to recognize Punta Arenas's
indigenous past, there's a shrine in the northern part of the cemetery
where the last member of the Selk'nam tribe was buried. Local legend
says that rubbing the statue's left knee brings good luck. ✉ *Av. Bulnes
949* ☎ *No phone* 🎫 *Free* ☉ *Daily dawn–dusk.*

Fodor's Choice **Isla Magdalena.** Punta Arenas is the launching point for a boat trip to see
★ the more than 120,000 Magellanic penguins at the **Monumento Natu-
ral Los Pingüinos** on this island. Visitors walk a single trail, marked
off by rope, and penguins are everywhere—wandering across your
path, sitting in burrows, skipping along just off the shore, strutting
around in packs. The trip to the island, in the middle of the Estrecho
de Magallanes, takes about two hours. To get here, you must take a
tour boat. If you haven't booked in advance, you can stop at any of
the local travel agencies and try to get on a trip at the last minute,
which is often possible. You can go only from December to February; the penguin population peaks in January and February. However
you get here, bring warm clothing, even in summer; the island can be
chilly, and it's definitely windy, which helps with the odor. If you like
penguins, you'll have a blast. If you don't like penguins, what are you
doing in Patagonia?

❶ Mirador Cerro la Cruz. From a platform beside the white cross that gives
this hill lookout its name, you have a panoramic view of the city's colorful corrugated rooftops leading to the Strait of Magellan. Stand with
the amorous local couples gazing out toward the flat expanse of Tierra
del Fuego in the distance. ✉ *Fagnano at Señoret* 🎫 *Free* ☉ *Daily.*

❺ Museo Naval y Marítimo. The Naval and Maritime Museum extols Chile's
high-seas prowess, particularly concerning Antarctica. Its exhibits are
worth a visit by anyone with an interest in ships and sailing, merchant
and military alike. The second floor is designed in part like the interior
of a ship, including a map and radio room. Aging exhibits include an
account of the 1908 visit to Punta Arenas by an American naval fleet.
Ask for a tour or an explanatory brochure in English. ✉ *Av. Pedro
Montt 981* ☎ *61/205–558* 🎫 *700 pesos* ☉ *Tues.–Sat. 9:30–5.*

❽ Museo del Recuerdo. In the gardens of the Instituto de la Patagonia,
part of the Universidad de Magallanes, the Museum of Memory is an
enviable collection of machinery and heavy equipment used during the
late-19th- and early-20th-century pioneering era. There are exhibits
of rural employment, such as a carpenter's workshop, and displays of
typical home life. ✉ *Av. Bulnes, Km 4 Norte* ☎ *61/207–056* 🎫 *Free*
☉ *Weekdays 8:30–11:30 and 2:30–6:30, Sat. 8:30–1.*

❹ Museo Regional de Magallanes. Housed in what was once the mansion
★ of the powerful Braun-Menéndez family, the Regional Museum of
Magallanes is an intriguing glimpse into the daily life of a wealthy

8

Punta Arenas

Angamos

Maipú

Sarmiento

Croacia

Mejicana

Carrera Pinto

Av. Colón

José Menéndez

Post Office

Pedro Montt

Waldo Seguel

Catedral

Roca

Fagnano

Errázuriz

Balmaceda

Av. Independencia

Port

Estrecho de Magallanes

Bulnes

Chiloé

Bories

Magallanes

Armando Sanhueza

Señoret

Av. España

Navarro

O'Higgins

Jorge Montt

Quillota

José Nogueira

21 de Mayo

Chiloé

Armando Sanhueza

Navarro

provincial family at the beginning of the 20th century. Lavish Carrara marble hearths, English bath fixtures, and cordovan leather walls are among the original bling. The museum has an excellent group of displays depicting Punta Arenas's past, from European contact to its decline with the opening of the Panama Canal. The museum is half a block north of the main square. ✉*Av. Magallanes 949* ☎*61/244–216* ✉*1,000 pesos* ⊙*Oct.–Mar., Mon.–Sat. 10:30–5, Sun. 10:30–2; Apr.–Sept., daily 10:30–2.*

⑥ Museo Salesiano de Maggiorino Borgatello. Commonly referred to simply as "El Salesiano," this museum is operated by Italian missionaries whose order arrived in Punta Arenas in the 19th century. The Salesians, most of whom spoke no Spanish, proved to be daring explorers. Traveling throughout the region, they collected the artifacts made by indigenous tribes that are currently on display. They also relocated many of the indigenous people to nearby Dawson Island, where they died by the hundreds (from diseases like influenza and pneumonia). The museum contains an extraordinary collection of everything from skulls and native crafts to stuffed animals. ✉*Av. Bulnes 336* ☎*61/241–096* ✉*1,500 pesos* ⊙*Oct.–Mar., Tues.–Sun. 10–6; Apr.–Sept., Tues.–Sun. 10–1 and 3–6.*

③ Palacio Sara Braun. This resplendent 1895 mansion, a national landmark
★ and architectural showpiece of southern Patagonia, was designed by French architect Numa Meyer at the behest of Sara Braun (the wealthy widow of wool baron José Nogueira). Materials and craftsmen were imported from Europe during the home's four years of construction. The city's central plaza and surrounding buildings soon followed, ushering in the region's golden era. The Club de la Unión, a social organization that now owns the building, opens its doors to nonmembers for tours of some of the rooms and salons, which have magnificent parquet floors, marble fireplaces, and hand-painted ceilings. After touring the rooms, head to the cellar tavern for a drink or snack. ✉*Plaza Muñoz Gamero 716* ☎*61/241–489* ✉*1,000 pesos* ⊙*Tues.–Fri. 10:30–1 and 5–8:30, Sat. 10:30–1 and 8–10, Sun. 11–2.*

NEED A BREAK? Tea- and coffeehouse, chocolate shop, and bakery, Chocolatta (✉*Bories 852* ☎*61/268–606*) is a perfect refueling stop during a day of wandering Punta Arenas. The interior is cozy, the staff friendly, and you can hang out, perhaps over a creamy hot chocolate, for as long as you like.

② Plaza Muñoz Gamero. A canopy of pine trees shades this square, which is surrounded by splendid baroque-style mansions from the 19th century. A bronze sculpture commemorating the voyage of Hernando de Magallanes dominates the center of the plaza. Local lore has it that a kiss on the shiny toe of Calafate, one of the Fuegian statues at the base of the monument, will one day bring you back to Punta Arenas. ✉*José Nogueira at 21 de Mayo.*

8

Patagonia's Penguins

As the ferry slowly approaches Isla Magdalena, you begin to make out thousands of black dots along the shore. You catch your breath, knowing that this is your first look at the 120,000 seasonal residents of Monumento Natural Los Pingüinos, one of the continent's largest penguin sanctuaries, a population that is at its height during the breeding season, which peaks in January and February.

But the squat little birds are much closer than you think. You soon realize that on either side of the ferry are large groups of penguins catching their breakfast. They are amazingly agile swimmers, leaping almost entirely out of the water before diving down below the surface once again. A few swim alongside the boat, but most simply ignore the intrusion.

Several different types of penguins, including the Magellanic penguins found on the gentle hills of Isla Magdalena, make their homes along the Chilean coast. For the thrill of seeing tens of thousands in one place, nothing beats Monumento Natural Los Pingüinos, open only from December to February. At this reserve, a two-hour trip by boat from Punta Arenas, the birds can safely reproduce and raise their young.

Found only along the coast of Chile and Argentina, Magellanic penguins are named for Spanish explorer Hernando de Magallanes, who spotted them when he arrived on these shores in 1520. They are often called jackass penguins because of the braying sound they make when excited. Adults, with the characteristic black-and-white markings, are easy to distinguish from the adolescents, which are a mottled gray. Also gray are the chicks, which hide inside their burrows when their parents are searching for food. A good time to get a look at the fluffy little fellows is when their parents return to feed them regurgitated fish.

A single trail runs across Isla Magdalena, starting at the dock and ending on a hilltop at a red-and-white lighthouse. Ropes on either side keep humans from wandering too far afield. The penguins, however, have the run of the place. They waddle across the path, alone or in small groups, to get to the rocky beach. Familiar with the boatloads of people arriving two or three times a week, the penguins usually don't pay much attention to the camera-clutching crowds. A few of the more curious ones will walk up to people and inspect a shoelace or pants leg. If someone gets too close to a nest, however, they cock their heads sharply from side to side as a warning.

An easier way to see penguins in their natural habitat is to drive to Pingüinera de Seno Otway, on the mainland about an hour northwest of Punta Arenas. It's open longer than Isla Magdalena—from October to March. Founded in 1990, the reserve occupies 2 km (1 mi) of coastline. There are far fewer penguins here—only about 4,000—but the number is still astounding. The sanctuary is run by a nonprofit group, which can provide English-language guides. Travel companies from Punta Arenas arrange frequent tours to the reserve.

–Pete Nelson

WHERE TO EAT

$–$$ ✕ **El Estribo.** Centered around a large fireplace used to grill the meats, this narrow restaurant is filled with intimate little white-clothed tables. The name means "The Stirrup," and the walls are adorned with bridles, bits, lariats, and all manner of stirrups. The longtime popularity of the place has more to do with its excellent regional food (which it ambitiously dubs *platos exóticos patagónicos*) than novelty of decor. More unusual preparations include rabbit Stroganoff and fillet of guanaco (a local animal that resembles a llama) in sherry sauce. There's also delicious spit-roasted lamb. For dessert try rhubarb pie—uncommon in these parts. ⊠*Ignacio Carrera Pinto 762, at Av. Magallanes* ☎*61/244–714* ⊟*No credit cards.*

$–$$ ✕ **La Leyenda del Remezón.** This cheerful little restaurant stands out because of its deliciously seasoned grilled fish and meats. The dining room is unpretentious and homey, with a welcoming fireplace, and the day's menu is scrawled onto a chalkboard; if you're lucky, it might include a delicious pisco-marinated goose. Although it's near the port, away from the main part of town, the terrific food and potent pisco sours (brandy mixed with lemon, egg whites, and sugar) make it a walk rewarded. ⊠*21 de Mayo 1469* ☎*61/241–029* ⊟*AE.*

¢ ✕ **Lomit's.** A fast-moving but friendly staff serves Chilean-style blue-plate specials at this bustling deli. In addition to traditional hamburgers, you can try the ubiquitous *completos*—hot dogs buried under mounds of toppings, from spicy mayonnaise to guacamole. Or seat yourself at the counter and treat yourself to a heavenly gelato. Try not to get too distracted by the televisions. Locals gather here for coffee and drinks, morning to midnight. ⊠*José Menéndez 722, between Bories and Av. Magallanes* ☎*61/243–399* ⊟*No credit cards.*

¢–$$$
★ **Parrilla Los Ganaderos.** You'll feel like you're on the range in this enormous restaurant resembling a rural *estancia* (ranch). The waiters, dressed in gaucho costumes, serve up spectacular *cordero al ruedo* (spit-roasted lamb) cooked in the *salón de parilla* (grill room); a serving comes with three different cuts of meat. Complement your meal with a choice from the long list of Chilean wines. Black-and-white photographs of past and contemporary ranch life are displayed along the walls. The restaurant is several blocks north of the center of town, but it's worth the small detour. ⊠*Av. Bulnes 0977, at Manantiales* ☎*61/214–597* ⊕*www.parrillalosganaderos.cl* ⊟*AE, MC, V* ⊗*Closed Sun.*

$$–$$$ ✕ **La Pérgola.** In what was once the sunroom and winter garden of Sara Braun's turn-of-the-20th-century mansion, La Pérgola has one of the city's most refined settings. A 100-year-old vine festoons the glass windows and ceiling. The photo-illustrated menu lists mainly Chilean seafood and meat dishes; you might start with fried calamari and then have whitefish in garlic sauce. The service is formal and attentive as in the rest of the Hotel José Nogueira, to which the restaurant belongs. ⊠*Bories 959* ☎*61/248–840* ⊕*www.hotelnogueira.com* ⊟*AE, DC, MC, V.*

8

¢   ✕**Pub Olijoe.** This tastefully designed two-floor bar is reminiscent of an upscale English pub, with paneled walls, ceiling, and bar, and reasonably priced drinks—especially during happy hour. Austral on tap is particularly tasty. Later in the evening, be warned, the music can get loud for conversation. It's a good joint for a pizza or *picoteos* (little snacks). Open until 2 AM. ⊠*José Errázuriz 970* ☎*61/223–728* ▤*No credit cards.*

¢–$$$ ✕**Puerto Viejo.** The paragon of stylish modern design, Puerto Viejo is
Fodor's Choice   down by the old port, appropriately enough. All-glass and untreated-
★   wood partitions cordon off the smoking section. Seafood is the specialty, but good lamb and steak are also available. Owned by a local farmers' association, its sister restaurant is Los Ganaderos. Reservations are recommended. ⊠*Av. Bernardo O'Higgins 1166* ☎*61/225–103* ⊕*www.puertoviejo.cl* ▤*AE, MC, V* ☉*Closed Sun.*

$$ ✕**Restaurant Asturias.** Rough-hewn wood beams and white-stucco walls are meant to evoke the Asturias region of Spain. The warmly lighted dining room is an inviting place to linger over *salmón papillote* (salmon poached in white wine with cured ham, cream cheese, and tomatoes), paella, or *congrio a la vasca* (conger eel—Chile's ubiquitous whitefish—in cream sauce). ⊠*Lautaro Navarro 967* ☎*61/243–763* ▤*AE, DC, MC, V.*

¢–$ ✕**Santino Bar-Resto.** This downtown bar has friendly service, good pizzas and crepes, and an excellent assortment of Chilean cocktails. It's most popular for its drinks; perhaps the most interesting libation is the beer that's frothed up with egg whites. It was nicknamed the "Shourtney" after a young couple from Texas and Uruguay, who declared their undying love for the egg beer—and for each other—at Santino. ⊠*Av. Colón 657, between Bories and Chiloé* ☎*61/220–511* ▤*AE, DC, MC, V* ☉*Closed Sun.*

$–$$$ ✕**Sotito's Restaurant.** A virtual institution in Punta Arenas, Sotito's has dining rooms that are intimate and cozy, with subdued lighting, exposed-brick walls, and wood-beamed ceilings. Locals gather to enjoy some of the best *centolla* (king crab) in the area. It's prepared in several imaginative ways, including a dish called *chupé,* with bread, milk, cream, and cheese. The restaurant is near the water, a few blocks east of Plaza Muñoz Gamero. ⊠*Av. Bernardo O'Higgins 1138* ☎*61/243–565* ⊕*www.chileaustral.com/sotitos* ▤*AE, DC, MC, V.*

$–$$ ✕**Taberna Club de la Unión.** A jovial, publike atmosphere prevails in this
Fodor's Choice   wonderful, labyrinthine cellar redoubt down the side stairway of Sara
★   Braun's old mansion on the main plaza. A series of nearly hidden rooms in cozy stone and brick have black-and-white photos of historical Punta Arenas adorning the walls. You're likely to hear ragtime and jazz on the stereo while you enjoy beers served cold in frosted mugs, tapas-style meat and cheese appetizers, sandwiches, tacos, pizza, fajitas, and carpaccio (the menu has more bar snacks than dinner entrées). The bar is affiliated with the Club de la Unión headquartered upstairs, and many members relax down here. Unfortunately, due to a lack of proper ventilation, this smoker-tolerant venue reeks of cigarette smoke. ⊠*Plaza*

Muñoz Gamero 716 ☎61/241–317 ▱*AE, DC, MC, V* ⊘*Closed Sun. No lunch.*

$–$$$ ✕**La Tasca.** Inside the Sociedad Española, on Punta Arenas's main square, is this rustically elegant Spanish restaurant, operated by the same owners as the legendary Taberna Club de la Unión. You can look out the windows of the gracious, wood-ceilinged dining room onto the plaza while enjoying a typical Chilean *vaina* (port, sherry, chocolate, cinnamon, and egg whites), followed by paella *con centolla* (with king crab). If you're ordering fish, keep it simple; some of the heavy cream sauces can be overwhelming. ✉*Sociedad Española, Plaza Muñoz Gamero 771, 2nd fl.* ☎61/242–807 ▱*AE, DC, MC, V.*

WHERE TO STAY

$ ▥**Hostal de la Avenida.** The rooms of this pea-green guesthouse all overlook a garden lovingly tended by the owner, a local of Yugoslav origin. Flowers spill out from a wheelbarrow and a bathtub, birdhouses hang from trees, and a statue of Mary rests in a shrine with a grotto. The rooms offer modest comforts for those on a budget. The ones across the garden, away from the street, are the newest. Beside them is a funky bar that Chilean poet Pablo Neruda would have approved of; it seems hunkered down for blustery winters. **Pros:** Quaint, simple, nice contrast to the big hotels. **Cons:** No Internet. ✉*Av. Colón 534* ☎61/247–532 ⤏*10 rooms, 6 with bath* ⌂*In-room: safe. In-hotel: bar, laundry service, public Wi-Fi* ▱*AE, DC, MC, V* ☍*CP.*

$ ▥**Hostal Oro Fueguino.** On a sloping cobblestone street near the obser-
★ vation deck at Cerro la Cruz, this charming little hostelry—tall, narrow, and rambling—welcomes you with lots of color. The first thing you notice is the facade, painted bright orange and blue. Inside are homey wall hangings and lamp shades made of eye-catching fabrics from as far off as India. The dining and living rooms are cheerful, and there's a wealth of tourist information. The warmth is enhanced by the personal zeal of the proprietor, Dinka Ocampo. **Pros:** Much of its charm comes from its quirkiness. **Cons:** Somewhat isolated. ✉*Fagnano 365* ☎61/249–401 ⊕*www.orofueguino.cl* ⤏*12 rooms* ⌂*Inroom: no a/c. In-hotel: laundry service, public Internet* ▱*AE, DC, MC, V* ☍*BP.*

$$ ▥**Hotel Isla Rey Jorge.** Lofty wood-framed windows let lots of light into the intimate rooms, decorated in mint and deep rose, at this English-style hotel with impeccable service. The hotel's richly toned *lenga* and *coigüe* woodwork in the lobby continues down into the popular basement pub, El Galeón. The hotel is just one block from Plaza Muñoz Gamero. **Pros:** Staff is friendly and efficient, inviting interior. **Cons:** Some rooms are rather indifferently appointed. ✉*21 de Mayo 1243* ☎61/248–220 or 61/222–681 ⊕*www.islareyjorge.com* ⤏*21 rooms, 4 suites* ⌂*In-hotel: restaurant, bar, airport shuttle, public Wi-Fi* ▱*AE, DC, MC, V.*

8

$$$ ⊡ **Hotel José Nogueira.** Originally the home of Sara Braun, this opulent
★ 19th-century mansion also contains a museum. The location—steps off
the main plaza—couldn't be better. Carefully restored over many years,
the building retains the original crystal chandeliers, marble floors, and
polished bronze details that were imported from France. Rooms are
stunning—especially on the third floor—with high ceilings, thick car-
pets, and period furniture. Suites have hot tubs and in-room faxes.
Pros: Central location, authentic. **Cons:** None really. ⊠*Bories 959*
🕾*61/711–000* ⊕*www.hotelnogueira.com* ⇄*17 rooms, 5 suites* ⭑*In-
room: safe, dial-up. In-hotel: restaurant, bar, laundry service, public
Wi-Fi* ⊟*AE, DC, MC, V.*

$$ ✕⊡ **Hotel Los Navegantes.** This unpretentious older hotel, just a block
from the Plaza de Armas, has spacious burgundy-and-green rooms and
a nautical theme (an enormous maritime map graces the lobby wall).
There's a charming dark-wood bar and a garden-view restaurant that
serves delicious roast lamb. **Pros:** Superb mattress and bedding quality.
Cons: Don't get burned by the radiators; few electrical outlets. ⊠*José
Menéndez 647* 🕾*61/617–700* ⊕*www.hotel-losnavegantes.com* ⇄*50
rooms, 2 suites* ⭑*In-room: safe. In-hotel: restaurant, bar, airport shuttle, public Wi-Fi* ⊟*AE, DC, MC, V.*

$$ ✕⊡ **Hotel Tierra del Fuego.** Just a couple of blocks from the main plaza,
this hotel is aging with grace. The place is clean and simple, with an
old-world pub that serves sandwiches and drinks into the wee hours.
Rooms are brightened by pretty rugs and marble bathroom sinks; some
even have kitchenettes. The prices are reasonable; it's a good value in
this category, especially given the amount of space you get. **Pros:** Close
to much of the town's action. **Cons:** Not the most romantic. ⊠*Av.
Colón 716* 🕾🕾*61/226–200* ⊕*www.puntaarenas.com* ⇄*26 rooms*
⭑*In-room: kitchen (some), Wi-Fi. In-hotel: bar, restaurant, public Wi-
Fi* ⊟*AE, DC, MC, V* ⦿*BP.*

NIGHTLIFE

During the Chilean summer, because Punta Arenas is so far south, the
sun doesn't set until well into the evening. That means that locals don't
think about hitting the bars until midnight. If you can't stay up late, try
the hotel bars, such as Hotel Tierra del Fuego's **Pub 1900** (⊠*Av. Colón
716* 🕾*61/242–759*), which attract an early crowd. The city's classic
speakeasy, **La Taberna Club de la Unión,** hops into the wee hours with a
healthy mix of younger and older patrons. Claustrophobes head to
Pub Olijoe's for a roomier option. If you're in the mood for dancing,
try **Kamikaze** (⊠*Bories 655* 🕾*61/248–744*) or the **El Templo** (⊠*Pedro
Montt 927* 🕾*61/257–384*) where the younger set goes to party until
dawn.

SHOPPING

You don't have to go far to find local handicrafts, pricey souvenirs, wool clothing, hiking gear, postcards, custom chocolates, or semiprecious stones like lapis lazuli. You will see penguins of every variety, from keychain size to larger than life. Warm wool clothing is for sale in almost every shop, but it isn't cheap. Unfortunately, few things are actually made in Chile—often a design is sent to England to be knitted and then returned with a handsome markup.

> ## HOLY GEOLOGISTS!
>
> You may find yourself having more conversations with more American geologists while in Puerto Arenas than you'd ever have a chance to at home. Middle-aged solo traveler? Geological consultant, most likely, brought in to advise on possible oil and methane gas deposits. They're generally itching for conversation, too.

Almacén de Antaño (⊠ *Av. Colón 1000* ☏ *61/227–283*) offers a fascinatingly eclectic selection of pewter, ceramics, mirrors, and frames. **Dagorret** (⊠ *Bories 587* ☏ *61/228–692* ⊕ *www.dagorret.cl*), a Chilean chain with other outlets in Puerto Montt and Puerto Natales, carries top-quality leather clothing, including *gamuza* (suede) and *gamulán* (buckskin), some with wool trim. **Quilpué** (⊠ *José Nogueira 1256* ☏ *61/220–960*) is a shoe-repair shop that also sells *huaso* (cowboy) supplies such as bridles, bits, and spurs. Pick up some boots for folk dancing.

PUERTO HAMBRE

50 km (31 mi) south of Punta Arenas.

In an attempt to gain a foothold in the region, Spain founded Ciudad Rey Don Felipe in 1584. Pedro Sarmiento de Gamboa constructed a church and homes for more than 100 settlers. But just three years later, British navigator Thomas Cavendish came ashore to find that all but one person had died of hunger, which some might say is a natural result of founding a town where there isn't any freshwater. He renamed the town Port Famine. Today a tranquil fishing village, Puerto Hambre still has traces of the original settlement, a sobering reminder of bad government planning.

WHAT TO SEE

About 2 km (1 mi) west of Puerto Hambre is a small white **monolith** that marks the geographical center of Chile, the midway point between northernmost Arica and the South Pole.

In the middle of a Chilean winter in 1843, a frigate under the command of Captain Juan Williams Rebolledo sailed southward from the island of Chiloé carrying a ragtag contingent of 11 sailors and eight soldiers. In October, on a rocky promontory called Santa Ana overlooking the Estrecho de Magallanes, they built a wooden fort, which they named **Fuerte Bulnes,** thereby founding the first Chilean settlement in the southern reaches of Patagonia. Much of the fort has been restored. ⊠ *5* *km (3 mi) south of Puerto Hambre* ☎*No phone* 🎫*Free* ⊙*Weekdays 8:30–12:30 and 2:30–6:30.*

The 47,000-acre **Reserva Nacional Laguna Parrillar,** west of Puerto Hambre, stretches around a shimmering lake in a valley flanked by hills. It's a great place for a picnic, if the weather cooperates. A number of well-marked paths lead to sweeping vistas over the Estrecho de Magallanes. ✉*Off Ruta 9, 52 km (32 mi) south of Punta Arenas* ☎*No phone* 🎫*650 pesos* ⊙*Oct. 16–Mar. 15, weekdays 8:30–5:30, weekends 8:30–8:30.*

PINGÜINERA DE SENO OTWAY

65 km (40 mi) northwest of Punta Arenas.

Magellanic penguins, which live up to 20 years in the wild, return repeatedly to their birthplace to mate with the same partner. For about 2,000 penguin couples—no singles make the trip—home is this desolate and windswept land off the Otway Sound. In late September the penguins begin to arrive from the southern coast of Brazil and the Falkland Islands. They mate and lay their eggs in early October, and brood their eggs in November. Offspring are hatched mid-November through early December. If you're lucky, you'll see downy gray chicks stick their heads out of the burrows when their parents return to feed them. Otherwise you might see scores of the adult penguins waddling to the ocean from their nesting burrows. They swim for food every eight hours and dive up to 100 feet deep. The penguins depart from the sound in late March.

The road to the sanctuary begins 30 km (18 mi) north of Punta Arenas, where the main road, Ruta 9, diverges near a checkpoint booth. A gravel road then traverses another fierce and winding 30 km (18 mi), but the rough trip (mud will be a problem if there's been recent rain) should reward you with the sight of hundreds of sheep, cows, and birds, including, if you're lucky, rheas and flamingos. The sanctuary is a 1-km (½-mi) walk from the parking lot. It gets chilly, so bring a windbreaker.

The best time to appreciate the penguins is in the morning before 10 AM, or the evening after 5 PM, when they are not out fishing. If you don't have a car, Comapa, like many other tour companies based in Punta Arenas, offers tours to the Pingüinera (⇨*By Boat in Patagonia & Tierra del Fuego Essentials*). The tours generally leave from Punta Arenas, return about 3½ hours later, and range in price from 7,000 to 10,000 pesos. ✉*Off Ruta 9* 🎫*2,000 pesos* ⊙*Oct.–Mar., daily 8–7.*

PORVENIR

30 km (18 mi) by boat from Punta Arenas.

A short trip eastward across the Estrecho de Magallanes, Porvenir ("Future"!) is the principal town on Chile's half of Tierra del Fuego. It's not much to speak of, with a landscape dominated by brightly painted

The Giants of Patagonia

Antonio Pigafetta was an Italian aristocrat who shelled out a great sum of money for the privilege of playing passenger on Ferdinand Magellan's famed circumnavigation, and his story is told in *Relazione del Primo Viaggio Intorno Al Mondo* (Reflections on the first voyage around the world). Among the most curious details of his book is its depiction of the native Patagonians as a race of giants. Patagonia itself, according to one etymological account, was named by Magellan as a remark upon the great size of the natives' feet ("Patagones" roughly translates as "bigfoots"). Pigafetta describes the initial encounter with the Patagones:

"One day we suddenly saw a naked man of giant stature on the shore of the port, dancing, singing, and throwing dust on his head. The captain-general sent one of our men to the giant so that he might perform the same actions as a sign of peace. Having done that, the man led the giant to an islet where the captain-general was waiting. When the giant was in the captain-general's and our presence he marveled greatly, and made signs with one finger raised upward, believing that we had come from the sky. He was so tall that we reached only to his waist ..."

Half a century later, in 1578, Sir Francis Drake's chaplain Francis Fletcher also wrote a manuscript that described meeting very tall Patagonians. In the 1590s, Anthonie Knivet, who had sailed with Sir Thomas Cavendish, claimed that he had seen dead bodies in Patagonia measuring over 12 feet in length. Soon the region of Patagonia was noted on maps as "Regio Gigantum."

The rumors of Patagonian giants were only definitively proven fictitious when the official account of Commodore John Byron's voyage appeared in 1773. This account revealed that Byron, also known as "Foul-Weather Jack," had indeed encountered a tribe of Patagonians, but that the tallest among them measured 6 feet, 6 inches. They were tall, but not 12-foot giants. The tribe that Byron met was probably the Tehuelche, who were later wiped out by the Rocca expedition in 1880.

8

corrugated-iron houses and neat topiary. Located at the eastern end of narrow Bahía Porvenir, it was born during the gold rush of the 1880s. After the boom went bust, it continued to be an important port for the burgeoning cattle and sheep industries. Today Porvenir is home to 6,000 inhabitants, many of whom are of Croatian descent. A signpost in the town even marks the distance to Croatia. There are a number of reasonable places to stay, but nothing noteworthy. We recommend **Hotel Rosas** (✉ *Philippi 196* ☎ *61/580–088*), with cozy, simple accommodations and a knowledgeable staff.

Porvenir's small **Museo Provincial Fernando Cordero Rusque** includes collections of memorabilia about subjects as eclectic as early Chilean filmmaking and the culture of the indigenous peoples. There are interesting photos of the gold rush and the first sheep ranches. The museum also functions as a tourist office. ✉ *Plaza de Armas* ☎ *61/580–098* 💲 *500 pesos* ⊙ *Weekdays 9–5, weekends 11–5.*

TIERRA DEL FUEGO

Tierra del Fuego, a more or less triangular island separated from the southernmost tip of South America by the twists and bends of the Estrecho de Magallanes, is indeed a world unto itself. The vast plains on its northern reaches are dotted with trees bent low by the savage winds that frequently lash the coast. The mountains that rise in the south are equally forbidding, traversed by huge glaciers slowly making their way to the sea.

The first European to set foot on this island was Spanish explorer Hernando de Magallanes, who sailed here in 1520. The smoke that he saw coming from the fires lighted by the native peoples prompted him to call it Tierra del Humo (Land of Smoke). King Charles V of Spain, disliking that name, rechristened it Tierra del Fuego, or Land of Fire.

Tierra del Fuego is split in half. The island's northernmost tip, well within Chilean territory, is its closest point to the continent. The only town of any size here is Porvenir. Its southern extremity, part of Argentina, points out into the Atlantic toward the Falkland Islands. Here is Ushuaia, the main destination, on the shores of the Canal Beagle. Farther south is Cape Horn, the southernmost point of land before Antarctica (still a good 500 mi across the brutal Drake Passage).

USHUAIA

596 km (370 mi) south of Río Gallegos, 914 km (567 mi) south of El Calafate.

At 55 degrees latitude south, Ushuaia (pronounced oo-swy-ah; the Argentines don't pronounce the "h") is closer to the South Pole than to Argentina's northern border with Bolivia. It is the capital and tourism base for Tierra del Fuego, the island at the southernmost tip of Argentina.

Although its stark physical beauty is striking, Tierra del Fuego's historical allure is based more on its mythical past than on reality. The island was inhabited for 6,000 years by Yámana, Haush, Selk'nam, and Alakaluf Indians. But in 1902, Argentina, eager to populate Patagonia to bolster its territorial claims, moved to initiate an Ushuaian penal colony, establishing the permanent settlement of its most southern territories and, by implication, everything in between.

When the prison closed in 1947, Ushuaia had a population of about 3,000, made up mainly of former inmates and prison staff. Today, the Indians of Darwin's "missing link" theory are long gone—wiped out by diseases brought by settlers, and by indifference to their plight—and the 50,000 residents of Ushuaia are hitching their star to tourism. The city rightly (if perhaps too loudly) promotes itself as the southernmost city in the world (Puerto Williams, a few miles south on the Chilean side of the Beagle Channel, is a small town). Ushuaia feels like a frontier boomtown, at heart still a rugged, weather-beaten fishing village, but exhibiting the frayed edges of a city that quadrupled in size in the '70s and '80s. Unpaved portions of R3, the last stretch of the Pan-American Highway, which connects Alaska to Tierra del Fuego, are finally being paved. The summer months—December through March—draw 120,000 visitors, and the city is trying to extend those visits with events like March's Marathon at the End of the World.

A terrific trail winds through the town up to the Martial Glacier, where a ski lift can help cut down a steep kilometer of your journey. The chaotic and contradictory urban landscape includes a handful of luxury hotels amid the concrete of public housing projects. Scores of "sled houses" (wooden shacks) sit precariously on upright piers, ready for speedy displacement to a different site. But there are also many small, picturesque homes with tiny, carefully tended gardens. Many of the newer homes are built in a Swiss-chalet style, reinforcing the idea that this is a town into which tourism has breathed new life. At the same time, the weather-worn pastel colors that dominate the town's landscape remind you that Ushuaia was once just a tiny fishing village, populated by criminals, snuggled at the end of the Earth.

As you stand on the banks of the Canal Beagle (Beagle Channel) near Ushuaia, the spirit of the farthest corner of the world takes hold. What stands out is the light: at sundown the landscape is cast in a subdued, sensual tone; everything feels closer, softer, more human in dimension despite the vastness of the setting. The snowcapped mountains reflect the setting sun back onto a stream rolling into the channel, as nearby peaks echo their image—on a windless day—in the still waters.

Above the city, the last mountains of the Andean Cordillera rise, and just south and west of Ushuaia they finally vanish into the often stormy sea. Snow whitens the peaks well into summer. Nature is the principal attraction here, with trekking, fishing, horseback riding, and sailing among the most rewarding activities, especially in the Parque Nacional Tierra del Fuego (Tierra del Fuego National Park).

As Ushuaia converts to a tourism-based economy, the city is seeking ways to utilize its 3,000 hotel rooms in the lonely winter season. Though most international tourists stay home to enjoy their own summer, the adventurous have the place to themselves for snowmobiling, dogsledding, and skiing at Cerro Castor.

GETTING HERE & AROUND

Arriving by air is the preferred option. Ushuaia's Aeropuerto Internacional Malvinas Argentinas (Peninsula de Ushuaia, 2901/431–232) is 5 km (3 mi) from town, and is served daily by flights to/from Buenos Aires, Río Gallegos, El Calafate, Trelew, and Comodoro Rivadavía. There are also flights to Santiago via Punta Arenas in Chile. A taxi into town costs about 7 pesos.

Arriving by road on the RN3 involves Argentinean and Chilean immigrations/customs, a ferry crossing, and a lot of time. Buses to/from Punta Arenas make the trip five days a week in summer, four in winter. There is no central bus terminal, just three separate companies.

There is no regular passenger transport (besides cruises) by sea.

ESSENTIALS

BUS   **Tecni-Austral** (✉*Roca 157* ☎*2901/431–408*). **Trans los Carlos** (✉*Av. San Martín 880* ☎*2901/22337*).

MAIL   **Ushuaia Post Office** (✉*Belgrano 96*).

VISITOR INFO   **Tierra del Fuego Tourism Institute** (✉*Maipú 505* ☎*2901/421–423*). **Ushuaia Tourist Office** (✉*Av. San Martín 674* ☎*2901/432–000* ⊕*www.e-ushuaia.com*).

WHAT TO SEE

The **Antigua Casa Beben** (Old Beben House) is one of Ushuaia's original houses, and long served as the city's social center. Built between 1911 and 1913 by Fortunato Beben, it's said he ordered the house through a Swiss catalog. In the 1980s the Beben family donated the house to the city to avoid demolition. It was moved to its current location along the coast and restored, and is now a cultural center with art exhibits. ✉*Maipú at Pluschow* ☎*No phone* 💳*Free* ⊙*Tues.–Fri. 10–8, weekends 4–8.*

Fodor'sChoice   Rainy days are a reality in Ushuaia, but two museums give you an
★   avenue for urban exploration and a glimpse into Tierra del Fuego's fascinating past. Part of the original penal colony, the Presidio building was built to hold political prisoners, street orphans, and a variety of other social undesirables from the north. In its day it held 600 inmates in 380 cells. Today it holds the **Museo Marítimo** (Maritime Museum), within Ushuaia's naval base, which has exhibits on the town's extinct indigenous population, Tierra del Fuego's navigational past, Antarctic explorations, and life and times in an Argentine penitentiary. You can enter cell blocks and read the stories of the prisoners who lived in them while gazing upon their eerie effigies. Well-presented tours (in Spanish only) are conducted at 3:30 daily. ✉*Gobernador Paz at Yaganes* ☎*2901/437–481* 💳*15 pesos* ⊙*Daily 10–8.*

At the **Museo del Fin del Mundo** (End of the World Museum), you can see a large stuffed condor and other native birds, indigenous artifacts, maritime instruments, and such seafaring-related objects as an impressive mermaid figurehead taken from the bowsprit of a galleon. There are also photographs and histories of El Presidio's original inmates, such as Simon Radowitzky, a Russian immigrant anarchist who received a life sentence for killing an Argentine police colonel. The museum is in the 1905 residence of a Fuegonian governor. The home was later converted into a bank, and some of the exhibits are showcased in the former vault. ✉*Maipú 173, at Rivadavia* ☎*2901/421–863* 💳*10 pesos* ⊙*Oct.–Mar., daily 9–8; Apr.–Sept., daily noon–7.*

Tierra del Fuego was the last land mass in the world to be inhabited—it was not until 9,000 BC that the ancestors of those native coastal inhabitants, the Yamana, arrived. The **Museo Yamana** chronicles their lifestyle and history. The group was decimated in the late 19th century, mostly by European diseases. Photographs and good English placards depict the unusual, hunched posture of the Yamana; their characteristic wobbly walk; and their way of hunting of cormorants, which were killed with a bite through the neck. ✉*Rivadavia 56* ☎*2901/422–874* ⊕*www. tierradelfuego.org.ar/mundoyamana* 💳*5 pesos* ⊙*Daily 10–8.*

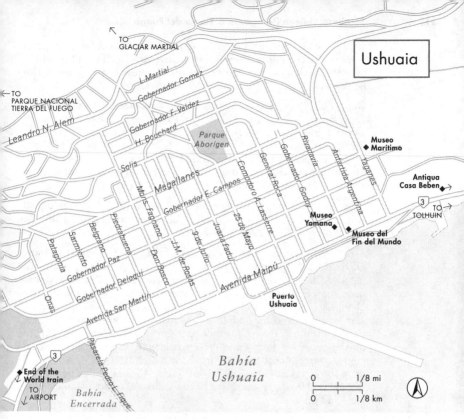

The **Tren del Fin del Mundo** (End of the World Train) takes you inside the Parque Nacional Tierra del Fuego, 12 km (7½ mi) away. The touristy 40-minute train ride's gimmick is a simulation of the trip on which El Presidio prisoners were taken into the forest to chop wood; but unlike them, you'll also get a good presentation of Ushuaia's history (in Spanish and English). The train departs daily at 9:30 AM, noon, and 3 PM in summer, and just once a day, at 10 AM, in winter, from a stop near the national park entrance. If you have a rental car, you'll want to do the round-trip, but if not, one common way to do the trip is to hire a *remis* (car service) that will drop you at the station for a one-way train ride, pick you up at the other end, and then drive you around the Parque Nacional for two or three hours of sightseeing (which is more scenic than the train ride itself). ⊠ *Ruta 3, Km 3042* ☎ *2901/431–600* ⊕ *www.trendelfindelmundo.com.ar* ✉ *95 pesos first-class ticket, 50 pesos tourist-class ticket, 20 pesos national park entrance fee (no park fee in winter).*

Tour operators run trips along the **Canal Beagle,** on which you can get a startling close-up view of sea mammals and birds on **Isla de los Lobos, Isla de los Pájaros,** and near **Les Eclaireurs Lighthouse.** There are catamarans that make three-hour trips, generally leaving from the Tourist Pier at 3 PM, and motorboats and sailboats that leave twice a day, once at 9:30 AM and once at 3 PM (trips depend on weather; few trips go in winter). Prices range 60 pesos–140 pesos; some include hikes on the islands. Check with the tourist office for the latest details; you can also book through any of the local travel agencies.

One good excursion in the area is to **Lago Escondido** (Hidden Lake) and **Lago Fagnano** (Fagnano Lake). The Pan-American Highway out of Ushuaia goes through deciduous beechwood forest and past beavers' dams, peat bogs, and glaciers. The lakes have campsites and fishing and are good spots for a picnic or a hike. This can be done on your own or as a seven-hour trip, including lunch, booked through the local travel agencies (75 pesos without lunch, 95 pesos with lunch).

One recommended operator, offering a comfortable bus, a bilingual guide, and lunch at Las Cotorras, is **All Patagonia** (⊠*Juana Fadul 26* ☎*2901/433–622 or 2901/430–725*).

A rougher, more unconventional tour of the lake area goes to **Monte Olivia** (Mt. Olivia), the tallest mountain along the Canal Beagle, rising 4,455 feet above sea level. You also pass the **Five Brothers Mountains** and go through the **Garibaldi Pass,** which begins at the Rancho Hambre, climbs into the mountain range, and ends with a spectacular view of Lago Escondido. From here you continue on to Lago Fagnano through the countryside past sawmills and lumber yards. To do this tour in a four-wheel-drive truck with an excellent bilingual guide, contact **Canal Fun** (⊠*Rivadavía 82* ☎*2901/437–395*); you'll drive *through* Lago Fagnano (about 3 feet of water at this point) to a secluded cabin on the shore and have a delicious *asado,* complete with wine and dessert.

Estancia Harberton (Harberton Ranch), consists of 50,000 acres of coastal marshland and wooded hillsides. The property was a late-19th-century gift from the Argentine government to Reverend Thomas Bridges, who authored a Yamana–English dictionary and is considered the patriarch of Tierra del Fuego. Today the ranch is managed by Bridges's great-grandson, Thomas Goodall, and his American wife, Natalie, a scientist and author who has cooperated with the National Geographic Society on conservation projects and operates the impressive marine mammal museum, Museo Acatushun (www.acatushun. com 5 pesos). Most people visit as part of organized tours, but you'll be welcome if you arrive alone. They serve up a tasty tea in their home, the oldest building on the island. For safety reasons, exploration of the ranch can only be done on guided tours (45–90 minutes). Lodging is available, either in the Old Shepherd's House (240 pesos per person with breakfast) or the Old Cook's House (210 pesos per person with breakfast). Additionally, you can arrange a three-course lunch at the ranch by calling two days ahead for a reservation. Most tours reach the estancia by boat, offering a rare opportunity to explore the **Isla Martillo** penguin colony, in addition to a sea-lion refuge on **Isla de los Lobos** (Island of the Wolves) along the way. ⊠*85 km (53 mi) east of Ushuaia* ☎*2901/422–742* ⊕*www.estanciaharberton.com* ✉*15 pesos* ⊙*By tour only, daily 9–7, last tour 5:30.*

★ If you've never butted heads with a glacier, and especially if you won't be covering El Calafate on your trip, then you should check out **Glaciar Martial,** in the mountain range just above Ushuaia. Named after Frenchman Luís F. Martial, a 19th-century scientist who wandered this way aboard the warship *Romanche* to observe the passing of planet Venus, the glacier is reached via a panoramic *aerosilla* (ski lift). Take the Camino al Glaciar (Glacier Road) 7 km (4 mi) out of town until it ends (this route is also served by the local tour companies). Even if you don't plan to hike to see the glacier, it's a great pleasure to ride the 15-minute lift (and hiking this stretch is unrewarding), which is open daily 10–5, weather permitting (it's often closed from mid-May until August) and costs 25 pesos. If you're afraid of heights, you can instead enjoy a small nature trail here, and a teahouse. You can return on the lift, or continue on to the beginning of a 1-km (½-mi) trail that winds its way over lichen and shale straight up the mountain. After a steep, strenuous 90-minute hike, you can cool your heels in one of the many gurgling, icy rivulets that cascade down water-worn shale shoots or enjoy a picnic while you wait for sunset (you can walk all the way down if you want to linger until after the *aerosilla* closes). When the sun drops behind the glacier's jagged crown of peaks, brilliant rays beam over the mountain's crest, spilling a halo of gold-flecked light on the glacier, valley, and channel below. Moments like these are why this land is so magical. Note that temperatures drop dramatically after sunset, so come prepared with warm clothing.

WHERE TO EAT

$–$$$ ✕**Arco Iris.** This restaurant in the center of town is one of the finest of the good-value *tenedor libre* (all-you-can-eat) parrillas on the main strip—nobody orders à la carte. Skip the Italian buffet and fill up instead on the spit-roasted Patagonian lamb, grilled meats, and delicious *morcilla* (blood sausage). It's all you can eat for 38 pesos. Sit by the glass wall to see the *parrillero* artfully coordinate the flames and spits. ⊠*Av. San Martín 96* ☎*2901/431–306* ▤*AE, DC, MC, V.*

$–$$$ ✕**La Cabaña Casa de Té.** This cottage, in a verdant wood of lenga trees beside the surge of a powerful river, overlooks the Beagle Channel and provides a warm, cozy spot for tea or snacks before or after a hike to the Martial Glacier—it's at the end of the Martial road that leads up from Ushuaia. Fondues are a specialty at lunchtime; at 8 PM the menu shifts to pricier dinner fare with dishes like salmon in wine sauce. ⊠*Camino Luís Martial 3560* ☎*2901/434–699* ▤*AE, DC, MC, V* ☯*Closed Mon.*

$$–$$$$ ✕**Chez Manu.** *Herbes de Provence* in the greeting room tip French
FodorśChoice quasi-celebrity chef Manu Herbin's hand: he gives local seafood a
★ French touch to diversify the Argentine gastronomy and create some of Ushuaia's most memorable meals. Perched a couple of miles above town, across the street from the Hotel Glaciar, the restaurant has grand views of the Beagle Canal. The first-rate wine list includes Patagonian selections. Don't miss the *trucha fueguina* (local trout) in white wine sauce, served with buttery rice cooked in fish stock, or the *centolla*

CLOSE UP

Next Stop: Antarctica

Antarctica. The White Continent. The last frontier of adventure travel. If you've come all the way to southern Patagonia, why not extend your journey, venture a bit farther south and catch a glimpse of the land of eternal winter at the bottom of the world?

Although tourism to Antarctica has increased dramatically in recent years, as the 2007 sinking of the cruise ship *Explorer* demonstrated, Antarctica is not a risk-free destination. Travel companies might offer gourmet meals and Pilates classes for passengers cruising off the Antarctic peninsula, but travelers should always keep in mind that luxury aside, the beauty of Antarctica is matched only by its isolation and utterly inhospitable environment. By all means, go to Antarctica, but choose your tour company with great care, searching out operators who prioritize safety, not price or amenities.

Most Antarctic cruises depart from Ushuaia, cross the Drake Passage and spend about a week cruising the Antarctic peninsula. The cruising season runs from November through March. Early season is best for viewing icebergs, while whales and other marine wildlife are especially plentiful in February and March. Most ships incorporate landings via Zodiac at various points along the peninsula, but remember that as with everything in Antarctica, these excursions are totally weather dependent.

The size of the cruise ship you take to Antarctica is an important and oft-overlooked consideration. Although large ships may offer more in the way of lectures and amenities, they have major drawbacks. There is a limit on the number of passengers who can disembark at any given attraction, so passengers on a large ship will have to take turns, and may miss out on the best landing points. Likewise, the sinking of the small *Explorer* notwithstanding, smaller ships are generally safer than the larger alternatives, because many are former icebreakers converted to cruise ships. One good one is the **Antarctic Dream** (⊕ *www. antarctic.cl*), a former Chilean navy vessel now operated by the Antarctic Shipping company.

Safety should always be your first priority, but if price is a sticking point, you can look into booking last-minute at a steep discount in Ushuaia. Doing so can save you thousands of dollars, but you will not be able to choose your ship with the proper care.

The **International Association of Antarctic Tour Operators** is an exemplary organization that promotes safe and environmentally friendly Antarctic tourism. Their Web site (⊕ *www. iaato.org*) is a good place to start your research.

—Tim Patterson

(king crab) au gratin. ⊠ *Camino Luís Martial 2135* ☎ *2901/432–253* ⊟ *AE, MC, V* ☉ *Closed Mon., May, and June.*

$–$$$ ✕ **Ramos Generales.** Entering this café on the waterfront is like entering a time machine transporting you back a hundred years. As you travel from room to room admiring the stories behind various antique relics (such as the hand-cranked Victrola phonograph), imagine that warehouses like this were not only providers of all kinds of products for the city's denizens, but also a point of social encounter. Try the submarino, a glorified hot chocolate which may prove the best one you've ever had. Goes well with a panini. ⊠*Maípu 749* ☎*2901/424–317* ⊕*www. ramosgeneralesushuaia.com* ⊟*AE, MC, V* ⊘*Closed Mon.*

$$–$$$$ ✗**Tia Elvira.** On the street that runs right along the Beagle Channel, this is an excellent place to sample the local catch. Garlicky shellfish appetizers and centolla are delicious, and even more memorable is the tender *merluza negra* (black sea bass). The room is decked out with nautical knickknacks that may seem on the tacky side for such a pricey place. The service is friendly and familial. ⊠*Maipú 349* ☎*2901/424– 725* ⊟*AE, DC, MC, V* ⊘*Closed Sun. and July.*

$$–$$$ ✗**Volver.** A giant king crab sign beckons you into this red tin restaurant,
★ which provides some major relief from Avenida San Martín's row of all-you-can-eat parrillas. The name means "return" and it succeeds in getting repeat visits. Newspapers from the 1930s line the walls in this century-old home; informal table settings have place mats depicting old London landmarks; and fishing nets hang from the ceiling, along with hams, a disco ball, tricycles, and antique lamps. The culinary highlight is king crab (*centolla*), which comes served with a choice of five different sauces. ⊠*Maipú 37* ☎*2901/423–977* ⊟*AE, DC, MC, V* ⊘*No lunch May–Aug.*

WHERE TO STAY

Choosing a place to stay depends in part on whether you want to spend the night in town, out of town several miles west towards the national park, or above town several miles uphill. Las Hayas Resort, Hotel Glaciar, Cumbres de Martial, and Los Yámanas have stunning views, but require a taxi ride or the various complimentary shuttle services to reach Ushuaia.

$$$ ▣**Los Acebos.** The new offering from the owners of Las Hayas (just down the winding mountain road), Los Acebos is a modern hotel surrounded by forests and mountains with a commanding view out to the Beagle Channel. Spacious and superclean rooms feature the same iconoclastic decor as Las Hayas, including the trademark fabric-padded walls. The restaurant serves international dishes in beautiful surroundings and in a warm, friendly atmosphere. The bar serves a variety of drinks, regional and international. Guests can imbibe by the lounge fireplace or in the game room. **Pros:** A great value for spacious and superclean rooms. **Cons:** A tad out of the way for a spaless facility. ⊠*Luis F. Martial 1911, Ushuaia* ☎*4393-0621/4750* ⊕*www.losacebos.com.ar* ⊅*56 rooms, 4 suites* ⌂*In-room: safe. In hotel: restaurant, room service, public Internet, gym, laundry, parking* ⊟*AE, MC, V.*

$$$$ ▣**Los Cauquenes Resort and Spa.** This resort hotel is more of a gated campus, with a series of buildings and cabanas along the Beagle Channel shore about 8 km (5 mi) west of town. Privileged beach access and sparse development in the Barrio Bahía Cauquén (for now) means a nature hike starts right outside your room. Request one on a higher floor, as many of the ground-floor rooms are partially underground. Rooms can get uncomfortably hot, and noise goes through the walls. Yet the water pressure is excellent, and the heated pool which flows

8

from inside to out is spectacular. The gym, sauna, and massage-relaxation studios are top-notch. On the relatively cheap menu of the restaurant Reinamora you will find the standard Patagonian lamb, rainbow trout, and a delicious king crab served with berries. **Pros:** Great amenities to soothe body and mind. **Cons:** No air-conditioning in rooms, thin walls can make for noisy nights. ⊠ *Reinamora s/n, Barrio Bahía Cauquén, Ushuaia* ☎ *2901/441–300* ⊕ *www.loscauquenesushuaia.com.ar* ⊷ *49 rooms, 5 suites, 13 cabanas* ⚲ *In room: safe. In-hotel: gym, pool, restaurant, bar, public Wi-Fi, parking* ⊟ *AE, MC, V.*

$$$$ ⊞**Cumbres de Martial.** This charming wood complex, painted fire-engine red, is high above Ushuaia at the foot of the ski lift that leads to the Martial glacier. Each spacious room has an extremely comfortable bed and a small wooden deck with terrific views down to the Beagle Channel. The *cabañas* are beautiful self-contained log cabins. There are also a teahouse and a small nature trail beside the Martial River. There is, however, no complimentary shuttle service to town, so you'll need to take a 10- to 15-peso taxi to access Ushuaia. **Pros:** Easy access to the glacier, views. **Cons:** You need to cab it to and from town. ⊠ *Camino Luís Martial 3560,* ☎ *2901/424–779* ⊕ *www.cumbresdelmartial. com.ar* ⊷ *6 rooms, 4 cabins* ⚲ *In-room: safe. In-hotel: restaurant, bar, laundry service, airport shuttle* ⊟ *AE, DC, MC, V* ☉ *Closed Apr. and May* ⧑BP.

$$ ⊞**Hostería Patagonia Jarké.** Jarké means "spark" in a local native lan
★ guage, and indeed this B&B is a vibrant addition to Ushuaia. This three-story lodge, cantilevered down a hillside on a dead-end street in the heart of town, is an amalgam of alpine and Victorian styles on the outside; inside, a spacious contemporary design incorporates a glass-roofed lobby, several living rooms, and breakfast room. Rooms have polished wood floors, peaked-roof ceilings, artisanal soaps, woven floor mats, bidets, Jacuzzi tubs, and lovely views. **Pros:** Feels like home. **Cons:** Steep walk home. ⊠ *Sarmiento 310,* ☎ *2901/437–245* ⊕ *www.hosteriapatagoniaj.com* ⊷ *15 rooms* ⚲ *In-room: safe. In-hotel: bar, laundry service, public Wi-Fi* ⊟ *AE, DC, MC, V* ⧑BP.

$$ ⊞**Hotel Cabo de Hornos.** Cabo de Hornos is a cut above other downtown hotels in the same price category. The rooms are clean and simple, and all have cable TV and telephones. The lobby-lounge is tacky and tasteful at the same time, decorated with currency and postcards from all over the world. Its old ski-lodge feel makes it a nice place to relax and watch *fútbol* with a cup of coffee or a beer. They also run a quaint local history museum. **Pros:** Good value. **Cons:** Nothing spectacular. ⊠ *San Martín at Rosas,* ☎ *2901/430–677* ⊕ *www.hotelcabodehornos.com.ar* ⊷ *30 rooms* ⚲ *In-hotel: restaurant, bar* ⊟ *AE, MC, V* ⧑CP.

$$$$ ⊞**Hotel del Glaciar.** Just above the Las Hayas hotel in the Martial Mountains, this hotel has the best views of Ushuaia and the Beagle Channel. The rooms are bright, clean, and very comfortable. After a long day in the woods, you can curl up on the large sofa next to the fire pit or make your way over to the cozy wood-paneled bar for a drink. Hourly shuttle buses take you to the town center. **Pros:** Old-style colonial atmosphere sets it apart from the modern behemoths on the mountain. **Cons:** Still very big. ⊠ *Camino Glaciar Martial 2355, Km 3.5,* ☎ *2901/430–640* ⊕ *www.hoteldelglaciar.com* ⌇ *119 rooms, 4 suites* ⟆ *In-hotel: restaurant, bar, laundry service, airport shuttle, public Internet* ⊟ *AE, DC, MC, V* ⦿| *CP.*

$$$$
★
⚏ **Hotel Fueguino.** A gleaming ultramodern addition to Ushuaia's downtown offerings, the Fueguino boasts all the amenities: conference center with four Internet stations, extensive gym and spa, shuttle service, multilingual staff, and some of the most thorough Wi-Fi coverage we've seen. Rooms feature custom Italian wood furnishings with stainless steel, leather accents, frosted glass, and blackout blinds. The Fueguino name is branded on every trinket you can think of, from bathrobes to shoe mitts. And whatever it's not stamped on is still top-of-the-line (even the bidets are Ferrum Marina). Beds with padded headboards and California-king-size mattresses are as firm as it gets. Downstairs the Komenk restaurant serves Mediterranean cuisine with Patagonian influences. A junior suite is worth the upgrade. **Pros:** Ultramodern sybaritic excess. **Cons:** Immediate vicinity a shambles, making this place a stark contrast with its environment. ⊠ *Gobernador Deloqui 1282,* ☎ *2901/424–894* ⊕ *www.fueguinohotel.com* ⌇ *50 rooms, 3 suites* ⟆ *In-room: safe. In-hotel: spa, gym, room service, public Internet, Wi-Fi, restaurant, bar* ⊟ *AE, MC, V.*

$$$$
⚏ **Hotel Los Yámanas.** This cozy hotel 4 km (2½ mi) from the center of town is named after the local tribe and offers a rustic mountain aesthetic. Some rooms have stunning views over the Beagle Channel, and all have wrought-iron bed frames, and are furnished with simple good taste. The expansive lobby, second-floor restaurant, games room with billiards, and sauna are just as welcoming. Never overlook the virtues of a 100-peso-per-hour massage. **Pros:** Top-notch gym. **Cons:** Questionable taste in lobby decoration. ⊠ *Los Nires 1850, Km 3,* ☎ *2901/445–960* ⊕ *hotelyamanas.com.ar* ⌇ *39 rooms, 2 suites* ⟆ *In-room: safe. In-hotel: restaurant, bar, gym, pool, laundry service, public Wi-Fi* ⊟ *AE, DC, MC, V* ⦿| *CP.*

8

$$$$
Fodor's Choice
★
⚏ **Hotel y Resort Las Hayas.** Las Hayas is in the wooded foothills of the Andes, overlooking the town and channel below. Ask for a *canal* view and, since the rooms are all decorated differently and idiosyncratically, sample a variety before settling in. All feature Portuguese linen, solid oak furnishings, and the Las Hayas trademark: fabric-padded walls. A suspended glass bridge connects the hotel to a spectacular health spa, which includes a heated pool, Jacuzzi, and even a squash court. The wonderful five-star restaurant Le Martial prepares an excellent version of *mollejas de cordero* (lamb sweetbreads) with scallops, and boasts the best wine list in town. Frequent shuttle buses take you into town. **Pros:** Four Internet stations, good restaurant. **Cons:** Decor doesn't suit everyone. ⊠ *Camino Luís Martial 1650, Km 3,* ☎ *2901/430–710, 11/4393–4750 in Buenos Aires* ⊕ *www.lashayashotel.com* ⌇ *85 rooms, 7 suites* ⟆ *In-room: safe. In-hotel: restaurant, bar, pool, gym, spa, laundry service, airport shuttle* ⊟ *AE, DC, MC, V* ⦿| *CP.*

$$$ ⊞ **La Tierra de Leyendas.** The Land of Legends is Sebas and Maia's honeymooners' delight. The couple put this adorable B&B together on the heels of careers in hospitality working for Marriott. The hotel is in the Estancia Río Pipo, on a wind-battered hill 4 km (2½ mi) west of town, in an area once inhabited by canoeist nomads. The five bedrooms—with names such as La Coqueta and La Mision—boast large windows facing the Beagle Channel or the snowcapped Andes; a cozy living room offers a book exchange, board games, video library, and glass display tables with antique arrows, bones, and currency. The restaurant has a topnotch gourmet menu—offering such exotic fare as *conejo a la cazadora* (stuffed Fuegian rabbit)—prepared by the owner. **Pros:** An extraordinarily quaint find for western Ushuaia. **Cons:** Insanely windy—hold on to your hat. ⊠ *Tierra de Vientos 2448,* ☎ *2901/443–565* ⊕ *www. tierradeleyendas.com.ar* ↪ *5 rooms* ⚷ *In-room: DVD, safe. In-hotel: laundry service, public Wi-Fi* ⊟ *AE, MC, V.*

NIGHTLIFE

Ushuaia has a lively nightlife in summer, with its casino, discos, and intimate cafés all close to each other. The biggest and most popular pub is **El Náutico** (⊠ *Maipú 1210* ☎ *2901/430–415*). **Bar Ideal** (⊠ *San Martín 393*) is a cozy and historic bar and café. **Kaitek Lounge Bar** (⊠ *Antartida Argentina 239* ☎ *2901/431–723*) is a place to eat until 2 AM, and to dance to pop music until 6 AM. **Tante Sara** (⊠ *San Martín 701* ☎ *2901/433–710* ⊕ *cafebartantesara.com.ar*) is a popular café-bar with a casual, old-world feel, in the heart of town, where locals kick back with a book or a beer (they pour Beagle, the local artisanal brew). During the day it's one of the few eateries to defy the 3–6 PM siesta.

PARQUE NACIONAL TIERRA DEL FUEGO

★   The pristine park, 21 km (13 mi) west of Ushuaia, offers a chance to wander through peat bogs, stumble upon hidden lakes, trek through native *canelo, lenga,* and wild cherry forests, and experience the wonders of wind-whipped Tierra del Fuego's rich flora and fauna. Everywhere, lichens line the trunks of the ubiquitous lenga trees, and lantern-like parasites hang from the branches.

Everywhere, too, you'll see *castoreros* (beaver dams) and lodges. Fifty beaver couples were first brought in from Canada in 1948 so that they would breed and create a fur industry. In the years since, however, the beaver population has grown to more than 50,000 and now represents a major threat to the forests, as the dams flood the roots of the trees; you can see their effects on the gnawed-down trees everywhere. Believe it or not, the government now pays hunters a bounty of 30 pesos for each beaver they kill (they need to show a tail and head as proof). To make matters worse, the government, after creating the beaver problem, then introduced weasels to kill the beavers, but the weasels killed birds instead; they then introduced foxes to kill the beavers and weasels, but they also killed the birds.

Visits to the park, which is tucked up against the Chilean border, are commonly arranged through tour companies. Trips range from bus tours to horseback riding to more adventurous excursions, such as canoe trips across Lapataia Bay. Another way to get to the park is to take the Tren del Fin del Mundo *(⇨above).* **Transportes Kaupen** (☎2901/434–015), one of several private bus companies, has buses that travel through the park, making several stops within it; you can get off the bus, explore the park, and then wait for the next bus to come by or trek to the next stop (the service only operates in summer). Yet one more option is to drive to the park on R3 (take it until it ends and you see the famous sign indicating the end of the Pan-American Highway, which starts 17,848 km [11,065 mi] away in Alaska, and ends here). If you don't have a car, you can also hire a private *remis* to spend a few hours driving through the park, including the Pan-American terminus, and perhaps also combine the excursion with the Tren del Fin del Mundo. Trail and camping information is available at the park-entrance ranger station or at the Ushuaia tourist office. At the park entrance is a gleaming new restaurant and teahouse set amidst the hills, **Patagonia Mia** (✉*Ruta 3, Entrada Parque Nacional* ☎*2901/1560–2757* ⊕*www.patagoniamia.com*); it's a great place to stop for tea or coffee, or a full meal of roast lamb or Fuegian seafood. A nice excursion in the park is by boat from lovely **Bahía Ensenada** to **Isla Redonda,** a wildlife refuge where you can follow a footpath to the western side and see a wonderful view of the Canal Beagle. This is included on some of the day tours; it's harder to arrange on your own, but you can contact the tourist office to try. While on Isla Redonda you can send a postcard and get your passport stamped at the world's southernmost post office. You can also see the Ensenada bay and island (from afar) from a point on the shore that is reachable by car.

Other highlights of the park include the spectacular mountain-ringed lake, **Lago Roca,** as well as **Laguna Verde,** a lagoon whose green color comes from algae at its bottom. Much of the park is closed from roughly June through September, when the descent to Bahía Ensenada is blocked by up to 6 feet of snow. Even in May and October, chains for your car are a good idea. No hotels are within the park—the only one burned down in the 1980s, and you can see its carcass driving by—but there are three simple camping areas around Lago Roca. Tours to the park are run by **All Patagonia** (✉*Juana Fadul 26* ☎*2901/433–622 or 2901/430–725).*

8

OUTDOOR ACTIVITIES

FISHING The rivers of Tierra del Fuego are home to trophy-size freshwater trout—including browns, rainbows, and brooks. Both fly- and spin-casting are available. The fishing season runs November–March; fees range from 10 pesos a day to 40 pesos for a month. Fishing expeditions are organized by the following companies. Founded in 1959, the **Asociación de Caza y Pesca** (✉*Av. Maipú 822* ☎*2901/423–168*) is the principal hunting and fishing organization in the city. **Rumbo Sur** (✉*Av. San Martín 350* ☎*2901/421–139* ⊕*www.rumbosur.com.ar*) is the city's oldest travel agency and can assist in setting up fishing trips. **Wind Fly** (✉*Av. 25 de Mayo 143* ☎*2901/431–713 or 2901/1544–9116*

⊕*www.windflyushuaia.com.ar*) is dedicated exclusively to fishing, and offers classes, arranges trips, and rents equipment.

MOUNTAIN BIKING
A mountain bike is an excellent mode of transport in Ushuaia. Good mountain bikes normally cost about 5 pesos an hour or 15 pesos–20 pesos for a full day. Bikes can be rented at the base of the glacier, at the **Refugio de Montaña** (⊠*Base Glaciar Martial* ☏*2901/1556–8587*), or at **D.T.T. Cycles** (⊠*Av. San Martín 903* ☏*2901/434–939*). Guided bicycle tours (including rides through the national park), for about 50 pesos a day, are organized by **All Patagonia** (⊠*Fadul 26* ☏*2901/430–725*). **Rumbo Sur** (⊠*San Martín 350* ☏*2901/421–139* ⊕*www.rumbosur.com.ar*) is the city's biggest travel agency and can arrange trips. **Tolkeyén Patagonia** (⊠*San Martín 1267* ☏*2901/437–073*) rents bikes and arranges trips.

SCENIC FLIGHTS
The gorgeous scenery and island topography of the area is readily appreciated on a Cessna tour. A half-hour flight (US$35, or 102 pesos per passenger; US$50, or 145 pesos for one passenger alone) with a local pilot takes you over Ushuaia and the Beagle Channel with views of area glaciers and snowcapped islands south to Cape Horn. A 60-minute flight (US$70 or 203 pesos per passenger; US$100 or 290 pesos for one passenger alone) crosses the Andes to the Escondida and Fagnano lakes. **Aero Club Ushuaia** (⊠*Antiguo Aeropuerto* ☏*2901/421–717* ⊕*www. aeroclubushuaia.org.ar*) offers half-hour and hour-long trips.

SKIING
Ushuaia is the cross-country skiing (*esqui de fondo* in Spanish) center of South America, thanks to enthusiastic **Club Andino** (☏*2901/422–335*) members who took to the sport in the 1980s and made the forested hills of a high valley about 20 minutes from town a favorite destination for skiers. **Hostería Tierra Mayor** (☏*2901/423–240*), **Hostería Los Cotorras** (☏*2901/499–300*), and **Haruwen** (☏*2901/424–058*) are three places where you can ride in dog-pulled sleds, rent skis, go cross-country skiing, get lessons, and eat; contact the Ushuaia tourist office for more information.

Glaciar Martial Ski Lodge (☏*2901/243–3712*), open year-round, Tuesday–Sunday 10–7, functions as a cross-country ski center from June to October. Skis can also be rented in town, as can snowmobiles.

For downhill (or *alpino*) skiers, Club Andino has bulldozed a couple of short, flat runs directly above Ushuaia. The newest downhill ski area, **Cerro Castor** (☏ *2901/422–244* ⊕*www.cerrocastor.com*), is 26 km (17 mi) northeast of Ushuaia on R3, and has 19 trails and four high-speed ski lifts. More than half the trails are at the beginner level, six are intermediate, and three are expert trails, but none of this terrain is very challenging for an experienced skier. You can rent skis and snowboards and take ski lessons. **Transportes Kaupen** (⇨*above*) and other local bus companies run service back and forth from town.

WHERE TO STAY

Dotting the perimeter of the park are five free campgrounds, none of which has much more than a spot to pitch a tent and a fire pit. Call the **park office** (☏*2901/421–315*) or consult the ranger station at the park entrance for more information. **Camping Lago Roca** (⊠*South on*

Parque Nacional
Tierra del Fuego

R3 for 20 km [12 mi] ☎No phone), within the park, charges 8 pesos
per person per day and has bathrooms, hot showers, and a small market. Of all the campgrounds, **La Pista del Andino** (✉Av. Alem 2873
☎2901/435–890) is the only one within the city limits. Outside of
town, **Camping Río Pipo** (☎2901/435–796) is the closest to Ushuaia (it's
18 km [11 mi] away).

PUERTO WILLIAMS

*75-min flight southeast from Punta Arenas; 82 km (50 mi) southeast
of Ushuaia, Argentina.*

On an island southeast of Ushuaia, the town of Puerto Williams is
the southernmost permanent settlement in the world. Originally called
Puerto Luisa, it was renamed in 1956 in honor of the military officer who took possession of the Estrecho de Magallanes for the newly
founded nation of Chile in 1843. Most of the 2,500 residents are troops
at the naval base, but there are several hundred civilians in the adjacent village. A tiny community of indigenous Yaghan peoples makes its
home in the nearby Ukika village.

Stop in at the Oficina de Turismo at Ibanez 130 (December–March,
weekdays 10–1 and 3–6 ☎61/621—011), but don't expect much

beyond maps. Accommodation offerings are simple and huddled around the center of town.

For a quick history lesson on how Puerto Williams evolved, and some insight into the indigenous peoples, visit the **Museo Martín Gusinde**, named for the renowned anthropologist who traveled and studied in the region between 1918 and 1924. ⊠*Aragay 1* 🕾*No phone* 🖅*500 pesos* ⊙*Weekdays 10–1 and 3–6, weekends 3–6.*

Weather permitting, **Aerovís DAP** (⊠*Av. Bernardo O'Higgins 891, Punta Arenas* 🕾*61/223–340* ⊕*www.aeroviasdap.cl*) offers charter flights over Cabo de Hornos, the southernmost tip of South America. Although the water looks placid from the air, strong westerly winds make navigating around Cape Horn treacherous. Over the last few centuries, hundreds of ships have met their doom here trying to sail to the Pacific.

HIKING

A hike to the top of nearby **Cerro Bandera** is well worth the effort if you have the stamina. The trail is well marked, but very steep. The view from the top toward the south to the Cordón Dientes del Perro (Dog's Teeth Range) is impressive, but looking northward over the Beagle Channel to Argentina—with Puerto Williams nestled below and Ushuaia just visible to the west—is truly breathtaking. Near the start of the trail, 3 km (2 mi) west of Puerto Williams, is the Parque Etnobotanico Omora visitor center (open daylight hours, www.cabodehornos. org), which got its name from the Yahgan word for hummingbird. In the Yahgan cosmology Omora was more than a bird; he was also a revered mythological hero. The Omora Foundation is a Chilean NGO dedicated to biocultural conservation in the extreme southern tip of South America. Their work led UNESCO to designate the Cape Horn Biosphere Reserve in June 2005. Within the park interpretive trails explore the various habitats of the Isla Navarino region: coastal coigue forests, lenga parks, nirre forests, sphagnum bogs, beaver wetlands, and alpine heath. Additionally, the Robalo River runs through the park and provides potable water to the town.

WHERE TO STAY & EAT

When you arrive in Puerto Williams, your airline or ferry company will recommend a few of the hospedajes available, then take you around to see them. With the exception of Lakutaia Hotel, all are rustic inns that also serve meals.

$$$$ ★ 🏨**Lakutaia Hotel.** From the people behind Punta Arenas's splendid José Nogueira comes this endearing venue, the most southern luxury hotel in the world. Hotel Lakutaia takes advantage of Navarino's beautiful surroundings to offer a range of unique outdoors activities including kayaking and trekking in Lauta, mountain biking, golf, horseback riding, sailing, walks to Castors Lagoon, and matches of Rayuela, a typical Chilean sport. Lukutaia also organizes ecological excursions to nearby fjords, mountains, indigenous settlements, the waterfalls in Robalo River, a Zodiac boat ride to the Cormorans Island, and a trip to Cape Horn. One of the most interesting trips visits millenary glaciers, fol-

lowing the same path covered by Darwin over 150 years ago. Another popular excursion is to Wulaia, where the indigenous Yaman tribe once thrived. The hotel's 24 double rooms are built with natural wood materials that fit perfectly with the forested world outside. Even the horse stables are impressive. The Lakutaia has a complete library-map room where you can find books and magazines with obscure details on the history and natural resources of the region. **Pros:** Offers a surprisingly impressive range of activities. **Cons:** Comes with a high price. ⊠*Seno Lauta s/n* ☎*61/621–020* ⊕*www.lakutaia.cl* ⇆*24 rooms* ⌂*In-room: no TV. In-hotel: laundry, restaurant* ▤*AE, MC, V* �ﾟ⦿ﾟ*CP.*

$ ⛩**Hostal Pusaki.** Run with Chilean hospitality, this humble hospedaje has comfortable rooms with up to four beds (including bunks). The dining room serves fine local fare. Dinner is especially pleasant if the fresh *ensalada de centolla* (king crab salad) is on the changing menu. **Pros:** As good a value as it gets in Puerto Williams. **Cons:** Facilities are spare. ⊠*Piloto Pardo 242* ☎*61/621–020* 🖷*61/621–116* ⇆*3 rooms without bath* ⌂*In-room: no a/c, no phone, no TV. In-hotel: restaurant* ▤*No credit cards* ﾟ⦿ﾟ*CP.*

NIGHTLIFE
Permanently moored at the main town dock is a small Swiss freighter listing slightly to port called the *Micalvi*. It's home to the rustic **Club de Yates** (⊠*Dockside* ☎*61/621–041*). Sailors stop off here for good company, strong spirits, and hearty food as they travel between the Atlantic and Pacific around Cape Horn. Stop by and mingle; you might meet Aussies, Brits, Finns, Russians, Swedes, or even the occasional American.

A world away from the cosmopolitan clubs of Santiago, **Pub El Pingüino** (⊠*Centro Commercial* ☎*No phone*) is a watering hole patronized by the town's civilians. Hours are irregular, but closer to the weekend it opens earlier and closes later.

8

Starting in Buenos Aires

WORD OF MOUTH

"I'm a *big* fan of BA. It's a huge city with lots to do. We've been there a few times, most recently for a couple of weeks to study Spanish. Nightlife? You bet. Culture? Yes. Locals? Friendly and outgoing. Food? Great. Prices? Dollar is still OK. Architecture? Sweet. Safe? Yes. Tango? Why not."

—JKinCALIF

www.fodors.com/forums

WELCOME TO BUENOS AIRES

TOP REASONS TO GO

★ **Dance the Night Away:** OK. This is the capital of tango, that most passionate of dances. But porteños also dance to samba, salsa, and DJ mixes. Regardless of the type of beat, rest assured it goes on until the wee hours.

★ **Shop Till You Drop:** High-quality silver and leather goods as well as fashionable clothing and accessories are available at world-class malls and boutiques. Open-air markets carry regional and European antiques and objets d'art as well as provincial handicrafts.

★ **Meat-ing Your Destiny:** The capital of cow country has enough parrillas (traditional grill restaurants) to satisfy even the most bloodthirsty.

★ **The Beautiful Game:** Top matches play out in Buenos Aires's colorful stadiums, stuffed to bursting with screaming futbol (soccer) addicts.

1 **Centro.** Locals use "El Centro" as an umbrella term for several action-packed downtown districts. Microcentro, the city's heart, bursts with banks, offices, theaters, bars, cafés, bookstores, and crowds. The area around Plaza and Avenida de Mayo is the hub of political life. Posh hotels, gleaming skyscrapers, and an elegant boardwalk make up Puerto Madero.

2 **San Telmo & La Boca.** The tango was born in these southern barrios. These days antiques stores and chic boutiques compete for space along San Telmo's cobbled streets. Just to the south, La Boca was originally settled by Italian immigrants. Now people come from all over for a snapshot of colorful but tacky Caminito or for a soccer match in Boca Juniors stadium.

3 **Recoleta & Almagro.** Today's elite live, dine, and shop along Recoleta's Paris-inspired streets. They're also often buried in the sumptuous mausoleums of its cemetery. Art galleries and museums are also draws. Gritty, working-class Almagro is known for its fringe theater pickings and tango scene, and the large Abasto shopping mall.

4 **Palermo.** Large Palermo has many subdistricts. If it's cool and happening, chances are it's in Palermo Viejo: boutiques, bars, restaurants, clubs, galleries, and hotels line the streets surrounding Plaza Serrano. The area across Avenida Juan B. Justo took the name Palermo Hollywood for the film and TV studios based here. There are two excellent museums (the MALBA and Museo Evita) in Palermo Chico, the barrio's northern end, also home to parks and the zoo.

GETTING ORIENTED

The world's ninth-largest city rises from the Río de la Plata and stretches more than 200 square km (75 square mi) to the surrounding pampas, Argentina's fertile plains. With more than one-third of the country's 39 million inhabitants living in or around Buenos Aires, it's clearly the country's hub as well as it's main gateway. The city's identity lies in its 48 barrios (neighborhoods)—each with its own character and history. Several generations of many families have lived in the same barrio, and traditionally people feel more of an affinity to their neighborhood than to the city as a whole.

Darsena A

Antepuerto

Dique 4

Dique 3

Dique 2

Dique 1

PUERTO MADERO

Reserva Ecologica

Darsena Sur

Av. Pedro de Mendoza

LA BOCA

Bransen

0   1/2 mile

0   1/2 kilometer

BUENOS AIRES PLANNER

No Time Like the Present

Fabulous wine, endless night-life, friendly locals, the best steak, rock-bottom prices . . . shaking off a stereotype can be hard. But when yours reads like a shopping list for indulgence, why bother? Whether they're screaming for a soccer team or enjoying an endless barbecue with friends, porteños are always demonstrating that enjoying the here and the now is what life is all about.

Visitor Info

The Web site of the city tourist board, **Turismo Buenos Aires** (⊕*www.bue.gov.ar*) has lively, downloadable MP3 walking tours in English. Bright-orange info booths at the airports and seven other locations provide maps and have English-speaking personnel.

The **South American Explorer's Club** (⊠*Estados Unidos 577, San Telmo,* ☎*11/4307–9625* ⊕*www.saexplorers.org*) is an American nonprofit that aims to help independent travelers in the region. The Buenos Aires' clubhouse has a map library; a book exchange; and a bulletin board.

Get Around Just Fine

Intriguing architecture, an easy-to-navigate grid layout (a few diagonal transverses aside), and ample window-shopping make Buenos Aires a wonderful place to explore on foot. Street cafés abound for when your feet tire.

Public Transit. Service on the *subte* (subway) is quick, but trains are often packed and strikes are common. Four of the six underground lines (A, B, D, and E) fan out west from downtown; lines C and H (only partly open) connect them. Single-ride tickets cost a flat 90¢. The subte shuts down around 11 PM and reopens at 5 AM.

Colectivos (city buses) connect the city's barrios and the greater Buenos Aires area. Ticket machines on board only accept coins (fares within the city are a flat 90¢). Bus stops are roughly every other block, but you may have to hunt for the small metal route-number signs: they could be stuck on a shelter, lamppost, or even a tree. Stop at a news kiosk and buy the *Guía T,* a handy route guide.

Taxis. Black-and-yellow taxis fill the streets and take you anywhere in town and short distances into greater Buenos Aires. Fares start at 3.10 pesos with 31¢ per 650 feet. You can hail taxis on the street or ask hotel and restaurant staffers to call for them.

Safety

Although Buenos Aires is safer than most Latin American capitals, the country's unstable economy means crime is a concern. Pickpocketing and mugging are common, so avoid wearing flashy jewelry, be discreet with money and cameras, and be mindful of bags. Take taxis as much as possible after dark. Police patrol most areas where you're likely to go, but they have a reputation for corruption, so locals try to avoid contact with them.

Protest marches are a part of life in Buenos Aires: most are peaceful, but some end in confrontations with the police. They often take place in the Plaza de Mayo, in the square outside the Congreso, or along the Avenida de Mayo connecting the two.

Tours

Ghosts, crimes, and spooky urban legends are the focus of the Buenos Aires Misteriosa tours run by **Ayres Viajes** (☎11/4383-9188 ⊕*www.ayresviajes.com.ar*).The super-personalized service—for tours in town and out—you get from Isabel at **Buenos Aires Tours** (⊕*www.buenosaires-tours.com.ar*)is almost heroic.For a local's perspective, contact the **Cicerones de Buenos Aires** (☎11/4431-9892 ⊕*www.cicerones.org.ar*), a free service that pairs you with a porteño to show you parts of town you might not see otherwise.Highly informed young historians from the University of Buenos Aires lead the cultural and historical tours at **Eternautas** (☎11/5031-9916 ⊕*www.eternautas.com*). It offers orientation tours, neighborhood walks, themed outings (e.g., Evita, the literary city, Jewish Buenos Aires), and excursions outside town.

A dynamic way to see the city's sights is on two wheels through **La Bicicleta Naranja** (☎11/4362-1104 ⊕*www.labicicletanaranja.com.ar*). You can rent a bicycle and gear to follow one of the routes on their excellent maps or go with a guide on general or theme trips.See Buenos Aires from the river on a 2½-hour sailboat tour with **Smile on Sea** (☎11/15-5018-8662 ⊕*www.smileonsea.com*). What better way to explore the waterways of the Tigre delta and Puerto Madero's docklands than from the water? **Puro Remo** (☎11/15-6397-3545 ⊕*www.puroremo.com.ar*)is a rowing club that offers guided kayaking and rowing tours (no experience needed).

Large onboard screens make the posh minibuses used by **Opción Sur** (☎11/4777-9029 ⊕*www.opcionsur.com.ar*)part transport and part cinema. Each stop on their city tour is introduced by relevant historical footage (e.g., Evita rallying the masses at Plaza de Mayo).You get serious insight into Buenos Aires' Jewish community on day tours run by Deb Miller's company, **Travel Jewish** (☎11/4106-0541 ⊕*www.traveljewish.com*).

Tick off the major sights and get the lay of the land on the basic three-hour bus tours run by **Travel Line** (☎11/4393-9000 ⊕*www.travelline.com.ar*).For tailor-made city tours contact **Wow! Argentina** (☎11/5239-3019 ⊕*www.wowargentina.com.ar*). Cintia Stella and her team can also arrange excursions all over Argentina.

When to Go 9

Remember that when it's summer in the United States, it's winter in Argentina, and vice versa. Winters (July–September) are chilly, though temperatures never drop below freezing. Summer's muggy heat (December–March) can be taxing at midday but makes for wonderful, warm nights. During these months (as well as in July for school holidays), Argentines crowd resorts along the Atlantic. Meanwhile traffic-free Buenos Aires has a host of city-sponsored concerts that bring people out into the sun and moonlight.

Spring (September–December) and autumn (April–June), with their mild temperatures—and blossoms or changing leaves—are ideal for urban trekking. It's usually warm enough for just a light jacket, and it's right before or after the peak (and expensive) season. The best time for trips to Iguazú Falls is August–October, when temperatures are lower, the falls are fuller, and the spring coloring is at its brightest.

Buenos Aires Temperatures

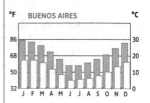

°F   BUENOS AIRES   °C

Updated by
Brian Byrnes,
Andy Footner
& Victoria
Patience

INCREDIBLE FOOD, FRESH YOUNG DESIGNERS, and a thriving cultural scene—all these Buenos Aires has. Yet less-tangible things are at the heart of the city's sizzle. Here, a flirtatious glance can be as passionate as a tango; a heated sports discussion as important as a world-class soccer match. It's this zest for life that's making Buenos Aires one of Latin America's hottest destinations.

EXPLORING BUENOS AIRES

Little remains of Buenos Aires's colonial days. This is due in part to the short lifespan of the adobe (mud and straw) used to build the city's first houses, and also to the fact that Buenos Aires's elite have always followed Europe's architectural trends. The result is an arresting hotchpotch of styles that hints at many far-off cities—Rome, Madrid, Paris, Budapest. With boulevards lined with palatial mansions and spacious parks, Palermo, La Recoleta, and some parts of the downtown area are testament to days of urban planning on a grandiose scale (and budget); San Telmo and La Boca have a distinctly working-class Italian feel.

CENTRO & ENVIRONS

Office workers, shoppers, sightseers, and traffic fill the streets around Centro each day. Locals profess to hate the chaos; unrushed visitors get a buzz out of the bustle.

❸ La Manzana de Las Luces *(The Block of Illumination).* More history is packed into this single block of buildings southwest of Plaza de Mayo than in scores of other city blocks put together. Among other things, it was the enclave for higher learning: the metaphorical *luces* (lights) of its name refer to the "illuminated" scholars who worked within. The block's earliest occupant was the controversial Jesuit order, which began construction here in 1661. The Jesuits honored their patron saint at the **Iglesia de San Ignacio de Loyola** *(Saint Ignatius of Loyola Church)* (⊠*Corner of Alsina and Bolívar).* The first church on the site was built of adobe in 1675; within a few decades it was rebuilt in stone. The Iglesia de San Ignacio is open to the public, but you can only visit the rest of Manzana de las Luces on guided tours led by excellent professional historians. Call ahead to arrange English-language visits. ⊠*Entrance and inquiries at Perú 272, Plaza de Mayo,* ☎11/4342– 6973 ⊠5 *pesos* ⊘*Visits by guided tour only; Spanish-language tours leave daily at 3, 4:30, and 6* PM; *call to arrange tours in English* Ⓜ*A to Plaza de Mayo, D to Catedral, E to Bolívar.*

❹ Plaza de Mayo. Since its construction in 1580, this has been the focal
★ point of Argentina's most politically turbulent moments, including the uprising against Spanish colonial rule on May 25, 1810—hence its name. Thousands cheered for Perón and Evita here; anti-Peronist planes bombed the gathered crowds a few years later; and there were bloody clashes in December 2001 (hence the heavy police presence and crowd-control barriers). Here, too, you can witness the changing of the

Grenadier Regiment guards; it takes place weekdays every two hours from 9 until 7, Saturday at 9 and 11, and Sunday at 9, 11, and 1.

The eclectic Casa de Gobierno, better known as the **Casa Rosada** (⊠*Hipólito Yrigoyen 219, Plaza de Mayo,* ☎*11/4344–3802* ⊕*www. museo.gov.ar* ☞*Free* ⊘*Weekdays 10–6, Sun. 2–6*), or Pink House, is at the plaza's eastern end, with its back to the river. It houses the government's executive branch (the president works here but lives elsewhere) and was built in the late 19th century over the foundations of an earlier customhouse and fortress. The balcony facing Plaza de Mayo is a presidential podium. Evita rallied the *descamisados* (the shirtless—meaning the working class) here, and Madonna sang her filmed rendition of "Don't Cry for Me Argentina." Check for a small banner hoisted alongside the nation's flag, indicating "the president is in." Ⓜ*Line A, Plaza de Mayo; Line D, Catedral; Line E, Bolívar.*

❺ **Teatro Colón.** Its magnitude, magnificent acoustics, and opulence (grander than Milan's La Scala) position the Teatro Colón (Colón Theater) among the world's top five operas. It has hosted the likes of Maria Callas, Richard Strauss, Arturo Toscanini, Igor Stravinsky, Enrico Caruso, and Luciano Pavarotti, who said that the Colón has only one flaw: the acoustics are so good, every mistake can be heard. The theater is currently dark owing to restoration work that's slated to end in 2010. Until then, tours of the theater—once very popular—are suspended, and performances are being held in other theaters. ⊠*Main entrance: Libertad between Tucumán and Viamonte; Box office: Pasaje Toscanini 1180, Centro,* ☎*11/4378–7100 tickets, 11/4378–7132 tours* ⊕*www.teatrocolon.org.ar* Ⓜ*D to Tribunales.*

SAN TELMO & LA BOCA

No longer do southern neighborhoods like San Telmo and La Boca play second fiddle to posher northern barrios. The hottest designers have boutiques here, new restaurants are booked out, and the south is also the linchpin of the city's tango revival, appropriate given that the dance was born in these quarters.

❶ **Calle Museo Caminito.** Cobblestones, tango dancers, and haphazardly
★ constructed, vividly painted conventillos have made Calle Museo Caminito the darling of Buenos Aires' postcard manufacturers since this pedestrian street and open-air museum–art market opened in 1959. Artists fill the block-long street with works depicting port life and tango, which is said to have been born in La Boca. It's all more commercial than cultural, but its embrace of all things tacky make it a fun outing. Many of La Boca's tenements have been recycled into souvenir shops. The plastic Che Guevaras and dancing couples make the shops in the **Centro Cultural de los Artistas** (⊠*Magallanes 861* ⊘*Mon.–Sat. 10:30–6*)as forgettable as all the others on the street, but the uneven stairs and wrought-iron balcony hint at what a conventillo interior was like. ⊠ *Caminito between Av. Pedro de Mendoza (La Vuelta de Rocha promenade) and Olivarría, La Boca* ☞*Free* ⊘*Daily 10–6.*

9

② **Estadio Boca Juniors.** The stadium that's also known as La Bombonera
★ (meaning candy box, supposedly because the fans' singing reverberates as it would inside a candy tin) is the home of Argentina's most popular club. Inside the stadium is **El Museo de la Pasión Boquense** (The Museum of Boca Passion), a modern, two-floor that chronicles Boca's rise from neighborhood club in 1905 to its current position as one of the world's best teams. On the tour, lighthearted guides take you all over: to press boxes, locker rooms, underground tunnels, and the field itself. ✉*Brandsen 805, at del Valle Iberlucea, La Boca,* ☎*11/4309–4700 stadium, 11/4362–1100 museum* ⊕*www. museoboquense.com.ar* ✇*Museum: 14 pesos. Stadium: 14 pesos. Museum and stadium: 22 pesos* ◷*Museum daily 10–6 except when Boca plays at home; stadium tours hourly 11–5; English usually available, call ahead.*

RECOLETA & ALMAGRO

For the most-illustrious families, Recoleta's boundaries are the boundaries of the civilized world. The local equivalents of the Vanderbilts throw parties in the Alvear Palace Hotel, live in spacious 19th-century apartments, and wouldn't dream of shopping elsewhere. By contrast Almagro to the southwest is a gritty, working-class neighborhood that spawned many tango greats.

⑥ **Cementerio de la Recoleta.** The ominous gates, Doric-columned portico,
Fodor'sChoice and labyrinthine paths of the city's oldest cemetery (1822) lead to final
★ resting place for the nation's most-illustrious figures, These 13½ acres are rumored to be the most expensive real estate in town. The cemetery has more than 6,400 elaborate vaulted tombs and majestic mausoleums, 70 of which have been declared historic monuments. The mausoleums resemble chapels, Greek temples, pyramids, and miniature mansions. Among the cemetery's highlights are the embalmed remains of Eva Perón, who made it (almost intact) here after 17 years of posthumous wandering, are in the Duarte family vault. The city government runs free guided visits to the cemetery in English on Tuesday and Thursday at 11. If you prefer an independent tour, the administrative offices at the entrance can provide a free map, and caretakers throughout the grounds can help you locate the more-intriguing tombs. These are also labeled on a large map at the entrance. ✉*Junín 1760, Recoleta,* ☎*11/4803–1594* ✇*Free.* ◷*Daily 8–6.*

⑦ **Museo Nacional de Bellas Artes.** The world's largest collection of Argen-
Fodor'sChoice tine art is displayed in this huge golden-color stone building. The 24
★ ground-floor galleries contain European art. Upstairs, the Argentine circuit starts in Room 102 with works from colonial times through the 19th century. Follow the galleries around to the right and through 20th-century art. Head straight for the first-floor Argentine galleries while you're feeling fresh, and keep the European collection for later. For English information, check out one of the MP3 audio guides (15 pesos) in the scant gift shop at the bottom of the stairs. ✉*Av. del Lib-*

ertador 1473, Recoleta, ☎11/4803–0802 tours (in Spanish) ⊕www.
mnba.org.ar ☒*Free* ⊙*Tues.–Fri. 12:30–7:30, weekends 9:30–7:30.*

PALERMO

Whether your idea of sightseeing is ticking off museums, flicking through clothing rails, licking your fingers after yet another long lunch, or kicking up a storm on the dance floor, Palermo can oblige.

⑩ **Museo Evita.** Eva Duarte de Perón, known universally as Evita, was the
★ wife of populist president Juan Domingo Perón. She was both revered by her working-class followers and despised by the Anglophile oligarchy of the time. The Museo Evita shies from pop culture clichés and concentrates on Evita's life and works, particularly the social aid programs she instituted and her role in getting women the vote. Evita's reputation as fashion plate is also reflected in the many designer outfits on display, including her trademark working suits and some gorgeous ball gowns. The museum's excellent guided visits are available in English but must be arranged by phone in advance. That said, laminated cards with just-understandable English translations of the exhibits are available in each room and at the ticket booth. ☒*Lafinur 2988, 1 block north of Av. Las Heras, Palermo,* ☎*11/4807–9433* ⊕*www.museoevita. org* ☒*10 pesos* ⊙*Tues.–Sun. 1–7* Ⓜ*D to Plaza Italia.*

⑧ **Museo de Arte de Latinoamericano de Buenos Aires** (MALBA, Museum of
Fodor's Choice Latin American Art of Buenos Aires). The fabulous MALBA is one of
★ the cornerstones of the city's cultural life. Its centerpiece is businessman and founder Eduardo Constantini's collection of more than 220 works of 19th- and 20th-century Latin American art in the main first-floor gallery. Young enthusiastic guides give great tours in Spanish; you can call ahead to arrange group English-language tours. ☒*Av. Presidente Figueroa Alcorta 3415, Palermo,* ☎*11/4808–6500* ⊕*www.malba.org. ar* ☒*12 pesos, free Wed.* ⊙*Thurs.–Mon. noon–8, Wed. noon–9.*

⑨ **Parque Tres de Febrero.** Known locally as Los Bosques de Palermo (Pal-
☾ ermo Woods), this 200-acre green space is really a crazy quilt of smaller
Fodor's Choice parks. Rich grass and shady trees make this an urban oasis, although
★ the busy roads and horn-honking drivers that crisscross the park never quite let you forget what city you're in. South of Avenida Figueroa Alcorta you can take part in organized tai chi and exercise classes or impromptu soccer matches. You can also jog, bike, or in-line skate here, or take a boat out on the small lake. ☒*Bounded by Avs. del Libertador, Sarmiento, Leopoldo Lugones, and Dorrego, Palermo* Ⓜ*D to Plaza Italia.*

9

WHERE TO EAT

Buenos Aires is the most cutting-edge food town in the Southern Hemisphere. Here, three things have come together to create a truly modern cuisine: diverse cultural influences, high culinary aspirations, and a relentless devotion to aesthetics, from plate garnishes to room decor.

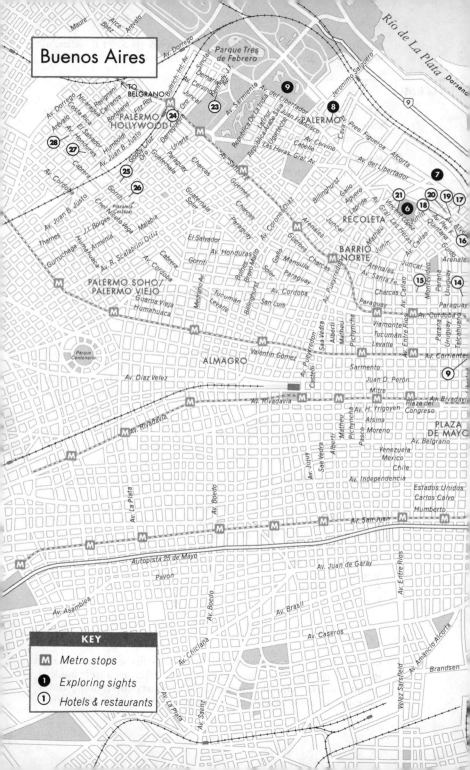

9

And yet, at their core, even the most modern international restaurants in Buenos Aires are informed by this city's appreciation of a good bottle of wine shared with friends and family over a long meal.

CENTRO & ENVIRONS

CENTRO

¢   **Confitería La Ideal.** Part of the charm of this spacious 1918 coffee shop–
CAFÉ   milonga is its sense of nostalgia: think fleur-de-lis motifs, timeworn European furnishings, and stained glass. No wonder they chose to film the 1998 movie *The Tango Lesson* here. La Ideal is famous for its *palmeritas* (glazed cookies), tea service, and the scores of locals and foreigners who attend milongas here. Tango lessons are offered Monday through Saturday at varying times throughout the day and night; concerts take place every evening except Tuesday and Thursday. ⊠*Suipacha 384, at Av. Corrientes, Centro* ☎*11/5265–8069* ⊕*www.confiteria ideal.com* ⊟*No credit cards* Ⓜ*C to C. Pellegrini, D to 9 de Julio.*

¢   **El Cuartito.** This porteño classic has been making pizza and empanadas
PIZZA   since 1934, and the surroundings have changed little in the last 70 years. The brusque waitstaff is part of the charm. Drop in for a slice at the *mostrador* (counter) or make yourself comfortable under the portraits of Argentine sporting greats for fantastic, no-nonsense food and cold Quilmes beer. Try a slice of *fainá* (like a chickpea-flour flat bread), one of the traditional Argentine variations on pizza. ⊠*Talcahuano 937, Centro* ☎*11/4816–4331* ⊟*No credit cards* Ⓜ*D to Tribunales.*

$ **Gran Café Tortoni.** In the city's first confitería, established in 1858, art
CAFÉ   nouveau decor and high ceilings transport you back in time. Tango star Carlos; writer Jorge Luis Borges; local and visiting dignitaries; and intellectuals have all eaten and sipped coffee here. Don't miss the *chocolate con churros* (thick hot chocolate with baton-shape doughnuts for dipping). Reserve ahead of time for the nightly tango shows; there's a 50-peso cover. ⊠*Av. de Mayo 825, Centro* ☎*11/4342–4328* ⊕*www.cafetortoni.com.ar* ⊟*AE, MC, V* Ⓜ*A to Perú.*

$$$$ **Tomo I.** The famed Concaro sisters have made this restaurant, on the
ARGENTINE   mezzanine of the Hotel Panamericano, a household name. The French-inspired menu has excellent fried, breaded calf brains. The chocolate tart oozes warm, dark ganache. White linen–covered tables set far apart in the romantic red room allow for quiet conversation. Service is tops. Reservations are recommended. ⊠*Carlos Pellegrini 521, Centro* ☎*11/4326–6698* ⊕*www.tomo1.com.ar* ⊟*AE, DC, MC, V* ☉*Closed Sun. No lunch Sat.* Ⓜ*B to Carlos Pellegrini, D to 9 de Julio.*

PUERTO MADERO

$$ **La Caballeriza.** Locals in the know come to this big, lively, informal steak
STEAK   house, where the prices are very reasonable for good, quality meat. Sip champagne at the friendly bar while you wait for a table. The parrilla is wood-fired, Uruguayan style, and the *asado de tira* (rack of beef short ribs) is a highlight, but you also can't go wrong with the classic *bife de chorizo* (bone-in sirloin or rump steak). There's another branch by the Recoleta mall next to the cemetery, but this one is superior. ⊠*A.M. de*

Justo 580, Puerto Madero ☎*11/4514–4444* ⊕*www.lacaballerizapuerto madero.com* ⊟*AE, DC, MC, V* Ⓜ*B to L.N. Alem.*

SAN TELMO & LA BOCA

SAN TELMO

¢ **Bar Dorrego.** Bar Dorrego probably hasn't changed much in the last
CAFÉ 100 years or so. Dark wood and politely aloof waiters set the stage; good coffee, *tragos* (alcoholic drinks), sangria, and snacks complete the scene. When the weather is warm, sit at a table outside, order a cold Quilmes beer and some salty peanuts, and soak in the scene. ⊠*Defensa 1098, at Humberto I, on Plaza Dorrego, San Telmo* ☎*11/4361–0141* ⊟*No credit cards* Ⓜ*C or E to Independencia.*

$$ **La Farmacia.** Mismatched tables and chairs, comfy leather sofas, and
ARGENTINE bright colors fill this cute, century-old corner house that used to be
☾ a traditional pharmacy. Generous breakfasts and afternoon teas are served on the cozy ground floor, lunch and dinner are served in the dining room, and you can have late-night drinks on the bright-yellow roof terrace. Arts and dance workshops are run upstairs, and the building has two boutiques selling local designers' work. The modern Argentine dishes are simple but well done, and the fixed-price lunch and dinner menus are deals. ⊠*Bolívar 898, San Telmo* ☎*11/4300–6151* ⊟*No credit cards* ☾*Closed Mon.* Ⓜ*C or E to Independencia.*

LA BOCA

$ **El Obrero.** For 50 years El Obrero has served juicy grilled steaks, sweet-
STEAK breads, sausages, and chicken. The blackboard menu includes *rabas* (fried calamari) and puchero. Try the *budín de pan* (Argentine bread pudding). This spot is popular with tourists and local workmen alike, so expect a short wait. La Boca is sketchy at night, so lunch is preferable; in any case, take a taxi. ⊠*Augustín R. Caffarena 64, La Boca* ☎*11/4363–9912* ⊟*No credit cards* ☾*Closed Sun.*

9

RECOLETA

$$$$ **La Bourgogne.** White tablecloths, fresh roses, and slick red leather chairs
FRENCH emphasize the restaurant's elegance. A sophisticated waitstaff brings
Fodor'sChoice you complimentary hors d'oeuvres as you choose from chef Jean-Paul
★ Bondoux's creations, which include foie gras, rabbit, escargots, chateaubriand, *côte de veau* (veal steak), and wild boar cooked in cassis. The fixed-price tasting menu is more affordable than à la carte selections and features a different wine with each plate. ⊠*Alvear Palace Hotel, Ayacucho 2027, Recoleta* ☎*11/4805–3857 or 11/4808–2100* ⌨*Reservations essential. Jacket and tie* ⊟*AE, DC, MC, V* ☾*Closed Sun. No lunch Sat.*

$$$$ **Duhau Restaurante & Vinoteca.** Just as the Palacio Duhau Hotel changed
MODERN the game of luxury in Buenos Aires, so has its eponymous restaurant.
ARGENTINE This wonderful spot serves some of the best food in the city, com-
Fodor'sChoice plimented with impeccable and friendly service. The menu is French-
★ inspired, but with proud touches of Argentine cuisine: sweetbreads

with Patagonian berries, king prawns from Tierra del Fuego, and trout from Bariloche. The beef is all certified Black Angus from the province of Santa Fe. The wine list reads like a book: more than 500 varieties are available. After dinner, visit the Cheese Room, which offers 45 different cheeses. ⊠*Av. Alvear 1661, Recoleta* ☎*11/5171–1340* ⊕*www.buenos aires.park.hyatt.com* ⊟*AE, D, MC, V* ⊘*No lunch weekends.*

$ **El Sanjuanino.** Northern Argentine fare is served at this long-estab-
ARGENTINE lished, if touristy, spot. El Sanjuanino is known for its tamales,
℃ *humitas* (steamed corn cakes wrapped in husks), and especially its empanadas, which crowds line up to take out for a picnic in the park (they're 20% cheaper to go). But they also make good *locro, pollo a la piedra* (chicken pressed flat by stones), venison, and antelope stew. Skip the boring, hamlike *lomito de cerdo* (pork steak). The decor includes hanging hams and a stuffed deer head, but the vibe is still fun. ⊠*Posadas 1515, at Callao, Recoleta* ☎*11/4804–2909* ⊟*AE, MC, V* ⊘*Closed Mon.*

PALERMO

PALERMO

$$ **Rio Alba.** In terms of quality, price, and charm, this is the best parrilla in
STEAK Buenos Aires. Period. It consistently serves the tastiest and most tender
Fodor'sChoice cuts of beef. The asado de tira is particularly good, as is the flavorful
★ entrana. Ask for a minigrill at your table to keep your meat warm; you're going to need time to finish the enormous servings. It's packed every night of the week. ⊠*Cervino 4499, Palermo* ☎*11/4773–5748* ⊟*AE, D, MC, V.*

PALERMO HOLLYWOOD

$ **El Encanto.** It's a sports, cinema, and theater museum *and* a fantastic
STEAK parrilla. Walls are covered with sports and film memorabilia, and glass cases are packed with trophies from soccer championships. The food is fantastic, too. The bife de chorizo and ojo de bife are top-notch, as are the salads and desserts. Service is touch-and-go, but the chaos and eclectic crowd make for an unforgettable evening. ⊠*Bonpland 1690, Palermo Hollywood* ☎*11/15–5809–2240* ⊟*No credit cards.*

PALERMO SOHO

$$$ **La Baita.** In a city filled with first- and second-generation Italians, it's
ITALIAN surprisingly hard to find a good Italian meal. Look no further than La Baita, a cozy corner spot in the heart of Palermo Soho that attracts highbrow porteños and Europeans. They do fantastic fresh pastas, and nice meat dishes. The main dining room is quaint, and some of the tables are too close together, but the romantic atmosphere, live music, and friendly service make up for it. ⊠*Thames 1603, Palermo Soho* ☎*11/4832–7234* ⊟*MC, V* ⊘*No lunch Mon.*

¢ **Club Eros.** A basic dining room attached to an old soccer club, Club Eros
ARGENTINE has developed a cult following for its downscale charm. The excellent fare at rock-bottom prices has begun to draw young Palermo trend-ies as well as older customers who have been loyal to the club for

decades. There's no menu, but you can confidently order a crispy milanesa (breaded meat cutlet), or, if available, a bife de chorizo and fries. Pasta sauces fall flat, but the flan is terrific. ✉*Uriarte 1609, Palermo Soho* ☎*11/4832–1313* ▭*No credit cards.*

WHERE TO STAY

Centro and Puerto Madero are teeming with international hotel chains, and most of them are well located. But once you close your door, it's easy to forget where you are. In San Telmo, hotels are primarily grand old mansions with soaring ceilings and impressive wooden doors. Across town in Palermo, it's a hipper, more urbane feel, but hotels are so new they haven't had time to develop their own character yet.

CENTRO & ENVIRONS

CENTRO

$$ **Buenos Aires cE Design Hotel.** This hotel drips coolness. The lobby's glass floor looks down to a small pool, just one example of the transparency theme here. Floor-to-ceiling windows afford amazing views, and mirrors are placed for maximum effect. Rooms have rotating flat-screen TVs that let you watch from bed or from one of the leather recliners. Mattresses are high and mighty and covered in shades of brown and orange. **Pros:** Supermodern and spacious suites; great location. **Con:** The basement lounge feels like, well, a basement. ✉*Marcelo T. Alvear 1695, Centro,* ☎*11/5237–3100* 🌐*www.designce.com* *21 rooms, 7 suites* *In-room: safe, kitchen, Ethernet, Wi-Fi. In-hotel: bar, pool, gym, laundry service, public Wi-Fi* ▭*AE, DC, MC, V* Ⓜ*D to Callao.*

$$ Fodor's Choice ★ **Marriott Plaza Hotel.** This Buenos Aires landmark brims with old-school style. Built in 1909 and renovated in 2003, the hotel sits at the top of pedestrian-only Florida Street and overlooks the leafy Plaza San Martín. The elegant lobby, crystal chandeliers, and swanky cigar bar evoke Argentina's opulent, if distant, past. Rooms are comfortable and clean, if not particularly spacious. **Pros:** Great prices; every area of the building offers a fascinating city view. **Cons:** The main lobby is small; check-in can be lengthy. ✉*Florida 1005, Centro,* ☎*11/4318–3000, 800/228–9290 in U.S.* 🌐*www.marriott.com* *313 rooms, 12 suites* *In-room: safe, Ethernet. In-hotel: 2 restaurants, room service, bar, pool, gym, concierge, laundry service, public Wi-Fi* ▭*AE, DC, MC, V* *BP* Ⓜ*C to San Martín.*

¢ **Milhouse Hostel.** This hostel goes the extra mile with pool tables, televisions, and concierge services. The house, which dates from the late 1800s, has been tricked out with funky artwork and accessories. Its three floors overlook a tiled patio and all lead out to a sunny terrace. Morning yoga classes may well be followed by rowdy beer-swilling *asados* (barbecues). At night, the surrounding streets can be dodgy, so take precautions. **Pros:** It's lovely and lively. **Cons:** It's a hostel; hygiene standards are sometimes below par. ✉*Hipólito Irigoyen 959, Centro,* ☎*11/4345–9604 or 11/4343–5038* 🌐*www.milhousehostel.com* *13 private rooms, 150 beds total* *In-room: no a/c, no phone, no TV, Eth-*

ernet, Wi-Fi. In-hotel: restaurant, bar, laundry facilities, parking (fee)
=*No credit cards* ⓘⓄⓘCP Ⓜ*A to Piedras, C to Av. de Mayo.*

PUERTO MADERO

$$$$ **Faena Hotel + Universe.** Argentine fashion impresario Alan Faena and
Fodor'sChoice famed French architect Philippe Starck set out to create a "universe"
★ unto itself. Rooms are feng shui perfect with rich reds and crisp whites.
Velvet curtains and Venetian blinds open electronically to river and city
views; velvet couches, leather armchairs, flat-screen TVs, and surround-
sound stereos lend more luxury. Other highlights are two excellent restaurants and an elaborate spa with a Turkish bath. **Pros:** Quite simply,
one of the most exhilarating hotels on the planet. **Cons:** An ever-present
"are you cool enough?" vibe. ✉*Martha Salotti 445, Puerto Madero,*
☎*11/4010–9000* ⊕*www.faenahotelanduniverse.com* ✒*110 rooms,
16 suites* ⚑*In-room: safe, DVD, Ethernet, dial-up, Wi-Fi. In-hotel: 2
restaurants, room service, bars, pool, gym, concierge, laundry service,
parking (fee), no-smoking rooms* ⊟*AE, DC, MC, V.*

SAN TELMO

$ **Gurda Hotel.** The Gurda will give you glimpse into what life was like at
Fodor'sChoice the turn of the 19th century. Seven rooms line the long, open-air hall-
★ way with exposed brick, green plants, and bamboo sticks. Each room
is named after something or someone decidedly Argentine—Jorge Luis
Borges, Malbec, Patagonia—with decorations to match. (In the Borges
room you can find volumes of his work and a colorful portrait of the literary legend.) Rooms are basic, but charming. **Pros:** The young friendly
staff can organize wine tastings with local sommeliers, and tango lessons. **Cons:** The entrance is on a busy street; the restaurant and bar
are noisy. ✉*Defensa 1521,* ☎*11/4307–0646* ⊕*www.gurdahotel.com*
✒*7 rooms* ⚑*In-room: safe, Wi-Fi. In-hotel: restaurant, room service,
bar, concierge, laundry service, parking (fee), no-smoking rooms* ⊟*AE,
DC, MC, V* Ⓜ*C to Constitucion.*

$$ **Moreno Hotel.** A gorgeous art deco building dating back to 1929, the
Fodor'sChoice Moreno's architects were posed with the challenge of restoring the 80-
★ year-old site without disturbing its original elements, like mosaic til-
ing and stained-glassed windows. The seven-floor hotel has spacious
and sexy rooms, each decorated in a color motif complete with chaise
lounges, Argentine cowhide rugs, and big fluffy beds. The top-floor
terrace has an outdoor fireplace, big wooden recliners, and amazing
city views. **Pros:** There's a top-notch restaurant and 130-seat theater
on-site. **Con:** Some rooms are just steps from the main lobby and eleva-
tor. ✉*Moreno 376,* ☎*11/6091–2000* ⊕*www.morenobuenosaires.com*
✒*39 rooms* ⚑*In-room: safe, refrigerator, Ethernet, dial-up, Wi-Fi.
In-hotel: restaurant, room service, bar, gym, concierge, parking (fee),
no-smoking rooms* ⊟*AE, MC, V* Ⓜ*A to Plaza de Mayo.*

RECOLETA & ALMAGRO

RECOLETA

$$$$ Fodor'sChoice ★ **Alvear Palace Hotel.** If James Bond were in town, this is where he'd hang his hat. In fact, Sean Connery *has* stayed here, because when it comes to sophistication, the Alvear Palace is the best bet in Buenos Aires. It has hosted scores of dignitaries since opening its doors in 1932, and although new and more-affordable hotels are making it something of a gray ghost, the Alvear is still swanky. It's all about world-class service and thoughtful touches. **Pros:** The lunch buffet is out of this world, and the French restaurant, La Bourgogne, is one of the city's best. **Cons:** You'll pay dearly to stay here. ✉*Av. Alvear 1891, Recoleta,* ☎*11/4808–2100, 11/4804–7777, 800/448–8355 in U.S.* 🌐*www.alvearpalace.com* *100 rooms, 100 suites* *In-room: safe, Ethernet, dial-up, Wi-Fi. In-hotel: 2 restaurants, room service, bar, pool, gym, concierge, laundry service, no-smoking rooms* *AE, DC, MC, V* *BP.*

$ **Art Hotel.** It has an impressive ground-floor gallery where exhibits of works by acclaimed Argentine artists change monthly. Rooms are classified as "small and cozy," "queen," or "king" and many have wrought-iron bed frames with white canopies. The building's 100-year-old elevator will take you to the rooftop patio, where there's also a hot tub. **Pro:** Its bohemian vibe will make you feel like you've joined an artists' colony. **Con:** Rooms are dark and somewhat antiquated. ✉*Azcuenaga 1268, Recoleta,* ☎*11/4821–4744* 🌐*www.arthotel.com.ar* *36 rooms* *In-room: safe, Ethernet. In-hotel: bar, laundry service, public Wi-Fi.* *AE, MC, V* Ⓜ*D to Pueyrredón.*

$ **Hotel Bel Air.** Given the fancy French-style facade, you could mistake the Bel Air for a neighborhood hotel somewhere in Paris. Inside, a more-modern feel takes over, with a round wood-panel lobby bar and a snazzy café that looks onto exclusive Arenales Street, dotted with art galleries, fashion boutiques, and furniture stores. Rooms have handsome wooden floors and simple but stylish furnishings in an array of earth-tone colors. **Pros:** Great price and location on a posh street. **Cons:** Staff is easily distracted; hallways and common areas are cramped. ✉*Arenales 1462, Recoleta,* ☎*11/4021–4000* 🌐*www.hotelbelair.com.ar* *77 rooms* *In-room: safe, dial-up, Wi-Fi. In-hotel: restaurant, room service, bar, gym, laundry service, airport shuttle, no-smoking rooms* *AE, DC, MC, V* Ⓜ*D to Tribunales.* *BP.*

$$$$ Fodor'sChoice ★ **Park Hyatt Palacio Duhau.** Its two buildings, a restored 1930s-era mansion and a 17-story tower, are connected by an underground art gallery and a leafy garden. The rooms are decorated in rich hues of wood, marble, and Argentine leather. Mansion rooms are larger and more charming. Sip a whiskey at the Oak Bar and visit the Ahin Spa, next to the city's largest indoor pool. **Pros:** Understated elegance; great restaurant; the 3,500-bottle Wine Library and "Cheese Room" are unique attractions. **Cons:** A long walk from one side of the hotel to the other; although elegantly decorated, common areas lack warmth. ✉*Av. Alvear 1661, Recoleta,* ☎*11/5171–1234* 🌐*www.buenosaires.park.hyatt.com* *126 rooms, 39 suites* *In-room: safe, Ethernet, dial-up,*

9

Wi-Fi, DVD. In-hotel: 2 restaurants, room service, bar, pool, gym, spa, concierge, laundry service ⊟AE, MC, V.

ALMAGRO

$$ **Abasto Plaza Hotel.** This place is *all* about the tango. Photos and paintings of famous musicians line the walls that surround the checked-marble dance floor, which is next to a boutique selling sequined skirts, stilettos, and fishnets. Suites each have their own dance floor for private lessons, or you can join other guests for nightly tango lessons and a live show. Rooms are large and elegant with—surprise—a tango theme. The enormous Abasto Shopping Center is across the street. **Pros:** If you're here to tango, this is your place. **Cons:** Tango overload is a real possibility; furnishings and bedding are tired. ⊠Av. Corrientes 3190, Almagro, ☎11/6311–4466 ⊕www.abastoplaza.com ⬳120 rooms, 6 suites ⌂In-room: Ethernet, dial-up, Wi-Fi. In-hotel: restaurant, room service, bar, pool, gym ⊟AE, DC, MC, V ⦿IBP Ⓜ B to Carlos Gardel.

PALERMO

$$ **Home Buenos Aires.** It oozes coolness and class. Each room is decorated with vintage French wallpaper and has a stereo, a laptop-friendly safe, and either a bathtub or a wet room. On-site there's a vast garden; a barbecue area; an infinity pool; a holistic spa; and a funky lounge bar where you can sip a cocktail and listen to mood music. **Pros:** Hip and fun; always has interesting guests. **Con:** Lots of nonguests come here to hang out, reducing the intimacy factor. ⊠Honduras 5860, Palermo Hollywood, ☎11/4778–1008 ⊕www.homebuenosaires.com ⬳14 rooms, 4 suites ⌂In-room: safe, Ethernet, Wi-Fi. In-hotel: restaurant, room service, bar, pool, spa ⊟AE, MC, V Ⓜ D to Ministro Carranza.

¢ **Giramondo Hostel.** The funky Giramondo has all a hostel needs: plenty of beds and bathrooms, a kitchen, a TV and computer lounge, and a patio, where backpackers from around the world grill up slabs of Argentine beef. The dark, dank underground bar serves up cheap drinks; it also has a small wine cellar. Giramondo is two blocks from buses and the subte on Avenida Santa Fe, so there's access to Palermo's pulsing nightlife and to downtown. **Pros:** They have the budget traveler in mind, and cater to short-term and long-term travelers. **Con:** The surrounding streets are chaotic and loud. ⊠Guemes 4802, Palermo Soho, ☎11/4772–6740 ⊕www.hostelgiramondo.com.ar ⌂In-room: no a/c, no phone, kitchen, no TV, Ethernet. In-hotel: bar, no elevator, laundry facilities ⊟No credit cards Ⓜ D to Palermo.

AFTER DARK

BARS & CLUBS

FodorśChoice **Bahrein.** Sheik—er, chic and super-stylish, this party palace is in a
★ 100-year-old former bank. Eat upstairs at Crizia, or head straight to the main floor's Funky Room, where beautiful, tightly clothed youth

groove to pop, rock, and funk. The downstairs Excess Room has electronic beats and dizzying wall visuals. For 500 pesos, get locked in the vault and guzzle champagne all night with strangers. ⊠*Lavalle 345, Centro* ☏*11/4315–2403* Ⓜ*B to Alem.*

★ **Le Bar.** Le Bar is a stylish addition to the Centro drinking scene. Up the stairs from the cocktail lounge is a clever sunken seating arrangement; farther still is a smokers' terrace. Office workers get the evening started; DJs start a bit later and play till 2 AM. ⊠*Tucuman 422, Centro* ☏*11/5219–8580.*

Bar 6. Somewhat of a Palermo Soho institution, Bar 6 suffers from the indifferent waitstaff that such a reputation demands. If you can get past that, it's a convenient Palermo meeting point (it opens at 8 AM), a stylish bar, and a decent restaurant. A DJ often plays good music in the evenings. ⊠*Armenia 1676, Palermo Soho* ☏*11/4833–6807.*

Cava Jufre. There aren't any wild nights at this wine bar, but gather around for plenty of earnest and good-natured appreciation of the output of lesser-known Argentinean bodegas. The decoration is simple and woody, and there's an impressive cellar downstairs. This is a good place to discover some new varietals—and do call ahead to see if there are any wine-tasting events planned. It's closed Sunday. ⊠*Jufre 201, Palermo* ☏*11/4775–7501* ⊕*www.lacavajufre.com.ar.*

Gran Bar Danzon. At this hot spot local business sharks and chic internationals sip wine and eat sushi by candlelight. It's extremely popular for happy hour, but people stick around for dinner and the occasional live jazz shows, too. The wine list and the appetizers are superb, as is the flirting. ⊠*Libertad 1161, Recoleta* ☏*11/4811–1108* Ⓜ*C to Retiro.*

The Kilkenny. A popular pub that spawned a whole street of imitators, the Kilkenny serves surprisingly good Irish food and has Guinness on draft. Celtic or rock bands play every night, entertaining the after-work crowd from nearby government and commercial buildings who come for the 8 PM to 11 PM happy hour. ⊠*Marcelo T. De Alvear 399, Centro* ☏*11/4312–7291* Ⓜ*C to San Martín.*

Fodor'sChoice
★ **Niceto.** The former home of the outrageous Club 69 boasts one of the city's most interesting lineups with everything from indie rock to minimal techno; it turns into one of the city's biggest cumbia venues every Wednesday at midnight with Club night Zizek. The larger main room with a balcony holds live shows and lots of dancing and there's usually something contrasting and chilled taking place in the back room, too. ⊠*Cnel. Niceto Vega 5510, Palermo Hollywood* ☏*11/4779–9396.*

TANGO

MILONGAS

La Catedral. Behind its unmarked doors is a hip club where the tango is somehow very rock. Casual milongas take place on Tuesday, Friday, and Saturday, and it's a cool night out even if you're not planning to dance. ⊠*Sarmiento 4006, doorbell 5, Almagro* ☏*11/15–5325–1630.*

Fodor'sChoice
★ **La Ideal.** Soaring columns and tarnished mirrors are part of La Ideal's crumbling old-world glamour. The classic tearoom hosts milongas organized by different groups in its first-floor dance hall every day

of the week. Many include live orchestras. ⊠*Suipacha 384, Plaza de Mayo* ☎*11/4601–8234* ⊕*www.confiteriaideal.com.*

FodorsChoice   **Salón Canning.** Several milongas call this large dance hall home. The
★   coolest is Parakultural, which takes place Monday, Wednesday, and Friday. Originally an alternative, "underground" milonga, it now attracts large numbers of locals (including longtime expats). ⊠*Av. Scalabrini Ortíz 1331, Palermo* ☎*11/4832–6753* ⊕*www.parakultural.com.ar.*

12 de Octubre *(El Bar de Roberto).* Cobweb- and dust-covered bottles line the walls of this tiny venue, with maybe the most authentic tango performances in town. From behind a heavy wooden bar, owner Roberto dispatches *ginebra* (a local gin) to old-timers and icy beer and cheap wine to students. When the singing gets going at 2 or 3 AM, it's so packed there's no room to breathe, but the guitar-and-voice duos manage gritty, emotional tango classics all the same. ⊠*Bulnes 331, Almagro* ☎*11/6327–4594* ⊙*Thurs.–Sat. after midnight.*

DINNER SHOWS

FodorsChoice   **Rojo Tango.** Five-star food, choreography, and glamour: you wouldn't
★   expect anything less from the Faena Hotel + Universe. Crimson velvet lines everything from the walls to the menu at the Cabaret, and tables often hold celebs both local and global. As well as classic tangos, the implausibly good-looking troupe does jazz-tango, semi-naked numbers, and even the tango version of Roxanne from *Moulin Rouge.* It's worth breaking the piggy bank for. ⊠*Martha Salotti 445, Puerto Madero* ☎*11/5787–1536* ⊕*www.rojotango.com.*

★   **El Viejo Almacén.** This place was founded by legendary tango singer Edmundo Rivero, but he wouldn't recognize the slick outfit his rootsy bar has become. Inside the colonial building lurks a tireless troupe of dancers and musicians who perform showy tango and folk numbers. ⊠*Balcarce 786, at Independencia, San Telmo* ☎*11/4307–6689* ⊕*www.viejo-almacen.com.ar.*

Starting in Santiago

Catedral Metropolitana, Plaza de Armas, Santiago

WORD OF MOUTH

"What to do in Santiago? If your tour doesn't take you to El Centro, go there yourself. Walk through the Plaza de Armas, braving the crowds on your way to the Mercado Central, perhaps for lunch at one of the seafood restaurants. Alternatively, spend an afternoon at the Feria de Artesenia by the Los Dominicos Church in Las Condes. You could also take the cable car up Cerro San Cristobel for stunning views, and lunch or dine at the Camino Real with the best wine list in Chile."   —toid

WELCOME TO SANTIAGO

TOP REASONS TO GO

★ **The Andes:** Ever-present jagged mountain peaks ring the capital. Wherever you go, you'll see them and remember that you are at the edge of the world.

★ **Great Crafts Markets:** Fine woolen items, expertly carved figurines, lapis lazuli jewelry, and other handicrafts from across the country are bountiful in Santiago.

★ **Museo Chileno de Arte Precolombino:** Occupying a lovely old building in the center of Santiago that used to be the *Real Aduana* (Royal Customs House), this museum's collection of indigenous pottery, jewelry, and artifacts is a joy for the eye.

★ **World-Class Wineries:** Santiago nestles in the Maipo Valley, the country's oldest wine-growing district. Some of Chile's largest and most traditional wineries—Concha y Toro and Santa Rita—are within an hour's drive of the city and so too is the lovely Casablanca Valley.

10

To LAS CONDES

PROVIDENCIA

1 Santiago Centro.
Santiago Centro, with the La Moneda Presidential Palace and its ministries and law courts, is the place from which Chile is governed and where you'll find most of the historic monuments and museums.

2 La Alameda. La Alameda, also known as Avenida Libertador Bernardo O'Higgins, marks the southern boundary of Santiago Centro and is lined with sights that include the San Francisco church and the ochre-colored Universidad de Chile. Farther east, past the base of the Santa Lucía hill, it changes its name to Avenida Providencia and then Avenida Las Condes.

3 Parque Forestal. A leafy park along the banks of the Río Mapocho gives this tranquil district its name. This is where you'll find the city's main art museums as well as, at its western tip, the bustle of the Mercado Central fish market and, on the other side of the river, the Vega and Vega Chica markets.

4 Bellavista & Parque Metropolitano. On the north side of the Río Mapocho, nestled in the shadow of the San Cristóbal Hill, Bellavista is Santiago's "left bank," a Bohemian district of cafés, small restaurants, crafts shops, aspiring art galleries, and one of the homes of Nobel poet Pablo Neruda.

5 Parque Quinta Normal Area. Slightly off the beaten track in western Santiago, the Quinta Normal park is not only one of the largest in the city but also home to four museums. Budget constraints are apparent in both the museums and the park itself but it's still a great place for a stroll, especially with children. On Sundays, you'll find plenty of Santiaguinos picnicking in the shade of its old trees.

GETTING ORIENTED

Pedro de Valdivia wasn't very creative when he mapped out the streets of Santiago. He stuck to the same simple grid pattern you'll find in almost all of the colonial towns along the coast. The city didn't grow much larger before the meandering Río Mapocho impeded these plans. You may be surprised, however, at how orderly the city remains. It's difficult to get lost wandering around downtown. Much of the city, especially communities such as Bellavista, is best explored on foot. The subway is probably the quickest, cleanest, and most economical way to shuttle between neighborhoods. To travel to more distant neighborhoods, or to get anywhere in the evening after the subway closes, you'll probably want to hail a taxi.

KEY

M *Metro stops*

i *Tourist information*

== *Cable Car Line*

SANTIAGO PLANNER

When to Go

Santiaguinos tend to abandon their city every summer during the school holidays that run from the end of December to early March. February is a particularly popular vacation time, when nearly everybody who's anybody is out of town. If you're not averse to the heat, this can be a good time for walking around the city; otherwise spring and fall are better choices, as the weather is more comfortable. Santiago is at its prettiest in spring when gentle breezes sweep in to clean the city's air of its winter smog and the trees that line the streets burst into blossom and fragrance.

Spring and fall are also good times to drive up through the Cajón del Maipo, when the scenery is at its peak. In fall, too, the vineyards around the city celebrate the *vendimia*—the grape harvest—with colorful festivals that are an opportunity to try traditional Chilean cuisine as well as some of the country's renowned wines. Winters in the city aren't especially cold—temperatures rarely dip below freezing—but days are sometimes gray and gloomy and air pollution is at its worst.

Eat Well & Rest Easy

Dining is one of Santiago's great pleasures. Everything from fine restaurants to informal *picadas*, restaurants that specialize in typical Chilean food, is spread across the city. Menus run the gamut of international cuisines, but don't miss the local bounty—seafood delivered directly from the Pacific Ocean. One of the local favorites is *caldillo de congrio,* the hearty fish stew celebrated by poet Pablo Neruda in his *Oda al Caldillo de Congrio* which is, in fact, the recipe. A *pisco sour*—a cocktail of grape brandy and lemon juice—makes a good start to a meal.

Lunch and dinner are served quite late—beginning at 1 pm for lunch, 7:30 or 8 pm for dinner. People do dress smartly for dinner, but a coat and tie are rarely necessary.

Santiago has more than a dozen five-star hotels, many of them in the burgeoning Las Condes and Vitacura neighborhoods. You won't find better service than at newer hotels such as the lavish Ritz-Carlton. But don't write off the old standbys such as Hotel Plaza San Francisco. Inexpensive small hotels are harder to find but they do exist, especially around the Calle Londres in the city center and in the Providencia district.

WHAT IT COSTS IN CHILEAN PESOS (IN THOUSANDS)				
¢	$	$$	$$$	$$$$
RESTAURANTS				
under 3 pesos	3 pesos–5 pesos	5 pesos–8 pesos	8 pesos–11 pesos	over 11 pesos
HOTELS				
under 15 pesos	15 pesos–45 pesos	45 pesos–75 pesos	75 pesos–105 pesos	over 105 pesos

Restaurant prices are based on the median main course price at dinner. Hotel prices are for two people in a standard double room in high season.

Language

Although staff at large hotels mostly speak adequate English and, in some cases, a little French and German, be prepared elsewhere for people to be helpful but to speak little or no English. Taxi drivers, except for the (very expensive) services provided by hotels, won't in general know English, and menus are mostly only in Spanish. Spanish-speaking travelers, even from other Latin American countries, will find that some words, particularly for food, vary.

Safety

Despite what Chileans will tell you, Santiago is no more dangerous than most other large cities and considerably less so than many other Latin American capitals. As a rule of thumb, watch out for your property but, unless you venture into some of the city's outlying neighborhoods, your physical safety is very unlikely to be at risk. Beware of pickpockets particularly in the Centro and on buses.

Other Practicalities

Navigation. In Santiago, it's easy to get your bearings because the Andes Mountains are always there to tell you where the east is. And, to make it even easier, the main districts you'll want to visit—the Centro, Providencia, and Las Condes—form the city's west–east axis, moving gradually up towards the mountains as they become more prosperous. This is the axis served by Line 1 of the subway.

Kids. Chileans love children and are quite likely to stop and admire them. Children are welcome in restaurants, except the most expensive ones at night, where they'll be admitted but raise eyebrows.

Tipping. In restaurants and for tour guides, a 10% tip is usual unless service has been deficient. Taxi drivers don't expect to be tipped but do leave your small change. Visitors need to be wary of parking attendants. During the day, they should only charge what's on their portable meters when you collect the car but, at night, they will ask for money—usually 1,000 pesos—in advance. This is a racket but, for your car's safety, it's better to comply.

Drinking Water. Tap water in Santiago is perfectly safe to drink, but its high mineral content—it's born in the Andes—can disagree with some people. In any case, a wide selection of still and sparkling bottled waters is available.

Getting Here & Around

Air Travel. Santiago's Comodoro Arturo Merino Benítez International Airport, often referred to simply as Pudahuel, is about a 30-minute drive west of the city. Taxis should cost around 16,000 pesos for a trip downtown. Hire one at the desks near customs, rather than using one of the services touted outside. Tickets for bus services cost around 1,500 pesos each at the same desks.

Car Travel. You don't need a car if you're going to stay within the city limits, as most of the downtown sights are within walking distance of each other. A car is the best way to see the surrounding countryside, however. The highways around Santiago are excellent and generally well signposted.

Subway Travel. Santiago's excellent subway system, the Metro, is the best way to get around the main part of the city but isn't very extensive. It is comfortable, inexpensive, and safe. The system operates weekdays 6 am–11 pm, Saturday 6:30 am–10:30 pm, and Sunday 8 am–10:30 pm.

Buses and taxis. Buses are relatively efficient and clean, although very crowded at peak times. Fares on the subway and buses are paid using the same prepaid smart card (most easily acquired in subway stations). No cash is accepted on buses. Taxis are reasonably priced and plentiful.

10

Updated by
Ruth Bradley

WHEN IT WAS FOUNDED BY Spanish conquistador Pedro de Valdivia in 1541, Santiago was little more than the triangular patch of land embraced by two arms of the Río Mapocho. Today that area, known as Santiago Centro, is just one of 32 *comunas* that make up the city, each with its own distinct personality.

Santiago today is home to more than 6 million people—nearly a third of the country's total population. It continues to spread outward to the so-called *barrios altos* (upper neighborhoods) east of the center. It's also growing upward, as new office towers transform the skyline. Yet in many ways, Santiago still feels like a small town, where residents are always likely to bump into an acquaintance along the city center's crowded streets and bustling plazas.

EXPLORING SANTIAGO

SANTIAGO CENTRO

In Santiago Centro you'll find interesting museums, imposing government buildings, and bustling commercial streets. But don't think you'll be lost in a sprawling area—it takes only about 15 minutes to walk from one edge of the neighborhood to the other.

Numbered bullets in the margins correspond to numbered bullets on the Santiago Centro & La Alameda map.

➊ Plaza de Armas. This square has been the symbolic heart of Chile—and
★ its political, social, religious, and commercial center—since Pedro de Valdivia established the city on this spot in 1541. The Palacio de los Gobernadores, the Palacio de la Real Audiencia, and the Municipalidad de Santiago front the square's northern edge. The Catedral graces the western side of the square. On any given day, the plaza teems with life—vendors selling religious icons, artists painting the activity around them, street performers juggling fire, and tourists clutching guidebooks. ⊠ *Compañía at Estado, Santiago Centro* Ⓜ *Plaza de Armas.*

➋ Catedral. Conquistador Pedro de Valdivia declared in 1541 that a house of worship would be constructed at this site bordering the Plaza de Armas. Check out the baroque interior with its line of arches topped by stained-glass windows parading down the long nave and the sparkling silver altar of a side chapel in the south nave. ⊠ *Plaza de Armas, Santiago Centro* ☏ *2/696–2777* ◷ *Daily 10–8* Ⓜ *Plaza de Armas.*

➌ Museo Chileno de Arte Precolombino. If you plan to visit only one museum
Fodor's Choice in Santiago, it should be the Museum of Pre-Columbian Art, a block
★ from the Plaza de Armas. The large collection of artifacts of the region's indigenous peoples is displayed in the beautifully restored Royal Customs House. The permanent collection, on the upper floor, showcases textiles and ceramics from Mexico to Patagonia. Unlike many of the city's museums, the displays here are well labeled in Spanish and English. ⊠ *Bandera 361, at Av. Compañía, Santiago Centro* ☏ *2/688–7348*

⊕ *www.museoprecolombino.cl* ✉ *Tues.–Sat. 3,000 pesos, Sun. free* ⊙ *Tues.–Sun. 10–6, public holidays, 10–2* Ⓜ *Plaza de Armas.*

LA ALAMEDA

Avenida Libertador Bernardo O'Higgins, more frequently called La Alameda, is the city's principal thoroughfare. Along with the Avenida Norte Sur and the Río Mapocho, it forms the wedge that defines the city's historic district.

❽ Biblioteca Nacional. Near the foot of Cerro Santa Lucía is the block-long classical facade of the National Library. Although it didn't move to its present premises until 1925, this library, founded in 1813, is one of the oldest and most complete in South America. The second-floor Sala José Toribio Medina (closed Saturday), which holds the most important collection of early Latin American print work, is worth a look. Three levels of books, reached by curved-wood balconies, are lighted by massive chandeliers. ✉ *La Alameda 651, La Alameda* ✆ *2/360–5200* ⊕ *www. dibam.cl* ✉ *Free* ⊙ *Apr.–mid-Dec., weekdays 9–7, Sat. 9–2; mid-Dec.– Mar., Sun.–Fri. 9–5:30* Ⓜ *Santa Lucía.*

❾ Cerro Santa Lucía. The mazelike park of Santa Lucía is a hangout for park-bench smoochers and photo-snapping tourists. Walking uphill along the labyrinth of interconnected paths and plazas takes about 30 minutes, or you can take an elevator two blocks north of the main entrance (no fee). The crow's nest affords an excellent 360-degree view of the city. Be careful near dusk as the park, although patrolled, also attracts the occasional mugger. ✉ *Santa Lucía at La Alameda, La Alameda* ✆ *2/664–4206* ⊙ *Nov.–Mar., daily 9–8; Apr.–Oct., daily 9–7* Ⓜ *Santa Lucía.*

❼ Iglesia San Francisco. Santiago's oldest structure, greatest symbol, and principal landmark, the Church of St. Francis is the last trace of 16th-century colonial architecture in the city. Construction began in 1586, and although the church survived successive earthquakes, early tremors took their toll and portions had to be rebuilt several times. Inside are rough stone-and-brick walls and an ornate coffered wood ceiling. ✉ *La Alameda 834, La Alameda* ✆ *2/638–3238* ⊙ *Daily 8 am–8 pm* Ⓜ *Santa Lucía, Universidad de Chile.*

❻ Palacio de la Moneda. Originally the royal mint, this sober neoclassical edifice designed by Joaquín Toesca in the 1780s and completed in

GOOD TO KNOW

There are few public restrooms in Santiago, which leaves many people begging to use the facilities in nearby restaurants and hotels. But Ecobaños operates four public restrooms in El Centro that are as clean as a hospital and as brightly lighted as a movie set. The uniformed attendants, constantly polishing the mirrors and wiping the floors, even wish you good day. All this for 260 pesos! They are located at Morandé and Huérfanos, Ahumada and Moneda, Ahumada between Compañía and Huérfanos, and Estado between Moneda and Agustinas.

10

1805 became the presidential palace in 1846 and served that purpose for more than a century. It was bombarded by the military in the 1973 coup, when Salvador Allende defended his presidency against General Augusto Pinochet before committing suicide there. The two central courtyards are open to the public, and tours of the interior can be arranged by e-mail with at least two days' notice. ⊠ *Plaza de la Constitución, Moneda between Teatinos and Morandé, La Alameda* ☎ *2/690–4000* ✑ *visitas@presidencia.cl* ⏲ *Daily 10:30–6* Ⓜ *La Moneda.*

④ **Plaza de la Constitución.** Palacio de la Moneda and other government
★ buildings line Constitution Square, the country's most formal plaza. The changing of the guard occurs every other day at 10 am within the triangle of 12 Chilean flags. ⊠ *Moneda at Morandé, La Alameda* Ⓜ *La Moneda.*

⑤ **Plaza de la Ciudadanía.** On the south side of the Palacio de la Moneda, this plaza was inaugurated in December 2006 as part of a program of public works in preparation for the celebration of the bicentenary of Chile's Independence in 2010. Beneath the plaza is the Centro Cultural del Palacio La Moneda, a new arts center that sometimes has interesting exhibitions but too often echoes with emptiness. The crafts shop there has top-quality work. ⊠ *Plaza de la Ciudadanía 26, La Alameda* ☎ *2/355–6500* ⊕ *www.ccplm.cl* ⏲ *Daily 10–7:30* Ⓜ *La Moneda.*

MAIN ATTRACTIONS ELSEWHERE IN THE CITY

PARQUE FORESTAL

⑪ **Mercado Central.** At the Central Market you'll find a matchless selection of creatures from the sea. Depending on the season, you might see the delicate beaks of *picorocos,* the world's only edible barnacles; *erizos,* the prickly shelled sea urchins; or heaps of giant mussels. If the fish don't capture your interest, the architecture may: the lofty wrought-iron ceiling of the structure, reminiscent of a Victorian train station, was prefabricated in England and erected in Santiago between 1868 and 1872. Diners are regaled by musicians in the middle of the market, where two restaurants compete for customers. You can also find a cheap, filling meal at a stand along the market's southern edge. ⊠ *Ismael Valdés Vergara 900, Parque Forestal* ☎ *2/696–8327* ⏲ *Sun.–Thurs. 6–5, Fri. 6 am–8 pm, Sat. 6–6* Ⓜ *Puente Cal y Canto.*

⑫ **Vega Chica and Vega Central.** From fruit to furniture, meat to machinery, these lively markets stock just about anything you can name. Alongside the ordinary items you can find delicacies like *piñones,* giant pine nuts found on monkey puzzle trees. If you're undaunted by crowds, try a typical Chilean meal in a closet-size eatery or *picada.* Chow down with the locals on *pastel de choclo,* a pie filled with ground beef, chicken, olives, and boiled eggs and topped with mashed corn. Be careful with your belongings. ⊠ *Antonia López de Bello between Av. Salas and Nueva Rengifo, Recoleta* Ⓜ *Patronato.*

⑩ **Museo de Artes Visuales.** This dazzling museum of contemporary art
★ displays one of the finest collections of contemporary Chilean art.

The building is a masterpiece: six gallery levels float into each other with the aid of Plexiglas-sided stairways. ✉*José Victorino Lastarria 307, at Plaza Mulato Gil de Castro, Parque Forestal* ☎*2/638–3502* ⊕*www.mavi.cl* ⌨*Tues.–Sat. 1,000 pesos (includes Museo Arqueológico de Santiago), Sun. free* ⊙*Tues.–Sun. 10:30–6:30* Ⓜ*Universidad Católica.*

BELLAVISTA & PARQUE METROPOLITANO

⓭ Cerro San Cristóbal. St. Christopher's Hill, within Parque Metropolitano, is one of Santiago's most popular tourist attractions. From the western entrance at Plaza Caupolicán you can walk—it's a steep one-hour climb—or take the funicular. Either route leads you to the summit, which is crowned by a gleaming white statue of the Virgen de la Inmaculada Concepción. If you come from the eastern entrance, you can ascend in the cable car or *teleférico* that leaves seven blocks north of the Pedro de Valdivia Metro stop. There is limited parking for 2,000 pesos at the Pío Nono entrance and free parking at the Pedro de Valdivia entrance. ✉*Cerro San Cristóbal, Bellavista* ☎*2/730–1300* ⊕*www.parquemet.cl* ⌨*Round-trip funicular 1,400 pesos; round-trip cable car 1,600 pesos* ⊙*Park: daily 8:30 am–9 pm. Funicular: Mon. 1–8:30, Tues.–Fri. 10–8:30, weekends 10–9. Cable car: Mon. 12:30–8:00, Tues.–Fri. 10:30–8:00, weekends 10:30–8:30* Ⓜ*Baquedano, Pedro de Valdivia.*

VITACURA

★ Museo de la Moda. This Fashion Museum, opened in 2007 by a son of Jorge Yarur Banna, one of Chile's most successful textile barons, hosts small exhibitions using a collection of clothes—mostly women's dresses—that dates back to the 1600s. Housed in the Yarur family's former home, which was designed by Chilean architects in the style of Frank Lloyd Wright in the early 1960s and decorated by a brother of Roberto Matta, one of Chile's most famous painters, the museum offers a fascinating insight into the lifestyle of the Chilean oligarchy in the run-up to the upheaval of Salvador Allende's socialist government and the ensuing military coup. The museum café serves excellent light meals and snacks at reasonable prices and, on weekends, has a special brunch menu. ✉*Av. Vitacura 4562 Vitacura* ☎*2/218-7271* ⊕*www. mmyt.cl* ⌨*3,000 pesos* ⊙*Tues.–Sun. 10–7* Ⓜ*No metro.*

10

WHERE TO EAT

Tempted to taste hearty Chilean fare? Pull up a stool at one of the counters at Vega Central and enjoy a traditional pastel de choclo. Craving seafood? Head to the Mercado Central, where you can choose from the fresh fish brought in that morning. Or try a trendy new restaurant in neighborhoods like Bellavista.

Remember that Santiaguinos dine a little later than the rest of us. Most restaurants don't open for lunch until 1. Dinner begins at 7:30 or 8, although most places don't get crowded until after 9. Many restaurants are closed on Sunday night.

BELLAVISTA

$$$
SEAFOOD
Fodor'sChoice
★

✕ **Azul Profundo.** When it opened, this was the only restaurant on this street near Parque Metropolitano. Today it's one of dozens of restaurants in trendy Bellavista, but its two-level dining room—with racks of wine stretching to the ceiling—ensure that it stands out in the crowd. Choose your fish from the extensive menu—swordfish, sea bass, shark, flounder, salmon, trout, and haddock are among the choices—and enjoy it *a la plancha* (grilled) or *a la lata* (served on a sizzling plate with tomatoes and onions). ⊠*Constitución 111, Bellavista* ☎*2/738–0288* ⌾*Reservations essential* ▤*AE, DC, MC, V* Ⓜ*Baquedano.*

$$$
CHILEAN
Fodor'sChoice
★

✕ **Como Agua Para Chocolate.** Inspired by Laura Esquivel's romantic 1989 novel *Like Water for Chocolate,* this Bellavista standout focuses on the aphrodisiacal qualities of food. One long table is actually an iron bed, with place settings arranged on a crisp white sheet. The food compares to the decor like the film version compares to the book: it's good, but not nearly as imaginative. *Ave de la pasión,* for instance, means Bird of Passion. It may be just chicken with mushrooms, but it's served on a copper plate. ⊠*Constitución 88, Bellavista* ☎*2/777–8740* ▤*AE, DC, MC, V* Ⓜ*Baquedano.*

$
CHILEAN

✕ **Galindo.** Join artists and the young crowd of Bellavista for traditional Chilean food in an old adobe house. This restaurant goes back 60 years when it started life as a canteen for local workmen and, although it gets crowded, it's a great place to try *pastel de choclo* or a hearty *cazuela,* a typical meat and vegetable soup that is a meal in itself. It also has the advantage of being open on Sunday. ⊠*Dardignac 098, Bellavista* ☎*2/777–0116* ▤*AE, DC, MC, V* Ⓜ*Baquedano.*

CENTRO

$$
CHILEAN
Fodor'sChoice
★

✕ **Blue Jar.** This restaurant, only a block from the Palacio de la Moneda, is an oasis of quiet on a small pedestrian street, and its food—simple but creative dishes using the freshest Chilean ingredients—appeals to locals and visitors alike, whether it's a sandwich, a salad and a bowl of soup, a full lunch, or a hearty breakfast. The menu changes monthly but not its hallmark hamburgers made from three different cuts of beef—one for flavor, one for texture, the other for color—with a little bacon fat added, and its wine list has some of Chile's most interesting labels at very reasonable prices. Reservations are advisable for lunch, particularly for an outside table. It closes at 8:30, so arrive early for evening drinks, sandwiches, and snacks. ⊠*Almirante L. Gotuzzo 102, at Moneda, Santiago Centro* ☎*2/696–1890* ▤*AE, DC, MC, V* ⊘*Closed weekends* Ⓜ*Moneda.*

$$
CHILEAN
★

✕ **Confitería Torres.** José Domingo Torres, a chef greatly in demand amongst the Chilean aristocracy of his day, set up shop in this storefront on the Alameda in 1879. It remains one of the city's most traditional dining rooms, with red-leather banquettes, mint-green tile floors, and huge chandeliers with tulip-shaped globes. The food, such as *lomo al ajo arriego* (sirloin sautéed with peppers and garlic), now comes from recipes by the mother of owner Claudio Soto Barría. A branch serves snacks and light meals in the Centro Cultural Palacio

La Moneda. ⊠*Alameda 1570, Santiago Centro* 🕾*2/688–0751* ⊟*AE, DC, MC, V* ☉*Closed Sun.* Ⓜ*Universidad de Chile.*

$ ✕**Donde Augusto.** What was once a simple seafood stand has taken
SEAFOOD over almost all the interior of Mercado Central. If you don't mind the
Fodor'sChoice unhurried service and the odd tear in the tablecloth, you may have the
★ time of your life dining on everything from sea urchins to baby eel. Go
for simple dishes like the *corvina a la plancha* (grilled sea bass), which
is mouthwateringly good. Get here early, as it closes at 5 pm Sunday–
Thursday and 6 on Saturday; it's open until 8 on Friday. ⊠*Mercado
Central, Santiago Centro* 🕾*2/672–2829* ⊟*AE, DC, MC, V* ☉*No dinner* Ⓜ*Puente Cal y Canto.*

PROVIDENCIA

$$ ✕**Aquí Está Coco.** The best seafood in Santiago is served here; ask your
SEAFOOD waiter—or friendly owner "Coco" Pacheco—which fish is the day's
Fodor'sChoice catch. This is a good place to try Chile's famous *machas* (clams), served
★ with tomatoes and Parmesan cheese, or *corvina* (sea bass) grilled with
plenty of butter. Don't miss the cellar, where you can sample wines
from the extensive collection of Chilean vintages. ⊠*La Concepción
236, Providencia* 🕾*2/235–8649* ♨*Reservations essential* ⊟*AE, DC,
MC, V* ☉*Closed Sun.* Ⓜ*Pedro de Valdivia.*

$$$$ ✕**Astrid y Gaston.** The kitchen is the real star here—every seat in the
CHILEAN pumpkin-color dining room has a great view of the chefs at work.
Fodor'sChoice You couldn't do better than start with the agnolotti, little pockets of
★ squid-ink pasta stuffed with king crab and cherry tomatoes. After that,
try one of the one-of-a-kind entrées, such as the lamb shank drenched
in *pisco* (a brandy distilled from small grapes) and served with three
kinds of yucca, or the parrot fish with tamarind and ginger. Make sure
to peruse the wine list, one of the best in town. Save room for one of
Astrid's desserts, such as the creamy confection called *suspiro limeña,*
"sigh of a lady from Lima": a meringue-topped dish of dulce de leche.
⊠*Antonio Bellet 201, Providencia* 🕾*2/650–9125* ♨*Reservations
essential* ⊟*AE, DC, MC, V* Ⓜ*Pedro de Valdivia.*

$$ ✕**Liguria.** This extremely popular picada is always packed, so you
CHILEAN might have to wait to be seated in the chandelier-lighted dining room
or at one of the tables that spill out onto the sidewalk. A large selection of Chilean wine accompanies such favorites as *cazuela* (a stew
of beef or chicken and potatoes) and sandwiches of *mechada* (tender
and thinly sliced beef). There are three branches in the neighborhood,
but each has its own personality. ⊠*Av. Providencia 1373, Providencia* 🕾*2/235–7914* ⊟*AE, DC, MC, V* ☉*Closed Sun.* Ⓜ*Manuel
Montt* ⊠*Pedro de Valdivia 047, Providencia* 🕾*2/334–4346* ⊟*AE,
DC, MC, V* ☉*Closed Sun.* Ⓜ*Pedro de Valdivia* ⊠*Luis Thayer Ojeda
019, Providencia* 🕾*2/231–1393* ⊟*AE, DC, MC, V* ☉*Closed Sun.*
Ⓜ*Tobalaba.*

10

WHERE TO STAY

Note that the 19% sales tax is removed from your bill if you pay in
U.S. dollars or with an overseas credit card.

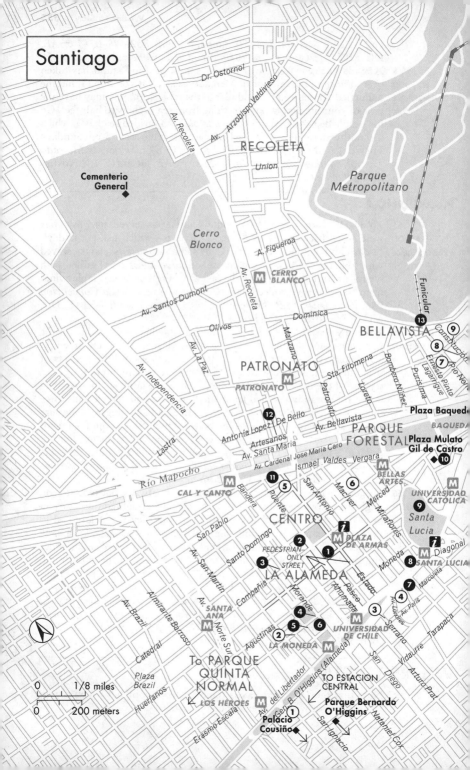

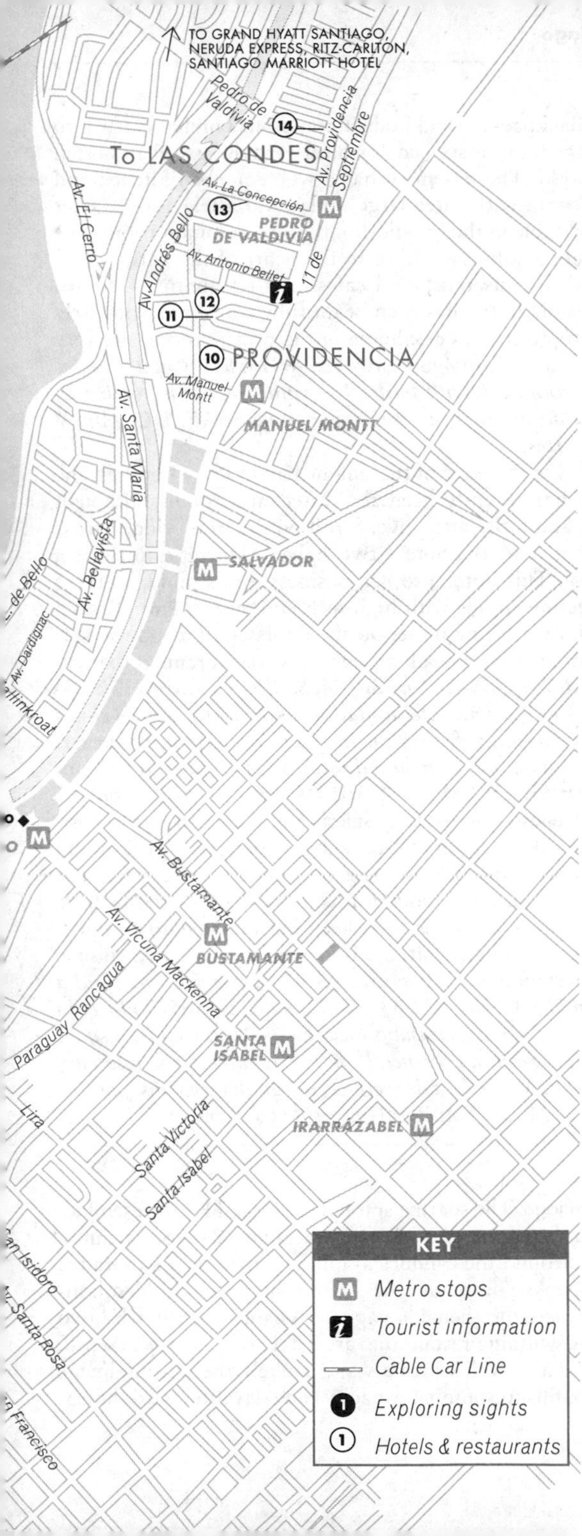
TO GRAND HYATT SANTIAGO, NERUDA EXPRESS, RITZ-CARLTON, SANTIAGO MARRIOTT HOTEL
Pedro de Valdivia
Av. Providencia
11 de Septiembre
To LAS CONDES
Av. La Concepción
PEDRO DE VALDIVIA
Av. El Cerro
Av. Andrés Bello
Av. Antonio Bellet
PROVIDENCIA
Av. Manuel Montt
MANUEL MONTT
Av. Santa María
Av. Bellavista
SALVADOR
Av. Dardignac
Av. Bustamante
BUSTAMANTE
Av. Vicuña Mackenna
Paraguay
Rancagua
SANTA ISABEL
Lira
Santa Victoria
Santa Isabel
IRARRÁZABEL
San Isidoro
KEY
Metro stops
Tourist information
Cable Car Line
Exploring sights
Hotels & restaurants

Exploring

Biblioteca Nacional 8
Catedral 2
Cerro San Cristóbal 13
Cerro Santa Lucía 9
Iglesia San Francisco 7
Mercado Central 11
Museo Chileno de Arte Precolombino 3
Museo de Artes Visuales 10
Palacio de la Moneda 6
Plaza de Armas 1
Plaza de la Ciudadanía 5
Plaza de la Constitución 4
Vega Chica and Vega Central 12

Restaurants

Aquí Está Coco 13
Astrid y Gaston 12
Azul Profundo 9
Blue Jar 2
Como Agua Para Chocolate 8
Confitería Torres 1
Donde Augusto 5
Galindo 7
Liguria 10

Hotels

Andes Hostel 6
Chilhotel 11
Hotel Fundador 3
Hotel Orly 14
Hotel Plaza San Francisco 4

CENTRO

$ **Andes Hostel.** Backpackers and budget-conscious families can ask to block off one of the four- or six-bed dormitories at this excellent hostel, opened in mid-2006. The basement has a well-equipped kitchen and pleasant dining room with three large tables and a television. Older kids love the pool table in the ground-floor lobby–common room. The location—opposite a subway station in the heart of the Parque Forestal, surrounded by museums, cool cafés, and restaurants—is hard to beat. **Pros:** This old house has been beautifully converted, spotlessly clean, great rooftop terrace. **Cons:** Some of the private rooms are very small. ⊠ *Monjitas 506, Santiago Centro* ☎ *2/632–9990* ⊕ *www.andes hostel.com* ↙ *6 rooms, 3 with bath; 9 dormitories* ⚒ *In-hotel: bar, public Wi-Fi, public Internet, no-smoking rooms* ☰ *AE, DC, MC, V* ⊗ *CP* Ⓜ *Bellas Artes.*

$$$ **Hotel Fundador.** On the edge of the quaint Barrio París-Londres, the Hotel Fundador has recently been renovated and rooms, although small, are bright and airily attractive. Stroll on the iron bridge across Calle Londres that links the hotel's two halves. Amenities include a small indoor pool. This hotel also has business on its mind, so there are plenty of meeting rooms with high-tech equipment. **Pros:** Tucked away from downtown traffic noise; on the doorstep of a subway station. **Cons:** Not an area for a stroll at night; few restaurants or bars in the immediate vicinity. ⊠ *Paseo Serrano 34, Santiago Centro* ☎ *2/387–1200* 🖷 *2/387–1300* ⊕ *www.hotelfundador.cl* ↙ *119 rooms, 28 suites* ⚒ *In-room: safe, dial-up, refrigerator. In-hotel: restaurant, room service, bar, public Wi-Fi, pool, gym, laundry service, parking (no fee), no-smoking rooms* ☰ *AE, DC, MC, V* ⊗ *BP* Ⓜ *Universidad de Chile.*

$$$ **Hotel Plaza San Francisco.** Across from Iglesia San Francisco, at this busi-
Fodor'sChoice   ness hotel you can take a dip in the sparkling indoor pool, work out in
★   the fitness club, or stroll through the art gallery. Recent redecoration has given the hotel a lighter, more modern touch. Its spacious rooms have large beds, and double-paned windows keep out the downtown noise. **Pros:** Helpful English-speaking staff, the Bristol offers interesting cuisine. **Cons:** Other good restaurants and bars are a Metro or taxi-ride away. ⊠ *La Alameda 816, Santiago Centro* ☎ *2/639–3832, 800/223–5652 toll-free in U.S.* 🖷 *2/639–7826* ⊕ *www.plazasanfrancisco.cl* ↙ *136 rooms, 9 suites* ⚒ *In-room: safe, refrigerator, Ethernet. In-hotel: restaurant, room service, bar, pool, gym, public Wi-Fi, laundry service, no-smoking rooms, parking (no fee)* ☰ *AE, DC, MC, V* ⊗ *BP* Ⓜ *Universidad de Chile.*

LAS CONDES

$$$$ **Grand Hyatt Santiago.** The soaring spire of the Grand Hyatt resembles
Fodor'sChoice   a rocket (and you shoot up a glass elevator through a 24-story atrium).
★   The rooms wrap around the cylindrical lobby, providing a panoramic view of the Andes. As you might guess from the pair of golden lions flanking the entrance, the theme is vaguely Asian, which is why two of the three award-winning restaurants are Thai and Japanese. (Senso, which is Tuscan, is also well worth a visit.) Duke's, the spitting image of an English pub, fills to standing capacity each day after work hours.

Pros: The garden is lovely, Atrium Lounge serves famed afternoon teas. **Cons:** Out of the way. ⊠ *Av. Kennedy 4601, Las Condes* ☎ *2/950–1234* 🖨 *2/950–3155* ⊕ *www.santiago.hyatt.com* 🛏 *287 rooms, 23 suites* ♿ *In-room: safe, refrigerator, Ethernet. In-hotel: 3 restaurants, room service, bar, public Wi-Fi, tennis courts, pool, gym, concierge, laundry service, parking (no fee), no-smoking rooms* ⊟ *AE, DC, MC, V* ⎮⊙⎮*BP* Ⓜ *No metro.*

$$ 🔡 **Neruda Express.** This "express" branch of the larger Hotel Neruda (on Avenida Pedro de Valdivia) has recently been redecorated and the rooms are tastefully modern, spacious, and luminous. Ask for one of the two suites on the second floor or one of the "superior" rooms on the ninth to 11th floors; they cost the same as a standard room. Although all windows have double glass, rooms on Avenida Apoquindo still get traffic noise; those at the back are quieter. **Pros:** On the edge of fashionable Las Condes. **Cons:** Fawlty Towers service has its charm but can also be very irritating. ⊠ *Vecinal 40, at Av. Apoquindo, Las Condes* ☎ *2/233–2747* 🖨 *2/232–1662* ⊕ *www.hotelneruda.cl* 🛏 *50 rooms, 2 suites* ♿ *In-room: safe, refrigerator, Wi-Fi. In-hotel: public Internet, laundry service, parking (no fee), no-smoking rooms* ⊟ *AE, DC, MC, V* ⎮⊙⎮*CP* Ⓜ *El Golf, Tobalaba.*

$$$$ 🔡 **Ritz-Carlton.** The rather bland brick exterior of this 15-story hotel belies the luxurious appointments within. Mahogany-paneled walls, cream marble floors, and enormous windows characterize the splendid two-story lobby, which faces a small leafy plaza just off busy Avenida Apoquindo. Elegant furnishings upholstered in brocade, and silk floral fabrics dominate the large guest rooms. Under a magnificent glass dome on the top floor you can swim or work out while pondering the panorama, smog permitting, of the Andes and the Santiago skyline. **Pros:** Prime location close to the main El Golf business and restaurant area. **Cons:** Almost the same comfort is available in other hotels at much lower prices. ⊠ *El Alcalde 15, Las Condes* ☎ *2/470–8500* 🖨 *2/470–8501* ⊕ *www.ritzcarlton.com* 🛏 *187 rooms, 18 suites* ♿ *In-room: safe, refrigerator, Ethernet. In-hotel: 2 restaurants, bar, room service, public Wi-Fi, pool, gym, concierge, laundry service, parking (no fee), no-smoking rooms* ⊟ *AE, DC, MC, V* ⎮⊙⎮*BP* Ⓜ *El Golf.*

$$$$ 🔡 **Santiago Marriott Hotel.** The first 25 floors of this gleaming copper tower house the Marriott. An impressive two-story, cream marble lobby has full-grown palm trees in and around comfortable seating areas. Visitors who opt for an executive room can breakfast in a private lounge while scanning the newspaper and marveling at the snowcapped Andes. There are wine tastings in the Latin Grill restaurant and theme evenings, with live music, in the Café Med. **Pros:** Excellent, friendly service in a spacious setting. **Cons:** In a suburban neighborhood, removed from the action. ⊠ *Av. Kennedy 5741, Las Condes* ☎ *2/426–2000, 800/468–4000 toll-free in U.S. and Canada* 🖨 *2/426–2001* ⊕ *www.santiagomarriott.com* 🛏 *280 rooms, 60 suites* ♿ *In-room: safe, refrigerator, Ethernet. In-hotel: 2 restaurants, bar, room service, public Wi-Fi, pool, gym, concierge, laundry service, parking (no fee), no-smoking rooms* ⊟ *AE, DC, MC, V* ⎮⊙⎮*BP* Ⓜ *No metro.*

10

PROVIDENCIA

$ 🛏**Chilhotel.** This small hotel is one of the few good midrange hotels in Santiago. For about what you'd pay for a dinner for two, you get a room that's clean and comfortable. Those overlooking the palm-shaded courtyard in back are especially lovely. It's in a funky old house, so no two rooms are alike. See a few before you decide. And talk about location—you're on a quiet side street, yet dozens of restaurants and bars are steps away. **Pros:** Excellent service closely supervised by owners; just a 10-minute Metro ride away from downtown sightseeing. **Cons:** Small rooms. ✉ *Cirujano Guzmán 103, Providencia* ☎ *2/264–0643* 🖷 *2/264–1323* ⊕ *www.chilhotel.cl* ⤳ *17 rooms* ⚭ *In-room: safe, refrigerator. In-hotel: restaurant, laundry service, public Wi-Fi, no elevator* ☰ *AE, DC, MC, V* ⫶◉⫶*BP* Ⓜ *Manuel Montt.*

$$ 🛏**Hotel Orly.** Finding a treasure like this in the middle of Providencia
Fodor's Choice is nothing short of a miracle. The shiny wood floors, country-manor
★ furnishings, and glass-domed breakfast room make this hotel as sweet as it is economical. Rooms come in all shapes and sizes, so ask to see a few before you decide. Cafetto, the downstairs café, serves some of the finest coffee drinks in town. **Pros:** Attractively decorated; excellent maintenance. **Cons:** Difficult to book on short notice. ✉ *Av. Pedro de Valdivia 027, Providencia* ☎ *2/231–8947* 🖷 *2/334–4403* ⊕ *www.orlyhotel.com* ⤳ *25 rooms, 3 suites* ⚭ *In-room: safe, refrigerator. In-hotel: restaurant, room service, laundry service, parking (no fee), public Wi-Fi, no-smoking rooms* ☰ *AE, DC, MC, V* ⫶◉⫶*BP* Ⓜ *Pedro de Valdivia.*

NIGHTLIFE

Bars and clubs are scattered all over Santiago, but a handful of streets have a concentration of such establishments. Try pub-crawling along Avenida Pío Nono and neighboring streets in Bellavista. The crowd here is young, as the drinking age is 18. To the east in Providencia, the area around the Manuel Montt Metro station attracts a slightly older and better-heeled crowd.

Note that establishments referred to as "nightclubs" are almost always female strip shows. The cheesy signs in the windows usually make it quite clear what goes on inside.

BARS & CLUBS

El Toro (✉ *Loreto 33, Bellavista* ☎ *2/737–5937*) is packed every night of the week including Sunday. The tables are spaced close enough that you can eavesdrop on the conversations of the models and other celebrities who frequent the place. For jazz, go to **Perseguidor** (✉ *Antonia Lopéz de Bello 0126, Bellavista* ☎ *2/777–6763*). At the base of Cerro Santa Lucía, **Catedral** (✉ *José Miguel de la Barra 407, Parque Forestal* ☎ *2/638–4734*) is a smart new bar, popular with the thirties crowd. It serves food but the same building also houses Opera, its upmarket restaurant partner. A secret meeting place during the Pinochet regime,

El Rincón de las Canallas (⊠*San Diego 379, Santiago Centro* ☏*2/699–1309*) still requires a password to get in (*Chile libre,* meaning "free Chile"). The walls are painted with political statements such as *Somos todos inocentes* ("We are all innocent").**Bar Yellow** (⊠*General Flores 47, Providencia* ☏*2/946–5063*) is a newer and more alternative place that has great food as well as drinks. Try the chips, and, if it's on the menu, the Thai soup with shrimp. And the staff really do speak English. Closed Sunday.

SHOPPING

AREAS

Vitacura is, without a doubt, the destination for upscale shopping. Avenida Alonso de Córdova is Santiago's equivalent of 5th Avenue in New York or Rodeo Drive in Los Angeles. "Drive" is the important word here, as nobody strolls from place to place.

Providencia, another of the city's most popular shopping districts, has rows of smaller, less luxurious boutiques. Avenida Providencia slices through the neighborhood, branching off for several blocks into the parallel Avenida 11 de Septiembre. The shops continue east to Avenida El Bosque Norte, after which Avenida Providencia changes its name to Avenida Apoquindo and the neighborhood becomes Las Condes.

MARKETS

Centro Artesanal Santa Lucía, an art fair just across La Alameda from the base of Cerro Santa Lucía, is an excellent place to find Aymara and Mapuche crafts. It's open daily 10–7.

Pueblito Los Dominicos (⊠*Av. Apoquindo 9085, Las Condes* ☏*2/201–9749* ⊕*www.pueblitolosdominicos.com*) is a "village" of more than 200 shops where you can find everything from fine leather to semiprecious stones and antiques. There's also a wonderful display of cockatoos and other live birds. It's open daily 10:30–8 in summer and 10–7 in winter. It's far from the main drag, so take a taxi, but an extension of the Metro, due in December 2009, will link it to Providencia and the Centro.

10

SPECIALTY SHOPS

HANDICRAFTS

Fodor'sChoice
★ **Artesanías de Chile** (⊠*Av. Bellavista 0357, Bellavista* ☏*2/777–8643* ⊕*www.artesaniasdechile.cl*), a foundation created by the wife of President Ricardo Lagos, is one of the best places to buy local crafts. The work is top quality and you know that the artisans are getting a fair price. The foundation also has shops in the Pueblito Los Dominicos and in the Centro Cultural Palacio La Moneda. The staff at **Pura** (⊠*Av. Isidora Goyenechea 3226, Las Condes* ☏*2/333–3144*) has picked out

SAMPLE ITINERARY

Santiago is a compact city, small enough that you can visit all the must-see sights in a few days. Consider the weather when planning your itinerary—on the first clear day your destination should be **Parque Metropolitano,** where you'll be treated to exquisite views from **Cerro San Cristóbal.** After a morning gazing at the Andes, head back down the hill and spend the afternoon wandering the bohemian streets of **Bellavista,** with a visit to Nobel laureate Pablo Neruda's Santiago residence, **La Chascona.** Check out one of the neighborhood's colorful eateries.

The next day, head to **Parque Forestal,** a leafy park that runs along the Río Mapocho. Be sure to visit the lovely old train station, the **Estación Mapocho.** After lunch at the **Mercado Central,** uncover the city's colonial past in Santiago Centro. Requisite sights include the **Plaza de Armas,** around which you'll find the Casa Colorada and the Museo Chileno de Arte Precolombino. Stop for tea in **Plaza Mulato Gil de Castro.** On the third day explore the sights along the **Alameda,** especially the presidential palace of La Moneda and the landmark church, **Iglesia San Francisco.** For a last look at the city, climb **Cerro Santa Lucía.** That night put on your chicest outfit for dinner in the trendy neighborhood of **Las Condes.**

expertly woven blankets and throws, colorful pottery, and fine leather goods. For everything from masks to mosaics, head to **Manos de Alma** (⊠ *General Salvo 114, Providencia* ☎ *2/235–3518*).

WINE

El Mundo del Vino (⊠ *Av. Isidora Goyenechea 2931, Las Condes* ☎ *2/584– 1172*) is a world-class store with an international selection, in-store tastings, wine classes, and books for oenophiles. It also has shops in the Alto Las Condes and Parque Arauco shopping malls and in Patio Bellavista. **La Vinoteca** (⊠ *Av. Isidora Goyenechea 2966, Las Condes* ☎ *2/334– 1987*) proudly proclaims that it was Santiago's first fine wineshop. It also has a shop at the airport for last-minute purchases.

UNDERSTANDING PATAGONIA

Spanish Vocabulary

SPANISH VOCABULARY

	ENGLISH	SPANISH	PRONUNCIATION
BASICS			
	Yes/no	Sí/no	see/no
	Please	Por favor	pore fah-**vore**
	May I?	¿Me permite?	may pair-**mee**-tay
	Thank you (very much)	(Muchas) gracias	(**moo**-chas **grah**-see-as)
	You're welcome	De nada	day **nah**-dah
	Excuse me	Con permiso	con pair-**mee**-so
	Pardon me	¿Perdón?	pair-**dohn**
	Could you tell me?	¿Podría decirme?	po-dree-ah deh-**seer**-meh
	I'm sorry	Lo siento	lo see-**en**-toh
	Good morning!	¡Buenos días!	**bway**-nohs **dee**-ahs
	Good afternoon!	¡Buenas tardes!	**bway**-nahs **tar**-dess
	Good evening!	¡Buenas noches!	**bway**-nahs **no**-chess
	Goodbye!	¡Adiós!/¡Hasta luego!	ah-dee-**ohss/** **ah**-stah **lwe**-go
	Mr./Mrs.	Señor/Señora	sen-**yor**/sen-**yohr**-ah
	Miss	Señorita	sen-yo-**ree**-tah
	Pleased to meet you	Mucho gusto	**moo**-cho **goose**-toh
	How are you?	¿Cómo está usted?	**ko**-mo es-**tah** oo-**sted**
	Very well, thank you.	Muy bien, gracias.	**moo**-ee bee-**en**, **grah**-see-as
	And you?	¿Y usted?	ee oos-**ted**
	Hello (on the telephone)	Diga	**dee**-gah
NUMBERS			
	1	un, uno	oon, **oo**-no
	2	dos	dos
	3	tres	tress
	4	cuatro	**kwah**-tro
	5	cinco	**sink**-oh

ENGLISH	SPANISH	PRONUNCIATION
6	seis	saice
7	siete	see-**et**-eh
8	ocho	**o**-cho
9	nueve	new-**eh**-vey
10	diez	dee-**es**
11	once	**ohn**-seh
12	doce	**doh**-seh
13	trece	**treh**-seh
14	catorce	ka-**tohr**-seh
15	quince	**keen**-seh
16	dieciséis	dee-**es**-ee-**saice**
17	diccisiete	dee-**es**-ee-see-**et**-eh
18	dieciocho	dee-**es**-ee-**o**-cho
19	diecinueve	**dee**-**es**-ee-new-**ev**-eh
20	veinte	**vain**-teh
21	veinte y uno/veintiuno	**vain**-te-**oo**-noh
30	treinta	**train**-tah
32	treinta y dos	train-tay-**dohs**
40	cuarenta	kwah-**ren**-tah
43	cuarenta y tres	kwah-**ren**-tay-**tress**
50	cincuenta	seen-**kwen**-tah
54	cincuenta y cuatro	seen-**kwen**-tay **kwah**-tro
60	sesenta	sess-**en**-tah
65	sesenta y cinco	sess-**en**-tay **seen**-ko
70	setenta	set-**en**-tah
76	setenta y seis	set-**en**-tay **saice**
80	ochenta	oh-**chen**-tah
87	ochenta y siete	oh-**chen**-tay see-**yet**-eh
90	noventa	no-**ven**-tah
98	noventa y ocho	no-**ven**-tah-**o**-choh
100	cien	see-**en**

ENGLISH	SPANISH	PRONUNCIATION
101	ciento uno	see-**en**-toh **oo**-noh
200	doscientos	doh-see-**en**-tohss
500	quinientos	keen-**yen**-tohss
700	setecientos	set-eh-see-**en**-tohss
900	novecientos	no-veh-see-**en**-tohss
1,000	mil	meel
2,000	dos mil	dohs meel
1,000,000	un millón	oon meel-**yohn**

COLORS

black	negro	**neh**-groh
blue	azul	ah-**sool**
brown	café	kah-**feh**
green	verde	**ver**-deh
pink	rosa	**ro**-sah
purple	morado	mo-**rah**-doh
orange	naranja	na-**rahn**-hah
red	rojo	**roh**-hoh
white	blanco	**blahn**-koh
yellow	amarillo	ah-mah-**ree**-yoh

DAYS OF THE WEEK

Sunday	domingo	doe-**meen**-goh
Monday	lunes	**loo**-ness
Tuesday	martes	**mahr**-tess
Wednesday	miércoles	me-**air**-koh-less
Thursday	jueves	hoo-**ev**-ess
Friday	viernes	vee-**air**-ness
Saturday	sábado	**sah**-bah-doh

MONTHS

January	enero	eh-**neh**-roh
February	febrero	feh-**breh**-roh
March	marzo	**mahr**-soh

ENGLISH	SPANISH	PRONUNCIATION
April	abril	ah-**breel**
May	mayo	**my**-oh
June	junio	**hoo**-nee-oh
July	julio	**hoo**-lee-yoh
August	agosto	ah-**ghost**-toh
September	septiembre	sep-tee-**em**-breh
October	octubre	oak-**too**-breh
November	noviembre	no-vee-**em**-breh
December	diciembre	dee-see-**em**-breh

USEFUL PHRASES

Do you speak English?	¿Habla usted inglés?	**ah**-blah oos-**ted** in-**glehs**
I don't speak Spanish	No hablo español	no **ah**-bloh es-pahn-**yol**
I don't understand (you)	No entiendo	no en-tee-**en**-doh
I understand (you)	Entiendo	en-tee-**en**-doh
I don't know	No sé	no seh
I am American/ British	Soy americano (americana)/ inglés(a)	soy ah-meh-ree- **kah**-no (ah-meh-ree- **kah**-nah)/in-**glehs(ah)**
What's your name?	¿Cómo se llama usted?	koh-mo seh **yah**-mah oos-**ted**
My name is . . .	Me llamo . . .	may **yah**-moh
What time is it?	¿Qué hora es?	keh **o**-rah es
It is one, two, three . . . o'clock.	Es la una./Son las dos, tres . . .	es la **oo**-nah/sohnahs dohs, tress
Yes, please/No, thank you	Sí, por favor/No, gracias	**see** pohr fah-**vor**/no **grah**-see-us
How?	¿Cómo?	**koh**-mo
When?	¿Cuándo?	**kwahn**-doh
This/Next week	Esta semana/ la semana que entra	**es**-teh seh-**mah**- nah/ lah seh-**mah**-nah keh **en**-trah
This/Next month	Este mes/el próximo mes	**es**-teh mehs/el **proke**-see-mo mehs

ENGLISH	SPANISH	PRONUNCIATION
This/Next year	Este año/el año que viene	**es**-teh **ahn**-yo/el **ahn**-yo keh vee-**yen**-ay
Yesterday/today/ tomorrow	Ayer/hoy/mañana	ah-**yehr**/oy/mahn-**yah**-nah
This morning/ afternoon	Esta mañana/ tarde	**es**-tah mahn-**yah**- nah/**tar**-deh
Tonight	Esta noche	**es**-tah **no**-cheh
What?	¿Qué?	keh
What is it?	¿Qué es esto?	keh es **es**-toh
Why?	¿Por qué?	pore **keh**
Who?	¿Quién?	kee-**yen**
Where is . . . ?	¿Dónde está . . . ?	**dohn**-deh es-**tah**
the train station?	la estación del tren?	la es-tah-see-on del trehn
the subway station?	la estación del tren subterráneo?	la es-ta-see-**on** del trehn la es-ta-see-**on** soob-teh-**rrahn**-eh-oh
the bus stop?	la parada del autobus?	la pah-**rah**-dah del ow-toh-**boos**
the post office?	la oficina de correos?	la oh-fee-**see**- nah deh koh-**rreh**-os
the bank?	el banco?	el **bahn**-koh
the hotel?	el hotel?	el oh-**tel**
the store?	la tienda?	la tee-**en**-dah
the cashier?	la caja?	la **kah**-hah
the museum?	el museo?	el moo-**seh**-oh
the hospital?	el hospital?	el ohss-pee-**tal**
the elevator?	el ascensor?	el ah-**sen**-sohr
the bathroom?	el baño?	el **bahn**-yoh
Here/there	Aquí/allá	ah-**key**/ah-**yah**
Open/closed	Abierto/cerrado	ah-bee-**er**-toh/ ser-**ah**-doh
Left/right	Izquierda/derecha	iss-key-**er**-dah/ dare-**eh**-chah
Straight ahead	Derecho	dare-**eh**-choh

ENGLISH	SPANISH	PRONUNCIATION
Is it near/far?	¿Está cerca/lejos?	es-**tah sehr**-kah/ **leh**-hoss
I'd like . . .	Quisiera . . .	kee-see-ehr-ah
a room	un cuarto/una habitación	oon **kwahr**-toh/ **oo**-nah ah-bee- tah-see-**on**
the key	la llave	lah **yah**-veh
a newspaper	un periódico	oon pehr-ee-**oh**- dee-koh
a stamp	un sello de correo	oon **seh**-yo deh korr-ee-oh
I'd like to buy . . .	Quisiera comprar . . .	kee-see-**ehr**-ah kohm-**prahr**
cigarettes	cigarrillos	ce-ga-**ree**-yohs
matches	cerillos	ser-**ee**-ohs
a dictionary	un diccionario	oon deek-see-oh- **nah**-ree-oh
soap	jabón	hah-**bohn**
sunglasses	gafas de sol	**ga**-fahs deh sohl
suntan lotion	Loción bronceadora	loh-see-**ohn** brohn- seh-ah-**do**-rah
a map	un mapa	oon **mah**-pah
a magazine	una revista	**oon**-ah reh-**veess**-tah
paper	papel	pah-**pel**
envelopes	sobres	**so**-brehs
a postcard	una tarjeta postal	**oon**-ah tar-**het**-ah post-**ahl**
How much is it?	¿Cuánto cuesta?	**kwahn**-toh **kwes**-tah
It's expensive/	Está caro/barato	es-**tah kah**-roh/
cheap		bah-**rah**-toh
A little/a lot	Un poquito/ mucho	oon poh-**kee**-toh/ **moo**-choh
More/less	Más/menos	mahss/**men**-ohss
Enough/too	Suficiente/	soo-fee-see-**en**-teh/
much/too little	demasiado/ muy poco	deh-mah-see-**ah**- doh/ **moo**-ee **poh**-koh

ENGLISH	SPANISH	PRONUNCIATION
Telephone	Teléfono	tel-**ef**-oh-no
Telegram	Telegrama	teh-leh-**grah**-mah
I am ill	Estoy enfermo(a)	es-**toy** en-**fehr**- moh(mah)
Please call a	Por favor llame a	pohr fah-**vor ya**-meh
doctor	un medico	ah oon **med**-ee-koh

ON THE ROAD

Avenue	Avenida	ah-ven-**ee**-dah
Broad, tree-lined boulevard	Bulevar	boo-leh-**var**
Fertile plain	Vega	**veh**-gah
Highway	Carretera	car-reh-**ter**-ah
Mountain pass	Puerto	poo-**ehr**-toh
Street	Calle	**cah**-yeh
Waterfront promenade	Rambla	**rahm**-blah
Wharf	Embarcadero	em-bar-cah-**deh**-ro

IN TOWN

Cathedral	Catedral	cah-teh-**dral**
Church	Templo/Iglesia	**tem**-plo/ee-**glehs**- see-ah
City hall	Casa de gobierno	kah-sah deh go-bee-**ehr**-no
Door, gate	Puerta portón	poo-**ehr**-tah por-**ton**
Entrance/exit	Entrada/salida	en-**trah**-dah/sah-**lee**-dah
Inn, rustic bar, or restaurant	Taverna	tah-**vehr**-nah
Main square	Plaza principal	plah-thah prin- see-**pahl**

DINING OUT

Can you	¿Puede	**pweh**-deh rreh-koh-
recommend a good	recomendarme un	mehn-**dahr**-me oon
restaurant?	buen restaurante?	bwehn rrehs-tow- **rahn**-teh?

ENGLISH	SPANISH	PRONUNCIATION
Where is it located?	¿Dónde está situado?	dohn-deh ehs-tah see-twah-doh?
Do I need reservations?	¿Se necesita una reservación?	seh neh-seh-see-tah oo-nah rreh-sehr- bah-syohn?
I'd like to reserve a	Quisiera reservar	kee-syeh-rah rreh-
table . . .	una mesa . . .	sehr-bahr oo-nah meh-sah . . .
for two people.	para dos personas.	pah-rah dohs pehr- soh-nahs
for this evening.	para esta noche.	pah-rah ehs-tah noh-cheh
for 8:00 p.m.	para las ocho de la noche.	pah-rah lahs oh-choh deh lah noh-cheh
A bottle of . . .	Una botella de . . .	oo-nah bo-teh- yah deh
A cup of . . .	Una taza de . . .	oo-nah tah-thah deh
A glass of . . .	Un vaso de . . .	oon vah-so deh
Ashtray	Un cenicero	oon sen-ee-seh-roh
Bill/check	La cuenta	lah kwen-tah
Bread	El pan	el pahn
Breakfast	El desayuno	el deh-sah-yoon-oh
Butter	La mantequilla	lah man-teh-key-yah
Cheers!	¡Salud!	sah-lood
Cocktail	Un aperitivo	oon ah-pehr-ee-tee-voh
Dinner	La cena	lah seh-nah
Dish	Un plato	oon plah-toh
Menu of the day	Menú del día	meh-noo del dee-ah
Enjoy!	¡Buen provecho!	bwehn pro-veh-cho
Fixed-price menu	Menú fijo o turistico	meh-noo fee-hoh oh too-ree-stee-coh
Fork	El tenedor	el ten-eh-dor
Is the tip included?	¿Está incluida la propina?	es-tah in-cloo-ee-dah lah pro-pee-nah

ENGLISH	SPANISH	PRONUNCIATION
Knife	El cuchillo	el koo-**chee**-yo
Large portion of savory snacks	Raciónes	rah-see-**oh**-nehs
Lunch	La comida	lah koh-**mee**-dah
Menu	La carta, el menú	lah **cart**-ah, el meh-**noo**
Napkin	La servilleta	lah sehr-vee-**yet**-ah
Pepper	La pimienta	lah pee-me-**en**-tah
Please give me	Por favor déme	pore fah-**vor deh**-meh
Salt	La sal	lah sahl
Savory snacks	Tapas	**tah**-pahs
Spoon	Una cuchara	**oo**-nah koo-**chah**-rah
Sugar	El azúcar	el ah-**thu**-kar
Waiter!/Waitress!	¡Por favor Señor/Señorita!	pohr fah-**vor** sen- **yor**/sen-yor-**ee**-tah

Travel Smart
Patagonia

WORD OF MOUTH

"Fewer people spoke English in Argentina than I
would have thought . . . and this is not me making an "ignorant American/Canadian" comment.
Most people we met—other than the front desk
staff at our hotels—did not speak a word of English. Given I do not speak a word of Spanish, this
sometimes made for some harrowing driving, tipping, paying, communicating experiences."

—jodicook

GETTING STARTED ARGENTINA

■ BY AIR

TO ARGENTINA

Flying times to Buenos Aires are 11–12 hours from New York, nine hours from Miami, 10½ hours from Dallas or Houston, and 13 hours from Los Angeles, via Santiago de Chile.

Aerolíneas Argentinas, the flagship airline, operates direct flights between Buenos Aires and New York JFK and Miami. At this writing, Aerolíneas flights are frequently prone to chronic delays due to industrial disputes.

Chilean airline LAN flies direct to JFK, Miami, and Los Angeles. There are direct flights from Los Angeles and Atlanta on Delta, and from Chicago on American. American also has nonstop service from JFK and direct service via Miami and Dallas from JFK, LaGuardia, and Newark. United flies from JFK via Washington, D.C. Continental connects Buenos Aires with Houston, Dallas, and Newark, sometimes via Panama City.

WITHIN ARGENTINA

Aerolíneas Argentinas and their partner Austral operate flights from Buenos Aires to more Argentine cities than any other airline, including daily services (often more than one) to Bariloche, Ushuaia, and El Calafate. The more reliable LAN also flies to these cities and a few others.

AIR PASSES

If you're flying into Argentina on Aerolíneas Argentinas, you're eligible for their Visit Argentina fares: these are regular tickets with a discount of 20%–30%. Aerolíneas Argentinas also participates in the Mercosur Air Pass (together with Austral Líneas Aéreas, Aerolíneas del Sur, and Pluna) that allows you to visit Argentina, Brazil, Chile, Uruguay, and Paraguay. Brazilian airline TAM's South America Pass works in a similar fashion but also includes Bolivia, Peru, and Venezuela, and is slightly more expensive.

If you are taking at least three flights within Argentina or South America in general, the OneWorld Alliance's (of which LAN Chile is a member) Visit South America pass can save money.

Airline Contacts Aerolíneas Argentinas (⊕ www.aerolineas.com.ar). **American Airlines** (⊕ www.aa.com). **Continental Airlines** (⊕ www.continental.com). **Delta Airlines** (⊕ www.delta.com). **LAN** (⊕ www.lan.com). **United Airlines** (⊕ www.united.com).

Airlines & Airports Airline and Airport Links.com (⊕ www.airlineandairportlinks.com).

Airline Security Issues Transportation Security Administration (⊕ www.tsa.gov).

Air Passes Mercosur Air Pass (Aerolíneas Argentinas ☎ 800/333–0276 ⊕ www.aerolineas.com.ar). **South America Pass** (TAM ☎ 888/235–9826 ⊕ www.tam-airlines.com). **Visit Argentina** (Aerolíneas Argentinas, ☎ 800/333–0276 ⊕ www.aerolineas.com.ar). **Visit South America Pass** (OneWorld Alliance ☎ 866/435–9526 LAN ⊕ www.oneworld.com).

AIRPORTS

BUENOS AIRES

Buenos Aires's Aeropuerto Internacional de Ezeiza Ministro Pistarini (EZE)—known as Ezeiza—is 35 km (22 mi) southwest of and a 45-minute drive from city center.

⚠ **Ezeiza has been plagued by problems. Faulty radar has led to all air traffic being controlled manually, which has caused huge delays. Underpaid airline staff have been on strike repeatedly. Local police even uncovered a luggage-theft racket here. At this writing things seem to have calmed, but you should still expect the unexpected.**

Most domestic flights operate out of Aeroparque Jorge Newbery (AEP). It's next to the Río de la Plata in northeast

Palermo, about 8 km (5 mi) north of the city center.

ELSEWHERE IN ARGENTINA

Several other airports in Argentina are technically international, but only because they have a few flights to neighboring countries; most flights are domestic.

Northern Patagonia's hub is Bariloche, which is 13 km (8 mi) west of which is the Aeropuerto Internacional San Carlos de Bariloche Teniente Luis Candelaria (BRC), known as the Aeropuerto de Bariloche. The gateway to southern Patagonia is Aeropuerto Internacional de El Calafate Comandante Armando Tola (ECA), 18 km (11 mi) east of El Calafate itself.

Airport Information Aeropuertos Argentinos 2000 (⊕www.aa2000.com.ar). Aeroparque Jorge Newbery (⊠Buenos Aires ☎11/5480–6111 ⊕www.aa2000.com.ar). Aeropuerto Internacional de Ezeiza Ministro Pistarini (⊕www.aa2000.com.ar). ORSNA (⊕www.orsna.gov.ar).

▌BY BUS

Most bus companies have online timetables; some allow you to buy tickets online or by phone. Web sites also list *puntos de venta* (sales offices). Most long-distance buses depart from Buenos Aires' Terminal de Omnibus de Retiro, which is often referred to as the Terminal de Retiro or simply Retiro. Ramps and stairs from the street lead you a huge concourse where buses leave from more than 60 numbered platforms. You buy tickets (be prepared to pay cash) from the *boleterías* (ticket offices) on the upper level; there are also two ATMs here. Each company has its own booth; they're arranged in zones according to the destinations served, which makes price comparisons easy. The terminal's excellent Web site lists bus companies by destination, including their phone number and ticket booth location. (*See individual chapters for information about local bus stations.*)

All long-distance buses have toilets, air-conditioning, videos, and snacks. The most basic service is *semi-cama,* which has minimally recleanable seats and often takes longer than more luxurious services. It's worth paying the little extra for *coche cama,* sometimes called *ejecutivo,* where you get large, business-class-style seats and, sometimes, pillows and blankets. The best rides of all are on the fully recleanable seats of *cama suite* services, which are often contained in their own little booth. Bus attendants and free drinks are other perks.

On services between nearby towns, you can usually choose between regular buses (*común*) and air-conditioned or heated services with reclining seats (*diferencial*). The companies that run local services rarely have Web sites—you buy tickets direct from the bus station.

Contact Terminal de Ómnibus Retiro (⊠Av. Antártida Argentina at Av. Ramos Mejía, Retiro, Buenos Aires ☎11/4310–0700 ⊕www.tebasa. com.ar).

▌BY CAR

If you don't fancy dealing with Argentine traffic yourself, you can also hire a *remis con chofer* (car and driver) in most cities. You can arrange this through hotels or local taxi companies.

GASOLINE

Gas stations are called *estaciones de servicio.* On long trips, fill your tank whenever you can, even if you've still got gas left, as the next station could be a long way away. Attendants always pump the gas and don't expect a tip, though most locals add a few pesos for a full tank. Credit cards aren't always accepted—look for signs saying *tarjetas de crédito suspendidas* (no credit cards).

Prices are often more expensive in the north of Argentina. South of an imaginary line between Bariloche and Puerto Madryn, gas is heavily subsidized and costs roughly half what it does elsewhere. GNC is compressed natural gas, an alternative fuel. Stations with GNC signs may sell only this, or both this and regular gas.

ROAD CONDITIONS

City streets are notorious for potholes, uneven surfaces, and poorly marked lanes and turnoffs. Many major cities have a one-way system whereby parallel streets run in opposite directions. Where there are no traffic lights at an intersection, you give way to drivers coming from the right, but have priority over those coming from the left.

Two kinds of roads connect major cities: *autopistas* (two- or three-lane freeways) and *rutas* (single- or dual-carriageways), *rutas nacionales* (main "national routes," indicated with an "RN" before the route number), both of which are subject to regular tolls. Autopistas are well-maintained, but the state of rutas varies hugely. In more remote locations, even rutas that look like major highways on maps may be narrow roads with no central division. Always travel with a map, as signposts for turnoffs are lacking.

Night driving can be hazardous: some highways and routes are poorly lit, routes sometimes cut through the center of towns, cattle often get onto the roads, and in rural areas *rastreros* (old farm trucks) seldom have all their lights working. Beware of *guardeganados* (cattle guards). They're often raised so that your car flies into the air if speeding. For highway-condition reports, updated daily, and basic routes in Spanish, contact La Dirección Nacional de Vialidad. A useful road-trip Web site is ⊕*www.ruta0.com*, which calculates distances and tolls between places and offers several route options. There are basic maps and some highway-condition reports (in Spanish) on the Web site of the Dirección Nacional de Vialidad (National Highway Authority).

Information Dirección Nacional de Vialidad (☎11/4343–8520 ⊕www.vialidad.gov.ar).

ROADSIDE EMERGENCIES

All rental car agencies have an emergency helpline in case breakdowns or accidents—some services take longer than others to arrive. The best roadside assistance is usually that of the Automóvil Club Argentina (ACA), which sends mechanics and tow trucks to members traveling anywhere in the country. If you have an accident on the highway, stay by your vehicle until the police arrive, which could take a while, depending on where you are. If your car is stolen you should report it to the closest police station.

Contacts American Automobile Association (AAA ☎800/564–6222 ⊕www.aaa.com). **Automóvil Club Argentino** (ACA ☎11/4808–4000 ⊕www.aca.org.ar). **Police** (☎101).

RULES OF THE ROAD

You drive on the right in Argentina, like in the United States. Seat belts are required by law for front-seat passengers. You must use your car lights on highways at all times. The use of cellular phones while driving is forbidden, and turning left on two-way avenues is prohibited unless there's a left-turn signal; likewise, there are no right turns on red. Traffic lights turn yellow before they turn red, but also before turning green, which is interpreted by drivers as an extra margin to get through the intersection, so take precautions.

Police tend to be forgiving of foreigners' driving faults and often waive tickets and fines when they see your passport. If you do get a traffic ticket, don't argue. Most tickets aren't payable on the spot, but some police officers offer "reduced" on-the-spot fines in lieu of a ticket: it's bribery and you'd do best to insist on receiving the proper ticket.

Paved highways run from Argentina to the Chilean, Bolivian, Paraguayan, and Brazilian borders. If you do cross the border by land you'll be required to present your passport, documentation of car ownership, and insurance paperwork at immigration and customs checkpoints. It's also common for cars and bags to be searched for contraband, such as food, livestock, and drugs.

RENTAL CARS

Daily rates range from 150 pesos to 280 pesos. This generally includes tax and 200 free km daily. Note that most cars have manual transmissions, so if you need an automatic, request one in advance.

Reputable firms don't rent to drivers under 21, and drivers under 23 often have to pay a daily surcharge of 10–15 pesos. Children's car seats are not compulsory but are available for 7–10 pesos per day. Some agencies charge a 10% surcharge for picking up a car from the airport.

Collision damage waiver (CDW) is mandatory and is included in standard rental prices. However, you're still responsible for a deductible fee—a maximum amount that you'll have to pay if damage occurs.

Check the policy to see if you can cross the border in your rental car.

Rental Agencies Alamo (☎810/999–25266, 11/4322–3320 in Buenos Aires ⊕www.alamo. com). **Avis** (☎810/999–12847, 11/4326–5542 in Buenos Aires ⊕www.avis.com). **Budget** (☎810/444–2834, 11/4314–7577 in Buenos Aires ⊕www.budget.com). **Dollar** (☎800/555–3655, 11/4315–8800 in Buenos Aires ⊕www.dollar.com). **Hertz** (☎810/222–43789, 11/4816–8001 in Buenos Aires ⊕www. hertz.com). **Localiza** (☎800/999–2999, 11/4813–3184 in Buenos Aires ⊕www. localiza.com).

ON THE GROUND ARGENTINA

■ COMMUNICATIONS

INTERNET

If you're traveling without a laptop, look for a *ciber* (Internet café) or *locutorios* (telephone and Internet centers). Expect to pay between 2 and 5 pesos per hour to surf the Web. Broadband connections are common.

You can find Wi-Fi in many hotel lobbies, libraries, business and event centers, some airports, and in public spaces—piggybacking is common practice.

Contact **Cybercafes** (⊕ www.cybercafes.com) lists over 4,000 Internet cafés worldwide.

PHONES

The country code for Argentina is 54. To call landlines in Argentina from the United States, dial the international access code (011) followed by the country code (54), the two-to-four-digit area code without the initial 0, then the five-to-nine-digit phone number. For example, to call the Buenos Aires number 011/4123–4567, you would dial 011–54–11–4123–4567.

Any number that is prefixed by a 15 is a cell phone number. To call cell phones from the United States, dial the international access code (011) followed by the country code (54), Argentina's cell-phone code (9), the area code without the initial 0, then the seven- or eight-digit cell phone number without the initial 15. For example, to call the Buenos Aires cell phone (011) 15/5123–4567, you would dial 011–54–9–11–5123–4567.

CALLING WITHIN ARGENTINA

Argentina's phone service is run by the duopoly of Telecom and Telefónica. Telecom does the northern half of Argentina (including the northern half of the city of Buenos Aires) and Telefónica does the south. However, both companies operate public phones and phone centers, called *locutorios* or *telecentros*.

You can make local and long-distance calls from your hotel (usually with a surcharge) and from any public phone or locutorio. At locutorios ask the receptionist for *una cabina* (a booth), make as many local, long-distance, or international calls as you like (a small LCD display tracks how much you've spent), then pay as you leave. Note that many locutorios don't allow you to call free numbers, so you can't use prepaid calling cards from them.

All of Argentina's area codes are prefixed with a 0, which you need to include when dialing another area within Argentina. You don't need to dial the area code to call a local number. Confusingly, area codes and phone numbers don't all have the same number of digits. The area code for Buenos Aires is 011, and phone numbers have 8 digits. Area codes for the rest of the country have three or four digits, and start with 02 (the southern provinces) or 03 (the northern provinces); phone numbers have six to nine digits.

For local directory assistance (in Spanish), dial 110.

To make international calls from Argentina, dial 00, then the country code, area code, and number. The country code for the United States is 1.

CALLING CARDS

Most *kioscos* (newsstands) and small supermarkets sell a variety of prepaid calling cards (*tarjetas prepagas*)—specify it's for *llamadas internacionales* (international calls).

Calling Card Information Telecom (☎ 0800/555–0030 ⊕ www.telecom.com.ar). **Telefónica** (☎ 0800/333–9000 ⊕ www.telefonica.com.ar).

MOBILE PHONES

All cell phones are GSM 850/1900 Mhz. If you have an unlocked dual-band GSM phone from North America and intend to call local numbers, buy a prepaid Argentinian SIM card on arrival—rates will be cheaper than using your U.S. network or than renting a phone. Alternatively, you can buy a basic pay-as-you-go handset and SIM card (*tarjeta SIM*) for around 110 pesos.

Cell numbers here use a local area code, then the cell phone prefix (15), then a seven- or eight-digit number. To call a cell in the same area as you, dial 15 and the number. To call a cell in a different area, dial the area code including the initial 0, then 15, then the number.

There are three main mobile phone companies in Argentina: Movistar, owned by Telefónica, CTI, and Personal. Their prices are similar but CTI is said to have better coverage, Movistar has the most users, and Personal is the least popular service. You can buy a SIM card from any of the companies' outlets; pay-as-you-go cards (*tarjetas de celular*) are available from kioscos, locutorios, supermarkets, and gas stations.

Cellular phones can be rented at the airport from Phonerental. A basic phone costs 20 pesos a week, outgoing calls are reasonable, but you pay 60¢ per minute to receive calls.

Contacts Cellular Abroad (☎800/287–5072 ⊕www.cellularabroad.com). **CTI** (⊕www.cti.com.ar). **Mobal** (☎888/888–9162 ⊕www.mobalrental.com). **Movistar** (⊕www.movistar.com.ar). **Personal** (⊕www.personal.com.ar). **Phonerental** (☎11/4311–2933 ⊕www.phonerental.com.ar). **Planet Fone** (☎888/988–4777 ⊕www.planetfone.com).

▮ CUSTOMS & DUTIES

Customs uses a random inspection system that requires you to push a button at the inspection bay—if a green light comes on, you walk through; if a red light appears, your bags are X-rayed (and very occasionally opened). In practice, many officials wave foreigners through. Officially, you can bring up to 2 liters of alcohol, 400 cigarettes, and 50 cigars into the country duty-free. That said, Argentina's international airports have duty-free shops after you land, and officials never take alcohol and tobacco purchased there into account. Personal clothing and effects are admitted duty-free, provided they have been used, as are personal jewelry and professional equipment. Fishing gear and skies present no problems.

Argentina has strict regulations designed to prevent the illicit trafficking of antiques, fossils, and other items of cultural and historical importance. For more information, contact the Dirección Nacional de Patrimonio y Museos (National Heritage and Museums Board).

Information in Argentina Dirección Nacional de Patrimonio y Museos (☎11/4381–6656 ⊕www.cultura.gov.ar).

▮ ELECTRICITY

The electrical current is 220 volts, 50 cycles alternating current (AC), so most North American appliances can't be used without a transformer. Older wall outlets take continental-type plugs, with two round prongs, whereas newer buildings take plugs with three flat, angled prongs or two flat prongs set at a "v" angle.

Brief power outages (and surges when the power comes back) are fairly regular occurrences, so it's a good idea to use a surge-protector with your laptop.

▮ EMERGENCIES

In a medical emergency, taking a taxi to the nearest hospital—drivers usually know where to go—can be quicker than waiting for an ambulance. If you do call an ambulance, it will take you to the nearest hospital—possibly a public one that may well look run-down; don't worry, though, as the care will be excellent. Alternatively you can call a private hospital.

For theft, wallet loss, small road accidents, and minor emergencies, contact the nearest police station. Expect all dealings with the police to be a lengthy, bureaucratic business—it's probably only worth bothering if you need the report for insurance claims.

American Embassy American Embassy (⊠ Av. Colombia 4300, Palermo, Buenos Aires ☎11/5777–4554, 11/5777–4873 after hours ⊕ http://argentina.usembassy.gov).

General Contacts Ambulance & Medical (☎107). **Fire** (☎100). **Police** (☎101). **All Buenos Aires Emergency Services** (☎911).

∎ HEALTH

MEDICAL CONCERNS

No vaccinations are required for travel to Argentina. However, the Centers for Disease Control (CDC), recommends vaccinations against hepatitis A and B, and typhoid for all travelers. A yellow fever vaccine is also advisable if you're traveling to Iguazú. Each year there are cases of cholera in northern Argentina, mostly in the indigenous communities near the Bolivian border; your best protection is to avoid eating raw seafood.

Malaria exists only in low-lying rural areas near the borders of Bolivia and Paraguay; cases of dengue fever, another mosquito-born disease, are also reported occasionally. The best preventative measure against both is to cover your arms and legs, use a good mosquito repellent containing DEET, and stay inside at dusk.

American trypanosomiasis, or Chagas' disease, is present in remote rural areas. There is no preventative medication for dengue or Chagas'. Children traveling to Argentina should have current inoculations against measles, mumps, rubella, and polio.

In most places in Argentina, including Buenos Aires, people drink tap water and eat uncooked fruits and vegetables. However, if you're prone to tummy trouble, stick to bottled water.

OTHER ISSUES

Apunamiento, or altitude sickness, which results in shortness of breath and headaches, may be a problem when you visit high altitudes. To remedy any discomfort, walk slowly, eat lightly, and drink plenty of fluids (avoid alcohol). If you experience an extended period of nausea, dehydration, dizziness, or severe headache or weakness while in a high-altitude area, seek medical attention. Dehydration, sunstroke, frostbite, and heat stroke are all dangers of outdoor recreation at high altitudes.

The sun is a significant health hazard, especially in southern Patagonia, where the ozone layer is thinning. Stay out of the sun at midday and wear plenty of good-quality sunblock. A hat and decent sunglasses are also essential.

Health Warnings National Centers for Disease Control & Prevention (⊕ www.cdc.gov/ travel). **World Health Organization** (WHO ⊕ www.who.int).

HEALTH CARE

Argentina has free national health care that also provides foreigners with free outpatient care. Although the medical practitioners working at *hospitales públicos* (public hospitals) are first-rate, the institutions themselves are often underfunded: bed space and basic supplies are at a minimum. World-class private clinics and hospitals are plentiful, and consultation and treatment fees and are low, compared to those in North America.

In nonemergency situations, you'll be seen much quicker at a private clinic or hospital, and overnight stays are more comfortable. Many doctors at private hospitals speak at least some English. Note that only cities have hospitals; smaller towns may have a *sala de primeros auxilios* (first-aid post), but you should try to get to a hospital as quickly as possible.

MEDICAL INSURANCE & ASSISTANCE

Consider buying trip insurance with medical-only coverage. Neither Medicare nor some private insurers cover medical expenses anywhere outside of the United States. Medical-only policies typically reimburse you for medical care (excluding that related to pre-existing conditions) and hospitalization abroad, and provide for evacuation. You still have to pay the bills and await reimbursement from the insurer, though.

Another option is to sign up with a medical-evacuation assistance company. Membership gets you doctor referrals, emergency evacuation or repatriation, 24-hour hotlines for medical consultation, and other assistance. International SOS Assistance Emergency and AirMed International provide evacuation services and medical referrals. MedjetAssist offers medical evacuation.

Medical Assistance Companies AirMed International (⊕www.airmed.com).**International SOS Assistance Emergency** (⊕www.intsos.com)**MedjetAssist** (⊕www.medjetassist.com).

Medical-Only Insurers International Medical Group (☎800/628–4664 ⊕www.imglobal.com).**International SOS** (⊕www.internationalsos.com).**Wallach & Company** (☎800/237–6615 or 540/687–3166 ⊕www.wallach.com).

OVER-THE-COUNTER REMEDIES

Towns and cities have a 24-hour pharmacy system: each night there's one *farmacia de turno* (on-duty pharmacy) for prescriptions and emergency supplies.

In Argentina, *farmacias* (pharmacies) carry painkillers, first-aid supplies, contraceptives, diarrhea treatments, and a range of other over-the-counter treatments, including drugs that would require a prescription in the United States (anti-

biotics, for example). Note that acetaminophen—or Tylenol—is known as *paracetomol* in Spanish. If you think you'll need to have prescriptions filled while you're in Argentina, have your doctor write down the generic name of the drug, not just the brand name.

▮ HOLIDAYS

January through March is summer holiday season for Argentines. Winter holidays fall toward the end of July and beginning of August.

Año Nuevo (New Year's Day), January 1. **Día Nacional de la Memoria por la Verdad y la Justicia** (National Memory Day for Truth and Justice; commemoration of the start of the 1976–82 dictatorship), March 24. **Día del Veterano y de los Caídos en la Guerra de Malvinas** (Malvinas Veterans' Day), April 2. **Semana Santa** (Easter Week), March or April. **Día del Trabajador** (Labor Day), May 1. **Primer Gobierno Patrio** (First National Government, Anniversary of the 1810 Revolution), May 25. **Día de la Bandera** (Flag Day), June 20. **Día de la Independencia** (Independence Day), July 9. **Paso a la Inmortalidad del General José de San Martín** (Anniversary of General José de San Martín's Death), August 17. **Día de la Raza** (European Arrival in America), October 12. **Inmaculada Concepción de María** (Immaculate Conception), December 8. **Christmas**, December 25.

▮ MONEY

You can plan your trip around ATMs—cash is king for day-to-day dealings. U.S. dollars can be changed at any bank and are widely accepted as payment. Note that there's a perennial shortage of change. Hundred-peso bills can be hard to get rid of, so ask for tens, twenties, and fifties when you change money. Traveler's checks are useful only as a reserve.

You can usually pay by credit card in top-end restaurants, hotels, and stores; the latter sometimes charge a small surcharge for using credit cards. Some establishments only accept credit cards for purchase over 50 pesos. Outside big cities, plastic is less widely accepted.

Visa is the most widely accepted credit card, followed closely by MasterCard. American Express is also accepted in hotels and restaurants, but Diners Club and Discover might not even be recognized. If possible, bring more than one credit card, as some establishments accept only one type. Throughout this guide, the following abbreviations are used: **AE,** American Express; **DC,** Diners Club; **MC,** MasterCard; and **V,** Visa.

Nonchain stores often display two prices for goods: *precio de lista* (the standard price, valid if you pay by credit card) and a discounted price if you pay in *efectivo* (cash). Many travel services and even some hotels also offer cash discounts—it's always worth asking about.

Prices throughout this guide are given for adults. Substantially reduced fees are almost always available for children, students, and senior citizens.

ATMS & BANKS

ATMs, called *cajeros automáticos,* are found all over Buenos Aires. There are two main systems. Banelco, indicated by a burgundy-color sign with white lettering, and Link, recognizable by a green-and-yellow sign. Cards on the Cirrus and Plus networks can be used on both networks.

Many banks have daily withdrawal limits of 1,000 pesos or less.

ATM Locations **Banelco** (⊕https://w3.banelco. com.ar).**Link** (⊕www.redlink.com.ar).

CURRENCY & EXCHANGE

Argentina's currency is the peso, which equal 100 centavos. Bills come in denominations of 100 (violet), 50 (navy blue), 20 (red), 10 (ocher), 5 (green), and 2 (blue).

Coins are in denominations of 1 peso (a heavy bimetallic coin); and 50, 25, 10, and 5 centavos. U.S. dollars are widely accepted in big-city stores, supermarkets, and at hotels and restaurants (usually at a slightly worse exchange rate than you'd get at a bank). You always receive change in pesos, even when you pay with U.S. dollars. Taxi drivers may accept dollars, but it's not the norm.

At this writing the exchange rate is 3.20 pesos to the U.S. dollar. You can change dollars at most banks (between 10 AM and 3 PM), at a *casa de cambio* (money changer), or at your hotel. All currency exchange involves fees, but as a rule, banks charge the least, and hotels the most. You need to show your passport to complete the transaction. ■TIP➔ **You may not be able to change currency in rural areas at all, so don't leave major cities without adequate amounts of pesos in small denominations.**

Exchange-Rate Information **O**anda.com (⊕www.oanda.com).**XE.com** (⊕www.xe.com).

▌ PASSPORTS

As a U.S. citizen, you only need a passport valid for at least six months to enter Argentina for visits of up to 90 days—you'll receive a tourist visa stamp on your passport when you arrive. You should carry your passport or other photo ID with you at all times. If you need to stay longer, you can apply for a 90-day extension (*prórroga*) at the Dirección Nacional de Migraciones (National Directorate for Migrations). The process takes a morning and costs about 100 pesos. Alternatively, you can exit the country; upon reentering Argentina, your passport will be stamped allowing an additional 90 days. Overstaying your tourist visa is illegal, and incurs a fine of $50, payable upon departure at the airport. If you do overstay your visa, plan to arrive at the airport several hours in advance of your flight so that you have ample time to take care of the fine.

Officially, children visiting Argentina with only one parent do not need a signed and notarized permission-to-travel letter from the other parent to visit Argentina. However, as Argentine citizens *are* required to have such documentation, it's worth carrying a letter just in case laws change or border officials get confused. Single Parent Travel is a useful online resource that provides advice and downloadable sample permission letters.

Contacts Dirección Nacional de Migraciones (✉ Av. Antártida Argentina 1355, Buenos Aires ☎ 11/4317–0237 ⊕ www.mininterior. gov.ar/migraciones).**Embassy of Argentina** (⊕ www.embassyofargentina.us).**Single Parent Travel** (⊕ www.singleparenttravel.net).

U.S. Passport Information U.S. Department of State (☎ 877/487–2778 ⊕ http://travel. state.gov/passport).

❚ SAFETY

CRIME

Argentina is safer than many Latin American countries. However, recent political and economic instability has caused an increase in street crime—mainly pickpocketing, bag-snatching, and occasionally mugging—especially in Buenos Aires. Taking a few precautions when traveling in the region is usually enough to avoid being a target.

Attitude is essential: strive to look aware and purposeful at all times. Don't wear any jewelry you're not willing to lose. Even imitation jewelry and small items can attract attention and are best left behind. Keep a very firm hold of purses and cameras when out and about.

Women can expect pointed looks, the occasional *piropo* (a flirtatious remark, usually alluding to some physical aspect), and some advances. These catcalls rarely escalate into actual physical harassment—the best reaction is to make like local girls and ignore it; reply only if you're really confident with Spanish curse words. Going to a bar alone will be seen as an open invitation for attention. If you're heading out for the night, it's wise to take a taxi.

In Buenos Aires, there's a notable police presence in areas popular with tourists, such as San Telmo and Palermo, which seems to deter potential pickpockets and hustlers. However, Argentinians have little faith in their police forces: many officers are corrupt and involved in protection rackets or dealing in stolen goods. At best the police are well-meaning but under-equipped, so don't count on them to come to your rescue in a difficult situation. Reporting crimes is usually ineffectual and is only worth the time it takes if you need the report for insurance.

The most important advice we can give you is that, in the unlikely event of being mugged or robbed, do not put up a struggle. Nearly all physical attacks on tourists are the direct result of them resisting would-be pickpockets or muggers. Comply with demands, hand over your stuff, and try to get the situation over with as quickly as possible—then let your travel insurance take care of it.

PROTESTS

Argentines like to speak their minds, and there has been a huge increase in strikes and street protests since the economic crisis of 2001–02. Protesters frequently block streets and squares in downtown Buenos Aires, causing major traffic jams. Most of them have to do with government policies. Trigger-happy local police have historically proved themselves more of a worry than the demonstrators, but though protests are usually peaceful, exercise caution if you happen across one.

SCAMS

Taxi drivers in big cities are usually honest, but occasionally they decide to take people for a ride, literally. All official cabs have meters, so make sure this is turned on. Some scam artists have hidden switches that make the meter tick over

Local Do's & Taboos

CUSTOMS OF THE COUNTRY

Welcoming and helpful, Argentinians are a pleasure to travel among. City-dwellers here have more in common with, say, Spanish or Italians, than other Latin Americans. However, although cultural differences between here and North America are small, they're still palpable.

Outside Buenos Aires, siestas are still sacrosanct: most shops and museums close between 1 and 4 PM. Argentines are usually fashionably late for all social events—don't be offended if someone keeps you waiting over half an hour for a lunch or dinner date. However, tardiness is frowned upon in the business world.

Fiercely animated discussions are a national pastime, and locals relish probing controversial issues like politics and religion, as well as soccer and their friends' personal lives. Political correctness isn't a valued trait, and just about everything and everyone—except mothers—is a potential target for playful mockery. Locals are often disparaging about their country's shortcomings, but Argentina-bashing is a privilege reserved for Argentinians. That said, some anti-American feeling—both serious and jokey—permeates most of society. You'll earn more friends by taking it in your stride.

GREETINGS

Argentinians have no qualms about getting physical, and the way they greet each other reflects this. One kiss on the right cheek is the customary greeting between both male and female friends. Women also greet strangers in this way, although men—especially older men—often shake hands the first time they meet some-

one. Other than that, hand shaking is seen as very cold and formal.

When you leave a party it's normal to say good-bye to everyone in the room (or, if you're in a restaurant, to everyone at your table), which means kissing everyone once again. Unlike other Latin Americans, porteños only use the formal "you" form, *usted,* with people much older than themselves or in very formal situations, and the casual greeting ¡Hola! often replaces *buen día, buenas tardes,* and *buenas noches.* In small towns, formal greetings and the use of *usted* are much more widespread.

LANGUAGE

Argentina's official language is Spanish, known locally as *castellano* (rather than *español*). It differs from other varieties of Spanish in its use of *vos* (instead of *tú*) for the informal "you" form, and there are lots of small vocabulary differences, especially for everyday things like food. Porteño intonation is rather singsong, and sounds more like Italian than Mexican or peninsular Spanish. And, like Italians, porteños supplement their words with lots and lots of gesturing. Another peculiarity is pronouncing the letters "y" and "ll" as a "sh" sound.

In hotels, restaurants, and shops that cater to visitors, many people speak at least some English. All the same, attempts to speak Spanish are usually appreciated. Basic courtesies like *buen día* (good morning) or *buenas tardes* (good afternoon), and *por favor* (please) and *gracias* (thank you) are a good place to start. Even if your language skills are basic and phrase-book-bound, locals generally make an effort to understand you. If people don't know the answer to a question, such as a request for directions, they'll tell you so. ■ TIP→ **Buenos Aires' official tourism body runs a free, 24-hour tourist assistant hotline with English-speaking operators, ☎0800/999-2838.**

OUT ON THE TOWN

A firm nod of the head or raised eyebrow usually gets waiters' attention; "*disculpa*" (excuse me) also does the trick. You can ask your waiter for *la cuenta* (the check) or make a signing gesture in the air from afar.

Alcohol—especially wine and beer—is a big part of life in Argentina. Local women generally drink less than their foreign counterparts, but there are no taboos about this. Social events usually end in general tipsiness rather than all-out drunkenness, which is seen as a rather tasteless foreign habit.

Smoking is very common in Argentina, but antismoking legislation introduced in Buenos Aires in 2006 has banned smoking all but the largest cafés and restaurants (which have to have extractor fans and designated smoking areas). Outside the city, you still get smoke with your steak. Most restaurants offer nonsmoking sections (*no fumadores*), but make sure to ask before you are seated. Smoking is prohibited on public transport, in government offices, banks, and in cinemas.

Public displays of affection between heterosexual couples attract little attention in most parts of the country; beyond downtown Buenos Aires, same-sex couples may attract hostile reactions.

All locals make an effort to look nice—though not necessarily formal—for dinner out. Older couples get very

dressed up for the theater; younger women usually put on high heels and makeup for clubbing.

If you're invited to someone's home for dinner, a bottle of good Argentinian wine is the best gift to take the hosts.

SIGHTSEEING

You can dress pretty much as you like in Buenos Aires: skimpy clothing causes no offense.

Argentinian men almost always allow women to go through doors and to board buses and elevators first, often with exaggerated ceremony. Far from finding this sexist, local women take it as a god-given right. Frustratingly, there's no local rule about standing on one side of escalators to allow people to pass you.

Despite bus drivers' best efforts, locals are often reluctant to move to the back of buses. Pregnant women, the elderly, and those with disabilities have priority on the front seats of city buses, and you should offer them your seat if these are already taken.

Children and adults selling pens, notepads, or sheets of stickers are regular fixtures on urban public transport. Some children also hand out tiny greeting cards in exchange for coins. The standard procedure is to accept the merchandise or cards as the vendor moves up the carriage, then either return the item (saying *no, gracias*) or give them money when they return.

Most Argentinians are hardened jaywalkers, but given how reckless local driving can be, you'd do well to cross at corners and wait for pedestrian lights.

more quickly, but simply driving a circuitous route is a more common ploy. It helps to have an idea where you're going and how long it will take. Local lore says that, if hailing taxis on the street, those with lights on top (usually labeled RADIO TAXI) are more trustworthy. Late at night, try to call for a cab—all hotels and restaurants, no matter how cheap, have a number and will usually call for you.

When asking for price quotes in touristy areas, always confirm whether the price is in dollars or pesos. Some salespeople, especially street vendors, have found that they can take advantage of confused tourists by charging dollars for goods that are actually priced in pesos. If you're in doubt about that beautiful leather coat, don't be shy about asking if the number on the tag is in pesos or dollars.

Advisories & Other Information Transportation Security Administration (TSA; ⊕www.tsa.gov).**U.S. Department of State** (⊕www.travel.state.gov).

TAXES

Argentina has an international departure tax of $18, payable by credit card or in cash in pesos, dollars, or euros. There's an $8 domestic departure tax, but this is often included in the price of tickets. Hotel rooms carry a 21% tax. Cheaper hotels and hostels tend to include this in their quoted rates; more expensive hotels add it to your bill.

Argentina has 21% V.A.T. (known as IVA) on most consumer goods and services. The tax is usually included in the price of goods and noted on your receipt. You can get nearly all the IVA back on locally manufactured goods if you spend more than 70 pesos at stores displaying a duty-free sign. You're given a Global Refund check to the value of the IVA, which you get stamped by customs at the airport, and can then cash in at the clearly signed tax refund booths. Allow an extra hour to get this done.

Tax refunds Global Refund (☎11/5238–1970 ⊕www.globalrefund.com).

TIME

Argentina is just one hour ahead of Eastern time for most of the year. Daylight savings time was introduced in 2007: clocks go forward one hour between December 31 and March 21 (summer in Argentina).

Time-Zone Information Timeanddate.com (⊕www.timeanddate.com/worldclock).

TIPPING

Propinas (tips) are a question of rewarding good service rather than an obligation. Restaurant bills—even those that have a *cubierto,* (bread and service charge)—don't include gratuities; locals usually add 10%. Bellhops and maids expect tips only in the very expensive hotels, where a tip in dollars is appreciated. You can also give a small tip (10% or less) to tour guides. Porteños round off taxi fares, though some cabbies who frequent hotels popular with tourists seem to expect more. Tipping is a nice gesture with beauty and barbershop personnel—5%–10% is fine.

TRIP INSURANCE

Comprehensive trip insurance is valuable if you're booking a very expensive or complicated trip (particularly to an isolated region) or if you're booking far in advance. Comprehensive policies typically cover trip-cancellation and interruption, letting you cancel or cut your trip short because of a personal emergency, illness, or, in some cases, acts of terrorism in your destination. Such policies also cover evacuation and medical care. Some also cover you for trip delays because of bad weather or mechanical problems as well as for lost or delayed baggage.

Another type of coverage to look for is financial default---that is, when your trip is disrupted because a tour operator, airline, or cruise line goes out of business.

Always read the fine print of your policy to make sure that you are covered for the risks that are of most concern to you.

Insurance Comparison Sites Insure My Trip. com (☎800/487–4722 ⊕www.insuremytrip. com). **Square Mouth.com** (☎800/240–0369 or 727/490–5803 ⊕www.squaremouth.com).

Comprehensive Travel Insurers Access America (☎866/729–6021 ⊕www. accessamerica.com) **AIG Travel Guard** (☎800/826–4919 ⊕www.travelguard.com) **CSA Travel Protection** (☎800/873–9855 ⊕www.csatravelprotection.com) **HTH Worldwide** (☎610/254–8700 ⊕www.hthworldwide. com) **Travelex Insurance** (☎888/228–9792 ⊕www.travelex-insurance.com) **Travel Insured International** (☎800/243–3174 ⊕www.travelinsured.com).

■ VISITOR INFORMATION

Buenos Aires has tourist information booths around the city and an excellent Web site. Each Argentine province also operates a tourist office in Buenos Aires, usually called the *Casa de [Province Name] en Buenos Aires.* The government umbrella organization for all regional and city-based tourist offices is the *Secretaría de Turismo* (Secretariat of Tourism). Their no-frills Web site has links and addresses to these offices, and lots of other practical information.

Limited tourist information is also available at Argentina's embassy and consulates in the United States.

Contact Argentine Secretariat of Tourism (☎800/555–0016 in Argentina ⊕www. turismo.gov.ar).

ONLINE RESOURCES

The like-minded travelers on Fodors.com are eager to answer questions and swap travel tales. The Web site of the *Buenos*

Aires Herald, the city's English-language daily, has lots of information on cultural events as well as news in the city and the rest of the country. Argentina Travel has general information on different aspects of Argentine culture and helpful travel tips, and Welcome Argentina has good overviews of Argentina's different regions. You'll also find information on the Argentina embassy Web site. Museo Nacional de Bellas Artes contains the world's biggest collection of Argentine art, and has lots of background on Argentine artists. Tangodata, the official tango site of the Buenos Aires city government, has lots of practical information and listings. Todo Tango is an excellent bilingual tango site with tango lyrics, history, and free downloads.

Argentine Wines is overflowing with information about Argentina's best tipple. Mundo Matero has everything you wanted to know about mate (a type of tea) but were afraid to ask.

All About Argentina Argentina Secretary of Tourism (⊕www.turismo.gov.ar). **Argentina Travel** (⊕www.justargentina.org). **Embassy of Argentina** (⊕www.embassyofargentina. us).**Fodors.com** (⊕www.fodors.com/forums). **Welcome Argentina** (⊕www.welcomeargentina.com.ar).

Culture & Entertainment Argentine Wines (⊕www.argentinewines.com). **Mundo Matero** (⊕www.mundomatero.com/yerba). **Museo Nacional de Bellas Artes** (⊕www.mnba.org. ar).**Tangodata** (⊕www.tangodata.gov.ar). **Todo Tango** (⊕www.todotango.com.ar).

Newspaper Buenos Aires Herald (⊕www. buenosairesherald.com).

GETTING STARTED CHILE

BY AIR

Miami (nine-hour flight), New York (11½ hours), and Atlanta (nine hours) are the primary departure points for flights to Chile from the United States, though there are also frequent flights from Dallas and other cities. Other international flights often connect through other major South American cities like Buenos Aires and Lima.

Here's the bad news: arriving from abroad, American citizens must pay a "reciprocity" fee of $130. The good news is that in addition to cash, credit cards are now also accepted. A departure tax of $18 is included in the cost of your ticket.

AIRPORTS

Most international flights head to Santiago's Comodoro Arturo Merino Benítez International Airport (SCL), also known as Pudahuel, about 30 minutes west of the city. Domestic flights leave from the same terminal.

Airport Information Comodoro Arturo Merino Benítez International Airport (☎2/690–1900 ⊕www.aeropuertosantiago.cl).

FLIGHTS

The largest North American carrier is American Airlines, which has direct service from Dallas and Miami; Delta flies from Atlanta. LAN flies nonstop to Santiago from both Miami and Los Angeles and with a layover in Lima from New York. Air Canada flies nonstop from Toronto.

LAN has daily flights from Santiago to most cities throughout Chile. Aerolineas del Sur (aka Air Comet Chile) and Sky also fly to most large cities within Chile.

Airline Contacts American Airlines (☎800/433–7300 in North America, 2/679–0000 in Chile). **Delta Airlines** (☎800/221–1212 for U.S. reservations, 800/241–4141 for international reservations, 2/690–1555 in Chile

⊕www.delta.com). **LAN** (☎800/735–5526 in North America, 2/565–2000 in Chile). **United Airlines** (☎800/864–8331 for U.S. reservations, 800/538–2929 for international reservations ⊕www.united.com).

Within Chile Aerolineas del Sur/Air Comet (☎600/625–0000 in Chile ⊕www.aircomet chile.cl). **LAN** (☎2/565–2000 in Chile). **Sky** (☎600/600–2828 in Chile).

▮ BY BOAT

Boats and ferries are the best way to reach many places in Chile, such as Chiloé and the Southern Coast. They are also a great alternative to flying when your destination is a southern port like Puerto Natales or Punta Arenas. Navimag and Transmarchilay are the two main companies operating routes in the south. Both maintain excellent Web sites with complete schedule and pricing information. You can buy tickets online, or book through a travel agent.

Information Navimag (✉Av. El Bosque Norte 0440, Piso 11, Las Condes, Santiago ☎2/442–3120 ⊕www.navimag.com ✉Angelmó 2187, Puerto Montt ☎65/432–300). **Transmarchilay** (✉Av. Providencia 2653, Local 24, Providencia, Santiago ☎2/234–1464 ⊕www.transmarchilay.cl ✉Angelmó 2187, Puerto Montt ☎65/270–430).

▮ BY BUS

Long-distance buses are safe and affordable. Luxury bus travel between cities costs about one-third that of plane travel and buses have wide reclining seats, movies, drinks, and snacks. The most expensive service offered by most bus companies is called *cama* or *semi-cama*, which indicates that the seats fold down into a bed. Service billed as *ejectivo* is nearly as luxurious.

Bus fares are substantially cheaper than in North America or Europe. Competing bus companies serve all major and many minor routes, so it can pay to shop around. Always speak to the counter clerk, as cutthroat competition may mean you can ride for less than the posted fare.

Tickets are sold at bus-company offices and at city bus terminals. Note that in larger cities there may be different terminals for buses to different destinations, and some small towns may not have a terminal at all. You'll be picked up and dropped off at the bus line's office, invariably in a central location. Expect to pay with cash, as only the large bus companies such as Pullman Bus and Tur-Bus accept credit cards.

Companies are notoriously difficult to reach by phone, so it's often better to stop by the terminal to check on prices and schedules.

Pullman Bus and Tur-Bus are two of the best-known companies in Chile.

Bus Information Pullman Bus (☎600/320–3200 ⊕www.pullman.cl). **Tur-Bus** (☎600/660–6600 ⊕www.turbus.com).

▌ BY CAR

Drivers in Chile are not particularly aggressive, but neither are they particularly polite. Plan your daily driving distance conservatively, as distances are always longer than they appear on maps. Obey posted speed limits and traffic regulations. And above all, if you get a traffic ticket, don't argue—and plan to spend longer than you want settling it.

AUTO CLUBS

El Automóvil Club de Chile offers low-cost road service and towing in and around the main cities to members of the Automobile Association of America (AAA).

Auto Club Information El Automóvil Club de Chile (⊠Av. Andrés Bello 1863, Providencia, Santiago ☎2/431–1000 ⊕www.automovil club.cl).

GASOLINE

Most service stations are operated by an attendant and accept credit cards. They are open 24 hours a day along the Pan-American Highway and in most major cities, but not in small towns and villages. Attendants will often ask you to glance at the zero reading on the gas pump to show that you are not being cheated.

RENTAL CARS

On average it costs 25,000 pesos (about $50) a day to rent the cheapest type of car with unlimited mileage. Hertz, Avis, and Budget have locations at Santiago's airport and elsewhere around the country. A locally owned Santiago company, United, lists slightly lower rates than the big chains on its Web site ⊕*www. united-chile.com*. Nearly all companies list higher rates (about 20%) for the high season (November to February).

To access some of Chile's more remote regions, it may be necessary to rent a four-wheel-drive vehicle, which can cost up to 48,000 pesos (about $100) a day. You can often get a discounted weekly rate.

An annoying fact about Chilean rental companies is that they often deliver the car to you with an empty tank. Ask about the nearest gas station, or your trip may be extremely short.

If you don't want to drive yourself, consider hiring a car and driver through your hotel concierge, or make a deal with a taxi driver for some extended sightseeing at a longer-term rate. Drivers charge an hourly rate regardless of the distance traveled. You'll often spend less than you would for a rental car.

You need your own driver's license, but not the International Driver's Permit (IDP), to drive legally in Chile. The minimum age for driving is 18. To rent a car you usually have to be 25, but a few companies let you rent at 22.

ROAD CONDITIONS

Between May and August, roads, underpasses, and parks can flood when it rains. It's very dangerous, especially for drivers who don't know their way around. Avoid driving if it has been raining for several hours.

The Pan-American Highway runs from Arica in the far north down to Puerto Montt, in the Lake District. Much of it is now two lane, or in the process of being widened, and bypasses most large cities. The Carretera Austral, an unpaved road that runs for more than 1,000 km (620 mi) as far as Villa O'Higgins in Patagonia, starts just south of Puerto Montt. A few stretches of the road are broken by water and are linked only by car ferries. Many cyclists ride without lights in rural areas, so be careful when driving at night. This also applies to horse- and bull-drawn carts.

RULES OF THE ROAD

The speed limit is 60 kph (37 mph) in cities and 120 kph (75 mph) on highways unless otherwise posted. The police regularly enforce the speed limit, handing out *partes* (tickets) to speeders.

Seat belts are mandatory in the front and back of the car, and police give on-the-spot fines for not wearing them. If the police find you with more than 0.5 milligrams of alcohol in your blood, you will be considered to be driving under the influence and arrested.

ON THE GROUND CHILE

■ ACCOMMODATIONS

The lodgings (all indicated with a ⊞ symbol) that we list are the cream of the crop in each price category. We always list the facilities that are available—but we don't specify whether they cost extra: when pricing accommodations, always ask what's included and what costs extra. All hotels listed have private bath unless otherwise noted. Properties indicated by ✗⊞are lodging establishments whose restaurant warrants a special trip.

It's always good to look at any room before accepting it. Expense is no guarantee of charm or cleanliness, and accommodations can vary dramatically within one hotel. If you ask for a double room, you'll get a room for two people, but you're not guaranteed a double mattress. If you'd like to avoid twin beds, ask for a *cama de matrimonio*. Many older hotels in Chile have rooms with wrought-iron balconies or spacious terraces; ask if there's a room *con balcón* or *con terraza* when checking in.

Hotels in Chile do not charge taxes to foreign tourists. Knowing this in advance can save you some cash. When checking the price, make sure to ask for the *precio extranjero, sin impuestos* (foreign rate, without taxes). If you are traveling to Chile from neighboring Peru or Bolivia, expect a bump-up in price. Everything in Chile is a bit pricier than in those two countries.

Also, note that you can always ask for a *descuento* (discount) out of season or sometimes midweek during high season.

HOTELS

Chile's urban areas and resort areas have hotels that come with all of the amenities that are taken for granted in North America and Europe, such as room service, a restaurant, or a swimming pool. Elsewhere you may not have television or a phone in your room, although you will find them somewhere in the hotel. Rooms that have a private bath may have only a shower, and in some cases, there will be a shared bath in the hall. In all but the most upscale hotels, you may be asked to leave your key at the reception desk whenever you leave.

RESIDENCIALES

Private homes that rent rooms, *residenciales*, are a unique way to get to know Chile, especially if you're on a budget. Sometimes residenciales are small, very basic accommodations and not necessarily private homes. *Hospedajes* are similar. Many rent rooms for less than $10. Some will be shabby, but others can be substantially better than hotel rooms. They also offer the added benefit of allowing you to interact with locals, though they are unlikely to speak English. Contact the local tourist office for details on residenciales and hospedajes.

LANGUAGE

Chile's official language is Spanish, so it's best to learn at least a few words and carry a good phrase book. Chilean Spanish is fast, clipped, and chock-full of colloquialisms. For example, the word for police officer isn't *policía*, but *carabinero*. Even foreigners with a good deal of experience in Spanish-speaking countries may feel like they are encountering a completely new language. However, receptionists at most upscale hotels speak English.

When giving directions, Chileans seldom use left and right, indicating the way instead with a mixture of sign language and *para acá, para allá* (toward here, toward there) instructions. At their clipped, rapid-fire rate, these often come off as two-syllable exchanges ("pa'ca," "pa'ya").

▌COMMUNICATIONS

INTERNET

Chileans are generally savvy about the Internet, which is reflected by the number of Internet cafés around the country. Connection fees are generally no more than $1 for an hour. Very few hotels have wireless connections, but almost all have Ethernet ports or a computer where you can get online.

If you're planning to bring a laptop computer into the country, check the manual first to see if it requires a converter. Newer laptops will require only an adapter plug.

Carrying a laptop computer could make you a target for thieves; conceal your laptop in a generic bag and keep it close to you at all times.

PHONES

The country code for Chile is 56. When dialing a Chilean number from abroad, drop the initial 0 from the local area code. The area code is 2 for Santiago, 58 for Arica, 55 for Antofagasta and San Pedro de Atacama, 42 for Chillán, 57 for Iquique, 56 for La Serena, 65 for Puerto Montt, 61 for Puerto Natales and Punta Arenas, 45 for Temuco, 63 for Valdivia, 32 for Valparaíso and Viña del Mar.

Mobile phone numbers are preceded by a number 9 (sometimes you'll see it written out as 09) or a number 8 (sometimes 08). Dial the "0" first if you're calling from a landline; otherwise drop it.

From Chile the country code is 01 for the United States and Canada, 61 for Australia, 64 for New Zealand, and 44 for the United Kingdom.

CALLING WITHIN CHILE

A 100-peso piece is required to make a local call in a public phone booth, allowing 110 seconds of conversation between the hours of 9 AM and 8 PM, and 160 seconds of talk from 8 PM to 9 AM. Prefix codes are not needed for local dialing.

To call a cell phone within Chile you will need to insert 200 pesos in a phone box.

Having numerous telephone companies means that Chilean public phones all look different. Public phones use either coins (and require a 100-peso deposit) or phone cards. Telefónica and other companies sell telephone cards, but many locals continue to use coins. If you will be making only a few local calls, it's not necessary to purchase a phone card.

Instead of using a public phone, you can pay a little more and use a *centro de llamadas,* small phone shops divided into booths. Simply step into any available booth and dial the number. The charge will be displayed on a monitor near the phone.

You can reach directory assistance in Chile by calling 103. English-speaking operators are not available.

CALLING OUTSIDE CHILE

An international call at a public phone requires anywhere from a 400- or 500-peso deposit (depending on the phone box), which will give you anywhere between 47 and 66 seconds of talking time. You can call the United States for between 39 and 76 seconds (depending on the carrier you use) for 200 pesos.

CALLING CARDS

If you plan to call abroad while in Chile, it's in your best interest to buy a local phone card (sold in varying amounts at kiosks and calling centers) or use a calling center (*centro de llamadas*). For calls to the United States, EntelTicket phone cards, available in denominations ranging from 1,000 to 15,000 pesos, are a good deal.

MOBILE PHONES

If you have a multiband phone (some countries use frequencies other than those used in the United States) and your service provider uses the world-standard GSM network (as do T-Mobile, AT&T, and Verizon), you can probably use your phone abroad. Roaming fees can be steep, however: 99¢ a minute is considered reasonable. And overseas you normally pay the toll charges for incoming calls. It's almost always cheaper to send a text message than to make a call, since text messages have a very low set fee (often less than 5¢).

If you just want to make local calls, consider buying a new SIM card (note that your provider may have to unlock your phone for you to use a different SIM card) and a prepaid service plan in the destination. You'll then have a local number and can make local calls at local rates. If your trip is extensive, you could also simply buy a new cell phone in your destination, as the initial cost will be offset over time.

Contacts Cellular Abroad (☎800/287-5072 ⊕www.cellularabroad.com) rents and sells GMS phones and sells SIM cards that work in many countries. **Mobal** (☎888/888-9162 ⊕www.mobalrental.com) rents mobiles and sells GSM phones (starting at $49) that will operate in 140 countries. Per-call rates vary throughout the world. **Planet Fone** (☎888/988-4777 ⊕www.planetfone.com) rents cell phones, but the per-minute rates are expensive.

▌CUSTOMS & DUTIES

You may bring into Chile up to 400 cigarettes, 500 grams of tobacco, 50 cigars, two open bottles of perfume, 2.5 liters of alcoholic beverages, and gifts. Prohibited items include plants, fruit, seeds, meat, and honey. Spot checks take place at airports and border crossings.

Visitors, although seldom questioned, are prohibited from leaving with handicrafts and souvenirs worth more than $500. You are generally prohibited from taking antiques out of the country without special permission (⇨ *Shopping*).

Information Chilean Embassy (✉1732 Massachusetts Ave. NW, Washington, D.C. USA ☎202/785-1746 ⊕www.chile-usa.org).

U.S. Information U.S. Customs and Border Protection (⊕www.cbp.gov).

▌EATING OUT

The restaurants (all of which are indicated by a ✗symbol) that we list are the cream of the crop in each price category. It is customary to tip 10% in Chile; tipping above this amount is uncommon among locals.

For information on food-related health issues, see Health below.

▌ELECTRICITY

Unlike the United States and Canada—which have a 110- to 120-volt standard—the current in Chile is 220 volts, 50 cycles alternating current (AC). The wall sockets accept plugs with two round prongs.

Consider making a small investment in a universal adapter, which has several types of plugs in one lightweight, compact unit. Most laptops and mobile phone chargers are dual voltage (i.e., they operate equally well on 110 and 220 volts), so require only an adapter. These days the same is true of small appliances such as hair dryers. Always check labels and manufacturer instructions to be sure. Don't use 110-volt outlets marked FOR SHAVERS

ONLY for high-wattage appliances such as hair-dryers.

Contacts Steve Kropla's Help for World Travelers (⊕www.kropla.com) has information on electrical and telephone plugs around the world. **Walkabout Travel Gear** (⊕www.walkabouttravelgear.com) has a good coverage of electricity under "adapters."

▮ EMERGENCIES

The numbers to call in case of emergency are the same all over Chile.

Foreign Embassies Chile (✉1732 Massachusetts Ave. NW, Washington, D.C. USA ☎202/785–1746).

Chile United States (✉Av. Andrés Bello 2800, Las Condes, Santiago ☎2/232–2600).

General Emergency Contacts Ambulance (☎131). **Fire** (☎132). **Police** (☎133).

▮ HEALTH

SHOTS & MEDICATIONS

All travelers to Chile should get up-to-date tetanus, diphtheria, and measles boosters, and a hepatitis A inoculation is recommended. Children traveling to Chile should have current inoculations against mumps, rubella, and polio. Always check with your doctor before leaving.

According to the Centers for Disease Control and Prevention, there's some risk of food-borne diseases such as hepatitis A and typhoid. There's no risk of contracting malaria, but a limited risk of several other insect-borne diseases, including dengue fever. They are usually restricted to forest areas. The best way to avoid insect-borne diseases is to prevent insect bites by wearing long pants and long-sleeve shirts and by using insect repellents with DEET. If you plan to visit remote regions or stay for more than six weeks, check with the CDC's International Travelers Hot Line.

In 2005 there was an outbreak of Vibrio parahemolyticus in Puerto Montt. The infection causes severe diarrhea and is caused by eating bad shellfish. You can consult ⊕*www.mdtravelhealth.com* for a country-by-country listing of health precautions that should be taken prior to travel.

Health Warnings Centers for Disease Control & Prevention (CDC ☎877/394–8747 (FYI-TRIP) international travelers' health line ⊕www.cdc.gov/travel). **World Health Organization** (WHO ⊕www.who.int).

SPECIFIC ISSUES IN CHILE

From a health standpoint, Chile is one of the safer countries in which to travel. To be on the safe side, take the normal precautions you would traveling anywhere in South America.

In Santiago there are several large private *clinicas* (clinics), and many doctors can speak at least a bit of English. Generally, *hospitales* (hospitals) are for those receiving free or heavily subsidized treatment, and they are often crowded with long lines of patients waiting to be seen.

When it comes to air quality, Santiago ranks as one of the most polluted cities in the world.

Visitors seldom encounter problems with drinking the water in Chile. Almost all drinking water receives proper treatment and is unlikely to produce health problems. If you have any doubts, stick to bottled water. Mineral water is good and comes carbonated (*con gas*) and noncarbonated (*sin gas*).

Food preparation is strictly regulated by the government, so outbreaks of food-borne diseases are very rare. But it's still a good idea to use the same commonsense rules you would in any other part of South America. Don't risk restaurants where the hygiene is suspect or street vendors where the food is allowed to sit around at room temperature. To be on the safe side, avoid raw shellfish, such as ceviche. Remember to steer clear of raw fruits and vegetables unless you know they've been thoroughly washed and disinfected.

OVER-THE-COUNTER REMEDIES
Mild cases of diarrhea may respond to Imodium (known generically as loperamide), Pepto-Bismol (not as strong), and Lomotil. Drink plenty of purified water or tea—chamomile (*manzanilla* in Spanish) is a good folk remedy.

You will need to visit a *farmacia* (pharmacy) to purchase medications such as Tylenol and *aspirina* (aspirin), which are readily available. Pharmacists can often recommend a medicine for your condition, but they are not always certain of the dosage. Quite often the packaging comes with no instructions unless the drug is imported, in which case it will cost two or three times the price of a local product.

▌ HOURS OF OPERATION

Many businesses close for lunch between about 1 and 3 or 4, though this is becoming less common, especially in larger cities. Most tourist attractions are open during normal business hours during the week and for at least the morning on Saturday and Sunday. Most museums are closed Monday.

HOLIDAYS
New Year's Day (January 1), Good Friday (March or April depending on year), Labor Day (May 1), Day of Naval Glories (May 21), Corpus Christi (in June), Feast of the Virgen de Carmen (July 16), Feast of the Ascension of the Virgin (August 15), Feast of St. Peter and St. Paul (June 29), Independence Celebrations (September 18), Army Day (September 19), Discovery of the Americas (October 12), All Saints Day (November 1), Immaculate Conception (December 8), Christmas (December 25).

Many shops and services are open on most of these days, but transportation is always heavily booked up on and around the holidays. The two most important dates in the Chilean calendar are September 18 and New Year's Day. On these days shops close and public transportation is reduced to the bare minimum or is nonexistent. Trying to book a ticket around these dates will be impossible unless you do it well in advance.

▌ MAIL

The postal system is efficient, and, on average, letters take five to seven days to reach the United States, Europe, Australia, and New Zealand. They will arrive sooner if you send them *prioritaria* (priority) post, but the price will almost double. You can send them *certificado* (registered), in which case the recipient will need to sign for them.

If you wish to receive a parcel in Chile and don't have a specific address to which it can be sent, you can have it labeled *poste restante* and sent to the nearest post office.

SHIPPING PACKAGES
A cheap, reliable method for sending parcels is to use the Chilean postal system, which although slow—up to 15 business days—is still reliable for sending packages weighing up to 33 kilograms (73 pounds).

Federal Express has offices in Santiago and operates an international overnight service. DHL, with offices in Santiago and most cities throughout Chile, provides overnight service. If you want to send a package to North America, Europe, Australia, or New Zealand, it will take one–four days, depending on where you're sending it from in Chile.

ChileExpress and LanCourier also offer overnight services between most cities within Chile.

Express Services ChileExpress (☎800/200–102). **DHL** (☎800/800–345).

Federal Express (☎800/363–030). **LanCourier** (☎800/800–400).

▌ MONEY

Credit cards and traveler's checks are accepted in most resorts and in many shops and restaurants in major cities, though you should always carry some local currency for minor expenses like taxis and tipping. Once you stray from the beaten path, you can often pay only with pesos.

Prices throughout this guide are given for adults. Substantially reduced fees are almost always available for children, students, and senior citizens.

ATMS & BANKS
Your own bank will probably charge a fee for using ATMs abroad; the foreign bank you use may also charge a fee. Nevertheless, you'll usually get a better rate of exchange at an ATM than you will at a currency-exchange office or even when changing money in a bank. And extracting funds as you need them is a safer option than carrying around a large amount of cash.

▌TIP➜ PIN numbers with more than four digits are not recognized at ATMs in many countries. If yours has five or more, remember to change it before you leave.

ATMs, or "cajeros automaticos," are widely available, and you can get cash with a Cirrus- or Plus-linked debit card or with a major credit card. Most ATMs in Chile have a special screen—accessed after entering your PIN code—for foreign-account withdrawals. In this case, you need to access your account first via the "foreign client" option. ATMs offer excellent exchange rates because they are based on wholesale rates offered only by major banks.

Banco de Chile is probably the largest national bank; its Web site ⊕*www.bancochile.cl* lists branches and ATMs by location if you click on the "surcur-

scales" (locations) link, then the "cajeros automaticos" link. Itua (⊕*www.itau.cl*), a Brazilian bank, recently bought all of the BostonBank locations in Chile and is also widely available. Citibank (⊕*www.citibank.com*) is another fairly common option.

CREDIT CARDS
Throughout this guide, the following abbreviations are used: **AE,** American Express; **DC,** Diners Club; **MC,** MasterCard; and **V,** Visa.

It's a good idea to inform your credit-card company before you travel. Otherwise, the credit-card company might put a hold on your card owing to unusual activity—not a good thing halfway through your trip. Record all your credit-card numbers—as well as the phone numbers to call if your cards are lost or stolen—in a safe place, so you're prepared should something go wrong. Both MasterCard and Visa have general numbers you can call (collect if you're abroad) if your card is lost, but you're better off calling the number of your issuing bank, since MasterCard and Visa usually just transfer you to your bank; your bank's number is usually printed on your card.

If you plan to use your credit card for cash advances, you'll need to apply for a PIN at least two weeks before your trip. Although it's usually cheaper (and safer) to use a credit card abroad for large purchases (so you can cancel payments or be reimbursed if there's a problem), note that some credit-card companies *and* the banks that issue them add substantial percentages to all foreign transactions, whether they're in a foreign currency or not. Check on these fees before leaving home, so there won't be any surprises when you get the bill.

Dynamic currency conversion programs are becoming increasingly widespread. Merchants who participate in them are supposed to ask whether you want to be charged in dollars or the local currency, but they don't always do so. And even if they do offer you a choice, they may well avoid mentioning the additional surcharges. The good news is that you *do* have a choice. And if this practice really gets your goat, you can avoid it entirely thanks to American Express; with its cards, DCC simply isn't an option.

Credit cards are widely accepted in hotels, restaurants, and shops in most cities and tourist destinations. Fewer establishments accept credit cards in rural areas. It may be easier to use your credit card whenever possible. The exchange rate varies by only a fraction of a cent, so you won't need to worry about whether your purchase is charged on the day of purchase or at some point in the future. Note, however, that you may get a slightly better deal if you pay with cash, and that some businesses charge an extra fee for paying with a non-Chilean (International) credit card.

Reporting Lost Cards American Express (☎800/528–4800 in the U.S., 336/393–1111 collect from abroad ⊕www.americanexpress.com). **Diners Club** (☎800/234–6377 in the U.S., 303/799–1504 collect from abroad ⊕www.dinersclub.com). **MasterCard** (☎800/627–8372 in the U.S., 636/722–7111 collect from abroad ⊕www.mastercard.com). **Visa** (☎800/847–2911 in the U.S., 410/581–9994 collect from abroad ⊕www.visa.com).

CURRENCY & EXCHANGE

The peso ($) is the unit of currency in Chile. Chilean bills are issued in 1,000, 2,000, 5,000, 10,000, and 20,000 pesos, and coins come in units of 1, 5, 10, 50, 100, and 500 pesos. Note that getting change for larger bills, especially from small shopkeepers, can be difficult. Make sure to get smaller bills when you exchange currency. Always check exchange rates in your local newspaper for the most current information; at press time, the exchange rate was approximately 475 pesos to the U.S. dollar.

Common to Santiago and other mid- to large-size cities are *casas de cambio*, or money-changing stores. Naturally, those at the airport will charge premium rates for convenience's sake. It may be more economical to change a small amount for your transfer to the city, where options

The U.S. State Department notes that travelers "should be aware that they might have difficulty using U.S. $100 bills due to concerns about falsification. The United States Secret Service has provided Chilean banks and local police with the tools and training needed to identify counterfeit U.S. currency. Although the training was very successful, many Chilean banks, exchange houses and business still refuse to accept the $100 notes. Whenever possible visitors to Chile should use traveler's checks or bring notes smaller than $50."

Currently, it's quite easy to figure out how much you're paying for something in Chile, as long as the U.S. dollar is equal to approximately 500 pesos: simply multiply what you're being charged by two (e.g., a 10,000-peso dinner is worth about 20 U.S. dollars).

Currency Conversion Google (⊕www.google.com). **Oanda.com** (⊕www.oanda.com) **XE.com** (⊕www.xe.com).

▌ PACKING

You'll need to pack for all seasons when visiting Chilean Patagonia, no matter what time of year you're traveling. Windbreakers, a sweater, long-sleeve shirts, long pants, socks, sneakers, a hat, a light waterproof jacket, a bathing suit, and insect repellent are all essentials. Light colors are best, since mosquitoes avoid them. A high-factor sunscreen is essential at all times, especially in the far south where the ozone layer is much depleted.

Other useful items include a screw-top water bottle that you can fill with purified water, a money pouch, a travel flashlight and extra batteries, a Swiss Army knife with a bottle opener, a medical kit, binoculars, and a pocket calculator to help with currency conversions. You can never have too many large resealable plastic bags, which are ideal for storing film, protecting things from rain and damp, and quarantining stinky socks.

PASSPORTS & VISAS

While traveling in Chile you might want to carry a copy of your passport and leave the original in your hotel safe. If you plan on paying by credit card you will often be asked to show identification or at least write down your passport number.

Citizens of the United States, Canada, Australia, New Zealand, and the United Kingdom need only a passport to enter Chile for up to three months.

Upon arrival in Chile, you will be given a flimsy piece of paper that is your three-month tourist visa. This has to be handed in when you leave. Because getting a new one involves waiting in many lines and a lot of bureaucracy, put it somewhere safe. You can extend your visa an additional 90 days for a small fee, but do this before it expires to avoid paying a *multa* (fine).

▌ SAFETY

The vast majority of visitors to Chile never experience a problem with crime. Violent crime is a rarity; far more common is pickpocketing or thefts from purses, backpacks, or rental cars. Be on your guard in crowded places, especially markets and festivals.

Wherever you go, don't wear expensive clothing or flashy jewelry, and don't handle money in public. Keep cameras in a secure camera bag, preferably one with a chain or wire embedded in the strap. Always remain alert for pickpockets, and don't walk alone at night, especially in the larger cities.

Volcano climbing is a popular pastime in Chile, with Volcán Villarrica, near Pucón, and Volcán Osorno the most popular. But some of these mountains are also among South America's most active volcanoes. CONAF, the agency in charge of national parks, cuts off access to any volcano at the slightest hint of abnormal activity. Check with CONAF before heading out on any hike in this region.

Many women travel alone or in groups in Chile with no problems. Chilean men are less aggressive in their machismo than men in other South American countries (they will seldom, for example, approach a woman they don't know), but it's still an aspect of the culture (they will make comments when a women walks by). It's a good idea for single women not to walk alone at night, especially in the larger cities.

Contact CONAF (☎45/298–221 in Temuco, 2/390–0125 in Santiago ⊕www.conaf.cl). **Transportation Security Administration** (TSA; ⊕www.tsa.gov).

▌ TAXES

An 18% value-added tax (V.A.T., called IVA here) is added to the cost of most goods and services in Chile; often you won't notice because it's included in the price. When it's not, the seller gives you the price plus IVA. At many hotels you may receive an exemption from the IVA if you pay in American dollars or with a credit card.

▌ TIME

Chile is one hour ahead of Eastern standard time and four hours ahead of Pacific standard time. Daylight saving time in Chile begins in October and ends in March.

Time Zones Timeanddate.com (⊕www.time-anddate.com/worldclock).

INDEX

NOTES

NOTES

NOTES

NOTES